For the Union and the Catholic Church

For the Union and the Catholic Church

Four Converts in the Civil War

MAX LONGLEY

McFarland & Company, Inc., Publishers
Jefferson, North Carolina

LIBRARY OF CONGRESS CATALOGUING-IN-PUBLICATION DATA

Longley, Maximilian, 1971–
For the Union and the Catholic Church :
four converts in the Civil War / Max Longley.
    p.   cm.
Includes bibliographical references and index.

ISBN 978-0-7864-9422-4 (softcover : acid free paper) ∞
ISBN 978-1-4766-1999-6 (ebook)

1. United States—History—Civil War, 1861–1865—Participation, Catholic.
2. United States—History—Civil War, 1861–1865—Religious aspects.
3. Catholics—United States—Biography. 4. Converts—United States—
Biography. 5. United States—History—Civil War, 1861–1865—Biography.
6. Catholic Church—United States—History—19th century. I. Title.

E540.C3L66 2015   973.7092'2—dc23   [B]   2015012046

BRITISH LIBRARY CATALOGUING DATA ARE AVAILABLE

© 2015 Max Longley. All rights reserved

*No part of this book may be reproduced or transmitted in any form
or by any means, electronic or mechanical, including photocopying
or recording, or by any information storage and retrieval system,
without permission in writing from the publisher.*

Cover Image: Men of an Irish-American regiment and
their chaplain pause before celebrating mass at
Camp Cass, Virginia, 1861 (Library of Congress)

Printed in the United States of America

*McFarland & Company, Inc., Publishers
Box 611, Jefferson, North Carolina 28640
www.mcfarlandpub.com*

To David

Table of Contents

Preface   1

1. "Every man, Catholic and non–Catholic, fell on his knees with his head bowed down"   5
2. *The End of Religious Controversy*   19
3. "I have the responsibilities, he the virtues"   28
4. "An heir-loom"   49
5. "The radical necessity of the Church"   65
6. "The Catholics ... will be found among the fastest friends of the Union"   80
7. "The devil ... comes to us as a philanthropist"   85
8. "Cowards fearing the light of day, and skulking beneath the cover of darkness"   101
9. "The Know-Nothings have inaugurated a new era"   113
10. "Framed, no doubt, for the express purpose of corrupting the faith of Catholic children"   121
11. "I wish that secession had never been thought of"   137
12. "Called upon by both sides to fight in the battles of the country"   145
13. "The nations of antiquity had slaves; where are those nations now?"   155
14. "Unless, *as a body,* we besiege Heaven with prayer, God will not be pacified"   168
15. "Waning of the prejudice against our religion, coming from the highest range of Protestant society"   184
16. "The most logical and effective assailants of slavery that these last three years have produced have been devout Catholics"   196
17. "If the general is crossing himself we are in a desperate situation"   201

18. "A mere inferential recognition, unconnected with political action or the regular establishment of diplomatic relations"   210

19. "Judea produced but one Judas Iscariot"   220

20. "The Bishop attributes to God what is an execrable violence of men"   231

21. "The only country in which the Pope could seek and find a suitable and secure Asylum"   243

Conclusion   253
Chapter Notes   255
Bibliography   282
Index   295

Preface

Four men—the brothers William and Sylvester Rosecrans, James Healy, and Orestes Brownson—came into the Catholic Church in the mid-1840s, just in time to experience the conflicts of the Civil War era. The events of that time provided what Barbara Tuchman might call a distant mirror with surprising reflections of the troubles of our own age.

Why follow four converts, rather than the "cradle Catholics" born in the country, or the increasingly dominant immigrant Catholics? A key reason is that I am myself a Catholic convert, with an accordingly heightened interest in the convert experience. Another reason is that our four converts' experiences in the Church began just as the controversies which would ultimately lead to war heated up. All four had significant roles to play in the dramatic events of the era.

Our converts' first two decades in the Church were marked by two important developments in the United States: increased division over slavery and a revival of traditional Protestant hostility toward Catholics. Our converts and other Catholics identified the basis of the latter problem, and their conclusion has been ratified by modern scholarship: there was a New England element in the population, descendants of the original Calvinist settlers of the region and now living in New England itself and in other states. Lacking the pure Calvinism of their ancestors, the new Puritans kept the conviction that the government ought to promote Godliness, which to many translated into a crusade against the evils of "Rum, Romanism and slavery," evils seen as connected as waves of Catholic immigrants came to the United States, drank, and voted for the party of slavery, the Democrats. Unlike the Puritanism-infused Whigs, Know-Nothings, and Republicans, the Democrats welcomed immigrants into their ranks.

The religious battles *in* the United States were not always *about* the United States. American Catholics and their opponents were not limited by domestic concerns, but fought over developments in Europe. To most Protestants and many Catholics, European radicals were the counterparts to the American revolutionaries, while to the Catholic hierarchy and intellectuals, the radicals were enemies to public order and to the Church herself. European divisions between Catholic conservatives and liberal Catholics were reflected in similar conflicts in the United States.

On one issue, the division was not between liberal Catholics and conservative Catholics, but between European and American Catholics. European Catholics, whether liberal or reactionary, were more antislavery than American Catholics. In what may be an early

1

example of American Catholic "dissent" against Church dogma, American Catholics minimized or explained away Rome's firm pronouncements on African slavery, which made clear that the theoretical justifications of slavery (e.g., self-sale, conviction of crime) did not justify seizing free Africans and shipping them across the sea to perpetual bondage. European Catholics' embarrassment and indignation at the persistence of African slavery in Europe's colonies and ex-colonies, in the face of Rome's condemnation of the enslavement of Africa's peoples, contrasted with the American Catholic attitude of tolerance of, or at least noninterference with, slavery. Only when the war began did some Catholics, such as our converts, embrace abolition.

Black Catholics existed at the intersection of anti–Catholic bigotry from Protestants and of antiblack bigotry from Irish Catholics. Harriet Thompson, a black Catholic in New York City, wrote a petition to Rome on the subject in 1853: "the church do leave the colored a prey to the wolf." Someone in Rome took note of the petition, but nothing seems to have come of it at the time, although papal censors decided to allow the antislavery novel *Uncle Tom's Cabin* to circulate freely in the Catholic world.[1]

This book shows members of the Catholic Church at their best, at their worst, and struggling in the twilight of moral ambiguity. I have tried to present their experiences as objectively as I can, but this does not mean I am morally neutral about what I describe. Overall, I will show a picture of a Church heroically struggling to build itself up in an often-hostile country, while struggling against the very real threat of the neo–Puritans.

History can record only inadequately what was probably the Church's greatest interaction with slavery—the penances and advice given by priests when hearing the confessions of slaves and masters. The dramas of priests ministering in slave states, in areas where the Catholic population was sparse and where Protestant masters were known to beat slaves for keeping the Sabbath, would themselves make a book were it not for the sanctity of the confessional. Such narratives would provide perhaps a better picture of the Church's activities than this book's depiction of the Church's public life, but we are rarely if ever able to know what went on behind that impenetrable veil.[2]

I have many people I need to thank (errors are mine, not theirs). I will start with the librarians and archivists who gave of their time to find manuscript sources: Lori Birrell and Melinda Wallington at the Department of Rare Books and Special Collections, University of Rochester (New York); Tammy Kiter and others at the New York Historical Society; Scott Taylor at the Special Collections Research Center at Georgetown University Library, Washington, D.C.; Dan Hinchen of the Massachusetts Historical Society; and the staff at the Rubenstein Library at Duke University in Durham, North Carolina, for access to the *Freeman's Journal* and the Louis Garesché papers.

I thank my friend Erica Haberman for the drawing of James McMaster.

For permissions for the use of images, I acknowledge Elizabeth Sudduth at the Irvin Department of Rare Books and Special Collections, University of South Carolina Libraries, Columbia, South Carolina; Polly Horn of the Myers Inn Museum, Sunbury, Ohio, Big Walnut Area Historical Society (she is a key compiler of information regarding William Rosecrans and his family); Claire Ballinger of the Maly Library, Athenaeum of Ohio–Mount Saint Mary's Seminary, Cincinnati, Ohio; Jennifer Ericson at the Abraham Lincoln Presidential Library and Museum, Springfield, Illinois; Susie Bock at the Special Collections

Department, University of Southern Maine, Portland; Christian Buat of the Site Remy de Gourmont; Steve Bartrick of Steve Bartrick Antique Prints and Maps and ancestryimages.com; and Christopher Welsh, CACHE' Historical and World Coins Web site.

I owe particular thanks to Chris Forsyth, Deanna Morgan, Jim Gard, Janice Fearinger, Janet Arlotta, Susan Callaghan, and Kathy Craig, who looked at my manuscript while it was developing and gave highly constructive criticism. I also thank my mother Elma Longley for proofreading.

1

"Every man, Catholic and non–Catholic, fell on his knees with his head bowed down"

As afternoon was moving toward evening on the battlefield of Gettysburg on July 2, 1863, the Irish Brigade was about to move into position, and Fr. William Corby, the chaplain, decided this was the time to offer a general absolution to his soldiers, lest they die before having a chance to confess their sins. While the din of battle came from the direction of Little Round Top, Fr. Corby stood on the "large rock" to address the men. He adjured the soldiers to do their duty, and to resolve to confess their sins the first chance they got, if they survived. According to an officer present, "every man, Catholic and non–Catholic, fell on his knees with his head bowed down." Fr. Corby then pronounced the words of absolution. The words "Dominus Noster Jesus Christus" competed with the noise of the nearby battle, and Corby concluded with "In nomini Patris, et Filii, et Spiritus Sancti, Amen." Both Catholic and Protestant soldiers remained kneeling while the formula of absolution was pronounced.[1]

The Irish Brigade then proceeded to that part of the battle area known as the Wheatfield. Amid the grain of the contested farmland a Reaper plied his deadly trade. Soldiers defending this part of the front remembered "a whirlpool of death." Over three hundred soldiers in the Irish Brigade were lost during this and other phases of the Gettysburg fighting. The survivors lived to see a Union victory and a withdrawal by the defeated Confederates.[2]

By July 1863, Catholics in the United States were as divided as other Americans. In the midst of a devastating civil war, Catholics in the North and South generally fought with their respective sections.

But at this time, the complexities and contradictions of Catholic life during the Civil War came to a head. Catholic soldiers were making heroic sacrifices on the battlefield at the same time that Catholics on the home front were sharing in the country's growing war weariness. Nothing highlighted the contrast more than the courage of the Irish Brigade at the battle of Gettysburg, Pennsylvania, in early July and the draft riots in New York in the middle of the month.

Catholic soldiers, especially Irish, served in many units on the Gettysburg battlefield. One of these units was the "Irish Brigade," made up of three New York Irish regi-

Statue of Father Corby at Gettysburg. The famous chaplain gave a general absolution to soldiers about to go into battle, knowing that many of them would be killed before they had the time to make a full confession (carptrash, Wikimedia Commons).

ments—including the famous "Fighting 69th" infantry regiment—and one regiment each from Massachusetts and Pennsylvania. When the brigade was first constituted, it had a few thousand men. Because of wartime casualties at Antietam, Fredericksburg, Chancellorsville, and elsewhere, that number was down to 530 as the Gettysburg fighting began.[3]

The Union forces were victorious at Gettysburg, and soon after that, on the Western front, Union general Ulysses Grant took the strategic Mississippi River town of Vicksburg.

Not all the Irish Catholic fighting spirit was thrown against the Confederates. There was growing discontent on the home front about the slow progress of the war, the emancipation of the slaves, and a new conscription law which threatened to take men from their homes and jobs to join the bloody fighting. As if by way of deliberate insult to the working classes, the law allowed draftees to purchase an exemption for $300, a sum available to the well-to-do but not to the average Irish worker.[4]

The trouble started in New York on July 13 with an attack by a mostly Irish fire company, its members newly liable to the draft, at the place where a draft lottery was being drawn. Rioters also attacked the state armory looking for weapons. The prowar Republican paper, the *New York Tribune*, was also threatened, and the riots devolved into lynching as mobs attacked and killed black victims and attacked the Colored Orphan Asylum.[5]

As New York's draft riots gathered strength so soon after the great display of Catholic military courage at Gettysburg, four American Catholics were in the midst of the great issues presented. All four had been in the Catholic Church for just under two decades, having converted to the minority religion in the face of prejudice from a heavily Protestant country.

One of these men—Fr. James Augustine Healy—was the first black American priest and a high-ranking one in Boston. He confronted, and embodied, key issues facing Catholics in the Civil War era. Union general William Rosecrans was the commander of the Army of the Cumberland in the Civil War's Western front. General Rosecrans's brother Sylvester was a bishop who served as the auxiliary (assistant) to the archbishop of Cincinnati. One of the four—Orestes Brownson—was the editor of a Catholic paper, often carving out his own line on many subjects (including the war and slavery) in conflict with the Catholic bishops.

On the Western front of the war, the pious, rosary-toting General William Rosecrans secured his position in Tennessee. General Rosecrans commanded the Army of the Cumberland, which he had lately led through a series of battles and flanking movements to capture most of Tennessee from the Confederacy. Having already advanced a considerable distance, Rosecrans was now halted while he consolidated his current position. His lines were extended, and he had a large number of men and horses to feed. A top graduate of West Point who had worked as an engineer in civil life, Rosecrans put his engineering skills to work clearing roads, building bridges, rebuilding railways, and establishing depots for military supplies.[6]

A proud Catholic convert, General Rosecrans made no secret of his religious proclivities, conducting religious discussions in camp alongside discussions of military affairs. His way of unwinding after a long day was to stay up into the early morning hours with his staff and visitors, discussing religious, literary, political, and military matters. His chief of staff, the officer-politician James Garfield, was treated to Rosecrans's discussions of his conversion and the glories of the Catholic faith. This took some getting used to on the part of the zealously Protestant Garfield, as did Rosecrans's "dirty-looking string of friars' beads" (rosary) and his frequent attendance at Mass. "He is the intensest religionist I ever saw," was Garfield's conclusion. "He is one of the most devotedly religious men I ever knew, and makes all his acts in the army a matter of religion."[7]

Nor was Rosecrans hesitant to mingle religion with antislavery views. The previous

Draft rioters clash with police at the headquarters of the prowar *New York Tribune*. "Charge of the police at the *Tribune* office," wood engraving in *Harper's Pictorial History of the Civil War*, vol. 2, p. 653 (Library of Congress, Reproduction Number LC-USZ62-47037 [b&w film copy neg.]).

year, campaigning in Kentucky, Rosecrans had dined with Bishop Martin Spalding of Louisville. General Rosecrans insisted on, in Spalding's words, "thrusting on us the odious subject of abolition." In April 1863, a widely published letter from the general said that the "destruction" of slavery was "ordained" by God. Criticized by Catholic editor James McMaster for his abolitionism, the general would later aver that the "traditions of the [Catholic] religion" didn't allow him to be an "apologist of the legal slave laws of our own land by which men and women are made cattle."[8]

Rosecrans didn't get in trouble because of his religion. At the time, the Northern suspicion of Catholics was in abeyance. However, Rosecrans got in trouble for another reason: his abrasive personality. He was possessed of a strong, and often justified, confidence in his own abilities, writing at length in his dispatches to rebut criticisms against himself. While beloved by his soldiers, and friendly and outgoing (if demanding) with his staff and outside visitors, in his relations with his superiors Rosecrans embodied the stereotype of the socially inept, arrogant, autistic engineer. He did not spare his military or civilian superiors from the criticism which he thought due them for their errors. Rosecrans didn't seem to care that his attitude was alienating the secretary of war, Edwin M. Stanton, and the rising star, General Ulysses Grant. So far, his string of successes in the field had protected him from reprisal.[9]

Now Rosecrans' superiors were telling him that he had to resume his advance into Confederate territory. They thought he was delaying too long, but Rosecrans thought he needed more time to secure his lines of supply, which were already overextended.[10]

In May, as he was beginning to consider how he could start his army moving again, Rosecrans received a visitor at his Murfreesboro headquarters. James Gilmore was a popular writer who ended up staying with the general and his staff for two weeks. Initially, Rosecrans thought Gilmore was gathering material for his writing. But there was another, hidden reason for the visit: Gilmore was involved in a plot by Horace Greeley and other Republicans to replace Abraham Lincoln as president by nominating someone else—someone like Rosecrans. By May 1863 William Rosecrans was the most successful Union commander, having won several battles and driven back the Confederates in the Western theater. He would make a better commander-in-chief than Lincoln, Greeley thought. And as a Catholic Democrat, he had a credibility with the Irish voters which the Republicans had never been able to attain.[11]

Before endorsing Rosecrans, however, Greeley wanted assurance on a key point: Would a President Rosecrans fight to the end to free the Southern slaves, as Greeley wished, or would he cut a deal with the Confederacy to let its states back into the Union while keeping their slaves? Greeley wanted Gilmore to visit Rosecrans and find out his attitude. If the general was willing to fight slavery without compromise, Gilmore was to convey Greeley's offer. Gilmore admired Lincoln and often met with the president, and was scheduled to meet with him again after seeing Rosecrans, but guiltily agreed to this treacherous mission.[12]

After a nerve-wracking railway journey, Gilmore reached Murfreesboro in safety and visited Rosecrans and his officers in their headquarters in a confiscated home. During one of his trademark lengthy discussions with Gilmore, Rosecrans gave Gilmore his view of the slave's future: "Give him the Bible and a spelling-book, freedom, and a chance for more than six feet of God's earth,—and let him alone." Rosecrans was also sympathetic to chief of staff Garfield's proposal to make soldiers of the freed slaves, and may have conveyed this to Gilmore.[13]

1. "Every man, Catholic and non–Catholic..." 9

Before going to see Lincoln, Gilmore carried out his mission to undermine the president. Satisfied that Rosecrans would fight to the end against slavery, Gilmore decided to approach the general about Greeley's proposition—would he let President Lincoln be replaced by President Rosecrans? Gilmore had had the opportunity to raise the issue with chief of staff James Garfield after nursing him though a several days' illness. Garfield, who had been elected to Congress the previous year and would in December leave the battlefield for legislative halls, thought his boss would make a great president and encouraged Gilmore to take the matter up with Rosecrans.[14]

Gilmore brought up the issue in one of his late night talks with the general. Rosecrans's reply, according to Gilmore's contemporary notes, was this: "My place is here. My country gave me my education"—referring to his training at the West Point officers' school—"and so has a right to my military services; and it educated me for precisely this emergency. So this, and not the presidency, is my post of duty, and I cannot, without violating my conscience, leave it. But let me tell you,

Portrait of Maj. Gen. William S. Rosecrans, officer of the Federal Army (Brady National Photographic Art Gallery, Washington, D.C., Library of Congress, Reproduction Number LC-DIG-cwpb–06052 [digital file from original neg.] LC-B8172–2001 [b&w film neg.]).

and I wish you would tell your friends who are moving in this matter, that you are mistaken about Mr. Lincoln. He is in his right place. I am in a position to know, and if you live you will see that I am right about him."[15] Gilmore left soon thereafter to talk to Lincoln about messages Rosecrans had entrusted to him, but not the message about the presidency. Lincoln wouldn't have to know about *that*.

Also in May, Rosecrans received a curious guest at his provost marshal's headquarters at Murfreesboro, Tennessee. Clement Vallandigham was a Democratic politician in General Rosecrans's home state of Ohio. Vallandigham had become a leader of those Democrats who called for an end to the war, and the general commanding in Ohio, Ambrose Burnside, arrested Vallandigham for an antiwar speech. Convicted by a military tribunal, Vallandigham was sentenced to imprisonment, which President Abraham Lincoln commuted to banishment—the Ohio peacenik was to be sent into Confederate territory. Secretary of War Edwin Stanton ordered Rosecrans to carry this banishment into effect.[16]

Near midnight on the 24th, after a trip by boat, rail and carriage, Vallandigham came under military escort to Rosecrans's provost marshal's office—a commandeered private house in Murfreesboro. The general attended the ceremony in which Vallandigham was handed over to him. He wanted to get a look at Vallandigham. The general and the politician argued, in a more or less friendly way, about the war. Rosecrans explained his view that good citizens must sustain the Union's war policy and oppose the slave-driving traitors of the Confederacy—a position he had advanced in public statements to the people of his (and Vallandigham's) home state of Ohio. Vallandigham replied by reiterating his support for an end to the war and a negotiated peace with the Confederacy, bringing about a reunion of the country by negotiation, not violence. To Vallandigham, the Emancipation Proclamation and other antislavery measures were unconstitutional obstacles to peace, interfering in the Southern states' right to order their own domestic institutions.[17]

According to a later account of the conversation, Rosecrans told Vallandigham that if the latter was left unguarded "my soldiers will tear you to pieces." Vallandigham replied that this indicated that Rosecrans and his men were "prejudiced and ignorant," and asked to be able to speak to the troops and change their minds—which Rosecrans declined to allow. Remarking that Vallandigham didn't "look like a traitor," Rosecrans told his soldiers to hand Vallandigham over to the Confederates. After daybreak, Rosecrans's soldiers brought their prisoner to the edge of Confederate lines, where the Confederates after some hesitation took Vallandigham into custody as a prisoner of war.[18]

In June, Rosecrans got his army moving after several months of consolidating his position. Meanwhile, on the home front, in William Rosecrans's native Ohio, the state faced a Confederate invasion and a political campaign by the supporters of the man the general had helped banish—Clement Vallandigham.

Sylvester Rosecrans, the general's brother, was the auxiliary bishop of Cincinnati, where he helped the incumbent archbishop, John Purcell, with his duties. These duties, as the two hierarchs saw them, included support for the Lincoln administration's war effort and its emancipation policies.

Archbishop Purcell and Bishop Rosecrans were fervent Union supporters, flying the American flag from the cathedral, visiting troops in the field, sending priests as chaplains and nuns as nurses to aid the Northern forces. Bishop Rosecrans was the archbishop's right hand, taking on his role as auxiliary bishop after officials of Pope Pius IX in Rome refused Purcell's request to retire.[19]

Archbishop Purcell spoke up for the Union from the beginning of the war, comparing secession to "the principle of private judgment"—a common Catholic term for Protestantism, and a damning accusation in that far from ecumenical age. In this statement, and in editorials in the pages of the diocesan organ the *Catholic Telegraph*—of which Sylvester Rosecrans was formerly coeditor—the heads of Cincinnati Catholicism made their views clear. Not only must the Union be restored, but slavery must be abolished in accordance with Lincoln's Emancipation Proclamation.

The *Catholic Telegraph* editorialized on April 8 against slavery, responding to needling from James McMaster's *Freeman's Journal,* which took the *Telegraph* to task for allegedly betraying Catholic principles with its abolitionist stance: "When [the Church] has not the legislative power in her hands she is patient, long-suffering, gentle. What she could not suppress she tolerated. But she found slavery little disposed to imitate her meekness." The Catholic Church flourished in the free states, but not in the slaves states, not even in the supposedly Catholic state of Louisiana, where the *Telegraph* was unaware of any Louisiana Senator or Congressman "who identified himself with the Catholic cause."[20]

The editorial went on to say that slavery was inconsistent with the proper flourishing of the Catholic faith. The editorial noted that some Southern ladies had burned copies of the *Telegraph* for its expressing such views, and sarcastically invited them to "prove their amiability and piety by doing so" again. Historically, the Church had promoted the elimination of slavery as promptly as circumstances would permit.[21]

The *Telegraph* then analyzed an incident from the New Testament epistle of the apostle Paul to Philemon. Although St. Paul had sent the Christian slave Onesimus back to his kind Christian master Philemon, he would not have returned a slave to a "Heathen master" or to a cruel master who split slave families by selling them down the river. This view was backed by papal condemnation of slavery.[22]

"Events have hurried on," the editorial declared, and "what the Church would not or could not do the politicians have done." American Catholics needed to accept that slavery was at an end.[23]

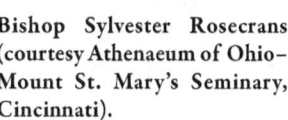

Bishop Sylvester Rosecrans (courtesy Athenaeum of Ohio–Mount St. Mary's Seminary, Cincinnati).

As for the draft, the *Telegraph* took a stance on that, too. Around the time of the preliminary Emancipation Proclamation, a *Telegraph* editorial declared in favor of conscription: "If you are drafted, *go you must*. When you talk of resisting the draft ... you make yourself not only ridiculous but criminal."[24]

Not all the bishops agreed with the militant antislavery Unionism of Archbishop Purcell and Bishop Rosecrans. Bishop Martin John Spalding of Louisville, Kentucky, thought the two prelates were not good representatives of Catholic views. Kentucky was part of the Cincinnati Archdiocese, and the diocese of Louisville was subject to Purcell. The bishop of Louisville had held his position since 1850 and was an influential figure within the archdiocese, which included the states of Ohio, Kentucky, Michigan, and Indiana. As the son of a slaveholding family, and as a bishop in politically divided Kentucky, a slave state wrested with difficulty from the Confederates, Spalding was inclined to take a different view of events than did those above him in the hierarchy.[25]

Spalding insinuated that Purcell was led into his political views by Bishop Rosecrans, who in turn was influenced by his general-brother. The latter was probably aiming at pleasing the powers that be in order to get a promotion (although General Rosecrans's hostile letters to his superiors militate against Spalding's interpretation).[26]

Spalding consulted with a friend of his, Archbishop Francis Patrick Kenrick of Baltimore, about educating officials in Pope Pius IX's Rome about the facts of the Civil War, as they were understood by Spalding. Kenrick was sympathetic to this plan. Baltimore was not only symbolically important to American Catholics as the country's oldest see, but like Louisville, it was in a border state, divided in sentiment between North and South. Kenrick's brother Peter was archbishop of St. Louis—and Missouri was another conflicted border state. Francis Kenrick, widely known among his colleagues for his learning, was the author of an influential work on moral theology, in which he advised that slavery was not inherently sinful so long as slaveholders did not abuse their power. Kenrick advised Spalding to explain the "facts" of the Civil War to Rome. "It is not very easy," said Kenrick, "for foreigners to understand the relation of the States to the General [federal] Government, which at other times was called the Administration, but which is now a truly absolute Government."[27]

Archbishop Kenrick was in the last weeks of his life by this time—he would die just after Gettysburg. With Kenrick's encouragement, Spalding contacted Alessandro Barnabo, head of the Congregation of Propaganda (responsible for mission territories, including the United States), alerting Barnabo to his coming essay. Spalding mailed the actual work from New York, without any identifying information on the package which could let the Lincoln administration trace the origins of the document.[28] Lincoln's agents were known to arrest administration critics, so Spalding was taking no chances.

Spalding's essay was written in Italian and gave an analysis which largely blamed the abolitionists and Republicans for the war. After giving his view that the Constitution established a voluntary union of states, Spalding avowed that the federal government could not wage war against a state. On whether there was a right of secession, as the Confederates claimed, Spalding professed merely to summarize the views of both sides, but his summary of the Union side was much shorter and less eloquent than his summary of the Confederate side. Summarizing the Confederate argument, he emphasized a point which was likely to resonate with the pope and his supporters: "Those very politicians who now clamor so much against the rebellion as the greatest sin in the book are the same men who in recent years have always been among the loudest patrons and advocates of each miserable European revolution, and the most devoted friends of Kossuth, Garibaldi, and nearly every other wicked charlatan of our times." The Hungarian revolutionary Louis Kossuth had rebelled against the Austrian government. The Italian revolutionary Giuseppe Garibaldi sought to overthrow the papal government in central Italy. Pope Pius was known for his opposition to Garibaldi and other revolutionaries in Europe.[29]

Spalding's letter continued. Slavery was "a social evil" even in the minds of "good and moderate men" in the South. But the problem of slavery had not been solved, because of "the dominant Protestant religion, which with its principles founded on private judgment as opposed to authority tending rather to division than to union." If the U.S. were Catholic, then the influence of Catholicism would have led to gradual emancipation, compensating the owners and educating the former slaves for the responsibilities of freedom. But the hypocritical Protestants of the North, in their "blind fanaticism"—the same fanaticism which led them to oppose the Catholic Church—insisted on "forced abolition," even though such a sudden measure would turn the unprepared slaves loose in a racist society: "Our philanthropists of the North wish certainly to see the slaves freed, but they wish by no means to have them among themselves. They are driven out with violence, not infrequently, and left to die of hunger." Spalding's criticism of slavery was not a mere tactical concession to bolster his case against the North—the bishop was expressing a criticism of slavery which he had also included in an 1855 book against his Protestant opponents. In that book, Spalding praised his Church for "slowly and cautiously" eliminating slavery in Europe and turning the serfs into free men.[30]

Spalding proceeded with his analysis: the fanatical abolitionists, by antagonizing Southerners, had thwarted the efforts of those "wise and moderate men" in the Southern border states who worked for "a *gradual* emancipation of the slaves." In self-defense, the Confederates were forced to take arms against Northern invaders. The North was fighting a "war of confiscation of property, of violent emancipation of the Negroes, of threatened and encouraged slave insurrection, of destruction and desolation of the vast and fair territory of the South, and finally of extermination of all the whites, and perhaps at the same time also of the Negroes themselves, if the revolt can not by any other means be suppressed." One hopeful development was the 1862 election results, in which Northern voters supported the Democratic Party—or as Spalding put it, voted "against the [Lincoln] government, and in favor of the Constitution."[31]

As Spalding saw it, the Catholic hierarchy in the United States, following its habits of political non-intervention, had limited itself for the most part to praying for peace. Some bishops, however, including "my Metropolitan" (Purcell) had gone beyond this spiritual role and backed the Northern position. These warlike bishops were wrong: "The Catholic Church, as most loving mother of all, must not be an enemy of anyone, nor even seem to be so." Whether the Union was broken or restored, the Church should heal the wounds of war, not exacerbate sectional hatreds as "the sects" (Protestants) did. The dominant Protestants in the North hated the Catholics, and it was even possible that the Northern leaders wanted to "attack the Catholic religion as soon as the revolt of the South is over." Spalding added a postscript denouncing the Northern draft law for subjecting Catholic priests to conscription.[32]

Spalding's report reached a Rome which was becoming skeptical of the Northern cause. The pope and his officials supported a reunited United States, which could serve as a counterweight to the power of Great Britain, which Rome saw as a foe. Nor could Rome give unqualified support to a proslavery rebellion. On the other hand, the growing casualties and Northern setbacks led the papal government to doubt that a military solution would be effective or humane. Pope Pius had called for a negotiated solution in October 1862, a plea which went basically unheard. Now the paper from influential Spalding offered the tempting prospect of a negotiated peace and a gradual abolition of slavery. The pope and his secretary of state, Cardinal Antonelli, took notice.[33]

While Archbishop Purcell and Bishop Rosecrans were getting outmaneuvered in Rome by one of their own Kentucky bishops, they faced war weariness on the part of the people of their own state of Ohio. To many Ohio Catholics, the peace advocacy of the Protestant politician Clement Vallandigham was more congenial than the militant Unionism and abolitionism of their own archbishop and his auxiliary bishop. After General Rosecrans sent Vallandigham into the Confederacy, the state Democratic Party rallied around the ex-congressman nominating him for governor. As the October 13 elections approached, Ohio's Democratic politicians did what Vallandigham no longer could—traveled the state to speak in his behalf. While the nominee moved to the British territory of Canada West (Ontario), north of Ohio, Democratic speakers and newspapers made the case for electing the exile in order to send a strong peace message to the Lincoln administration. Vallandigham's message resonated with the Irish and German Catholics of Ohio. Traditionally Democratic in sympathy, tired of the war, resentful of the draft, fearing competition for manual labor jobs from the freed slaves, these Catholic voters were often inclined to agree with Vallandigham's critique of the war and of emancipation, rather than with the antislavery, prowar views of their spiritual shepherds.[34]

To respond to the threat of Vallandigham and to counter his appeal among Ohio

Catholics, the archdiocese went into action to support the Republican candidate, John Brough. Bishop Sylvester Rosecrans in particular worked to promote Brough among skeptical Catholic voters.[35]

In mid–July, Ohio received an unwelcome visitor in the form of John Hunt Morgan, dashing Confederate cavalry commander. Crossing Union lines, Morgan and his men rode into Indiana and thence into southern Ohio, clearing away the felled trees laid across their path by state militia under General Ambrose Burnside, commander of this part of the Union lines. They stole horses from the farms they passed and generally spread panic through the area. Boats stopped traveling the Ohio River, and authorities declared martial law in many places, including Cincinnati.

As chancellor of the Boston diocese, James Augustine Healy faced the possibility that the Irish Catholics of Boston might emulate their brethren in New York and stage riots of their own. Boston's bishop, John Fitzpatrick, was in Belgium to assist American diplomats in that country. As the highest ranking diocesan official remaining in Boston, Healy had to confront day-to-day problems such as the threatened riots.

Healy was also the first black priest ordained in the United States. He and his brothers and sisters went into the Church's service after being brought back to the ancestral religion of his white father. Rising in the ranks, Fr. Healy saw himself not as a racial champion, but as a faithful servant of the Church and its predominantly Irish Catholic faithful. The Irish Catholics, as it happened, were strongly antiblack, at a time when the Massachusetts Protestant establishment (with many of whose members Healy was on good terms) was antislavery and, to an extent, sympathetic with certain black aspirations. Healy's Irish flock had its own tensions with the Protestant establishment, not least from clashes over racial issues. But so far, the Boston Irish hadn't objected to Healy, as one of their spiritual shepherds, taking their interests in hand.

Father James Healy, who became a bishop after the Civil War (courtesy African American Collection of Maine, Jean Byers Sampson Center for Diversity in Maine, University of Southern Maine Libraries).

The Irish North End neighborhood had sent many volunteers to the war who had been killed or wounded in battle, and the inhabitants' restiveness might now deploy against the government which was demanding additional, and apparently unequal, sacrifices. "It will be strange to me," wrote Fr. Healy, "if we escape some such trouble" as was afflicting New York. Trouble indeed erupted in the North End on July

14, as a mob arose in response to a federal conscription agent trying to summon draftees. Governor John Andrew called out troops in response.[36]

Fr. Healy heard reports that two priests had denounced the conscription law in "words calculated to inflame the minds of their hearers" and that "an Irish society" meeting in a Catholic church had cheered Confederate president Jefferson Davis. Fr. Healy was not the highest-ranking diocesan official in the bishop's absence—that would be Vicar-General John Williams—but it was Healy who undertook to handle the crisis of the threatened riots.[37]

Bishop Fitzpatrick had worked out riot protocols during prewar disturbances—have priests go to trouble spots and calm down turbulent people, discourage public gatherings which might degenerate into mobs. This was not the only time the Church had sent out its ministers to soothe the storms of popular passion—clerics had helped defuse potential draft riots in Pennsylvania in the previous year, and a belated effort would be made in New York along the same lines.[38]

Fr. Healy enjoyed positions of trust as rector of the cathedral and chancellor of the diocese. His diocese's trust in him, however, did not always translate into egalitarian views on racial questions. The diocesan newspaper, the *Pilot,* though on the local level it supported sending black and white Boston children to the same schools, supported antiblack policies on the federal level. *Pilot* editorials before the war called for enforcement of the federal Fugitive Slave Act, an enactment widely deplored in Massachusetts. When the U.S. Supreme Court, presided over by the Catholic Chief Justice Roger Taney, declared that blacks could not be citizens, the *Pilot* accepted the decision "out of respect to the profound learning, distinguished abilities, and high character of the judges." This at a time when Fr. Healy, like other leaders in the diocese, was championing the citizenship rights of naturalized Irish immigrants.[39]

When the war began, the Catholic leadership in Massachusetts supported the North. The Protestant establishment in the Bay State, previously fans of the Catholic-baiting Know-Nothings, temporarily warmed to the Catholic population and its spiritual leaders.[40]

In May 1862, Bishop Fitzpatrick left the United States for Europe, supposedly to recuperate from the chronic illness which often led him to delegate duties to others, like Fr. Healy. While supposedly convalescing, Bishop Fitzpatrick stayed at the American legation in Belgium, helping represent the Union government in that largely Catholic country. With the bishop away, Fr. Healy continued his pre-existing social and political contacts with members of the local Protestant establishment.[41]

Another priest was watching Fr. Healy's efforts: Fr. Hilary Tucker, a war skeptic from Missouri who served at the cathedral and had been replaced by Fr. Healy as rector (the priest responsible for those who attended Mass at the Cathedral). In a personal diary, Fr. Tucker discussed many things which annoyed him about the priest who had replaced him. To Fr. Tucker, Fr. Healy was "very ambitious, very proud"—even rebuking ex-rectors for unspecified misconduct—and too mindful of ingratiating himself with the laity. As Bishop Fitzpatrick's stand-in, Fr. Healy mingled a good deal with the elite of wartime Boston, Catholic and WASP, including the mayor, Frederick Lincoln (probably no relation to the president). "He does not know himself," wrote Tucker. "He has too high an opinion of himself and his abilities, great as they certainly are."[42]

Fr. Tucker blamed the war on Protestant fanatics, especially in New England. The New England clergy, in his view, were "seasoned with the spirit of [Reformation Calvinist leaders] John Calvin, John Knox, and the devil; father of them all—out of which elements we have double distilled New England puritanism, the Elixir of Hell; and its citizens." In a diary entry of July 4, 1863, while the battle of Gettysburg was going on, Tucker said that every Massachusetts family had a member who was wounded or slain on that battlefield, and he denounced the "accursed puritanic abolition clergy" for applauding a speaker (Oliver Wendell Holmes, Sr.) who compared suffering in the cause of antislavery to the sufferings of Christ.[43]

For all his private posturing, Fr. Tucker was no Iago scheming against his colleague. Instead, he found some things to admire, and even formed a friendship of sorts. Fr. Healy invited Fr. Tucker along on family outings with Fr. Healy's siblings who lived in the suburb of Newton. Fr. Tucker didn't have family in Boston and was glad to tag along with his colleague's family. It may well be that Fr. Tucker's gripes about Healy were part of a more general misanthropy which he would have expressed toward a priest of any race who was in a position of authority over him.[44]

Fr. Tucker deplored the $300 exemption as making the war a "rich man's war but a poor man's fight," hitting much harder on the "poor hod-carrier" than the "rich millionare." Despite this heated rhetoric, however, Fr. Tucker was against the rioters. The Boston rioters were "most dangerous, and even criminal." Fr. Tucker and others in Boston watched to see if efforts by those like Fr. Healy could prevent a recurrence of the riots.[45]

Orestes Brownson was in an awkward position as one of the few Catholics to belong to the Republican Party. Most Catholics, lay and clerical, were Democrats. According to Brownson's own explanation, much of the blame for this situation belonged to the Republicans, or at least to many of the party's most prominent figures. Republican organs like Horace Greeley's *Tribune* often endorsed many of the pernicious "isms" of the day. The Republican New York *Times* was no better, having said that after conquering the South, the federal government should turn its attention to crushing the Catholic Church.[46] Attitudes like this, as Brownson pointed out, only confirmed Catholic voters in their opposition to the Republican Party and their loyalty to the Democrats.

Brownson, then, was fairly lonely in his role as a Catholic editor supporting the Republican Party. Brownson used his *Quarterly Review*, as well as public speaking opportunities, to promote the cause of the Union and abolition, and urging a more vigorous prosecution of the war. In 1862, he ran as a Republican for a congressional seat in New Jersey, but lost along with many Republican candidates in the Democratic resurgence of that year. Brownson also shared his advice in meetings with government officials, including President Lincoln.

Orestes Brownson, from the frontispiece of vol. I of his *Works* (Detroit: Thorndike Nourse, 1882).

Even before Lincoln's Emancipation Proclamation, Brownson broke with his own archbishop, John Hughes of New York, to demand that the abolition of slavery be added to the North's war aims. Archbishop Hughes, who supported the war but opposed abolition, had struck back at Brownson for his dissent, further isolating the editor.

Brownson had not always been for emancipation. In much of the antebellum period, he blamed the abolitionists for disturbing the peace of the country. As the war approached, Brownson changed his position, as he changed his position on many issues throughout his career, and blamed the South for trying to push slavery on the country. When war broke out he became an abolitionist. In February 1863, Brownson wrote to Senator Charles Sumner (R-MA), a leading Congressional abolitionist: "We ... are more in need of statesmanship than generalship, though much we need of both." Lincoln was well intentioned but "weak, ignorant and wrongheaded." A new Republican president was needed, but it wasn't clear who.

Slavery was not the only issue on which Brownson had changed his views over the course of his career. Throughout his life, Brownson had frequently changed his position on the most fundamental issues. At various points in his career, he had been a Protestant minister, an unbeliever, a transcendentalist, a conservative Catholic, and now a liberal Catholic. Whenever he changed his mind, however, Brownson strenuously defended his new opinion, with the same fervor as someone who had always been of the same mind.

Speaking to an enthusiastic crowd at Washington's Willard Hotel, Brownson reviewed his arguments for freeing the slaves, but he reassured his hearers that he did not support civil equality for black people. As in his *Review*, Brownson said that black people were inferior to whites and should voluntarily resettle in some foreign country or U.S. territory, where they could work out their destiny without having to "struggle against the prejudices of race."[47]

The issues of the Civil War were not the only points on which Brownson courted controversy. On the one hand, his support for a powerful papacy was highly provocative in a country skeptical of papal authority. On the other hand, Brownson, a Vermont Yankee by origin, antagonized the majority of Catholics, who were of Irish and German immigrant origin, by his demands that they assimilate into the American community.[48]

In 1863, Brownson was just recovering from some run-ins with Rome over issues such as Catholic education, the status of the territories ruled by the pope, and even the condition of the damned in hell.[49]

In Ireland, Archbishop Paul Cullen fumed about Catholic converts like Brownson. To Cullen, Brownson's *Review* had too much influence over Catholics in Ireland and England. Rome should keep this heterodox Yankee in check. Archbishop Cullen took credit for blocking Brownson from getting a professorship at a proposed Catholic university in Ireland to be run by another convert, Englishman John Henry Newman.[50]

There was evidence that Hughes was correct and that Brownson was losing his influence in America. After his conversion, his *Review* received the endorsement of many U.S. bishops. A papal emissary had commended Brownson's *Review* in a report to Rome. But as Brownson gave voice to his controversial views, he alienated many of his readers. One Catholic subscriber to his *Review* wrote him angrily, declaring that he (the subscriber) had been unsuccessfully trying to cancel his subscription. While the South had merely been trying to defend its Constitutional rights, the correspondent complained, Brownson (and Archbishop Hughes as well) was damaging and discrediting the Church's position: "You have destroyed all the good you have accomplished and the church instead of prospering will lose ground in your midst so soon as the government settles down once more into a peace." Brownson was aiding Northern fanatics by supporting the "present administration" and its unpatriotic policies. The correspondent, a physician, compared the Union government to a "patient" needing to be cured of its political condition. The situation would get better "if there was any other man at the head of the Government" than Abraham Lincoln. The correspondent signed himself "Most respectfully, Samuel A. Mudd, M.D."[51]

Not all the subscription-cancellers were as militant as Mudd—later an associate of President Lincoln's assassins. Mudd was only one of many who canceled their subscriptions, bringing Brownson and his family into a state of poverty.[52]

Undeterred, Brownson persisted in defending his new changed views. In addition to poor leadership from President Lincoln, Brownson saw disloyalty throughout the North. The source of this disloyalty was the Democratic Party. To Brownson, there was certainly such a thing as a loyal Democrat, but the mainstream of that party was under the control of disloyal elements who promoted peace with the Confederacy.[53]

Not that Brownson spared his fellow Catholics from all blame. He estimated that almost all of the Catholic journals in the country—except his own, of course—were at best of unreliable loyalty to the Union.[54]

Now that we have seen what our four protagonists were doing at a crisis point of the Civil War, it is time to go back to the mid-1840s, when these four men all converted to the Catholic faith. A soldier, a student, an ex-slave, and a spiritual pilgrim entered the American Catholic Church just as the Church and the country were about to encounter grave issues which threatened to split both down the middle. Our four converts were almost immediately thrown into this maelstrom.

2

The End of Religious Controversy

Leaving the dominant Protestant religion and culture of the mid–19th century United States and exchanging it for the unpopular and suspect Catholic Church was not an easy thing. Converts did not act from a desire for popularity. A convert needed to be convinced of the truth of the Catholic faith, and have the courage and perhaps, stubbornness to hold to his faith in the face of antagonism. William Rosecrans showed these characteristics of courage and stubbornness even in his early, Protestant years, and his stubborn and proud nature would have only been reinforced by tales of his ancestors.

William Rosecrans's family had something of a warrior tradition in Norway and Denmark. One Erik, the son of Niels Iversen, is said to have received a rose wreath from the pope in 1325. Erik copied the wreath onto his coat of arms and named himself "Rosenkrantz," meaning "rose wreath."[1]

One Harman Hendrik Rosenkrants left Bergen, Norway for New York in the mid–17th century. A descendant, Daniel Rosenkrans, was born in Pennsylvania in 1737. In the American Revolution, Daniel became a captain, fighting in Pennsylvania's Wyoming Valley. Both Daniel and his wife had had harrowing escapes from hostile Indians. A child, also named Daniel, was born to them in 1773. Official documents began listing the family name as "Rosecrans." Daniel then married Thankful Wilcox, and in 1808 moved to the new state of Ohio. Daniel acquired a farm in Delaware County in the center of the state, and in addition to farming worked as a physician.[2]

Dr. Daniel Rosecrans was a Universalist, believing that all humans go to heaven. His wife Thankful was a Methodist. Thankful agreed to let the doctor's fellow universalists meet in their house in exchange for the doctor extending hospitality to Methodist circuit riders when they came by. One of the doctor's sons, the young Crandall Rosecrans (b. 1794) served in the War of 1812 under General William Henry Harrison, ending the war as a captain. In 1816, Crandall married Jemima Hopkins, who was related to Samuel Hopkins, a Rhode Island patriot who had signed the Declaration of Independence. The newlyweds soon had a son, Chauncey, who died in infancy. In 1819, another son, William Starke, was born.[3]

The family lived in a rural part of Delaware County—so rural that the young William could hear the prolonged howling of wolves. When William was two, Crandall moved from the family farm to a new farm in what became Homer, Ohio, in neighboring Licking County. Here Crandall worked as a storekeeper and tavern owner as well as a farmer, and found time to run a potash factory. William was joined by three younger brothers, the youngest of whom was Sylvester, born in 1827. William helped out in his father's store, as well as clerking in other area stores. He already showed signs that he was going places, as another clerk later recalled.[4]

Later, at West Point, William would write about his family: "I have a mother who loves me well. A father whose fortune is his father's blessing, his own hands and my good mother. Father is strong-willed, self reliant man who is popular and well respected in spite of his 'iron will' and hot temper." Those who came to know William would recognize him in his description of his father.[5]

There was later a remarkable uncertainty as to whether William had ever been baptized. In 1886 William wrote to the Rev. L. W. Mulhane, who was compiling an account of William's career, about "a vague tradition" that "a Protestant or Wesleyan Methodist minister" had baptized the infant William, at Thankful's insistence.[6]

William had an early fascination with military matters, perhaps not surprising given the numerous soldiers among his ancestors, whose exploits would likely have been recounted by Crandall, himself a veteran. William organized the neighbor boys and his own younger brothers into a pretend army company, and led his troops into battle with cornstalk weapons. He developed a personal motto, "Lick not get licked."[7]

William went sporadically to school, but he had a great deal of what we now call home schooling, studying under his father's guidance and also on his own initiative. With paternal encouragement, he learned arithmetic and algebra, borrowing books from a local school and from neighbors. He memorized the Declaration of Independence at age 6—learning the text from a copy on the wall of the house. Crandall was a fan of the military hero General Andrew Jackson, and William caught the enthusiasm, learning about the battle of New Orleans, Jackson's famous triumph over the British.[8]

One book William borrowed from a neighbor was the novel *Thaddeus of Warsaw*, by Jane Porter. After borrowing the lengthy book, he became ill. So William spent his illness reading the book. Taken up in the story, he was disappointed to find that the last few pages were missing. After getting his health back, he decided to earn enough money to get a complete copy of his own. He worked in his father's store for three months so that he could buy and finish the novel.[9]

The novel which so inspired William was full of adventurous scenes likely to appeal to an adolescent boy. It also set forth Thaddeus as a moral exemplar, and William later showed many of the same attitudes as that of Porter's protagonist.

The title character, Thaddeus Sobieski, was based on Tadeusz Kościuszko, a Polish volunteer in the American Revolution who later fought a last-ditch, vain effort to keep his own country free. Like Kościuszko, Thaddeus takes up arms for his country's freedom at the beginning of the book, is defeated, and goes into exile. While struggling in poverty, Thaddeus risks his freedom to save a fellow exile, saves the life of a woman and her child, and rescues a wife from a brutal husband. Porter's story is specifically intended to portray the protagonist, based on the admired Kościuszko, as a model of virtue. As Porter put it, Kościuszko showed "neither pride nor vanity" while successful, and when fortune turned against him "the weakness of passion, never sinks the dignity of his fortitude, neither does the firmness of that virtue, blunt the amiable sensibility of his heart."[10]

Like Kościuszko, Thaddeus in the novel combines military and civic virtues, fighting as a noble and chivalrous Christian warrior. One character (Thaddeus's half-brother) praises him in these terms: "Though deprived of the splendor of command; though the eager circle of friends no longer cluster round him; though a stranger in this country, and without a home.... I see the heir of a princely house, who, when mankind have deserted him, is yet encompassed by his virtues."[11]

The novel contrasts Thaddeus's Christian virtues with the corruptions of a modern world which discards Christianity in favor of modern doctrines—doctrines of the perfectibility of mankind and a limited or irrelevant sovereignty of God. Such notions lead people to abandon morality. "By such gradations," wrote Porter, "the progress of depravity is accomplished." Christianity, not arrogant modern humanistic ideas, develops humility and "upright character." Porter was a Protestant who referred casually to "papist[s]" and "monkish beadsmen," but her critique of modern civilization echoed that of many Catholics.[12]

At 15, William got a job with a storekeeper named George Arnold. The intellectually curious William impressed others. He chauffeured a prominent attorney, T. W. Barkley, to the state capital of Columbus. Barkley was impressed by William's intelligence and knowledge, and urged him to pursue a higher education. William talked the matter over with his father, but prospects appeared limited. The Rosecrans family didn't have the resources to send William to college, so another option presented itself. Intelligent young men—if they could get political sponsors—could receive an education at the military academy at West Point, New York, courtesy of the taxpayer.[13]

In a country living in the shadow of Andrew Jackson and a suspicion of anything that looked antidemocratic, West Point struck many opponents as the nursery of an American aristocracy. To supporters, the academy was a training ground for excellent military leaders. And because it had a strong engineering curriculum—one of the few schools in the country to teach the subject—graduates often had civilian careers with private companies who needed engineering skills.[14]

Young William first approached Alexander Harper, the local congressman. He walked fifty miles to keep his appointment with Harper, who offered to help if William could provide evidence of his academic and physical fitness and moral character. William did this, but his application was delayed as Harper sought a place at the academy for his own son. Eventually Harper forwarded the application materials, but by this time William had grown impatient. William wrote directly to Joel R. Poinsett, the secretary of war. Poinsett agreed that William would make a good cadet, and got him admission to the academy on condition that he passed the entrance exam. After some exam preparation at nearby Kenyon College, William passed the test and was admitted to West Point. The new cadet was admitted in 1838, as a member of the Class of 1842.[15]

From the very beginning, cadets were subject to a strict regimen. The equivalent of freshman orientation was an encampment in the field where the new cadets, under the not-always-benevolent supervision of the upperclassmen, lived in tents and underwent military drills in their new gray uniforms. After this introduction to the military life, the new academy students moved into their spartan dormitories—iron bedsteads had just been introduced—and began their formal training. Cadets rose early to study, going in to breakfast at 7:00 a.m.

They marched into their classrooms at 8:00 a.m. and had class until 4:00, with a lunch break at 1. Then it was drill until sunset. Instruction was in various subjects—mathematics, French, ethics, chemistry, mineralogy and geology, natural and experimental philosophy (physical sciences), drawing, civil and military engineering and the art of war, and practical military engineering.[16]

William's most important instructor at the academy was Dennis Mahan, professor of civil and military engineering and the art of war. Mahan was a son of Irish Catholic immigrants, though his father had converted to Episcopalianism and raised him in that faith. Mahan was a stern instructor who was respected and feared, rather than loved, by most of his students. Through his classes, and through his considerable influence over the academy's curriculum, Mahan insisted on cadets getting academically rigorous instruction. He made sure his students learned how to build fortifications and defensive lines—he would write a widely used textbook on the subject.[17]

To Mahan, as he later put it, America was a "warlike" country, but "the least military" of "the civilized states of Christendom." Properly trained officers could change that, serving as commanders in victorious campaigns to spread American influence and territory. Winning required more than skill in building fortifications, thought Mahan; it required the ability to wage offensive war. Having studied in France, Mahan was a fan of the military campaigns of Napoleon Bonaparte. Like the emperor, Mahan advocated going on the offensive by waging a war of movement and "carrying the war into the heart of the assailant's country." In one respect, Mahan disagreed with the Corsican general: to Mahan, offensive operations and the seizure of territory could be done with minimal casualties. With flanking moves and deception, with the use of good intelligence gathering and the denial of intelligence to the enemy, with adaptation to fluid battlefield conditions, Mahan believed a good general could outmaneuver and defeat the enemy without the massive bloodshed associated with the Napoleonic wars. "*To do the greatest damage to our enemy with the least exposure to ourselves*, is a military axiom lost sight of only by ignorance to the true ends of victory," Mahan wrote. Mahan's ideal was of troops led by "a bold, energetic, but prudent leader," which was the kind of officer he wanted to produce through his training.[18]

William absorbed Mahan's teachings, not only in class but in an extracurricular Napoleon Club for which Mahan recruited his best students. William was of this superior group. Mahan's select cadet study circle studied the campaigns of the professor's favorite general, and they tried out their principles during the summer encampments, when classroom recitations gave place to field exercises. William also, through Mahan's influence, commenced a lifelong study of Napoleon's campaigns and those of another famous military leader, Frederick the Great, king of Prussia.[19]

Also influential in William's life at West Point were his classmates, mainly fellow members of the class of 1842. One of his roommates was a Southerner named James Longstreet, a fun-loving cadet popular with his fellows. Longstreet was almost as low in his academic rankings as William was elevated. And Longstreet's exuberant behavior frequently got him demerits, in contrast to the straight-arrow William. The academy regulated the behavior of students, punishing them for such behavior as slovenly dress or maintaining facial hair—the latter regulation did not have a long-lasting effect on these future Civil War officers. Cadets were also punished—if they were caught—for smoking, card playing, drinking, or going to an off-campus tavern to escape the wretched school food. Missing Sunday chapel was also punishable.[20]

One incident which could have gotten William in trouble involved a quarrel over a lady—another cadet challenged him to a duel over the issue. As the challenged party, William could choose the method of dueling, and he chose pistols at six paces. The other cadet blanched at this highly risky procedure and backed down. William had carried his point with courage and boldness.[21]

For the first-year cadets, official discipline was supplemented by hazing ("devilment") on the part of the upperclassmen. Formally forbidden, hazing was nevertheless a part of the West Point experience. The pranks of sadistic upperclassmen went from insults to mock capital trials, and occasional assaults. As an upperclassman, William played a trick on a younger cadet named Ulysses Grant, telling him he had to abandon his position guarding a pump. Many graduates recalled their hazing experience as a useful if informal training in how to adapt to unexpected challenges.[22]

For one cadet, however, the "devilment" he received was not welcome then or later. Julius Garesché, who was a year ahead of William, was of French heritage and had been born in Cuba. His father was Protestant and his mother was Catholic. His parents' marriage contract stipulated that Julius was to be raised Protestant, but while attending Catholic Georgetown University, Garesché decided to accept his mother's faith rather than his father's. His father gave Garesché and his brothers permission to join the Church, and his father would himself join the Church on his deathbed.[23]

Coming to West Point in 1837, Garesché received his traditional hazing as a plebe, with the special bonus of being singled out for his Catholic faith. As time went on, though, Garesché won respect from his classmates for his sincerity and piety. Reportedly the faculty gave Julius special leave to observe his Easter duty—according to William's later recollection, the only cadet to be given such permission. In his last year as a cadet, the faculty appointed Julius as an instructor in French, in which he was fluent.[24] William and Julius appear to have befriended each other, even though William was a year behind Garesché. Friendship with a sincere and committed Catholic, who patiently endured and overcame the hardship of being in a minority religion, would certainly have affected William. The unpopularity of Catholicism at West Point was in many ways a reflection of the hostility of the dominant Protestant culture, and was a warning sign to anyone contemplating a career as an officer that joining the Church was not a very good career move.

In 1842, William graduated fifth in his class. His class standing entitled him to choose which part of the army he would serve in, and William chose the Corps of Engineers. He also chose Ann Elizabeth Hegeman, a girl from a prominent New York family whom he began courting. Ann herself was the daughter of Judge Adrian Hegeman. William met Ann at a graduation party, and determined to seek her hand, which would prove to be a year-long quest.[25]

His first assignment after graduation was Fortress Monroe, Virginia, as the engineering officer responsible for supervising the building of harbor works at Hampton Roads. After about a year of this, he came back to West Point as a professor, teaching engineering and "philosophy" (physical sciences) and working as a quartermaster and commissary for the school. Mahan's influence can probably be detected here—William ended up as the first assistant professor of engineering, assisting Mahan himself. Accompanying his new position was a new rank—First Lieutenant Rosecrans proceeded to instruct the new generation of cadets.[26]

As William courted Ann, she urged him to focus more seriously on religion. William wrote Ann in 1842 that his "religious feelings are daily changing?, becoming broader [and] deeper," adding, "I do not, and perhaps I shall never belong to any Christian sect." If Ann was concerned that William was not going to take spiritual matters seriously, she need not have worried. Indeed, his growing religious preoccupation was taking him in directions she might not like. Writing Ann in 1843, William said that "my mind grows daily more and more Catholic." In Episcopal terminology, "Catholic" could mean High Church, a movement within Episcopalianism itself for greater liturgical traditionalism. If this was William's meaning, his Catholic tendencies soon moved him further, toward the real thing. His marriage to Ann, though, was in the Episcopal Church, being solemnized in New York City's St. Paul's Episcopal Chapel.[27]

William's spiritual discontent was not appeased. He became convinced that God existed and had revealed Himself, but which of the various religions had received the fullness of the divine revelation? Of the religious groups making claim on mankind's spiritual allegiance, which one was the true Christian church? William reconstructed his spiritual quest in 1863, during his late night conversations with James Garfield at his military headquarters. From a perspective of nearly twenty years, William remembered his prayerful searching in the mid–1840s. Could an "authorized supernatural teacher" be found among the Protestants, in the Orthodox Church, or with the Catholics? William prayed for guidance: "When I knelt down, I felt ashamed, and thought quite likely I was a damned fool, but then I remembered it was one of the experiments and so I prayed on, though it seemed to me no more than talking to a stick or stump."[28]

It was around his time as a professor, according to a later account by his daughter Anita, that William met an elderly Irishman who was traveling the country selling books and papers. He sold William a lengthy work of Catholic apologetics called *The End of Religious Controversy*. Said the officer-professor: "I've read about every religion but the Catholic & I believe I'll investigate that for a change."[29]

John Milner, the author of *The End of Religious Controversy*, was a priest and bishop in England, involved in the struggles of the Church in the United Kingdom. Milner helped secure a close semblance of equal rights for Catholics in Great Britain and Ireland, achieved in 1829, three years after his death. *The End of Religious Controversy* was one of the numerous books, tracts, and articles published by the contentious churchman, and was aimed at replying to Protestant criticism of the Catholic Church.[30]

The Protestant critics against whom Milner's book was aimed raised the points which were common in anti–Catholic circles—that Catholics worshipped Mary and the saints, they were subversively undermining the authority of governments, they violated religious freedom, they disregarded the Bible, and so on. Milner tackled these accusations with verve.

Catholics did not reject the Bible, Milner said, but upheld "the Bible and tradition, taken together." The traditions of the Church, and the declarations of popes and Church councils, established the proper interpretation of scripture and tradition. Just as the secular law had its authorized interpreters, "judges and magistrates," so did scripture and divine law have its authorized interpreters in the Church.[31] The Church's decisions on religious questions were like secular courts' decisions on legal questions.

In contrast to Catholics, who could get authoritative guidance from their Church on questions involving their faith, Protestants were left adrift, on the pretext that every Christian could interpret the Bible for himself. This Protestant approach "has always produced endless and incurable dissentions, and of course errors; for truth is one, while errors are numberless."[32]

The Catholic Church, said Milner, "still constitutes *the main stock of Christianity.*" It has "endured and overcome the persecutions and heresies of eighteen centuries." To this day, God continued to perform miracles confirming the divine nature of the Church; "fresh miracles of a recent date continue to be proved with the highest degree of evidence." Despite Protestant cavils, there were verified instances of miracles performed by the likes of St. Francis Xavier and other missionaries who had spoken in tongues and even raised the dead.[33]

Milner enumerated the numerous European countries in which Catholicism prevailed "notwithstanding the revolutionary persecution which which the Catholic religion has endured and is enduring." Africa, the Middle East, and Asia were full of Catholics. Latin America was a Catholic region, and Louisiana and Canada had large Catholic areas. There was no single Protestant sect which was so spread out through the world, validating St. Augustine's remark that "there are heretics every where, but not the same heretics every where."[34]

To Milner, Protestantism had not arisen from a renewed zeal for Christianity, but "in consequence of the politics of princes and statesmen, the avarice of the nobility and gentry, and the irreligion and licentiousness of the people." Yet Protestants pretended that their movement was the revival of a purer Christianity![35]

Concerning the saints, Milner deplored the "misrepresentation" of the Church's stance. Catholics did not worship saints. In seeking the intercession of the saints, Catholics were "merely honoring those *whom God honors.*" If we can ask for the prayers of the living, we can ask for the prayers of the saints in Heaven.[36]

Regarding religious persecution, Milner allowed that the civil governments in some Catholic countries had persecuted heretics as a matter of state, but he said this was not required by Church doctrine. The Church herself did not execute heretics—when it turned convicted heretics to the civil authorities for punishment, it did so with a recommendation of pardon. Modern Catholic states allowed liberty to Protestants—the pope himself received Protestant visitors. In those historical circumstances when Catholic authorities had repressed heretics, the heretics were dangerous rebels and criminals. Under Queen Mary—the 16th-century monarch whose burning of Protestants was seared into the historical consciousness of the English—the Protestants had preached rebellion against the government. But even so, Queen Mary should have acted differently: "Still, I grant, persecution was not the way to diminish the number or the violence of the enthusiastic insurgents." The last Catholic king of England, James II, tried to end persecution of Catholics and many Protestants but "lost his crown in the cause of toleration." a riposte to Protestants, to whom the "Glorious Revolution" overthrowing James II in 1688 was widely seen as a victory over Catholic tyranny. Milner turned around the Protestants' persecution accusations and enumerated example after example of Protestants persecuting Catholics—and other Protestants. The Protestants were not such champions of religious freedom as they pretended! Protestant persecution was worse than the Catholic variety, anyway, said Milner, since Catholics acted in defense of their "*ancient religion*" against "incalculable disorders, and sanguinary contests," while Protestants "persecuted in behalf of *new systems*," oppressing those who held to the old faith as well as mistreating fellow Protestants—persecuting those who allegedly read the Bible the wrong way, contradicting the supposed Protestant principle of letting people interpret the Bible for themselves.[37]

One of Milner's arguments seemed particularly suited to William's concerns. While non–Catholics are "*carried about by every wind of doctrine*," Milner wrote, Catholics "never experience any apprehension whatsoever" concerning "the road they are in." Catholics, especially converts from Protestantism, experienced "peace and security" rather than their previous "doubts and fears." Further, "great numbers of Protestants" joined the Catholic Church on their deathbeds, while Protestants had not been able to show any examples of Catholics concerting to Protestantism while their death impended.[38]

William may have been able to talk about his concerns with George Deshon, his fellow graduate who had also obtained a professorship at West Point. Deshon went on to convert and to be a prominent Paulist priest, so his conversation would have been interesting. But Deshon was not a Catholic yet. Around this time, William sought out someone who *was* Catholic—his friend Julius Garesché. The newly commissioned officer, who graduated a year ahead of William, was now an officer with Company K of the 4th Artillery. From July to November 1842, Garesché served at Fortress Monroe, probably at the time when William had newly been sent there. This would have been an excellent opportunity for the two to renew their friendship, and possibly discuss spiritual matters.[39]

William Rosecrans as an engineering officer (digital image © **Big Walnut Area Historical Society, reprinted by permission**).

Garesché was sent to Fort McHenry in Baltimore. According to Julius's son and biographer Louis, William came to Fort McHenry in 1843 on a visit. As Louis wrote much later, William "had a conversation with Julius on some points of the [Catholic] Religion that he did not fully comprehend, and was given by [Julius] such a plain and satisfactory explanation that his doubts were dispelled and his ignorance entirely removed."[40] This later account by a loyal son may have exaggerated the role Julius played in William's conversion, but the influence of William's pious friend would have been considerable.

William finally decided to join the Catholic

Church in 1845. There was one difficulty, in that it wasn't clear if he had ever been baptized. The Catholic Church insists on baptism for those who join her, but she does not allow anyone to be baptized twice, which would be a sacrilege. A common practice in the American Catholic Church was to baptize American converts *sub conditione,* that is, preceding the ceremony with the phrase "if thou art not yet baptized," so that the convert was getting baptized only if he needed to be. Such was the course adopted in William's case, as he recalled later to Fr. Mulhane.[41]

Questions concerning ultimate things were forced on William and Ann ("Anne" as he spelled her name). In 1845, they had a son, William, who died shortly after birth. A similar tragedy befell another son, James Addison. If anything could concentrate a mourning father's attention on matters of life and death, this would.[42]

In May 1846, Congress declared war on Mexico. Rather than sending him to the front, William's superiors assigned him to engineering work in various cities, supervising the building of harbors in Virginia and Rhode Island—and earning a reputation for garrulity on religious matters—while his former roommate James Longstreet was winning renown serving in combat under Generals Zachary Taylor and Winfield Scott. William's brother Henry also served in the war. In Newport, Rhode Island, William used his engineering skills to help build St. Mary's Church in the city. Bishop Fitzpatrick of Boston, whose diocese included Newport, referred to William as "Lieut. Rosecranz a very pious convert." Milo Hascall was more hostile, calling William a "crank" who talked excessively about religion. "No night was ever so dark and tempestuous, that he would not brave the tempestuous seas of Newport Harbor to attend Mass."[43]

Meanwhile, by mid–1846, Anne Rosecrans had become very ill. It is not clear if this sickness was connected with the stress of her husband's religious change, or the death of her children, or both, though there were certainly conflicting pressures on her from William on one hand and her Episcopalian mother on the other. During her illness, she had visions of hell. Whatever the content of her visions, they inspired her to join her husband in the Catholic Church, becoming in her way as much a zealot as William. When she thought herself on the verge of death, she sent messages to her relatives and friends urging them to consider the Church, too.[44] Anne survived, and so did her religious influence, as shown by the case of her brother-in-law Sylvester.

3

"I have the responsibilities, he the virtues"

William Pursues His Brother

Religious matters continued to trouble the Rosecrans family. William's younger brother Sylvester, after a great deal of inner conflict, followed his beloved brother William into the Catholic Church, where he grew in the faith and ultimately stepped out of William's shadow as he embarked on a clerical career.

Still a Protestant, Sylvester was enrolled in 1843 in Kenyon College, an Episcopal institution in Gambier, Ohio. Sylvester seems to have done very well at Kenyon, possibly being in the top of his class. But he was not necessarily very religious at the time he enrolled. Writing to William in June 1843, Sylvester asked, "Is there a God?" "I seek truth" about religion, Sylvester added, "and you [William] are my only intimate." Sylvester wrote William from the college in January 1846 to express his shock at his brother's conversion: "There was the overturning of so many of my own opinions derived from you," Sylvester confessed, "prejudices (perhaps ignorant and presumptuous)" against the "deadly practical errors in the Roman Branch of the Church, which I have been taught were there, are deep-rooted & to disturb them makes my whole moral being rock to & fro."[1]

Suffering from the illness during which she ended up joining the Church, William's wife Anne wrote to Sylvester, begging her brother-in-law to follow her husband and herself to the Church of Rome. Responding to his sister-in-law's plea, a troubled Sylvester wrote to William. Asking after Anne's health, he said he had been "astonished" and "deeply affected" by her plea. "It seemed to me that the net in which I am being drawn towards 'what is now called the Catholic Church' is strengthening and closing around me before I can see by whose hands it is drawn."[2]

William persistently pressed Sylvester to join the Church but Sylvester was not ready. His desire for secular achievement warred with his spiritual impulses. He was repelled by the fact that "the generality of mankind did little more than obtain what they could eat and drink, or at most, enjoyed; the pleasures of travelling, of society, of music, of magazines and poetry reading—in short of the senses—I thought to find some other way." He thought that seeking greatness was the route to a higher sort of life. Sylvester gave a Junior Speech to his fellow Kenyon students on the importance of this quest for greatness. He appears to have contemplated a political career.

Not yet persuaded that the Catholic Church was for him, Sylvester still had a "Protestant respect" for "the white-robed army of [Catholic] martyrs." Someone (likely William) sent him "my first Catholic book," a volume by 18th-century English bishop Richard Challoner (possibly Challoner's *Grounds of Catholic Doctrine*). Sylvester read the book, but only when nobody else could see him do so. Hiding the book in a drawer of his college room, Sylvester feared that his roommate might find it. "The proofs ... of the truth of the Catholic religion multiplied upon me until finally I believed in its authority before I was instructed in its doctrines." Trying to avoid the pull toward the Church, Sylvester tried to find consolation in "sensual gratifications" and the "company" of others, the sort of pleasure-loving people who had previously disgusted him. William kept sending him letters pressing the claims of the Church, but "I received [the] letters with a pang, read them hastily, answered them with labor and forgot them as soon as possible." "Old Rector Smith" pressed him to be baptized and confirmed, but "his address froze me" and Sylvester refused. He was in anguish: "Here I have waited a year; am I going to wait until my death? I sat up very late that night and felt very unhappy."[3]

On William's invitation, Sylvester came to West Point in summer 1846 to visit. Sylvester met William, Anne, Anne's mother, and some of the officers and their relatives. "My shackles, one by one, dropped off. The things I used to love grew dimmer in my remembrance." Sylvester read a book by the priest Martin Spalding (future bishop of Louisville and the Rosecrans brothers' future adversary) giving a Catholic view of the German Reformation. He also read part of a history of the Reformation in England. William had probably suggested these works.[4]

Sylvester made his last visit to an Episcopal church. The week after that, William persuaded him to attend Mass at the Catholic Church near the academy. Sylvester didn't particularly know what was happening during the Mass, his knowledge of the Church being mainly theoretical. He did not see the Elevation of the Host, but bowed with he saw others doing so. He kept going to Mass. "I continued to read Catholic books a little, though I considered it really a bore, and to hear William talk."[5]

After the brothers had bathed in a nearby river, William suggested that Sylvester was ready to be baptized. This made Sylvester reflect (as he said later) that "if I have to choose between Religion and no Religion, I will take Religion." He agreed to be baptized—"the die was cast." William said, "what ever other prayers you say, I would like to have you say the Hail Mary," which Sylvester got on his knees and did. At Mass that day, Fr. Villani "asked me some eight or nine questions." That afternoon, Fr. Villani baptized Sylvester, hastily recruiting a "Mr. Phalen and [a] Mrs. Lawson" as godparents. Sylvester did not feel a sense of spiritual exultation at the baptism (or so he reflected two years later, in his then mood of self-reproach). Interestingly, after Sylvester's death, William remembered being the godfather, with his wife Anne as the godmother. This mistake may reflect William and Anne's great influence over Sylvester, as opposed to the actual godparents whom Sylvester does not seem to have seen much afterwards.[6]

The Priesthood Pursues Sylvester

In 1845, Sylvester transferred to St. John's College, a Jesuit institution in New York later to become Fordham University. The course work was largely a repeat of that at Kenyon, giving Sylvester time to futher consider his position some more. Walking near Long Island Sound one day, Sylvester felt revulsion toward his habits and associates. He threw away the tobacco he was carrying and gave up that weed. "I was exceedingly disgusted with my companions. They were so young and so boyish."[7]

The Jesuit fathers at St. John's gave spiritual advice, and Sylvester began to think of the priesthood. This would mean giving up his political ambitions, taking on a humble and obscure life of service in some remote location, and suffering the indignity of "my equals ... pass[ing] me by as their inferior[,] as an unknown individual!" Yet serving as a priest would help him escape the "insignificance," "stillness" and "nonelessness" of life. Writing in the third person, he wrote: "when friends are falling around him like autumn leaves and the fondly cherished hope of years is faded forever, he can twine his bleeding heartstrings about the one object above, and still triumphantly hope."[8]

Returning to West Point for the Christmas holiday, Sylvester made his confession and took his first Holy Communion in the chapel. He later reflected on the "tepidity" he felt at the time. On New Year's of 1847, William impressed his brother by giving up a round of social calls with an old professor when he learned Mass would be celebrated nearby—William wrote a note of apology and went to Mass instead.[9]

During a walk near the Hudson, William "cautiously" broached the subject of Sylvester entering the priesthood. Sylvester replied that he did want to be a priest and had already written his parents for permission. William rejoiced, and their parents agreed to Sylvester's plan. Returning to St. John's, Sylvester did well enough to be selected to give the commencement address, what Sylvester later called "my never-to-be-forgotten speech," whose favorable reception left him "intoxicated with vanity."[10]

After graduation, Sylvester went with his brother on a retreat, a Jesuit practice by which members of the order, and sympathetic laypeople, were led through a period of prayer and reflection based on the spiritual exercises of Ignatius Loyola, Reformation-era founder of the order. Inviting the Rosecranses seems to have been the idea of Jesuit Priest Augustus Thebaud with the idea of persuading Sylvester to be a Jesuit priest. Sylvester was as usual impressed by what he saw as William's superior piety. Said Sylvester admiringly, "He had a mind to sieze [sic] upon the vast principles of Religion[,] to penetrate its sublime maxims, and the strength and steadiness of nerve to apply them unflinchingly to himself, more necessary for me perhaps than it was for him."[11]

Sylvester disappointed Fr. Thebaud by refusing to become a Jesuit, though he "concluded anew" to pursue the priesthood outside the order (priests can belong to religious orders or they can be "secular," living in the world without affiliation with an order). Sylvester noted that he had "a great repugnance to living in N.Y. and to becoming a Jesuit also." He did not elaborate, but potentially relevant was the fact that, of all the Catholic religious orders, the Jesuits were the most hated and suspected in the Protestant world. Many Catholics were suspicious of them too, due to their perceived militancy and single-minded devotion to the pope. There were Jesuits and Jesuit institutions throughout America, and they still inspired suspicion. As an example of this climate of suspicion, the flagship newspaper of the Boston diocese, influenced by Protestant mistrust, had changed its name from *The Jesuit* to the *Boston Pilot*.[12]

Sylvester went to Ohio and made an unsuccessful attempt to convert his parents. Then he went to Cincinnati, Ohio to follow up on his choice of vocation. "And finally, I was dropped in Cincinnati at the corner of 8th and Western Row, on a rainy day in November."[13]

Conspiracy Theories and Religious Hostility

As an Ohioan, Sylvester came under the authority of Bishop John B. Purcell of the Diocese of Cincinnati, who had been bishop since 1833. The diocese was then a broad area including the states of Ohio, Kentucky, parts of the Northwest Territories, and the state of Michigan (including much of the modern Midwest). Much of this was frontier territory. The Cincinnati see retained authority over Kentucky, thus bringing the Church hierarchy in Cincinnati in contact with the spiritual affairs of a slave state.[14]

Purcell and his diocese had already acquired some fame, for good or ill, outside Catholic circles. The diocese was the subject of a Protestant conspiracy theory of Catholic subversion in America. The source of the theory was the diocese's fundraising effort. In need of money for the growing diocese, Purcell and his predecessor sought aid from Europe. From 1823 to 1869, the diocese obtained the equivalent of $120,000 from the Association for the Propagation of the Faith, a society in Lyons, France. This charitable organization was funded by the voluntary contributions of European Catholics who sought to help the Church in mission territories like the United States.[15]

The diocese obtained a lesser amount from the Society for the Propagation of the Faith of the American Missions, also known as the Leopoldine Association—about $50,000 between 1830 and 1885, much of it by 1837. The Leopoldine Association was founded in 1829 by the emperor of Austria and the king of Bavaria in response to pleas for aid from Purcell's predecessor, Edward Fenwick. Cincinnati got the lion's share of the aid, though other U.S. dioceses received some assistance also. The Leopoldine Association was headquartered in Vienna, capital of the Austrian Empire, and initially was under the auspices of the archbishop of Olmutz, who happened to be the emperor's brother. The association was named after an Austrian archduchess. Only subjects of the Austrian Empire could be members, and they were required to make prayers and weekly donations for aid to the beleaguered Church in America.[16]

The Leopoldine Association got the attention of anti–Catholics in America. To many Protestants, the involvement of the reactionary Austrian Empire, bulwark of the European monarchist status quo, in American missions was highly sinister. Catholicism was spreading in the Western territories, many of which were in the Cincinnati diocese—was this a coincidence? Protestant minister Lyman Beecher, father of Harriet Beecher Stowe, was one of those who sounded the alarm. The Beechers in general would be active against both Catholicism and slavery up to the time of the Civil War. Lyman published a popular 1835 pamphlet, *A Plea for the West,* which laid out the details of the alleged Catholic conspiracy.[17]

Beecher was already known to Catholics. In 1834, he delivered a violently anti–Catholic speech in Boston, shortly before a mob attacked and burned an Ursuline convent in nearby Charlestown, in response to a false rumor about a nun being kidnapped. The rioters were acquitted and the Massachusetts legislature never voted compensation.[18]

In his pamphlet, Beecher denied any intent to suppress American Catholics' religious freedom, and he disavowed and deplored the Charlestown riot in which he was implicated. But, said Beecher, Americans had to take action in response to dangerous Catholic designs against their country. The Leopoldine Association, said Beecher, was a device by which the Austrian emperor and his "creature," the pope, intended to send uneducated Catholic "pauper immigrants" from Europe, "like the locusts of Egypt," to settle in the lands of the American West. The conspiracy would use Catholic schools and other means to win converts and allies in the Protestant community, including the press, the bar, doctors, merchants, and unprincipled politicians seeking votes from the new immigrants. The object of the sinister conspiracy, to which the hierarchy in the Midwest was privy, was to have the duped immigrants and converts vote to undermine American institutions, uniting the state with the Catholic Church and establishing the Inquisition in the United States.[19]

As to the motive for the alleged conspiracy, Beecher cited the Austrian emperor's chief minister, Klemens von Metternich, architect of the Austrian-dominated, conservative, monarchist order of things in Europe, hated in America as a repressive reactionary. Beecher said that Europeans were growing restive under this order—reactionaries and Catholics were losing European support—and America threatened the decrepit old order in Europe. So the Catholic conspirators meant to overthrow America's free institutions.[20]

Beecher's pamphlet proved highly popular. Many Americans perceived a threat to the settlement and Americanization of the West—first from Catholics and later from an alleged Slave Power conspiracy. Lyman Beecher was not alone in warning against the Catholic menace. In articles of his own, artist-inventor Samuel Morse telegraphed his belief in a Catholic conspiracy in which the Leopoldine Association played a central role. Like Beecher, Morse said that Austria, fearing the influence of free institutions in America, had a "grand scheme" to use Catholicism for subversive purposes and subvert American liberty. Beecher and Morse were honest fanatics, and their works were highly influential, but other anti–Catholic writers trafficked in sensationalism and outright fabrications. Authors like the phony ex-nun Maria Monk made out like the bandits they sometimes were with popular accounts of lecherous monks and nuns, goings-on in the confessional, and so forth. As one magazine put it, "the abuse of the Catholics is a regular trade, and the compilation of anti–Catholic books ... has become a part of the regular industry of the country, as much as the making of nutmegs, or the construction of clocks." But thanks to Beecher and Morse, Bishop Purcell's diocese received more than its share of unwelcome Protestant attention.[21]

While faced with the bigotry of Lyman Beecher, Bishop Purcell was pleasantly surprised to find that the minister's daughter was more fair-minded toward the Church. Harriet Beecher (later Harriet Beecher Stowe) was a teacher at Cincinnati's Western Female Institute, run by her sister Catherine. A geography textbook written by Harriet was included in the curriculum. Purcell made a visit to the institute and he appreciated the establishment and Harriet's textbook. As Harriet explained: "[Purcell] spoke of my poor little geography, and thanked me for the unprejudiced manner in which I had handled the Catholic question in it." The building housing the Beecher sisters' academy would briefly be used by the diocese as a hospital in the 1850s.[22]

The Cincinnati diocese got national attention again about a year and a half after Beecher's pamphlet. The Rev. Alexander Campbell of Virginia encountered Bishop Purcell in a series of 1837 debates. Campbell argued that the Catholic Church was a false church, while Purcell replied in the Church's defense. A meeting of Cincinnatians proclaimed Campbell the winner. The proceedings of the debates were published as a lengthy book. This was one of several Catholic–Protestant debates throughout the country, held in the scholarly pugilistic manner of such discussions. Sylvester Rosecrans was headed for a diocese where the Catholic–Protestant divide in the country was particularly relevant.[23]

Sylvester Leaves for the Rome of Pio Nono

Sylvester now lived in the Cincinnati diocesan headquarters—he was "half wild," he said later. But Bishop Purcell was impressed by the new convert's potential, and decided that he should be trained for the priesthood in Rome, the capital of the Catholic world and believed to be a less hostile environment than Cincinnati. The seminary to which Sylvester was to be assigned was the College of the Propaganda. The Congregation of the Propaganda, established in the 17th century, was responsible for spreading the faith into new lands and supervising the Church in mission territories. Propaganda had jurisdiction over the American Catholic Church and nominated the American bishops the pope appointed—such as Purcell.[24]

"One dark dreary night"—December 11, 1847—Sylvester departed from Cincinnati. Purcell saw him off. Sylvester went through Indiana, where "the lights in the farmhouses vividly reminded me of home. But I did not feel discouraged." In a couple of weeks, as Christmas was approaching, Sylvester was in New Orleans, whence he took a ship to Italy. At the request of Bishop Purcell, New Orleans bishop Anthony Blanc paid for Sylvester's trip.[25]

When he left the country, Sylvester did not anticipate how much events then going on in Europe would affect Catholics in the United States. Events in contemporary European politics would reverberate over the world, as radical forces attacked and turned against a new pope who was initially sympathetic to liberal reform. The split between this pope and his potential allies would change the relations of the Church to the world, feed mutual suspicion between American Catholics and other Americans, and foment discord within the American Church itself. In the lead-up to the Civil War, these divisions heightened the mutual hostility of American Catholics and an increasingly influential Northern Protestant movement of social reform—a movement which was at the center of the crusade against slavery.

Yet the whole thing started on a hopeful note, with Americans showering praise on the new Pope Pius IX. The end of 1847, when Sylvester left the United States, was a time of American optimism about Pius IX, known affectionately (or otherwise) to many Italians as "Pio Nono." A good deal of liberal and nationalist hope focused on the former Giovanni Maria Mastai-Ferretti, bishop of Imola in the Papal States. Since succeeding to the See of Peter in 1846, Pope Pius went in a different direction than did his conservative, or even reactionary, predecessor, Gregory XVI. The popes ruled a broad swathe of central Italy known as the Papal States—one of several countries into which the Italian peninsula was then divided.

In his capacity as ruler of the Papal States, Pope Gregory had faced down revolutionaries, blocked proposals for reform, governed through priests, and even stopped the building of railways (in order to protect local craftsmen from competition from imported goods). Gregory was seen as a symbol of opposition to the modern world. Pius, in contrast, granted amnesty to political prisoners and exiles, started railway construction, stopped requiring the Jews of Rome to attend annual Christian sermons, and began allowing a limited role for laypeople in the administration of the Papal States. An Italian patriot, Pius wished a benediction upon his homeland; "O Lord God, bless Italy," he said in a moment of enthusiasm. Pius's example inspired liberal nationalists throughout the European continent to fight against the conservative—and in some cases foreign—regimes which ruled them. Many Italian nationalists, like the priest Vincenzo Gioberti, envisioned the pope as the head of a federation of all the countries of then divided Italy.[26]

Across the Atlantic, Americans hoped that their Revolution would inspire other peoples, including the Italians, to embark on their own national liberation movements. The pope appeared to be an excellent candidate to bring the spirit of 1776 to the Italians—he was basically viewed as George Washington in a fancier hat. On November 29, shortly before Sylvester left on his journey, a convention of New York notables and thousands of people met in the Broadway Tabernacle, filling the building to capacity, to pass a resolution of support for the new pope. The sponsors of the meeting signed a resolution supporting Pius. The resolution proclaimed that "the noble attitude of Pius IX, is in entire harmony with the spirit of that universal Christian Church, whose mission on the face of the earth has ever been to elevate man, to sustain the oppressed, and to humanize the oppressor." The numerous signatories included editor Horace Greeley and Reform Rabbi Max Lilienthal.[27]

Bishop John Hughes of New York appeared by invitation, basking in this unusual demonstration of support from the Protestant (and Jewish) communities. New York mayor William Brady praised the pope's "efforts for the regeneration of his people." Others praising Pius as a champion of Italian nationalism were former president Martin van Buren, Secretary of State (and presidential aspirant) James Buchanan, and Benjamin Butler (Massachusetts politician and future Civil War general). Rallies elsewhere in the country, as well as praise in the press, identified the pope with the liberation of Italy and the overthrow of Italy's Austrian oppressors (who occupied the northern part of the peninsula and influenced many of Italy's states).[28]

At Frascati

Sylvester's activities in the first half of 1848 are hard to follow. It appears that, rather than go directly to Rome, he went to Frascati, twelve miles southeast of Rome, where he carried out spiritual exercises preparatory to moving to the College of the Propaganda. In June 1848 he started a journal, which initially focused on his spiritual experiences in Frascati and recollections of his conversion. Recounting his conversion story, he retrospectively praised his brother's constantly pestering him to join the Church. Sylvester had found such pressure quite annoying at the time, but now he said: "Thank God for inspiring [William] with such perseverance!" "I have the responsibilities, he the virtues," sighed the jealous brother.[29]

Political turmoil was roiling the Papal States, and indeed all Europe. Throughout

Europe, partially inspired by Pope Pius's reformism, liberals and nationalists rose up against established governments. Klemens von Metternich, the Austrian minister who sought to maintain the reactionary status quo in Europe, grumbled that he had planned for everything except a liberal pope. The Hungarians rose up against Austria, the Germans rose up against their various principalities or demanded that their rulers support their national cause, the French overthrew King Louis-Phillippe, Chartists in England marched in London, and Irish rebels attacked British power. In Italy, liberal and radical nationalists began agitating for political changes in the various countries, from Piedmont, Parma, Modena, Tuscany, and the Austrian provinces in the north; to Naples in the south—with the Papal States in the middle. The king of Piedmont, Charles Albert, went to war with Austria in hopes of driving the hated Austrians out of the Italian territories of Lombardy and Venetia. Throughout the Italian peninsula, nationalistic Italians cheered on the war and in some cases sought to join it.[30]

In the Papal States, many of the people cheering on Pope Pius's reforms wanted the pontiff, as an Italian patriot, to become the head of an Italian Confederation and join the war against the Austrians. Pope Pius had a conflicting perspective which put him at odds with the Italian nationalists. Possessed of a worldwide vision which went beyond Italy to the Catholic fold throughout the world, the pope incurred criticism from nationalist-minded Roman politicians for a lack of single-minded attention to the crisis facing the Italian peninsula. In the words of historian Owen Chadwick, Pius's "cabinet ministers said that they could not get near him to get vital decisions out of him about the affairs of State, because he was closeted with an official from the Curia [roughly, the Papal cabinet] to discuss the disciplinary case of some monk or nun in America." Pius, who had gone on a diplomatic assignment to Chile before himself becoming pope, had a strong concern for the affairs of the universal Church outside his own country, even in the far-off western hemisphere.[31]

A pope who wanted to be a truly catholic—universal—leader was not going to head a political movement focused solely on a single country—even his beloved Italy. Ironically, it was the would-be modernizers and radicals who wanted to impose a narrow, parochial vision on Pio Nono, seeking to turn him into a petty Italian prince focusing his attention on local wars—after the model of the Renaissance popes. In a further irony, liberals in the United States (as in other countries) also endorsed this limited vision of the pope's duties—they wanted Pio Nono to be just another an Italian princeling, at the expense even of American affairs. Not realizing the conflict between the pope's duties and the local concerns of Italian nationalists, many Americans were setting themselves up for disappointment and anger if the pope repudiated the nationalists and radicals.

Sylvester and his fellow students in Frascati naturally shared the universal, not the particularistic, vision of the Church. They were training to be priests in their various home countries—not in the pope's own neighborhood. The students began to get hints of the political turmoil. In late June, he and his fellow American students "went out and encountered a spy," apparently an Italian nationalist opposed to the Catholic Church and the papal regime. Learning that the students were Americans, the man gave them "voluble compliment[s]." Yet he had a "serpent of a tongue," and "harangued against priests and everybody." "Why do you make yourself priest? Why?" the man asked one of the students.[32]

On September 6, Sylvester wrote a curious entry in his journal, declaring, "I have had a little experience," and applying the text "put not your trust in princes"—this meant "not only that the potentates of the earth are not to be trusted, but also that no one is to act for you; no one must be allowed to lead you by the nose." Sylvester did not specify who had been previously "lead[ing] [him] by the nose," whether it was a priest, professor, or maybe William. But Sylvester was in another of his spiritually down moods. When writing the brief memoir of his conversion in his journal, reaching the part where he was "not discouraged" during his journey to Italy, he added, "God help me!" He used the same exclamation on September 13: "Whatever of deep intent I ever had seems to be gone and I seem to be resigned to living a harum-scarum life here notwithstanding the stern trials and the fearful hour that waits me hereafter. God help me!"[33]

Stimulated by purported democratic clubs, enthusiastic mobs of Romans demonstrated "in support" of the pope—actually to pressure the pope to fight the Austrians and appoint ministers sympathetic to war and radicalism. The pope's own general, Giacomo Durando, without Pius' approval, issued a proclamation which called, in effect, for a crusade to "exterminate" the Austrians, whom he called "the enemies of God and of Italy." Durando's proclamation forced the pope's hand. Pius would have to take a forthright stand supporting or opposing his general. Though an Italian patriot, Pius did not want to lend his spiritual authority to a war of aggression, compromising his position as a universal pastor. Nor did he want to provoke Austrian Catholics to go into schism.[34]

The pope gave a public "Allocution" on April 29, 1848, in which he rejected the idea that he would start an aggressive war against Austria or lead an Italian republic. Fervent Italian nationalists, and liberals in America and Europe, were shocked by what they saw as a betrayal of the hope of secular liberation. The nationalists and radicals redoubled their pressure in the Roman streets, seeking to force prowar ministers on Pius. In a proclamation responding to the attacks, Pius borrowed from the Latin liturgy the anguished cry of Christ addressing earlier ungrateful crowds: "Popule meus, quid feci tibi" ("My people, what have I done to you?").[35]

Meanwhile, the United States for the first time appointed a minister resident, effectively an ambassador, to represent the country in the Papal States. Congress had approved the establishment of this position in the first flush of enthusiasm over the pope's reform program. The first minister who was appointed, Jacob L. Martin, soon succumbed to the fevers which regularly afflicted Rome during the summer. Consul Nicholas Brown was now the only American representative on the scene—consuls were low-level diplomatic officials responsible for looking after American citizens, but supposedly without power to deal with matters of state. America had had consuls in Rome for decades. Brown was an enthusiast for the cause of Roman radicalism, and forgot his duties sufficiently to devote his diplomatic correspondence to praise of the radical cause, rather than the humdrum business he was supposed to be restricted to. Brown's views did not represent those of the state department (the recipient of Brown's missives), but nevertheless represented a current of opinion in the United States sympathetic to European nationalist movements, perceiving such movements as parallel to America's own revolutionaries of 1776.[36]

In Frascati, geographically close to Rome but politically remote, Sylvester confronted his own spiritual anguish. On September 15, thinking back to when he decided to be a priest, Sylvester wrote that his "feelings then" were different from "those into which I have worked myself now." From the earlier time, he recalled "a very great calmness in my resolution to advance in virtue. I had then deeply impressed in my mind the shortness of our worldly existence and the eternity of our existence hereafter, and hence the absolute necessity of virtue and the necessity of nothing but virtue. Hence the calmness with which I determined after my half-hour's meditation to foresee and provide against the dangers of the day." In his next day's journal, Sylvester noted: "This morning I received God within me. He came to unite Himself to and to change me into Himself."[37]

On September 30, Sylvester noted in his journal how impressed he had been to witness the religious devotion of the "poor peasants": "How many of these poor men will have a rank far far above those who look at them and smile at their ludicrous appearance in the Church." His exercises at Frascati were halfway over and he couldn't wait for them to end. "I have been pulled hither and thither too much already."[38]

Dramatic events in Rome during November sealed the separation of the pope and the radical movement among the Romans. Seeking a way out of his political dilemmas, the pope finally turned to Pellegrino Rossi as his prime minister. Rossi supported a league of Italian states and peace with Austria. He began repressing crime, corruption and disorder in Rome and the rest of the Papal States. The radicals were outraged at Rossi's policies, and some of them got together to plot how to put Rossi out of the way.[39]

On November 15, assassins surrounded Rossi and slit his throat. The killers fled the scene of this daylight murder, committed in the midst of great crowds. Supporters of the assassins serenaded Rossi's widow in her house, proclaiming, "Blessed be the hand that stabbed Rossi." Many Romans, far from deploring the murder, celebrated it as the death of a tyrant.[40]

After Rossi's murder the mob surrounded Pius's Quirinal Palace, and in the battle between the mob and the pope's troops, a priest standing at the window was shot to death. Pius yielded to mob pressure and appointed a radical ministry, while accepting a "Civic Guard," run by the radicals, to patrol Rome and guard the pope's person. Abandoned by many of his erstwhile friends, surrounded by murderous mobs, Pius decided to escape.[41]

On November 22, Sylvester recorded "good news"—a letter from William announced that their mother, their sister Lydia, and their brother Henry had either joined the Catholic Church or would soon do so. This was "certainly due to the prayers and exertions of William." "How often [William] has labored for our conversion," reflected Sylvester. "With what faith as of the 'dark ages' he had asked the prayers of others!"[42]

On November 24, Pope Pius disguised himself as a parish priest and escaped the Quirinal Palace in a carriage. The pope took asylum across the border from the Papal States in the town of Gaeta, in the conservative and sympathetic kingdom of Naples.[43]

Liberation or Sacrilege?

In December, in what seems to have been Sylvester's final spiritual retreat at Frascati or the first retreat in Rome, the topic was "a happy death. The first meditation was on the sanctity our calling requires as Christians, Priests, Apostles."

American Consul Nicholas Brown had another happy death in mind—someone else's

Mob attack on the papal palace at the Quirinal. "The Insurrection at Rome.—Attack on the Pope's Palace." *Illustrated London News,* **2 December 1848, p. 337 (courtesy Anthony P. Campanella Collection of Giuseppe Garibaldi, Irvin Department of Rare Books and Special Collections, University of South Carolina Libraries, Columbia).**

death—in a December dispatch to Secretary of State James Buchanan. Brown, like some other Americans, wrote in praise of Rossi's murder, pointedly noting that it took place "within a few yards of the spot where Caesar expired," and claiming that with the killing "the keystone of the arch of corruption" had been "removed." Brown "bitterly ... regretted" Pius's flight, saying the pope had been in no danger: "No personal violence was attempted or initiated against him. His hated advisors alone were aimed at." Brown's dispatch showed the willingness of American sympathizers to blame the pope for any conflicts the Church had with the forces of "modernity," regardless of who the actual aggressors were.[44]

It was around this time that Sylvester finally entered Rome, soon after the pope had left it, in order to live and study at the College of the Propaganda. This institution, located on Rome's Piazza di Spagna, was founded in 1622, to train students from non–Christian or heretical countries for the priesthood, envisioning that the new priests would go back to their homelands to spread the true faith. The college included the Museo Borgia, donated by a cardinal of the name who presided over Propaganda in the 18th century.[45]

On December 11, Sylvester was "disturbed a little by a crowd of people ... screaming like crazy persons." On December 27 he began his journal with "Quotidie morior" ("I die daily," apparently a self-reproach at his spiritual sluggishness). He explained how he wrote William "answer[ing] his questions about my Communion, said a little to encourage him in his pursuit of virtue, &c"—the first time Sylvester mentioned in his journal any advice or encouragement from him to William rather than the other way around. In a final page of the letter, as he summarized it, Sylvester updated Ann ("Annie") about several matters, including "news of the Pope's Edict." This edict was issued by Pius in his exile, explained that he had been driven from Rome, and designated ministers to run things in his absence. The decree was posted on the walls of Rome but promptly torn down. The Roman authorities ignored this decree, and at year's end called for elections to a constituent assembly to decide the future status of the Papal States.[46]

A tour guide to Rome, published in 1871, said that the students at the College of the Propaganda underwent an "annual examination" in January, with "poetry and speeches in their several languages, accompanied also by music, as performed in their respective countries," an examination which "few travelers who are then in Rome omit to attend." Whether or not any travelers attended such exercises in January 1849, the attention of the Romans was focused instead on a New Year's Day proclamation by the pope, by which Pius prohibited Catholics from taking part in the upcoming elections. Pius said it was forbidden to deprive the pope of his temporal sovereignty of the Papal States, citing a decree of the Reformation-era Council of Trent that anyone who stole Church property would be automatically excommunicated.[47]

From the perspective of the pope, and of faithful Catholics like Sylvester, the revolution in the Papal States was more than a change of government—it was the sacrilegious spoliation of Church property. In this view, the Italian territory ruled by the papacy wasn't a normal country, but a sacred trust administered by the Church, like its other property. Outside meddling with the government of these sacred territories was like stealing a consecrated vessel or turning a church building into a stable. It was sacrilege—a literally damnable meddling with divine things. Here, perhaps, was one of the greatest gaps between the perspective of Pio Nono and his supporters and the perspective of nationalists, liberals and radicals, who thought the revolutionaries in the Papal States had the right to change their government, even to the point of taking the country away from the pope altogether.[48]

For the next couple of months, the only entries Sylvester made in his journal pertained to the "retire[s]" (retreats) held at the college. Throughout this time, though, as he later said, he was "bother[ing] his head ... with political affairs." A consituent assembly was elected for the Papal States, dominated by radicals. A minority of the electorate in Rome and elsewhere in the Papal States took part in the elections, defying the papal ban on participating. American consul Brown nevertheless saw the constituent assembly as representing the whole people and deplored "the dread abyss, so recklessly opened between the unhappy Pontiff and his people."[49]

Consul Brown didn't wait for a reconciliation, but sided with the revolutionaries. On February 5th, wearing the uniform of his office, he joined the members of the constituent assembly as they proceeded to their meeting hall in the *Cancellaria*. On February 9, The constituent assembly proclaimed the Papal States to be a republic, leaving the pope his "spiritual power" but no sovereignty over his own lands. On the 11th, consul Brown offered the Republican authorities his "warmest congratulations," and attended a Te Deum in Saint Peter's, presided over by Republican priests.[50]

The pope's new foreign minister Cardinal Giacomo Antonelli, on February 18, sent requests to four Catholic powers—Austria, France, Spain and Naples—asking them to drive the revolutionaries out of Rome and restore the pope's rule. The fate of the Papal States was the business of the whole Catholic world, and now was the time for faithful Catholics to reclaim the pope's patrimony from radical usurpers. All four countries began mobilizing to send troops into the Papal States—Austria after securing its dominant position in the penninsula at the battle of Novara to the north of the Papal States.[51]

The leading intellectual of Italian unification, Giuseppe Mazzini, arrived in Rome on March 5. The assembly soon appointed him to a "triumvirate" which he dominated—basically he became dictator of the new republic. Mazzini had no particular experience, except in working in European revolutionary societies and writing about his ideals. He was a romantic dreamer who envisioned not only the political unity of Italy, but a "religious transformation" to unite all mankind in a new faith. This post–Catholic religion would be centered on a "Rome of the People," which would be the spiritual center of a new Europe as well as headquarters of a sort of European parliament. Of course, to realize this beautiful dream it would first be necessary to overthrow the power of the Church.[52]

A new American minister to Rome arrived on April 2. Outgoing Secretary of State James Buchanan took no notice of consul Brown's fanboy dispatches about the Roman revolutionaries. Buchanan instructed the new minister to Rome, Lewis Cass, Jr. (son of an influential Senator of the same name), to take a wait-and-see attitude toward the Roman Republic, not recognizing it until it had clearly established its independence. In other words, Cass was to ascertain whether the republic could withstand the invading foreign armies. Mazzini and his colleagues courted Cass assiduously, urging him to recognize the new Roman regime, but Cass did not take the bait. Brown, meanwhile, wrote in a dispatch praising the republic that "the Papacy, I regret to say it, is fallen, morally fallen, forever"—a sentiment coming to be held unofficially by many Americans though not by their government.[53]

On behalf of the American bishops, Archbishop Eccleston of Baltimore invited the exiled pope to come to the United States to preside at the hierarchy's forthcoming provincial council. Pope Pius declined the invitation, saying that "existing times and circumstances" precluded acceptance.[54]

Besieged

Easter Sunday in 1849 fell on April 8. Sylvester and other Propaganda students went on a Holy Week retreat, where the first of the assigned meditations, as Sylvester put it, "was on the use of grace derived from the tears which our Savior shed over Jerusalem." Jesus had wept over the impending ruin of the city of Jerusalem, which was thus punished for rejecting Him and killing the prophets. The students would certainly be reminded of another ungrateful city which had expelled Christ's vicar and faced its own punishment.[55] Sylvester was about to have a vivid experience of war and rebellion—an experience which would shock and frighten him. He would carry that memory with him even after leaving Rome.

The republic's authorities took over St. Peter's, recruiting an army chaplain and a Republican priest freshly arrived from Bologna, named Allesandro Gavazzi, to celebrate Easter Sunday services in place of the absent pope. Gavazzi had been active in the revolutionary movement in his home city of Bologna, in the northern Papal States. He moved to Rome and was made almoner-in-chief of the Republican army, disregarding his own Church's leadership and its desire to overthrow the Republic. A friar named Ugo Bassi, whom Gavazzi met in Ancona (again in the northern Papal States) also came to Rome.[56]

In the last week of April, French troops arrived at Civita Vecchia, the Papal States' Mediterranean port, and began marching toward Rome. Sylvester noted this, and referred to the Roman Republic's authorities and their supporters as "these madmen" and "these wretches" who were going to bring "evils ... upon the city." As to why they were fighting for this desperate cause, "perhaps God lets them harden their hearts in order that their chastisement may be more signal. Or they may be so mad as for the name of liberty they want to die.... God forgive them and save them!"[57]

The Mazzini regime did not disabuse Sylvester of his negative view of its activities. The regime confiscated some Church property for the alleged purpose of helping poor priests—though consul Brown exultantly wrote that the confiscation was in response to the pope's opposition to the Republic. Mazzini's government also confiscated Church buildings for military purposes. As reported by American transcendentalist and journalist Margaret Fuller, the pope's former Quirinal palace would be used to house the wounded in the forthcoming battles. Convents were also confiscated, which Sylvester deplored, speaking particularly about the convent of his namesake, St. Sylvester, which Sylvester saw cleared of its 40 nuns to make room for troops. "A line of carriages" took the nuns away while a crowd and Civic Guards stood watch.[58]

Margaret Fuller was the correspondent of Horace Greeley's influential *New York Tribune*. In her dispatches, Fuller strongly defended the Roman Republic and denounced the pope and his allies for trying to destroy it. Fuller's new husband was a member of the Republic's Civic Guard, part of the forces defending the city. Fuller was a friend of Mazzini, who relied on her to defend his nationalist crusade before the world. Bishop John Hughes of New York acknowledged her influence on American opinion, sarcastically declaring that no foreign ambassador had recognized the Republic except Fuller, "the female plenipotentiary who furnishes the *Tribune* with diplomatic correspondence." The *Catholic Magazine* denounced "the Protestant press" and "our secular journals," such as the *Tribune,* for supporting "seditious" and "mobocratic" revolutions in Europe.[59]

Hughes, meanwhile, denounced the "murderers" and "wicked men" who ran the rogue Roman Republic. The faithful gave $25,978.24 in support of the pope—Bishop Hughes raised $6,000 of it. This was part of a revived institution of "Peter's Pence" by which Catholics could contribute directly to the support of the pontiff. Protestant Americans saw this as raising funds in support of reactionaries battling a free government. Thus the battles between Pius IX and his Italian enemies enhanced suspicions between American Catholics and their non–Catholic fellow citizens.[60]

A famous revolutionary leader, Giuseppi Garibaldi, marched into Rome with his troops, and they made themselves at home in the St. Sylvester convent. Garibaldi was a flamboyant figure from north Italy who had fought in civil wars in Latin America, learning guerrilla warfare tactics. Bringing followers from throughout Italy, as well as a few sympathetic foreigners, Garibaldi wished to lend his sword to Mazzini, his compatriot and rival. Garibaldi's sketchy religious views made Mazzini look orthodox in comparison, and Garibaldi bore a strong hatred towards priests. Sylvester had heard rumors of the arrival of Garibaldi and his "assassins."[61]

When Sylvester and some other students went for a walk on the 29th, "some grenadiers ... insulted [them] as [they] passed along." That evening "a mob took the Cardinals' carriages out to make barricades with. Four or five went for ours.... Al fuoco, al fuoco (to fire, to fire!), they cried there and we thought they were going to put fire to the college."[62]

The French reached the gates of Rome on April 30, but the Roman soldiers beat back the overconfident French. From his limited vantage point, Sylvester noted: "Drums were beating and the wildest confusion filling the city." That afternoon there was "a rattle of musket shots which lasted for some time. Then about us began to rain the 'viva' through the city that the French were beaten." The citizens illuminated their windows; "even [the students' windows] have lamps sitting outside. Mine fell by the way into the street and was lost."[63]

The lighting of victory lamps was apparently a placatory gesture by the students to avoid a mob attack on the college. The seminarians were in the awkward position of being inside a besieged city and sympathizing with the besiegers—they saw the Republicans as socialist infidels, and the invading foreign forces as liberators. There were many papal sympathizers like Sylvester and his compatriots in Rome. Dealing with this embarrassing fact, Mazzini was aware of the economic and public relations problems of killing or expelling the Republic's numerous internal opponents. Mazzini may have been a fanatic, but he was not stupid, and he had a lingering affection for the Catholic Church. He did not want any massacres or proscriptions of his opponents.[64]

Not all the revolutionaries were as easygoing as Mazzini, and political assassins were at work throughout the Republic killing priests, monks and nuns, and Papal supporters. So far, these outrages had mainly been in the territories outside Rome, but during and after the battle of the 30th, the hand of the assassin again reached into Rome itself. A Roman mob seized two alleged Jesuits and tore them to pieces.[65]

Even more sinister was a terrorist named Callimaco Zambianchi. An exile from the Papal States under the prior pope, Zambianchi availed himself of Pius's amnesty and moved back. He took part in an assassination campaign in revolutionary Bologna until Fr. Alessandro Gavazzi and Ugo Bassi, the two Republican religious figures, restored law and order in the city and drove Zambianchi to take another role in the revolution. Leading a contingent of revenue police near the Neapolitan border, Zambianchi arrested some priests and laity on subversion charges and sent them to Rome for punishment. He was outraged when the Roman authorities set the suspects free, and he decided that he would administer his own form of justice. He had his chance when he and his men were deployed to Rome to help defend the city. During the battle of May 30 he shot a passing Dominican. His troops were then quartered in the poor Trastavere quarter, where he officiated at the murders of numerous priests and monks—the numbers are unclear, with claimed deaths ranging from six to ninety. The Mazzini government stopped the killing spree in time to prevent the death toll rising higher, but the regime was unable or unwilling to have Zambianchi arrested. Zambianchi later joined Garibaldi's army, justifying Sylvester's epithet of "assassins."[66]

Word of the murders soon drifted back to the Propaganda College, underlining the insecure situation of Sylvester and the seminarians. With their very lives on the line, it is hardly surprising that Sylvester proclaimed himself and the other students "willing, nay wish, for the French to enter the city." Sylvester continued reflecting in his journal: "The devil is working hard and Europe is going to Barbarism; we shall see, or other generations shall see." Sylvester added, "When will the French the Spanish and the Austrians enter?" He then reproached himself for his timidity, enjoining himself to show "fortitude, humility, [and] simple [single?] mindedness." Yet he worried about the "horrid stories" the students' mothers would hear.[67]

Sylvester wrote William on May 9 "not to be anxious," but his own anxiety, expressed in his diary, was peaking: "I thought something of going away today.... If I had money of my own I would certainly go tomorrow." But this would disappoint the heads of the college, "as I have tried so lately the temper of the superiors about this I hesitate." He assured himself that the Roman regime would not last—"the sovereigns of Europe cannot stand long this fire in their midst."[68]

A new approach of the reinforced French army was heralded by "great excitement" on May 11. "We feel tolerably secure" at the college, wrote Sylvester, although "the soldiers will probably enter the buildings to fire from the [college] windows" and had already set up "bags of dirt" to throw from those windows.[69]

A French negotiator, Ferdinand de Lesseps (later the builder of the Suez Canal) came to Rome, negotiated a cease-fire, and entered into peace talks. The guns were silent from May 17 to June 1.[70]

Meanwhile, developments in the northern Papal States were unfolding which would ultimately affect Sylvester and the whole American Church. The Austrians took Bologna and reinstated the pope's cardinal legate, Gaetano Bedini. Sylvester would hear more from the cardinal in future, but for now he focused on affairs in Rome. He resolved to stop writing his account of the siege: "I fear that I shall remember too much of these villainous affairs."[71]

De Lesseps signed another agreement with the Republic—a proposed peace deal—on May 31, but the French general, Charles Oudinot, repudiated the deal and the cease-fire on the following day. On June 3, French troops defeated Roman forces at Villa Corsini. Sylvester changed his mind about covering political events to write what he knew of the battle: "the hospitals are full of wounded." The authorities took twelve beds from the college, apparently for the wounded.[72]

The perception gap between Sylvester and the supporters of the Republic is shown by a letter from English poet Arthur Hugh Clough to a friend around this time. Clough said that priests were not being harmed—they were going about the city normally as if nothing was happening. Confession was still being administered at St. Peter's. "There is nothing to deserve the name of 'Terror.'" True, some pamphlets had appeared calling for the assassination of alleged enemies of the Republic, but the government had promptly suppressed these.[73] The Propaganda College students, hearing reports of assassinations—even if deplored by Mazzini—could hardly share Clough's confident belief that there was no terrorism worth the name.

Mail service to the college partly resumed. The students got copies of *L'Univers*, a hardcore propapal ("ultramontane") French newspaper. They read with pleasure, perhaps from that paper, a speech by the Spanish prime minister (probably Ramón María Narváez) defending his country's military intervention in favor of the pope. Sylvester praised the speech's "vastness of view and deep earnest religious spirit truly noble." In Sylvester's view, this was the best defense of the pope he had yet seen.[74]

The sound of gunfire provided a backdrop to the students' activities. French shells sailed into the poor Trastavere district—when they heard an approaching shell, the inhabitants would exclaim, "There goes another Pio Nono!" The women and children would toss live shells into the Tiber in a patriotic effort to protect their community.[75]

The students at the college now faced the threat of eviction from their dwelling. The Mazzini government ordered citizens fleeing from the Trastavere to be sheltered in houses and palaces in the better parts of the city, further away from the shelling. On June 14, when the shooting was "unusually sharp," Sylvester learned that the government had tried to take over the college to house some Trastavere refugees, which would have made the students homeless. The rector of the college appealed to American consul Nicholas Brown, who "us[ed] his influence with Mazzini" and prevented the seizure. "The Rector was very grateful to [Brown], and invited him to come and see us." Brown's vocal support of the republic may have paid off. Despite his support for the republic and opposition to the papacy, Brown had done his consular duty by intervening on behalf of vulnerable students, including American citizens.[76]

On June 21, the French captured two key bastions inside the walls of the city. The end was approaching. During the battle, Sylvester wrote that "the bombs were clashing around at a fine rate. They seemed sometimes to break very near." Learning that the Republicans had incurred a serious and bloody defeat, Sylvester wrote: "God help the poor mortals that thus perish under the anathema of his Church and convert the rest of them." By laying hands on the lands and property of the Church, Sylvester believed, the revolutionaries incurred excommunication—their souls were in danger of eternal perdition.[77]

The government tried again to take over the college. This time the rector called on the American ambassador Cass, who "had a firm squabble" with the government over the issue. This would have been an informal discussion, since Cass did not recognize the Republic. But since Mazzini was courting Cass's favor, the ambassador may have had extra influence. In any case, the students stayed in their building, though the rector, pressed to at least donate part of the college, let the government use "the Cardinal's part"—presumably the Museo Borgia—as "an act of charity." So in all likelihood, a group of Trastavere refugees sheltered in the elegant and richly appointed rooms built by Cardinal Borgia. Sylvester wrote that "Mr. Cass has conducted himself very nobly in this affair."[78]

"The 'gentlemen of the Reformation,'" as Sylvester insultingly called the Republican authorities, "have hopes yet. In spem contra spem"—in hope against hope. On June 29, Sylvester wrote sarcastically about a "panegyric" which "Gavassi"—Fr. Alessandro Gavazzi—had given for one of Garibaldi's slain officers. The rebel priest had "compare[ed] him [the officer] to all the saints and martyrs and [gave] him the crown of heaven," Sylvester contemptuously reported.[79]

Consul Brown, believing the war over, tendered his resignation, while boasting that he had been "serviceable to my countrymen and others"—possibly an allusion to his intervention on behalf of Sylvester and his fellow students.[80]

Early on the 30th, the students "were wakened by the bombs crashing around us." Going outside to check on what was going on, Sylvester overheard two citizens: "'It isn't much!'

says one. 'Not much! Not much!' said the other astounded; 'Why it rains [bombs]!'" "All is quiet now," Sylvester concluded, "though about noon there was a terrible firing." Many of the students who lived on the upper floors moved to the recitation room to make their beds for the night. "The corridor is full of benches."[81]

The defenders of Rome finally gave up. Garibaldi and the assembly rejected Mazzini's proposal to fight to the death in the streets of the city, and Mazzini resigned. The Republican authorities agreed on surrender terms—Garibaldi and his troops would have two days to get out of the city, after which the French would be admitted unopposed. On July 3, thousands of French soldiers poured into Rome. Sylvester saw about two thousand marching past the college, as well as others patrolling nearby. Some of the soldiers broke up a pro–Republican demonstration at a café frequented by radicals—"that infamous hole of assassins," as Sylvester called it. "In our part of the city all was quiet and ill-concealed exaltation." Sylvester concluded his journal entry: "Deo gratias. Deo gratias. Deo gratias. Deo gratias. Deo gratias." Thanks be to God.[82]

Graduation

Garibaldi fled with several thousand men and his chaplain, Gavazzi's friend Ugo Bassi. Garibaldi escaped the pursuing armies, but he lost most of his men to desertion or capture by the Austrians. Many of the deserters became bandits. Bassi, who did not desert, was captured near Bologna, and was brought to that city for an Austrian court martial and death sentence. Garibaldi spent a brief time in exile in the United States.[83]

The American and English consuls provided papers to many of the other former Republican leaders, allowing them to escape Rome and the French dragnet. At Margaret Fuller's

Sylvester and his fellow students were relieved when the French liberated Rome from the revolutionaries. "The Last Attack on Rome by the French." *Illustrated London News,* 28 July 1849, p. 53 (courtesy Anthony P. Campanella Collection of Giuseppe Garibaldi, Irvin Department of Rare Books and Special Collections, Thomas Cooper Library, University of South Carolina Libraries, Columbia).

urging, minister Cass provided false papers to Mazzini, who fled to England, and to Fr. Gavazzi, who was disgusted with the pope for opposing the republic. The rebel priest also blamed the pope's legate in Bologna, Gaetano Bedini, for allegedly sharing responsibility for the death of Ugo Bassi. Gavazzi left the Church, turned Protestant, and became an anti–Catholic propagandist based in London. This was by no means the last time that Sylvester and other American Catholics would hear of Gavazzi or Bedini.[84]

To many Americans, the pope's honeymoon was over. His supposed betrayal of Italian nationalism gave him a new image as an enemy of liberty. An angry Margaret Fuller wrote after the failed Roman revolution, "Not only Jesuitism must go, the Roman Catholic religion must go.... The influence of the clergy is too perverting, too foreign to every hope of advancement and health." Fuller planned to publish a book on the subject of the Roman Republic's rise and fall. However, Fuller, her young child, and her manuscript drowned when the ship on which she sailed back to America wrecked off the coast of Long Island. Despite the loss of Fuller and her book, her *Tribune* correspondence helped fix in American Protestant minds the image of a Church irrationally hostile to freedom and liberalism. Meanwhile, to American Catholics, the defeat of Mazzini and Garibaldi was cause for rejoicing. Bishop Hughes ordered a Te Deum.[85]

While waiting to return to Rome, the pope appointed three cardinals—the "Red Triumvirate"—to administer the restored Papal Territories. The Austrians kept order in the north of the Papal States, the French in Rome and the area around it. Sylvester was gratified to see the disarming of the pro–Republican Civil Guard. He attended a Te Deum celebrating the pope's restoration. "We walked out to St. John Lateran's for the first time in 75 days," Sylvester wrote on July 10. Minister Cass exchanged compliments with Cardinal Della Genga, one of the Triumvirate, who thanked Cass for not hastily recognizing the republic and declared that Pius was (as Cass put it) "an enthusiastic admirer of America, and its institutions." The papal government, on Cass's request, agreed to permit American Protestants in Rome to worship freely.[86] American Protestants at home might be growing more resentful of the pope and the Church over which he presided, but on the diplomatic level, relations stayed on an even keel.

The other revolutionary movements in Europe—in Germany, Hungary, Ireland, and England—had been crushed by this time. Only France experienced an enduring change of regime, and that was to replace a king with a president—who was soon to proclaim himself Emperor Napoleon III.[87]

Sylvester's journal entries became sparser over the next few months. Apparently the war had at least partly interrupted the normal course of studies at the college, and with the return of peace the students had to work more consistently. Sylvester noted on September 7 that the constraints on his activities—"you must conform yourself in all things"—limited his journal writing. His journal entries again became far less frequent.[88]

Pope Pius returned to Rome on April 12, 1850. In the same month, he met with Minister Cass, and thanked the diplomat for his humanitarian actions during the French siege (perhaps alluding to the protection of the Propaganda College). The pope also told Cass of his admiration for the United States, and his gratitude to American Catholics for their support in the recent difficulties. Over the next few years, while not repeating the political reforms of his early papacy, Pius presided over a decade of respectable economic progress and low taxes (defense being handled largely by the French and Austrians). His main preoccupation, however, remained events throughout the Catholic world—building up the Church and expounding her doctrines. On a personal level, the pope was pleasant and approachable. He liked to walk around Rome, greeting artists and prominent visitors. He continued his interest in the Church's affairs throughout the world, and his interest in promoting the cause of the Church in countries far from Europe led some to call him the "Missionary Pope."[89]

The pontiff was scarred by his experience with reform, revolution, and nationalism. He had reached out to reform forces in his own territories, only to be violently rebuffed—he experienced the death of his moderate prime minister, a murderous mob attack on his palace, his own exile from Rome, and the takeover of the Eternal City and his other territories by what he saw as a gang of brigands. He had seen purported liberals cheer bloodthirsty assassins, and nationalism invoked as a rationale for pitting Catholics against each other. He no longer wanted any part of liberalism or nationalism, and fulminated against liberal authors and doctrines. His suspicion also extended to theological idea which he saw as flirting with liberalism.[90]

Pius IX. R. de Cesare, *The Last Days of Papal Rome: 1850–1870* (Boston: Houghton Mifflin, 1909).

As Pope Pius and the Church were pushed into political reaction, many people in America, and in other countries, turned against him. In many of the same circles where he had been lauded as a champion of reform and a free Italy, he was now excoriated as an enemy of freedom and an ally of tyrants. There were also people within the Church who thought he had gone too far in his reaction against modern radical movements. Many of America's evangelical Protestants were suspicious of what they saw as the aggression of the again reactionary Church. While still in exile, Pius IX established a Catholic hierarchy in England for the first time since the Reformation, provoking opposition even in America. Closer to home, in September 1850, the pope turned several U.S. bishoprics into archbishoprics, an elevation in rank reflecting a petition from the American hierarchy in 1849 and Pius's continuing interest in mission territories like America. The new archdioceses were St. Louis, New Orleans, New York ... and Cincinnati. Bishop Purcell came to Rome in 1851 so he could formally be elevated to the rank of archbishop. On Palm Sunday, Sylvester attended Mass and took Communion, then accompanied Purcell to St. Peter's, where they sat "just behind a row of Bishops and Archbishops dressed in Copes and Chasubles." Pope Pius entered, "borne on the shoulders of about sixteen men." Sylvester noted "the waving of plumes, and diamonds flashing on the mitres and vestments of Archbishops, Bishops, Patriarchs, Abbots." Pius performed the Palm Sunday service and distributed Communion to the high-ranking prelates, the diplomats, and "the lords and gentlemen who had tickets for the occasion.... The long procession of Palms was exceedingly beautiful, the palms waving above all the way down to St. Peter's."[91]

In 1852, Sylvester graduated from the College of the Propaganda with a doctorate in theology and prepared for his ordination on June 5. "These hands," the awestruck Sylvester wrote on May 17, "that are now employed in writing are the hands of one soon to be ordained Priest!" On the eve of his ordination, Sylvester made a final entry in his journal: "Tomorrow the Holy Ghost will descend upon me and I shall receive in all its fullness the terrible power over the Mystical and Real Body of Jesus Christ. The Holy Ghost will descend upon me as upon the Apostles in the Supper Room and I shall be transformed."[92]

The *Catholic Telegraph*, newspaper of the Cincinnati archdiocese, published an announcement of Sylvester's new honors, informing the readers of the new priest who would soon be in their midst.[93]

The 25-year-old priest had been strengthened by adversity. The crisis of the Church amid Rome's turbulence had tied Sylvester closer to his faith. Sylvester had acquired practical experience about living in a community dangerously hostile to the Church. He had experienced more of war than his brother had in the army. Finally, he had witnessed the disruption and chaos of a rebellion.

4

"An heir-loom"

Up from Georgia

Late in March 1844, two passengers, one from Georgia and the other from Massachusetts, fell into conversation on a steamer from Washington, D.C., to New York. One of the passengers was a planter from Georgia named Michael Healy. The Irish immigrant had a plantation near Macon worked by about fifty slaves. He often came north on business, but on this occasion he also had other matters to deal with.[1]

The passenger from Massachusetts was John Bernard Fitzpatrick, the newly-consecrated titular bishop of Callipolis (Gallipoli, now in Turkey). Fitzpatrick's real job was not to serve in that disused see, but to assist the bishop of Boston, who had the Dickensian appellation of Benedict Fenwick. Fitzpatrick, as a priest, had been a protégé and trusted assistant to Bishop Fenwick, and as the latter grew old and ill, Fenwick had asked for the assistance of a coadjutor, or assistant bishop with the right of succession—Fenwick had Fitzpatrick specifically in mind. The Massachusetts native was accordingly made bishop at a comparatively young age—he was in his early thirties. Fitzpatrick was on his way back to Massachusetts from Washington, D.C., where Bishop Fenwick had done the consecration himself.[2] The encounter between Michael Healy and Bishop Fitzpatrick was significant for the history of two developments in American Catholicism—the growing number of Irish Catholic immigrants and the confrontation of the American Church with slavery.

As Michael Healy talked to the new bishop, he explained the peculiar situation he was in. It had to do with the upbringing of his children. Michael and one of his slaves, Eliza, lived as man and wife. The couple had nine surviving children, who were themselves slaves under Georgia law because slave status followed the status of the mother. This sort of situation was unusual—not the part about the master having children by his female slaves, but the part where Michael and Eliza held themselves out as married. As with other slave states, both the law and social custom in Georgia clamped down hard on marriage across the racial line, much less across the line demarcating free whites and enslaved blacks. Joseph Henry Lumpkin, soon to be the state chief justice, expressed his disgust at interracial unions: "which one of us has not narrowly escaped petting one of the pretty little mulattoes belonging to our neighbors as one of the family?" Michael Healy would qualify as one of the people who would provoke the chief justice's ire. Perhaps Michael kept people from knowing his wife's race—but he did not hide the fact that she was his wife. In 1847, the local paper, the *Georgia Telegraph,* ran lists of people who had letters waiting for them at the local post office, and Mrs. Eliza Healy was one of those listed.[3]

The South's harsh attitude to interracial marriage was not unique. In Bishop Fitzpatrick's own state of Massachusetts, the legislature had repealed the law against interracial marriage only in the previous year (1843). Many Bay Staters were still hostile to the concept. Ex-president John Quincy Adams of Massachusetts, just before undertaking numerous antislavery causes as a congressman and lawyer, wrote in 1835 with respect to Shakespeare's famous play about a tragic interracial marriage: "The great moral lesson of the tragedy of Othello is that black and white blood cannot be intermingled in marriage without a gross outrage upon the law of Nature; and that, in such violations, Nature will vindicate her laws."[4]

The situation in the Catholic Church was different. The Church recognized marriages between men and women of different races, and between slaves and free people—so long as the free spouse knew the slave spouse's status. For the Church, the only potential issues with Michael and Eliza's marriage were the religious difference—Michael may have been a baptized, if nonpracticing, Catholic, and Eliza may have been a Protestant—and the apparent informality of the marriage.[5]

Michael Healy's concern about his children stemmed from the fact that Georgia law, unlike the Church, did not recognize interracial marriages and regarded his wife and children as slaves and all his children as bastards. Indeed, as writer Lydia Maria Child summarized the problems of a fictional Georgia slaveholder in one of her novels, "the laws of Georgia restrained humane impulses by forbidding the manumission of a slave. Consequently, he must either incur very undesirable publicity by applying to the legislature for a special exception in this case, or [the slave] must be manumitted in another State."[6]

It was rare for the Georgia legislature to pass such exceptions. The legislature made clear its purpose to avoid ending up with more "free persons of color" in Georgia. Not only would it be embarrassing to lay his personal business before the solons, but it was unlikely that Michael could have persuaded them to free ten slaves at once. Not only was he forbidden from freeing his wife and children while they remained in Georgia, he couldn't legally give his slave children the right to work for themselves. And even teaching blacks and "mulattoes," like his children, to read and write would be a crime. Georgia slaves were supposed to remain ignorant, kept in hard bondage for life.[7]

This left the loophole mentioned by Lydia Child—Michael could send his children out of Georgia to be educated in the North, preparing them for an adult life of freedom outside Georgia. If this were to be done, it should be done while Michael's children were still young enough to get a basic education, and while Michael himself was still alive. To have his children educated properly, and to protect them from enslavement after he died, Michael decided to bring his older children north.[8]

The eldest child, James Augustine Healy, along with some brothers and sisters, were accordingly brought to Flushing, New York, and later to New Jersey, to be taught in Quaker schools. This solved two problems: the laws of these Northern states recognized Michael's children as free, and the Quakers (unusual for the time) were willing to let black students into their schools. The problem was that, by 1844, 14-year-old James was about to complete his course of education with the Quakers, so the question was where he and his brothers should study next. And his sisters were coming up as well.[9]

As it turned out, the diocese of Boston had an educational opportunity which was as race neutral as that of the Quakers. As Fitzpatrick explained to an interested Michael Healy, Bishop Fenwick had recently founded a new Catholic college, Holy Cross. Bishop Fitzpatrick said that Michael Healy's children would be welcome at the new institution. Among other considerations, the bishop was probably thinking about reclaiming Michael for the Church and rescuing his children from the darkness of infidelity. Michael had probably been born a Catholic in Ireland, but if so he drifted away from the Church and left his family unbaptized. The unbaptized Healy children—from the eldest, James (b. 1830) on down—were infidels both in theory and in fact. And for each of his sons in college Michael Healy was well off enough to afford the tuition—$150 per year in 1840s money for each son.[10]

Holy Cross College had opened only the previous year. For Bishop Fenwick, a Jesuit soaked in the order's respect for education, Holy Cross College was the culmination of many years' exhausting effort. Under the presidency of a Jesuit priest, Thomas Mulledy, S.J., the institution was up and running and had just begun taking in students.[11]

Michael Healy's Bishop Grapples with Slavery

Michael Healy's territorial bishop was not Fitzpatrick, but the bishop of Charleston, who until recently had been John England. Michael would have been able to follow some of the Church's affairs in the *Georgia Telegraph* newspaper in nearby Macon. It is likely that the *Georgia Telegraph* was Michael's window on the world, when he could spare time from his other concerns. In a time when newspapers were a primary source of information, and even of literary enjoyment, the probability is high that Michael followed the affairs of his erstwhile church in that periodical's pages—and a surprising number of items in his local paper dealt with Catholic affairs. So if the *Telegraph's* articles are an indication of the topics which engaged Michael's attention, then following the *Telegraph's* coverage of the Church would help illuminate Michael's milieu.[12]

Michael was classed among the area's "wealthy farmers" in a *Telegraph* article of December 14, 1841. Michael's spiritual life had not been as vigorous as his interest in hogs, but as a Catholic, even a lapsed one, Michael Healy, as a Georgia resident, came under the jurisdiction of Bishop John England of Charleston. (The Church's position in the South was even more tenuous than in the North. There were a few well-settled Catholic communities—e.g., in Maryland and Louisiana—and some moderately well-served urban parishes, but the rural parishes were short of priests and the people there did not always receive the degree of spiritual attention they merited.) Bishop England came to the United States from Ireland, where as a priest he had criticized the British government. He was reassigned to the United States and made a bishop in 1820. The Charleston diocese included North Carolina, South Carolina, Georgia, and the then-territory of Florida. England made fervent defense of American Catholics against the attacks and bigotry of Protestant figures, including politicians. The *Telegraph* printed some of these political letters, and after England's death it ran a letter from a sympathetic Protestant praising the bishop's defense of "his persecuted church."[13]

One aspect of England's career that didn't make it into the columns of the Georgia *Telegraph* was the bishop's complicated relationship with the issue of slavery. In private correspondence, England abhorred "the condition of the slaves" in the United States, and called slavery "the greatest moral evil that can desolate any part of the civilized world."[14]

Coincidentally or not, Bishop England's legal advisor was an antislavery Catholic: a judge from North Carolina named William Gaston, who died in January 1844, two months before the fateful meeting between Michael Healy and Bishop Fitzpatrick. Gaston was surprisingly successful in winning public office in the slaveholder-dominated Tar Heel State—not only was the political establishment willing to overlook an apparent ban on Catholic office-holding in the state constitution, it was willing to overlook Gaston's strong denunciation of slavery in a speech to the sons of the elite at the University of North Carolina in 1832. Addressing the state's future movers and shakers, Gaston said they had the "duty" to work for the "mitigation" and "ultimate extirpation" of slavery. Slavery "stifles industry and represses enterprise" and "poisons morals at the fountain head." As a judge, Gaston made rulings protecting slaves and affirming the citizenship of free black people. Gaston also made an unsuccessful attempt to protect free black citizenship as a delegate to a North Carolina constitutional convention. He was considered, and rejected, for a post on the U.S. Supreme Court. The seat ended up going to Roger Taney, another Catholic lawyer.[15]

Bishop England faced the same hard questions as his legal advisor, but he did not confront the issue with Gaston's directness and boldness. England, while bishop, had also been the papal representative in Haiti, a country founded by rebelling slaves. One of the nuns in his see city was black. None of this made him popular in Charleston, a hotbed of proslavery sentiment. The final straw was when England supervised the creation of schools in Charleston which educated free blacks. This was not the only such Catholic school to be founded in the United States—black schools had been founded in Washington, D.C., and in Baltimore, though sometimes not outlasting the zealous priests who founded them. In Charleston, there was a newly militant attitude among the whites which set itself against any education for blacks. A Charleston mob in 1835 went to the post office and burned abolitionist literature. The mob members then discussed attacking Bishop England's residence and even lynching the bishop, whose activities led them to link him with the abolitionists.[16]

England rallied a militia band, the Irish Volunteers, to defend the episcopal premises. The lynch mob never showed up. England, who blamed the abolitionists for provoking this backlash, denounced them and gave up his black schools in order to placate the local establishment.[17]

Events in Rome soon made England's position, and that of other bishops, even more difficult. The British government sought the support of Pope Gregory XVI in fighting slavery in the Catholic territories of Brazil and Cuba, which continued to import slaves seized in Africa. Pope Gregory was receptive to this appeal. A confirmed reactionary, he was proud of the Church's record of cleansing Europe of slavery during the Middle Ages, while deploring Europeans' later adoption of slavery in their colonies. Before becoming pope, as head of Propaganda, Gregory had supervised Catholic missionary activity in those continents afflicted by slavery, and he was aware of the difficulties the institution posed in trying to win over the peoples of those lands. Not wishing to single out Brazil and Cuba, but desiring to launch a spiritual attack on the slave traffic, Pope Gregory in 1839 issued an apostolic letter to the whole Catholic world. This letter, *In Supremo Apostolatus*, denounced the enslavement of black people and the slave trade from Africa, "that inhuman traffic ... in contempt of the rights of justice and humanity." Gregory rejoiced that, under Christian influence, "there are no more slaves in the greater number of Christian nations." But things had deteriorated since the antimodern Pope's beloved Middle Ages; "afterward," some Catholics "did not hesitate to reduce to slavery Indians, Negroes and other wretched peoples," or buy slaves from slave traffickers. Gregory cited many of his predecessors who had issued thundering condemnations of the enslavement of American Indians and Africans. Now Pope Gregory reiterated this stance. Catholics were not only forbidden to enslave anyone or engage in the slave trade, but they could not even "defend [it] as permissible," or "publish or teach" anything contrary to this papal decree. The encyclical did not speak expressly about the obligation of Catholics to work for the abolition of slavery, though the pope's approval of the Church's prior influence in ending the institution in the past hinted heavily that Catholics should oppose it in the future.[18]

Bishop Fenwick of Boston believed that *In Supremo* would "place our southern bishops in no very pleasant situation." Bishop England in Charleston felt the pressure of Southern suspicion of the pope's apparent meddling with slavery, which many interpreted as an abolitionist appeal. Secretary of State and Democratic vice presidential candidate John Forsyth sent a letter to Georgia Democrats citing *In Supremo* and accusing the pope of conspiring with the British to attack American slavery. England used the occasion of Forsyth's letter to publish several articles on slavery in his diocesan organ, the *Catholic Miscellany*. The purpose of these articles was to deny that the Catholic Church's doctrines entailed waging a war against American slavery—though England was careful not to say slavery was a good thing, as Southern spokesmen were beginning to say at the time.[19]

The bishop angrily denied that his namesake country had anything to do with the pope's letter—though the British had in fact prompted it. Bishop England analyzed the pope's decree and argued that it applied only to the African slave trade, and did not forbid slavery, or the sale of slaves, in America. This was a convenient idea, since American law, while allowing slavery in many states, banned the African trade, thus conforming to the bishop's interpretation of *In Supremo*. Pope Gregory's letter didn't conflict with American slavery, said England, because if it did American bishops would have made an antislavery statement at their recent meeting, but they hadn't. Finally, England recalled an audience he had with Pope Gregory in 1836. Then the pope had allegedly said: "Though the southern states of your union have had domestic slavery as an heir-loom ... they are not engaged in the *Negro traffic*."[20]

In successive articles in this *Catholic Miscellany* series, Bishop England reviewed in great detail the Church's attitude toward slavery, starting with apostolic times. As England put it, "the Savior did not repeal the permission to hold slaves, but ... he promulgated principles calculated to improve their condition, and perhaps, in the process of time, to extinguish slavery." This meant a gradual process—perhaps taking many generations. England didn't think it was possible to abolish slavery "now" in South Carolina. It was "for the legislature and not for me" to decide about abolition in the future. The bishop died soon after his slavery articles were published. While England had suggested a gradual end to slavery, he had done it in such a deferential manner, and in the context of an attack on the abolitionists, so that the slavery forces were willing to accept him as one of their own.[21]

American Catholics Break with Catholics Across the Atlantic on Slavery

An anonymous "Son of Erin" wrote to the *Georgia Telegraph* in 1843 to denounce the powerful Irish crusader Daniel O'Connell, known as "The Liberator" for his crusade to free Irish Catholics from British oppression. O'Connell's crusade had led to Britain in 1829 recognizing equal rights for Catholics in its empire, and now O'Connell, backed by supporters in Ireland and America's Irish diaspora, was campaigning for Irish home rule (then called "Repeal"). Macon's *Telegraph* covered these campaigns, and wished "God speed" to Repeal. The paper did not identify the "Son of Erin," but his literary style would probably put him in the planter, professional, or business classes, rather than among the railway workers. As for his reasons for anonymity, that could be from a desire to avoid antagonizing the local Irish with harsh words against the Liberator, or from some other cause which deterred him from putting his name before the public. Given the comparatively small numbers of the better-off Irish Americans in the area, the letter could have been by Michael Healy or someone known to him.

O'Connell's crusade for Irish freedom was not what angered the "Son of Erin." In his July 4 letter, the anonymous correspondent denounced another of O'Connell's crusades—his campaign for the abolition of slavery, in which the Liberator invoked the pope to call on Irish Americans to campaign against slavery in their new country.

O'Connell was one of several Catholics outside the U.S. who believed slavery to be incompatible with the Church's teachings. Nicholas Bergier in France, Bishop Johann Sailer in Switzerland, Abbe Dugoujon (a missionary in the French Caribbean colony of Guadeloupe), and Jaime Balmes (a vigorous Catholic apologist in Spain) were authors, both lay and clerical, who denounced slavery as contrary to Holy Scripture and the Church's traditions. R. R. Madden, an Irish Catholic who served on an English-Spanish antislave trafficking court in Cuba, and who came to the United States as an expert witness on behalf of the slaves in the *Amistad* case, was also active in fighting slavery. O'Connell, though, was the one who had the most clout in America because of his influence with the growing Irish American Catholic community.[22]

As an Irish priest, Bishop England had been a valued ally and friend of O'Connell. Now, living as he did in the middle of a slaveholding community determined to preserve its peculiar institution, England thought that his old friend did not appreciate the delicate nature of the slavery question in the South, which as England saw it made immediate abolition—as opposed to more gradual emancipation—impossible. England was also angry at what he saw as the British government's hypocrisy, keeping the Irish in subjection while campaigning for the freedom of blacks.[23]

O'Connell's denunciations of slavery were reprinted in American abolitionist publications, in an exception to the anti–Catholic hostility of many abolitionists. Along with 60,000 other Irish people, Protestant and Catholic, O'Connell signed an 1843 address to Irish immigrants in America, urging them to use their "moral and political power" to oppose American slavery.[24]

Though Irish Americans supported O'Connell's battle for Irish freedom, they did not like his attempt to recruit them into abolitionism. Irish Americans did not want to associate themselves with a divisive antislavery campaign which they linked to their former English overlords. Antislavery advocates in America seemed to them to be Catholic-baiting Protestants (several of Lyman Beecher's children were examples) or even hardcore heretics whose very status as Christians was dubious (abolitionist William Lloyd Garrison and Unitarian leader William Ellery Channing were examples). As James Healy's brother Sherwood later put it, "those in modern times who pity the negro hate the church." There was an economic factor as well—the Irish poor competed with free blacks for menial jobs, and didn't like the thought of more freed blacks adding to the competition.[25]

This opposition among Catholics was encouraged by the fact that the traditional center of gravity of the American Church—along with its eldest sees, Baltimore and New Orleans—was in the South. Skepticism of abolitionism was not limited to the Irish in the South, but extended to the much greater population of Irish in the North, where the Church's new center of gravity in its population was emerging. Bishop John Hughes of New York, an Irish native, had written antislavery verses as a young landscaper at Mt. St. Mary's Seminary in slaveholding Maryland. But as a Philadelphia priest, Hughes befriended William Rodrigue, who became his brother-in-law, and Mark Frenaye, a merchant who supported Hughes' church-building projects. Both Rodrigue and Frenaye had escaped from the murderous slave rebellion in Santo Domingo, where enraged former slaves massacred whites. The lesson Hughes drew from his friends' hair-raising stories was that immediate emancipation would lead to disaster. Not even a personal conversation on the subject with O'Connell himself swayed Hughes, although O'Connell achieved the rare feat of "silencing" the bishop with his eloquence. Hughes wrote that Americans of Irish birth ought to "repudiate [O'Connell's] address with indignation."[26]

O'Connell's abolitionist commitment was soon put to the test. In Cincinnati, Irish-American supporters of home rule wrote to O'Connell in 1843 to contribute a donation to the Irish freedom movement ... and to denounce abolitionism. Slavery was bad, said the Cincinnati letter, but the American abolitionists were the Church's "bitter[est] enemies," and slaves lived in a "state of degradation" such that freeing them at once would be disastrous.[27]

An angry O'Connell responded to the letter from Cincinnati during a rally in Ireland. To the Cincinnati Irish, he said, "it was not in Ireland you learned this cruelty." As O'Connell saw it, Pope Gregory's decree prohibited American slavery, even under Bishop England's narrow interpretation that the document applied only to the slave trade. Didn't states in the Upper South breed slaves for sale to the Deep South cotton states? This was just as bad as the African slave trade, and came under the pope's prohibition on slave trafficking. O'Connell's comment ought to have struck home, since the internal slave trade was very conspicuous in the South and publicized by abolitionists in the North. "If you be Catholic," said O'Connell, "you should devote your time and best exertions to working out the pious intentions of his Holiness."[28]

Abolitionists retained the hope that the diaspora Irish would line up behind Ireland's liberator. Boston abolitionists William Lloyd Garrison and Wendell Phillips held a meeting in their city's Faneuil Hall to publicize O'Connell's speech and attempt to recruit the Irish for abolitionism. They sought to combine the Irish home rule cause with the antislavery crusade. In addition to praising O'Connell, Phillips offered "three cheers for the abolitionist

Pope Gregory XVI," eliciting the desired response. On an earlier occasion, Phillips had praised the Church for lacking race prejudice, citing Fr. George Paddington, a black priest studying for the priesthood in Rome "with none to sneer at his complexion." Phillips did not mention some additional details. Fr. Paddington, an Irish-born black man, had been ordained in Haiti by Bishop England before going to Rome to continue his studies. While Fr. Paddington had been well received in Ireland, he described the United States as the "cursed land of slavery." The Irish audience in Boston, unimpressed by the example of their black countryman, applauded two other speakers who repudiated O'Connell and Pope Gregory, disavowing any support for abolitionism.[29]

William George Read, an influential Catholic layman and friend of Bishop England's, arranged for the publication of the late Bishop England's slavery articles in book form. Read wrote in an introduction that O'Connell had "misconstrue[d]" Pope Gregory's decree as being against slavery. O'Connell himself blew any remaining chance of connecting with the American diaspora in a March 1845 speech. He called on Britain to support Irish home rule, promising in exchange that the Irish would become loyal to the London government. Backed by the supportive Irish, "the throne of Victoria can be made perfectly secure—the honor of the British empire maintained—and the American eagle, in its highest point of flight, be brought down." Irish Americans rushed to affirm their defense of the "American eagle." O'Connell followed up this bridge-burning speech with another, warning Americans that if they went to war with Britain, the latter would send black troops to the South to promote slave revolts. Eager to prove their loyalty to the United States, Irish Catholic leaders again rejected O'Connell's anti–American antislavery activism as kow-towing to the hated British and opening the Irish immigrants, through guilt by association, to charges of radicalism and disloyalty to American institutions. As a group of Irish immigrants in Philadelphia protested to O'Connell as early as 1838, his anti–American remarks would cause "our native American citizens" to view the American Irish "jealously and suspiciously." The Philadelphia epistle averred that Irish Americans "bear true allegiance to the country that has adopted them and are ever ready to serve her."[30]

O'Connell's avowals of British patriotism didn't work with the authorities. He served a term in British prison for his home rule campaign. During this time, a devastating fungal blight hit the Irish potato crop, leading to massive starvation and the emigration of many of the survivors to the United States, in wave after desperate wave. A weak and sick O'Connell went on a journey in 1847 to see Pius IX. He died en route, and had most of his body buried in Ireland, but this faithful Catholic had his heart buried in Rome. Hopes of the Irish American Catholics joining an antislavery campaign seem to have died with him.[31]

The Irish Americans settled into their antiabolitionism. Their reasons were numerous—the competition of the Irish poor with free blacks for blue-collar jobs, Irish affiliation with the immigrant-friendly but proslavery Democratic Party, and a characteristic immigrant desire to integrate themselves into the American community by rejecting radical attacks on American institutions. Ironically, Irish effort to fit in by repudiating antislavery activism had the effect, among many antislavery Northerners, of provoking additional prejudice against the Irish immigrants as supporters of an un–American and immoral practice.[32]

By 1848, Michael Healy was president of the Hibernian Society and headed up its St. Patrick's Day celebration. In all likelihood, Michael had returned to the Church. And with the education of his children in the North satisfactorily arranged, he would have felt confident in taking a more prominent role in public affairs. After all, the mere fact of having black families in defiance of local mores did not stop powerful Georgia whites from being integrated into the power structure, in some cases even going into politics. The Hibernian Society toasts ripped into Britain for making the Irish into "slaves" and subjecting them to "starvation" in the Famine. The late hero-statesman, Daniel O'Connell, was toasted, but there was also a toast to "the American eagle," a reference hard to miss after O'Connell had ruffled the feathers of that bird. Healy offered a toast to "Thomas Jefferson, the disciple of liberty." The banquet represented an Irish-American consensus, North and South: honoring O'Connell as a martyr to Irish liberty, respectfully brushing him aside to the extent he tried to advocate liberty for American slaves.[33]

Despite his apparent integration into Macon society, Michael Healy advertised his plantation and slaves for sale, declaring that he "wish[ed] to change his business." No sale seems to have been consummated before his death, but his ads show that he may have been seeking to close up shop as a planter.

Other American Catholics Grapple with the Idea of Slavery

On May 21, 1844, the *Georgia Telegraph* reported that "the most terrible Riots that have ever been known in the country" had erupted in Philadelphia. Irish Catholics and anti–Catholic "Nativists" had fought in the streets, and the nativists attacked Irish houses and buildings, as well as a Catholic church, burning it to the ground. In July, there was another flare-up, chronicled by the *Telegraph* and only suppressed by the state military forces.[34]

The riot was the culmination of Catholic-Protestant tensions, but the immediate cause was a dispute over the use of the Bible in government schools. School authorities required all students, even Catholic students, to read from the Protestant King James Bible. The bishop of Philadelphia, Francis Patrick Kenrick (the future archbishop of Baltimore), asked that Catholic pupils be allowed to read from the Douay translation instead. The school committee exempted Catholics from reading the King James without allowing the Douay version. This compromise, acquiesced in by Kenrick, was too much for the anti–Catholic element in the city, who started trouble about the supposed suppression of the King James version. This trouble culminated in the riots of 1844. Kenrick took a limited defensive posture—it was not his nature to take an aggressive stance.[35]

Kenrick was known and esteemed, not for his militancy, but for his great learning. He employed that learning in a book on moral theology he published in 1840. The book was intended to be studied by priests and future priests to help them do their duty when sinners came to them in the confessional. Kenrick's work laid out what constituted mortal sins which Catholics must confess to their priests, along with the proper penances to impose for such sins. Among the topics covered in this comprehensive work were the duties of masters and slaves. Kenrick's discussion of slavery manifests the same timidity which he showed in his confrontation with his Philadelphia enemies.[36]

Kenrick could draw upon a list of Church fathers and moral theologians who had addressed slavery. Early Church fathers like St. Gregory of Nyssa, St. John Crysostom, and

Gregory the Great had suggested that slavery fell short of the Christian ideal and urged owners to gradually emancipate their slaves. Papal declarations repeatedly denounced the traffic in Indian and black slaves. Under the influence of leaders like these, reflected throughout the Church, slavery had been purged from much of Catholic Europe by the end of the Middle Ages, though St. Thomas Aquinas still wrote that slavery could be valid in this fallen world, as a consequence of sin, though in violation of the natural law. Traditional Catholic teaching held that there were several legitimate grounds on which people could be enslaved. Kenrick adopted this view of legitimate slavery. One ground for enslavement was conviction of a crime. Another ground was capture in a just war. A third rationale was self-sale to a master. The final, most shaky reason was being the child of a slave. The theologians, and Kenrick, did draw an important distinction—a slave was not the property of the master, since no human being could own another as property. Instead, the master had the right to the *labor* of his slave only.[37]

Slaveholders had duties under the natural law and the divine law which went beyond the positive laws of the slave states. Kenrick said that masters were obliged to respect slave marriages, even if the slaves got married against the master's wishes—slave states, in contrast, did not recognize marriages among slaves. Husbands and wives, said Kenrick, could not be arbitrarily sold away from each other, nor children from their parents—though slave states allowed this. Catholic masters had to provide at least some education in the fundamentals of the faith, and afford slaves relief from manual labor on Sundays and holy days (if this could be done without giving idle slaves the occasion for revolt). While masters were permitted to whip their slaves for certain misbehavior, they were not allowed to inflict disproportionate punishments, or mutilation.[38]

Masters were also required to provide slaves with food, clothing, and shelter in exchange for their labor, though they should not give food that was too rich and luxurious—as if that were a danger. While the master could recover runaway slaves, a fugitive slave who confessed his sins to a priest should be absolved without being required to return to his master—the harsh fate of recaptured runaways made it unfair for a priest to order the slave to return to servitude.[39]

Kenrick faced a difficulty. His theoretical defense of slavery did not seem to apply to slavery as it actually existed in the United States. American slaves were subject to breakup of their families, were denied religious education, were subject to excessive punishments, and generally treated worse than Kenrick's idealized version of slavery would allow. There was also the question of whether American slaves were actually slaves at all under the standards Kenrick articulated. The ancestors of American slaves had not all been convicted of crimes, nor had they all voluntarily sold themselves into servitude. The capture of slaves in Africa had met the consistent denunciation of the popes, so such captures could hardly be defended on just-war grounds. If the slaves' ancestors had not been legitimately enslaved, then even the Church's teachings on the legitimate grounds for slavery would seem to mean American slaves were entitled to be free men and women. So it appeared that American slaves were illegitimately held in servitude.[40]

Yet Kenrick was not the sort of person to throw down the gauntlet at an entire social system. The bishop who shrank from conflict with anti–Catholic nativists in his own city was not going to preach the destruction of America's well-established slave system. Kenrick got around the theological problems of slavery's legitimacy by arguing that slavery in America had persisted a long time, and that a hasty emancipation of the slaves would cause social disruption—so the existence of slavery was justified by long practice and by the public interest. Having patched over the gaps in his proslavery argument, Kenrick called for deference to the slave system. For instance, while he deplored the laws against educating slaves, Kenrick urged that "nothing be done" in defiance of these laws.[41]

There were other Catholics in the United States who in some way or other faced the dilemma of slavery. The first notable example is one of the Founding Fathers, Charles Carroll of Carrolton, member of a powerful Maryland Catholic family and signer of the Declaration of Independence—indeed, the last surviving signer of the Declaration, dying in 1832 at the age of 95. Carroll was more than a cafeteria Catholic—he spent his youth in France being educated by Jesuits before returning to America to be a leader of the patriot cause in Maryland.[42]

Despite owning a large plantation with slaves, Carroll recognized the need to free his country from slavery's curse. With independence won, Carroll served in the Maryland legislature and cosponsored a bill to eliminate slavery in that state. The bill failed. Later in his career, Carroll was active in the American Colonization Society, which sought to colonize freed slaves in Africa—the U.S. set up a colony in Liberia in West Africa where many freed slaves were settled (some American priests were briefly assigned to serve the small Catholic population), but there was not a significant enough number of settlers to put a dent in the American slave population. Carroll was aware of the problems of slavery, but was frustrated by the continued agitation about the issue at the time of the Missouri crisis in 1820. Slavery "is admitted by all to be a great evil," he wrote; "let an effectual mode of getting rid of it be pointed out, or let the question sleep forever." Shortly after Carroll's death, William Lloyd Garrison and other abolitionists rose up to demand unconditional abolition of slavery—without requiring the former slaves to leave their homes in the United States. Garrison was frustrated at the popularity of slaveholders like Carroll.[43] It was this more militant phase of the antislavery movement which triggered the riots in Charleston and elsewhere.[44]

Charles Carroll's cousin John was the first Catholic bishop in the U.S., rising to be archbishop of Baltimore, the first and de facto most prestigious see in the country (the pope rebuffed the American hierarchy's efforts to raise Baltimore's status de jure). Bishop England's diocese of Charleston was carved out of the late Bishop Carroll's archdiocese. John Carroll, too, had reservations about slavery. Writing to a priest who had moral reservations about serving in a slaveholding community, Bishop Carroll wrote to express his own doubts about slavery while telling the priest to stay at his post. After all, the priest might have the opportunity, in the course of his ministry, to alleviate the condition of the slaves. Bishop Carroll also got involved in the question of the large number of slaves owned by the Jesuit order in Maryland, who worked the several plantations the order owned. The issue caused internal turmoil among the Jesuits because of the moral problems of slaveholding, the question of whether the Jesuits should own so much land in the first place, and the financial needs which could be met by selling off these assets. In 1838, the Maryland Jesuits sold off their slaves, mainly to Louisiana, in some cases separating husbands and wives in violation of clear Catholic doctrine. Carroll's successor, Bishop Eccleston, raised concerns about the transaction, and the local provincial who ordered the sale resigned. In Boston, then–Bishop Benedict

Fenwick wrote his brother George to deplore the "extraordinary news" about the "poor Negroes."[45]

A Catholic attorney developed a respectable antislavery record during the early part of his career. He set his own slaves free. In 1819, he defended a Methodist preacher, Jacob Gruber, who made a passionate antislavery speech at a Maryland camp meeting and was charged with stirring up a slave insurrection. Defending the Methodist reverend, the attorney defended Gruber's antislavery views. The lawyer called slavery "a blot on our national character," which should be "gradually, wiped away." The lawyer was Roger Brooke Taney, who later went over to the proslavery side.[46]

How did American Catholics, in practice, carry out their duties with respect to slavery? A study of Catholic slaveholders in a Missouri county tried to shed some light on that question. The less zealous Catholic slaveowners behaved like their Protestant neighbors, but among the more observant Catholics some points of difference could be observed. Observant Catholics were less likely than the Protestant owners to emancipate their slaves (as allowed by Missouri law, which was more permissive than Georgia law). At the same time, the observant Catholic owners were more likely to respect family ties between husbands and wives, or parents and children. Sometimes the Church solemnized marriages between slaves even when the masters had refused consent—showing a greater regard for slave marriages than the masters and the laws which reflected their attitudes. The local Vincentian seminary—like priests and religious throughout the country—had a reputation, deserved or otherwise, for treating their slaves leniently. The Vincentians were known to buy slaves who had been separated from their spouses or children, in order to reunite their families. In Louisiana, a state formerly settled by Catholics and retaining some French Catholic influence on its laws, a statute against selling slave children under ten away from their mothers provided better protection to slave families than was the case in more fully Protestant states.[47]

Holy Cross

The Quaker education of James Healy, son of Michael, had prepared him sufficiently for his new Catholic college that he was allowed to skip the equivalent of freshman year, which for him reduced the normal six-year course of study to five years.

Holy Cross College was located in Worcester, Massachusetts. The Massachusetts legislature (general court), skeptical of Catholics, refused to grant a charter to Holy Cross until the end of the Civil War, so the degrees it awarded were technically issued by Georgetown College, a Jesuit institution in Washington, D.C., that later became Georgetown University (Patrick Healy, by then a Jesuit priest, would become president of the institution in 1873). One of the opponents of chartering Holy Cross was an editor named Henry Wilson, who in 1849—the year of James's graduation—declared that no school which discriminated based on religion (other than a theological seminary) should receive the benefit of a charter.[48]

The Holy Cross curriculum provided three academic tracks—ecclesiastical, commercial, and professional. All Healy brothers chose the professional curriculum, and all but one of them were destined ultimately for ecclesiastical or commercial work. The professional course was meant to create well-rounded Christian gentlemen, with the requisite knowledge to serve their fellow man. This was in line with the Jesuit tradition of higher education for those destined for the elite. The inculcation students received in religious topics would prepare those students who wanted to join the priesthood for the additional training they would receive. The foreign languages included the usual Greek and Latin as well as French. Instruction in the modern sciences, history, and public speaking were also included. All the classes were supposed to be suffused with religious training as the priest-professors taught the connection between each subject and the principles of the Catholic faith. Each year, in accord with Jesuit practice, there was a retreat where students were guided in meditation on spiritual subjects. It was at one of these retreats—on November 18, 1844—that James and his brothers Hugh, Patrick, and Sherwood were baptized. They were confirmed the following June by Bishop Fitzpatrick.[49]

The professors also sought to promote strict discipline. The daily routine was very specific: rise at five for Mass, study, breakfast, classes, dinner, more classes, with a couple short breaks, study, say the rosary, by which time it was after eight, then free time until bed at 9 p.m. In accordance with best educational practices at the time, teachers could reinforce their authority by beating recalcitrant students, or at least smacking them on the head to make sure they paid attention in class. Punishment might also include forced memorization of large chunks of Latin poetry. Holy Cross still showed signs of its recent construction—the scaffolding around the main building had not been fully dismantled. James joined some of the student groups, took part in literary exercises, and made friends with many of his fellow students, to the extent of feeling free to comment on them in his journal. James also, as the eldest, kept track of the activities of his younger brothers Hugh, Sherwood, and Patrick. James recorded in his journal that he had become addicted to cigars, trying in vain to break the habit. He also repeated in his journal what he regarded as a hilarious story in a Boston paper about "a negro preacher" of the Protestant persuasion.[50]

The strain of academic life could be relieved by squirrel hunting in the local countryside, or swimming or skating (depending on the season) in local rivers. There were also shows in Worcester which the students were apparently allowed to attend—Jesuits have traditionally encouraged wholesome entertainments, and these shows *may* have qualified.[51]

While generally well liked by their young comrades, the Healys seem to have received a few racial slights during their time in Worcester, which rankled. James later wrote that "our condition is much more generally known about Boston than I had ever supposed," referring apparently to the siblings' multiracial status and partial slave ancestry. Sherwood and Patrick were darker than James, precluding any possibility that James, known as their brother, would be mistaken for a well-tanned white person.[52]

In 1846, Bishop Fenwick died, and his coadjutor, the Healys' initial sponsor, John Fitzpatrick, became the new bishop of Boston. By this time, the Healy boys had befriended Fr. George Fenwick, brother of the late bishop and the college's instructor in classical languages. Since the age of seven, James had been at various schools far away from his family's Georgia home. At Holy Cross, during college holidays, rather than return to their father's Georgia plantation, the Healys stayed with the relatives of priests in the Boston area. While Michael Healy came north occasionally on business, and may have visited his children, the Church became James's new family.[53]

There were legal reasons not to come back to Georgia. Georgia law regarded the Healy children as free, but insisted that they exercise their freedom outside the state. Recognizing the freedom of former slaves whom their former masters had settled in the North, the laws of Georgia banned these freed people from coming back to the state. The Georgia legislature wanted to limit the free black population, and it enacted that "free persons of color" could not come to the state. Lest there be any doubt in the Healys' case, another Georgia law prohibited free blacks who had lived outside Georgia (except in neighboring slave states) to return. In short, masters had to send their slaves outside the state in order to free them—to keep from increasing the free black population—and once gone, the former slaves could not come back—they could be arrested and fined every month that they did so (the fine was $100 for each conviction, and the free black would have to work it off if he couldn't pay it).[54]

So the Healy children were legally banished from their home state. They could, of course, take their chance on ignoring the law. Powerful Georgia planters sometimes defied the laws by sheltering their black families from official notice, and Michael Healy may have been able to pull this off, as he had been able to get away with publicly proclaiming Eliza his wife. Yet there would always be the possibility that some officious or resentful person would start a prosecution, as had been known to happen. The Healys chose not to take these risks.[55]

Unable to go back home to their parents even on school vacations, James and his brothers adopted Fr. George Fenwick as a father figure, seeking his advice on important personal matters and addressing him as "Dad." James recorded how he and Fr. Fenwick "had some talk ... about my future destiny." It may have been during these talks that James crystallized his eventual desire to enter the priesthood. He grew so attached to his new spiritual family that he appeared to think it noteworthy that he "recognized" a photograph of his mother Eliza "after so long an absence from home."[56]

Whether coincidentally with his inclination for the priesthood or not, James took an interest in the college's public speaking class. "I make it a constant practice to speak upon every question proposed," he wrote in his journal on one occasion. In the particular instance he spoke of, "I was rather beaten." But that was not his fault: "I had the weakest side." These are the words of someone who had at least some confidence in his eloquence. James placed first in his class and played a key role in his class's graduation in July 1849.[57]

Prominent guests at this event included the recent convert Orestes Brownson (watching the graduation of his son John) and Fr. Theobald Mathew, an Irish priest. Fr. Mathew, famous for his crusade against drinking, was at the beginning of a U.S. tour. While he had signed the Irish antislavery letter, he was able to convince skeptical Americans that in his tour he would denounce only the slavery of drink—not the slavery of slavery. The country was in the middle of a divisive debate on the status of slavery in the extensive territories recently acquired from Mexico, and foreigners meddling in the matter would not be welcomed. Reassured that the priest would not interfere during his tour with America's delicate domestic affairs, both the U.S. House and the Senate gave Fr. Mathew the privileges of their floors—symbolic honors granted to distinguished persons. After attending the Holy Cross graduation, Fr. Mathew would spend over a year traveling across America—including the South—giving his temperance sermons and administering abstinence pledges to many in his enthusiastic audiences.[58]

Thanks to his academic standing, James Healy was chosen to give the valedictory address for this first full Holy Cross graduation ceremony. He worried about the speech's reception. The night before, "I was quite melancholy & walked about all alone until bed time thinking of tomorrow." The address seemed to be a success. James showed the rhetorical skills of which he had boasted in his journal. He explained why the students of Holy Cross had chosen the school: "here we are taught to practice the faith of ages," as opposed to the present age's spirit of "anarchy and licentiousness." He thanked the professors for "the most uniform and unvarying kindness." He appealed to his audience: "Education is not a path of flowers unaccompanied by its thorns. It is a steep and arduous height you dare when you begin your upward course. Years pass over you like a dream; you spring up into men, while you are yet upon the journey; but never be discouraged! Still onward and upward you must proceed if you wish for success." As tears filled his eyes, Healy declared: "Today I cease to be a student.... Fellow students (and it is the last time I shall ever address you by that endearing name) fellow students, farewell!"[59]

Then came the granting of degrees to the top students, of whom James Healy was first. John H. Brownson, son of Orestes, was second (his brothers William and Henry Brownson had been baptized alongside the Healy brothers), and Hugh Healy was fourth.[60]

At a post-graduation banquet, as James noted in his journal, he and other students "layed in something to keep our *spirits* up"—though not in front of Fr. Mathew, who had left to give a proabstinence speech in Boston. That evening, James and his brothers, with a friend, went into Worcester to celebrate the day's events. They watched a minstrel show performed by the popular Ethiopian Serenaders. James commented in his journal that he and his companions "laughed a great deal," but noted that the minstrel show was not a high-class act—there was "too much noise" and "too much foolery."[61]

James had spent the formative period of his adolescence at Holy Cross College, and was now to depart for further study in other lands. Bishop Fitzpatrick, perhaps seeing a younger version of himself in his young proselyte, decided that the best way to train James Healy for the priesthood was to send him to the same institutions at which Fitzpatrick himself had studied, beginning at the Seminary if St. Sulpice in Montreal, Canada. James' French studies at Holy Cross probably made him fluent enough in that language to get along in the French-speaking, Catholic part of Canada. Later in life, others noted James's excellent fluency in French.

A preliminary, embarrassing issue had to be gotten out of the way first, both for James and for his brothers Sherwood and Patrick, who would be training with the Jesuits. By canon law, only men born in lawful wedlock could be ordained as priests (this rule was designed to block the illegitimate sons of priests from being ordained). If they were illegitimate, there would be no point in any of the Healy brothers commencing priestly training. The marital status of Michael and Eliza Healy raised some problems because there was no official record of it, plus there was a religious difference between the two, Michael apparently being Catholic. It was hardly surprising that no record of the marriage would exist, since Georgia law prohibited marriage between black and white people. And there had been no church wedding ceremony. But, as James wrote to his spiritual "Dad," Fr. George Fenwick, "Father assured me that he and Mother were really married." James was still anxious about the situation, as he explained to Fr. Fenwick: "it is not all certain that my mother was baptized"—

a potential stumbling block if Michael had received that sacrament, since marriages between the baptized and the nonbaptized were problematic. James hoped that Fr. Fenwick would "not ... give the affair any chance of becoming public." The racial difference between Michael and Eliza was not a problem in the eyes of the Church. As for the apparent informality of the marriage ceremony, in most of the U.S., an area regarded as mission territory where practices were less formal than in Europe, a man and woman could get married merely by having an informal ceremony away from any church and without any priest. In fact, Bishop Kenrick in his manual of moral theology *encouraged* this informal method of marriage in the case of interracial unions—a priest presiding over such a marriage would scandalize the white community, endangering the priest's relationship with his neighbors.[62]

Bishop Fitzpatrick did not leave a record of his reasoning, but he seems to have believed that Michael and Eliza's marriage was perfectly valid. So James Healy set out for Canada to begin his studies for the priesthood.

Down to Georgia

Michael Healy concluded his life as a respected local citizen of the Macon area. He entered some of his horses in the spring meeting race near Macon in April 1849. Articles in the *Georgia Telegraph* began criticizing the pope's suppression of freedom in his domains—so contrary to the ideas of the liberty-loving people of Georgia. But the *Telegraph* correspondents, like many Southerners, balanced their anti–Catholic suspicions against their gratitude to Church spokesmen—especially in the North—for fighting the growing anti slavery movement. An article in the May 14, 1850, Georgia *Telegraph*, reprinted from the *New York Express*, indicated this tendency. The article summarized an antiabolitionist speech by a Catholic priest. Fr. Jeremiah Williams Cummings, of St. Stephen's Parish in New York City, was a friend of Orestes Brownson, the Massachusetts convert, and an advocate for what he considered reforms in the American Church. The *Telegraph* article paraphrased Fr. Cummings as suggesting that slavery would "die out of itself" over time, and would do so all the quicker if the Church increased its influence in America. But Fr. Cummings devoted considerable attention to denouncing the crusade of foreign abolitionists (and, by extension, the American variety) for the immediate freedom of the slaves. Using a homespun image, the priest compared abolitionists to the man who burned his barn to roast a pig. Michael Healy may have been too distracted to pay attention to the report of Fr. Cummings' speech. His wife Eliza died on May 19, 1850—five days after the article was published in the *Telegraph*. Michael did not outlive his wife for long—he died on August 29, 1850.[63]

5

"The radical necessity of the Church"

An otherwise excellent book on Orestes Brownson's life has a misleading title, referring to Brownson as a "religious weathervane." While it is true that Brownson frequently changed direction, switching dizzyingly from one religious and political view to another, he was not a weathervane. A weathervane changes with the prevailing winds, but Brownson went against the wind as often as he went with it. His own intense grappling with the biggest problems of life dictated his changes, rather than changes in spiritual and intellectual fashion.

Vermont's rocky soil was not as fertile as that in the western states, but the social climate was fertile in producing idiosyncratic people and movements. In Vermont could be seen, in perhaps the strongest form, a strain of fervor for unorthodox religions and causes which also affected New England, along with the western part of New York. This region would soon be called the "burned-over district" because its people responded to frequent religious revivals in the area, indicating a spiritual hunger that insisted on being fed, not necessarily with conventional fare but with fare that appealed to the people's earnestness and sincerity.[1]

Orestes Brownson was born into this environment in 1803, in Stockbridge, Vermont. His father, Sylvester Augustus Brownson, died when Orestes was young, leaving his mother, Relief Metcalf Brownson, to cope with five children and little income with which to care for them. Relief ultimately sent the children to be cared for by other families, Orestes to a family named Huntington in nearby Royalton. His later scramble to support himself, and his early family situation, may have contributed to an unsociable, intense nature which made it hard for him to get along with others. As the narrator in his autobiographical novel *Charles Elwood* put it: "Poverty is a stern master, and when combined with talent and ambition, often compels us to seem wanting in most of the better and more amiable affections of our nature."[2] Probably unable to afford school, Orestes largely educated himself, acquiring an enormous fund of knowledge as time went on, until he became the most educated, and the least schooled, of our four converts.

Orestes's family seems to have been surrounded by spiritual seekers and eccentrics. Judging from what appears to be an autobiographical description in Orestes's 1854 novel *The Spirit-Rapper,* Orestes as a boy knew "an idle, shiftless lad" named Joseph Smith, as well as Smith's family. Later, Smith claimed to have received divine revelations which led to the founding of the Church of Latter Day Saints (Mormons). Orestes's brother Oran joined the Mormons, and some of the Mormon leaders tried to convert Orestes as well.[3]

From the very beginning, Orestes was absorbed in spiritual matters. As his narrator explained in *Charles Elwood:* "My first lesson was the catechism, and my earliest delight was in reading religious books, conversing with religious people, and thinking of God and heaven." As a teenager, he had a conviction of sin and a religious conversion. He relapsed into religious doubt, then he accepted the stern Calvinism which had been inherited from New England's founders. He was baptized in 1822 at the Ballston Center (New York) Reformed Presbyterian Church, a congregation in the strict Covenanter tradition. Depending on whether one accepts Brownson's account in his 1857 memoir *The Convert,* or the indignant reply by Reuben Smith, who had been pastor at the time, the congregation at this time either resolved to avoid contact with "sinners" who fell short of Calvinist purity, or simply "renewed our church covenant" and resolved "to attempt more separateness from the world." By this time, Orestes had moved back with his family, who were living in Ballston Spa, near Ballston Center. He was glad, he wrote in a journal, that God had saved him from "dashing my speculative brains against the rocks of infidelity," as rejection of Christianity was called at the time.[4]

Meanwhile, Orestes had been studying writings by Universalists, and apprenticed himself to a printer who followed that religion. Universalism was centered in New England and upstate New York. Its members were farmers and humble people served by small-circulation journals and itinerant preachers. Under the Universalist theology, there was no hell, and everyone ended up in heaven after they died.[5]

Brownson worked briefly as a teacher and tutor. In this capacity, he visited the home of John Healy in Camillus, New York—John's daughters needed a tutor, and Brownson filled that role. In his frequent visits, Brownson fell in love with one of the daughters, Sally. Like a modern Abelard without the unpleasant side effects, Brownson wooed and won his pupil, and they married in 1827.[6]

By this time, Brownson had left teaching, and joined the Universalists as a preacher, ministering to scattered congregations of Universalists in the Finger Lake area of upper New York State, earning modest payments from such congregants as he had. He also wrote for, and in 1829 took on the editorship of, a Universalist journal, *The Gospel Advocate and Impartial Investigator.*[7]

Brownson began giving sympathetic coverage to Fanny Wright, a Scottish radical and feminist who as an activist and an itinerant speaker advocated many of the ultraradical causes of the day, from abolition of slavery, to married women's rights to easier divorce and birth control, to opposition to religion. Praised by Brownson and other radicals, Wright was known in less supportive circles as "The Great Red Harlot of Infidelity." What Brownson's wife thought of this connection with Wright, and later other female reformers like Margaret Fuller, is unclear. Based on hints he later dropped in his novel *The Spirit-Rapper,* Brownson may have excited suspicion that he had some romantic attachment to these fiery, unconventional females. In his memoir *The Convert,* Brownson expressed lingering affection for Wright—though her views were wrong and dangerous, she showed courage and consistency, and "many who condemn her have been and are greater sinners than she."[8]

Around this period, Brownson later claimed in *The Convert,* he was part of a secret conspiracy to form the country's children into a different mold by establishing state-run schools to indoctrinate them. However this may be, Brownson later backed away from his support for state education. While believing that the government should provide educational opportunities for the poor, he felt this should not entail compulsory attendance laws or taking control of schools away from parents and local communities, as reformers like Massachusetts education commissioner Horace Mann were advocating. Brownson continued this educational philosophy as a Catholic, denouncing state-run education as a form of state worship, or "statololatry."[9]

The Universalist leadership didn't like Brownson promoting Wright in their paper, and his parishioners were not fans, either. Nor did they like signs of a growing skepticism toward traditional Christianity, even the watered-down traditionalism of the Universalists. Brownson got fired as editor of the *Goepel Advocate* in late 1829. He declared that he was not a Universalist any longer, and he was accordingly "disfellowshipped."[10]

In this "infidel" phase, Brownson went through considerable mental torment. As he later put it, losing one's childhood faith is "a fearful change," the loss of "all that has been familiar to us ... what is this different in reality from that event that men call death?" But his anguish did not stop his editorial and political activities. He coedited a New York paper called the *Genessee Republican and Herald of Reform* for about a year from 1830 to 1831. Identifying with the working classes, he supported a third-party movement, the Workingman's Party, which sought to inspire a political revolt by the workers against the dominant parties.[11]

Brownson's sojourn in the wilderness of infidelity came to an end as he became converted to another brand of Christianity—Unitarianism. Unitarianism was, socially, many steps up the ladder from Universalism. The Unitarian movement had captured much of Boston's elite, in a reaction to the traditional Calvinism of the Bay State. Unitarianism was particularly powerful in Boston, towards which city Brownson was drawn. As Harriet Beecher Stowe (daughter of a Calvinist minister) noted, "Unitarianism reigned in [Calvinism's] stead," controlling the judiciary, Harvard University, the literary world, and "all the elite of wealth and fashion." Denying the divinity of Christ, expressing skepticism of literal biblical interpretation, Unitarianism was launched as a formal movement with a sermon by the clergyman William Ellery Channing. Channing emphasized the inherent goodness of humanity and the possibility of continual improvement. Brownson was inspired by Channing's works, naming a son William Ellery Channing Brownson. Brownson became editor of another paper, *The Philanthropist*, which combined advocacy of reform with religious discussion reflecting the editor's new Unitarian views.[12]

Serving as pastor in various towns, Brownson the new Unitarian minister preached in such congregations as he could find, continuing his advocacy of the workers' movement. He drew inspiration, though he did not slavishly emulate the early French socialist Saint-Simon. He became editor of the *Boston Reformer* magazine in 1836.[13]

The Unitarian preacher was highly influenced in spiritual and philosophical matters by several French writers, such as Victor Cousin, Benjamin Constant, and Félicité Robert de Lamennais (who left the Catholic Church after Pope Gregore XVI's antiliberal encyclical *Mirari Vos*). Brownson drew on these Gallic sources to prepare a vision of religious reform for Americans. As Brownson modestly put it to his friend George Bancroft, "I am trying to democratize religion and philosophy." This project was embodied in a book called *New Views of Christianity, Society and the Church*, which was considered important enough to get more buzz, and to outsell, Ralph Waldo Emerson's *Nature* published in the same year. The world needed a new religious synthesis, explained Brownson, a synthesis which properly balanced the spiritual and materialist elements. Christianity had gradually developed toward this synthesis, through historical stages such as the Reformation and the founding the Unitarian movement. Now, a new religion needed to emerge, and would probably burst forth first in the United States, preparing the way for "UNION" and "PROGRESS," since it was through the Christian religion that society was to be reformed.[14]

Another Unitarian minister, George Ripley, was a good friend of Brownson's—Brownson later said Ripley was the most influential Protestant in his life. With Ripley's and Channing's help, Brownson was appointed to minister to Boston's poor, and he ended up based in the Masonic Hall, where there was also a Unitarian "School for Human Culture." Brownson, as a man of poor origins who continued to advocate strongly for the poor, was an excellent messenger for the Unitarian gospel in a climate where Unitarianism was associated with the favored classes.[15]

Brownson looked the part of a powerful intellectual. A large and strongly built man of six feet, he was always happy to let whoever he was talking to know what he thought, eschewing the social graces in favor of blunt talk. He could work into the early morning on his articles, sermons, and his public lectures. As historian Philip Gura says, Brownson's "regimen was Spartan: he frequently worked until three in the morning, ate little (but drank strong coffee all day long), and at a time when temperance was in the air, already had sworn total abstinence. His only noted vice, besides being cantankerous, was chewing tobacco."[16]

An English visitor, Harriet Martineau, was impressed by Brownson on a visit to Boston and recorded her impressions in 1837. Deploring the conformism and insincerity of most ministers, she gave Brownson as an example of a new and better type of cleric. She called Brownson "a strong man, full of enlarged sympathies" who appealed to "the earnest spirits of the city and the day," who demanded "the whole truth" from ministers, not "abstract and inappropriate services." Martineau said that the establishment of Brownson's ministry was "an eloquent sign of the times."[17]

Brownson's son Orestes, Jr., was nine years old when Martineau's description of his father appeared. The boy, several decades later, left his own impression of his famous father: "in a great loose silk dress [he] used to preach with all the serious earnestness of life & death." The junior Orestes said that his father "impressed me with an idea of fear; that I can never overcome—His whole soul was in his metaphysical, philosophical & theological studies and he saw not that what interested him could not interest his son Orestes."[18]

By this time the Workingman's Party looked like a dead end to Brownson. A third party movement wasn't going to dislodge the two-party duopoly of Democrats and Whigs, so Brownson decided to work for reform through activities in the Democratic Party. His friend George Bancroft, an historian and Democratic Party politico who combined political pragmatism with idealized visions of public uplift, got Brownson a patronage job from Democratic president Martin van Buren. Brownson was appointed Steward (administrator) of the Marine Hospital in Chelsea. The income from the position was welcome to Brownson and his family, but to preserve his independence, he obtained assurances that he could publish his opinions without risking his job, no matter how inconvenient those opinions might be. This independence was useful, because Brownson's radicalism was reinforced by a severe economic downturn in the same year he got his new job, and he was determined to speak out on what he considered the capitalistic roots of the disaster.[19]

Many of Boston's Unitarians intellectuals sparked a new transcendentalist movement, eschewing Unitarianism's hyper-rationalism and trying to appeal to the heart as well as the head. Leading transcendentalists began meeting at a "club" in 1836. Ralph Waldo Emerson attended these meetings, as did journalist Margaret Fuller, who would later cover the revolution in Rome. Several "club" members were Unitarian ministers, like Brownson, the abolitionist Theodore Parker, whose extreme theological liberalism would later lead him away from the Unitarian ministry, and Brownson's close friend George Ripley, whose spiritual searching would lead him to the utopian community at Brook Farm. Brownson's comrades found him brilliant, but hard to get along with, focused more on pressing his own views than listening to what others had to say, and becoming angry when contradicted. Brownson stopped coming to the gatherings in 1837.[20]

Years later, after having long cast off the transcendentalists and other radicals in favor of the Church, Brownson would summarize the views of some of his earlier radical associates (voiced by the character Priscilla) as seeking to "emancipat[e] the state from the church, man and society from the state, and woman from man and society." While professing zeal for uplifting the human race, they did not show much affection for individual humans. With respect to slavery, for example, "all were of course abolitionists, or friends of the blacks, and therefore excluded studiously the negroes from their gatherings." In 1838, after Brownson left the group, an escaped slave named Frederick Douglass came North, attained prominence as an abolitionist, and many white reformers associated with him. Nonetheless, some white abolitionists were indeed uncomfortable with blacks, including fellow abolitionists like Douglass.[21]

Though no longer going to the transcendentalists' "club," Brownson kept up relations with these advanced-thinking people, and with others abroad. One summer he tutored a young man named Henry David Thoreau in German. When a young man named Charles Sumner visited Brownson's favorite philosopher Victor Cousin in Paris, the philosopher expressed a particular interest in Brownson, indicating that Brownson's interest was reciprocated.[22]

Brownson shifted from his working-class paper, the *Boston Reformer,* and put forth a more intellectual sort of publication. In 1838 Brownson founded the *Boston Quarterly Review*. While occasionally running articles by the likes of Theodore Parker and others, most of the content was furnished by Brownson himself, writing on philosophical, theological, and political topics.[23]

Brownson began a correspondence with South Carolina senator John C. Calhoun, a fellow Unitarian but, more significantly, a prominent statesman and political theorist. Calhoun had led his state's resistance to a federal tariff, which South Carolina proclaimed unconstitutional, facing down federal threats until Congress agreed to lower the tariff rates and end the crisis. To Calhoun, each state must have the power to block any action of the federal government deemed by that state to be unconstitutional. The alternative was to let a majority tyrannize over the minority. Calhoun's doctrine of nullification also allowed states like South Carolina to protect slavery from federal interference, slaves not being a minority entitled to protection under Calhoun's theories. Furthermore, Calhoun's doctrine of the equality of the states meant that citizens of slave states should be able to bring their slaves into federal territories, so that the institutions of each state would receive equal respect from the federal government—a doctrine pregnant with discord for the republic. Calhoun became a subscriber to the *Boston Quarterly Review,* saying, "It contains a vein of original thinking beyond most of our periodicals."[24]

Brownson shared Calhoun's concern about majority tyranny, but not because of a love of slavery. If the federal government was allowed to aggrandize power at the expense of the states, Brownson thought, the wealthy classes would use federal power to further oppress the workers. The battle to help the workers needed to be fought at the state level. This allowed for an alliance between Northern reformers and Southern planters. Brownson's correspondence with Senator Calhoun picked up, with at least one personal interview, and Brownson became one of Calhoun's Northern friends and allies, while Calhoun wrote Brownson about his crusade to restore constitutional government. Brownson told Calhoun in 1841 that the latter was "a sort of spiritual father, to whom I am indebted for nearly all the correct political views I have."[25]

In an article in the April 1838 issue of the *Boston Quarterly Review,* Brownson addressed

Before joining the Catholic Church, Brownson associated with prominent people in the unorthodox political and spiritual movements of the day. For instance, Henry David Thoreau was a pupil of Brownson (Thoreau's statue is seen next to a reconstruction of his Walden Pond cabin) (photograph by Matito, Flickr).

5. "The radical necessity of the Church"

the slavery question. He was still against slavery, unlike Calhoun, but he differed from the abolitionists in that he believed that the responsibility for dealing with the slavery problem rested with the Southern states, not with Northerners. Under the Constitution, the North had no business with Southern slavery. The slavery question was a distraction from the important issues facing the country—the capitalist system which oppressed the Northern workers was worse than slavery. This article provoked an attack by William Lloyd Garrison, whose paper the *Liberator* accused Brownson of betraying the cause of the slaves.[26]

It was not unusual for supporters of the labor movement at the time to disavow the abolitionists. Unlike the slaves, the Northern workers had no assurance that their employer would feed and clothe them, or care for them in their old age. A satirical poem printed in several workers' movement newspapers portrayed two young women, daughters of a powerful capitalist, who bemoaned the plight of the slaves, while, unheeded, one of their father's workers starved to death:

> Their tender hearts are sighing
> As Negroes' woes are told:
> While the white slave was dying,
> Who gained their fathers' gold.[27]

Brownson's boldest step in defense of the workingmen was an essay in the *Boston Quarterly Review* about the Christian obligation to oppose the existing labor system. The article was titled "The Laboring Classes." In this July 1840 article, Brownson portrayed the sufferings of the workers and the indifference of the ruling classes, and offered his analysis of the causes and cures of the situation. The article contended that there was such a mutual antagonism between the workers, seeking a fair share of the world's wealth, and the capitalists and their hangers-on, seeking to retain their unjust privileges, that the two groups were approaching outright warfare. This anticipated the class war doctrines preached by Karl Marx eight years later in his *Communist Manifesto.* Unlike Marx, Brownson did not think class warfare was inevitable. The community could avoid this result by a politico-spiritual renewal, in which the church, through the state, actively promoted social justice. One of Brownson's specific proposals was to abolish inheritance, so that every generation began with the same amount of property, with no invidious distinctions in property ownership based on birth.[28]

The program of "The Laboring Classes" could most plausibly be carried out by the Democrats, figured Brownson. Indeed, some radicals praised the article as expressing what the Democratic Party ought to be advocating. Calhoun also had words of praise. "The Laboring Classes" indeed became a campaign document—but for the Whigs, opponents of the Democrats. Supporters of the Whig presidential candidate, General William Henry Harrison, used Brownson's article to paint the Democrats as radical extremists who would wage war on property rights. When incumbent Democratic President Martin Van Buren lost to Harrison in November 1840, many Democrats blamed Brownson's article for his defeat—including, as Brownson understood it, Van Buren himself.[29]

After Van Buren lost the presidency, Brownson lost his job at the Chelsea Marine Hospital. More significantly, he lost his faith in the wisdom of the people. The aristocratic Whigs, in addition to circulating Brownson's article, had run a populist campaign featuring showmanship and singing (and drinking), and the voters had fallen for it. This showed

Brownson that the people as a mass could be foolish, or even oppressive, and could disregard the public interest.[30]

Another editor was impressed with Brownson's championing the cause of the common man. John O'Sullivan was the editor of the *Democratic Review* in New York. Widely viewed as the originator of the term "Manifest Destiny," O'Sullivan championed the cause of democracy and labor. He liked what he saw in Brownson's radical preaching, his "Laboring Classes" essay and his prior activism in the Workingman's Party. Early in 1842 the two made a deal by which the editors would work together on the *Democratic Review*. They signed an agreement by which Brownson, as coeditor, would have independence to write as he wished, without having to clear it with O'Sullivan, and vice versa.[31]

Brownson was not a good fit for a paper whose founding editor, along with most of the readers, believed in the sovereignty and wisdom of the people as embodied in majority votes. In editorials, Brownson alternated between philosophical discussions which the practical-minded O'Sullivan and his readers found too abstruse, and denunciations of the "mischievous nonsense" about the wise and virtuous public. The people, regardless of social class, "are *not* competent to govern themselves." A popular vote was not a panacea—as with Harrison's victory in 1840, "the Haves always carry it over the Have-nots." Brownson explained that America was a constitutional republic, not a pure democracy, with the Constitution's authority based "under the Church, [on] the authority of God." "*Concurring majorities*," Calhoun's principle of the states blocking bad federal measures, were the basis of the Constitution, not pure majoritarianism. The people could not act except as the "supreme authority" allowed. O'Sullivan found it necessary to print articles expressing his disagreement with Brownson's viewpoint. O'Sullivan could not help but be impressed by Brownson's intellect and sincerity, but thought he was fundamentally mistaken. "The young Liberal," pronounced O'Sullivan, "so often becomes metamorphosed into the old Conservative." As Brownson lost faith in the people, the subscribers were losing faith in him and O'Sullivan—the circulation of the *Democratic Review* went down, partly in response to the new coeditor's articles. Finally, Brownson and O'Sullivan negotiated an amicable divorce. Nothing daunted, Brownson established a new periodical of which he was the sole editor—*Brownson's Quarterly Review*, whose first issue appeared in January 1844.[32]

Along with these political problems, Brownson was undergoing yet another religious evolution. His study, particularly of the French philosopher Pierre Leroux, led him to a new conception of the Church, which he articulated in a book, *The Mediatorial Life of Jesus*. To Brownson, the transcendentalists seemed unmoored from community and tradition. Brownson countered with the portrait of a Church embodying God's presence in history and forming the basis of social solidarity and reform. The social cohesion of the Catholic Middle Ages gave Brownson a glimpse of an alternative to the individual-centered theology and social views of too many Unitarians and transcendentalists. Brownson wanted a form of Catholicism without the pope. He published sympathetic discussion of Trinitarian doctrine, and wrote to Channing to criticize his Unitarian teachings, though Brownson continued to hold his Unitarian pulpit.[33]

At this point, Brownson began meeting with a young man named Isaac Hecker. Hecker's family ran a successful New York flour business and he was interested, like Brownson, in reform movements and the candidacy of Calhoun. But young Isaac wanted more—he was tormented by ill-defined but powerful spiritual yearnings. When Brownson gave one of his lectures in New York, the Heckers looked him up and Brownson became a friend of the family. Isaac would visit Brownson's Chelsea home for spiritual discussions. Isaac's brother John encouraged these meetings, hoping that the more mature Brownson could give the confused Isaac some direction. Brownson initially prompted Isaac to attend Channing's sermons, and encouraged Isaac's plans to live on Brook Farm where George Ripley was residing. Isaac was circulating in some of the same transcendentalist circles as Brownson, but was dissatisfied like him.[34]

Isaac's experiences on Brook Farm did not satisfy his spiritual aspirations. Like Brownson, he felt a divine pull toward a fuller life. But he wondered: "How can I be assured of the reality of my experiences?" While Brownson's learned and intense talk inspired Isaac in his spiritual searching, and helped Isaac with many of his questions, the elder Brownson with his commitment to theological inquiry and intellectual rigor contrasted with Isaac's more internal and contemplative faith. Isaac wrote that he was awestruck by the "profound truths rushing forth from [Brownson's] brain," but noted also that Brownson "never moves my heart," and because of his "peevish" nature, "he defeats but will never convince an opponent." But the two different men were moving in similar directions. In 1843, Brownson was at a point where he meant "to preach the Catholic doctrines and administer the sacraments" without joining the Catholic Church.[35]

Hecker was, as he later put it, Brownson's "disciple." But the influence was not one way. In their later recollections, both Brownson and Isaac gave each other credit for their respective journeys toward the Catholic Church. The long conversations in Chelsea were bearing fruit. After unsatisfying consultations with Bishop John Hughes and an Episcopal priest, Isaac learned that Brownson was getting ready to become Catholic, and Brownson told Isaac that "your devotion must be regulated and directed by the discipline of the Church."[36]

As Brownson moved away from the Unitarian Calhoun theologically, he continued to support the senator politically. As Calhoun began exploring a presidential candidacy, he rallied supporters, including Brownson. In the January 1844 of his new *Brownson's Quarterly Review*, Brownson published an article praising the "pure and upright" Calhoun, though technically declining to endorse him for president. Brownson particularly praised Calhoun's doctrine of state sovereignty and his fight for the principle of state nullification against the federal tariff law.[37]

Calhoun subscribed to the *Brownson's Quarterly Review* and "heartily approve[d]" Brownson's summary of the Senator's nullification views. Calhoun disappointed Brownson by deciding not to seek the Democratic nomination for president. Brownson did not accept Calhoun's withdrawal, publishing an April 1844 article urging the South Carolinian to run as an independent, fighting under "the old republican [states' rights] flag of '98, all torn and tattered as it may be."[38] Calhoun didn't take up the invitation.

Along with political disappointment, Brownson was moving toward what he considered a major spiritual advancement, as he sought out the bishop of Boston for instruction in the Catholic faith. Bishop Fenwick passed Brownson along to Bishop Fitzpatrick, then Fenwick's coadjutor. Fitzpatrick taught the eager inquirer the principles of St. Thomas Aquinas's scholastic theology, a detailed system which differed from the editor's previous philosophical guides. The intellectual rigor of the scholastic method and tradition appealed to Brownson, and Fitzpatrick was well positioned to give such instruction, being himself steeped in this knowledge. Fitzpatrick also taught from St. Augustine. Bishop Fitzpatrick was somewhat suspicious of Brownson's eccentric background of continually shifting views, so different from the bishop's experience of being reared in the Church from his youth. Determined to become fully Catholicized and to receive challenging, rigorously orthodox training, Brownson eagerly took Fitzpatrick's instruction and became a sort of disciple. Brownson even asked, successfully, to submit any theological discussion in his *Review* to Fitzpatrick's revision and censorship, to keep the *Review* on an orthodox course.[39]

In May 1844, in a move which ought not to have surprised anyone, Brownson quit his position as a Unitarian minister. In the July *Brownson's Quarterly Review* came an announcement which also wouldn't have surprised those following the editor's career. Brownson was going to join the Catholic Church.[40]

"We know not what new light may break in upon our minds," wrote Brownson, "but, so far as at present informed, we are compelled, by what seems to us to be the force of truth, to look upon the separation of the reformers from the Roman communion, in the sixteenth century, as irregular, unnecessary, and, we must add, as a serious calamity to Christendom." Brownson wrote of "the radical necessity of the Church."[41]

On October 20, 1844, the Catholic Church received Brownson as a convert. Normally this would be a wrenching experience in becoming alienated from former Protestant friends, but Brownson later claimed that, since he hadn't made deep friendships in the Boston intellectual community, he had all the fewer ties to sever. Hecker had preceded Brownson by two months. Brownson's wife and children followed soon thereafter. Once her husband led her into the Church, Sarah Brownson became a devout follower of her new faith. "I love every thing Catholic," she wrote a friend, "and with God's help I will live and die a Catholic." Brownson credited Isaac Hecker in helping Sarah, like himself, accept Catholicism.[42]

"I feel that I am a pioneer in opening and leading the way," said the intense Isaac Hecker later. "I *smuggled myself* into the *Church,* and so did Brownson." Brownson's friend George Ripley left Brook Farm as the utopian community failed, and went to work as a journalist. Ripley never came over to the Church, but his wife Sophia, continuing the spiritual search which inspired their living at Brook farm, converted, again encouraged by Isaac Hecker.[43]

Brownson's Quarterly Review was now a militant Catholic organ, featuring frequent attacks on Protestants and putting the Church forward as the only source of salvation, and the only guarantor of a sound political and social order, answering the anti–Catholic polemicists in a militant and unsparing tone. The *Review* turned on Brownson's former transcendentalist and radical associates, one article proclaiming that "Protestantism Ends in Transcendentalism" (which was not a compliment). The editor firmly turned his back on his earlier views. He did not abandon reform ideas, but put them strictly second after affairs of the spirit. Bishop Fitzpatrick had urged boldness on Brownson, though this may have been as unnecessary as urging fierceness on a tiger. Protestants largely dropped their subscriptions.[44]

Brownson received an offer to edit another paper, the *Freeman's Journal* in New York. This organ of Archbishop Hughes had vigorously championed the cause of the Church against the Protestant-run Public School Society, a private group which, with New York City subsidies, monopolized government-funded education in the city. Hughes, through the *Freeman's Journal*, supported New York's Whig governor, William Henry Seward, in a hard-fought campaign to transfer control of the public schools from the Public School Society to local boards under the supervision of a City Board of Education. While ultimately not a satisfactory answer to the need for Catholic education, this new law, and Hughes's willingness to work with Seward, caused an unusual alliance between the two men.[45]

The *Freeman's Journal* reflected Bishop Hughes's own confrontational attitude toward the Church's enemies. When New York's churches were threatened with attack in the wake of the riots in Philadelphia in 1844, Hughes posted guards at the churches and told the mayor that if any Catholic churches were burned, New York would be burned like Moscow in the Napoleonic wars. The *Freeman's Journal* published an extra edition to rally Catholics and get the nativists to back off. The extra proclaimed that the local government's promises to protect Catholic property was "all MOONSHINE." Therefore, "LET EVERY MAN BE PREPARED TO DEFEND HIMSELF AND HIS PROPERTY." Coincidentally or not, rioters did not touch New York's Catholic churches, sparing New York a repeat of the Philadelphia riots.[46] This was the sort of uncompromising stuff that appealed to Hughes—but where could he find an editor after his own mind who could continue the paper with that style of writing?

Isaac Hecker and Orestes Brownson encouraged each other in their respective journeys to the Catholic Church. Hecker later became a prominent priest, and founder of a religious order. Here Fr. Hecker is shown at a ripe old age (Walter Elliott, *The Life of Father Hecker* [New York: Columbus Press, 1891]).

After the *Freeman's Journal* had run through a few editors, Hughes in mid–1846 entrusted the editorship to Fr. James Roosevelt Bayley. Bayley in turn allowed much of the material to be written by James McMaster, a convert who had grown up in a militant Scots Presbyterian household. McMaster had studied for the Episcopalian ministry, fallen under the influence of the high church Oxford Movement, and joined the Church. During the service to receive McMaster into the church, the convert held his candle too close to the one of the priests, setting the priest's hair on fire. McMaster later joked that "if I don't set fire to something more than that it will be a pity."[47]

Fr. Bayley was giving up the editorship of the *Freeman's Journal*, and offered the editorship to Brownson. Bayley thought that with Brownson at the helm, the *Freeman's Journal* would be in "good, safe hands." Brownson declined, saying that Bishop Fitzpatrick of Boston, who supervised Brownson's *Review*, "understands managing me" and "I dare not trust myself away from his direction." Brownson averred himself "a Bostonian" and "a Yankee," in context meaning someone of New England heritage, whose style would not be suited to a New York journal. Nor did Brownson think he could run a "brilliant, racy, popular" paper such as the

Freeman's Journal needed to be. As a "hater of democracy," Brownson suggested, he would not have the "compliance" toward the people which would be required of the *Journal's* editor.[48]

So, unable to find anyone else as well qualified as McMaster, Hughes finally agreed to sell the *Freeman's Journal* to the ex–Covenanter. From mid–1848, McMaster was the owner of the *Freeman's Journal* and put his own stamp upon it—taking a militant tone suitable to a paper defending Bishop Hughes's views.[49]

In his political articles, Brownson was not under episcopal supervision, and was free to develop his own ideas. Catholic principles, as Brownson saw them, were a necessary antidote to the excessive individualism, and hatred of authority, which he saw in Americans, including especially his former associates among the reformers and radicals. Lawlessness could undermine the whole structure of civilization, imperiling everything, including liberty. Brownson continued the Calhounism he had commenced while he was a Unitarian minister, applying the senator's doctrines. This brought Brownson into the midst of the controversy over the Mexican war. When the war commenced in early 1846, Brownson at first kept quiet. He was against the conflict, seeing it as a war of aggression, but he did not wish to undermine his own country—and certainly not to raise any question of Catholic dual loyalties. Embarrassingly, while there were numerous Catholic soldiers who fought bravely and well in the American army against Mexico, some Irish Catholics in the American army deserted and joined the Mexican army in the so-called San Patricio (Saint Patrick) Batallion.[50]

John Hughes, bishop, then archbishop, of New York, was the foremost Catholic prelate of his era (photograph by Mathew Brady and Levin Corbin Handy, Brady-Handy Photograph Collection, Library of Congress, Reproduction Number LC-DIG-cwpbh-02511 [digital file from original neg.]).

Brownson finally spoke out about the Mexican war in his July 1847 issue. He denounced the war as aggression against Mexico, sharing a viewpoint for once with many antislavery New Englanders including his former pupil Thoreau. Unlike Thoreau and the others, Brownson endorsed Calhoun's theory that the Constitution, based on the equality of all the states and their several institutions, protected slaveholders' right to bring slaves from slave states into any territory taken from Mexico. Brownson foresaw that the issue of territorial slavery would prompt discord—the "antislavery party" would try to prevent the South from exercising its Constitutional rights, followed by an attack on the slave system in the South itself, "and immediate emancipation or civil war will be the alternative—both bad, and one hardly more to be deprecated than the other." The way to avoid such a situation would simply be not to take any Mexican territory, precluding a dispute over the status of slavery in those territories.[51]

Calhoun, who had continued his fruitful relationship with Brownson, thought the latter's piece was the only recent article to deal properly with the issue of the Mexican War, and arranged to have Brownson's article circulated in South Carolina. Congress and the president did not take Brownson's advice—in 1848, after Mexico's defeat, the United States acquired an extensive territory from Mexico, and a North/South dispute indeed arose over the status of slavery in the new conquests.[52]

After Calhoun's death in March 1850, Brownson continued his defense of Calhoun's principles. Yet Calhounite ideas of state sovereignty, which critics denounced as revolutionary, coexisted in Brownson's mind with a strong defense of established governments against what he deemed the existential threat of modern radicalism.[53]

A controversy between the forces of rebellion and the interests of duly constituted government under law, as Brownson saw it, erupted in Massachusetts. As Brownson had predicted, the quarrel

James McMaster, Orestes Brownson's fellow convert-editor, became the owner of the Catholic *Freeman's Journal* in New York City (drawn by Erica Haberman from a digital image of a public-domain painting by Sister Angelico Dolan, reproduced by permission of Erica Haberman, digital image reproduced by permission of Pat McNamara).

over slavery in the territories taken from Mexico split the country between North and South, causing fears of disunion and civil war. In 1850, Congress compromised the issue by passing a series of measures granting various concessions to both North and South. One of the compromise measures was a beefed-up Fugitive Slave Act, making it easier for the federal government to recover slaves who had fled from their masters, returning them to the South. Northern opponents of the law called the new statute unconstitutional and ungodly, sometimes preaching resistance to it. During the debate over the compromise measure, William Henry Seward, Whig Senator and former governor of New York, invoked a "higher law" governing federal policy on slavery in the federal territories and requiring the exclusion of slavery therefrom. Seward's well-publicized phrase was soon applied to the Fugitive Slave Act, either to deny its moral validity or to mock those who would resist it.[54] To Calhounites like Brownson, for whom the Constitution guaranteed the right to hold slavery in the territories, Seward's invocation of the higher law was an attack on the Constitution itself, and resistance to the Fugitive Slave Act was of a piece with such lawlessness.

In January 1851, Brownson wrote an article on the "higher law." While there was such a thing as a higher law, a law of God superseding human enactments, the Fugitive Slave Act did not violate this higher law. It was the Catholic Church, and the Church alone, which could decide what the law of God required, thus avoiding anarchy—with everyone deciding what God wanted—on the one hand, or despotism—where people obeyed every human enactment however unjust—on the other hand. The Protestants' problem was that, lacking an authoritative Church, they had to either decide on an individual basis what laws to obey, which would be anarchy, or obey all laws, which would be "statolatry"—the worship of the state. By avoiding these extremes, Catholics are "at once freemen and loyal subjects."[55]

Soon, Brownson again called forth his editorial eloquence against his old associate, the Unitarian minister Theodore Parker. In 1851, the federal government seized a fugitive slave named Thomas Sims in Boston. Abolitionists and local blacks tried to organize a rescue, rouse the people against the seizure of Sims, and enlist the state courts against the federal slave-catchers, all to no avail. Sims was shipped back to Georgia, and Parker preached a sermon blaming the sins of the people for the fate of the captured runaway.[56]

To Brownson, the true sinners were not those who allowed the fugitive slave law to be enforced, but those who resisted the law by trying to "intimidate the authorities" and using lawyers to seek to "evade the law." Northern radicals, on religious grounds, denied the moral force of the fugitive slave law. Brownson argued that laws were to be presumed Godly unless proven otherwise, and the moral force of a law could not be at the mercy of the "private judgment" of every individual. Brownson said he opposed slavery as much as "the free soilers"; he would not have introduced slavery into the country if it did not exist, but it did exist, and trying to abolish it in present circumstances would lead to "a greater evil." Brownson opposed the lawless "principles and methods" of the abolitionists—like the Puritans they were, they were recklessly trying to "make this world a paradise," leading to the opposite result. Lawful authority had to be maintained: "The supremacy of law is as necessary to secure the freedom of the slave when emancipated, as to preserve the freedom of the master now."[57]

Massachusetts and the rest of the North, as Brownson saw it, were dominated by freesoilers—who wanted to exclude slavery from the federal territories. Freesoilers were as bad as abolitionists to Brownson's way of thinking, and just as dangerous. Here Brownson was not thinking only of slavery, but of the entire agenda of the radical intellectual crowd of which he used to be a member. If given their head, the radical forces would not stop with abolition, but would impose "the most frightful despotism, under the name of liberty, that it is possible to conceive." Of his former radicalism, Brownson reflected: "Alas! Men are often powerful to do evil, but impotent to repair it." The country needed the "conservative influence" of the South to counterbalance Northern radicalism and "preserve civilized society."[58]

Brownson thought that even politicians who supported the compromise of 1850 and opposed Northern radicalism were, inconsistently, sowing the seeds of future trouble and lawlessness by sympathizing with radical revolutionaries in Europe. In the turbulent years of 1848 and 1849, European rebels had risen up against established governments, earning cheers, usually at a distance, from American sympathizers—including Brownson's former New England comrades. Not only did these Americans praise the temporary overthrow of the pope in his domains, they supported the uprisings in the extensive Austrian empire, especially by the Hungarian nobility which sought autonomy or independence for their central European homeland. A key leader of this revolution was Louis Kossuth, who ran the rebel Hungarian government until the Austrians, with Russian assistance, crushed Hungarian resistance and restored Imperial authority.[59]

Brownson believed that the same disorganizing anarchist/despotic tendencies which he saw in domestic politics were reflected in the European revolutions and the American reaction to them. The modern world "sympathizes with every rebel," he noted sourly in 1849. In 1851, the United States government dispatched a ship to bring Kossuth to America from his Turkish exile, and the Hungarian revolutionary received an ecstatic reception. Brownson was livid. He wrote that Kossuth and the other European revolutionaries were "enemies of the human race," part of a "grand conspiracy" to overthrow "every legally constituted government in the civilized world." The Fillmore administration, so helpfully conservative at home, seemed to be compensating by expressing a dangerous sympathy with revolutionaries abroad. The United States was at risk of becoming "the second, or the bottle-holder, of universal rebeldom."[60]

Brownson's attitude as a convert, and for that matter throughout his life, was expressed in his 1857 memoir *The Convert, or, Leaves from my Experience*:

> I hated what is called policy then, and I have no fondness for it even yet. A man's life-blood is frozen in its current, his intellect deadened, and his very soul annihilated, by the everlasting dinging in his ears by the wise and prudent, more properly the timid and selfish, of the admonition to be politic, to take care not to compromise one's cause or one's friends. My soul revolts, and revolts even to-day, at this admonition. Almost the only blunders I ever committed in my life were committed when I studied to be politic, and prided myself on my diplomacy.[61]

6

"The Catholics ... will be found among the fastest friends of the Union"

Winding Up Affairs in Georgia

Michael Healy's will left his property to his family and designated three executors—one of whom, Robert Hardeman, was a judge. The executors were to sell off the estate and send the proceeds to a friend of Michael's, the New York businessman John Manning, to provide for the children, including James Healy. The executors seemed dedicated to carrying out Michael's wishes, despite the color of the beneficiaries. Michael Healy had no "official" white wife and children to compete with his black family—a frequent cause of inheritance disputes—and no such disputes arose.

The will still had to be probated, and Hugh Healy, the second-oldest child and the oldest still in the United States, handled this and some other business. Hugh was one of the minority of the Healy children who did not go into the priesthood or a religious order—he went into business in New York under John Manning. Hugh went down to Georgia to handle the estate, bring the youngest three Healy children north, and provide a suitable gravesite for Michael and Eliza.

In the eyes of Georgia law, Hugh was a free person of color, and could be arrested for daring to return to the state. Yet the influential executors of Michael's will may have smoothed Hugh's path, helped him to avoid arrest, probate the will, and bring the three youngest Healy children up North, where they were duly baptized.[1]

While in Georgia, Hugh also arranged the erection of a tombstone for his parents' grave. Together in death as in life, Michael and Eliza are buried side by side in a final act of defiance to racial caste.[2]

In a Tuscan Dungeon

In early 1853, Protestant activists took up the cause of two Protestants from the Grand Duchy of Tuscany, a Catholic kingdom in Italy. Francesco and Rosa Madiai, husband and wife, were convicted in 1852 of proselytizing on behalf of Protestantism, committing what the prosecution called an "inadvertently political" offense against Tuscany, whose government feared Protestants not only as heretics but as potential Italian nationalist rebels.

The couple got approximately three-year sentences. Evangelical Protestants in Britain took up the case.[3]

In early 1853, the Madiai agitation came to the United States, as meetings in many cities held rallies inspired by the American and Foreign Christian Union, a Protestant group which set itself to oppose Catholic influence and evangelize the backward Romanists. A large rally was held in New York City's Metropolitan Hall. The call for the meeting said that the Madiais were in prison merely for reading the Bible.[4]

Another initiative of the American and Foreign Christian Union, building on its campaign for the Madiais, was to call for the United States to crusade for religious freedom around the world, and to make treaties with other governments safeguarding the religious freedom of American Protestants. Senator Lewis Cass (father of the American minister to the Papal States) took up this cause, urging that America take the lead in promoting "freedom of conscience" throughout the world.[5]

Archbishop John Hughes of New York went to the New York Madiai rally, and he had had enough. The archbishop wrote a lengthy letter in the *Freeman's Journal,* the Catholic periodical edited by convert James McMaster,

Rosa Madiai and her husband, Italian Protestants, were condemned to prison in the Catholic kingdom of Tuscany, in Italy. Protestant activists in England and American took up the Madiais' cause. Archbishop Hughes believed that pro–Madiai activists were hypocrites who were unfairly stirring up Protestant passions against American Catholics ("The Misses Senhouse," eds., *Letters of the Madiai, and Visits to their Prisons* [Philadelphia: Presbyterian Board of Publication, 1853]).

denouncing the new movement for Protestant freedom abroad. To Hughes, the Madiai campaign was an anti–Catholic initiative led by the hypocritical British establishment which oppressed Irish Catholics. The prelate rejected the idea that the Madiais had merely been punished for reading the Bible, a bizarre slur against the Church, which had developed and nurtured the Bible in the first place.[6]

Different countries, said Hughes, should respect each other's internal affairs. While the U.S. did not have Tuscany's laws against Protestant proselytism, it had other laws against the free exercise of conscience, suppressing the polygamous Mormons in the West and abolitionists in the South. If the United State could protest to the Tuscans about human rights violations, the Tuscans could protest the burning of the Charlestown convent in Massachusetts.[7]

Hughes also deplored the Protestant agitation for stirring up ill will between Protestants and Catholics in the U.S., even though American Catholics had nothing to do with events in Tuscany. Catholics had won their right to religious freedom by their courageous fight for freedom in the American Revolution, and they might be called upon to fight for freedom again. In prophetic mode, Hughes said,

> The time may come, and perhaps sooner than is expected by our wisest public men, when the United States will have need of the support of all her citizens. Who can tell whether the future of the country may not reveal dangers, either from foreign enemies or from internal divisions which will test the loyalty and fidelity of every citizen of whatever religion? In such an emergency the Catholics, in spite of the denunciations to which they have been lately exposed, will be found among the fastest friends of the Union and the bravest defenders of the soil.[8]

Soon after this, the Tuscan government commuted the Madiais' sentence to banishment and the couple moved to Switzerland. An agent for the American entertainer P. T. Barnum wrote to a prominent English defender of the Madiais, offering to "exhibit" them in the U.S.: "I have no doubt they would draw fair audiences in our northern States, where the Protestant feeling runs strong." This offer apparently went nowhere, but the agent's business sense (or that of his boss) was correct—there was a strong "Protestant feeling" in the North which was determined to manifest itself against the Catholic Church.[9]

A Visit from the Cardinal

When Sylvester Rosecrans came back from Rome in 1853, he was assigned to St. Thomas Church in Cincinnati, then transferred to be an assistant priest at the cathedral. Impressed at the young priest's theological training, Archbishop Purcell made Sylvester a professor at Mt. St. Mary's of the West in Cincinnati, the seminary which at the archdiocesan council of 1855 would soon be elevated to chief seminary of the diocese. The 1855 decree made five of the bishops into a governing board (except the bishops in remote Detroit and upper Michigan)—thus Purcell along with the bishops of Cleveland (Ohio), Covington (Kentucky), Louisville (Kentucky) and Vincennes (Indiana) supervised the curriculum of the school.[10] But as of 1853, the new priest's worries were more than academic.

In June 1853, Cardinal Gaetano Bedini, designated by the pope as the pontiff's ambassador to Brazil, made a stopover in the United States in what was supposedly a trip to Brazil.

Ugo Bassi, the rebel friar who fought his pope, was a hero to nationalist Italians, especially after the Austrians executed him. Another renegade friar, Allessandro Gavazzi, came to the United States to whip up hatred against papal emissary Cardinal Gaetano Bedini, whom Gavazzi blamed for Bassi's death (George Macaulay Trevelyan, *Garibaldi's Defense of the Roman Republic* [London: Longmans, Green, 1908]).

The diplomatic mission was largely a cover story. Bedini's main purpose in visiting the United States was to make a survey of the U.S. Church, report what he saw, and suggest improvements. Bedini was also expected to try to reconcile some schismatic parishes with their local bishops (he failed at this). The American bishops were not entirely happy with having a high-ranking prelate poke into their affairs, but they had to cooperate with someone sent by the pope.[11]

If the Catholic authorities were ambiguous about the visit, many anti–Catholics were enraged. The renegade priest Allesandro Gavazzi, whom Sylvester Rosecrans had come across in Rome, appeared in New York City under the sponsorship of the anti–Catholic activists of the American and Foreign Christian Union. The former priest delivered what McMaster described as a "ferocious discourse," his fiery words and black garb riveting his hearers' attention. Gavazzi disclaimed being a mere Protestant—he was "a destroyer" out to extirpate the Catholic Church.[12]

Alessandro Gavazzi, renegade priest and self-proclaimed "destroyer" of the Catholic Church (J. W. King, *Allessandro Gavazzi: A Biography* [London: J. W. King, 1857]).

When it came to Cardinal Bedini, Gavazzi's rhetoric grew even more heated. The cardinal's mission in the United States, Gavazzi claimed, was to undermine American liberties. Gavazzi called the cardinal "the bloody butcher of Bologna" and blamed him for the execution of Garibaldi's chaplain, Ugo Bassi, during the revolution in the Papal States, even though the execution had been carried out by the Austrians.[13]

Hostile crowds in Boston burned the emissary in effigy and mobbed him in many of the places he visited, such as Wheeling, Virginia, and Pittsburgh, Pennsylvania. In Baltimore, someone fired bullets into the room where the Cardinal was staying. In New York, Italian exiles formed a plot to assassinate Bedini. One of the conspirators confessed the existence of the plot and gave a warning to the cardinal. The informer's colleagues promptly killed him.[14]

Shaken by this threat against his life, Bedini nevertheless published a letter in the *Freeman's Journal* denying any wish to pursue the would-be Italian assassins. "It is not by any means my wish to pursue anyone with the sword of justice. My life is in the hands of God rather than in those of men. My ministry is wholly one of peace and pardon. My heart is for loving even those that hate me."[15]

The cardinal was nevertheless quite nervous about the way events were turning out. Traveling to Canada, he shared a train carriage with Gavazzi, though the two foes did not speak to each other. In Canada Bedini faced angry hecklers. He returned from Canada "in a state of terrible trepidation," according to Bishop Fitzpatrick of Boston, but soon recovered "a feeling of greater security."[16]

The political establishment in the U.S. was generally friendlier. President Pierce and Postmaster General Campbell (a Catholic) met with Bedini. Pierce sent a Navy ship to bring Bedini to some of his Western destinations.[17]

As Cincinnati got ready for a visit from the cardinal, Fr. Sylvester Rosecrans sought to get another Catholic visitor. Now the clerical director of the Men's Catholic Literary Institute, Rosecrans wrote Brownson to renew a speaking invitation. Sylvester reminded Brownson of some philosophical discussions the two had previously had.[18]

Bedini's visit to Cincinnati caused more of a stir than Brownson. On December 21, Bedini came to the city and visited the seminary. He presumably also paid a visit to the new cathedral, erected the previous year. He would have met Fr. Rosecrans, who was part of the archbishop's entourage.[19]

Cincinnati was still simmering over the issue of Catholics in the schools. Also, many of the German immigrants who lived in Cincinnati were "forty-eighters" who had fled from the revolutions in their own country and hated Bedini as a symbol of political reaction. When Bedini arrived in Cincinnati, a German paper called the *Hochwächter,* in passages later translated into English by the *Catholic Telegraph,* incited its Teutonic readership against the visiting prelate. The *Hochwächter* urged that its readers "not do less" against Bedini than people in Europe had done against various counterrevolutionaries—the examples cited included three alleged enemies of the people who had been lynched by mobs. "Is there no ball [bullet], no dagger, for a monster whose equal was never on earth?" the paper chillingly inquired.[20]

On Christmas Eve, German demonstrators marched toward the cathedral and the nearby archbishop's residence next door. The marchers were estimated at around five hundred men and a hundred women. According to Archbishop Purcell's later recollections, as the mob was attacking the archbishop's house and smashing the windows, Sylvester descended the staircase and faced the rioters, helping to disperse them. If this occurred, Sylvester had some aid. Cincinnati police went to meet the mob, shots rang out, and a couple policemen and several Germans were wounded. One of the Germans was killed.[21]

Several alleged rioters were arrested, along with the publisher of the *Hochwächter,* but authorities dismissed the charges on the ground that a specific intent to attack Bedini could not be proven. Then the tables turned as suspicious Protestants came to see the police as tools of the Catholics who had unjustly attacked a group of peace-loving Germans. Several of the police were prosecuted—albeit unsuccessfully—on assault charges for their attacks on mob members. Police chief Lukens lost his job.[22]

Returning to New York in early 1854, Bedini slipped away unobtrusively and took ship for Europe, avoiding a hostile welcoming committee of New York Protestants. The U.S. government, through its minister in Rome, regretted the riotous mobs. The pope's secretary of state, Cardinal Antonelli, blamed the disorders on foreigners and exonerated the American government.[23]

Bedini submitted his report to Rome. Among other things, the emissary reported that Cincinnati's was among several "well managed" seminaries, but that the best way to train American priests was by setting up an American College in Rome.[24]

7

"The devil ... comes to us as a philanthropist"

The Angel Gabriel and the Pope

Orestes Brownson was in Boston, planning a move to New York, but for now he remained in the Puritan citadel.[1] He was prepared to tackle some of the currently simmering issues in the country. And sometimes the issues came to him.

A bizarre figure named John S. Orr came to Boston. A native of British Guiana, Orr was partially of black descent, though apparently such a background didn't stop him from winning a following among the whites in the places he visited. Orr wore a white robe and heralded his speeches by sounding a brass horn, giving him the nickname of the "Angel Gabriel." Orr went on tour around the Northeast, leaving destruction in his wake. Orr and his followers tried to burn a Catholic church in Boston—they were thwarted by the police, but they would not disperse until the police let them take the cross from the roof and burn it. The police also thwarted Orr and his mob in New York City, but Orr had better luck in Nashua, New Hampshire; Bath, Maine; and Syracuse, New York—attacking the Irish quarter in the first city and destroying one church each in the other two. Harassed by local officials, Orr took his agitation to Scotland and to his native British Guiana, stirring up more trouble and earning himself a prison sentence in the latter place.[2]

Brownson's Liberal Turn

A nutty and dangerous Archangel Gabriel imitator wasn't the only issue Brownson was grappling with at this time.

Quarrels among French Catholics led to a dramatic showdown between Brownson and a fellow bearded convert-editor—James McMaster. Brownson was sympathetic to a liberal French Catholic named Charles Montalembert, and McMaster championed a reactionary Paris editor, Louis Veuillot. Veuillot edited the newspaper *L'Univers*, the Catholic newspaper which had consoled Sylvester Rosecrans during his days in revolutionary Rome. In the pages of *L'Univers,* Veuillot waged war against anyone he deemed disloyal to the pope. Veuillot frequently mocked the idea of representative government and democratic freedoms.[3]

Montalembert, a frequent correspondent of Brownson's, defended the pope as vigorously as did Veuillot, earning honors from Pius IX for defending the pontiff's rule over the Papal States. But Montalembert did not share Veuillot's hatred for republican institutions—he supported such institutions and opposed Napoleon's rule. Montalembert also thought that the best way to defend Catholic interests in France was not through Napoleon's dubious alliance with the Church, but by establishing a regime of religious freedom for the Church and other religious groups. In his letters to Brownson, Montalembert denounced Veuillot as a tool of despotism who discredited Catholicism by linking it to a politically reactionary agenda.[4]

In an April 1853 article, "The Ethics of Controversy," Brownson described Veuillot's *L'Univers* as "more brilliant than solid ... imprudent and rash." A proper respect for the pope included respect for the bishops—a respect *L'Univers* did not show. Catholic journalists needed to be under the supervision of their bishops, Brownson scolded, and must accept correction if a bishop told an editor that the editor was wrong. This criticism would be applicable to Brownson himself in a few years. *L'Univers*, said Brownson, was "erect[ing] absolutism into a dogma of faith." Free institutions were best for the Church: "we have never found the Church free save in free states." This anticipated a famous saying Montalembert would utter a decade later, supporting "a free church in a free state."[5]

When McMaster published a response in defense of Veuillot, Brownson in turn wrote several drafts of a private response to McMaster. In the version he ultimately seems to have sent, Brownson reproached McMaster for his uncharitable and hostile tone toward Brownson. Brownson professed to be indifferent to McMaster's attitude toward him. But if McMaster was to wage war, let him make an honest avowal.[6]

In August, Fr. Isaac Hecker, Brownson's and McMaster's mutual friend, wrote Brownson to say he had always been interested in uniting the Church's American champions. Hecker had met with McMaster and several other gentlemen, who agreed to advance their ideas in the *Freeman's Journal*. These men were to meet in two weeks. Perhaps not coincidentally, Fr. Hecker suggested that Brownson come to New York. Fr. Hecker may have been trying to effect some sort of reconciliation.[7]

MONTALEMBERT

Charles de Montalembert, leading French liberal Catholic and friend of Orestes Brownson. Montalembert is known today for his idea of "a free Church in a free state" (Jules Claritie, et al., *Le Plutarch Populaire Contemporaine illustré* [Paris, Librairie Centrale, 1870], between pp. 12 and 14).

The Power of the Pope

Brownson was also striving to defend the supremacy of the spiritual power over worldly, temporal power. This was not simply an abstraction, but a matter of fundamental importance. To Brownson, American individualism was excessive, ignoring both human and divine laws. American Catholic politicians were arguing that they could separate their religion from their politics, or even defy the pope and the hierarchy on political question Brownson said this tendency manifested itself in European affairs as well—Americans continued to wrongly sympathize with the defeated revolutionaries of 1848, equating their own revolutionary principles with these European uprisings denounced by the Church. Consistent with these revolutionary sympathies, Americans continued down their antinomian, anti institutional, law-defying road. The spiritual power of the pope was needed in order to inculcate obedience to duly constituted authorities.

Not that existing governments were good, Brownson hastened to add—they were oppressive. In Europe, ever since the Reformation, both Catholic and Protestant governments had fallen into dictatorship—Brownson called it "caesarism." Brownson saw a tendency to "statolatry"—worship of state power at the expense of the spiritual world. The thing about the European revolutionaries was that they were not fighting for freedom, but would simply replace

Louis Veuillot was an aggressive ultramontane Catholic journalist who inspired James McMaster (digital image of photograph by Vincent Gogibu, http://www.remydegourmont.org/vupar/rub2/veuillot/notice.htm, reprinted by permission).

dictatorship by monarchs with dictatorship by the people—"democratic caesarism." So despite the oppressions of despotic regimes in Europe, the Church had no choice but to uphold the power of the established governments against "the madness of the liberals"—it was necessary to "protect the people from the revolutionists, who would destroy them." Thus, Brownson held that revolutionary anarchy was just the flip side of tyranny.[8]

To Brownson, the twin evils of lawlessness and caesarism were not confined to Europe, but were growing in the U.S. The country started out well with the American Revolution, which to Brownson had been based on good principles, establishing a balanced government with a proper separation of government institutions and a proper balance of central and local authority. This was in accord with the balanced government practices of the Middle Ages, he believed, whose division of authority among monarchs and the estates of the realm, and between central and local authority, Brownson admired. But the good medieval setup in the United States had been undermined since 1789—the year the French Revolution started. Since then, both the federal and state governments had shown expanding centralizing tendencies. America was headed for a bureaucratic dictatorship governing in the name of the majority. As Brownson put it vividly in his 1854 novel *The Spirit-Rapper*, the demonic spirits who stirred up the European revolutionaries did not need to foment revolution in the United States, which was already descending into "complete individualism or ... absolute social despotism," in accordance with the diabolical plan.[9]

To Brownson, the world faced these problems because it either ignored spiritual values or artificially separated the spiritual life from everyday activities, and (what was the same thing for Brownson) refusing to accept the spiritual guidance of the Catholic Church on issues which touched on politics. Separating religion from politics, as many world leaders, Protestant and Catholic, were doing, was "political atheism" as far as Brownson was concerned. An example of this, from Brownson's viewpoint, is provided by Thomas Francis Meagher. Meagher had taken part in an abortive revolution in Ireland in 1848, earning a conviction of treason and sentence of transportation to Van Dieman's Land in Australia. Escaping from Down Under, Meagher ended up in New York, where he was much feted. In addition to his law practice he undertook lecture tours of the country, talking up Irish revolution.[10]

In early 1854, Meagher spoke in San Francisco about "Catholicism and Republicanism." Meagher denounced "some men"—unnamed but certainly including Brownson—who would subvert liberty in the name of religion, as with the 1848 revolutions, which Meagher praised. Archbishop Hughes remonstrated with Meagher, who grudgingly toned down his support of the 1848 uprisings.[11] Brownson, like other Catholic editors, rebuked the popular Irish hero for repudiating the authority of his Church, which opposed the European uprisings.

Brownson said the Church could "declare and apply" the law of God "to kings and princes, states and empires, as well as to individuals, in public as well as in private matters." Under the historical precedents Brownson analyzed, the pope's powers were broad enough to include the deposition of oppressive rulers, relieving their subjects of their duty of obedience. So if the popes could call on subjects to *resist* their secular rulers, by the same token they could require *obedience* to secular rulers when, as now, dangerous revolutionaries were trying to upend society.[12]

The pope's deposing power was, to Brownson, simply a side issue—not something the pope needed to use right then, when he needed to focus on inculcating obedience to established authorities. It was simply one example of the Church applying its spiritual power to political issues. Denying the deposing power would rope off a large part of politics from the spiritual domain of the Church—the very thing the revolutionaries were trying to do![13]

Now in a bizarre reversal, Brownson's opponents attacked him, the noted counterrevolutionary, as a political subversive. Brownson faced a replay of the 1840 situation when the Whigs used his "Laboring Classes" essay to denounce the Democratic Party to which he belonged. Brownson's defense of the deposing power, however theoretical, reinforced Protestant suspicion of Catholics. Brownson could not have given more of an eye-poking provocation to paranoid Protestants if he had tried. Many Catholics thought Brownson's conclusions unnecessarily provocative—and perhaps wrong.

Seared into the collective memory of Anglo-American Protestants was Pius V's 1570 bull *Regnans in Excelsis*, declaring the popular Protestant English queen Elizabeth I deposed and calling on her subjects to overthrow her. King Phillip II of Spain invoked this bull when he sent his famous armada against England. Conventional Protestant thinking also unfairly associated the popes with Guy Fawkes, a Catholic terrorist whose thwarted plot was actually repudiated by the pope. Brownson's article pressed all the Protestant buttons—papal dominance, foreign invasion, Catholic subversion, papal pretensions to worldly supremacy.[14]

Many Catholic critics distanced themselves from Brownson. There had been a longstanding quarrel within the Catholic world over the pope's power regarding temporal affairs. A powerful faction—associated with the Gallican group in France—denied that the pope could unseat rulers, and posited a broad area of temporal, political matters where popes could not meddle. While acknowledging that the popes had exercised the deposing power in the Middle Ages, these critics either said the popes had been wrong, or argued that the pope had been exercising this power with the consent of the rulers of time—a situation which did not apply in modern Europe or the United States. Hence, he could no longer depose earthly governments. The critics also felt Brownson's discussion of the question, whatever its merits, was highly inopportune at a time when nativists were seeking just such evidence as Brownson's articles to impugn the loyalty of American Catholics.

Thomas Francis Meagher was an Irish revolutionary, an escapee from British custody, an American lawyer and statesman, and later a Civil War general (W. F. Lyons, *Brigadier General Thomas Francis Meagher* [New York: D&J Sadlier, 1870]).

At least three Catholic journals came to Brownson's support—the *United States Catholic Miscellany* of Charleston, the *Propagateur Catholique* of New Orleans, and the *Shepherd of the Valley* of St. Louis. But bishops who had lent their names to Brownson's *Review*—such as John Purcell in Cincinnati, who wanted his name removed from a list of episcopal endorsers of the journal, and Martin Spalding in Louisville—were angry at the truly bad timing of these articles. Even the pugnacious John Hughes of New York—who normally didn't shrink from a clash with Protestants—told Brownson in reference to two of his papal-power articles that "whilst all things are lawful, some things are inexpedient," paraphrasing 1 Corinthians 6:12.

In an exasperated reply to the critics in April 1854, Brownson protested that "properly speaking, our *Review* has never claimed or defended any temporal or civil power or jurisdiction at all for the pope out of the ecclesiastical states [the Papal States of central Italy]." The Pope had "judicial and declarative" power to say if a "prince" has so far violated natural or divine law as to lose the right to rule. Yet the pope only had spiritual sanctions—such as excommunication—to enforce his decrees; he had no army except in his own dominions.

Historically, said Brownson, the popes had not abused their power—they had sometimes erred in the direction of too much deference to worldly rulers, but had never behaved oppressively in the other direction. "It is far safer to err on the side of the spiritual than on the side of the temporal, and in exaggerating the powers of the church, than in exaggerating those of the state. The temporal as distinguished from the spiritual has all the passions and inclinations of human nature in its fallen state to support it, and is never in danger of being unduly depressed."

Rise of the Know-Nothings

P.T. Barnum's agent was right when he commented in 1853 that "the Protestant feeling runs strong" in "our northern states." The country, particularly in the North, experienced a surge of anti–Catholic incidents in this year. It started off symbolically on March 6, and the target was a piece of marble that Pius IX had contributed to the United States for use in building the Washington Monument. Some anti–Catholics stole the marble from a storehouse and likely cast it into the Potomac. The New York *Crusader* praised the thieves for their alleged service to Protestant America.[15]

A rash of attacks on churches and assaults on priests were erupting across the North in 1854. John "Angel Gabriel" Orr was just the beginning. Mobs burned around twelve Catholic churches, damaged others, and interrupted services. Priests were assaulted while trying to reach dying people and provide them with the last rites. In Newark, New Jersey, a procession of Orangemen (Irish Protestants) and others claimed they had been attacked as they passed a Catholic Church. The Orangemen and their associates responded to the alleged aggression by burning the church down. The priest narrowly rescued the Blessed Sacrament from the sacrilegious mob. In Ellsworth, Maine, Catholics suffered attacks from mobs, the schools and the judiciary: a mob tarred and feathered a local priest, Fr. John Babst, and rode him out of town on a rail.[16]

On top of these outbreaks, a convention representing a new political movement met on May 11, 1854. The organization was called the Order of the Star Spangled Banner, which organized itself as the Native American Party ("Native American" meaning born in the United States—it had no reference to the indigenous peoples). Organized as a secret society, the party held initiation ceremonies for its members, who had to pledge to oppose Rome and support the party's candidates. Asked about their group's operations, members were supposed to tell nonmembers, "I know nothing." So the group was nicknamed the Know-Nothings. In the South, the new movement attracted enough support to keep the national Know-Nothing organization neutral on slavery. But some of the Northern Know-Nothings were agitated by the antislavery sentiment growing in the North at the time, seeing slavery as an evil alongside Catholicism. These Know-Nothings organized their activism, as they put it, around "Rum, Romanism and Slavery." This strong current of antislavery, antialcohol nativism was among what could be called the Northern Puritan element. Protestant New Englanders and New England-descended citizens in the Midwest had a heritage of Calvinist suspicion at anything hinting of Popery. Though their Calvinist dogmatism had been considerably watered down since the days of Cotton Mather, they shared the old Puritan emphasis on enforcing social morality. They had been mainstays of the Whig Party, but as that party collapsed under the pressure of the slavery issue, they began seeking other political vehicles. In 1854 the Know-Nothings seemed to many of these neo–Puritans to be the best fit for their politics and ambitions.[17]

The Puritan bloc would have agreed with Cincinnati Presbyterian minister Charles Boynton that "Puritanism, is but another name for Apostolic Christianity. Puritanism, Protestantism, and True Americanism are only different terms to designate the same set of principles." They would have concurred with Edward Beecher, son of Lyman and a Catholic baiter like his father, that America was "chosen by God to enjoy the honor of being the receptacle of Puritan ideas." Indeed, the crusading neo-Puritan version of nationalism required that the whole country be made over into the image of Puritan New England and subject to New England Puritan values—Protestantism, antislavery, and an interventionist government to reshape the habits of the public. This meant rejecting the supposedly inferior and wicked cultures of the South and of the Catholics. Not coincidentally, winning this moral crusade would also mean the Puritan New England element would recover the dominance it had possessed before the New England-based Federalist Party had been displaced by the Democrats earlier in the century.[18] American Catholics were realistic, not paranoid, in seeing a hostile Puritan bloc arrayed against them as well as against the South.

To the Puritan nativists, their religio-political views were true Americanism, and the antagonists of true Americanism were the proslavery faction ... and the Catholic Church. As for the latter, it had waged a war against freedom and true religion since the days of the Emperor Constantine—the pope and his minions were trying to revive in Europe and America the papist darkness which purportedly existed in the Middle Ages. "The Roman Catholic Church in America is anti-American, antiliberal," accused John Breckenridge.[19]

Another issue—linked in the minds of many nativists to the Catholic issue, was the issue of drink—the "Rum" in "Rum, Romanism and Slavery." Protestant America was by modern standards a community of drunkards—alcoholic beverages until quite recently had been the only sanitary drinks available, and Americans of all classes indulged to an extent which in the 21st century would be deemed acute alcoholism. As Protestant reformers joined temperance movements and tried to come off their collective bender, they turned their attention to the drinking habits of Catholics. While many Catholic figures—such as Fr. Mathew—promoted temperance, and even some legal limits on the liquor business, the nativists still linked the Irish Catholics to whiskey and the German Catholics to beer. Catholics were almost unanimously united against Prohibition legislation—another strike against Catholics in the minds of the newly sober activists who formed a small but determined minority in the Protestant community.[20]

The Irish Question

In 1853, Brownson met a young Catholic named John Acton, who would become famous as a historian of the Church and a supporter of the "liberal" Catholic group. Acton was impressed by Brownson and his mentor Bishop Fitzpatrick. The nineteen-year-old got in touch with prominent English convert John Henry Newman, who was trying to establish a university in Dublin, to recommend Brownson as a professor at the proposed institution. Newman agreed to extend the offer, looking past a quarrel with the American editor over the question of the development of Catholic doctrine. At first Brownson modestly declined the professorship—"I am a plain, untutored backwoodsman"—but when the offer was renewed, Brownson became more receptive to the idea. By this time, though, his writings had antagonized prominent Irish leaders and clerics, and he never got the job.

Brownson saw the Irish as essentially Christian and resistant to the ideological errors of the day: "the philanthropists have not much to hope from Ireland. Pat will sometimes live and talk as an unbeliever, but he has a singular propensity to die a Christian."[21] Brownson also, though, rejected efforts to suggest that the "the Celt"—the Irishman—was more pious or holy than those like himself who were "descended from the old Puritan stock."

But other articles from 1854 got Brownson the reputation of being antiimmigrant. He did this by fairly bluntly calling attention to some of the political and social problems among recent Irish immigrants.

The German Catholic immigrants tended to settle in the Midwest, and the Irish immigrants pouring in the country tended to settle in the Northeast. From the peak of the potato famine in 1847 until 1854, over 100,000 Irish came to the United States each year. The population of New York grew to about one-fourth Irish—and this was only persons of Irish birth, not counting American-born citizens of Irish ancestry. The city's Catholic population was growing to half of the whole.[22]

Many of these poor immigrants brought social problems with them. In New York, Irish immigrants lived in crowded, unhealthy tenements. In the district called Sweeney's Shambles, one adult out of five died between 1854 and 1856. Tuberculosis was "the natural death of Irish immigrants," according to Archbishop Hughes. Yet the tenants held on desperately to their homes, prioritizing rent over other expenses, to avoid being thrown into the street by their landlords. They had been accustomed to bad housing and cruel landlords in rural Ireland, so this was hardly a new experience. But the very poor did tax the local governments' charities.[23]

Some of the immigrants were lumpenproletarians involved in crime and disorder. About half of all convicts in 1850 were of foreign birth. Drunkenness among many immigrants was noticeable, despite the best efforts of Fr. Matthew. Riots sometimes erupted among the immigrants—including fighting among rival groups from the same country.[24] It is not as if the immigrants invented crime and rioting, yet these problems were highly visible, and did nothing to improve the image of the new arrivals.

Brownson's first foray into the controversy was in a July 1854 article about the common schools (government-run schools). Brownson deplored the common school laws, as he had done before his conversion. He explained that these laws took away from the parents the responsibility for the education of their own children. The states, by centralizing control over these schools and taking control from local communities, were manifesting the same "democratic caesarism" which Brownson saw threatening Europe.[25]

In the meantime, though, speaking as a Catholic, Brownson urged his Catholic readers to send their children to the common schools. Whatever their flaws as harbingers of tyranny, the common schools could do Catholic schoolchildren a service by assimilating them to American culture. And exposing Catholic children to Protestantism at school would help inoculate them against Protestant proselytizing when they became impressionable adults.[26]

Then Brownson backtracked, professing himself unable, as a layman, to second-guess bishops who chose to set up Catholic schools in their dioceses. Brownson's own bishop—John Fitzpatrick of Boston—was an outlier in following the editor's suggested policy of deliberately throwing Catholic children into the vortex of public school education. While praising Fitzpatrick's approach, Brownson tried to technically steer clear of criticizing the policies of the other bishops, which had after all been approved at episcopal conferences.[27]

The *Catholic Telegraph*, coedited by Fr. Rosecrans, accused Brownson of doing what he had tried to disavow—defying the authorities of his church in the field of education.

Not only were the American bishops (with Fitzpatrick dissenting) promoting the building of parochial schools, but Pope Pius had made statements against mixed Protestant and Catholic education in Ireland. The pope's views would also apply to the United States, said the critical editors. The *Telegraph*, at the same time, noted that Catholics in Cincinnati willingly paid their school taxes, even after a political defeat of the previous year denied the Church any share in those taxes for its own schools.[28]

Then came Brownson's articles on the Know-Nothings and the Irish immigrants. Here, Brownson made clear that the new party was animated by anti–Catholic bigotry. In line with Catholic criticism of anti–Catholic movements, Brownson was charging even the "Native Americans" with being under foreign Protestant influence. It was the flip side of Brownson's argument which proved controversial. The Know-Nothings drew on "two powerful sentiments;—the sentiment of American nationality alarmed by the extraordinary influx of foreigners, and the anti–Catholic sentiment." The proper Catholic response was to disarm the Know-Nothings by separating the religious issue from the immigrant issue. For this to happen, Catholics would have to avoid "gratuitous offense" to American national sentiment. This could not occur so long as Catholic immigrants had "foreign sentiments, attachments, associations, habits, manners, and usages," giving native Protestants the impression "that Catholicity itself is foreign to the real American people." Brownson's solution: the Irish Catholic immigrants should assimilate to the dominant Anglo-Saxon culture in the United States, no longer parading their distinctiveness in ways offensive to the majority. "It is idle for our Irish Catholic friends to pretend that they are contributing nothing to strengthen the dangerous radical tendencey of the country. They do it by the facilities they afford to the machinations and intrigues of demagogues, not, we readily admit, by their radical convictions or intentions."

Brownson's views on this topic had evolved. In 1845, he suggested that only the Catholicism of the Irish prevented them from integrating into American society. Now, with the upsurge of post-famine immigration, Brownson had changed his views. He addressed the Irish in blunt terms: "It is for you to conform to us, and not for us to conform to you. We did not ask you to come here; we do not force you to remain." Catholics needed to renounce foreign associations and deal with the "miserable rabble" who came with the immigrants, discrediting Catholicism with their drunkenness and crime.

These articles caused a severe backlash. Brownson's British friend George Clerk voiced some of the gentler criticisms in a letter: "you have seemed too sweeping in your denunciation, and ... you have seemed to justify by your pen, the brutal acts of violence against Irish Catholics, of which your countrymen have been guilty, and in the perpetuation of which they show themselves as thorough adepts as the Protestants of England and Scotland." The Irish would have been even more incensed had they known of an 1849 letter Brownson wrote to McMaster, in which the former said the Irish "are but one or two removes from the state of barbarians." Also, "in external decorum and the ordinary moral and social virtues ... [the Irish are] the most deficient class in our community."[29]

Fr. Sylvester Rosecrans probably contributed as coeditor of the *Catholic Telegraph* to a critical article. This article, ironically, criticized Brownson as a "neophyte" who made inflated and provocative claims on behalf of the Church. Sylvester Rosecrans, however, was in fact a more recent "neophyte" than Brownson, being two years younger in the faith than the latter. But regarding these newspaper quarrels, the *Telegraph* said there should be "a spirit of moderation—an unwillingness to take offense, to condemn flippantly, without hearing both sides."[30]

Brownson experienced more blowback from his articles from Archbishop John Hughes of New York. The archbishop wrote to him to criticize his articles on papal power and the Irish, and invited the editor to a personal conference. This would probably not be a tea-and-conversation conference—Hughes's nature was to lay down the law, not to engage in dialogue. Brownson replied that he had duly submitted the articles to bishop Fitzpatrick for theological examination, but that Hughes had the power to destroy the *Review*. If the archbishop wanted to run a rebuttal, he could do so. Hughes wrote back affirming his belief in Brownson's good faith, while mentioning that *Review* subscribers had contacted him about the articles. The bishops of Hughes's archdiocese cautioned the faithful in fall 1854 not to assume that a Catholic paper had the endorsement of the local bishops and priests.[31]

Archbishop Hughes's views on Brownson's *Review* would be laid out a couple years later in a speech on the Catholic press. Certain papers, said Hughes, promoted invidious divisions between foreign-born and native-born Catholics—a personal issue for Hughes, who had been born in Ireland but become an American citizen. American law knew no distinction between foreign-born and native-born citizens, so why should professedly Catholic papers make such distinctions? "The learned Dr. Brownson" (Brownson had received an honorary doctorate) was clearly included in Hughes's criticism of certain convert-editors who spoke with "a boldness in the ear of their countrymen which few persons trained from infancy in the Catholic Church would have felt warranted to employ."[32]

With the famously combative Hughes taking issue with his articles, calling them inexpedient and uncharitable, Brownson had a sign that his combative nature had reached great heights. Brownson wrote to his fellow Catholic editors to emphasize that, as he saw it, his article on the Native Americans was written to defend Catholics of foreign origin from nativist assaults.

The Pandora's Box of Slavery Is Opened

Harriet Beecher Stowe's bestselling antislavery novel, *Uncle Tom's Cabin*, had begun circulating in an Italian translation in the Papal States. Stowe's father and two of her brothers were known as hardcore Catholic-bashers. In Rome, however, Mrs. Stowe's antislavery activity was viewed in a favorable light. When someone complained about the alleged Protestant tendencies of the book, the Church's Congregation of the Index, responsible for censoring anti–Catholic works, decided to approve the circulation of the book in Catholic lands. The Congregation was probably influenced by a report from a consultor (reviewer) that the novel attacked the evils of slavery.[33]

The Puritan element in the Know-Nothing party was also interested in the slavery controversy. Despite the risks of alienating the Southern part of the party and the Northern moderates, many Northern Know-Nothings pushed back against what they saw as Southern aggression on slavery's behalf. Some of these Know-Nothings saw Catholicism and slavery as twin evils—comparable conspiracies to keep people in bondage, physical and spiritual.

Other Northern Know-Nothings were opportunists, caring less for nativism than for fighting slavery, and seeing the Know-Nothing party as the best vehicle to promote their agenda now that the northern Whigs had collapsed.

Nativists were offended by the political proclivities of the Irish immigrants. The Democratic Party and its operatives recruited the Irish, and the Irish responded with loyal support for the Democratic party, which had traditionally drawn support from the foreign-born and rejected the elitist social engineering of the Northern Whigs. Some states didn't even require that voters be citizens, and where citizenship was a prerequisite to voting, Democratic Party pols saw to the prompt naturalization of the newcomers, sometimes disregarding the five-year waiting period imposed by federal law.[34]

Other Northern opponents of slavery joined a new party which was calling itself Republican, but at this time it was unclear which party was the wave of the future in the North. What was clear to most people was that many Northerners were getting riled up at apparent proslavery aggression.

The revival of the slavery controversy was largely attributable to a bill in Congress known as the Kansas-Nebraska Act. This bill, sponsored by Senator Stephen Douglas (D-Illinois) and supported by the Democratic Pierce administration, organized much of the American West into two new territories, Kansas and Nebraska. Slavery had been barred from these territories since the Missouri Compromise of 1820, but the Kansas-Nebraska bill proposed to repeal the Missouri Compromise and leave the question of slavery to territorial settlers. Many Northerners objected to this bill for allowing the introduction of slavery into an area where even the South had previously agreed to keep it illegal.

Opponents of slavery, including Harriet Beecher Stowe, organized a petition of New England ministers against the Kansas-Nebraska bill. The petition, which gained 3,050 signatories, protested against the Kansas-Nebraska measure "in the name of Almighty God, and in his presence." Enactment of the bill, said the petition, would "expos[e] us to the righteous judgments of the Almighty." A similar petition from 504 midwestern Protestant clergy was also presented to Congress. Senator Douglas and his Southern supporters were outraged at the "political preachers" who signed this petition, accusing them of violating the separation of church and state. The Catholic Church was introduced into the debate when Southerners praised the Catholic clergy for staying out of politics and refusing to follow the example of their Northern Protestant colleagues by meddling in the slavery controversy. Indeed, despite their praise of the "separation of church and state" when this was useful to denounce the Catholics, many Protestant ministers had taken upon themselves the responsibility as serving as the nation's moral conscience, leading the country in the paths of righteousness. By the time the Kansas-Nebraska Act passed—May 30, 1854, just under three weeks since the first national Know-Nothing meeting—nativists in the North had another grievance against the Church—this time for its *abstention* from politics in a cause favored by the antislavery contingent.[35]

At the same time that President Pierce was signing the controversial Kansas-Nebraska Act, events in Boston pushed New Englanders and other Northerners even further into the antislavery camp. A federal commissioner (magistrate) in Boston, Edward Greely Loring, ordered a fugitive slave named Anthony Burns to be returned to his master. An abolitionist mob attacked the courthouse where Burns was being held. In the melee, the mob was beaten back, but a part-time federal marshal, James Batchelder, died. Escorted by soldiers and militia, Burns was marched through a protesting Boston, with buildings draped in black, to a ship which carried him back to slavery. Abolitionists later purchased Burns's freedom.[36]

One of the state militia units which escorted Burns, the Columbian Artillery, was predominantly Irish. The Burns unrest took place soon before the signing of the Kansas-Nebraska Act, and shortly after the national Know-Nothing meeting. Again Catholics—Irish immigrants, to boot—were found on the wrong side of the slavery controversy just as the issue was becoming central to the ideas of the Northern Puritan element.

Brownson, in Boston, was at the center of the antislavery agitation. In the October 1854 issue of his *Quarterly Review*, he addressed this growing controversy. He attacked the Northern antislavery faction, but his reasoning was different from that of militant Southern slavery supporters. The South now believed slavery was a good thing, but Brownson was open to a gradual amelioration and abolition of the institution over the long term, mainly at the South's own initiative. Meanwhile, the Northern antislavery group and their plans of immediate emancipation, with no compensation to the masters, should be resisted and masters should, as a general rule, be allowed to recover their fugitive slaves in the North.[37] As a good Calhounite, Brownson opposed both abolitionism and the free-soil program, which would leave slavery alone in the South while blocking its expansion into the West.

Brownson, in this 1854 article, reiterated the position he laid out in 1851. As with many of Brownson's articles, this one was in the form of a review. The works reviewed were some speeches by Massachusetts senator Charles Sumner against the Fugitive Slave Act in the wake of the Burns case. To Brownson, the Northern abolitionists and free-soilers, far from being friends of freedom, would endanger the republic with their policy of immediate emancipation, which would promote the very centralization and "democratic caesarism" which Brownson had constantly written against.[38]

Brownson assured his readers that he was "as much opposed to slavery" as Sumner and his colleagues. The slave "has an immortal soul as precious as my own, and he may reign with the saints in heaven, while I may be doomed to suffer eternally with the devil and his angels in hell." But abolitionists and free-soilers endangered the "constitutional order." Brownson said that "the best practical condition of the negro race here is, for the present at least, that of slavery." He did not exclude the possibility of African Americans being gradually eased out of slavery, but he cited his favorite politician, John C. Calhoun, in support of the slaves' current status. Brownson enunciated his claims: the free blacks were in a "degraded" condition, said Brownson, and if the slaves were freed immediately, they would sink to the same level of degradation. Slaves were allegedly treated better than the white workers whose exploitation Brownson had famously denounced. Brownson acknowledged that there were evils in the slave system, but these evils, as he saw it, consisted in the lack of proper Christian instruction for the slaves, and the ability of owners to disrespect slave marriages and sell husbands away from wives, and parents from children. The South would probably have corrected these problems already, Brownson claimed, if abolitionist agitation hadn't forced them to focus on defending, not reforming, slavery. Brownson was open to the idea of compensated emancipation of the slaves but it was the South, not the North, which should take the initiative in transitioning to a nonslave society. Even if slavery was unjust, a state, having encouraged slavery, could not "take advantage ... of its own wrong"

7. "The devil ... comes to us as a philanthropist"

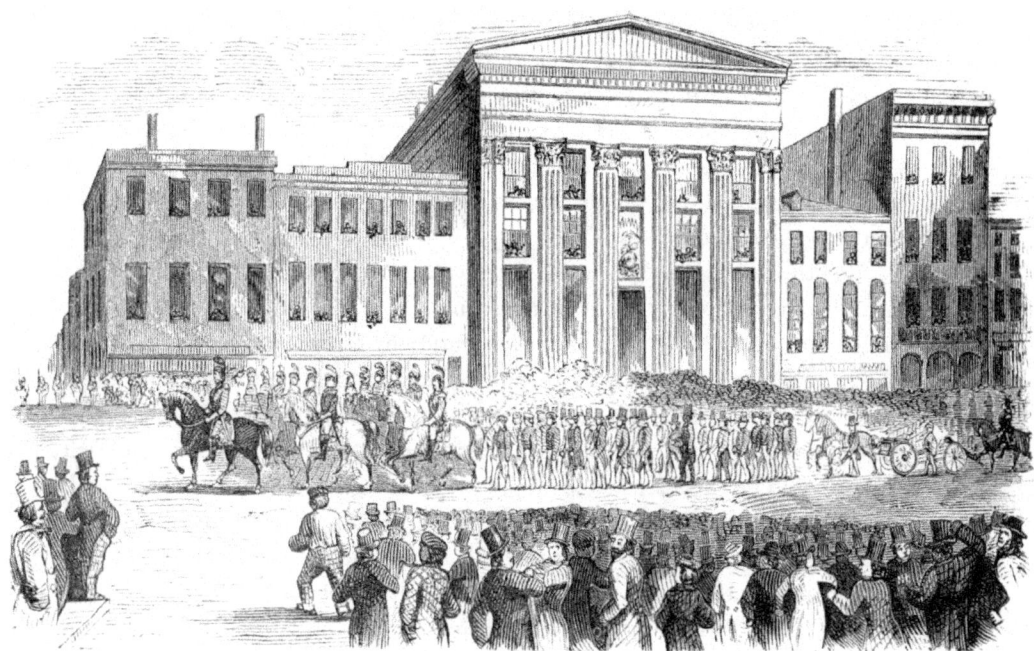

"It was not in Ireland you learned this cruelty," was the cry of the late Daniel O'Connell against Irish-Americans' alliance with slaveholders. In Boston, an Irish-American militia unit, the Columbian Artillery, helped escort Anthony Burns back to slavery, much to the outrage of many Massachusetts Protestants, whose leanings toward the anti–Catholic Know-Nothing party were increased ("Marshal's posse with Burns moving down State Street," in Charles Emery Stevens, *Anthony Burns: A History* [Boston: John P. Jewett, 1856]).

by freeing a slave without compensation—any state which abolished slavery would have to pay "full indemnification" to the former masters.

Northerners could play a limited rule where fugitive slaves were concerned. If a fugitive slave came to a free state, either the master should have the right to recover him or the community should "pay his ransom"—i.e., compensate the owner for the value of the slave. The Catholic Church had followed this course—paying ransom for slaves whom Catholics could not in conscience send back to their masters. Brownson's use of the term "ransom" was deliberate—Catholic doctrine did not allow one human being to own another, so the term "purchase" would have been inappropriate. A master was entitled only to the labor of a slave, not the possession of his body, as Brownson clarified. Southern slave law, in contrast, saw slaves as property. To Brownson, the Fugitive Slave Act simply embodied the principle of Northern "non-intervention" in the affairs of the slave states. Northern citizens and officials weren't required to help masters recover their slaves, though they were required to "suppress ... resistance" to the master's efforts of recovery.

Sumner said that the Fugitive Slave Law "takes away that essential birthright of the citizen, trial by jury" by giving adjudicatory powers to a federal commissioner. But as Brownson interpreted the law, an alleged slave claiming his freedom "has the benefit of a jury secured to him" in the slave states. Brownson had not invented his legal analysis out of whole cloth. Many jurists endorsed it, including Commissioner Loring in the Burns case.[39]

Sumner also attacked the Fugitive Slave law as "in derogation of the rights of the states" because it assigned slave-catching responsibilities to the federal government. The U.S. Supreme Court had ruled the other way, denying states the right to hinder the return of fugitives, and according to Brownson, Senator Sumner had no business assailing the Constitutionality of a law on grounds which had been rejected by the U.S. Supreme Court. If the Court's Constitutional interpretations could be second-guessed, the result would be "tantamount to no government at all."[40]

Brownson's theological analysis at first seemed like a defensible reading (though not the only possible reading) of Catholic doctrine, insofar as it did not endorse slavery and made room for the ultimate abolition of the institution by way of compensated emancipation, while rejecting immediate emancipation. Abraham Lincoln, until the events of 1862 and 1863, also supported gradual emancipation with compensation to the masters. The main problem was that slavery, as it existed in the United States, was derived from the African slave trade which had met repeated condemnations from Rome—thus Brownson's analysis ought to have started with the fundamental illegitimacy of American slavery.[41]

When Browson tried to apply his theological ideas to the American situation, he made several errors which invalidated his defense of the Fugitive Slave Act and his critique of Senator Sumner. While Brownson admitted that by divine law a master could lose hit title to a slave "by inhumanity, or the denial to the slave of his moral freedom," Brownson did not acknowledge that the Fugitive Slave Act contained no provision for sheltering slaves who had been the victim of cruel treatment. Nor did he point out that the law made no provision for "ransoming" fugitive slaves. Abolitionists had indeed tried to "ransom" Burns in Boston by purchasing his freedom from his owner, but federal officials blocked this attempt. The abolitionists were ultimately able to "ransom" Burns from his master, but only after Burns had been in a slave prison in Virginia for a considerable time.[42] To Brownson, even if he knew these facts, the details of the Burns case did not matter so much as the political principles underlying the Fugitive Slave Act. The abolitionists, after all, had ultimately been able to "pay [Burns's] ransom," albeit after a delay not contemplated by Brownsonian principles.

A more important area on which Brownson was not fully informed was in his claim that Southern states guaranteed a jury trial to people held as slaves but claiming to be free. There was a serious problem of free blacks being kidnapped and enslaved, but persons held as slaves did not necessarily have the right to a jury trial. Indeed, some slave states would not even hear an alleged slave's claim to freedom unless some white person vouched for the claim. The Tennessee Supreme Court threw out the claims of thirteen slaves who had supposedly been emancipated by the Alabama legislature, because no white person had stepped forward to endorse the claim. Even where no white endorsement was required, courts generally had the right to reject what they deemed nonmeritorious freedom claims without invoking a jury, with the petitioner, if black, bearing the burden of making the case that he might not be a slave.[43]

And this says nothing about the practical obstacles to a slave trying to access the courts of his master's state. In the previous, year, 1853, a black man named Solomon Northrup published a memoir titled *Twelve Years a Slave*. As someone who followed literary trends, Brownson ought to have been aware of the book. Northrop's narrative describes how he was lured from New York, where he was free, kidnapped, and illegally held as a slave in Louisiana. As the title indicates, it was twelve years before he was able to get free. He feared retaliation if he pressed his claim in a Louisiana court, and he only did so after getting the support of white friends in New York and several prominent statesmen.[44] So for many persons held as slaves, as Brownson ought to have been aware, it was naive to assume that they could get a Southern jury together to adjudicate their claim to freedom, without the belated intervention of numerous powerful whites.

A Novel and a Conspiracy Theory

Brownson saw the Northern antislavery activists as a more urgent threat to the republic than slavery itself. He published a remarkable novel in 1854 in which he lumped the anti slavery activists and other reformers together as hypocritical "philanthropists" who endangered the country and were literally inspired by diabolical forces. At a time of widespread conspiracy theories—Protestant conspiracy theories about Catholics (targeting Brownson himself), Northern conspiracy theories about the South, and Southern conspiracy theories about the North, Brownson put forward a conspiracy theory to top them all. The novel *The Spirit-Rapper; An Autobiography* is a dramatic story which is frequently interrupted by the speeches of the protagonists, speeches which explain the author's viewpoint. The book does not present its characters as fully developed individuals, but as representatives of various schools of thought.

The novel portrays two phenomena and links them. The first phenomenon was the wave of spiritualism in the United States where alleged mediums like the Fox sisters in New York claimed to contact the ghosts of the dead. Brownson believed these spiritual manifestations were sometimes real. The other phenomenon was the revolutionary movement in Europe in 1848. Both of these movements were inspired by demonic spirits, in Brownson's telling.[45]

The narrator of the book becomes a spiritualist (or "Mesmerist") and receives messages from spiritual forces which turn out to be demons. Possessed of a Faustian/Frankensteinian desire that he "might make myself the Messiah of the nineteenth century," the narrator helps promote his diabolical "spiritualism" while involving himself in social reform movements. The narrator gets involved with various "philanthropists and world-reformers," who are based on the people Brownson hung out with in his preconversion days. These "philanthropists" are characterized by "love of mankind in the abstract ... [and] the most sublime hatred or indifference to all men in particular." A pious Protestant minister named Cotton vainly tries to warn the narrator away from his new associates, warning that "the devil ... comes to us as a philanthropist" the better to deceive people into accomplishing his evil purposes.[46]

The narrator gets together with a woman he calls "Priscilla" (named after a second-century heretic). Priscilla is based on some of Brownson's former female reformer-associates like Fanny Wright. Priscilla recruits the narrator more fully into the "philanthropist" racket, and in turn the narrator uses his diabolical powers to put Priscilla under his spiritual control.[47]

With his "slave" Priscilla, the narrator travels to Europe, where he, other diabolically-influenced conspirators, and various naive dupes, spark the revolutions of 1848. Unfortunately for the narrator and the other devilish conspirators, however, "the friends of religion and society [in Europe] were more numerous and more energetic than we had believed," and the European revolutions fail.[48]

Giving up on his hope for revolutionizing Europe, the narrator in *The Spirit-Rapper* brings Priscilla back to the United States in 1849, plotting to replace American Christianity with spiritualism. Saddened by how Priscilla has deteriorated under his influence, he releases her from his spell, and she returns to her husband. Then the narrator himself, persuaded by an apparently Catholic character, gives up his diabolical associates and embraces true Christianity (probably meaning Catholicism, though the novel isn't explicit). Priscilla's husband, thinking the narrator is having an adulterous relationship with her, gives him a fatal wound, leaving him just enough time to finish his memoirs, i.e., the novel.[49]

In December, Pope Pius IX proclaimed the doctrine of the Immaculate Conception of the Blessed Virgin Mary. Rome did not invent the concept of the Virgin being exempt from original sin—that doctrine was widespread among the people and among many theologians—but the papal decree in December made such belief mandatory for all Catholics. In Catholic eyes, this event was a high point in Church history.

From the worldly standpoint in America, however, the end of 1854 was not such a good time. Throughout the North, the new Know-Nothing Party won astonishing victories, taking over entire states in New England and winning large blocs in the legislatures of other states. The American Church had a bumpy ride ahead.

Another bumpy ride awaited Brownson and his political sparring partner Thomas Francis Meagher. In November, the two were traveling in Michigan on what were presumably lecture tours. The two prominent Catholic figures were in the same passenger train when a gravel train hit it. Forty-seven passengers died, but Brownson and Meagher escaped and then went to work saving other surviving passengers from the debris. Brownson published praise for his fellow traveler's heroism.

The elections in the same month, and the Know-Nothing victories, were signs that Catholics needed to work together to extricate their church from the political train wreck it had experienced.

8

"Cowards fearing the light of day, and skulking beneath the cover of darkness"

In Paris

From Montreal, James Healy went to Paris to complete his priestly training. He attended a seminary run by the same order which ran the Montreal institutions—the Sulpicians. The Healys' sponsor, Bishop Fitzpatrick, was an alumnus of the Paris institution, as were other prominent leaders of the U.S. Church. With his knowledge of French, James would be able to take advantage of the training offered.[1]

The seminary was located in the fashionable St. Germain neighborhood in Paris, but seminary life was somewhat more austere than that of most of their affluent neighbors. One former student called the seminary "a community in which habits of almost monastic retirement were allied to the studious activity of a university." The approximately 300 students were under a strict disciplinary regime, whose rules were explained to them twice a year by the head of the Sulpicians. Early rising, scripture studies, practicing the liturgical celebrations they would have to know as priests, and strict propriety in conduct, including abstaining from alcohol, were all required (Healy finally had to meet Fr. Mathew's standards). The students were to a great extent on the honor system, being deemed responsible adults who would comply with the rules without being minutely supervised. Bishop Fitzpatrick had clearly felt confident in Healy's sense of responsibility in meeting the demands of the seminary.[2]

The seminary maintained a priestly ambience, seeking to accustom its students to the duties of a clerical state somewhat apart from the world. The Sulpicians celebrated two feasts peculiar to their order—the feasts of the Interior Life of Jesus and of the Interior Life of Mary. This emphasis on spiritual contemplation was reinforced by a July celebration of La Sacerdoce do Notre Seigneur—the Priesthood of Our Lord. To reinforce the focus on the interior, priestly life, students were not allowed to read newspapers, lest they be distracted from their studies and spiritual preparation by news of the world. They could learn about outside events from their professors, who *were* allowed to read newspapers, but they were kept at some distance from the exciting events of French politics as the French emperor Napoleon III, nephew of the original Napoleon, consolidated his power and got involved in a war with Russia.[3]

Some peculiarities of the seminary instruction taught a lesson of humility which was different from what Healy had experienced at Holy Cross. There was no ranking of students, no academic honors. There were public oral examinations, but these were not formally graded. The students were expected to work at their studies from spiritual zeal, not a desire to excel vis-à-vis their compatriots. This was certainly a significant change for Healy, who had been a top student at Holy Cross and been singled out for honors on that account. There was a practice of students giving readings and even sermons during meals, to be evaluated later, and this would have provided an opportunity for Healy to demonstrate his eloquence.[4]

Except for access to newspapers, relations between students and instructors were on a fairly egalitarian plane. The professors lived in the same quarters as the students, sat with the students at meals, and socialized with them as equals. Students also had access, though not strictly as equals, to the head of the Sulpicians, Joseph Carrière, who gave great attention to his role as supervisor of the seminary. The modestly dressed and simple-living Carrière shared in the rigors of Sulpician discipline which the students and faculty had to observe. He led the spiritual exercises which were often expected of students during their meals in the refectory. He was highly popular and approachable, and his door was open to students who sought advice and spiritual counseling, and he was known for his willingness to provide this assistance very broadly. He had a good deal of familiarity with affairs in North America, being responsible for both the Montreal seminary and Mt. St. Mary's Seminary in Baltimore, the first Catholic higher-education institution in the U.S. Carrière had even visited the United States in 1829, going on a tour of inspection of the Sulpician institutions and serving as a theological consultant at the First Council of Baltimore held that year. It was in 1829 that the archbishop of Baltimore, presumably in consultation with Carrière, established the first black order of nuns in the U.S., the Oblate Sisters of Providence. So Healy had, at the head of his seminary, a sympathetic figure with knowledge of America and its racial situation, who could alleviate the loneliness of studying in a foreign land.[5]

As a scholar Carrière had opposed the liberal religious ideas of Félicité Robert de Lamennais, a prominent liberal Catholic, who left the Church after Pope Gregory XVI denounced liberal ideas of freedom of the press and freedom of religion in his encyclical *Mirari Vos* (1832). Lamennais's friend Montalembert remained in the Church and kept some of Lamennais's liberal ideas alive in the French Church, and in the American Church through correspondents like Orestes Brownson. Carrière had a more conservative, traditionalist attitude, submitting to correction from Rome when it found errors in his extensive writings on marriage. After this, his scholarly reputation only increased. Carrière's scholarship and expertise on the validity of marriage under Catholic canon law may have been helpful to James Healy in his later work handling marital matters for the Boston diocese. More significantly, Healy may have been influenced by Carrière's conservative religious orientation as opposed to the liberal orientation of the likes of Montalembert and Brownson.[6]

While Healy was studying in Paris, the bishops of Bordeaux province issued a declaration rejoicing in the abolition of slavery in France's colonies, which had taken place in 1848. The assembled bishops said that the former slaves, "although of a different color, are our brethren in Adam and in Jesus Christ, and ... were held in hard slavery, to the destruction of their souls."[7]

While Healy was away, a tragedy hit his family. His brother Hugh, the aspiring merchant who had helped handle the Healy estate in Georgia, saw off Sherwood at New York harbor when Sherwood left in 1853 to join James at the Sulpicians in Paris. Struck by a ship while in a rowboat in the harbor, Hugh fell into the water and caught a deadly chill. Before he died, Hugh asked if his spiritual "Dad," Fr. Fenwick, was praying for him.[8]

On June 10, 1854, at a ceremony at Notre Dame Cathedral, James Healy became Fr. James Healy as he was ordained a priest by the archbishop of Paris, Marie-Dominique-Auguste Sibour. (The archbishop was stabbed to death a few years later by a renegade priest.)[9]

Soon after Fr. Healy was ordained, Bishop Fitzpatrick, who was in Europe trying to recover his health, met in Paris with the new priest. The bishop had been subject to attacks of some sort which greatly affected his constitution, and he was trying vainly to get cured by a European vacation. The bishop probably spoke to Fr. Healy of the need for him to serve in Boston, a prospect which made Fr. Healy nervous, but he went with his bishop back to Boston. In a later letter to his "Dad," Fr. Fenwick, Fr. Healy opened up his heart about the climate in Boston. Describing himself in the third person, Fr. Healy said he was "a poor outcast on a throne of glory which ill-becomes him." His black heritage was "generally known" among Boston Catholics, and if he could have found a better place to be "I should have desired never to show my face in Boston."[10]

There was little time for self-pity—Fr. Healy was put to work assisting the head of Boston's House of the Angel Guardian, a diocesan home for troubled and homeless boys. He had only a brief time of service at that institution, however, before Bishop Fitzpatrick called on him for other assignments. He became Bishop Fitzpatrick's secretary, responsible for drafting the bishop's official papers and letters. Fr. Healy moved to the Franklin Street rectory beside the cathedral so he could be close to the bishop.[11]

Fitzpatrick continued to suffer from the malady he had unsuccessfully tried to alleviate during his European tour. Still weak and exhausted from his work, Fitzpatrick had an attack at the end of March—his official journal breaks off suddenly on March 29 after Fitzpatrick wrote only a couple of words. While delegating some major decisions to his friend Fr. John Williams, the bishop increasingly relied on Fr. Healy for the routine work of the diocese, letting the young priest take over its everyday functions. Fitzpatrick appointed Fr. Healy to a newly established position in the diocese—that of chancellor, making Fr. Healy responsible for much of the work of an extensive diocese.[12]

By early 1855, the new priest had all these duties placed on his shoulders just as the Boston diocese and the faithful began experiencing a serious crisis, perhaps one of the worst in its history. The ailing bishop and his flock were at the epicenter of a political explosion which installed the militantly anti–Catholic Know-Nothings in power.

Slavery Complications

Fr. Healy remained legally exiled from his old home state of Georgia, due to that state's laws against the admission of free persons of color. Both James and his father Michael were exiled from their native lands—Michael died a voluntary exile from Ireland, buried in a foreign grave, and James was banished from the state where his parents' grave was located.

Like Hugh, James might have braved the risk of arrest and gone back to Georgia, but the law would have always hung over him while he was there (and as of 1859, he would not simply have been arrested and fined if caught, he would have been sold into slavery).[13]

Michael Healy's executors faithfully carried out the stipulations of the patriarch's will. As they sold off the estate, they had the proceeds sent to New York, where John Manning (Hugh Healy's business mentor) distributed the money to the Healy children. Ultimately, a total of $51,000 or more was disbursed—around three-fourths of a million dollars in today's money. In addition to the sale of land and buildings, some of these proceeds came from the sale of Michael Healy's slaves. In a couple cases, the executors separated slave families by sale, in contravention of Catholic doctrine.[14]

While the executors were selling off the slaves, a complication arose. Margaret Phillips, one of Michael Healy's former slaves, claimed that she and her children were legally free under the will of a former master in Maryland. A white man named John Knight sought freedom for Phillips and her children. The justices of the state supreme court threw out Knight's case on a technicality, while suggesting that, in any event, Georgia's antiemancipation law prevailed over Maryland law and that Phillips and her children were still slaves. The estate later sold Margaret and her children separately.[15]

Know-Nothings in the Bay State

Fr. Healy took on his new assignment with Bishop Fitzpatrick as the Know-Nothing party established complete political dominance over Massachusetts and sought to enact its agenda into law. From his new front-row seat, Fr. Healy could watch the action and do what little he could to help his bishop respond to the thorough takeover of his state by a militantly anti–Catholic faction. Massachusetts was not alone, though it had the most virulent case of Know-Nothingism as 1854 turned into 1855. In many of the Northern elections of 1854, the Know-Nothings made astonishing gains. The Know-Nothings won decisively in Massachusetts and Pennsylvania. They were highly influential in the political coalitions which won in Ohio, Illinois, and Maine. They controlled the People's Party which won in Indiana. They ran even with the two other parties in the New York elections. The Northern elections showed that, in the words of a member of the displaced Whig party, "Roman Catholicism is feared more than American Slavery." Slavery was involved in the elections, though—two-thirds of the U.S. House members elected on the popular platform of opposition to the Kansas-Nebraska Act were also members of Know-Nothing lodges. Know-Nothings were now the main opposition party to the Democrats in the North—the new Republican Party lagged behind.[16]

Massachusetts voters elected Know-Nothings to all forty of the seats in the state Senate and installed a 389–4 Know-Nothing majority in the state house. Most of these members of the legislature—the General Court—were new to politics with only six senators and thirty-four representatives having a prior record of officeholding.[17]

The Massachusetts legislature got to work at once after meeting in early 1855. Above the speaker's podium in the state house of representatives, a Latin motto was inscribed. In conformity with its antiforeign policy, the Know-Nothing legislature had the inscription removed and replaced with an English translation: the Latin language was too foreign, and too Catholic, and was one of many things which had to be expunged from the state.[18]

The Know-Nothing legislatures of Rhode Island and New Hampshire petitioned Congress to provide penalties for anyone who brought criminals or paupers into the country. A nativist representative duly proffered such a bill in the U.S. House of Representatives, but it was rejected on Constitutional grounds—the federal government did not have the power to physically exclude immigrants, it was claimed.[19]

The new Know-Nothing governor of Massachusetts, Henry Gardner, prompted state officials to throw about a thousand people, overwhelmingly immigrants, out of the government's almshouses, and to send about a third of these back to Europe. The governor also dissolved all militia units made up of Irish-Americans, taking their equipment and taking over their armories (Connecticut's government took similar action). The militiamen were not only considered too Catholic and too foreign, but in Massachusetts there was lingering resentment at the Columbian Artillery, the Irish militia unit which helped send Anthony Burns back into slavery.[20]

The legislatures in Massachusetts, Maine, Rhode Island, and Connecticut prohibited state judges from naturalizing foreigners, so that citizenship applicants would have to use the federal courts. To limit voting by presumably ignorant immigrants, Connecticut imposed a literacy test for voters, and the Massachusetts legislature started the process toward amending the state constitution for the same purpose (the literacy test would finally be imposed in 1857, under Republican rule).[21]

The Massachusetts General Court considered another, more radical proposal to address the immigrant vote. Under a proposed amendment to the state constitution, naturalized citizens would have to wait twenty-one years after their naturalization before being able to vote. This measure had overwhelming legislative support, but fortunately for the Irish Americans, the proposal had to be dropped due to drafting errors—probably a result of the unusually low number of lawyers (eleven) among the solons.[22]

Further Know-Nothing initiatives involved the much-vexed school question, and hit particularly hard in Boston where Bishop Fitzpatrick eschewed the establishment of parochial schools and encouraged Catholics to send their children to the government-run common schools. The General Court passed a law requiring daily Bible readings in the common schools, and the Bible had to be "the common English version"—in other words, the King James edition whose Protestant origins made it abhorred by Catholics. While Catholics had their own English translation in the form of the Douay-Rheims edition, Protestants tended to think that anyone who rejected the King James was rejecting the Bible itself. In Boston, the School Committee added more requirements by compelling reading of the Lord's Prayer by teachers, and declared that pupils ought to be required to recite the Ten Commandments as well—all in the version spelled out in the King James.[23]

A state constitutional amendment, approved by voters in 1855, closed the door to any government aid to Catholic schools. The amendment provided that tax money raised for common-school purposes could only be given to municipal-run schools, and that these tax funds "shall never be appropriated to any religious sect for the maintenance exclusively of its own schools."[24]

Revisiting the trusteeship dispute which had played out in so many other states, the

General Court took from Fitzpatrick the legal power to administer parish land in his diocese, placing authority in the hands of lay trustees. The legislature also elected a prominent Know-Nothing, Henry Wilson, to the U.S. Senate to serve alongside Charles Sumner, the Republican. Despite later attempts to play down Wilson's Know-Nothing membership as mere political expediency, Wilson was a strong nativist who had opposed a charter for James Healy's alma mater, Holy Cross. He also supported a two-year waiting period for naturalized citizens seeking the right to vote. Thus, like many Northern antislavery politicians, Wilson had an anti–Catholic record.[25]

To the Massachusetts Know-Nothings, the opposition to Catholicism and Catholic immigrants was only part, although a very important part, of a broad reformist agenda. In the Puritan tradition, the party's members wanted to use the government to promote righteousness across the whole range of evangelical Protestant concerns. A busy General Court increased state spending on public institutions, tightened regulation of liquor, increased penalties for corruption in office, secured the property rights of married women, broadened the protections afforded to poor debtors, and reformed the criminal justice system. It passed public health and antimonopoly laws targeting large business enterprises. To pay for these various projects, the legislature greatly increased taxes and the state debt.[26]

Of the three holy causes of Rum, Romanism, and Slavery, slavery remained, and the Massachusetts Know-Nothings did not neglect it. The General Court enacted a Personal Liberty Law aimed against the federal Fugitive Slave Act and those who had enforced it. State officials, specifically including the state militia (the dissolved Columbian Rifles had not been forgotten), could not cooperate in sending back fugitive slaves. State judges were not allowed to help the federal government return fugitives. Another law desegregated the common schools of the state, which had previously been segregated by race. As to the latter reform, the Boston *Pilot* said that Catholic families sent their children to school with blacks, while the upper crust, despite theoretically supporting racial equality, sent their own children to all-white schools.[27]

The response of the Boston diocese to the Know-Nothing onslaught was at first rather tame. For much of 1854, the perpetually unhealthy Bishop Fitzpatrick was away in Europe trying to recuperate. In his absence, the editor of the *Boston Pilot,* Fr. John Roddan, was reading Orestes Brownson's conciliatory articles in his capacity of theological censor. Perhaps influenced by these articles, Fr. Roddan took a subdued tone in the *Pilot,* urging the Boston Irish not to provoke the nativists. To Fr. Roddan, Brownson was engaged in constructive criticism of Irish vices, and "ought to be regarded as a friend, not as an enemy." With Fitzpatrick's return from Europe and the establishment of a Know-Nothing government, Fr. Roddan took his paper in a more confrontational direction, denouncing the measures emanating from the General Court.[28]

The nativist legislature provoked backlash from Protestants as well as Catholics after the legislature established a committee to look into convents, seminaries, "and other institutions of like character." Years of propaganda about Catholic institutions, such as the phony *Awful Disclosures of Maria Monk* and the rumors leading to the attack on the Charlestown convent, suggested to nativists that there might be sinister secrets in the nooks and crannies of Church institutions. The "Nunnery Committee" set about its work, visiting Fr. Healy's alma mater, Holy Cross, as well as two schools in Lowell and Roxbury run by the Sisters of

Notre Dame. The investigators had nothing but praise for Holy Cross during their visit to Worcester—it probably didn't hurt that they used their budget from the state to buy wine during their visit to that town.[29]

Then, dropping in unannounced on the Roxbury school, the committee members and some associates accompanying them rummaged around in the various rooms and closets, while the bemused and startled nuns and students looked on. While investigating the Lowell school, the committee members again charged their alcohol to the state treasury. More than this, they also billed the taxpayers for entertaining a certain Mrs. Patterson, a lady known for sharing her favors with men.[30]

The *Daily Advertiser* and other non–Catholic journals exposed the unsavory activities of the Nunnery Committee. An effort to expose the dirty secrets of the Catholic Church had boomeranged into an exposure of the dirty secrets of many Know-Nothings—and this exposure was particularly embarrassing because of the party's attempts to promote temperance and to discourage vice. The legislators in Boston were sufficiently embarrassed that they pulled the plug on the Nunnery Committee and expelled the chairman, Joseph Hiss, from the House.[31]

Know-Nothingism in New York

In the fateful elections of 1854, the New York Know-Nothings, after a campaign of about a month, got one-third of the vote, which gave them the balance of power in a politically fragmented state. Two Know-Nothing legislators, James Putnam and Erastus Brooks, struck against the Church with the support of the other legislators. Brownson, soon to move to New York himself, probably followed the ensuing controversy.[32]

By New York law, church property used for public worship—at least if the title was in the name of the church—had to be controlled by local lay trustees, not by the bishops of the church. The American Church had moved beyond the trusteeship system, with the bishops decreeing that these properties should be under episcopal control. Archbishop Hughes did not fully implement these decrees, but he did buy up some bankrupt parishes whose debts were so overwhelming as to force judicial sales. Since the Church hierarchy could not own the properties in its own right, Hughes acquired these parish properties as an individual owner. Meanwhile a schismatic parish in Buffalo, whose trustees had been excommunicated for insisting on the sole right to run their property, petitioned the legislature, which responded by enacting a law proposed by Putnam and Brooks. The new statute, speaking in general terms but unmistakably aiming at Archbishop Hughes, prohibited the prelate from acquiring any more parish property, even in his personal capacity, and provided that at Hughes's death all parish property he owned would pass to a corporation run by the local trustees, or if there was no such corporation, to the state until the trustees could incorporate and acquire the property.[33]

Brooks and Hughes entered into a vigorous controversy in the secular newspapers over the extent of Hughes's property holdings, and Hughes defended his side with his acid pen, hurling sarcasm and accusations of dishonesty against the nativist legislator. Hughes's attitude alienated Protestant readers, only bolstering their support for the Putnam and Brooks law.[34]

In the meantime, Hughes published conciliatory letters in James McMaster's *Freeman's*

Journal, giving Catholics a more peaceful message than he was giving to his Protestant foes. In the March 28 *Freeman's Journal,* shortly before the law was adopted, Hughes said that the bill "would certainly inflict very great injury on us in our rights of conscience, and in our rights of property," since each religious group should have the right to govern itself according to its own rules. But the bill would have the inadvertent beneficial effect of rallying sympathy from fair-minded Protestants, and causing "many who have hitherto been lukewarm Catholics" to grow closer to their embattled Church. In the meantime, Hughes, for once, urged his flock to remain quiet and avoid agitation.[35]

Differing Catholic Responses

While many Catholics were facing off against the Know-Nothings and their supporters on the political plane, other Catholics were encountering their foes on the battlefield of ideas.

The scholarly archbishop of Baltimore, Francis Patrick Kenrick, went public with his disagreement with Orestes Brownson's provocative views. Kenrick published *A Vindication of the Catholic Church* in 1855. A lady in the gallery slipped a copy of this work—or a version of it—to Representative Joseph Chandler of Pennsylvania, a Catholic, while the latter was giving a speech on papal authority. The archbishop devoted some attention to disavowing and dismissing Brownson's writings: "Most assuredly I dissent from [Brownson], if he claim for the Pope any claim to interfere with our civil allegiance." Brownson had shown "his usual independence" in upholding papal power, but his "speculation" was only that "of an individual." Kenrick admitted that he had previously praised Brownson (in 1846) "in terms of high commendation of his zeal and ability in defense of the Catholic faith, which he had embraced but two years before." Neither Kenrick nor the other bishops who endorsed Brownson, however, had meant to endorse everything Brownson might say. In any event, Kenrick was confident that Brownson, "as well as every other Catholic in the [United] States, in the hour of trial will be found the devoted supporter of our National and State institutions."[36]

Kenrick laid down what he considered the true doctrine of papal power—the view which Brownson dismissed as "Gallicanism" (subordinating the Church to the state). The doctrine of the deposing power, said Kenrick "has long ceased to be advocated even in Rome itself." Medieval popes, in deposing secular rulers, had acted under "medieval principles of jurisprudence" no longer applicable in "the actual state of society." In deposing rulers, the medieval popes had asserted the same principles as the authors of the American Declaration of Independence in calling on subjects of a temporal government to reject their oppressor, especially if the oppressor (like Elizabeth I of England) had violated an oath to uphold the Catholic faith. In America, of course, the rulers did not take any oath to uphold the Catholic Church, so they could not be deposed for being anti–Catholic. In the modern age, in rejecting tyrannical governments, "men act on their own sense of right," without consulting the pope, as with America's Declaration of Independence.[37]

In early January, Know-Nothing representative Nathaniel Banks of Massachusetts took to the floor of the U.S. House of Representatives (of which he would soon become speaker) to denounce papal pretensions. Banks cited Orestes Brownson's *Review* articles defending the power of the popes to depose secular rulers. Joseph Chandler rose to reply. Chandler was a lame-duck Whig representative from Pennsylvania who had been rejected by the voters after converting to Catholicism, amid nativist charges of dual loyalty. Chandler's reply to Banks denied that Brownson's ideas represented the true doctrine of the Church. Chandler said that "religion is a personal matter," and that the pope could not "interfere with the political relations of any country" outside the Papal States. If the pope should send an invasion force to this country, American Catholics, and Chandler himself, would resist the invaders. Chandler cited numerous Catholic authorities who—as Chandler saw it—denied that the pope, in modern circumstances, could absolve subjects of their allegiance to their sovereigns: the late Bishop England of Charleston, Archbishop Kenrick of Baltimore (who had supplied Chandler with some of his arguments), the archbishops of New York and Dublin, the Council of Baltimore, various French Gallican writers, the faculties at several Catholic universities, and papal authorities.[38]

As a rebuttal to Representative Chandler, Protestant divine John M'Clintock published a pamphlet arguing that the Pennsylvania senator had misstated the true Catholic doctrine on the popes' temporal power. "Listen then to your best writer," M'Clintock taunted Catholics as he cited passage after passage from Brownson's ultramontane articles in his *Review*. M'Clintock quoted from an 1849 letter from the American bishops, published in every issue of the *Review*, praising the publication. While acknowledging that Brownson had recently declared that he himself, not the bishops, bore responsibility for his opinions, M'Clintock still tried to pin Brownson's views on the U.S. hierarchy: "It would be unjust and ungenerous, in them, to the highest degree, to abandon [Brownson]. He holds the *true* papal doctrine, and vindicates it manfully."[39]

The publicity which Protestant attackers gave to Brownson's ultramontane views was upsetting to many bishops, especially since, as M'Clintock noted, the bishops' 1849 letter of endorsement continued to be printed in the *Review*. The pope wasn't going to make a decree to overthrow the U.S. government, so why provoke paranoia by defending the pontiff's right to do so? Several American prelates, including Archbishop Purcell in Cincinnati, got in touch with Francis Patrick Kenrick of Baltimore, urging him to lean on Brownson and get him to stop printing the embarrassing endorsement letter. Kenrick did as requested early in 1855, formally alerting Brownson to the concerns of various bishops that the six-year-old letter would be construed as their endorsement for ideas which they in fact disapproved of. Brownson continued to include the 1849 letter in the *Review* for another year, when he stopped reprinting it.[40]

Brownson had no intention of backing off from the controversy. To Brownson, Chandler's speech, which posited such a rigid separation between religion and politics, was wrong in principle even though there was no practical danger of a papal decree against American institutions. Chandler, by minimizing the pope's power even in theory, was simply another Catholic politician trying to limit his religion to private devotion while feeling free to behave like an atheist where affairs of state were concerned. It was not fitting to respond to nativist lies by artificially constraining the scope of the spiritual realm, as Chandler had done. If some bishops didn't have the stomach to confront Chandler's errors, Brownson would continue at the task.

In his April 1854 *Review*—the same issue where he assumed sole responsibility for his views—Brownson reviewed two anti-Catholic books which had come out that year and which denounced papal pretensions as dangerous to America's republican institutions. These books were *The Papal Conspiracy Exposed,* by Edward Beecher, and *Romanism in America,* by Rufus W. Clark, both Protestant ministers.[41]

Brownson denounced Clark as "ignorant" and "untruthful," possessed of "satanic cunning." Clark accused Brownson's *Review* and the *Freeman's Journal* of preaching the extermination of Protestants, which Brownson indignantly denied. Clark attributed America's greatness and political freedom to Protestantism, but Brownson said the country's greatness was due to the country's "natural resources" and "fertility of our soil," and the inheritance from "Catholic England." Protestantism itself was hostile to religious liberty—the only European countries with true religious freedom were Catholic states like "France, Belgium and Austria." In any case, religion was about eternal salvation, not worldly prosperity.[42]

Brownson started off slowly in the review of Edward Beecher's book, pointing out that the author was the son of the Catholic-baiting Lyman Beecher, the brother of "the really able and independent Henry Ward Beecher, and the brother of the world-renowned or world-notorious Harriet Beecher Stowe, author of *Uncle Tom's Cabin*." Brownson indignantly proclaimed, "We probably know as much about the subject [of papal conspiracy] as [Edward Beecher] does, and our word is as good as his; and we tell him and our countrymen that there is no papal conspiracy in the case, and that the only conspiracy we know of is that of Protestantism in the Know-Nothing movement, to deprive Catholics of their political and civil rights, or perhaps to exterminate them, or to expel them from the country." Brownson wrote that "sensible people" would come to realize the weakness and dishonesty of such Protestant arguments, and Americans would soon have to choose "between Catholicity and no religion."[43]

Returning to the well-worn argument over papal power, Brownson again defended his position that the pope had a "judicial" power to decide whether a government had, by violations of the natural law, forfeited its right to rule, but this power did not mean the Church was the source of the U.S. government's authority—that authority came from natural law. Since the U.S. Constitution was in full conformity with the natural law, the pope wasn't going to depose American governments—"the papal authority is and can be terrible only to tyrants." Brownson respected his opponents in the American Church who denied the pope's power over secular governments, but in Brownson's view, intelligent Protestants would respect the integrity of a full-blown ultramontane like himself rather than the half measures of "Gallican" Catholics.[44]

American Catholics did not seek to persecute Protestants, said Brownson—it was the "demented" Protestants who were at the time persecuting Catholics—burning Catholic institutions, taking their orphans away from their ancestral faith, mobbing and shooting Catholics, and otherwise taking away Catholic rights. American Catholics were enduring a Protestant persecution like the persecutions of pagan Rome, but as with those earlier persecutions, Catholics would emerge victorious: "Let men like Dr. Beecher, Rev. Rufus W. Clark, and the host of puritanical ministers at the head of the violent movements against Catholics, reflect on the fate of the persecuting pagan emperors, and remember that they who were most responsible for them are they on whom the divine vengeance will fall swiftest and heaviest."[45]

8. *"Cowards fearing the light of day"* 111

Frontispiece to *Papal Conspiracy Exposed*, by Edward Beecher (brother of Harriet Beecher Stowe), contrasting Christ riding a donkey with the pope borne on a litter (Edward Beecher, *The Papal Conspiracy Exposed, and Protestantism Defended, in the Light of Reason, History and Scripture* [Boston: Stearns, 1855]).

Bishop Martin John Spalding of Louisville took up the literary cudgels against the Know-Nothings. Rather than siding with either Archbishop Kenrick and Congressman Chandler on the one hand, or Brownson on the other, Bishop Spalding straddled the issue of papal power. Spalding "cared not to inquire" whether past popes' decrees of deposition against secular rulers was based on an inherent papal power (as Brownson claimed), or delegated to the popes by the "people and princes" of the time (as Kenrick and Chandler contended). In the past, the pope had indeed used his power to declare the deposition of secular rulers, and "every exercise of [the deposing power] was a blow aimed at tyranny, and struck for the rights of the people." But that was all in the past—"the claim to [the power] has been abandoned" from three hundred years.[46]

Spalding turned the antipapal rhetoric of the Know-Nothings and their supporters against them, arguing that it was Protestant ministers, not Catholic priests, who meddled in American politics. Spalding said that Catholic clergy didn't get involved in politics, unlike Protestant ministers who were often "either abolitionists or freesoilers, ultraists or politico-religious alarmists." In a swipe at the Protestant ministers who petitioned against the Kansas-Nebraska Act, Spalding added that Catholic priests did not "venture, either collectively or individually, to address huge remonstrances to Congress, threatening vengeance in the name of Almighty God, unless certain political measures were either passed or repealed!"[47]

To Spalding, the Know-Nothings were "cowards fearing the light of day, and skulking beneath the cover of darkness." Despite their avowed defense of native-born Americans, the Know-Nothings consorted with turbulent Protestant immigrants, "the spawn of foreign revolutions," "the blood-stained Irish Orangemen [Protestant militants] and the truculent German infidels." The Know-Nothings embodied the same spirit of Protestant persecution which had assailed the Church in England, Holland, Germany and Switzerland, and even in America, as instanced by the Philadelphia riots, the burning of the Ursuline convent in Massachusetts, and the exclusion of Catholic priests from many almshouses. Far from endangering civil liberty, the Church had built the foundations of freedom. Catholic Maryland was the first American colony to have religious freedom. It was "in the good old Catholic times, in the middle ages" that the Church had bestowed on English civilization the boons of "trial by jury, *habeas corpus*, stationary courts, and the principle ... that taxes are not to be levied without the free consent of those who pay them." The Church's influence had abolished "that odious feature, common to every pagan society—domestic slavery" in Europe. "Without violence—without any sudden shock to the social system," the Church had also abolished serfdom as well. This was in implied contrast to the Northern evangelicals' destructive push for immediate emancipation, a point Spalding would elaborate on in 1863 when he wrote his memorandum to the pope.[48]

By 1855, Brownson was writing to his friend, Fr. Jeremiah Cummings, that he would be backing off from his ultramontane defense of papal power. "It seems it is necessary for the peace of the Church that I should make way for the Chandlers to defend Catholicity on Gallican principles." Church authorities included Chandler's speech in textbooks for Catholic schools. Despite Brownson's courageous defense of papal power, American Catholics had retreated before the Know-Nothing attacks in an attempt to show themselves to be good Americans.[49] It is noteworthy that Catholic leaders associated loyalty to the country with an unwillingness to agitate the slavery issue.

9

"The Know-Nothings have inaugurated a new era"

To New Jersey

After putting his October 1855 *Review* to bed, Orestes Brownson moved to New York to get out from under the supervision of Bishop Fitzpatrick of Boston. Now, however, it was as if he had stepped out of the frying-pan into the fire. Archbishop Hughes was far from being a fan of Brownson. The Irish-born prelate found the upstart convert irritating and prone to embarrass the Church. The strain between the two strong-minded Catholics showed in 1856, when Brownson and Hughes clashed during a ceremony at St. John's University, where both men were speakers.[1]

Brownson sought a buffer between himself and the authoritarian Archbishop Hughes, but he did not want to move his home base too far from the key city of New York. Brownson resolved this problem by moving to Elizabeth, New Jersey, which was still in Hughes's archdiocese but was under Bishop James Roosevelt Bayley of the suffragan diocese of Newark. Elizabeth was in eastern New Jersey, but close to New York City. Staten Island was nearby to the southeast, and Newark and its bishop nearby to the northeast.[2]

James Roosevelt Bayley's career showed that he was potentially more sympathetic to Brownson than was Hughes. Hughes was born a Catholic in Ireland, and was naturally at odds with a Yankee convert who published biting criticisms of Irish immigrants. Bayley, in contrast, was a native-born convert who, like Brownson, had paid a price for changing his old Protestant milieu to a Catholic one. His grandfather James Roosevelt had cut him out of his will because of his change of religion, and though the grandson contested this in court, he finally lost in the New York Court of Appeals. Reportedly, Bayley resignedly remarked that "it will be all the same a hundred years hence." Archbishop Hughes put the matter in more explicitly spiritual terms: Bayley "took the Lord for his portion and for the lot of his inheritance, and the world took him at his word and left him no other."[3]

Bayley was not as scholarly as the self-taught Brownson, but he was an eloquent speaker and would have a quote from Samuel Johnson for just about any occasion. One difference with Brownson was Bayley's dedication to setting up Catholic schools in his diocese—he ultimately wanted "every Catholic child in the state in a Catholic school." In this he was far more typical of the bishops of the time than Brownson's former bishop, Fitzpatrick of Boston.[4]

Meanwhile, Brownson was in demand as a lecturer, traveling to speak in places like

Cincinnati and Louisville (in Purcell's archdiocese), Pittsburgh, Milwaukee, Chicago, Mobile and New Orleans on topics like "Catholicity and Civilization" and "Why I am not a Protestant." Despite, or because, of the active anti–Catholic movement in the country, audiences continued to be interested in a no-holds-barred exposition of the Church's position.

Return to Civilian Life

While Brownson was establishing a new base for his career of writing and speaking, Lieutenant William Rosecrans was dissatisfied. His income as an army officer was not as much as he wanted for the support of a large family. Ann Rosecrans had money from her wealthy family, but "living on his wife" (as Sylvester bluntly put it) was not a satisfactory situation for a proud and ambitious man. William looked around for better jobs. There was a vacant professorship at the Virginia Military Academy. Lt. Rosecrans sought that position, but it went instead to Thomas Jackson, the future "Stonewall."[5]

Lieutanant Rosecrans considered leaving military for literary pursuits in the service of the Church. He spoke to Cininnati's Catholic Institute in 1853, urging the compatibility between Catholicism and American institutions, in contrast to nativist propaganda. In a letter to Sylvester, William raised the possibility of setting up a Catholic bookstore in Cincinnati. The Archdiocesan newspaper, the Catholic *Telegraph,* was in need of an editor, and William contemplated this position as well. The *Telegraph* had been founded two decades previously to combat the anti–Catholic propaganda of the likes of Lyman Beecher and Samuel Morse. In line with this purpose, the paper defended the Church against her many foes, a combative attitude suited to an aggressive convert like William. Sylvester, rather than his brother, ended up working on the *Telegraph,* assisting Fr. Edward Purcell as editor. Fr. Purcell was the brother of Archbishop Purcell. (One of Edward Purcell's activities was to serve as a banker for members of the flock, flouting Church canons against such activities by priests).[6]

Active in encouraging Catholic devotion among his Catholic fellow officers, William encouraged a devotion to the Sacred Heart of Jesus—he was one of the officers who formed the Confraternity of the Sacred Heart to encourage such devotion. The prefect of Propaganda, Cardinal Giacomo Fransoni, inspired by William's "singular zeal in performing the duties of the Catholic Faith," gave the young officer a gold medal.[7]

In 1863, he applied to Secretary of War Jefferson Davis for permission to leave the army. Davis was reluctant, and granted William a few months' leave instead, expressing the hope that "before [the leave] expires you will probably change your mind." William was persistent, and Secretary Davis finally accepted his resignation. Perhaps the secretary hoped Rosecrans would return to the army later.[8]

Now a civilian, William set himself up as an engineer and architect in Cincinnati. He kept his eye on opportunities, and saw the potential of the coal in western Virginia (modern West Virginia). He took a supervisory and engineering job with the Canal River Coal Company, perceiving the profitability of the Coal River, where as one may guess the presence of coal had long been noted. The coal in the area could be refined into paraffin for lanterns and oil to lubricate machinery. The problem was the cost of shipping the coal, once mined, down the Coal River—a considerable expense given the obstacles to navigation.[9]

William drew up a plan to turn the Coal River into a navigable canal with a series of locks. Construction began, and as something of an expert on the topic, William spoke to a convention of coal operators who were looking a way to improve navigation on the Kanawha River. The state legislature meanwhile set up the New Coal River-Slack Water Navigation Company, with majority stockholding by the state and with William as president. William supervised the beginning of the canal's construction, and the project was well under way by 1857, when the peripatetic engineer went back to Cincinnati.[10]

Traveling through western Virginia, William acquired some familiarity with the geography of the area. This would prove valuable when he returned as the military liberator of the western Virginia population, which resented the domination of the eastern Virginian slave aristocracy. On slavery, William later said that before the war he opposed that "beastly system" as contrary to Catholic principles, but was against the abolitionists.[11]

Sylvester Faces More Violence

Around this period, Sylvester had another personal experience of Cincinnati's turbulence. Returning home from teaching at the seminary, Sylvester encountered two criminals, one of whom shot the priest-professor, embedding a bullet in his body. Sylvester returned home and began trying to take the bullet out himself. Biographer Richard Clarke says laconically that Sylvester was "discovered" by an unnamed person who sent for a doctor to have the bullet out.[12] A couple guesses as to the identity of the person who found Sylvester doing home surgery would be his brother or his sister-in-law, but the account does not say.

The archdiocese and its flock faced renewed attacks in this Know-Nothing period. A man claimed that Purcell had boasted of controlling the votes of 6,200 people, whose names were written in a book. Purcell gave an affidavit that the charge was false. As in New York, the Catholics and Protestants clashed over the government-run schools, which held readings from the Protestant King James Bible and, Purcell claimed, taught anti–Catholic doctrines. Yet Catholics had to pay taxes to support these "common schools."[13]

Fourteen percent of Ohio's population was born abroad. Most of this new population was German. The Cincinnati archdiocese received most of the country's German immigrants,

Bishop James Roosevelt Bayley of Newark, New Jersey. Bayley lost a large inheritance when he converted to Catholicism. As a suffragan bishop of New York's archbishop John Hughes, Bayley was more sympathetic to Orestes Brownson than was Hughes (photograph by Mathew Brady and Levin Corbin Handy, Brady-Handy Photograph Collection, Library of Congress Prints and Photographs Division, Reproduction Number LC-DIG-cwpbh–02675).

as the New York archdiocese and the Boston diocese received most of the Irish immigrants. Germans tended to be farmers or artisans. This Irish immigrants in the archdiocese gravitated to proletarian jobs like canal worker.[14]

A whole district in northern Cincinnati was called Over the Rhine, reflecting the German population that lived there. The "Rhine" was in fact the Miami-Erie Canal. The Cincinnati Germans were actually more numerous than the Irish in the city, and the German quarter with its shops and beer gardens (provocative to the growing prohibitionist movement associated with nativism) excited the interest and suspicion of the English-speaking, native-born population.[15]

Many of the Germans were faithful Catholics, but a large number among them were influenced by the abortive 1848 revolutions in their homeland. Many German immigrants in the United States sought to promote European revolutionary, and anticlerical, principles in their new country.[16]

Many of the German liberals and revolutionaries formed *Turnverein*, or *Turner* organizations, to promote self-help and radical causes. The Cincinnati archdiocese, seeking to provide the Germans with more appropriate outlet for their sociable and charitable impulses, allowed the formation of Catholic *Vereins*. The non–Catholic, antireligious *Turner* were nonetheless quite influential, as were the radical journals which sprung up, like the *Hochwächter* which had pleaded for a bullet or dagger to be used against Cardinal Bedini. Again, the archdiocese tried to counteract the effects of the radical German papers by sponsoring its own paper, the *Wahrheits-Freund* (Friend of Truth), a German-language counterpart to the *Telegraph*.[17]

In March 1855, delegates from radical German groups throughout Ohio met in Cincinnati and approved a statement of principles ("Cincinnati Platform") which coincided with Know-Nothing concerns on some points. The Cincinnati Platform endorsed compulsory education in government schools and insisted that "the Pope's exercise of power in the United States through the medium of bishops and other agents be ended," and that Jesuits be deemed "enem[ies] of the Republic."[18]

In Cincinnati, an "American Reform" slate of candidates took over the municipal government in 1854. To get the support of Protestant and "infidel" Germans, the reform candidates focused on Catholic-bashing while playing down the antiimmigrant rhetoric. They also de-emphasized prohibition, so as not to scare off German beer drinkers.[19] But the potential for an alliance between Cincinnati nativists and anti–Catholic German immigrants was squandered in an antiimmigrant mayoral campaign.

Know-Nothings nominated James Taylor, editor of the *Cincinnati Times,* in the April 1855 mayoral election. The Germans did not have a friend in Taylor, who whipped up his supporters against the immigrants. There were clashes between Germans and nativists on election day, and on the following day, after Taylor's defeat by Democrat James J. Faran, a Know-Nothing mob invaded the Over-the-Rhine area. The mob destroyed ballots in a couple of German wards, and would probably have rampaged all over the German neighborhoods if the Germans hadn't organized into militias to repel the invaders. The defenders had a cannon, and fired a warning shot over the attacking mob. Several people were killed in the invasion.[20] If an anti–Catholic party was going to win German votes, it would have to distance itself from these sorts of conflicts.

A council for the Cincinnati archdiocese met in 1855, dealing with the affairs of the Church from Michigan in the North to Kentucky in the South. The council's decrees did not address the Know-Nothing threat, focusing on internal Church discipline and the need for a provincial seminary.[21] The meeting, however, would have given bishops the chance to compare notes with Purcell on the growing nativist menace.

The antislavery and anti–Catholic movements overlapped in Ohio. Ohio voters turned against slavery in the wake of 1854's Kansas-Nebraska Act. Most of these voters joined the Know-Nothings, mixing hostility to the Peculiar Institution with hostility to the Church of Rome. Riding this tide, an 1855 convention of Republicans and Know-Nothings met in Columbus in July to nominate a "fusion" ticket—most of the Republican delegates were members of Know-Nothing lodges. Salmon P. Chase, a well-known Republican antislavery politician who, though not a Know-Nothing, had signaled his opposition to "papal influences and organized foreignism," was nominated for governor. The other nominees on the state ticket were Know-Nothings. Chase won the governorship, while the Know-Nothing candidates captured the statewide offices they sought.[22]

Because of the Chase ticket's nativist coloration, otherwise sympathetic Germans opposed to slavery had withheld their votes from the victorious fusionists.[23] Chase felt his Know-Nothing associates to be something of an incubus on his ambitions—he wanted to pick up the votes of the non–Catholic Germans as well as Know-Nothings, and this would mean avoiding attacks on immigrants as such, while throwing in just enough antislavery anti–Catholic policies to attract votes from both non–Catholic Germans and native anti–Catholics.

The slavery question heated up in Ohio as two dramatic cases brought the evils of slavery forcibly to the attention of Ohio citizens. The state and federal authorities fought over an alleged fugitive slave named Rosetta Armstead, with the Ohio judiciary defending her as a free woman and federal officials defying the state and sending Armstead into slavery. More shocking to public opinion was the case of Margaret Garner, who when seized as a fugitive slave in January 1856 killed one of her daughters and tried to kill her remaining three children to prevent their becoming slaves. The Republican legislature responded in 1857 by strengthening the state's personal liberty laws to protect alleged slaves from being sent South.[24] Slavery began to seem a greater threat to the state than the Whore of Babylon.

While Know-Nothings in Ohio were casting their lot with the antislavery forces, the Kentucky nativists were proslavery and were suspicious of immigrants as a threat to the institution. As Know-Nothings fought the Germans, both they and the radical Germans targeted the Catholics. Many Louisville Germans were radical "forty-eighters" who put forward a radical "Louisville platform" denouncing both Catholicism and slavery, and inspiring other radical German statements like the one in Cincinnati. Kentucky nativists, who supported slavery, also feared the Teutonic immigrants for the threat they posed to the Peculiar Institution. The one point where the nativists agreed with the radical Germans was on denouncing the Catholics. They supported the government schools and opposed Bishop Spalding, who denounced the compulsory Protestant Bible readings in those schools and wanted education taxes to be fairly apportioned among denominational schools. Sylvester and others in Cincinnati would have learned from Spalding about affairs in this part of the archdiocese, since Kentucky was subject to Cincinnati. Hammered from anti–Catholics on both sides, Bishop

Spalding began a series of public speeches and publications defending the Church, culminating in his voluminous *Miscellanea*. Seeking to rebut anti–Catholic accusations by telegraphic entrepreneur Samuel Morse, Spalding asked William Rosecrans for "further facts, & references" to counter the bigoted businessman.[25]

The Know-Nothings took over the Louisville city government in the April and May elections in 1855. This control allowed the local school board to fire all the Catholic teachers except one in the government schools. The influential Louisville *Journal* editorialized on the issues in the forthcoming election of August 6 by announcing that "the Pope seeks to rule this country." Public disturbances with the Know-Nothings on one hand and the Irish and Germans on the other roiled the waters as the new elections approached.[26]

When August 6 arrived, Know-Nothing city leaders limited the number of polling places in their districts and sent parties of men to chase away Irish and Germans from the courthouse where they tried to vote. Voters carrying the yellow-colored ballots of the Know-Nothing party were allowed to pass unmolested.[27]

In the morning, Irish ruffians killed a man. Around midday, Know-Nothings began wandering into the German area of town, burning houses. At least one Know-Nothing and one German were killed. Seeing the situation worsen, Bishop Spalding gave the keys to the cathedral to the mayor, cleverly making the Know-Nothing leader responsible for the safety of Catholic property. When mob members gathered around a church near the cathedral, believing Catholics had weapons there, Mayor Barbee appeased the unruly citizens by inspecting the church and finding it free of arms.[28]

From the church the freeborn American citizens went to a German brewery, broke in, drank the beer, and in their inebriated state decided to set fire to the building. In the afternoon, a Know-Nothing mob in the Irish quarter went to the Irish neighborhood known as Quinn's Row. Armed Irishmen were initially able to defend their homes, but some of the mob set fire to houses, burning down twelve of them with many of their residents in them, and killing some Irish who survived the inferno and tried to escape. When the fire department arrived, mob members threatened to cut the fire hoses if there was any attempt to put out the fires in the Irish

In 1856, the Know-Nothings nominated Millard Fillmore for president. Anti-Catholic and antiabolitionist, Fillmore had been president before, when he signed the compromise measures of 1850 which sought to resolve the slavery issue. Fillmore's 1856 nomination was brought about by a coalition of Southern Know-Nothings and centrist Northern Know-Nothings who wanted to finesse the slavery issue. Large numbers of Northern Know-Nothings, especially from the Puritan element in the population, rejected Fillmore as soft on slavery and began migrating to the Republican Party (*Biography of Millard Fillmore* [Buffalo: Thomas and Lathrops, 1856]).

homes. After these Louisville riots, Bishop Spalding took a two-year break from his literary labors.[29]

The Know-Nothing Party Splits

The antislavery group in the Know-Nothing Party, which dominated New England and which had helped elect Chase in Ohio, faced opposition from Southerners and from Northerners who wanted to conciliate the South on slavery. The Know-Nothings met in Philadelphia in June 1855 to draw up a national platform. Southerners and a minority of conciliatory Northerners provided a majority vote for a platform which ducked the slavery dispute. Most of the Northern Know-Nothings protested what their Southern and centrist colleagues had done, issuing an "Address to the People of the United States." The antislavery Know-Nothings wanted the restoration of the Missouri Compromise line, which would have banned slavery in the federal territories of Kansas and Nebraska.[30]

The *New York Times* was pleased by the Northern Know-Nothings' stance. The paper wanted Northerners to oppose any efforts to legalize slavery in the vast territories of Kansas and Nebraska. To the *Times*, the antislavery Know-Nothings were the first politicians to represent the interests of Northern voters on this issue. "The Know-Nothings are entitled to the credit of having been the first to meet the aggressive proslavery spirit with manly courage.... Their noble adherence to principle, we are sure, will be held in everlasting remembrance.... The Know-Nothings have inaugurated a new era."[31]

Centrist and Southern Know-Nothings did not want their party starting a new antislavery era. Seeking a middle road on slavery, they backed former President Millard Fillmore, signer of the 1850 compromise measures on slavery. If anything, Fillmore despised the anti slavery forces as much as he opposed Catholics, blaming both Catholics and abolitionists for the Whig defeat in 1844, which "[shook] my confidence in our ability to sustain a free government." In 1855 he wrote to deplore "the corrupting influence which the contest for the foreign vote is exciting upon our election[s]." He saw the Know-Nothings, into whose ranks he was initiated in a private ceremony, not only as a way to organize the antiforeign movement, but as a "truly national party, which shall *ignore* this constant and distracting issue of slavery."[32]

When the Know-Nothing presidential nominating convention met in Philadelphia in February 1856, the Southerners and centrist Northerners again had a majority. They nominated Fillmore on a platform which took a waffling position on slavery. They also voted to seat Catholic delegates from Louisiana. These were not exactly zealous Catholics, but dissenters of French descent who opposed their own hierarchy. Thomas Semmes had written to Brownson a year previously describing Catholic New Orleans citizens, in terms which suggested why some of them would become Know-Nothings: "The men are generally infidels, tho' the women are pious Catholics. The Catholics themselves are what may be termed liberals, and a vast number of them are Catholic in sentiment, tho' not I am sorry to say, in practice."[33]

A large number of Northern Know-Nothings rejected Fillmore, denounced the national party's slavery stance and its acceptance of Catholic delegates, and met for their own convention in New York. Managed by politicians like Henry Wilson, who wanted to lead the Northern Know-Nothings into the Republican fold, the new convention endorsed John C. Frémont, the Republican candidate for president. The Northern Know-Nothings nominated a separate candidate for vice president, a sign that the two organizations were still nominally distinct. However, most Northern Know-Nothings began a pilgrimage to the Republicans.[34] American Catholics watched as their enemies helped swell the ranks of the new and growing Republican Party in the North.

10

"Framed, no doubt, for the express purpose of corrupting the faith of Catholic children"

Rights That Catholics Are Bound to Respect?

In the 1856 presidential election, the Know-Nothing Fillmore carried only one state, Maryland, while the Northern members of his party voted for the Republican Frémont in great numbers. The winner of the election was James Buchanan, the Democrat, who not only carried the slaveholding states (apart from Maryland) but several key Northern states including his home state of Pennsylvania. Frémont won a plurality of the Northern vote, with the Republican candidate winning New England, New York, the Upper Midwest. and Ohio.[1]

Brownson indicated another of his famous changes of position in 1857, when he began to turn against the South on the slavery question. In the January issue of the *Review,* Brownson continued to see abolitionists as a threat to national unity, but now he thought the Southern advocates of slavery posed another danger. Brownson said that the country's "sectional, slave-holding minority" was seeking to control the country. This minority was plotting to establish a slave republic by extending slavery into federal territories and even conquering Latin America for slavery. "We do not reproach [the South] for her slavery, but we owe her no aid beyond letting it alone where it is." Brownson expounded his new constitutional theory—in the absence of positive law to the contrary, slavery was not permitted in any given community, and Congress could not legislate with respect to slavery. This meant that slavery was not allowed in the federal territories, and Congress could not extend the institution there. The South's pro-slavery policy represented a regression, "the progress of the whole civilized world since the introduction of Christianity has been towards the abolition of slavery," not toward its extension as the South wanted. If Buchanan pursued a sectional policy by favoring the South, he would provoke the growth of a Northern sectional party which would win the presidency in 1860.[2]

Brownson returned to his theme in the April issue, in an article which he apparently started in early March or thereabouts. He obviously received some blowback from his January article from Southerners and their supporters. Brownson was disappointed that Southerners should react this way—he hadn't changed his views on slavery since 1838, when as a Protestant he wrote his essay declaring that the North should leave Southern slavery alone. He still believed that the antislavery crowd was worse than the South because of its support of a consolidated federal government. Brownson said that the only way his opinion had changed was in his view that slavery in the territories was unconstitutional. This was, he admitted, a change from his 1847 essay on "Slavery and the Mexican War," where he supported the right of slaveholders to bring slaves into the federal territories. This latter view, he said, was no longer operative for him, because in 1854, he was "assured that the supreme court had decided that slavery is a local institution, existing only by virtue of the positive law—a fact of which I was unaware in 1847." Today, Brownson held his antislavery opinions regardless of what the Supreme Court might say. "We are faithful to the principles we learned from Mr. Calhoun and the state-rights party, which has always been our party; but we arrive, we grant, at a different conclusion from that insisted on by our masters." Calhoun, and Brownson at an earlier date, had thought the Constitution *protected* territorial slavery regardless of what Congress decided, and Brownson's current view was that the Constitution *prohibited* slavery in the territories even if Congress purported to legitimize it.[3] Aside from this minor difference, Brownson was still a Calhounite.

Brownson had gone this far in his essay when he learned of the Dred Scott decision by the United States Supreme Court on March 6. In an opinion by the Catholic Chief Justice Roger Taney, the Court took the Calhounite line, and not Brownson's antislavery variant of that line. The Court averred that Congress could not exclude slavery from the federal territories, and thus the Missouri Compromise and any other Congressional statute purporting to ban territorial slavery was unconstitutional. The Court also declared that black descendants of American slaves—even free blacks—could not be citizens. Democrats seized on this decision to argue that the Republican Party's policy of banning slavery in the territories was illegitimate.[4]

Brownson did not like the *Dred Scott* opinion, since it contradicted his view that slavery could not legally exist in the federal territories. The denial of black citizenship was also wrong, and it was too bad that a Catholic Chief Justice had ignored the Catholic principle of the unity of humanity. The decision was "more in accordance with the teaching of Aristotle"—who wrote that certain people were slaves by nature—"than with the teachings of the Gospel." Blacks were "no doubt inferior to the white race," but they still had human dignity. Slavery was not a black-only institution, since both blacks and whites could be reduced to slavery if human laws warranted it. But in the absence of some positive law enslaving them or reducing their civil rights, black people had the same rights as whites. Brownson knew that, by criticizing the *Dred Scott* decision, he seemed to be contradicting his repeated calls for obedience to the Supreme Court's constitutional interpretations, so he made clear that his duty as a "loyal citizen" required him, albeit under protest, to accept the Court's decision as an alternative to disunion. Yet Northern public opinion would grow more hostile to the South as a result of this decision, which would be seen as another step in the Southern campaign to dominate the country. "We almost fear for the safety of the Union. Yet we believe Almighty God has great designs with regard to the American people, and we will trust in his good providence to carry us safely through the present crisis, the most dangerous that has as yet occurred in our history."[5]

Brownson's erstwhile supporter, the Boston *Pilot,* editorialized against Brownson that the Supreme Court was a legal tribunal and must uphold the law "whether it squares with the Gospel or not." Brownson also encountered other critics after his slavery essays in January and April. As Brownson later described it, "a committee from highly respectable and most influential gentlemen in this city" met Brownson to urge him to retract, or at least to stop insisting on, his antislavery views. The *Review* started losing subscribers on account of its antislavery politics. An economic downturn that began later in 1857 also could not have helped Brownson's bottom line.[6]

The Buchanan administration did not follow Brownson's suggestions, instead seeking to turn the Kansas territory into a slave state over the objections of a majority of the white settlers. The slavery agitation reached boiling point, and the Republicans sought to win the Northern states on their platform of resisting the expansion of slavery into new territories. Voters who opposed slavery on moral grounds, and/or wanted white settlers to be free to move into the western territories without competing with slaves, were the natural constituency for the Republicans, who focused on this issue as well as traditional Whig issues like public works projects.[7]

There were some consolations for Brownson amid the backlash against his politics in 1857. He received letters from or about converts who attributed their embrace of Catholicism to the influence of the *Review*. A priest named Fr. William Cumming wrote to thank him for curing him of his "Gallican" views and persuading him to adopt the propapal ultramontane position. In May Brownson spoke in Baltimore under the auspices of Archbishop Kenrick. An illness, perhaps brought on by the strains of the job, began to affect him.[8]

The Know-Nothings Reach Their Sell-by Date

To secure a hold on the North, the Republicans needed the votes of the former Know-Nothings—those who were concerned about slavery as well as about Rum and Romanism. At the same time, it wouldn't do to scare off the non–Catholic German voters with the sort of immigrant-bashing so popular with many nativists. It was also time to tone down the antialcohol policies—the Germans might not vote Republican if it meant giving up their beer.[9]

Bishop Timon of Buffalo believed that the toned-down Catholic-baiting of the Republicans was even more insidious than the open hostility of the declining Know-Nothings: "There seems to be an anti–Catholic twang in much of what they [the Republicans] write and say. A moderate anti–Catholic party with a concealed warfare would do us much more harm than the brutal force and open warfare of the K[now]N[othings]."[10]

The experience of an Illinois politician illustrates the kind of straddling that Republicans had to do. Abraham Lincoln supported a Republican platform in Illinois which denounced discrimination "on account of religious opinions, or in consequence of place of birth." This did not stop him, however, from accepting the support of Simeon Francis, editor of the pro–Lincoln *Illinois State Journal* and a member of the Know-Nothing order. Francis published an article during the 1858 Senate race between Lincoln and Stephen A. Douglas. The article linked the Catholic Church to the proslavery wing of the Democratic Party, as indicated by the headline: "The Two Despotisms—Catholicism and Slavery—Their Unity and Identity." Lincoln used humor and lawyerly evasion to avoid committing himself for or against the Know-Nothings. Punning on the members' self-description as Native Americans, he joshed, "do they not wear breech-clouts and carry tomahawk?" Falling short of full political courage, Lincoln said in general terms that he supported anything good in the Know-Nothing program and opposed anything bad in it.[11]

It was not in a public statement, but in a private letter (to his friend Joshua Speed), that Lincoln unburdened himself of his actual antinativist views. Many Americans deny that blacks are created equal, and the Know-Nothings would make "foreigners and Catholics" the next victims, Lincoln wrote.[12]

Whall Between Church and State

The chancellor of the Boston diocese, Fr. James Healy, was a busy man—as any American priest would be in that era of too few priests to serve a growing Catholic population. Fr. Healy's duties included the usual ones of presiding at Mass, delivering homilies, and taking the confessions of the flock. When the Protestant elite of Boston went to summer at nearby Nahant, taking their Irish Catholic servants with them, Fr. Healy went to Nahant to minister to the servants' spiritual needs. While there, he rubbed shoulders with the "Brahmins" of Boston (as Oliver Wendell Holmes, Sr., referred to the community's leaders and members of its established families—invoking the metaphor of the superior Brahmin caste in Hinduism). Developing good social relations with many of the Brahmins, Fr. Healy was in a position to give these people an example of the learned, nonimmigrant side of Catholicism. If they were as free of color prejudice as they claimed, than Fr. Healy's African-American origins would not have fazed them.[13]

Fr. Healy's duties as the Boston diocese's first chancellor included handling marital cases. The priest whose parents' own marriage had been of unclear status now ruled on the validity of others' marriages and considered requests for dispensations for Catholics to marry outside the faith.[14]

To accustom the priests and the flock to the new office, Fr. Healy had to set some ground rules, confining personal appointments to scheduled hours of the day. Since Bishop Fitzpatrick remained ill, Fr. Healy did a lot of the bishop's work, such as keeping up the official journal, handling correspondence, and in many cases ghostwriting the bishop's letters.[15]

The recent epicenter of the Know-Nothing movement, Massachusetts was turning into a Republican state as the voters chose a Republican-controlled legislature in the 1856 elections, while electing Nathaniel Banks, a Know-Nothing-turned-Republican, as governor in 1857. Nativism was not forgotten, even as the Republicans shifted most of their focus to the slavery issue. The Republican legislature proposed a two-year disenfranchisement for naturalized citizens—in the May 1859 election the voters would decide whether to add this provision to the state constitution.[16]

Soon before this election, Know-Nothingism gave more signs that it was still not extinct in Massachusetts. The Boston School Committee required that the pupils recite the ten commandments—in the King James translation—every week. In Boston's Eliot School, the teacher asked one day—March 7, 1859—that a student named Thomas Whall recite the

Protestant ten commandments in accordance with the School Committee decree. Young Whall refused, and his father had several conferences with the principal and members of the city school committee. Fr. Bernardine Wiget of St. Mary's in the Irish North End, where the Elliot School's Catholic pupils worshipped, told the children that Sunday not to recite from the Protestant Bible, and that any pupils who dared to do this would have their names read out from the altar. Parishioners adopted a resolution telling the children "not to be ashamed, but to be proud of their holy religion ... and ... recite their own Catholic prayers." On Monday, March 14, the teacher again demanded that Whall do the recitations. When Whall refused, assistant principal McLaurin Cook beat the recalcitrant child with a rattan cane during several intervals over a half-hour period, a couple times telling Whall to soak his wounded hands in water before submitting to further beating.[17]

About one hundred students were expelled and about three hundred left the school. Whall's father brought a criminal complaint against assistant principal Cook, charging assault and battery. Cook's lawyer said that Fr. Wiget, a Swiss immigrant, "comes to us from a foreign land to instruct us in our laws." Judge Sebeus Maine of the Boston Police Court acquitted the cane-wielding schoolmaster.[18]

"The mind and the will of Wall [sic] had been prepared for insubordination and revolt by his father and the priest," thundered the judge. The judge insinuated that sinister forces were at work: "May not the innocent pleading of a little child for its *religion in school*, if granted, be used like a silken thread, to first pass that heretofore impassible gulf which lies between *Church and State*, and when one secured, may not stronger cords be passed over it, until cables, which human hands cannot sever, shall have bound *Church and State together forever*?"[19] With this poetic expostulation, the judge rejected any bridge-building, and affirmed that Thomas Whall's punishment was legitimate.

Some Protestants supported Whall on religious-freedom grounds. Fellow Catholics praised him. Catholics in Covington, Kentucky (in Martin John Spalding's bishopric under the archdiocese of Cincinnati) sent Whall a gold cup. Many of Boston's Protestant leaders, however, were indignant against the Church. Unitarian pastor Arthur Buckminster Fuller (brother of Margaret Fuller) took an uncompromising stand in favor of the Protestant Bible in the common schools, linking the threat of Catholic domination to the other concerns of Puritan evangelicals: "Intemperance and slavery would quickly be overcome if Romanism ceased to exert her influence to uphold them both."[20]

Bishop Fitzpatrick responded to the crisis with a letter to the Boston School Committee. Fr. Healy may well have had a hand in the drafting, given the uncertain state of the bishop's health and his frequent assignment of such tasks to the chancellor. Fitzpatrick had every reason to be indignant—he was alone among American Catholic bishops in urging his flock to send their children to the common schools rather than establishing parochial schools for them. After all this, to be repaid with compulsory Protestant exercises in the schools, now enforced by beatings—it was enough to affect his peaceable temper. Fitzpatrick clarified in his letter that he had always opposed the Protestantizing of the common schools, but had not previously expressed his opposition for fear of stirring "angry passions" and "violent acts." Fitzpatrick still did not envision establishing parochial schools to resolve these clashes, writing in his journal that providing Catholic schools to his flock was "plainly impossible." Venting his true feelings at the "bigots" who ran the state, he privately fumed that the King

James Bible laws "were framed, no doubt, for the express purpose of corrupting the faith of Catholic children." Other bishops had managed to raise funds for Catholic schools, but Fitzpatrick, a supporter of common schools, stuck with his position. Fitzpatrick's assimilationist approach received a boost when, in Boston city elections soon after the Whall case, voters chose several Catholics, including a priest, to serve on the school committee.[21]

Nevertheless, a modern study comparing census data in Boston—Bishop Fitzpatrick's bailiwick where students went to the common schools—and Chicago—with the more dominant influence of the parochial-school approach—showed that Bishop Fitzpatrick's accomodationist attitude toward public schools was in error. According to 1860 census figures, Boston, where 85 percent of schoolchildren were in the common schools, had fewer poor Irish school-age children in school than did Chicago. In the latter city, there was a more equal balance between public school and private school attendance, and more poor Irish children went to school (either public or private) than in Boston. The Chicago Catholic press promoted the parochial schools as against the common schools, with the *Western Tablet* warning parents that if they send their children to the government schools, those children, having lost their salvation due to the anti–Christian instruction, would "rise up at the last dread day of account to curse you in all the unavailing repentance and bitterness of final despair."[22]

Whether in response to the Whall agitation or otherwise, the voters in May 1859 amended the Massachusetts constitution to require immigrants to wait for two years after naturalization before they could vote. Since this was a Republican-sponsored amendment, Republicans in other states were embarrassed. Disenfranchising immigrants was all very well in Massachusetts, where the Irish immigrants outnumbered the Germans, but further west, the non–Catholic Germans whom the Republicans were courting were the key immigrant voting bloc and did not appreciate antiimmigrant laws. These Germans needed to be cultivated if the Republicans were to take the White House in 1860.[23]

Republican leaders in the Midwest disavowed the two-year amendment. In Illinois, the Republican leadership thoroughly washed its hands of the measure, which the Democrats were trying to pin on Republicans. One of the Illinois Republicans who disavowed the two-year amendment was Abraham Lincoln, the former Whig Congressman whose growing national fame made him a presidential prospect. In his great care for the German Protestant vote, Lincoln bought up a German paper in Springfield, the *Staats-Anziger*. In mid–May, Lincoln exchanged correspondence with the editor, Theodore Canisius, which was widely republished. Lincoln put a considerable distance between himself and the newly adopted disenfranchisement law in Massachusetts. In true states' rights fashion, Lincoln said he would not "scold" the "sovereign and independent state of Massachusetts" about its law. But while implying that he had no right to interfere with Massachusetts's business, he opposed such laws elsewhere: "I am against [the two-year law's] adoption in Illinois, or in any other place, where I have a right to oppose it."[24]

Chancellor Healy in Boston meanwhile responded to information about restrictions on the Church in the Boston Navy Yard. Navy policy raised obstacles for seamen who wished to go to Mass on Sunday. Acting as Bishop Fitzpatrick's surrogate, Fr. Healy prepared a letter to Navy Secretary Isaac Toucey, giving a lengthy review of the situation and asking for relief.[25]

William Rosecrans's Friend Julius Gareschè Addresses Public Controversies

An article by "Catholicus" appeared in the May 22, 1858, *Freeman's Journal,* the New York Catholic paper edited by James McMaster. The letter, titled "Executive Power Over the Army," said nothing specifically about Catholic concerns. But as the author's pseudonym suggested, the rights of soldiers were a matter of special concern to Catholics, after Massachusetts's Know-Nothing governor, Henry Gardner, disbanded the Irish Catholic Columbian Rifles militia unit.[26]

Perhaps some echoes of this Massachusetts controversy influenced the article "Executive Power Over the Army": whether the president had the power to dismiss a military officer without charge or trial. The author, "Catholicus," was Captain Julius Gareschè, William Rosecrans's fellow Catholic and fellow West Point graduate. Gareschè had aquired legal training as well as military experience, and had been raised to the position of assistant adjutant general in Washington, D.C., but his career had experienced a hiccup a few years earlier when his commanding officer on the Texas frontier kept him under administrative arrest without trial and threatened to put derogatory information in his file. Insisting on a hearing, Gareschè achieved exoneration of his superior's charges, only to face new complaints that he was allegedly favoring Catholic soldiers. These complaints did not reach the disciplinary stage.[27]

In Washington, as in Texas, Gareschè had developed the reputation of a pious Catholic layman, giving his time and money to charity and helping Washington, D.C.'s poor and sick of all races. Despite his good repute, he did not seem inclined to sign his own name to an article suggesting that his commander-in-chief might have limited powers. As "Catholicus," Gareschè in his article went into a lengthy legal analysis explaining that arbitrarily discharging military officers was contrary to law. The article explained some practical dangers, as well, in entrusting the president with such power.[28]

Letting the president remove army officers for any reason, the article contended, would turn the army into an "instrument of oppression" such as the Founding Fathers feared. An officer subject to arbitrary dismissal would be "degrade[ed] ... into a mere creature and instrument of the President's will." A president could use the threat of dismissal to induce army officers to obey illegal orders. "Is there no question now before the country," Gareschè asked significantly, "out of which such a case might grow?"[29]

In his September 1859 issue, Brownson published an article on divorce by "J. P. G."—Captain Julius Gareschè again. Himself in a loving marriage strained by financial problems and the death of some of his children, Gareschè appreciated the value of strengthening marital ties. Not only was divorce contrary to the Bible, but it had ill social effects. Gareschè was alarmed by the campaign for allowing divorce for "incompatibility of temper." Nor could divorce be limited to more "reasonable" grounds than incompatibility—concessions to divorce would bring the country on a "slippery precipice" toward sexual anarchy.[30]

With liberalized divorce, claimed J. P. G., there would be a "universal corruption of morals." Husbands and wives would feel free to desert each other, driven apart by the normal stresses of marriage and the attractions of other potential spouses. The propensity to divorce would be passed through the generations, until divorce became routine and accepted. Single parenthood would be increased—and boys raised by single mothers and girls raised by single fathers would not get the support they needed to prepare for adulthood. The affection of parents for children would decline. Divorce encouraged "polygamy and the grossest sensuality"—the Mormons had sprung up in states with liberalized divorce laws. Waiting in the wings were the free love advocates and their plans for the destruction of the institution of marriage altogether, along with the contraception and abortion which would accompany such a situation.[31]

Catholics v. Jews

In 1858 and 1859 a dispute over the breakup of a family in the dominions the pope ruled as a monarch—the Papal States of central Italy—spilled over into the United States, increasing the alienation between American Catholic and their Protestant—and Jewish—fellow citizens. The quarrel also accentuated differences between Catholic Americans and their countrymen over the status of the pope, with many Catholic zealously defending the pope's rule over his lands and other Americans cheering on Italian nationalists who were seeking to put the whole peninsula under a single secular government.

In June 1858, the Inquisition in Bologna, in the northern papal territory of the Romagna, seized a seven-year-old Jewish boy, Edgardo Mortara, from his parents. The Inquisition believed that, as an infant, the boy had been baptized by the family's servant girl when she thought him on the point of death. Edgardo was brought to Rome, under the eye of Pius IX himself, to be raised as a Catholic. Jewish leaders in Europe asked European governments to protest, which they did. Foremost among the critical governments were the expansionist northern Italian kingdom of Piedmont, which had territorial designs on the papal domains, and Piedmont's ally Great Britain, whose policy was to concern-troll for alleged papal misgovernment in order to delegitimize Pius's rule. The British criticism was exaggerated—the Papal States were undergoing a period of low taxes and modest economic growth, and its people hadn't starved en masse as had the subjects of certain countries. Of greater concern to Pius was the criticism of the French and Austrian governments—French armies helped protect the southern part of the pope's domains, while the northern part, including Bologna, was guarded by the armies of Austria.[32]

Jewish protests crossed the Atlantic to America, where the Jewish community, though 150,000 strong, was not politically united. Various Jewish leaders, including Rabbi Isaac Meyer Wise in Cincinnati, wrote to President James Buchanan asking him to intervene in the case, as European countries had already done, and to ask that little Edgardo be returned to his parents. Protestant sympathizers and the secular press also publicized the cause and denounced the pope's government for splitting up a family for religious reasons.[33]

The protests to Buchanan were in vain. Secretary of State Lewis Cass declared that the case did not warrant American intervention. In a December 1858 letter to Jewish petitioners, Cass expressed his personal view that the treatment of the Mortaras was "an inexcusable act of cruelty" but said that "it becomes us to maintain the same reserve towards other Countries which we expect them to observe towards us." Cass went on to say that if the United States could protest human rights abuses in Europe, European powers could protest such abuses in the United States.³⁴ In other words, American slavery would be vulnerable to foreign complaints if countries were allowed to concern themselves with each others' affairs.

Near the end of December 1858, the fast-disappearing Know-Nothing party in New York tried to fan the dying embers of their organization into a flame by taking up the cause of Mortara's parents. This stance may have helped boost the party's influence. In the 1859 elections, the New York Know-Nothings endorsed a mix of Democratic and Republican candidates. All but one of these candidates won victories.³⁵

Archbishop Francis Kenrick of Baltimore thought that he should make a contribution to the Church's defense in the Mortara case. Kenrick submitted an article on the subject to Brownson, and Bishop O'Connor of Pittsburg wrote with some additional points. Kenrick and O'Connor had strongly criticized Brownson's view that the pope could depose secular rulers, but the prelates had kept the lines of communication open with the influential editor, and were accustomed to submitting material to the *Review*. The Mortara article was to be anonymous.³⁶

The article, published in the *Review*'s April 1859 issue, made an uncompromising defense of the papacy's actions in the Mortara case. The blame for losing his son rested with young Mortara's father for hiring a Christian servant in violation of a law prohibiting such things: "If [the servant] used an opportunity to baptize the child, he must blame himself for employing her." "We yield to no one," protested the article, "in our devotion to religious liberty, and in the present state of the world, at least, we believe the only true policy is for the constitution and laws to leave truth and error alike free." The Mortara case presented "a conflict of rights"—the rights of the parents over the child on the one hand, and young Edgar's rights on the other. Having been baptized a Christian, thanks to his father's lawbreaking, Edgar had become a Christian through supernatural grace and had the right to a Christian upbringing, which he would not receive in a Jewish household where his religion was held in contempt. If he were sent back to his parents, "his religious liberty would be manifestly endangered, since he would be unable to resist parental influence."³⁷

Citing examples from England, America, and Russia, the article showed how government authorities often took children away from parents, including Catholic parents, who were deemed unfit. The United States, certainly, had no business complaining about the internal affairs of foreign countries. Secretary Cass was out of line even expressing a personal opposition to the treatment of the Mortaras: "Our own 'domestic institutions' are quite as unintelligible to those of other countries, and far more liable to become the matter of censure: but whatever individuals may opine in regard of them, we know of no instance in which men in authority denounce them."³⁸ Since "domestic institutions" was a common euphemism for slavery, the article's meaning was clear—Secretary Cass shouldn't be criticizing the human rights speck in other countries' eyes while American had the plank of slavery in its own eye.

What, then, in the article's view, accounted for the fuss being raised about the Mortara case? Some of the culprits could be readily identified: "The Jews ... having to a great extent control of the press in Germany and other countries," were playing up this case. The main problem, though, had to do with the designs of foreign powers. The kingdom of Piedmont-Sardinia, together with England and France, was using the Mortara case "to hold the temporal government of the Pope up to public execration" so as to justify seizure of the territory of the central Italian Papal States.³⁹

The article then moved into a discussion of the pope's role as ruler of the Papal States. It is not clear if this part of the article, which later got Brownson in trouble, had been prepared by Kenrick or whether it had been inserted by Brownson on his own—probably the latter. The situation of the pope's Italian subjects, said the article, was "not intolerable, and is in fact superior to that of the people in most European States." But in contrast to the attitude of Pope Pius and many in the U.S. hierarchy, who conveived of the Papal States as a sacred trust belonging to the Church, the article declared that the pope ruled his territories in a purely secular capacity, and was not infallible in governing the territories, as he admittedly was in spiritual affairs.[40]

Other Catholic journals waded into the Mortara case, again citing the issue that President Buchanan and Cass had indirectly, albeit clearly, alluded to: American slavery. How could the United States government possibly grant the Jewish petitions and complain to another government about the separation of families? The *Catholic Telegraph*, coedited by Sylvester Rosecrans, ran in translation an article from *L'Univers,* the ultramontane French paper edited by Louis Veuillot: European governments never urged the United States "that the negroes of the slave states should in future be treated like Christians and human beings, and that at any rate when a family was sold it should be sold to one master." The *Telegraph's* translation was reprinted in other American Catholic papers. James McMaster's *Freeman's Journal* opined "that the Jews have as much natural right to circumcise a Catholic child, without parental consent, as Christians have to baptize a Jew child," that is, no right at all. Still, the U.S. government shouldn't open a can of worms by complaining to the pope. McMaster imagined a situation in which, after the American ambassador complained to the pope abour the Mortara case, the papal government raised concerns about an American slave whose family had been separated by sale. McMaster noted that "*every* government has its own embarrassing questions."[41]

Engineers and Educators

William Rosecrans left his project in western Virginia after it was well started, and ended up setting up an oil refinery in Cincinnati, on Columbia Street. He took council from Abraham Gesner, who had invented and patented a procedure for distilling oil. William produced the oil for lanterns, which were used for illumination, but his oil did not sell well because it dirtied the wick. William conducted experiments to produce a clear oil which burned cleanly. An explosion in the lab one day set a fire which William was able to put out. He was, however, burned badly on the face. The nuns of the Ursuline Convent and Academy in Columbia, South Carolina, prayed for his recovery, a fact which the nuns recalled later when they themselves faced the threat of their institution being burned. It took a year and a half before William was healed, and a scar remained on one side of his face, turning up his mouth on that corner to look like an eerie smile. He would always insist on being photographed on the nonburnt side of his face after that.[42]

William was not taken out of action by the accident. He managed to make a clear oil of the kind he was seeking, and while he was at it he came up with a couple new kinds of lamps, including a lantern which used a round wick. He found a new way to make soap.[43]

William, however, was not neglecting the spiritual side of life. He wrote, however, a letter to the New York Catholic editor James McMaster in January 1858. Writing from Newport, Rhode Island, the engineer sent the editor a $4.50 check for a translation of a book of daily spiritual meditations (written by a Pere Griffet), with the remainder of the check to pay up his subscription to the *Freeman's Journal*. McMaster, William said, had won an impressive reputation for his hard-hitting editorials in defense of the Catholic faith. William praised McMaster for improving his (McMaster's) work and making it stronger and deeper.[44]

In August 1859, William wrote again to McMaster. He was back in Cincinnati and in somewhat worse straits than before. He could not afford to renew his subscription until he had paid the creditors of his business. He did send five dollars to settle the account of an unnamed relative and friend.[45]

Apparently in light of his financial condition, William applied for a professorship at yet another military academy, the Louisiana Military Institute. He believed that there had just been a vacancy in April 1860. As it happened, the professor who was supposedly going to resign—William T. Sherman—had decided to stay, so this opportunity fell through and William remained in civilian life for the moment.[46]

More Challenges for the Church in Ohio

Salmon Chase had presidential ambitions, and his re-election as governor of Ohio would be a first step toward that end. Chase's focus remained slavery, not nativism, and he wanted to sideline the Know-Nothings who had helped him win in 1855 but who, in their decline, were a source of embarrassment. The state Know-Nothings were pressing for a one-year disenfranchisement of naturalized citizens, a measure which would alienate immigrant voters, including the large numbers of liberal and Protestant Germans. Chase, rather than back this radioactive bill, gave the Know-Nothings another bill they wanted, giving lay trustees control over church property. This new law had the potential for giving the Church some of the same hassles in Ohio to which it was subject in some other states like New York and Massachusetts. To Chase, the key point was that the bill was anti–Catholic without being antiimmigrant. Chase's strategy of courting non–Catholic immigrants worked, barely, as Chase was re-elected governor in 1857 by a narrow margin.[47]

Like the rest of the country, the Cincinnati archdiocese suffered from a shortage of priests. In the past two decades, the number of dioceses in the country had increased almost threefold while the Catholic population grew from 600,000 to 3.1 million. American-born priests were not enough to meet the need, and missionary priests often had to be recruited from Europe.[48] Archbishop Purcell wanted to train more American-born priests for service in his archdiocese, to address the shortage and perhaps also to avoid having a preponderance of foreigners in a Church which was under attack for alleged foreign allegiances.

Archbishop Purcell had made various attempts to provide for the education of future priests, at one point in the 1840s having the seminarians reside at his own household while he imparted to them such learning as he could. He sent some seminarians to St. Mary's Seminary in Emmitsburg, Maryland, and of course sent Sylvester to Rome. The seminary of Mt. St. Mary's of the West in Cincinnati, named in 1855 as the archdiocesan seminary, and where Sylvester Rosecrans taught, was supposed to solve the longstanding problem.[49]

Mt. St. Mary's was supposed to operate on a freestanding basis, not being connected to any college. This was a new development, since the American Church's custom was that a seminary would be attached to a college, which often taught students from the equivalent of early grade school to the postsecondary level. Under this sort of arrangement, the seminarians had much of the responsibility for teaching, supervising, and disciplining the students at the college, a system which led to criticism. With their job of training the college boys and keeping them out of trouble, the seminarians had reduced time for their own studies, reinforcing the trend of turning newly minted priests loose on the country with limited academic training. Critics like Fr. William Barry, rector of the Cincinnati seminary, criticized this situation. Many Church leaders did not think the limitations of priestly training were much of a problem, since as they saw it, America did not need scholar-priests, but decent pastors who practiced simple living and who stayed off the bottle. And whatever their limitations, the seminaries had a reliable source of funding from the tuition paid by students at the associated college, many of whom were from Protestant families—the Catholic colleges were strongly subscribed. This in itself was a cause for criticism, due to a fear that seminarians might be so demoralized by contact with their worldly students that they might reconsider their priestly vocation.[50]

The Cincinnati seminary was supposed to be a freestanding institution without connection with a college, but this turned out to be impracticable. By 1856, it was clear that it would not be possible to keep the seminary afloat without the tuition revenue of an associated college. Archbishop Purcell then attached a college to the seminary. To run the new St. Mary's College, Purcell picked Fr. Sylvester Rosecrans, while keeping Sylvester in his position as professor at the seminary until 1860. It appears that by this time Rosecrans was developing a reputation as a scholar. Biographer Richard H. Clarke waxed eloquent: "No heresy in philosophy or theology could escape the searching and analytical power of his naturally strong and admirably trained mind. Of him, in this connection it was well said, 'He was a school-man to whom Albertus Magnus would have pointed with pride. He was a theologian, whom St. Thomas Aquinas would have loved.'"[51]

Archbishop Purcell and Sylvester's admiring biographer were not the only ones who perceived such qualities in Sylvester. The last was on the short list for heading a new institution, an American College to be set up in Rome. The project of a separate college for American seminarians in the Eternal City was a favorite of Archbishops Hughes and Kenrick. It was also one of the recommendations Cardinal Bedini made after his tour of the United States. A Roman College would result in more priests, give them a "more solid education," and provide a thorough education to many priests who would ultimately be appointed bishops. Pope Pius IX enthusiastically backed this recommendation, notifying several American bishops of his decision when they were in Rome in 1854 for the declaration of the dogma of the Immaculate Conception, and reiterating his wishes in a letter to the bishops in the following year.[52]

When Cincinnati held its Provincial Council in 1855, the bishops opposed the project of an American College. The archdiocese was just starting its own scheme of theological education, with Mt. St. Mary's of the West, and after having gone through so many vagaries of experimentation with various educational schemes, they did not want Rome to impose a new one. But the pope had already made up his mind. Not that the Western bishops lacked zeal for education—at the same council they decreed that priests, if the local situation allowed, must set up parochial schools for the education of children—failure to do so would be a mortal sin.[53]

Rome solicited nominations from the bishops for rector of the proposed American College. Their Graces nominated fifteen candidates in total. Archbishop Kenrick nominated three candidates—one of whom was Rosecrans (Kenrick spelled his name "Rosecranz"). Kenrick's recommendation was significant because he was one of the American College's most zealous advocates, in contrast to the unenthusiastic Purcell. The Roman rector job, however, ultimately went to Fr. William McCloskey.[54]

The rector of the Cincinnati seminary was a twenty-five-year-old priest named William Barry. No sooner had he been made rector than he became a frequent contributor to *Brownson's Quarterly Review* on the subject of Catholic education. With Brownson cheerleading, Fr. Barry called for reforms of seminarian training, calling for a sort of ladder of seminaries from the diocesan to the archdiocesan to the national level, plus the American College in Rome. Repeating the old arguments for freestanding seminaries, Fr. Barry, said the colleges ought to be separate from the seminaries—the option which the archdiocese had been forced to give up for lack of money. As to the quality of the colleges, Barry said, "We fear that our Catholic colleges in this country have failed to be living, intellectual bodies ... as consequently to send forth into the world living men capable of grappling with and mastering the living questions of the day." Whether this applied to the college Sylvester ran, Fr. Barry did not say. So that no aspect of education in the Cincinnati archdiocese would go unexamined, Brownson in July 1859 denounced an anti–public school pastoral letter in Cincinnati. It is not certain how Archbishop Purcell took this criticism, but he received at least one letter denouncing the young reformer, Fr. Barry.[55]

The Papal States and the United States

The attention of the American public, such at least as could be spared from slavery, turned to a large extent to Italy. The furor over the Edgardo Mortara case died down—Edgardo later became a priest and lived until 1940[56]—but the public was interested in the upsurge of the Italian national movement, which had the pope's territories in its crosshairs. Also targeted by the nationalists were the Kingdom of Naples, taking up the southern half of Italy, and several small states in the north. Austrian possessions in Italy were also slated for "liberation." The Papal States, with their central location, were necessarily on the annexationist agenda of the national movement, because the nationalist dream involved a unified state including the center of the peninsula—especially Rome with its historical associations.

Upon the failure of the antipapal revolution of 1848–49, many Protestant Americans—inclined to sympathize with nationalist movements—were in sympathy with the defeated revolutionary government of Mazzini and Garibaldi. They ultimately wanted to see Italy united under a single government, with the pope's authority in the center of the peninsula overthrown. But in the 1850s both the Church and its temporal control of the Papal States persisted.[57]

Many Americans saw misgovernment, not reform, as the hallmark of the Papal States. The Protestant polemicist Theodore Dwight—already known to Catholics for helping write Maria Monk's phony memoir of imagined Catholic crimes—was an advocate for the overthrow of the allegedly corrupt and oppressive government of the Papal States. Dwight published a virulently antipapal account of the Roman revolution of 1848–49. In 1859, he published a translation of the memoirs of Guiseppi Garibaldi, the guerrilla leader who had commanded the military forces of the defeated Republic while Sylvester Rosecrans was in Rome. Garibaldi was contemplating a new expedition to "liberate" Italy and the Papal States, and Dwight praised the general for opposing "the cruelties of Popery" "with the clearness of a theologian."[58]

Many American nativists thought that the overthrow of the pope's power in Italy would weaken the Church throughout the world, including in the United States. The American and Foreign Christian Union, dedicated to Protestantizing Italy, propagandized for the cause of Italian unification and helped the revolutionaries who were plotting for that outcome. The *Daily Times* of New York cheered the northern Italian Piedmontese government, which as it slavered greedily over the pope's territories closed numerous convents and monasteries in Piedmontese territory.[59]

By early 1859, dreams of "liberating" the Papal States seemed close to fulfillment. Napoleon III—the adventurer-emperor of France—went to war against Austria alongside the Piedmontese, and the two countries drove the Austrians out of most of the Italian penninsula. This meant that that Pope's northern territories—the Romangna, the Marches and Umbria, comprising most of the land area, wealth and population of the Papal States, lost their protective Austrian garrison, leaving the area vulnerable to Piedmontese aggression. A revolutionary government seized the Romagna and awaited French approval to attach itself to Piedmont. The government of Piedmont began fomenting rebellions in the Marches and Umbria, softening them up for invasion. In the South, the guerrilla chief Guiseppe Garibaldi, invaded the southern Italian kingdom of Naples and conquered his way up southern Italy. Garibaldi made no secret of his wish to take Rome.[60]

Speaking to the students at the new American College on the Feast of St. Francis de Sales, January 29, 1860 (the college had been founded on December 8, 1859), the pope reiterated the idea that his central Italian territories were a sacred trust belonging to the Church. The pope said he could not yield his claim to these territories even if he wanted to, and he certainly had no wish to hand over his states to the hated Piedmontese regime. As Pius was aware, the Piedmontese government was attacking the Church, closing monasteries and turning out the monks and nuns, banishing bishops from their sees, all this while hypocritically proclaiming its dedication to religious freedom (as in the Mortara affair).[61]

In the July 1860 issue of his *Review*, Brownson continued his straddle on the pope's temporal domains. Property given to the Church was in fact given to God, and this included the Papal States. Still, Brownson expressed some sympathy for the aspirations of the Italian nationalists who wanted to unite the peninsula, including the Papal States, under a single government. The Pope's possession of his territories was not "indispensable" to his independence, and so the loss of these territories would not threaten the Church.[62]

10. *"Framed, no doubt, for ... corrupting the faith"* 135

Piedmont sent troops into the northern Papal States on September 11, 1860. At the battle of Castelfidardo, the Piedmontese army defeated the outnumbered papal troops, including the brave foreign volunteers known as Zouaves. Garibaldi handed over southern Italy to Piedmont. Having availed itself of the tools of aggression so familiar to the modern era—contrived crises, phony plebiscites—Piedmont ruled almost the whole Italian peninsula, including the northern Papal States. The only territories outside Piedmont's grasp (in addition to Austrian-held Venetia) were five of the pope's Mediterranean provinces, including the city of Rome. Piedmont's ally France protected this remainder of the pope's territory from Piedmontese aggression—despite his support for Italian unification, the Emperor Louis Napoleon could not afford to abandon Rome and forfeit French Catholic support. Italy was about to be proclaimed a single Piedmont-ruled kingdom—Piedmontese prime minister Camillo Cavour declaring in October that Rome would one day be the capital.[63]

To Pope Pius, the loss of his northern territories was more than a political setback; it was an attack on the Church itself, an attack he could not recognize or accept. The Church's right to the Papal States was non-negotiable, and was indeed linked to the papacy's spiritual power. The Papal States were a literally sacred trust, "a part of the robe of Jesus Christ, which remained whole even on the hill of Calvary," as Pius protested to the Piedmontese

Italian monument celebrating the defeat of outnumbered papal troops at the 1860 battle of Castelfidardo, which led to the annexation of the northern Papal States by King Victor Emmanuel's Kingdom of Piedmont. Only Rome and its environs remained under Papal rule. American Protestants celebrated Pope Pius IX's defeat, while American Catholics raised funds to support the Pope in his difficulties (by Roby Ferrary from Castelfidardo [Flickr]).

King Victor Emmanuel. As Pius explained to the Emperor Napoleon himself: "I cannot concede what is not Mine."[64]

The American Church agreed with the pope on the sacredness of his territories. After the pope returned to his restored territories in 1850, Archbishop Hughes announced that the pope ruled his states by divine right, and said that the pope's temporal sovereignty was necessary to his independence. When Piedmont took over the northern Papal States in 1860, Catholics held indignant meetings in several cities, including Cincinnati. Archbishop Hughes ordered collections in all the churches in his archdiocese to help the pope. Archbishop Francis Kenrick of Baltimore in 1860 issued a pastoral letter calling for all parishes in his province to hold collections for the pope. Writing to his brother Peter, bishop of St. Louis, who had also raised funds for the pope, Archbishop Kenrick said that the money should be sent to Fr. McCloskey, the rector of the American College, who would give it to the pope or to the prefect of Propaganda.[65]

Outside of the Catholic community, American reaction was quite different. There were meetings throughout the country to celebrate Italy's unification at the expense of the pope and other states on the Italian peninsula. A public meeting in New York celebrating Piedmontese and Garibaldian victories attracted numerous movers and shakers in the business world, including at least three men who had taken part in the 1847 meeting honoring Pius IX. Now these same men were celebrating the pope's loss of most of his territory.[66]

Some in Rome were still in sympathy with the United States despite many Americans' sympathy with the Piedmontese. In November, John P. Stockton, the U.S. minister to the pope's government, spoke with Cardinal Antonelli, the papal secretary of state. During a conversation focused on the Italian crisis, Cardinal Antonelli offered his view that (in Stockton's rendering) "the United States was the only free country in the world."[67]

The divide between Catholics and non–Catholics was widening again. But slavery at home was taking Americans' attention away from events abroad. In September 1859, Democratic California Senator David C. Broderick, an antislavery leader—and a Catholic—was killed in a duel with a slavery supporter. In October 1859, John Brown and other antislavery militants raided Harpers Ferry in western Virginia in an unsuccessful attempt to prompt an uprising among the slaves. Brown's December 2 hanging did not stop the controversy—Brown's supporters included prominent abolitionists, and Southerners tried to link Brown's raid to the Republican Party.[68] As 1860 progressed, the implications of these events came to assume greater importance to Americans than debates over Papism.

11

"I wish that secession had never been thought of"

Catholic Democrats—who made up the overwhelming majority of Catholics—could only watch as the Republicans picked up the votes of non-Catholic Northerners. In a remarkable political feat, the new party won support in 1860 from both nativists and from many non-Catholic immigrants. What both groups had in common was their suspicion of the South and, in many cases, their suspicion of Catholicism. The Republicans basically wrote off the Catholic vote. They still wanted the immigrant Protestant vote. Protestant immigrants from England, Scotland, Wales and Ulster were already pretty firmly in the Republican camp. That left the Germans. While German Catholics voted like Irish Catholics—overwhelmingly Democratic—the Protestant Germans were a mixed bag. Republicans had to show the Protesant Germans, and the "forty-eighters," that they did not object to foreign immigrants as such, and that Protestants born abroad could trust the new party.[1]

The Know-Nothings were basically finished as a separate party in the North, despite the we're-not-dead-we're-just-resting rhetoric of some of their more optimistic members. After the massive Northern Know-Nothing migration to the Republican Party, the Know-Nothing rump got together with ex-Whigs to form the Constitutional Union Party. The focus of the CUP was not nativism or Catholicism, but keeping the country together by downplaying the slavery issue. The party's target voters were the former Know-Nothings and Whigs of the South, plus Northerners who had voted for the Know-Nothing candidate Millard Fillmore in 1856. These voters, worried now about slavery rather than Romanism, were skittish about Republicans' radical reputation.[2]

The Republicans wanted the support of these Fillmore voters. The Republican-controlled House of Representatives in 1860 selected William Pennington, a Republican and ex-Know Nothing, as speaker. Republican bigwigs in New York, such as Horace Greeley, even proposed a fusion of Republicans and Know-Nothings. This idea was too much for other Republicans, but the party elders had other ideas for bringing the Fillmore voters onboard. They could appeal to this bloc by adopting a more moderate image on slavery and endorsing federal public-works projects.[3]

Senator William Henry Seward of New York was the leading Republican candidate for president, but he had two problems which cost him the nomination—roughly, he was buffeted by Know-Nothings from both ends. For one thing, many people considered Seward too confrontational with the South on slavery. This might alienate swing voters, among

"The Boat that Rides in Safety," cartoon from the Republican Party's *Wide-Awake Pictorial,* November 1, 1860. Washed out of their boat, the anti–Catholic Know-Nothings are permitted to get in the Republican Party boat. The caption quotes the Republican crew: "Take you in! well, yes; if you don't kick up a row in the boat—take a seat in the stern and be quiet. Not otherwise." Not mentioned in the cartoon is the fact that many influential ex–Know-Nothings had been in the Republican Party's "boat" for several years by 1860. Catholics noted indignantly the large ex–Know-Nothing contingent in the Republican Party (courtesy Abraham Lincoln Presidential Library & Museum, reprinted by permission).

whom the former Fillmore voters of 1856 figured prominently. On the other hand, the ex–Know-Nothings who had already migrated to the Republican Party distrusted Seward's Catholic ties. Long memories of the school struggles of the 1840s, when Seward sided with Archbishop Hughes in support of education reform, influenced nativist thinking. Former Know-Nothing Thaddeus Stevens of Pennsylvania, who as a strong antislavery man might have been sympathetic to Seward, rejected him on nativist grounds. "Pennsylvania," said Stevens, "will never vote for a man who favored the destruction of the common-school system in New York to gain the favor of Catholics and foreigners."[4]

With Seward out of the way, second-tier candidates could compete for the presidential nomination, which the Republicans gave to Abraham Lincoln in their May convention. The accompanying party platform called for keeping slavery out of the federal territories. The platform also upheld equal rights for those of foreign birth. This was designed to appeal to the Germans. While one nativist deplored this "Dutchification" (Germanization) of the platform, most of the former Know-Nothings in the party remained loyal, supporting the Republicans for their slavery stance.[5]

The Democrats broke into Northern and Southern factions, with the Northern Democrats nominating Lincoln's Illinois debating partner, Stephen Douglas. The Southern Democrats nominated John C. Breckenridge. The Breckenridge faction wanted the federal government to put all its power toward supporting slavery in federal territories, while the Douglas faction would, at least de facto, leave the matter up to white settlers in the territories.[6]

Brownson's Endorsement of Lincoln

In the July 1860 *Review*, Brownson discussed the pending presidential race. He started out by deploring what appeared to be many subscription cancellations, deploring the censoring effect of public opinion. Brownson said he tried to keep political partisanship out of the *Review* to avoid distraction from the periodical's "more important religious and philosophical purposes."[7]

The essay charged right ahead and went into politics anyway. Brownson deplored the allegiance of Catholics to the Democratic Party. The Democrats might from time to time get a "nominal" or "indifferent" Catholic into office. Because of public pressure, no serious Catholic, "publicly associated with the defense of Catholic interests," could get elected. So the Catholic officeholders who remained were, by implication, an unworthy lot, perhaps seeking office to get a living.[8]

Democrats, Brownson said, appealed to Irish Catholics not as Catholics, but by ethnic appeals. This was counterproductive, he added, since it encouraged the Irish to cling to their foreign origin and fail to acquire "American habits and associations." Such ethnic appeals had brought the country to the "verge of ruin."[9]

By denying any inherent link between Catholicism and any particular party, Brownson was warming up for an announcement which was hardly going to endear him to many of his remaining subscribers. He endorsed Abraham Lincoln, the Republican, for president. Previously, Brownson said, he had only supported Democratic Party candidates. But on the vital issue of slavery, it was the Republicans who came closest to advocating the correct policy. Both the Northern and Southern wings of the Democratic Party had embraced the cause of slavery, differing only in the lengths they would go to promote the institution. Logically applied, the Democratic position that there was nothing wrong with slavery would entail reopening the African slave trade, and what Catholic could endorse such a thing?[10]

Brownson reiterated what he considered the true constitutional position, which he had already explained in 1857. Congress could not legislate regarding slavery in the territories. In the absence of valid legislation on the topic, the natural condition of human beings—freedom—reasserted itself, making slavery unconstitutional in the federal territories. This would limit slavery to those Southern states which specifically authorized the institution.

He thought the Republicans were hardly ideal, given the strength of the abolitionist element in the party. Brownson continued to oppose Northern abolitionists for meddling with slavery in the South as opposed to blocking its extension. But Republicans were less bad than the Democrats. While the Republican Party was wrong to claim a congressional power over slavery, this was "a respectable error" which was at least an error in the correct—antislavery—direction.[11]

Brownson anticipated that the South would secede from the Union in the event of Lincoln's election. He admitted in his essay that he had formerly looked to the South's powerful planters as an aristocratic counterbalance to the excesses of universal suffrage. In his "hatred of democracy," Brownson said, he had been "half reconciled to the existence of slavery." But instead of putting the brakes on Northern mob rule, the Southern ruling classes had allied with Northern demagogues and worsened the problem they ought to have cured: "we therefore hold [the South] to a great extent indirectly responsible for the democracy that now threatens the whole country with ruin."[12]

For a prominent Catholic intellectual to endorse the Republican Party was sufficiently shocking. This caused backlash from Brownson's Catholic subscribers. Apart from slavery, some of the other opinions he published in his *Review* provoked backlash from other quarters—Brownson's own archbishop and Rome itself.

Complaints to Rome

The July 1860 graduation exercises at Fordham University featured what was becoming a tradition—a clash between Brownson and Archbishop Hughes. From the podium, with Brownson in the audience, Hughes praised Brownson as "one of the strongest thinkers we have amongst us, and one of the best writers in the English language"—provoking applause. The archbishop then undertook to contradict what Brownson and certain contributors—apparently Fr. Barry—had said about the quality of education in Catholic universities. Catholics had founded Europe's great universities, so the faithful need no be ashamed about the quality of their institutions. Hughes referred to the situation in Ireland, where the hated British were trying to entice Catholics into Protestant universities but faithful Catholics were trying to build up a Catholic university. Despite his criticisms, Hughes told the audience that they should all subscribe to the *Review*.[13]

The next issue of the *Review*, in October, was absolutely packed with articles guaranteed to provoke. One article included, among other things, a discussion of the Papal States. Brownson returned to his theme that the pope's right to rule the Papal States was a "secular right" not connected to his spiritual functions. The Piedmontese government had no right to commit aggression against the Papal States, as it was currently doing, but the pope should voluntarily allow his States to be absorbed in a united Italy, freeing the people of the territory from "slavery or perpetual nonage."[14]

In another essay, Brownson criticized the philosophy taught in Catholic (and Protestant) universities. Brownson put in a plug for his favorite Italian philosopher, the late Vincenzo Gioberti (d. 1851), who had many philosophical and theological enemies in the Church. He was also politically unpopular in Rome for advocating Italian unification—though his proposed Italian federation would have had room for the pope, Gioberti's plans challenged the pope's sovereignty over his States. Gioberti's works had been placed on the Index of Forbidden Books because of his politics, but Brownson felt free to rely on Gioberti for his nonpolitical, philosophical writings.[15]

In "Rights of the Temporal," the same October 1860 essay in which Brownson challenged the theological basis of the pope's right to the Papal States, Brownson doubled down and defended what he considered the rights of the laity as against the hierarchy. He criticized the Church hierarchy's stance in the church-property dispute, he defended Fr. Barry's animadversions on Catholic education, as well as Brownson's own right as a layman to criticize Church authorities. The Church did not form a "mutual admiration society," and laymen such as Brownson were not "interlopers or nullities." The Church's leaders should take warning from "the rise and continuance of Protestantism." "If the laity are not frankly recognized, and freely permitted to do whatever laymen can do," this would provoke an overreaction in which the laity would "usurp the special functions of the clergy themselves."[16]

Brownson's priest friend, Fr. Jeremiah Cummings, made a contribution to the October issue entitled "Vocations to the Priesthood." Fr. Cummings criticized the lack of native-born, properly trained American priests. America had once received "first rate" priests who were forced out of France and Ireland by the political turbulence of the 1790s. Today, though, the French and Irish bishops kept their good priests at home, so that foreign priests serving in America were mediocrities cranked out by "cheap priest factories" in Europe.[17]

In another article, Brownson called for a more charitable view of the founders of Protestantism than was customary in Catholic polemics. Going up to the present, Brownson found that there were still things about Catholicism which rightfully repelled Protestants, and which was unattractive to the more intelligent Catholics. In "this city"—presumably New York—successful men who grew up Catholic had become only "nominal" members of the Church, believing that a man's being Catholic meant "surrendering his manhood, and denying his natural sense of right and wrong."[18]

Public criticism of the October issue came in the Catholic and Irish press. Archbishop Hughes had replaced McMaster's *Freeman's Journal* with a new publication, the *Metropolitan Record*—edited by John Mullaly—as his official organ. The archbishop ran a sarcastic attack in the *Record* on the philosophical, ecclesiological, and educational philosophy of Brownson's recent articles and mocked Brownson for having excessive confidence in his own wisdom and in "his American birth."[19]

Apparently with some pride, Brownson on October 18 wrote to his son Henry (soon to be associated in the editorship of the *Review*) that the October issue had "kicked up a bobbery, and made the Archbishop [Hughes], they say, perfectly frantic." All in all, the October issue was "one of the best I have ever sent out."[20]

William Elder, bishop of Natchez, Mississippi, was a friend of Brownson's, and wrote to object to specific points in the October *Review*, as well as the overall belligerent tone: "we ought to try as far as possible not to call forth censures unnecessarily, because they cause divisions, and divisions cause weakness." Brownson's friend Charles Montalembert, the liberal French Catholic, also wrote. In his October 16 letter, Montalembert seconded the criticism of Catholic education—Montalembert had tangled with the French government and the Church in the cause of independent Catholic schools. But Montalembert disagreed with Brownson's stance on the Papal States. The Italian enemies of the pope, like the French revolutionists, had good objectives, but like the French in their Revolution their choice of bad means had lost them the blessing of God.[21]

A priest in Chicago, John McMullen, wrote Brownson an angry letter of criticism. Brownson had visited Chicago in the previous year and stayed in the bishop's residence while the Catholic community "doted on" him with "real love," as Catholic artist Eliza Starr put it at the time. When Brownson visited Chicago on a lecture tour in 1859, the star-struck Starr met with him. She observed his hearty, infectious laugh. "They had a good deal of fun with the big old Doctor, whose very bulk they loved." He told "very ludicrous" tales of his days as a Universalist and Unitarian minister. The lecture itself was "over the heads of a great many" in the audience. Starr herself was inspired by at least one part of the speech: Brownson "was combating the idea that Catholicity degrades human nature; and after a train of proofs of its constant care to save the soul from degradation, he burst into a strain of angelic eloquence, upon the immortality she gives to the body, the powdered bones, the scattered dust of the good Christian, hinting at the union between our dying bodies and that divine and mystical body, which is our Viaticum." Fr. McMullen's attitude was quite the reverse of Starr's. His letter concluded with what Brownson took to be a threat to report the editor to Rome. Brownson, in a lengthy and heated reply, affected to believe that "some mutual enemy must have written me in your name." In spiritual matters, Brownson said, he was bound to obey the priests and bishops, but not in temporal matters: "we will obey the priest only so far as in obeying him we are obeying God." To the Irish Fr. McMullen Brownson thundered about the difference between liberty-loving Americans and authority-loving foreigners. Americans saw clerics as "ministers of the law," not dictatorial rulers. Such was the spirit of "Americans of the old stock," like Brownson himself, "who have the real American national character." Thus McMullen's censures "affect me less seriously than he probably supposed they would." As to the suggestion of denouncing him to Rome, he would welcome any Roman correction. "I am a Catholic; a Catholic I am determined to live and die. Err I may; a heretic I may be, as a *formal* heretic I never was. It will cost me nothing to retract any error authority may point out in any of my writings."[22]

Someone—possibly Fr. McMullen—did indeed report Brownson's work to Rome. Cardinal Barnabo of the Congregation of the Propaganda, which supervised mission territories such as America, wrote to Fr. Cummings. The New York priest was to inform his friend Brownson that the complainants thought the articles were "deeply offensive to the sincere Catholic heart."[23]

Secession Winter

On November 6, Abraham Lincoln swept the North. Southern voters almost unanimously opposed him, as did Catholics, Brownson notwithstanding. With a broad coalition of Northern Protestants, Lincoln was able to take all the Northern electoral votes except for a minority of electors in New Jersey who voted for Douglas.[24]

Lincoln won the most votes in the New England states and those states which had large New England-descended populations. Lincoln won the Fillmore voters of 1856, who generally distrusted Catholics and foreigners and wanted to steer a middle course on slavery. Lincoln also won substantial support from Protestant immigrants, but not Catholic ones.[25]

Republican George W. Julian, not himself a Know-Nothing, later gave a broad view of the role of the Know-Nothings in the formation of the Republican Party in the late 1850s. Former Whigs and Democrats, as Julian explained it, "generally made their exodus from their former political masters under cover of Know-Nothingism, which served them as a sort of 'underground railroad.'" One of the many reasons they came over to the Republicans was "the signal rout of the organized crusade against foreigners and the Pope" and the replacement of that crusade by the campaign against slavery.[26] Apart from Brownson, Catholics distrusted the victorious party which provided such a welcome haven for their enemies.

Once the election results were known, South Carolina, followed by other states in the Deep South, seceded from the Union. By the time of Lincoln's inauguration on March 4, 1861, seven states had voted to break off from the country: South Carolina, Alabama, Mississippi, Florida, Louisiana, Georgia, and Texas. In April, these states, organized as the Confederate States of America, attacked Fort Sumter, a federal fort in Charleston harbor. President Lincoln called out the militia to suppress the "rebellion," prompting the secession of four more slave states: Virginia, North Carolina, Tennessee, and Arkansas.[27]

While these exciting events were going on, Brownson continued to deal with criticism of his articles on the Papal States, education, and other Catholic issues. In a letter of November 29, 1860, Bishop J. H. Luers of Fort Wayne, Indiana, writing to Brownson about his October *Review*, suggested that, to avoid aggravating matters, Brownson stop discussion of "nationalities, or any other exciting question," and instead pursue "useful and instructive" topics, of which the bishop gave some examples—"Theology, Philosophy, Geology Literature ... the Catholic view of Slavery, &c. &c." Luers's letter was probably one of the very few instances at that juncture when any American was urged to stay away from controversial topics and take up slavery instead.[28]

Brownson wrote Fr. Cummings on January 11, 1861, knowing that the letter would find its way to Rome. If what he wrote was wrong, Brownson said, he would submit to correction. "I can assure his eminence [Cardinal Barnabo] that I have no pride of opinion to gratify, and that the Holy See will always find in me a docile and obedient subject."[29]

Brownson's January issue was apparently an attempt to clarify the points where he had been challenged. Brownson did not appear particularly "docile and obedient" from the standpoint of his critics. Brownson called for Italy to become a confederation under Piedmontese leadership, with the pope getting compensation for the loss of his territories. Fr. Barry returned to the education question, mocking Hughes's defense of Catholic colleges and denouncing the grade-school-to-university format of some of these colleges. Fr. Cummings reiterated his position that American-born priests would get a better reception in America than priests educated abroad. Brownson added an article in defense of his position, and made an announcement that discussion of the controversial issues was closed. Brownson was angry at the denunciations he had met with in the Catholic press, at the misrepresentations his critics made of his views, and the uncharitable attacks against him personally. Archbishop Hughes had even suggested that Brownson was to blame for the way others had misinterpreted him![30]

As the country drifted into war, Brownson's literary collaborator, and sometime theological sparring partner, Archbishop Francis Patrick Kenrick of Baltimore, experienced up close the divisions of church and country. Baltimore was the country's oldest see. The fabled Mason-Dixon line, separating North and South, was the archdiocese's northern border. As the nation was splitting up all around him, Francis was characteristically working on a scholarly project: an English translation of the Pentateuch, the first five books of the Bible. Archbishop Kenrick occasionally turned to Brownson for suggestions. Brownson wanted to use the King James translation as the basis of a Catholic translation. The archbishop intended to make at least some use of the King James, but Rome insisted on using the Latin (Vulgate) translation as a point of departure. Brownson was more a fan of a translation being put out by his English friend John Henry Newman—Kenrick hoped to get his translation out before Newman could publish his. By the end of 1860, Francis was winding down his work on the Pentateuch.[31]

Francis' position as archbishop of the oldest American see gave him some de factos prominence, and bishops and priests wrote him for advice. Showing the caution which marked his nature, Francis tried to minimize offense to either side, though as a supporter of the Union even a retiring scholarly nature such as his could not fully avoid giving provocation. The priests at the Baltimore cathedral refused to pray for the U.S. authorities, so Kenrick read the prayers in person. As the archbishop read the prayer for the Union, many people in the pews walked out, and some of those remaining made noises as if to obscure the objectionable words.[32]

Maryland secessionists attacked federal troops and burned bridges. In response, the Lincoln administration locked up suspected secessionists without trial. Archbishop Kenrick commented that the federal commander, Benjamin Butler, "has allowed no looting of civilians or of ourselves. He has imprisoned those whom he mistrusts with no regard for constitutional rights."[33]

Francis Kenrick shared his fears with the poet Eliza Allen Starr, an artist and drawing teacher in Chicago. Starr first became interested in the Church when visiting Philadelphia while Francis was bishop, and converted in 1854. Francis arranged for the publication of many of her pieces in the *Catholic Mirror* of Baltimore. He also wrote to her with spiritual advice.[34]

In August, Francis wrote to Miss Starr that the *Catholic Mirror* had grown hostile to the Union and was probably not a good place to run any more of her poems. The archbishop regretted the pro-Confederate stance of his supposed diocesan organ. "The sympathies of Marylanders generally are with the South, especially as we are treated as a conquered people. I do not interfere, though from my heart I wish that secession had never been thought of. Shall we ever again be a united people?"[35]

12

"Called upon by both sides to fight in the battles of the country"

Dueling Teachings from One Bishop

Just before the war started, a Southern bishop gave a sermon which was both a defense of, and a warning to, the Confederate states in their approach to slavery. Augustin Verot, the vicar apostolic of Florida, spoke at the St. Augustine parish church on January 4, 1861. Aspiring to guide the country in this crisis, the bishop had his sermon published.[1]

The subsequent history of this sermon shows that it could be used by both sides of the slavery debate. James McMaster's Southern-sympathizing *Freeman's Journal* printed the sermon on June 18, 1864, to justify McMaster's view of slavery "as a human arrangement for the common good." In contrast, the *Catholic Telegraph* of Cincinnati, in December 1865 (around the time the Thirteenth Amendment was ratified and slavery finally abolished), printed the sermon to support "our own complete justification for and unqualified condemnation of Negro Slavery."[2]

The published version of the sermon, a slightly revised version of the preached version, was basically divided into two parts. The first part attacked the abolitionists, whom Verot blamed for the secession crisis. Slavery was not a "moral evil" as abolitionists claimed, but has "received the sanction of God, of the Church, and of society at all times, and in all governments." The second part of the sermon laid out the rights of the slave, and warned the Confederate states that God would set His face against them if they disregarded these rights.[3]

Verot explained how, in his view, slavery was consistent with Christianity. The equality of human beings as taught by the Bible was spiritual equality, not the equality of condition advocated by "agrarians and anarchists." The canon law of the Church "recognizes Slavery, and countenances masters in retaining possession of their slaves." In any case, the slaves would be harmed by "sudden and abrupt manumission."[4]

The South faced "a conspiracy against justice and truth ... headed by fanatical preachers," nativist, Northern Protestant abolitionist ministers, who hated the Catholic Church as well as the South. Verot allowed that slavery could be abolished by law, and admitted that this had happened "in the greater part of Christian nations." (What Verot unfortunately failed to note was what Pope Gregory XVI had said about this development in his 1839 letter *In Supremo Apostolatus*. Pope Gregory had specifically praised the gradual abolition of slavery in Europe, credited it to Christianity, and blamed "men ... blinded by the desire of sordid gain" for reversing this moral progress by enslaving Indians and Africans.)[5]

Verot's sermon, about halfway through, shifted emphasis and turned to the abuses of slavery in the South. The African slave trade was "the worst of piracies" and should never be revived. Persecuting the "free colored population" was a "crying, cowardly, infamous tyranny," Verot added, citing the laws of certain states which enslaved or banished free blacks (Fr. Healy's native Georgia had such laws). Verot also denounced white sexual predation against slave women and free black women: "who knows whether the Almighty does not design to use the present disturbances for the destruction of frequent occasions of immorality, which the subservient and degraded position of the slave offers to the lewd." The bishop also denounced masters for interfering with slave marriages and separating slave families by sale. Verot reminded his audience that masters had to feed, clothe, and house their slaves, and provide them the means of religious instruction. The Confederacy ought to have a "servile" code outlining the duties and rights of masters and slaves and protecting slaves from the abuses outlined in the sermon. Verot warned that "if these wrongs be persevered in, this may be the reason why the Almighty, in his justice and wise severity, may sweep slavery out of the land, not because slavery is bad in itself, but because men will abuse it from wanton malice."[6]

Verot sent a copy of the sermon to Archbishop Kenrick in Baltimore for his review. Verot anticipated that the U.S. bishops would soon hold a new council, and that such a council should adopt decrees to protect the rights of "the poor slaves on our plantations." There was no such council during the war.[7]

In July, Pope Pius made Verot the bishop of Savannah, while letting him continue in the post of apostolic vicar of Florida. This promotion did not indicate full approval of Verot's sermon—someone in Propaganda wrote on an Italian translation that "not everything can be affirmed."[8]

Massachusetts Decides It Needs the Catholics After All

As the leaders of Massachusetts geared up for war, they set aside their previous dislike of the Catholics and the Irish and recruited them. The diocesan authorities in Boston, including Chancellor James Healy, helped with the effort, forming an alliance which would have been deemed implausible before the war.

Republican governor John Albion Andrew, an abolitionist lawyer, had some fences to mend if he wanted to reach out to the Irish Catholics. The diocesan organ, the Boston *Pilot,* had warned its readers in 1860 not to vote Republican, because of the two-year disenfranchisement law for immigrants approved by Republican legislators and voters. When President Lincoln issued his call for troops, Massachusetts faced the awkward situation of having suppressed Irish militia companies during the peacetime Know-Nothing fervor. Fortunately, many Irish immigrants were still receptive to recruiting appeals, from a mix of motives including proving Irish valor, saving democracy for future generations, showing loyalty to the Union and rebuking nativist slurs, earning pay for their families, partaking in an adventure, and getting military experience in preparation for waging war against

England. Distinctly *not* among the Irish-American motivations for war was a desire to abolish slavery. Republicans and abolitionists were seen as de facto disunionists whose agitation of the slavery issue had helped provoke the war. Now that the war had begun, Patrick Donahoe's *Pilot,* the diocesan organ, called for suppressing the rebellion and urged the Irish to volunteer.[9]

Thomas Cass, former commander of the Columbian Rifles, had formed a private, unofficial military organization, the Columbia Association, after the Know-Nothings suppressed his company. The association was made up of former Columbian Rifles and kept up its drills without state sanction. Now that war was begun Cass was allowed to recruit an Irish regiment, the Ninth Massachusetts Infantry, from his association and from additional volunteers. The Ninth paraded in Boston Common, serenaded by Irish songs and wielding green flags along with more conventional military banners. Governor Andrew tried to bridge mutual suspicions between Irish and non–Irish, praising the Irish troops as fellow citizens. Yet echoes of old divisions could be heard even in this honeymoon period. After the Ninth Regiment had departed for the front, a Boston Protestant was overheard remarking, "There goes a load of Irish rubbish out of the city."[10]

Governor Andrew now authorized another Irish unit. Ambitious would-be officers were recruiting volunteers for what became the Twenty-Eighth Regiment. Bishop Fitzpatrick, editor Patrick Donahoe of the *Boston Pilot,* and Chancellor James Healy promoted and coordinated the recruiting. The Church proved a channel of communication between Governor Andrew and the Irish community, though not always a successful one. Governor Andrew wrote Bishop Fitzpatrick to ask about the qualifications of certain candidates for officer in the Irish units. Fitzpatrick, perhaps with Fr. Healy's advice, wrote that he was "unacquainted with most of the ... candidates," and that he didn't know enough about the rest to comment on their qualification as officers. The significant fact is that in the former center of Know-Nothingism, a Protestant governor was creating Irish Catholic regiments and consulting with the Church on the officers.[11]

Whether due to the Church's recommendations or otherwise, the officers and men of the Irish regiments would show considerable courage when it came to fighting the enemy, showing their mettle in many battles, especially on the front between Washington and Richmond. Unfortunately, these soldiers also showed a marked tendency to fight among themselves. Rivalries among the officers were not abated by the intervention of the Church, as prominent leaders and would-be leaders vied for officer positions.[12]

While one Protestant Massachusetts company took a temperance pledge before marching to the front, to others in the military, Protestant as well as Catholic, the issue of drinking vs. fighting was not either/or but both/and. Many officers developed reputations as drinkers, and many soldiers matched the officers. The Irish officers and soldiers did not hesitate to reinforce stereotypes by combining hard drinking with hard fighting.[13]

The Catholic/Protestant honeymoon period was illustrated by the appointment of Catholic chaplains for the Irish regiments. Two priests, Thomas Scully and Charles Egan, ministered to the spiritual needs of the Ninth Regiment, and two more priests, Nicholas O'Brien and Lawrence McMahon, were assigned to the Twenty-Eighth. Catholics in other Massachusetts regiments had more difficulty getting chaplains. Governor Andrew heard reports that, in some Protestant-dominated regiments, the Catholic soldiers were not afforded access to Catholic worship. In a public letter, the governor said he hoped that the officers would facilitate Catholic worship rather than restrict it.[14]

Bishop Fitzpatrick's health remained an issue, and was of concern throughout the Boston diocese. Chancellor Healy wrote to a frequent correspondent, Bishop Francis McFarland of Hartford, Connecticut, saying that Fitzpatrick's health had improved, but that Fitzpatrick was constantly warned that excessive activity would make his condition worse.[15] Being in the thick of Civil War recruiting probably added to the strain of the bishop's job, making Fr. Healy all the more indispensable.

Buckeyes at War

Archbishop Purcell summoned an archdiocesan council to meet in 1861. It met on April 28, as the war got under way. Shortly before departing for the Cincinnati council, acting Bishop J. H. Luers of Fort Wayne wrote Bishop Peter Paul Lefevere of Detroit with the latest gossip: the archbishop was going to ask for a coadjutor, probably Sylvester Rosecrans. The council also turned to the current crisis of the Union. Archbishop Purcell told the assembled bishops: "In the midst of the most formidable preparations of our fellow-citizens for mutual destruction, the Church in her peaceful meeting gives us a glimpse of the peace of the Heavenly Jerusalem."[16]

Very soon, appeals for peace gave way to support for the troops. Perhaps after some initial wavering, Purcell decided to wholeheartedly support the Union war effort. It wasn't an easy decision. In 1859, the head of the St. Mary's Seminary, Fr. John Quinlan, had been replaced by Fr. Barry and transferred to Mobile, Alabama, to be its bishop, emphasizing the true universality of the Church in a divided country. But Purcell had made his choice and proclaimed: "The President has spoken and it is our duty to obey him as head of the nation." Purcell flew the U.S. flag over the cathedral and encouraged recruiting. Two professors at the seminary, E. P. Scammon and Dr. Charles O'Leary, set the example by volunteering, becoming a general and an army surgeon, respectively.[17]

Amid this crisis, Archbishop Purcell left on June 30 for Rome. He needed to make his once-in-ten-years visit to the pope, and he wished to be allowed either to resign or have the aid of Sylvester Rosecrans as coadjutor, that is, an assistant bishop with the right of succession at Purcell's death. The recent archdiocesan council had refused to back either request. The other bishops did not want anyone as young as Sylvester—he was only thirty-four—to be appointed to such a position and be designated as Purcell's successor. In Rome, Purcell was again denied his request to resign, but the archbishop put forward Sylvester's name persistently enough that Rome began considering young Rosecrans as a bishop—if not as a coadjutor, perhaps as an auxiliary. Auxiliary bishops help their senior bishop without having the right to succession. Perhaps as a consolation for having his resignation refused, Pope Pius made Purcell's mother a countess and appointed him to the Noble Society of Rome.[18]

William Rosecrans heard the call for support of the Union. As in Massachusetts, the Union relied on the state government in Ohio to raise troops. Governor William Dennison asked Rosecrans to be a civilian assistant to the man Dennison picked to command the Ohio forces, the engineer and former army officer George B. McClellan. William got to work supervising the building of a makeshift military camp named after the governor. Camp Dennison was about thirteen miles north of Cincinnati, and the soldiers from Ohio and Indiana went there to train. The soldiers slept on the bare ground—Rosecrans refused to install bunks and floors in what was supposed to be a temporary camp.[19]

William left Cincinnati after the camp was constructed. He was looking to buy weapons and to get a military commission for himself. Winfield Scott, the overall Union commander, and other officers recommended William for the post of brigadier general of volunteers. Salmon Chase, the former Ohio governor now serving as secretary of the treasury, contributed a recommendation. Meanwhile, Governor Dennison offered to make Rosecrans the chief engineer of Ohio, supervising necessary military construction in the state while holding a colonel's position. Exhibiting what would become his special approach to making friends and influencing people, William refused the offer in a blunt letter. Rosecrans wrote Dennison that "I must go with our people to the front," rather than live an easy life in Cincinnati and "enjoy the many opportunities for having a finger in 'fat contracts.'"[20]

The War Department sent William his brigadier general's commission on May 16. William's old friend Julius Garesché, serving as assistant adjutant general, enclosed a friendly note. Garesché contrasted William favorably with political, "Republican" generals.[21]

The Cincinnati archdiocese was particularly forward in getting spiritual and material aid to the troops. Before the war, a group of Sisters of Mercy had been brought to Cincinnati from Ireland by a zealous convert, Sarah Peter. In a visit to Kinsale, Ireland, the wealthy widow had offered the then-respectable sum of $4,000, which was a fourth of all she had, and the proceeds of her life insurance policy. Purcell gave assurances that the sisters would be supplied with these necessities of life. In 1857 a group of these nuns came to Cincinnati to work at their callings of teaching and nursing. Now that the war was begun, their own building became a hospital where they attended to the sick and wounded.[22]

Other Cincinnati nuns took up the call to serve. The Sisters of Charity of St. Vincent de Paul, founded by Elizabeth Ann Seton (today recognized as a saint), had a longstanding presence in Cincinnati. They busied themselves with teaching and nursing, with several of them serving at the St. John's Hotel for Invalids. In the St. John's Hotel, assisted by doctors, the nuns attended to the sick of all faiths, many of whom traveled from outside the city, charging them according to what they were able to pay. Sister Anthony O'Connell, the procuratrix of the community, served as head of St. John's. Shortly before the war, the Cincinnati *Daily Commercial* expressed its admiration of Sister Anthony; she was "like Florence Nightingale. It is beautiful to see her pass around the sick, giving spiritual consolation to one, and bodily comfort to another."[23]

To commemorate the 200th anniversary of the death of St. Vincent de Paul, Pope Pius allowed the Sisters of Charity dedicated to his name in Europe and America to observe a jubilee on a day they selected. The Cincinnati Sisters of Charity chose March 25, the Feast of the Annunciation. Archbishop Purcell officiated at a High Mass and the nuns renewed their vows.[24]

Sister Anthony and five other nuns went to the soldiers training at Camp Dennison. The Cincinnati *Commercial* praised the nuns in peace as it had in war: "Sister Anthony and a number of Sisters of Charity are acting as nurses and do much of the cooking for the sick, who are thus supplied with palatable food prepared in the very best manner by those whose lives are devoted to such labor. The services of these good women cannot be estimated. They are the Florence Nightingales of America."[25]

The *Catholic Telegraph* appealed to its readers to donate in support of the nuns' labors: "The visit of the different hospitals is equal to a journey of two or three miles. There are about 12,000 men in the encampment. The Sisters have to walk in mud and water over their shoe-tops in heavy rains to attend their no sinecure duties."[26]

William was concerned about getting the Catholics among his troops access to the ministrations of their religion. He consulted with Fr. William Barry, rector of the Cincinnati seminary, on the subject. Due to the shortage of priests, getting chaplains for the Catholic soldiers, and giving soldiers opportunities to get together for worship, was difficult even for a commander who shared these soldiers' religion.[27]

Federal and Ohio authorities worried about that part of Virginia which was across the Ohio River, and decided to send a military force into that area. In western Virginia's mountainous country, with many poor whites and few slaves, the people were resentful of the planter establishment of eastern Virginia. Most of the counties in the region voted against secession, and pro–Union politicians were setting up a provisional government. Confederate troops were advancing into the area, threatening the Union loyalists and a key railroad line. William's brigade consisted of the 23rd, 24th, 25th and 26th Ohio regiments, almost 2,000 in all. With his fellow generals Thomas Morris and Charles Hill, there were three brigades. As the United States troops poured across the Ohio river into Virginia, they at first met little resistance. The Confederates withdrew to more defensible positions, with a minor skirmish in early June.[28]

A young soldier in the Ninth Indiana Volunteer Regiment, who had worked on an abolitionist newspaper and briefly attended the Kentucky Military Institute, later described the experience of the midwestern boys who invaded the Appalachian country. Ambrose Bierce wrote of his sojourn in western Virginia as the "halcyon days" of the war, where casualties were low and the armed tourists were rewarded with the sight of "dim blue billows, ridge after ridge interminable, beyond valleys full of sleep." The sunsets were romantic, "the level rays projected from the trunk of each giant pine a wall of shadow traversing the golden haze to eastward until light and shade were blended in indistinguishable blue." Less romantically, Bierce described the wild pigs devouring the bodies of slain soldiers.[29]

The invading federal troops were entering the diocese of the bishop of Wheeling, Richard W. Whelan. The creation of the Wheeling diocese, roughly corresponding to the future state of West Virginia, had been largely the idea of Whelan himself, when as bishop of Richmond he did missionary work with the Catholics among the hardy western mountaineers, working sometimes with his own hands to build the Wheeling cathedral. He became the first bishop of Wheeling in 1850. When riots threatened during the visit of Bishop Bedini to Wheeling in 1853, Whelan sent word that rioters who entered the cathedral grounds would be shot.[30]

Whelan was not so war-minded against the South. He was not sympathetic to the would-be Union liberators of his diocese. The bishop refused to fly the United States flag over his cathedral, on the grounds that only the flag of God should be placed there. Whelan wrote to the prowar Archbichop Hughes in May 1861, saying that the U.S. should recognize Confederate independence rather than follow the war agenda of the Republican Party.

Bishop Whelan said Catholics shouldn't back "the party that contains the most deadly enemies, abolitionists, infidels, and red republicans." During the war, fearing he would be seized as a hostage by Union authorities, Bishop Whelan prepared a letter of protest to be published in the *Freeman's Journal* in that eventuality—which never transpired. Despite the bishop's position, the Sisters of St. Joseph, a local order of nuns in Wheeling made independent by Bishop Whelan, cared for the wounded of both sides at the Athenaeum building, near William's headquarters. The Atheanaeum doubled as a prison for suspected subversives. Bishop Whelan celebrated daily Mass for the approximately ten nuns in their hospital before they went on their daily rounds among their patients. Despite suspicions against Bishop Whelan and his nuns, the faithful and selfless service of these sisters improved the reputation of the Catholic Church.[31]

The Northern invaders in Virginia wanted to attack a Confederate position called Rich Mountain. The Confederates,

West Virginia historical marker crediting William Rosecrans with the Union's 1861 Rich Mountain victory, "decisive in McClellan's N. W. Virginia campaign" (Brian M. Powell [CC-BY-SA-3.0 (http://creativecommons.org/licenses/by-sa/3.0)], via Wikimedia Commons).

dug in at this elevation, did not expect an attack from the south, believing that this would be impractical since there did not seem to be any paths an army could use. Here is where the Union loyalties of the western Virginians proved helpful. The Hart family had a farm at the top of Rich Mountain, and a son of that family, David Hart, came to the Union camp to offer some assistance. He knew a path unknown to the Confederates, a path coming from the south where an attack was least expected. William suggested that his brigade should go up this path and attack from the south, while McClellan would follow up the attack with an assault from the north.[32]

William's forces went quietly up the path, seeking the element of surprise. One of the horses broke the silence with neighs and snorts. An incensed William cursed, declaring that the horse should be beheaded. (William later explained his habit of profanity to James Garfield: "I do still curse and damn when I am indignant, but I never blaspheme the name of God.") The horse's noise did not alert the Confederates, and William carried off the surprise attack as planned, driving the enemy away. The Confederate commander surrendered the next day.[33]

Rosecrans expected McClellan to close the military pincers by attacking the Confederates from the North. Instead, McClellan remained motionless, listening to the battle, fearing that the Confederates were too strong to attack. When McClellan learned that William had won at Rich Mountain, he wrote a glowing report, praising William's prowess, though he thought William had not fully exploited the victory. McClellan also gave himself plenty of credit for Rich Mountain and a follow-up victory at Carrick's Ford. "We have annihilated the enemy in western Virginia," he boasted.[34]

The victory William won for his superior had an unfortunate side effect. After the humiliating defeat of Union troops at Bull Run outside Washington, Lincoln fired the disgraced general McDowell and chose McClellan to command the Union forces in the area between Washington and Richmond, crediting McClellan with the victories in western Virginia and hoping for more victories of the same kind, which McClellan did not produce—perhaps because he no longer had William in his command. Lincoln gave William the command of Union troops in western Virginia now that McClellan had been promoted.[35]

William worked at building fortifications, inspiring his men, and working at their training. The journalist Whitelaw Reid called the general "nervous and active in all his movements, from the dictation of a dispatch to the tearing and chewing of his inseparable companion, his cigar ... he seemed never to grow weary, and never to need sleep." William was "easy of access" and "inspired ... confidence in the rank and file." A different witness to William's activities reported that "he is in his saddle almost constantly ... he takes his meals as often on horseback as at his table," and he rarely slept. Writing to the people of western Virginia, William essayed his eloquence. "If you stand firm for law and order and maintain your rights, you may dwell together peacefully and happily as in former days." William could have been thinking of his "former days" as a civilian in the area. The *Catholic Telegraph* printed some of the general's inspiring words.[36]

There were still Confederate forces in western Virginia under the command of Robert E. Lee. Lee had twenty thousand men at his command while Rosecrans had under half that. Still, Rosecrans boasted to journalist Whitelaw Reid that he would triumph over Lee's "splendid plan." Torrential rains poured on the area, making maneuvers difficult. William wrote his wife to put some religious perspective on the weather and the campaign: "How shameful to complain of the little crosses of daily life when war compels men to sleep on the cold ground, stand in rain, and go out with life in hand, not knowing when they will return. Oh, my own sweet wife, let us humble ourselves." Lee had his own problems with the torrential rains, which made his planned assaults difficult, along with the personality clashes between Lee and the political generals he supervised. At Carnifex Ferry, Rosecrans's troops clashed with troops under the command of one of these politicos, John B. Floyd. Floyd withdrew. Writing his wife, William knew whom to credit for the victory—the Lord, and the intercession of the Virgin Mary. Lee wanted to attack the Union troops at their key post at Cheat Mountain. When the attack came the outnumbered federals held on. The defeated Lee left for other assignments. Western Virginia was liberated from Robert E. Lee, thanks to William, and a pro-union government organized itself, preparing the way for the future state of West Virginia.[37]

Wounded soldiers returning to Cincinnati from the western Virginia campaign were sent to the Sisters of Charity at St. John's Hotel, in Cincinnati. There were already rumblings that Dorothea Dix, who aspired to control the nursing service, would interfere with the nuns. Meanwhile, the sisters cared for the wounded warriors along with the attending physicians. The wounded piled up, requiring the nuns to use most of the available space for beds.[38]

Archbishop Purcell, after performing a Pontifical Mass in Rome on August 15, left Europe to return to his turbulent see. Back in Cincinnati, he toured his archdiocese's orphanages, hospitals, and schools. No retirement for him![39] He was probably waiting for the pope to assign him Sylvester Rosecrans as an assistant.

News of William's victories had some trouble getting out to people in the Church. On September 20, Fr. William McCloskey, rector of the American College in Rome, wrote Archbishop Purcell, reporting a rumor that William was pinned down by General Lee and running low on water.[40]

Bishop Spalding in Louisville, Kentucky, was as misled as Fr. McCloskey in Rome. On September 27, Spalding wrote to Purcell to express his relief that the pope had not accepted Purcell's resignation. Believing that Sylvester Rosecrans had been rejected as coadjutor, he was relieved, since he considered Sylvester too young. As for Sylvester's brother, Spalding had heard that William's troops had been surrounded and the general captured.[41] Spalding's willingness to accept these reports showed that the bishop was no fan of the Rosecrans brothers.

More Bishops Contribute to the Debate

John Hughes, Brownson's archbishop, articulated his views on the issues of the civil war in response to an article by his old friend, Bishop Patrick Lynch of Charleston, South Carolina. Lynch's diocese had recently received nearly 100 slaves from a parishioner's will, indicating his own stake in the slavery controversy. In a public letter to Hughes in early August 1861, Lynch outlined what he considered the South's grievances against the North—and Northern Protestants. While Archbishop Kenrick of Baltimore claimed Lynch had predicted that the Southern confederacy could not survive, in public Lynch was more bullish about the Southern cause. Lynch declared that the South was driven to secession by Northern aggression against slavery. Northern Protestants made "antislavery" into "a religions dogma" which they "carr[ied] into politics." "We, as Catholics, might everywhere smile at this additional attempt to 'reform' the teachings of our Savior."[42]

Bishop Hughes published a reply in the *Metropolitan Record* on August 23. He made clear that his objection to the Confederacy was not because of slavery as such, but because he opposed secession. Hughes praised the "temperate" tone of Lynch's letter in contrast to the rhetoric of other South Carolinians. "The nature of your ministry and mine necessarily implies that we should be the friends of peace." Hughes sympathized with the South concerning the North's fanatical attacks on slavery: "the South has had much reason to complain." Hughes's personal opinion was that conventions in North and South should work on conciliation proposals to pave the way for peace.[43]

Still, Hughes denied that the South was justified in seceding. The Confederate states had no legitimate grievance, having enjoyed their full rights under the U.S. Constitution. All that the North wanted to do in the war was restore the country's "ante bellum" condition—no interference with slavery was intended. Hughes implied that if the Democratic Party in the North were to unite, they could block the radicalism of the Republicans and put the country back on a sounder course.[44]

Hughes blamed the slave trade on the hated British, who had vetoed colonial American limits on the trade. While the U.S. Constitution left Southern slavery to the Southern states, "the word [*slavery*] itself was not used in any of the paragraphs found in the Magna Charta of our government."[45] While trying to divorce the North's war effort from abolitionism, Hughes did not endorse slavery.

Hughes then addressed another of Lynch's contentions—that the North was luring immigrants to their deaths by recruiting them for military service. In fact, Catholic immigrants owed a duty of loyalty to the United States for making them citizens, and military volunteers were fulfilling that loyalty. As to the South, Hughes suggested there was as much nativist bigotry in the South as in the North. Hughes said that Irish immigrants "are called upon by both sides to fight in the battles of the country," and would get no gratitude for their sacrifice. "Still, whether in peace or war, take them all in all, they are as true to the country as if they had been born on its once free and happy soil."[46]

Another bishop gave a proslavery sermon, this time prompting a complaint to Rome. Augustus Mary Martin was the bishop of the Natchitoches diocese in northern Louisiana, with a sparse Catholic population. Martin grew up in France, influenced by the liberal Catholics de Lammenais and Montalembert. On August 21, 1861, he issued a pastoral letter in French concerning *la guerre du Sud pour son Independence* (the Southern war for independence).[47]

Bishop Martin, unlike Bishop Verot, made only a brief reference to the abuses of slavery, waxing almost lyrical in defense of the institution as it existed in the United States. The pastoral started by crediting God with the enslavement of Africans—"children of the race of Canaan"—so that they could be cared for by their owners, who had the responsibility of being their "shepherds and fathers." In exchange for giving up their freedom, "which they are unable to defend and which would kill them," the slaves were entitled to have their masters feed them and give them religious instruction. Slavery was "an eminently Christian work" and "the redemption of millions of human beings," bringing them to "the light of the Gospel." The enemies of slavery were Northern Puritans and other foes of the Church.[48]

The Congregation of the Propaganda received a complaint about the pastoral, and sent the document along to the Congregation of the Index, which was responsible for protecting the faithful from heretical or immoral writings.[49] As the case proceeded through the papal bureaucracy, the war provoked by slavery continued in America.

13

"The nations of antiquity had slaves; where are those nations now?"

Problems with Rome: Papal States, Foreign Priests, Catholic Education

In Elizabeth, New Jersey, where Brownson lived, the primary newspaper, the *New Jersey Journal,* declared: "From all parts of the country comes up the sound of gathering armies, and through the streets of our cities is heard the tramp of soldiers and the hurried muster of troops." A Rhode Island artillery corps, going through the town, met an enthusiastic reception by Elizabethans: "Great was the excitement here among all our citizens, and many were the souveniers left by the gallant soldiers behind, in the way of handkerchiefs and rings and buttons cut from their uniforms, and given to our fair damsels who were watching the transfer at the depot." A Mexican War veteran in Elizabeth, David Hatfield, raised a company of his townsmen and went to the fighting, carrying a sword and sash presented by Elizabeth citizens at a farewell ceremony in May. Major David Hatfield died a year later while fighting on the northern Virginia front.[1]

Brownson would be caught up in the issues of the war, but he also continued to deal with reactions to his writings on other issues. Cardinal Barnabo, the prefect of Propaganda, thought Brownson's remarks on the Papal States were offensive to Catholics and contrary to the position of the American bishops. While Barnabo acknowledged that the Church encouraged the recruitment of native-born priests, he did not believe this excused the harsh tone of Cummings's articles on foreign priests published in Brownson's *Review*. However, having received Brownson's explanations and Cummings's promise not to write again on priestly education, Barnabo believed that the editor had made proper submission and the matter could be considered closed. Fr. William McCloskey, rector of the North American College in Rome, believed that the attempt to condemn Brownson had been blocked by Barnabo's "good sense and sympathy with such an old hero."[2]

In correspondence with his friend Bishop William Henry Elder of Natchez, Mississippi, Brownson explained that he considered himself ill-treated by the Catholic press—instead of approaching him personally, his episcopal critics and their editorial allies had launched attacks in print which either misrepresented his views or blamed him for the misrepresentations of others. "The article on the Rights of the Temporal was inspired, to some extent dictated, and revised and approved by a dignitary of the Church. Numerous alternations were made at his suggestion. Moreover I presented the main points in confession

155

with my confessor, a Jesuit, a professor of theology, and one of the ablest theologians I ever met. I made the subject a matter of prayer, and offered up my communion four times while writing it, for light of guidance." Brownson blamed Archbishop Hughes for his problems—but "I cannot accept the Archbishop of New York as my consultor. His advice I cannot respect, and I am not under his jurisdiction."[3] Brownson seemed to be setting his archbishop against his local bishop, James Roosevelt Bayley of Newark, who was probably the "dignitary" who was reviewing Brownson's work and serving as a buffer between the editor and Hughes.

Bishop Bayley certainly seemed better disposed to Brownson than Archbishop Hughes was. In January 1861, the bishop sent an invitation asking Brownson to be on the board of trustees of Seton Hall College, an institution Bayley had founded and was in the process of incorporating. Brownson wrote back in February cheerfully accepting the proffered position. The trustees were an advisory body, but in appointing Brownson, Bishop Bayley was showing the former a good measure of confidence, including possible sympathy with Brownson's ideas about Catholic education.[4]

War Hawk

The July 1861 issue of *Brownson's Quarterly Review* contained an essay titled "The Great Rebellion." To Brownson, things were looking up for the Union cause. This was a great change from the beginning of the year, when secession seemed triumphant and "the great bulk of the people seemed to be wholly engrossed in trade and speculation, selfish, and incapable of any disinterested, heroic or patriotic effort. What wonder, then that we were despondent, without hope for the future?" But the North's patriotic uprising in support of the war was better than Brownson expected.[5]

Brownson clarified his states' rights Calhounism by specifying that the federal government, though one of "express and delegated powers ... formed by sovereign states, by mutual compact," was a true national government, supreme within its sphere, and entitled to demand allegiance from the people. Brownson also averred that he had always opposed slavery "as a man, as a philosopher, as a Christian, and as a statesman." It was "a flagrant violation of those rights of man on which our republic professes to be founded, no less than of that brotherhood of the human race asserted by the Gospel." Like most Northerners, Brownson had wished that the Southern states would abolish slavery, but instead the South had adopted a rule-or-ruin policy of promoting the expansion of that iniquitous institution. Contrary to fear-mongering secessionist politicians, the Republicans did not seek to abolish Southern slavery, "but to resist the aggressions of the slaveholders upon the equal rights of the nonslaveholding states." What was the root cause of the rebellion? "The people of the slaveholding states have rebelled against the federal government because the majority of the people of the nonslaveholding states differ from them in opinion on the subject of slavery, and insist on treating black men, as well as white men, as belonging to the human family, in a word, as men created with rational and immortal souls and redeemed by the passion and death of our Lord; because, in fact, we include them in the great brotherhood of humanity." Brownson did not want the war to be a "war of liberation" to free the slaves, and he would not know what to do with the slaves if they were freed. But if the South prolonged the fighting, the North would be "roused and embittered" and "slavery must go."[6]

The war "will be the thunder-storm that purifies the moral and political atmosphere." It was a judgment of God to bring Americans back to their duty. The war would reinforce the importance of allegiance to legitimate government. Admiration for the destructive "democratic doctrines of European liberals" meant that Americans had "forgotten that freedom is impossible without order, and order impossible without authority, and authority able to make itself respected and obeyed."[7]

The North would win, but only after "a long, severe, and bloody struggle." It would take a "long and severe" war entailing "great privations and manifold sufferings," to bring home "the practical lessons of the war."[8] At a time when many people were predicting a quick end to the war, Brownson had injected a shot of cold realism, and Catholic willingness to confront suffering, into the discussion.

A friend of Brownson's, Fr. Augustine Hewit, a priest serving in Fr. Hecker's Paulist order, indicated that at least one important person was pleased with the *Review* article on the war. The pope's consul general in New York City, Louis B. Binsse, had high praise for the article, said Fr. Hewit. Binsse was a prominent New York merchant and sought to keep Rome updated on American developments. Six months later he would send optimistic reports about Northern prospects in the war.[9]

Binsse's praise showed that if the July issue had confined itself to the "Great Rebellion" essay, papal officials would not have been offended. However, Brownson strayed from discussion of the Civil War in order to tackle more controversial topics.

Problems with Rome: Papal States, Condition of the Reprobate

In the same July issue which contained his essay "The Great Rebellion," Brownson returned to the question of the Papal States, again roiling traditionalist sensibilities. Another article concerned polemical literature. Brownson was unhappy with the way Catholic apologists went about defending their faith. He thought the apologists' methods were obscurantist and reactionary. Brownson suggested other ways to promote the faith to modern men. In the course of this discussion, Brownson offered, tentatively, a theological proposition which he considered open to investigation. It could be permissible, Brownson suggested, to believe that the damned in hell gain some mitigation to their punishment, reaching "natural beatitude" (or approaching it without ever reaching it, according to his son Henry's later interpretation). Brownson may have been influenced by his former universalism in hoping for some amelioration in the condition of the damned. But he was not reverting fully to universalism—he was not suggesting that everyone goes to heaven upon their death or attain the vision of God vouchsafed to those in Heaven—as universalists taught. But Brownson's suggestion was still fairly controversial for Catholics.[10]

Bishop William Henry Elder of Natchez, Mississippi, continuing his habit of comparatively friendly criticism, wrote Brownson about the July issue. Somehow a copy of the *Review* had gotten through the hostile military lines and reached Bishop Elder in the heart of the Confederacy, and Elder's reply similarly managed to reach Brownson in the North.

Bishop Elder, a Confederate supporter, declined to get into a debate on the "Great Rebellion" article, focusing instead on the non-war-related material Brownson had published. Elder continued to object to Brownson's tone, such as his denunciation of many priests' lack of education. Rather than rail against these priests, suggested the bishop (who acknowledged that many priests were not learned), Brownson could undertake constructive criticism. Another of Brownson's unfortunate habits was disavowing objectionable interpretations of his articles only after the article was criticized, rather than clarifying issues in the article itself. Elder said that busy bishops didn't always have the opportunity to approach Brownson privately about their concerns, as Brownson preferred. The Catholic press, which criticized Brownson, did not represent the bishops' views in all matters. As to Brownson's speculations on hell, Bishop Elder declared that Brownson had not paid enough respect to the historic teachings of the Church. "It is true that you only *ask* questions. But you are not so inexperienced in Rhetoric and human nature as not to know that interrogations convey statements as clearly as direct assertions"—and Brownson's questions conveyed doubt as to the eternal punishment of the damned. Brownson should have stated a clear position rather than by "vague expression" challenge traditional teachings. If the confessor Brownson mentioned in his December letter had signed off on the "Polemics" (hell) article, then "he is not a safe man for you to entrust your conscience to." Elder warned Brownson against intellectual pride—he should "take a more kindly view of the spirit of Catholics," and "consider and profit by serious strictures, even when you think them unwarrantably harsh, extracting the truth for your present profit, and offering up the bitterness for your future reward."[11]

Cardinal Barnabo was not amused when he received complaints of the July issue. The Cardinal thought Brownson had, back in January, apologized for his inappropriate comments and speculations. Now, wrote Barnabo to Fr. Cummings in an irritated tone, Brownson was not only repeating his bad ideas but coming up with new ones. The status of the Papal States should not be agitated as Brownson was doing, and the eternity of hell's torments was an article of faith which was not subject to debate. Barnabo wrote to Archbishop Hughes asking Brownson's old foe to bring the editor into line, protecting the faithful, and the youth, against Brownson's errors.[12]

Brownson again wrote a letter of submission at Cummings's request, which Cummings again forwarded to Barnabo. Once again, Barnabo was more or less satisfied with Brownson's contrite remarks. The cardinal wrote Hughes that Brownson had shown the right attitude and a willingness to correct his errors, even if his retraction was not theologically complete. Before getting this letter, Hughes responded to Barnabo's earlier, harsher letter. Hughes said that formal action against Brownson was not called for. Unlike Barnabo, who acted from respect to Brownson as an "old hero," Hughes was less inspired by admiration for Brownson and more by the practicalities of the situation. Hughes agreed with the criticism of Brownson's July article but resignedly remarked that "I don't think it would be very useful to open up a dispute with Brownson. He likes to argue." Hughes believed that Brownson was far less influential now than he used to be—he had pretty much dropped into obscurity and most Catholics had stopped reading him. Since Brownson moved to New York, Hughes had declined to oversee Brownson's work, and the latter had associated with a circle of clever priests who wanted to impose their ideas of reform on the Church, in "faithful imitation of Lammenais' school in Paris." But these priests had lost influence, and now none of the New

York priests supported Brownson except for Fr. Cummings. Picking a fight with the now-obscure Brownson would unnecessarily stir up matters, and the Catholic faithful were too wise to be corrupted. Hughes wrote at the same time to Brownson, paraphrasing his response to Barnabo in far gentler terms and averring that "as to your personal orthodoxy as a Catholic I have not the slightest doubt."[13] And there the matter rested. Unlike the other articles, Brownson's articles on the war did not provoke inquiries from Rome. Hughes, on the other hand, would clash with Brownson over the *Review's* war articles.

The stress of these controversies, the loss of subscribers for the *Review* because of his attitude toward slavery and the war, plus illness, led Brownson to a momentous decision—he would quit publishing his *Quarterly Review*. Archbishop Francis Patrick Kenrick of Baltimore wrote in late September that "Brownson, tired out with contradiction, and suffering from his eyes, will give up his work in the month of October. He will be in need of the means to sustain life. It would be an excellent thing to fix a pension for him of at least six hundred dollars a year. If the Bishops favor this, it can be done easily." Kenrick may have been thinking of tapping into the convert fund, which had been replenished that year. The converts' fund was initially set up because some converts, before joining the Church, had been Protestant clerics with wives and children, but after their conversion were ineligible for the Catholic priesthood because of their marriages. One such convert was Levi Silliman Ives, who left his position as Episcopal bishop of North Carolina to become Catholic, greatly embittering his former Episcopal colleagues. Another convert was Jedediah V. Huntington, another former Episcopal priest, now a professional writer, some of whose novels sold respectably despite (or because of) being criticized by Brownson as salacious. But since as he admitted to Brownson, Huntington disliked immigrant Catholics, he did not tap into this important market, and could not keep himself out of poverty with his writing. Francis Kenrick gave Huntington some jobs and charitable contributions, engaging in an extensive correspondence with the novelist. Like Huntington and Ives, Brownson was a former Protestant minister barred by marriage from the priesthood. But by the end of October 1861, Brownson's spirits picked up. His wife Sarah wrote to the wife of a family friend that Orestes would continue publishing. The Church did not have to dip into the convert fund for Brownson.[14]

Between the July and October issues, Brownson considered the slavery question which he deemed to be at the heart of the war. Abolitionists, including some Republicans, wanted the North to take advantage of the war in order to eliminate slavery. Congress and the Lincoln administration had to balance this with the need to conciliate proslavery supporters of the Union. While not following a fully abolitionist policy, the North adopted some measures which began eroding slavery. Slaves escaping into the lines of the Union army were not returned to their masters, on the grounds that they were enemy property subject to Union control, although the ultimate status of these "contrabands" as slaves or free was left ambiguous. Congress explicitly liberated slaves who did work for the Confederate military, allowing these slaves to enjoy full freedom if they reached the Union lines.[15]

At the end of August, the commanding general in Missouri tried to expand the federal government's limited slave-liberation policy. John C. Frémont had been the Republican candidate in 1856. At the end of August, Frémont issued a proclamation declaring the slaves of pro–Confederate owners to be free.[16]

Frémont's proclamation provoked a political crisis, with the strong antislavery men calling on President Lincoln to back Frémont. However, Lincoln was not ready for a step as radical as this from his grandiose general. Lincoln required Frémont to modify his proclamation so as to free only slaves covered by the 1861 Confiscation Act—that is, slaves employed in the Confederate war effort—rather than freeing all slaves owned by Confederate supporters. To many opponents of slavery, Frémont was a liberator and Lincoln a timid reactionary.[17]

Like other Americans, Brownson was alert to these developments. As the former supporter of John C. Calhoun pondered this issue, he received a message from France. A prominent French Catholic had just finished a book on slavery. This book was responsive to events in the United States—and to some extent, to events in France as well. Emperor Napoleon III of France leaned toward the Confederacy, relying on divisions in the United States to allow room for French adventurism in Mexico. The liberal opposition in France, partly in response, took up the antislavery cause. The French public was primed by *Uncle Tom's Cabin*, and by denunciations of slavery by French authors like Victor Hugo, to detest American slavery. To opponents of the emperor, the fact that the regime was playing footsie with the Confederacy provided another reason to criticize the South's institutions. Given the Imperial censorship, criticizing abuses in a foreign country was easier than criticizing abuses by the emperor. The liberals' criticism of American slavery resonated with the French public, as Confederate emissaries noted sorrowfully. Even Louis Veuillot's antiliberal newspaper, *L'Univers,* was against slavery. The emperor himself, who was somewhat responsive to public opinion, had to tread delicately.[18]

Augustin Cochin was part of the liberal Catholic movement like his friend Montalembert. Cochin was a politician as well as a prolific author and editor. He had just completed a two-volume work, *L'Abolition de l'Esclavage* (the abolition of slavery). His correspondence with Brownson began in 1857, when Cochin started, with Montalembert's encouragement, the research which led to his book. Cochin wrote to Brownson asking for advice on the U.S. section of the books. On July 21, 1861, Cochin mailed Brownson the completed work, asked that it be reviewed, and asked if there could be an English translation. Cochin was confident that the South would be defeated.[19]

The first of Cochin's two books was about the results of emancipation in those countries which had abolished slavery. Contrary to proslavery propaganda, Cochin argued that freeing the slaves had led to good results, not social disruption and chaos. Cochin's second volume discussed the effects of slavery itself throughout the world, including in the United States. The volume also gave the author's view of Catholic doctrine on slavery. The Church over time "tempers, restrains, guards, and by degrees shakes slavery." By "this great and slow work," slavery had been virtually eliminated in Europe by the Middle Ages. Sadly, as European Christians established colonies in the Americas and elsewhere, there was a deplorable "relapse" as the colonists adopted slavery. Through the application of Christian principles, and not otherwise, said Cochin, slavery would be ended in the New World as well as the old: "Slavery was not abolished before [Christianity], it is not abolished outside of it, it will not be abolished without it."[20]

Inspired by Cochin's work, Brownson published an article entitled "Slavery and the War" in the October 1861 issue of the *Review*. Here Brownson declared support for abolition.

Formerly, Brownson announced, he had opposed abolition in order to preserve the Union—now he was for abolition for the same reason. The Lincoln administration had been using "timid and half-way measures" against an enemy which was trying to extend slavery throughout the country. The Union needed a rallying cry, and liberty would rally the people more than the administration's current lame and inadequate slogans. The struggle between North and South would end in one section imposing its "labor system" on the other, and since freedom was better than slavery, freedom should win. The Confederates wanted "the Union reconstructed on the basis of slavery." Such a compromise peace was unacceptable; it would simply leave the possibility of future secession. And such a "paganized republic" based on slavery would be immoral and unsustainable. "The nations of antiquity had slaves; where are those nations now? ... [T]he fate of all slaveholding nations [should] be a warning" to Northern compromise advocates. God would "avenge the slave." Getting rid of slavery would be an "act of long delayed justice." "Most fearful will be [God's] judgments upon us, if we neglect the opportunity, and fail to avail ourselves of the right" to abolish slavery. The Union had the Constitutional power to free slaves as a war measure, even in loyal states, though in the latter case the government should "pay the ransom" of slaves of loyal owners. Military necessity required treating slaves as "free and loyal citizens," regardless of whether it alienated "lukewarm friends" of the Union. Cochin's work showed that slavery could be abolished "without any serious detriment, even to the former slave proprietors."[21]

"The church has tolerated slavery, where she lacked the power to abolish it; but her whole history proves that she sets her face against it, and uses all the means at her disposal, without shocking the public peace, or creating tumults and disorder, to prepare the slave for freedom, and to secure his ultimate emancipation."

Antiwar Catholics were the "dupes of pretended patriots, but real traitors."[22] The government should not be tender toward its opponents in the North or the South, and Brownson did not care if Lincoln acted unconstitutionally so long as he upheld the Union. "Traitors and friends of traitors have no constitutional rights," so the government should "silence every voice raised against the right of the government to vindicate and preserve the Union by force of arms."[23]

Brownson's article received considerable praise in the Republican press. Horace Greeley's New York *Tribune* received it warmly. The veteran abolitionist William Lloyd Garrison praised the essay in his *Liberator*. Cochin's work also received a boost thank to Brownson's essay.[24]

Yet Archbishop Hughes was so incensed at Brownson's "Slavery and the War" that he forgot his own advice—to ignore Brownson and refuse to give him more attention. Hughes wrote a rebuttal to Brownson and published it, unsigned, in the *Metropolitan Record*. This article reiterated the position Hughes took in his letter to Bishop Lynch—the war was being fought to restore the Union, not to abolish slavery. Hughes's ostensibly anonymous article, entitled "The Abolition View of Brownson Overthrown," rejected Brownson's views as well as those of Cochin, whose book Brownson had reviewed: "Augustin Cochin knows nothing of what slavery is in the United States." Hughes's article said that "the constitution of the country, the laws of the State, regard [the slaveholder's] title to his slaves as not less legitimate than his title to the land." Hughes protested that he did not support slavery, and would oppose introducing it into free territory, but he rejected the idea of fighting the war for "the philanthropic nonsense of abolitionism." Gradual abolition, with the transition to freedom supervised by the ex-masters, was preferable to immediate emancipation. Immediate abolition would "destroy the relation between [slaves] and their masters," and moving to the North would not help the ex-slaves' condition, since the free blacks' "feelings [are] outraged on every corner of our streets."[25]

These were fairly familiar arguments against immediate emancipation. Then Hughes waded into doctrinally doubtful waters. The African rulers, who would otherwise kill their captives, enslaved them instead and sold them to America. If "slavers at the dock should buy them off at $1.25 a head from the massacre of their barbarous tyrant, would they be doing wrong?" While a "genuine Christian" or a "decent man" would not engage in the African slave trade, "it is difficult to discover in the purchases [of trafficked Africans] any moral transgression of the law of God or of the law of man where that traffic is authorized."[26]

Hughes did acknowledge the downside of slavery, specifically the fact that the children of slaves were themselves enslaved and that slave families could be disrupted by sale. At the same time, Hughes blamed the abolitionists for endangering the country: "Sometimes it has appeared to us that abolitionism ... stands in need of a strait jacket and the humane protection of a lunatic asylum."[27]

In unpublished notes, Hughes gave further expression to his views. The slave trade was wrong and under the condemnation of the Church. But the Church did not require that slaves be returned to their "primitive condition" in Africa—they could end up worse off. The master was "not individually responsible" for the condition of his slaves, but he "should treat his slaves with all humanity and Christian care and protection." Hughes vividly expressed his view that Southern slaves were better off than Northern free blacks: "If Heaven had permitted me to have been born in Africa or in America as the son of an African slave, I should sooner remain in Southern bondage than avail myself of the opportunity of Northern freedom. In the South I should know my place."[28]

In a letter to Secretary of War Simon Cameron, Hughes was indignant at the idea that his flock might be made to fight an abolitionist war: "The Catholics, so far as I know, whether of native or foreign birth, are willing to fight to the death for the support of the constitution, the Government, and the laws of the country. But if it should be understood that, with or without knowing it, they are to fight for the abolition of slavery, then, indeed, they will turn away in disgust from the discharge of what would otherwise be a patriotic duty."[29]

Hughes wrote his old friend William Seward that he had responded to Brownson to prevent the "vast mischief" abolitionism would do to the war effort. The government should not put "new firebrands of division" into the ranks of loyal Southerners. "It will be time enough to regulate this unhappy question of slavery when the war shall have terminated." Either because of or in spite of Hughes's antiabolitionist stance, Seward sent the archbishop to Europe to represent the Union case. He started in France.[30]

Diplomacy and John Hughes did not mix well together. His reputation preceded him. The Parisian paper *Le Monde* published the *Metropolitan Record* article in translation. French liberals were upset. There were reserves of sympathy in France for the cause of the slave, but not for a foreign squabble over disputed territory, which is how the French saw Hughes's summarizing the issues of the American Civil War.[31]

While mingling with the French elite, Hughes spoke with Augustin Cochin, the man whose work on slavery had been the ostensible occasion for this dispute. Cochin tried to persuade Hughes that the latter's article was doing damage to the Northern cause. Hughes told Cochin that he had not signed any articles—a technically accurate quibble, though Hughes acknowledged to Seward his authorship of the unsigned article. Cochin tried to repair the damage caused by the *Metropolitan Record* article, with an item in Cochin's newspaper, *Le Correspondant*. This paper was the main organ of the Catholic liberals who opposed the emperor. Cochin's paper declared in an ambiguous manner that Hughes was not responsible for the *Metropolitan Record* piece, reiterating that the article was unsigned and had been translated in France without Hughes's permission. The article was for an American, not a French audience, explained *Le Correspondant*, and had simply tried to promote peace. Cochin was trying to help the archbishop—and the French liberals—out of the public relations thicket into which Hughes's response to Brownson had led. Hughes's diplomacy may have recovered from this setback. As Cochin wrote to Brownson, Hughes not only pointed out he hadn't signed the article, the archbishop called slavery a plague and an injustice.[32]

Brownson, in his newfound position as an abolitionist, began to make new friends, or old ones. Most notable was Charles Sumner, the abolitionist Massachusetts Senator and former target of Brownsonian ire. Before the war, Brownson had denounced Sumner's antislavery ideas as dangerous to the Republic. Now the newly minted abolitionist befriended his erstwhile foe. As early as October 1861, Brownson was writing to Sumner, and the two began corresponding on political issues and on more personal topics. Brownson lobbied for military positions for a friend, and for his son Edward ("Ned"). It was an unlikely alliance—the aloof, aristocratic egalitarian Sumner and the prickly Catholic convert Brownson. Sumner was inspired by the ideals of the French Revolution, an event which to Brownson epitomized the horrors of modern spiritual and political errors. Yet the two men worked together in urging the Lincoln administration toward a stronger antislavery policy. Brownson worked with other abolitionists as well. He was invited to share a Boston speaking platform with one of these, Gerrit Smith, who had egged on Frémont's emancipation policy and had been a member of the "Secret Six" supporting John Brown.[33]

In the January *Review*, Brownson took some thwacks at his nemesis Archbishop Hughes. With a combination of caution and sarcasm which did little to conceal his dislike of the prelate, Brownson singled out slavery as the cause of the war: "if there had been no slavery in the country, there would have been no rebellion, and no rebellion, no war."[34]

Brownson added that he and the archbishop had a disagreement over whether military necessity justified abolition—Brownson believed there was a military necessity to free the slaves, and Hughes denied this. If Brownson was wrong, then four million slaves "for whom, as well as for us, our Lord was incarnated, suffered and died on the cross, would be converted from slaves to freemen." If Hughes was wrong, then through its failure to abolish slavery "the integrity of the nation itself would be destroyed" and "liberty ... would in all probability be henceforth rendered impossible on this continent. Evidently, then, it would be better that the administration should err with us than err with [Hughes]."[35]

"Were [Hughes] to see his way clear," Brownson cattily remarked, "he would labor as earnestly and as persistently for the abolition of slavery as those abolitionists themselves, against whom he so vehemently directs his cutting irony and his biting sarcasms. To say less would be to doubt his Catholic spirit, and his devotion to the religion of which he is regarded as so bright an ornament and so illustrious a champion."³⁶

Brownson went on to say that Hughes's antiabolitionist stance hurt Hughes' reputation and "places our religion in a false position." Hughes's "war upon the antislavery party," though sincere and honest, "seems to us now fitted only to give indirectly, if not directly, aid and comfort to the enemies of the United States; and we have no doubt that, were we to adopt it, we should find ourselves suddenly arrested for treason, and sent to keep company with some of our old friends at Fort Warren [a federal military prison in Boston harbor]." Loyal citizens must be united—they should focus on the Confederate enemy, not make swipes on their abolitionist allies. Everyone "must choose either the Lord's side or the devil's side.... He who is not with us is against us." In hindsight, Brownson thought he should have probably listened more to the abolitionists before the war—their moral and practical insights about slavery were more on-target than Brownson had been willing to acknowledge.³⁷

Brownson defended the North, especially his native New England, as being more American than the South. It was too bad that many Catholics, with their Southern associations and sympathies, did not recognize this superiority. "The interests of Catholicity are linked with the cause of freedom ... an antislavery Protestant is worth more than a pro-slavery Catholic."³⁸

Brownson turned his sarcastic invective against Hughes's words that seemed to sympathize with the African slave traders. The passage on the slave trade looked like "an apology" for it. But that couldn't be what Hughes had meant! Hughes must have been speaking loosely, in a "popular newspaper style." He must not have meant to endorse the African trade, because Pope Gregory's decree of 1839 had pronounced excommunication against anyone who said such things. Surely the archbishop would not "expose himself to excommunication and deposition" by thus defying the papacy and the doctrines of the Church!³⁹

While denouncing his archbishop, Brownson developed ties to General Frémont, author of the controversial antislavery proclamation in Missouri. Brownson's family physician was Henry S. Hewit, brother of Fr. Augustine Hewit. Henry, a veteran, rejoined the army when the war started and got assigned to St. Louis, where he was under Frémont's command before being assigned to the front.⁴⁰

Brownson wrote Sumner about hastening a commission for his son Edward ("Ned"), whom Lincoln had nominated for an officer's position. The young man had arranged to serve on the staff of General Frémont. Lincoln had by now removed Frémont from command in Missouri, sending him to command the forces in western Virginia, where he would replace the triumphant General William Rosecrans who had been given a new assignment.⁴¹

In the April 1862 issue of *Brownson's Quarterly Review* came the article "State Rebellion, State Suicide." Backing off somewhat from his position that the Confederates were conspiring to extend slavery throughout the country, Brownson still insisted that slavery was at the root of the rebellion and that true peace could only come by one section imposing its system on the other. So if the North wanted to have peace while keeping its free-labor system, it would have to impose that free-labor system and abolish slavery throughout the country. Ending the war with slavery intact simply meant waiting for the next rebellion to break out. Reiterating the position he had held since 1857, Brownson added that the existence of slavery could be maintained only by positive law. The Confederate states (all the slave states except Missouri, Delaware, Maryland and Kentucky), by arraying themselves against the United States, had thrown themselves back into the state of nature. And with the reversion to the state of nature, the relation of slave and master was also abolished, since neither the law of nature nor federal law recognized slavery. The federal government could not re-institute slavery if it wanted to. The federal government had no choice but to recognize and enforce the freedom of the ex-slaves. Contrary to these principles, the Lincoln administration continued to recognize Confederate slavery and refused to accept that the states had self-destructed. This was at the same time too tender to the rebels and a violation of states' rights, because it allowed the federal government to reconstruct the seceded states based on a pro-Union minority rather than based on the votes of the entire people. A country where the central government could do this was "a consolidated or centralized republic," not the limited republic of the framers.[42]

Brownson's article put a Catholic spin on the antislavery ideas promoted by many abolitionists and Republicans. Before the Civil War, these politicians, lawyers, and activists had argued that the American Constitution derived from the law of nations, which in turn came from the natural law. By the natural law, freedom was the proper condition of man, and only positive law in the slave states could make an exception to this principle. Outside of jurisdictions whose laws specifically recognize slavery, there could be no slaves, and any slave who left a slave jurisdiction became free. Wherever the federal government exercised exclusive authority—in the territories, on the high seas, in the District of Columbia—slavery could not legally exist or receive federal encouragement. Even the fugitive slave clause, under the strictest antislavery thinking, could not be enforced by the federal government, but was the responsibility of the states. As the slogan went, freedom was national and slavery was sectional. Abolitionist politician Salmon Chase had helped develop these constitutional/natural law theories, and at the time of Brownson's article, as a member of Lincoln's cabinet, Chase, like Sumner, was making a point very similar to Brownson's: the seceded states, by dissolving their relations to the Union, had reverted to the status of territories, and as with other federal territories, slavery was not entitled to federal recognition. In the Senate, Charles Sumner had introduced resolutions endorsing the same position, known as state suicide—influencing Brownson's article, as Brownson acknowledged in a letter to Sumner.[43]

Another article in the April 1862 *Review* took up an issue where Brownson differed from Sumner—the question of what to with the slaves when they were freed. To Brownson, the answer was to colonize them outside the United States. Sumner was a racial egalitarian who rejected the idea that black people should be colonized outside the country. Sumner and other "radical" Republicans rejected colonization as a denial of equal rights to free blacks. But others in the Republican Party, including President Lincoln, wanted to colonize the freed blacks in Africa or Latin America, at least on a voluntary basis, for the same reasons cited by Brownson in his article—avoiding racial strife and letting the two races work out their destinies separate from each other. Lincoln recommended voluntary colonization in his annual message to Congress in December 1861. The president remarked, "I am so far behind the Sumner lighthouse, that I will stick to my old colonization hobby."[44]

In his colonization article, Brownson declared that, in voting for Lincoln in 1860, he was not focused on the interests of the slave, but on opposition to the agenda of the slave power. He had not overlooked the injustice of slavery, but he had "not given it in [his] calculations all the weight it deserved." He knew that abolitionists (he was probably thinking of Sumner) were opposed on humanitarian grounds to resettling the slaves out of the country, and he respected these humanitarian concerns. But justice to the nonslaveholding whites of the South, who did not want to live among freed slaves, indicated the need for separation. While affirming the common origin of all human beings, in accordance with Catholic orthodoxy—and rejecting the "polygenist" views of the likes of the distinguished scientist Louis Agassiz of Harvard, who believed that the "superior" whites and the "inferior" blacks had been separately created (Brownson's erstwhile patron—the intellectual Bishop Fitzpatrick had listened to at least one presentation from Agassiz). Brownson accepted the scientific "monogenist" view that blacks, while descended from the same ancestors as whites, were racially inferior. To Brownson, all races partook of original sin, but the blacks had degenerated furthest from their common origin. Whites and blacks could not live together on terms of equality, wrote Brownson, so it was best to separate them. All freed slaves were the "wards" of the federal government, which as guardian could order the former bondmen sent to another country. But Brownson disavowed any compulsion—like Lincoln, he supported "voluntary emigration." Most freed blacks would choose to leave without compulsion, so long as the U.S. set up a good destination country where black people could exercise "civil and political rights." Brownson wrote Sumner that he would not spend much effort promoting his voluntary colonization ideas, which he thought would work out naturally. Brownson also apologized for trespassing on Sumner's territory with the state-suicide article.[45]

Even in the South, Catholic leaders believed in the common origin of all human beings, rejecting the idea of the whites as a natural master race and the blacks being condemned as a servile class suited only to slavery. The French-language *Propagateur Catholique,* organ of Archbishop Odin of New Orleans, early in 1862 affirmed that whites, under proper conditions, could be subject to slavery just as much as blacks. Racially based theories of slavery "flatter our pride" but are false, said the paper. Bishop Elder, on March 24, wrote Archbishop Odin to denounce a book published in Richmond by one T. W. MacMahon, affirming that whites and blacks were separately created as a master class and a servant class respectively. Bishop Elder wanted such ideas to be formally discountenanced, because of the common origin of all humans. The federal seizure of New Orleans at the end of April may have distracted Archbishop Odin from such a project.[46]

Brownson's sons, Ned and Henry, went into the army, showing that Brownson would share in the sacrifices he urged on the country as a whole. Henry went to the Army of the Potomac to serve in the Third Artillery. Ned, his officership nomination smoothed by Senator Sumner, became a lieutenant, also fighting on the northern Virginia front. Orestes had not wanted his son Ned to be a soldier, but since Ned was set on it, the editor pressed his new friend Sumner to promote the young man's military career. The Senate considered Ned's nomination to serve as aide-de-camp to General John Charles Frémont in the Mountain Department, with the rank of captain. The senators approved Ned's nomination, just as Senator Sumner had assured Orestes it would.[47] Orestes and Frémont were both premature abolitionists, a stance for which they had been both praised and denounced. Now Ned served to bind the editor and the general even closer.

But Ned had precious little time to work with Frémont. Frémont had taken up his new command in Wheeling, western Virginia, in March 1862, replacing William Rosecrans. Rosecrans had managed to defeat Robert E. Lee in western Virginia; Frémont faced off against another formidable opponent, Thomas "Stonewall" Jackson. Frémont would not fare as well against a Confederate hero as William Rosecrans had done.[48]

Frémont was one of three generals whose armies had faced Stonewall Jackson in the Shenandoah Valley. Jackson, by burning bridges and engaging his enemies on favorable terms, was able to beat Frémont. The Pathfinder was no match for the former professor.[49]

It was mid-June when Ned got to Frémont's headquarters in Mount Jackson, Virginia. He was appointed "postal director," and he was "treated with the utmost deference by all the officers and men." It took a few days before he met Frémont himself, though. On June 25 Ned wrote that he had had his first meeting with Frémont, who allowed him to get a new horse.[50]

And that was basically the end of Ned's service under General Frémont. Lincoln removed Frémont from command on June 27. Ned wrote his sister Sarah that "all Frémont's Staff are beheaded with [sic]," including himself. Ned had contacted Sumner with a view to a new assignment; until then, Ned would be on General Banks's staff. As for Frémont, he now had the title of general, but no troops. He lived in New York City and in Washington, still the object of affection and admiration to his staff and to the radicals.[51]

In the January and April 1862 issues of his journal, Brownson distanced himself from the American hierarchy. He declared that he would send each issue to Rome for correction, in case it contained errors, but that he would give the criticisms of American bishops only such heed as the merits of the criticism warranted. "No single bishop can define the faith, or condemn an opinion as heretical, on his own authority; nor can all the bishops of a province, nor all the bishops of a nation, assembled in plenary council, nor all the bishops of the world, without the Pope, the successor of Peter." A bishop could ban the *Review* from his diocese, assuming he did it out of spiritual not political motives, and Brownson's own ecclesiastical superiors could excommunicate him "on legal grounds, for legal reasons, or otherwise his interdict is of no force and does not bind us." Bishops could not forbid him from publishing his *Review*, though his bishop could order him to remove material deemed spiritually dangerous, until Brownson could get the bishop's decision corrected "by an appeal to the supreme court"—i.e., Rome. He acknowledged that submission in such a case, until Rome could correct the error, was "essential to order."[52] Brownson was not going to leave the Church or defy the pope, but he would submit to the pope and Roman officials instead of the unreliable American hierarchy.

14

"Unless, *as a body*, we besiege Heaven with prayer, God will not be pacified"

A New Bishop

On March 25, 1862, the Feast of the Annunciation, Sylvester was consecrated as bishop. Archbishop Purcell was the principal consecrator, assisted by Bishop Spalding of Louisville and Bishop Luers of Fort Wayne, Indiana. Sylvester's formal title was bishop of Pompeiopolis. Many of his former seminary students, who were now serving as priests, got together to get the new bishop a pectoral cross, which Sylvester received during the ceremony. In a speech afterward, Sylvester noted the gift: "I beg you not to forget your promised prayers in my behalf, that, as I wear the Cross you gave outwardly on my breast, I wear the Redeemer's cross deeply on my heart, and never at any moment forget that, whether God requires it all at once, or only [piecemeal], *bonus pastor animam suam dat pro ovibus suis* [the good shepherd lays down his life for his sheep]."[1]

Pompeiopolis, of which Sylvester was now the bishop, is in Turkey, on the southern coast, in the province of Cilicia. The Roman general Pompey had named the city after himself, and made it a home for reformed pirates he had conquered and set to honest labor. By the 19th century, the city was depopulated, known only to the Church, to tourists, and to readers of the tourists' travelogues. John Carne, who visited in the 1830s, wrote of collapsed pillars that were "partly overgrown by the thickets and rank foliage: their appearance in so lone a situation is desolate and mournful: there are no dwellers near them, either shepherds or peasants."[2]

Residing in his uninhabited diocese may have involved a relaxed work schedule, but Sylvester was not expected to go to Pompeiopolis. The latter was a titular see, *in partibus infidelium,* and Sylvester was appointed to it so that he could have a bishop's rank, doing the work of a bishop while serving under Purcell. Sylvester soon had the management of the Cincinnati archdiocese because, promptly after Sylvester's consecration, Purcell left for Rome for the second time in two years.[3]

Purcell wished that Sylvester could have been appointed coadjutor bishop, with the right of succession, but instead Sylvester had been designated an auxiliary bishop without succession rights. Purcell still hoped that Sylvester would ultimately be promoted to coadjutor. At the banquet after Sylvester's consecration, Purcell quoted John 12:26 from the Latin vulgate Bible, "Qui mihi ministrat me sequatur," which in the Church's Douay-Rheims

English translation is, "If any man minister to me, let him follow me." Purcell left the archdiocese in the hands of the bishop he hoped would follow him as archbishop. As Sylvester assumed his new duties as acting head of a huge archdiocese, he kept his teaching position at the Cincinnati seminary. When he wasn't touring the archdiocese, he combined his episcopal duties with his teaching duties. Sylvester was willing to take an enormous workload on his shoulders—laying down his life piecemeal—as his flock experienced the effects of war on the battle front and on the home front.[4]

Touring the archdiocese, with outside visits to Pittsburgh and Boston, Sylvester performed his episcopal duties, consecrating churches and supervising priests. Sylvester kept Purcell posted on developments in the archdiocese, and on William's military activities.[5] The tour of the archdiocese was probably meant to accustom the priests and people—and possibly the other bishops—to the fact that they had an auxiliary bishop who had their metropolitan's confidence.

Sylvester issued a pastoral letter dedicating the archdiocese to the Sacred Heart of Jesus. This was timely, with so many young men of the archdiocese going off to war. The Cincinnati Archdiocese undertook to provide physical aid to soldiers of all denominations, and spiritual aid to the Catholic soldiers. After the devastating Battle of Shiloh in April 1862, the states and the Union authorities sent medical aid for the wounded—8,400 federal and 8,000 Confederate. Sarah Peter, the wealthy Cincinnati laywoman, arranged to send some

When Rome made Sylvester Rosecrans a bishop, it appointed him to the titular see of Pompeiopolis, a deserted city in Turkey, *in partibus infidelium*. Appointment to this vacant bishopric left Sylvester free to serve as an auxiliary bishop in the Archdiocese of Cincinnati. "Ruins of Soli or Pompeiopolis—Asia Minor" engraved by J. H. Kernot after a picture by W. H. Bartlett, published in *Syria, The Holy Land, Asia Minor &c. Illustrated*, 1837 (courtesy of antiqueprints.com).

of the Sisters of the Poor of St. Francis to the Tennessee battlefield to bring the wounded to hospital. Mayor George Hatch of Cincinnati asked Archbishop Purcell to send some Sisters of Charity, the same order which had tended to the wounded at Camp Dennison the previous year. These sisters assigned one-third of their members, who had experience working with Irish plague victims, to attend to the injured at Shiloh. A transport bringing the wounded from Shiloh threatened to sink, and the captain told Sister Anthony O'Connell and her colleagues to escape. They refused, inspiring the doctor to stay as well: "Since you weak women display such courage, I too, will remain." The Cincinnati nuns worked tirelessly in field hospitals on the various Western battlefronts, on hospital ships, and their order's St. John's Hospital in Cincinnati, where they attended to wounded Confederates as well as wounded Union soldiers.[6]

As was the case throughout the armies, the nuns won the confidence and respect of many of the doctors, patients, and observers. On the Tennessee front, where many Ohio soldiers served, the sisters worked in the cold, traveling among widely separated, ramshackle battlefield hospitals filled with infected soldiers. But like other nuns they kept to their duties. The Protestant Mary Livermore, who worked with Catholic nuns during her stint with the U.S. Sanitary Commission, praised the nuns highly: "Sick and wounded men watched for their entrance into the wards at morning, and looked a regretful farewell when they separated at night." One anti–Catholic injured soldier, who initially wouldn't look at or communicate with the Cincinnati sister who was dressing his wounds, ended up accepting baptism into the Church.[7]

Shortly before Purcell departed for Rome, he got a letter which Cardinal Barnabo at the Propaganda had sent to the various U.S. archbishops. Barnabo eased the situation regarding Catholic chaplains. In general, priests need the permission of local bishops to operate in their bishops' dioceses. But how to address the situation of chaplains traveling with the armies, who were approved in one diocese but marched with their soldier flock into another diocese because of the fortunes of war? When they entered a new diocese, said Barnabo, the chaplains would be able to perform their priestly functions temporarily without the approval of the local bishop, until that bishop had the opportunity to examine the chaplain's qualifications and decide if he was worthy of serving in the new diocese. Purcell sent this instruction along to the bishops of his archdiocese. Barnabo made clear that he was not taking sides in the war, but was trying to make sure that Catholics in the military, "whether of the northern or southern army ... may not be deprived of any opportunity of receiving the sacraments, especially at this time when the necessity is so urgent." Soldiers should not die unshriven. Purcell had already sent three priests to minister to the Catholic troops, and encouraged priests to volunteer for this service, but there remained a shortage of chaplains for the Catholics in the Union armies. General William Rosecrans struggled with the difficulties of the shortage, while the Protestant soldiers had numerous pious institutions offering them, at least, uplifting literature as well as preachers.[8]

Purcell and Sylvester brought the Church into the political arena in support of the Northern war effort. The Ohio Republicans and the War Democrats fused to form the Union Party, supporting the war and generally endorsing Lincoln's war policies. The new party took the governorship in 1861 and commanded legislative majorities. The new governor, David Tod, and the legislature called for the unconditional defeat of the Confederates.

The Unionists' 1862 campaign for congressional seats and some state offices focused on rallying citizens on the home front to back the commander-in-chief. Archbishop Purcell and Bishop Rosecrans supported the Union Party and promoted its fortunes in the *Telegraph*.[9]

The Democratic opposition did not, at this juncture, oppose the war so much as oppose certain policies the Republicans were pursuing in the alleged interest of bolstering the war effort. The Democrats particularly targeted Republican restrictions on the civil liberties of their opponents. Under leaders like Clement Vallandigham, Ohio Democrats presented themselves as defenders of liberty versus Republican oppression. When a Republican gunman murdered a Democratic editor, Vallandigham and others played up the case as an instance of a Democrat being martyred for his principles.[10]

Another target of the Democrats was the Republican policy of freeing slaves. 1862 was a banner year for emancipatory legislation by the Republican Congress, which stopped the army from returning fugitives, freed the slaves in the District of Columbia (with an appropriation to voluntarily resettle free blacks outside the country), affirmed in a nonbinding resolution a willingness to compensate any state which adopted "gradual abolishment of slavery," banned slavery in federal territories, and passed a strengthened Confiscation Act, which proclaimed freedom to all slaves of rebels—not simply those slaves who were used to help the Confederate war effort. This new law embodied the same policy that General Frémont had tried to carry out in Missouri the previous year, and which he had gotten in trouble for adopting. In an August speech to a black delegation, Lincoln called slavery "the greatest wrong inflicted on any people" while sticking to his position that part of the solution involved shipping black people out of the country: "But for your race among us, there could not be war."[11]

Fears of black interstate migration, echoed by Democrats, continued to affect Ohioans. A mob in Cincinnati threw rocks and eggs at an abolitionist speaker, Wendell Phillips. Congressman Samuel Cox asked his colleagues, "Is Ohio to be Africanized?" Rioting broke out in Cincinnati on July 10 as workers—largely Irish—opposed efforts by employers to hire runaway slaves and other black people for laboring jobs. Irish mobs attacked the black part of town, and blacks staged a retaliatory raid into the Irish area. The *Telegraph* editorialized that black competition was "fast undermining white labor along the Ohio. It is a question of bread and butter or starvation to thousands and nothing is more easily understood than jealousy [apprehension] in such a vital ma[tt]er."[12]

While Democrats denounced the administration's antislavery policies, antislavery leaders and activists urged Lincoln to do more. Abolitionists—whose ranks swelled as the war continued—pleaded with the president to free all the slaves in the Confederacy, regardless of whether their owners were loyal to the Union or not. To one group of Protestant petitioners, who urged emancipation on him, Lincoln in reply urged delay and repeated an old anti–Catholic legend. Lincoln's letter said that proclaiming freedom for slaves who were held in enemy-occupied territory would be "inoperative, like the Pope's bull against the comet." A popular Protestant myth was that 15th-century Pope Callistus III had issued a decree (bull) excommunicating Halley's Comet. The reality was that Pope Callistus issued no such bull. The comet story got quite a boost from Lincoln's endorsement, and Lincoln's remark continues to be quoted in histories without acknowledging that there was no such papal bull.[13]

The president did agree that an emancipation decree was necessary, but to avoid having it be as useless as Pope Callistus's mythical bull, he decided to wait for a Union victory so he could act from a position of strength. The battle of Antietam was such a victory, though not as thorough a victory as initially reported. So on September 22, Lincoln issued his preliminary Emancipation Proclamation. In it, the president promised that he would free all the slaves in Confederate-held areas on January 1, 1863—whether the owners were loyal to the United States or not, and without any mention of compensation.[14]

To Democrats, this new decree was horrible—turning a war for the Union into a war to free the slaves, inviting a slave insurrection like the one in San Domingo, and loosing a torrent of free slaves into the North. The question was particularly salient in Ohio, where the Democrats appealed to hostility against free blacks coming into the state and taking blue-collar jobs. This was the logical consequence of abolitionist policies, said the Democrats, and would only get worse if the Republicans stayed in office.[15]

As if to ratchet up the outrage, two days after his emancipation decree Lincoln issued another proclamation suspending habeas corpus throughout the country, which seemed to Democrats like offering freedom to black people while taking freedom away from white people.[16]

Another controversial administration policy was a federal militia law which passed in July 1862. The law was a thinly disguised draft, since states would have to conscript men if they couldn't fill their quotas voluntarily. Governor Tod proclaimed a draft on October 1. The draft began provoking resistance, particularly in some rural areas. War taxes were high, and the economy was hurting as the Mississippi was closed by the war, interfering with a traditional route for Ohio's food and manufactured products.[17]

The Democrats defeated the Union party in Ohio's congressional and state elections, part of a midterm Democratic surge.[18]

Triumphs in Mississippi

William Rosecrans, commanding troops in western Virginia, showed his engineering background as he invented an Army ambulance which brought wounded soldiers from the battlefield while giving them a smoother, less bumpy ride than regular wagons. The new design was adopted throughout the U.S. Army, and even in Europe. William mitigated the effects of a typhoid outbreak among his men by making hospital tents where the victims survived better than they did in crowded in private houses.[19] This sort of thing undoubtedly contributed to the popularity William was always able to win with his troops.

But the War Department replaced William with John C. Frémont, fresh from his controversial stint in Missouri. After being thus replaced, William's first assignment was in a subordinate role in the army he had formerly commanded. Chafing against these restrictions, he came up with a plan for Northern victory by coordinating federal forces in western and northern Virginia. The new secretary of war, Edwin Stanton, disliked this meddling in his business, and accused William of insubordination. An exchange of angry letters between Stanton and William turned Stanton into William's enemy for the rest of the war. This did not stop William from getting a promotion to command an army on the Western front, in Tennessee and northern Mississippi. His commander was Ulysses S. Grant. The Western armies had recently fought two actions commanded by Grant—the capture of Fort Donelson and the bloody battle of Shiloh.[20]

William's soldiers included not only Catholics but Protestants, not only Irish but militantly liberal Germans. Robert McCook, a law partner of radical German leader (and lapsed Catholic) Johann Stallo, raised the Ninth Ohio Infantry Regiment from among the Cincinnati Germans, many from the radical *Turnverein*, and McCook's unit fought well at Rich Mountain. For a brief time, McCook's adjutant was Stallo's friend August Willich, a genuine communist and former associate of Karl Marx (whom Willich broke with in part because Marx was too violent). Willich soon became commander of a regiment of Indiana Germans, which served under Rosecrans on the western front.[21]

The Union troops occupied Corinth, Mississippi, strategically important because it was on a key railroad line. Rosecrans, assigned to this sector, worked on strengthening the defenses which had initially been put up by the Confederates. To help with this work he employed some of the fugitive slaves who had reached his camp—perhaps the earliest use of black people in military work of this kind in the war. Confederate general Sterling Price wanted to retake Corinth and perhaps win back Tennessee. Price seized the town of Iuka to the east of Corinth.[22]

Grant, probably at Rosecrans's suggestion, came up with a plan to defeat the Confederates at Iuka. Rosecrans would come up from the south and west, and Grant would send General Edward Ord to attack from the North. Capturing Price in a pincers movement might even crush Price's army.[23]

Two roads went into Iuka from the south and west. Rosecrans moved his troops up the western road, to keep his men together, reckoning that if his troops were divided between the two roads, they would be more vulnerable if Price struck before the federals were ready. Dragging a large army along the road took longer than the plan allowed for, and Rosecrans notified Grant he was running late. Grant told Ord to hold off attacking until he could hear the sound of battle, which would be the sign that Rosecrans had started his part of the planned joint attack.[24]

On September 19, 1862, William struck against Iuka. His army and the Confederate forces were more or less evenly matched. At the end of the battle, Price withdrew from Iuka, escaping down the trail William had avoided when coming up. Meanwhile, General Ord did not hear the sounds of the battle—an oversight attributed by some analysts to a phenomenon known as "acoustical shadow"—and so Ord did not close the northern part of the pincers as the battle plan called for. Iuka was a victory, but it didn't end with the destruction of Price's army as planned.[25]

Grant later accused William of confusing the battle plans by being late, of letting Price escape, and of failing to promptly pursue the Confederate general. William replied that he had kept Grant up to date on his movements, that it would have been reckless to divide his forces between two roads to block a possible escape, and that the problem was Ord's failure to join the attack according to the battle plan. Stationed at a nearby town, Grant had not communicated directly with Rosecrans for a long time during the course of the battle, and Rosecrans blamed the lack of communication for the absence of a complete victory. This marked the beginning of Grant's quarrel with Rosecrans.[26]

Grant's anger at Rosecrans may not have had much to do with military tactics at all. Part of Grant's delay in communicating with Rosecrans can be attributed to an exaggerated report of the contemporaneous Union victory at Antietam. The report said Lee's Northern Virginia army had been destroyed, and Grant sent Price a demand for surrender, now that the Confederate cause was supposedly lost. The time it took for Grant to receive Price's indignant refusal could have contributed to the delay in getting Ord to move. The Cincinnati *Commercial* ran a denunciation of Grant's inaction: "how did the enemy get away? ... *Hellish Whiskey* was the whole cause." In short, the paper said Grant was too drunk to order any aid to be sent to Rosecrans at Iuka—maybe Grant had held a premature celebration of the imagined destruction of the Confederacy. Grant blamed William for the *Commercial's* article. Grant was known to overindulge on occasion, but to this day historians don't know for sure whether Iuka was one of those occasions. Bishop Sylvester Rosecrans had no doubt, writing his brother: "The awful charge against Grant in today's *Commercial* is not so surprising as it is disgusting. I am afraid it is true."[27]

The Confederates decided to retake Corinth from the federals. Confederate general Earl Van Dorn said "the attack on Corinth was a military necessity" but that he faced "that astute soldier General Rosecrans ... one of the ablest generals of the United States army." Rosecrans knew an attack was coming somewhere along his line, and in Corinth he put his black engineers to work building up the interior lines of defense.[28]

Battle of Corinth, Currier and Ives, 1862 (Library of Congress, Reproduction Number LC-USZC4–2086 [color film copy transparency], LC-USZ62–3276 [b&w film copy neg.]).

14. *"Unless,* as a body, *we besiege Heaven..."*

When the Confederates attacked on October 3 and 4, they initially drove back Corinth's Union defenders. William rallied his men, riding from one part of the battle line to another. When some of his men broke and ran, William ran among them, crying, "Soldiers! Stand by your country!" rebuking the runaways and smacking them with the flat end of his sword. One soldier later said William "was one of the most fearless officers I ever saw in battle.... How he escaped [death] God only knows." To some soldiers who stood their ground in the face of the enemy bullets, William literally took off his hat to honor "men as brave as these." William re-formed his lines, and the Confederates spent themselves in vain attacks against the new positions. The Southerners finally gave up, withdrawing so rapidly as to leave many of their supply wagons behind. Confederate general Van Dorn lost an estimated 4,838 men (killed, wounded, etc.) and Rosecrans lost 2,520. The men cheered their victorious general, crediting him with their triumph.[29]

Again, William won a battle. Again, Grant said William didn't do enough to exploit the victory. It took a few hours for the federal command to realize the Confederates had withdrawn from Corinth. When William began chasing after the Confederate troops, Grant ended up calling him off. The end result of Iuka and Corinth was to injure the Confederate cause; Price and Van Dorn's attempts to recover losses in Tennessee and Mississippi failed. Rosecrans had beaten them in two battles where the Southern forces outnumbered his own.[30]

Lincoln took William out from under Grant's command and promoted him from brigadier general to major general of volunteers, and appointed him to head the Army of the Cumberland, which was responsible for Union operations in Tennessee east of the Ohio River, and for any invasion of the northern parts of Alabama and Georgia. For the moment, Tennessee was the key point. Not easily satisfied even with a promotion, Rosecrans complained that he was now junior to other generals with less experience in the war, and he protested "the injustice of the position to which my junior rank would consign me." William managed to get his promotion back-dated so as to give him the necessary seniority. Moving to his new headquarters in Bowling Green, Kentucky, on November 1, William wrote Sylvester about how he hoped to manage things: "It would be a great thing for us if the rebels would come and fight us near our base. For the only remedy for the evil is *fighting*. We must crush their power."[31]

Even with a commander of their own religion, whose brother worked to provide material and spiritual support to the army, William's Catholic soldiers still did not have enough chaplains. Civilian pastoral needs and the limited number of priests were obstacles to giving Catholic soldiers the same spiritual aid as the Protestants. Throughout the Union army, there were only 40 official chaplains officially serving 200,000 Catholic soldiers. The Army of the Cumberland was served by three Catholic priests. In contrast, the Methodists in the Army of the Cumberland had 32 chaplains, and the Baptists and Presbyterians had 6 each. But Catholic Chaplains had ready access to William's headquarters, which one critic described as "a resort for priests."[32]

It may have been around this time that William's men came up with a song:

> Old Rosy is our man,
> Old Rosy is our man,
> He'll show his deeds, where'er he leads.
> Old Rosy is our man.[33]

Rome and Washington

On a hillside near Nagasaki, Japan, soldiers bound twenty-six people to crosses and slew them with spears. It was 1597, and the victims were Catholics—European missionaries as well as Japanese people whom they had converted. This marked the beginning of an era of martyrdom for Japanese Catholics. It wasn't until the 19th century before Christianity became legal again in Japan, at which time underground "Kirishitan" (Christians) began revealing themselves again.[34]

The twenty-six martyrs of Nagasaki had been declared "blessed," or worthy of reverence in certain circumstances, in 1627. Now Pope Pius IX meant to declare them saints, worthy of public veneration in all churches. The pope invited the bishops of the world to Rome, to attend the June 8, 1862, canonization ceremony. At least 255 bishops came, including fifteen from the United States. Purcell was one of these latter, and the odds are that he either kept his close friend Sylvester current about events or briefed him after returning to the United States. John Hughes was also present, combining his diplomatic mission to Europe with his spiritual visit to Rome. As Hughes put it to Seward, "there is scarcely a day in which I have not occasion to make known to distinguished strangers the true state of the case" in the Civil War. Everyone in Rome acknowledged, claimed Hughes, that the North had "virtually, though not actually" won.[35]

Arriving around the same time as the bishops, the new American diplomatic minister to the pope arrived in Rome. When the prior minister had left at the beginning of the Lincoln administration, Lincoln appointed Rufus King, but King went to the front as an officer instead of to Rome. Seward and Lincoln did not place a high priority on relations with Rome, so King's replacement, Alexander Randall of Wisconsin, did not arrive until around June of 1862. Until that time, W. J. Stillman, the American consul in Rome, held the fort. Stillman met in January with Cardinal Antonelli, the papal secretary of state. This was in the midst of the crisis about the U.S. seizure of the British ship *Trent*. Antonelli warned that this was not a propitious time for America to fight Britain, which sought (in Stillman's paraphrase) "to strike a deadly blow when we were in a measure crippled." Britain was unpopular in Rome because of its attempt to strip the pope of his territories, and some Roman officials wanted a U.S./British war. Antonelli had a different view, also inspired by anti–British sentiment, hoping that the United States would serve as a counterweight to British influence "once at peace with ourselves" and not before. When the *Trent* affair was resolved, Antonelli said he still wished the U.S. "should in some way cripple England" (Stillman's paraphrase).[36] This would presuppose a re-united United States.

Randall had his first interview with the pope on June 6, 1862, two days before the canonization ceremony for the Japanese martyrs. The minister brought a letter from Seward. Seward's letter said that the U.S. and the papacy should avoid interfering in each others' affairs, implicitly comparing possible British or French mediation in the Civil War with the pope's own problems with foreign aggression. "Intrusion by a foreign nation, anywhere" hurts the "friends of freedom" and "impair[s] the unity of the States exclusively interested." Seward said that most American priests and bishops were "true patriots" who had "given aid to that Government, by whose strong arm, they have been protected in the practice and enjoyment of their religious faith and worship." Randall reiterated Seward's point, praised

Hughes for promoting the American cause, and urged Pius to promote loyalty among American Catholics. At this time, with the good reports they were receiving about Northern successes, Roman officials were indeed rooting for a quick Northern victory, so that a united America could serve as a counterweight to the papacy's enemies. The pope's reply to Seward's letter was warm, expressing appreciation at the trust which Lincoln had shown in Hughes, noting the "equality" of "all forms of religious worship" in the U.S., and praying for the country and her rulers. Around this time, Cardinal Antonelli established a new papal consulate in San Francisco. Randall reported that the other American bishops in Rome also promoted the Northern cause.[37]

Reports that Pius would use the occasion of the bishops' assembly to call a church council proved unfounded, but the pope did take advantage of the bishops' presence to raise some important issues. On June 9, the day after he canonized the Japanese martyrs, Pius addressed the bishops and denounced the self-proclaimed Italian Kingdom, run by King Victor Emmanuel, for its aggressions

Cardinal Giacomo Antonelli, the papal secretary of state, sympathized with the Union, seeing a reunited U.S. as a counterweight to Britain, the pope's foe (R. de Cesare, *The Last Days of Papal Rome: 1850–1870* [Boston: Houghton Mifflin, 1909], opposite p. 345).

against his territories, accusing the Italian rulers of teaching an atheistic doctrine of *might makes right* and of persecuting the Church. Most of the assembled bishops issued a statement expressing solidarity with the pope in his confrontation with the Victor Emmanuel government. The pope also circulated a draft document for comment by the bishops. This document was a condemnation of modern doctrinal errors, many of which stemmed from what Pius saw as the dangerous, militantly anti–Catholic radical and liberal movements in Europe. Bishop Michael Domenec of Pittsburgh, noting language which seemed critical of democracy, feared the possibility of a conflict with American institutions.[38] Domenec probably expressed the views of many in the American hierarchy—the Church had long struggled with a reputation of being un–American, and an attack on European radicalism and liberalism could be seen as a denunciation of American institutions as well. Pope Pius did not publish the draft at this time.

As the bishops of the world left Rome for their home dioceses, the political fortunes of both the United States and the papacy became clouded. Union forces suffered several defeats on the key Northern Virginia front—the victory at Antietam was balanced out by defeats at Second Manassas and Fredericksburg. Prospects for a quick Northern victory seemed less likely. At the same time, the pope had his own difficulties as his remaining ter-

Silver papal medal issued in Rome in 1862 on the occasion of the canonization of the twenty-six Japanese martyrs and Michael de Sanctis. As bishops gathered from all over the world for this event, Archbishop John Hughes of New York lobbied them on behalf of the Union cause in the U.S. Civil War. The Latin inscription on the medal reads, in English: "The citizens of Rome (render homage to) the bishops from all over the world, fathers and protectors of the Catholic name, who, after defending the rights of the papacy and everywhere acting as advocates of Roman Catholic affairs, heeded the summons of Pope Pius IX and, on June 8, 1862, attended his conferment of heavenly honors upon the newly-elevated saints" (digital image and English translation © Christopher Welsh, CACHE Historical and World Coins Web site, http://www.cachecoins.org, reprinted by permission).

ritories (Rome and environs), guarded largely by the unreliable French and by a reliable but small force of foreign Catholic volunteers. Emperor Napoleon of France made friendly gestures to Victor Emmanuel, who was threatening the papal domains. A guerrilla army under Garibaldi tried to attack the Papal States, but Victor Emmanuel restrained what he considered a premature move.[39]

Rome continued to hope for the reunification of the United States, with the reunited nation balancing out other great powers, but as the prospects for a Northern victory seemed to grow dim, the pope and his officials began leaning toward the idea of reunification through North/South peace negotiations. The attempt at a military solution seemed to be bleeding both sides dry, causing much human suffering and weakening what ought to be a strong country.[40]

Lincoln's Emancipation Proclamation actually helped turn the pope and his men against the Northern war effort. It showed that the North was aiming at conquest of the South, not a negotiated peace. For some, the change of opinion was rapid. In the two months prior to the proclamation, the papacy's quasi-official newspaper, *L'Osservatore Romano,* argued that a compromise solution allowing gradual, compensated emancipation would be best, but since neither side was willing to yield, the North was more in the right than the proslavery South. The paper rejected the idea of foreign recognition of the Confederacy. In the two months after the proclamation, however, *L'Osservatore* virtually turned on a dime and denounced Lincoln, castigating the president's decree as a piece of trickery which didn't even free any slaves (since the border slave states and the Union-occupied parts of the Confederacy were left untouched). The proclamation would instead incite massacres of the whites. Freedom for the slaves "will not come about from the benevolent initiative of the North," the newspaper now proclaimed. The "intelligent and chivalrous" Confederates, once they became independent, could be expected to come up with "a peaceful (but serious and solid) solution to this issue," following "the example of France and England," which had abolished slavery gradually and with compensation to the owners. After the Democratic victories in the November congressional elections, *L'Osservatore* compared the hapless Republicans to the radicals of the French Revolution, and said "the Union is definitely done for" and the American people had grown tired of the fighting. Now the paper supported the idea of French intervention.[41]

The pope did not go so far as to avowedly back his unofficial newspaper's call for great-power intervention. Instead, in October Pius sent a pastoral letter to Archbishop Hughes, who was back in New York, and to one of Hughes's Southern counterparts, Archbishop Jean-Marie Odin of New Orleans. The pastoral said that the pope was "greatly afflicted" by the "destructive civil war" and its "slaughter, ruin, destruction, devastation, and ... other innumerable and ever-to-be deplored calamities." Pius urged the two prelates, "as far as compatible with the nature of the holy ministry," to urge both sides to make peace. "We are influenced by no political reasons, no earthly considerations, but impelled solely by paternal charity, to exhort them to tranquility and peace."[42]

The pope took up this theme again in a November meeting with Richard M. Blatchford, Randall's replacement as American minister. Pius said that although the North would not accept mediation by one of the great powers, it might listen to a peace proposal from a minor power without designs on America and with a minuscule military—a power like the papacy. In a follow-up meeting with Cardinal Antonelli, the papal secretary of state affirmed to Blatchford his support for a strong, united America. The great powers of Europe wanted the U.S. weakened, and if he (Antonelli) were an American, he would (in Blatchford's paraphrase) "do everything in my power to preserve the strength of the Nation undivided ... surrender[ing] for the moment every minor question of policy and interest for the preservation of the Union and of its political power." If the South won, Antonelli believed, the United States would be reduced to the condition of one of the countries of South America.[43]

Archbishop Purcell returned from Rome to the Cincinnati archdiocese in August 1862. At the beginning of September, soon after getting back and shortly before President Lincoln's preliminary Emancipation Proclamation in September, Purcell gave a speech on the war. Until then the *Telegraph*, edited by the archbishop's brother Edward, was skeptical about emancipation, but now, perhaps at Sylvester's urging, Archbishop Purcell tore into slavery. Part of the reason for the war, Purcell suggested, was the South's failure to come up with a plan for gradual emancipation. The Southern states could have allowed for gradual emancipation, on a timeline of fifty years or even a century. Instead, the South had doubled down on defending slavery into the indefinite future. "A people could not long survive the fatal contrast between the Declaration of Independence and the Constitution of the United States, the one asserting that all men are born free, sovereign and independent, that the other millions may be slaves." Since the South hadn't accepted gradual abolition, the timetable of freedom should be accelerated: the Union, as a war measure, ought to free the slaves, thus bringing the war to end within three months. The *Telegraph* and its German counterpart, the *Warheits Freund,* took up the crusade, denouncing slavery as contrary to Catholic principles. The *Telegraph* debated with other Catholic papers, like the *Freeman's Journal,* over slavery.⁴⁴

A Curse and a Proclamation

While the pope was urging peace, William prepared for war. In November and December 1862, he sought to get his Army of the Cumberland in fighting shape in preparation for striking a blow against the Confederates. He enforced discipline, worked to improve his supply lines, and to get more rations. He bombarded the War Department with demands for more cavalry, concerned about the superior cavalry available to the Confederates under Generals Morgan and Longstreet.⁴⁵

After Arthur Ducat, William's chief of staff, became too sick to serve, William wanted to recruit his fellow West Point graduate Julius Garesché to his command staff. Shortly before the war, Garesché raised money for the embattled Pius IX and considered joining the pope's foreign volunteers, but he remained in the adjutant general's office. When the war came, Garesché was senior assistant to Adjutant General Lorenzo Thomas. Garesché spent most of his time working, convincing his boss of his indispensability. In what remained of his free time he continued his charitable rounds in Washington for the St. Vincent de Paul Society, ministering to smallpox victims during an outbreak. When a black Washingtonian was dying of smallpox, Garesché's cared for the man, and after the man's death served as the sole mourner at his funeral. Pursuant to a vow he had made, each day he read a chapter of Thomas à Kempis's *Imitation of Christ,* a famous Catholic devotional work which instructed the reader to patiently and joyfully bear the tribulations God sends. Garesché's son Louis later wrote that Garesché worked hard to get an artillery officer's commission for a man whose father was "a *bigoted* Presbyterian minister"—so that Julius could "do [the minister] good for evil, by heaping coals

Julius P. Garesché, William Rosecrans' friend and comrade in arms. The two Catholics disagreed over abolition. General Rosecrans supported Lincoln's Emancipation Proclamation, while Garesché opposed it. Meanwhile, Garesché was warned that, as divine punishment for his uncharitableness toward his Confederate kinsmen, he would die in his first battle (from the frontispiece to the biography by Julius' son Louis Garesché [Philadelphia, J. P. Lippincott, 1887]).

of fire on his head." Julius's efforts to get himself posted to the front were thwarted by Adjutant General Thomas and by Garesché's own wish to start at a lower rank so he could work his way up through battlefield triumphs.[46]

William, with Garesché's permission, persuaded the War Department to give his old friend a position as chief of staff for the Army of the Cumberland, where he would serve as Rosecrans's right hand. The order went through on November 5. Adjutant General Lorenzo Thomas valued Garesché's work too much to want him to go, but he was not there when this decision was made, and it was too late for him to get it reversed.[47]

Garesché's sense of duty was torn between staying in the army and leaving it. Julius Garesché was against the "snarling curs of Abolition," but believed in fighting for the Union. His relatives were not so enthusiastic. His brothers Alexander and Ferdinand in Missouri opposed the Northern war effort. His cousin Bauduy helped make gunpowder for the Confederate army. Julius would have resigned his commission if his brothers joined the Confederate armed forces, lest he risk committing fratricide, but this brothers assured him that they did not plan to enlist.[48]

Julius Garesché believed that the Emancipation Proclamation would provoke murderous slave insurrections such as the revolt in Santo Domingo, where his family formerly owned plantations (Archbishop John Hughes of New York also had friends and family who had fled the Santo Domingo uprising, contributing to Hughes's antiabolitionist stance). Garesché planned to resign from the army if the Emancipation Proclamation was carried out. This image from *France Militaire* (1833), by Victor Hugo's brother Abel, portrays one of the many massacres of whites which occurred during the Santo Domingo slave rebellion (Abel Hugo, *France Militare. Histoire des Armées Françaises de Terre et de Mer de 1792 à 1833*, Tome Premier [Paris, Chez Delloye, 1833], between pp. 260 and 261).

There was another issue which might provoke Garesché into resigning. He was opposed to making the war into a campaign to free the slaves. He believed in gradual emancipation, but thought that immediate liberation would be a disaster. His family, on his mother's and father's sides, had owned plantations on the then–French colony of Santo Domingo, where murderous slave insurrections resulted in massacres of the whites and confiscation of their property as the insurgents established the independent countries of Haiti and ultimately the modern Dominican Republic. As late as 1888, Julius's son Louis was applying to the French government to be compensated for the losses the family had suffered from the rebelling slaves nearly a hundred years previously.[49]

Slavery formed a potential source of tension between Julius and William. Around the time of the Emancipation Proclamation and Archbishop Purcell's abolitionist speech, William began writing his wife, and telling others, about his support for emancipation, both as a blow to the immoral system of slavery and as a war measure to defeat the South. Writing to his wife Anne, William waxed Biblical about the slaves escaping into his encampments: "Our lines are to them the Canaan of their deliverance and rest." William's political sponsor, Secretary Chase, wrote him urging support for the Emancipation Proclamation, but this urging was probably redundant for the strong-willed William, who was not accustomed to mold his opinions to suit his superiors. Julius Garesché wrote his wife that his old friend's emancipationist views would not affect their close relations: "I was told that I would find [William] a crazy abolitionist: but, though his tendencies are somewhat in that direction, it is rather through a Catholic sentiment that he is so, and we will, therefore, thoroughly understand each other on this point."[50]

There was yet one more factor which could have, but did not, dissuade Julius from going to the front. For years, he had premonitions of death—not unusual for a soldier, but he had several near-death experiences when he was on leave from the army. He was nearly drowned in a river on one occasion, and was almost run over by a train on a different occasion.[51]

Then there was an incident in late 1861 which accentuated the omens of doom. Julius lost his temper, cursing his Confederate relatives for their support for the Confederacy. Whatever the nature of this curse, around August 1861 a holy woman told Julius's brother Frederick, a Jesuit priest and her confessor, that she had a divine revelation about Julius's fate. Because he sinned by cursing his relatives, Julius would die in eighteen months, during his first battle, but he would be spiritually prepared for that event, and God would take care of his loved ones. When Frederick wrote Julius about this, upsetting the latter's wife, Julius assured her that as a staff officer in Washington, he was not in a position to die in battle as foretold. Mrs. Garesché was angry at her priestly brother-in law for doing a "horoscope," but she was reassured that this prophecy was foolish.[52]

In September 1862, Garesché wrote to the antiwar editor James McMaster, with a personal note and with a letter to be published in McMaster's *Freeman's Journal*. The letter called for "an organized system of Catholic prayers" to avert the "threatening ruin" of the country. "Unless, *as a body*, we besiege Heaven with prayer, God will not be pacified. Oh! why do not our bishops come forward, and set this on foot?"[53]

Garesché renewed his *Freeman's Journal* subscription and asked that any money left over be used for the country's cause. Garesché also alluded to President Lincoln's antislavery proclamation of eight days' earlier (Garesché's letter to *Freeman's Journal* was written September 30). Lincoln had promised that on January 1 of 1863, he would issue a decree freeing all the slaves in those states which remained "in rebellion" against the United States. Garesché deplored Lincoln's catering to the abolitionists. This, plus the devastation wrought by the Union armies in Virginia, had given new spirit to the Confederates, who had raised new armies and were currently victorious. The abolitionists truly deserved the title of traitors, Garesché believed. As to the *Freeman's Journal,* "I cannot do without your paper. Every week, when I receive it, I feel cheered and, for a while, think there is yet *hope* for our poor country—but, in a day or two, I lose the impression, and the dark blank future rises before me."[54]

According to accounts by members of the Garesché family, Garesché continued to hope that the Democratic victories in the 1862 elections would deter Lincoln from issuing his final emancipation decree on January 1. If Lincoln went ahead with his plans and issued his order as promised, Garesché intended to resign his commission. Meanwhile, Garesché drafted a proclamation on William's behalf offering leniency to Kentuckians who had been compelled to join the Confederates, or who had been "carried away" by "natural sympathies." The "desolating and unnatural war" must end. As he settled into his duties at General Rosecrans's headquarters, Garesché was looking toward January 1 with interest and concern.[55]

15

"Waning of the prejudice against our religion, coming from the highest range of Protestant society"

Massachusetts

In February 1862, the Massachusetts state senate voted to appoint Bishop Fitzpatrick to Harvard University's board of overseers. Seeking to put a Catholic bishop on the board of this key institution of the Protestant establishment was quite a gesture of outreach to Catholics, but the appointment was blocked in the state house at Fitzpatrick's own insistence. The bishop wrote that he simply had too much work to do already and would not be able to spare the time for the Harvard position. The *Pilot*, in reprinting the bishop's letter, averred that fact the offer was made showed the "waning of the prejudice against our religion, coming from the highest range of Protestant society."[1]

The state legislature made another key gesture toward the Irish Catholic population, modifying the Bible-reading laws and practices under which Catholic children in the common schools had been obliged to read from the Protestant King James Bible. Under the new law, the schools would "require no scholar to read from any particular version [of the Bible], whose parent or guardian shall declare that he has conscientious scruples against allowing him to read therefrom." The *Pilot* was happy to note the Bay State's act of justice to its "adopted citizens in this hour of national trial." The law did not obviate all Catholic concerns, however. Irish Catholic leaders in Lowell complained to the *Pilot* in June and July that municipal authorities did not recognize their schools: a state constitutional amendment of 1855 banned the use of school funds for sectarian purposes. The correspondents protested this "bigotry and injustice."[2] But the injustice was not remedied.

Bay Staters also helped soldiers' wives and children, struggling with the loss of their breadwinners at the front. In 1861, Colonel Cass of the Ninth Regiment complained to Governor Andrew that donations to soldiers by the rich Brahmins of Boston had omitted the Irish. Since that time, public authorities and private charities in Massachusetts provided aid for all soldiers' families. A statute of 1861, as well as state and local bounties for enlistment, gave partial compensation to families for the loss of their breadwinners. The benefits were attractive enough that people from other states tried to enlist in Massachusetts. A March 1862 statute provided state accounts where soldiers could deposit part of their pay for the benefit of their families. Soldiers used the system to send $3 million back to their families.[3]

Another sign of legislative favor was to come. The legislature proposed in 1862 to repeal the clause in the state constitution imposing a two-year waiting period before naturalized citizens could vote. Changes to the Massachusetts constitution needed to be approved in two successive legislative sessions, and the legislature again approved the proposal in 1863. The matter came before the voters on April 6, 1863, and the voters accepted it. Naturalized citizens would again be able to vote as soon as they obtained their citizenship. Another pillar of the Know-Nothing legislative agenda was pulled down.[4]

Bishop Fitzpatrick's health problems had grown sufficiently bad that he needed to go to Europe to recuperate. At least, that was one of the reasons given for his departure from the United States in May 1862. Writing to his friend Bishop Francis McFarland of Hartford, Connecticut, Fr. Healy noted in a postscript that Bishop Fitzpatric's health had improved.[5] Whatever his medical condition, Fitzpatrick had enough energy while in Europe to help the Union cause.

Before leaving, Fitzpatrick designated his good friend Fr. John Williams as the acting head of the Boston diocese, thus making Fr. Williams vicar general. At the same time, the bishop delegated to Chancellor Healy the primary responsibility for dealing with the secular authorities. Fitzpatrick gave Fr. Healy, not Fr. Williams, a power of attorney to act in civil matters. At Fitzpatrick's request, Governor Andrew gave Fr. Healy a seven-year commission as a justice of the peace, allowing him to execute necessary legal documents. U.S. citizenship was a prerequisite to holding this job, so Governor Andrew was recognizing Fr. Healy as a full American citizen, disregarding the U.S. Supreme Court's *Dred Scott* decision, which excluded blacks from citizenship. So much for the *Pilot's* deference to the "learned" Supreme Court justices![6]

Bishop Fitzpatrick's first stop was Rome, to attend the canonization ceremony for the Japanese martyrs. While there, he was one of a handful of American bishops consulted by Fr. William McCloskey, rector of the American College in Rome. Fr. McCloskey wanted financial help for his institution. While it was embarrassing to beg for money while the country, and the U.S. church, were themselves in a bad state, Fr. McCloskey received some encouragement in his efforts.[7]

Fitzpatrick was not in perfect health and Fr. McCloskey even received a report of the bishop's death. The report was exaggerated; the Boston bishop traveled through France and ended up in Brussels, Belgium.[8]

Henry S. Sanford, the American minister resident in Belgium, was a well-off New York businessman whose diplomatic enterprises extended beyond the small country to which he was posted. With the approval of Secretary of State Seward, Sanford used his diplomatic post as a base for counteracting Confederate initiatives throughout Europe. Using government and personal funds, he recruited consuls and private detectives to ferret out Confederate agents, trying to block them from commissioning warships. He bought up arms and equipment so that the Confederates couldn't get them. He ran a pro–Northern propaganda operation, hiring journalists when he could in order to get his message out to European readers.[9]

Before encountering Bishop Fitzpatrick, Sanford was entrusted with a negotiation with one of the Church's most dedicated enemies. Early in the war, Guiseppe Garibaldi, then popular among non–Catholic Americans and liberal Europeans for his "liberation" of southern Italy, suggested that he might heed a request from the United States to serve as a Union commander. President Lincoln thought that thus capitalizing on Garibaldi's popularity would give the North's cause a needed morale boost and inspire European support. Seward instructed Sanford to approach the Redshirt leader with the offer of a major general's commission. In late 1861, Garibaldi professed to be interested. He may have sincerely wanted to be a Union general, but he also used the threat of leaving Italy as leverage so that Italian nationalists would press him to stay and win Rome from the pope. But King Victor Emmanuel, probably wanting Garibaldi out of his hair, gave his blessing to Garibaldi's proposed American adventure. Other Italian nationalists protested the idea of their beloved leader going abroad. Garibaldi may have decided to refuse the U.S. position by imposing impossible conditions, or else he received an exaggerated impression of the responsibilities Lincoln was offering him. Not only did Garibaldi insist on being the commander of all the Northern armies, he wanted the power to free the slaves when he chose. When the Lincoln administration rejected these megalomaniacal conditions, the negotiations ended. Before the negotiations fell through, the press in the United States and Europe gave widespread coverage to the abortive Northern offer. These reports raised the indignation of Julius Garesché, who wrote to a prominent pro–Union prelate (probably Hughes) with a dramatic plan: If Garibaldi took the job, Garesché and a couple other top officers "over whom [Julius] had great influence" (as Julius's son Louis later put it) would resign. It's not clear if William Rosecrans was part of this plan. The threat of Catholic officers resigning receded as Garibaldi kept his focus on fighting the pope, but this episode shows the horror felt by Catholics like Garesché against serving with a man they saw as a sacrilegious bandit.[10]

Giuseppe Garibaldi, "liberator" of Italy and deadly foe of the pope and the Catholic Church, was considered for a generalship in the Union armies. Rumors of the negotiation prompted some Catholic officers to consider resigning. Garibaldi ultimately decided not to fight in the American Civil War (George Macaulay Trevelyan, *Garibaldi and the Making of Italy: June–November 1860* [London: Longman's, Green, 1914]).

Bishop Fitzpatrick did not seem bothered by Sanford's negotiations with Garibaldi. Writing to Senator Sumner, Fitzpatrick called Sanford "an efficient patriot in the highest sense." Sanford returned the compliment in writing to Seward. In predominantly Catholic Belgium, Fitzpatrick was influential with the capital's "ultra Catholic community," according to Sanford. Describing Fitzpatrick's "charming, genial manners," Sanford said the cleric "strengthened our cause with that class which had been the most prejudiced against us." Bishop Fitzpatrick circulated among the people. The Boston prelate found the Belgians friendlier to the Union than other Europeans. Fitzpatrick described the North's "host of [Belgian] friends in all classes and ranks of society."[11]

Fitzpatrick's activities attracted the notice of Ambrose Dudley Mann, a Confederate emissary based in Belgium. Mann, an optimist who tended to see Europe as supportive of the Confederacy, reported that the Belgian Catholic clergy were on the South's side, along with the Catholic papers in the country. Still, Mann said that Fitzpatrick was active in advocating for the Northern cause, "occasionally" serving as "the chief" of the American legation.[12] Mann's report seems plausible in light of Sanford's busy schedule dealing with matters throughout Europe—Fitzpatrick would be a good deputy for Belgian matters when Sanford was otherwise occupied.

Fr. Healy, meanwhile, was in Massachusetts, serving as Fitzpatrick's deputy in key secular matters. As he continued his regular priestly duties, he also continued his involvement with the military, political, and economic affairs of his flock. Before the state set up government accounts where the troops could deposit their pay, the soldiers sent their paychecks to Fr. Healy for safekeeping or for disbursement to families. Fr. Healy was also one of the Irish community leaders consulted by Governor Andrew in the very competitive business of selecting officers for Irish regiments.[13]

Soon after the bishop's departure, a pastoral emergency arose, as an appeal came from the 28th Massachusetts for a chaplain. At this time the 28th was stationed in South Carolina, and many of them were dying of disease. In these circumstances, the soldiers were worried about their souls. According to one account, the administrator—a description which seems to match Fr. Williams rather than Fr. Healy—discussed the letter at a meeting of the clergy, a meeting at which Fr. Healy was probably present. South Carolina was in a separate diocese—under the authority of the secessionist Bishop Lynch—and the administrator said he could not order a priest to go there. Volunteers, though, were apparently acceptable, and Fr. Lawrence McMahon, recently ordained, offered himself. By the next week, Fr. McMahon was with the 28th at Hilton Head, South Carolina. The regiment was going into battle at James's Island, and up to the very moment the troops went into the battle, Fr. McMahon heard the soldiers' confessions. He followed the regiment to northern Virginia, where it joined the Irish Brigade in place of the non–Irish 29th Massachusetts. Fr. McMahon served the spiritual needs of many Catholic soldiers outside the regiment, such was the need for Catholic chaplains. After serving in many campaigns, Fr. McMahon returned to Boston where he collapsed from exhaustion and illness in the doorway of the bishop's house. He had to recuperate before returning to his duties.[14]

Having Catholic chaplains was important to the Irish soldiers, as reflected in recruiting appeals. Col. Cass died at the battle of Malvern Hill in July 1862, shortly after Bishop Fitzpatrick's departure. While Governor Andrew sorted through various letters from quarrelsome candidates vying to replace Cass as commander of the Ninth Regiment, a regimental recruiting poster went up to find Irishmen to replenish the ranks. The poster contained appeals to ethnic pride regarding the "unconquerable nationality" of the Irish, as well as assurances of a bounty, pensions for themselves or their families if they were wounded or died ("What employer, let us ask, does the like?") and higher pay "than that for which many of you toil at laborious drudgery, equally, if not more dangerous, than the field of honor and glory." One subheading in raised type made a more spiritual promise: "In this regiment you will have A CHAPLAIN OF THE OLD FAITH."[15]

Priests from Massachusetts and other states ministered to the Irish Brigade during its long service, which in 1862 meant enduring the boredom, sickness, mud, and bloodshed of the northern Virginia front. With services held in tents, and altars made up of "cracker boxes," the chaplains performed daily Mass when the army wasn't on the move, and heard confessions. During battle, as Fr. William Corby put it, chaplains had to be "'within gun shot,' and ready to serve [the soldiers] at a moment's notice." For example, during the battle of Fredericksburg, a captain with whom Fr. Corby had just then been talking (about their good luck in avoiding injury), was mortally wounded by a cannonball within ten feet of the priest, who rushed over to hear the officer's confession. The captain died that night.[16]

After Antietam, where Meagher's Irish Brigade lost 60 percent of its fighting force after courageously holding out against the enemy, Fr. Corby went among the wounded administering Communion to those who needed it. "In doing so, I was obliged to carry it to them, as they lay here and there on the straw, unable to move—stepping over some, and walking around others. Those ready to receive were pointed out by a good soldier, or each made a sign for himself."[17]

On rare occasions, a chaplain could hold a full-fledged military Mass. Fr. Corby described the military celebration, somewhat different from what civilians were accustomed to: "A military signal, either by drum or bugle, is given at the proper time, and orders are passed along the line to 'fall in!' Once in ranks, all the regiments march under orders of their respective officers to the 'church tent.' ... During the more solemn parts of the Mass the soldiers 'present arms'—an act of the highest respect—while outside, at the time of the Consecration (if we are not in the presence of the enemy) cannons boom in various directions; going forth like thunder in the heavens, to represent, as it were, the voice of God, or at least to speak of the presence of Him who rules from above, amid the crash of nations. Thus we see how God is served, even in camp."[18]

The Massachusetts Irish regiments had their chaplains—Fr. McMahon of the 28th (before his collapse) and Frs. Scully and Egan (successively) for the 9th. Chaplains did a full day's work of celebrating Mass and hearing confessions in their own units. Irish Brigade chaplains also rode to nearby encampments to serve Irish soldiers in other units without their own Catholic chaplains. Their spiritual aid could go even further—writing letters for the illiterate soldiers, Catholic and Protestant, to their loved ones at home and reading letters which came from home.[19]

In an example of ecumenical outreach, Fr. Corby tells of a German-American soldier condemned to death for desertion. He had been raised by Protestants but had never been baptized. After talking to a Protestant chaplain who was indifferent to whether the soldier was baptized or not, Fr. Corby persuaded the soldier to undergo the sacrament, which he did half an hour before being shot.[20]

In early 1862, the institutional support for the Irish soldiers expressed from newly

15. *"Waning of the prejudice against our religion"*

Ninth Massachusetts Infantry Camp near Washington, D.C., 1861. This photograph was taken just before the chaplain celebrated Mass. The American Catholic Church was hard pressed to provide chaplains for Catholic soldiers in the Union armies (Library of Congress, Reproduction Number LC-DIG-ppmsca-34231 [digital file from original item, bottom], LC-USZC4-4605 [color film copy transparency], LC-BH8255-80 [b&w film copy neg.]).

friendly quarters like the Massachusetts establishment was reciprocated in the form of Irish American support for the Union cause. As non–Irish officers mingled with the Irish troops, some discovered for the first time that they had some Irish in them. During a Christmas dinner, some officers of the Ninth laid claim to Irish heritage. Major Patrick Guiney, Cass's successor, said such claims were largely "blarney, but true of some of them." Non-Irish members who were recruited to fill in Irish regiments had an extra incentive for such "Blarney" as they dealt with the ethnic tensions of fitting in in such an unaccustomed environment.[21]

The Irish troops on the northern Virginia front needed all their courage as they entered the bloody conflicts of 1862. Despite the high casualties of the Irish Brigade at Antietam, the Irish admired their commander, George McClellan. President Lincoln, though, thought McClellan too cautious and slow to act against the enemy. Lincoln removed McClellan and replaced him with Ambrose Burnside. The replacement of their popular general was bad enough for the Irish American soldiers, but things got much worse when Burnside took the army, and its Irish Brigade, to the Confederate-held town of Fredericksburg, Virginia.[22]

There were already ominous signs that Irish American enthusiasm for the war was waning. By fall, the 28th Massachusetts and 69th New York regiments were among the ten regiments with the most combat deaths. The Irish Brigade as a whole was among the three hundred Northern units with the most casualties (killed, wounded, captured, missing). In July 1862, General Meagher addressed an enthusiastic crowd in a recruiting meeting. He rebuked some hecklers who said the "black Republicans" (antislavery Republicans) should do the fighting. He urged the cheering crowd to "one more effort, magnanimous and chivalrous for the Republic." The cheering was not matched by commensurate enthusiasm for volunteering. One of Meagher's own aides, Captain James B. Turner, wrote at this very time to his unemployed father, who was considering becoming a soldier for the income, warning him of "the mingled fatigue, exposure and want of proper nourishment ... being cursed and cuffed about by some vulgar wretch in authority ... soldiering in any capacity you must give up."[23]

The Emancipation Proclamation was another problem for the Irish, despite a one-time indication that Irish Americans might be sympathetic to it. Marching from Harpers Ferry, site of John Brown's abortive slave liberation raid, the Irish Brigade sang "John Brown's Body," a popular song which says that the soul of the dead abolitionist is "marching on."[24] This temporary enthusiasm, however, did not reflect Irish-American opinion on abolition. Large numbers opposed Lincoln's proclamation.[25]

Meanwhile, at Fredericksburg, the Confederates sat behind a stone wall at Marye's Heights. The Confederates commanded the field in front of them with their guns. "A chicken could not live in that field when we open on it," proclaimed Colonel Edward Porter Alexander of the defending force. This was close to the truth. As the Irish soldiers rushed toward the wall the Southerners mowed them down. The attack was so brave, yet so doomed, that even Confederate general George Pickett was moved. "Your soldier's heart," Pickett said in a letter to his wife, "almost stood still as he watched those sons of Erin fearlessly rush to their death. The brilliant assault ... was almost beyond description."[26]

"It is well that war is so horrible," said General Robert E. Lee, the Southern commander, after his victory at Fredericksburg, "else we should grow too fond of it." If the victor thought the battle was horrible, how much worse did the North view it, especially the Irish of the North. To many Irish Americans, the Lincoln administration was throwing away Irish lives for the benefit of the rich and the abolitionists. In a letter published in the *Irish American*, a captain in the 88th New York wrote, "Oh! It was a terrible day. The destruction of life has been fearful, and nothing gained.... Irish blood and Irish bones cover that terrible field today.... We are slaughtered like sheep, and no result but defeat.... I do not know what disposition will be made of us now in our shattered condition."[27]

Even before Fredericksburg, the Boston *Pilot* endorsed the idea of an armistice followed by peace talks. In December and January, the time of Fredericksburg and the final Emancipation Proclamation, the *Pilot* ran editorials denouncing emancipation as unconstitutional and dangerous, inciting the slaves to bloody revolt. "The suppression of abolitionism is necessary to save the Union," Patrick Donahoe's paper said. Even an Irish War Democrat, Richard O'Gorman, denounced the Emancipation Proclamation as part of a policy to create between North and South "such a Union as that between Great Britain and Ireland."[28] This was not a compliment to the Lincoln administration's war aims.

Fr. Hilary Tucker, whom Fr. Healy replaced as rector of the cathedral in Boston, was more out of place in Boston than Healy was. The Missouri-born Tucker had been a priest in Quincy and Chicago, Illinois, before being assigned to Boston, but he never lost his slave-state attitudes. On July 4, 1862, he wrote in his diary that he had heard a report that General McClellan had been defeated. He hoped the report was true. He denounced Massachusetts prowar politicians. Senator Sumner, wrote the priest, deserved hanging. Governor Andrew was "a fanatick with no mind of his own except as influenced by a Baptist minister." Fr. Tucker was, however, favorably impressed by a sermon that Bishop Sylvester Rosecrans delivered in Boston—Sylvester's commitment to the Union cause did not cloud Fr. Tucker's judgment in the matter. Fr. Tucker criticized Fr. Healy in his diary, though the Tucker diary did not mention Fr. Healy's race.[29]

Stones River

With his initial headquarters at Bowling Green, Kentucky, William moved to Nashville and worked on keeping his army supplied and his lines of supply rebuilt and secure. William drove himself at least as hard as he drove his aides, which was hard. Garesché rivaled Rosecrans in industry. Rather than sleeping at the end of a hard day's work, Rosecrans would discuss philosophy and religion with Garesché and the others.[30]

The correspondent "W. D. B." who covered William's army for the Cincinnati *Commercial*, described the experience of riding with the general on his inspections of the army and the countryside. William

> wander[ed] over the field of thought and speculation—nevertheless pursuing persistently the great object, of his contemplation as the helm which governed his reflections ... the mercury of his spirits rises into playfulness, which develops itself in merry familiar quips and jests with his subordinates, and none laugh more pleasantly than he.... All of nature to him is admonition of God. Such is his abhorrence of infidelity, that he would banish his best loved officers from his military household, should any presume to intrude it upon him. He is wont to say he has no security for the morality of any man who refuses to recognize the Supreme Being. Religion is his favorite theme, and Roman Catholicism to him is infallible. In his general discussions of religion, he betrays surprising acquaintance with the multifarious theologies which have vexed the world, and condemns them all as corruptions of the true doctrines of the Mother Church. His social conversations of this character are seldom indulged with his cherished guest, Rev. Father [Jeremiah] Trecy, with whom he is always en rapport, but he is ever ready to wage controversy with any other disputant. But argument with him on his faith, had as well be ended with the beginning, save for the interest with which he invests his subject, and the ingenious skill with which he supports it. Ambling along the highway in a day's journey, unless some single theme of business absorbs him, he will range through science, art, and literature with happy freedom and ability. You do not listen long before you are persuaded that you hear one who aspires ambitiously beyond the mere soldier.... Ten hours' trotting with him, though a sore trial of flesh, is richly repaid by instruction received, and the happy recollections which his companions afterward find stored in their memories.[31]

Rosecrans's priority was keeping his army supplied, and building up enough rations that he would be able, when ready, to march for several days without relying on his unreliable supply lines. With his own cavalry outnumbered, he feared that John Hunt Morgan, Nathan Bedford Forrest, and their Confederate horsemen would run up behind him and cut off his forces from their support. So William cautiously waited, readying his forces and securing his rear. Lincoln and his cabinet wanted a prompt battle, and they grew impatient with what they saw as William's delay. William's immediate superior, General Henry Wager Halleck, put the matter bluntly. The Confederates could not be allowed to hold middle Tennessee, which the Union had possessed in July. Such a gain of territory could provoke France and England to intervene against the Union. Moving into Confederate territory, Halleck told William, could well mark a "turning point in our foreign relations." So "your movements have an importance far beyond mere military success." Secretary of the Treasury Salmon P. Chase, the former Ohio governor who until now had promoted William's career, rebuked William for his "tarrying at Nashville."[32]

William was not expecting to tarry for long. He wrote his wife, "I put my trust in God and the intercession of our Lady. It may be that by my hands he will work out the deliverance of the poor negro from his bondage." He urged Anne: "Let us pray that God may deliver those captives now bought and sold like beasts. I will hope in Him [that] I will remember that He has redeemed them at the same cost as those whose skins are white."[33]

William finally decided to move when he heard that Confederate general Braxton Bragg had sent infantry to besieged Vicksburg, Mississippi, and launched much of his cavalry on a raid further north. William gave orders for an advance. At nighttime on Christmas day, he met with his staff to outline his plans. Underlining his enthusiasm, he slammed a mug of hot toddy on Garesché's table and cried, "We move tomorrow, gentlemen! We shall begin to skirmish, probably as soon as we pass the outposts. Press them hard! Drive them out of their nests! Make them fight or run! *Fight them! Fight* them! Fight, I say!"[34]

William's army was now on the move, approaching Confederate-held Murfreesboro, Tennessee, and the nearby Stones River. The plan was to fake out Bragg by making the federal right wing look stronger than it was, then to attack with the left wing. Major General Alexander McCook (of the same fighting family as Robert McCook, who commanded the German regiment raised by Johann Stallo) would protect the right wing and hold on with his small

Mass at Stones River (John Fitch, *Annals of the Army of the Cumberland* [Philadelphia: J. P. Lippincott, 1864], opposite p. 327).

15. *"Waning of the prejudice against our religion"* 193

forces while the real attack proceeded on the left. As it happened, Bragg had a similar plan—to strike with *his* left against the Union right. William sent a proclamation to his troops: "the eyes of the whole nation are upon you.... Be cool! I need not ask you to be brave." On the evening of December 30, the military bands of the two sides played rival tunes—"Hail Columbia" and "Yankee Doodle" for the Federals, "Dixie" and "The Bonnie Blue Flag" for the Southerners. The bands of both sides ended by playing "Home Sweet Home," reflecting a shared preference for where the soldiers would rather to be.[35]

William and Julius Garesché, at dawn the following day, December 31, went to a tent to receive Communion at the hands of their priest, William's friend Fr. Jeremiah Trecy. Almost twenty years later, William wrote that "I never saw Garesché look so bright and animated, as he appeared during all that morning." Bragg started the battle with an attack on the Union's right flank under McCook. In his

"Majr. Genl. William S. Rosecrans: at the Battle of Murfreesboro [Stones River], Jany. 2nd 1863," Currier and Ives (Library of Congress, Reproduction Number LC-USZC2-2807 [color film copy slide]).

headquarters in the middle of the battlefield, William heard reports that McCook was being driven back. At first, this did not disrupt his plans. But messenger after messenger came up to him, like in the opening of the Book of Job, each bringing bad news. It turned out that McCook's inadequate troops were being routed—General August Willich (Karl Marx's old associate) had been captured. William realized at last that he would have to change his plans to avoid utter defeat. Instead of an attack on Bragg's right, William would have to reinforce McCook's men and rally them to return to the fighting.[36]

Now William decided he would need to supervise the fighting personally. "Mount, gentlemen," he ordered his staffers, and he and his aides, including Garesché and Fr. Trecy, began riding on horseback from one part of the battle to another. Garesché would occasionally read from a "small book," presumably *The Imitation of Christ,* but William was "too busy" to note this. Finding the Confederates breaking through at one point in the line, William turned to Colonel Samuel W. Price, who held a ford over the river.[37]

"Will you hold this ford?" William asked Price.

"I will try, sir."

Wrong answer. "Will you hold this ford?" William repeated.

"I will die right here," Price replied.

"Will you hold this ford?" William asked once more.

"Yes, sir," answered Price.

"That will do," William said, and rode to another part of the field.[38]

William supervised the moving of a battery here, urged soldiers on to the attack there, rallied and reinforced McCooks's men on the right, and inspired the soldiers by his presence. Colonel Hans Heg wrote of what he saw of his commander: "I saw him while riding to and fro at furious rates, the sweat pouring down his face, his clothes splattered over with blood, and I could not help expressing my gratitude to Providence for having given us a man that was equal to the occasion—a general in fact as well as in name." William often stood on elevated ground near the enemy, and in the enemy's full view, in order to get a better perspective on the battlefield, and the soldiers loved him for thus risking his life along with them.[39]

Another Catholic officer, Phillip Henry Sheridan, was on the battlefield. He fought hard to defend the right wing and prevent its collapse. He was finally driven back, and William found Sheridan with a smoke-covered face, cursing loudly. "Watch your language," William rebuked Sheridan. "Remember, the first bullet may send you to eternity." Sheridan replied that he had to swear to keep his men's respect. William then gave orders for the disposition of Sheridan's troops. Sheridan did not die, and went on to win fame on the northern Virginia front.[40]

At one point, when William and his staff were again in an exposed position and getting shot at by the enemy, Garesché pleaded with William not to risk his life like this. "Never mind me," William cooly replied. "Make the sign of the cross and go in." One of the soldiers, in a later letter, enthused: "Where the fight raged hardest, where the men fell fastest, there was Rosencranz [sic], encouraging and directing."[41]

As William and his aides rode toward the center of the battlefield, with Garesché riding close enough to touch William's knee, a shell tore off Garesché's head. Only part of the jaw was left. The adjutant's blood spurted upwards. Garesché's horse carried the body around twenty steps before the dead man fell on the ground at the feet of the others' horses. Much of Garesché's blood fell on William's coat, but William was too absorbed to notice. When told of his friend's death, William simply remarked, "We cannot help it, brave men die in battle. Let us push on, this battle must be won." Later, William removed the buttons off his uniform and placed them in an envelope labeled "Buttons I wore the day Garesché was killed." At the end of the day, one of the commanders recovered Garesché's body. The dead man was carrying the book which he read daily during life, Thomas à Kempis's *Imitation of Christ*.[42]

That day's battle concluded with the Union forces still intact, thanks to William's efforts. A Union rout had been prevented, and now a council of war met to decide what to do next. William ultimately decided to continue the battle, perhaps in part because of an accident. When William rode out to examine the nighttime battlefield, he saw what he took to be Confederate campfires on a possible retreat route; in fact, it was federal men burning campfires in violation of William's curfew orders. In any case, William decided the Union forces should stand their ground.[43]

15. *"Waning of the prejudice against our religion"*

While the armies were battling on New Year's Eve, President Lincoln in Washington signed a bill to create a new state, West Virginia, out of the mountainous, pro–Union areas of western Virginia. The people of the new state largely owed their liberation from Confederate domination to William's campaign in 1861. As a condition of statehood, the bill required the gradual emancipation of the slave population, a condition which the people of the proposed new state would have to accept before attaining statehood (the Emancipation Proclamation did not cover the proposed new state).[44] William's liberation of western Virginia had led to the liberation of slaves.

New Year's day, 1863, was fairly quiet, with both sides building up their positions in preparation for resuming the battle, and burying the dead. In Washington, Abraham Lincoln signed the final Emancipation Proclamation, fulfilling his September promise to declare the slaves in rebel-held territories to be free. This was the contingency under which Garesché had resolved to quit the army, but now Garesché was dead. Bragg sent a message claiming that he had won a victory the previous day.[45]

Bragg had bragged prematurely. On the 2nd, William's army repulsed the Confederate attacks. Bragg decided he could no longer stay in his present position. He withdrew from Murfreesboro. William heard Mass, then sent his army into the now-vacated town. "Thank God and our Lady for the victory," William wrote to Anne. In his report of the battle, Rosecrans prayed in Latin to give glory to the Lord alone for the victory.[46]

Both sides incurred heavy casualties in this battle. William lost 13,000 men to death, wounds or capture. This reflected one of the highest Union casualty rates in the battles of the war. But it was a victory, at a time when Union forces on other fronts incurred humiliating defeats. "God bless you, and all with you," wrote President Lincoln. "Please tender to all, and accept for yourself, the nation's gratitude for your and their skill, endurance, and dauntless courage." Lincoln was still on the subject several months later: "I can never forget, whilst I remember anything, that about the end of last year and the beginning of this, you gave us a hard-earned victory, which, had there been a defeat instead, the nation could scarcely have lived over." Lincoln was especially glad that the victory "check[ed] ... a dangerous [defeatist] sentiment which was spreading in the North." Even Secretary of War Stanton seemed to forget his enmity to William: "there is nothing you can ask within my power to grant to yourself or your heroic command that will not be cheerfully given." A headline in the *Chicago Tribune* announced "a Complete Victory," and the Louisville *Journal* proclaimed that Rosecrans "is the only [Union general] that knows how to fight a battle." William's hometown papers in Cincinnati, the *Gazette* and the *Commercial,* were full of praise.[47]

William had lost his best friend and comrade, but he had reached the height of his popularity. He probably took away the lesson that waiting to advance until his army was ready and his supply lines were clear would bring good results—despite the nagging from above to move prematurely. He also experienced the fruits of fame, buoyed up by praise from a fickle public.

16

"The most logical and effective assailants of slavery that these last three years have produced have been devout Catholics"

The Life of a Catholic Abolitionist

"I am bound to be Aide to somebody," Ned Brownson wrote to Sarah. He was transferred to Washington, where he unsuccessfully tried to pull strings to get Frémont another generalship position. Ned did not accomplish anything for his former commander, but he became aide to a General Casey, and then was appointed aide de camp to Colonel Hunt, who commanded the Third Artillery in the army defending Washington. The latter assignment, Ned thought, gave more chances for glory. He no longer wanted to be returned to Frémont's command, although the question was moot because Frémont had no command and was cooling his heels in New York.[1]

Ned's father Orestes saw himself as an embattled supporter of the Union among hostile Catholics. Brownson's son Henry, paraphrasing his father, later said, "if he had not been a New Englander by birth and descent, or if he had been willing to denounce his Puritan ancestors as a set of psalm-singing hypocrites without a single virtue, he would have been a great favorite with Catholics, and if he had been willing to make his *Review* a tender to the New York *Freeman's Journal*, he had no doubt that [editor James] McMaster would have been a sta[u]nch Union man, for 'he is,' [Orestes] said, 'a man incapable of acting from other than personal or sectional prejudices, and we have sometimes fancied he would rather go *below*, than enter heaven with a Yankee, or as other than chief of his clan.'"[2]

By this time, Brownson was openly affirming his pride in his New England heritage. In his response to Archbishop Hughes, he quoted "a noble young Irish gentlemen" who rejected the call of a Southern Senator (Judah Benjamin, later a member of Jefferson Davis's cabinet) to reconstruct the Union without New England: "Yes, you may exclude New England, but at the expense of excluding your brains." Brownson proceeded, in his own voice, to praise his native region: "The New England mind, the New England spirit and energy, took the lead in resisting British tyranny and oppression, in creating the American nation; and it is still in New England that survives in greater purity and vigor than elsewhere, the genuine American national life.... New England is not only the head, but the heart of America....

Liberty, when retired from all the rest of the Union, will still find a home there." Brownson rejoiced, however, that Northern Catholics, despite their adherence to the Democratic Party and their prejudice against Republicans and New Englanders, "have nobly volunteered to fill the ranks of our army, and generously shed their blood in defense of the Union."[3]

Controversies over Brownson's theological and Church-related articles continued. The bishop of Philadelphia, James Frederick Wood, published a letter in the diocesan newspaper declaring that the *Quarterly Review* was not a genuine Catholic publication. When Brownson learned of this, he wrote Wood to protest. If the bishop objected to what he wrote, why not write him directly with the specific objections? Bishop Wood wrote back to say that his action was not meant personally, but Wood thought he had a duty to his flock to warn them against the *Review*.[4]

While taking up the cause of his old family physician in May 1862, Brownson took the opportunity to express some optimism about the war. Dr. Henry S. Hewit was on General Ulysses Grant's medical staff, but reporter Whitelaw Reid of the Cincinnati *Gazette* published accusations that the doctor was unreliable, incompetent, and intemperate. Grant let Hewit go in April. Hewit complained about this to Brownson and asked his old patient to take the matter to Secretary of War Edwin Stanton. Brownson wrote to Senator Sumner, asking him to forward a plea to Stanton. Hewit, Brownson said, had a gruff and unsympathetic-seeming manner, but was a very compassionate man with a heart of gold (which is probably how Brownson envisioned himself, as well). In the letter to Sumner, Brownson reflected on the war, saying he thought the North had basically won. The only worry now was that the North might make an improper compromise with the South.[5]

Developments in the English Catholic world, among Brownson's allies there, reached across the Atlantic. The English convert-run Catholic paper, *The Rambler*, was to be replaced with a quarterly called *Home and Foreign Review*, under the same management, including Brownson's friend Lord Acton. The editor of the new *Review*, Richard Simpson, heard that Brownson was discontinuing his own *Review* and contacted Brownson's friend Fr. Isaac Hecker to see if Brownson might agree to be a contributor to the English periodical. *The Rambler* had been known as liberal by Catholic standards, earning opposition from the English hierarchy for that reason. Liberalism of course meant different things by Catholic standards then than by secular ones. In his letter, Simpson said the new periodical would oppose democracy and revolution, as well as oppose oppression by the pope's central Italian government. Writing directly to Simpson, Brownson again indicated that reports of his *Review*'s demise were exaggerated. So long as he had his own *Review*, Brownson would not contribute to other periodicals. He did express sympathy for Simpson and his other liberal Catholic friends in England, suggesting that his English counterparts faced the same struggle against the "oscurantisti" (Catholic reactionaries) that Brownson himself did. But Brownson thought Simpson would prevail. Brownson said he himself had once been one of the oscurantisti, and credited Simpson with getting the courage to take up the liberal Catholic cause.[6]

In July 1862, Brownson published the essay "What the Rebellion Teaches." Repeating his constant theme of the duty of obedience to constituted authority, he reproached Americans for their confused ideas on the right of revolution. Americans had preached the rightness of rebelling against constituted authority when it came to European countries, and now faced a similar rebellion in the South. "Either the theory which you have insisted on in the case of all foreign revolutions is untenable, or you are wrong in attempting to enforce the laws of the Union over states that do not choose to obey them." Many Northerners supported the right of the pope's subjects in central Italy to rebel and join the Piedmont state, yet some of these same Northerners denied the right of the South to rebel against the United States and form their own country! Some of the same people who wanted Jefferson Davis hanged supported "Garibaldi, that prince of freebooters," perhaps to the extent of wanting him to command the Union armies! Yet "even Jefferson Davis, John B. Floyd, or Gideon Pillow"—the latter two being Confederate generals—were better than Garibaldi, who "was not worthy to be named in the same breath" with these Southern leaders. Though he opposed Victor Emmanuel's aggression on behalf of a united Italy, Brownson still hoped for a united Italy as well as a rebuilt American Union. The era of small states was gone, and "great states" were the only ones which could get by in the modern world.[7]

"The doctrine [of secession] has been lurking in the American mind from the first," said Brownson, advocated by New England states in the War of 1812 as well as by Southern states now. The doctrine of "state sovereignty," which justified secession, was "incompatible with the stability of government, and especially with the maintenance of the life and integrity of the nation." Yet this dangerous doctrine had been held by indisputable American patriots. This situation illustrated "the danger of false theories," their damaging influence, and the importance of counteracting such false theories with correct ideas. So much for the "self-complacent men" who denounced people like Brownson as "abstractionists" merely for trying to "call attention to first principles."[8]

Despite occasional military incompetence and treason, the Union had fielded an army and navy and was making great strides against the enemy. Brownson admitted that "the war has corrected many of our [my] own prejudices." He was pleased that "universal suffrage," about which he had formerly been skeptical, had "vindicated itself." The courage of immigrant soldiers also set Brownson at ease about the influence of the foreign born. "The sturdy Germans of the West" and "the brave and impulsive Irish" were redeeming their reputations. There were a disproportionate number of Catholics in the army. No "sane" person could revive nativism now.[9]

Brownson disavowed both the unlimited divine right of rulers to rule and the unlimited divine right of subjects to rebel. The former was a heresy of such eras as that of Louis XIV of France or the Stuart rulers of England. The latter was a heresy of such revolutionary fanatics as Mazzini. In reality, governmental power was a "trust" confided in the people by God, and delegated by the people to a government of their choice. Once the government is established, it rules by divine right so long as it keeps within the constitution which governs it, and rebellion is "a sin against God." In the case of "tyranny or oppression," though, the people could resist and replace the oppressive government. "The condemnation of the Southern seceders is that they have resisted the federal government in the exercise of its legitimate powers, without having a single act of tyranny or in contravention of the constitution to allege against it." This was the true "dialectic" theory which "harmonizes the two extremes" of caesarism and mob rule.[10]

Also in the July issue, Brownson published the essay "Confiscation and Emancipation." He defended Senator Sumner's ideas of the war and emancipation. Repeating earlier arguments, Brownson said the rebellion was not simply a criminal insurrection, as the administration seemed to think, but a war of the revolting states against the federal government, and the federal government had the same powers against the enemy states as in the case of a foreign war. This included the power to seize rebel property, force the rebels to pay for the war, and the power to free the slaves, who were in any event already free under the "state suicide" theory. Rebels had no right to compensation for their slaves, and anyway the federal government had no business compensating slave masters in the states because the federal government wasn't responsible for the existence of slavery in those states. In Washington, D.C., the federal government *was* responsible for the existence of slavery, so it properly compensated the loyal masters when freeing the slaves. Recurring to his sentiments of 1854, Brownson said that a government which established and encouraged slavery owed loyal slave masters a duty of compensation. Brownson repeated that he wanted the issue of slavery considered separately from the question of what to do with the slaves once freed. The Union should set the slaves free and only then debate their fate. Now that the war had given the U.S. a chance to purge itself of the "national sin" of slavery, emancipation should be adopted. Brownson reiterated that he preferred voluntary emigration of black people to some place where they wouldn't have to deal with white prejudice: "we look forward to such emigration as the final solution of the negro question." There was no need to fear that the freed slaves would starve to death from laziness, as slavery supporters claimed; black people were better able to support themselves without their masters than their masters were able to support themselves without the slaves.[11]

Brownson made another contribution to emancipation during 1862. Augustin Cochin's two-volume work, *L'Abolition de l'Esclavage*, had influenced Brownson's own views in his abolitionist essay of October 1861. To Brownson, Cochin's work deserved an American audience, given its relevance to the great struggle going on in the country. Brownson sent a copy or copies of Cochin's work to Mary Louise Booth, a Catholic literary figure and a friend of Brownson's daughter Sarah. The thirty-year-old Booth had come to Brooklyn as a young woman, making vests by day to earn a living and writing by night. She attained respectability and profitability by getting a reporting job at the *New York Times* and writing an extensive history of New York, published in 1859. Booth was also a skilled translator, having converted a pro–Northern French work into English in the course of a single week. With Cochin's approval, Booth set to work translating the first volume of *L'Abolition*, the volume which spoke of the good effects of emancipation. As Booth worked on the translation, Pope Pius awarded Cochin a knighthood, a promising sign that the Church's highest authorities approved his antislavery works.[12]

Booth's translation of Cochin's Volume I, entitled *The Results of Emancipation,* hit the shelves in January 1863. This was perfectly timed with Lincoln's Emancipation Proclamation at the beginning of the month. A well-researched book showing that emancipation would have good consequences, rather than leading to the disasters feared by opponents, was well calculated to boost the antislavery cause. Northern journals praised the book and its helpfulness to the fight against slavery.[13]

The *Atlantic Monthly* was full of praise for the book and for Catholic freedom lovers:

It is worth while to note that the most logical and effective assailants of slavery that these last three years have produced have been devout Catholics,—Augustin Cochin in France and Orestes A. Brownson in America. And while we think that it would require a goodly amount of special pleading to clear either the Catholic Church or most Protestant sects from former complicity with this iniquity, we heartily rejoice that those liberal men who intelligently encourage and direct the noblest instinct of the time are the exclusive possession of no form of religious belief.[14]

17

"If the general is crossing himself we are in a desperate situation"

Waiting

One officer, Emerson Opdycke, wrote in his diary shortly after William Rosecrans's victory at Stones River that he was impressed with his commander: "Our western armies are nearly always successful; would to Heaven the eastern army was equally so for then this rebellion would soon end."[1]

President Lincoln, Secretary Stanton, and William's immediate superior, General Halleck, pressured William to start moving against the enemy. On March 1, Halleck, with Stanton's approval, sent Rosecrans and his other generals an offer—the first commander to win "an important and decisive victory" would get rewarded with "a major generalcy in the Regular Army." William's sense of honor was offended at the offer. "Does [Halleck] seek to bribe me to do my duty?" shouted William on getting Halleck's telegram. Not content with this verbal outburst, William wrote an indignant letter to his superior: "Have we a general who would fight for his own personal benefit, when he would not for honor and the country?"[2] Angry letters like this did not endear William to his superiors.

William thought he had good reason not to start an advance. He was in hostile territory, with his supply lines endangered. Guerrillas and the superior Confederate cavalry could interfere with his supplies and starve his army if he overextended himself. As with the time before Stones River, it was necessary to get the Army of the Cumberland in proper shape before attacking the enemy and winning victories. William bombarded Washington with requests for more cavalry to meet the Confederate horsemen and secure his lines. His requests were rebuffed. He wasn't even allowed to form his own cavalry from his infantry troops.[3]

William worried about his supply lines, given the tendency of Confederate armies and guerrillas to destroy roads and railway bridges. He set to work furnishing a supply depot in Nashville, near his lines, so that he could have two or three months' worth of supplies available without having to bring the supplies over long distances. William also built up his army's defenses. He fortified Murfreesboro. He wanted the Army of the Cumberland to be in tiptop shape, and it was. He improved the transportation of sick soldiers for medical treatment, and he improved sanitary conditions. The disease rate dropped 9.8 percent in 1863 from what it had been in 1862 under William's predecessor, Major General Buell. A medical officer from Washington, Lieutenant Colonel Frank H. Hamilton praised William's work. "Col.

Hamilton ... said Rosecrans' army is cleaner, and better policed than the army of the Potomac."[4]

By late May, William's army was told to be in readiness for an advance. Emerson Opdycke met chief of staff James Garfield, who introduced Opdycke to William. Opdycke wrote his wife that he was "much pleased" with his commander: "he appears to have more brain force than I had before thought him possessed of; he looks finely, and seems to think very highly of Gen. Garfield." At the time, Garfield seemed to reciprocate this esteem.[5]

William arrested Fr. Emmeran Bliemel, a Confederate-sympathizing priest in Nashville, and interned him at Camp Chase in Ohio. Fr. Bliemel later served as a Confederate chaplain until he was decapitated by a cannonball in 1864 while ministering on the battlefield in Jonesboro, Georgia.[6]

William imposed a stern policy in Union-occupied Tennessee. He seized civilian property he believed he needed for his army, and imposed loyalty oaths on the inhabitants. The *Freeman's Journal* correspondent in Nashville was caught by these security measures. E. E. Jones, former editor of a Tennessee paper called *Spirit of the Times,* wrote dispatches to the *Freeman's Journal* from Nashville denouncing the allegedly oppressive security measures aimed at the civilian population. He wrote under the pseudonym "Charles" or "Charlie." The victims of federal policies, said Jones in the early summer of 1863, belonged to the "best families of Tennessee." Rosecrans had Jones arrested in June, then released him under condition that he not write on "absorbing topics"—that is, criticism of the war and the military—while his case was under consideration. So Jones wrote articles about a Dominican school near Nashville. By July 18, the *Freeman's Journal* was receiving dispatches from a correspondent writing under the name "Ralph."[7]

William's monitoring of subversion was under the superintendence of William Truesdail, head of the military police for occupied Tennessee. While Truesdail was efficient in rooting out disaffected citizens and traffickers with the enemy, he also appears to have done some corrupt dealing in his own behalf, and civil governor Andrew Johnson conveyed some complaints about such behavior to William. The general dismissed these complaints as coming from "smugglers and unscrupulous Jews, who have been detected in contraband trade, and their property confiscated." Some Jewish merchants had indeed sought to trade illicitly with the Confederacy. While William's generalizations about Jews were offensive, he limited his animadversions to guilty persons, and did not proceed as far as General Grant, who banished all Jews from his command until overruled by President Lincoln.[8]

The Army of the Cumberland finally began its advance on June 24, 1863. A heavy rain began pouring at the same time, making the roads extremely muddy and hard to travel over. But Opdycke proclaimed that "the whole Army of the Cumberland is in motion. The rebels are retreating." Opdycke wrote his wife that "Gen. Rosecrans (and indeed the whole army) seems to be in fine spirits; every private in it is sure of victory, though I do not think that we shall meet the enemy for some time yet."[9]

William followed a risky strategy, probably based in part on what he learned at West Point from Dennis Mahan. William divided his army, relying on various ruses to deceive Confederate general Braxton Bragg about where Union forces were concentrated. Bragg was duly fooled, and lost control of Middle Tennessee through being outflanked, not through the standard series of bloody battles by which Civil War victories were usually obtained. By the time he entered Tullahoma on July 3, William's casualties were 83 or 84 deaths and 486 injured, missing or captured—very small by the bloody standards of the war. Indeed, William thought, precisely because the victory was so bloodless it didn't get the attention it deserved, in contrast to the hard-fought Union victories during this same period in Vicksburg and Gettysburg.[10]

Bragg retreated to the city of Chattanooga, an important railway junction and an important key to the Confederate position. Again, William waited, securing his supply lines and pestering the War Department for more cavalry. A frustrated Halleck again prompted William to move: "There is great disappointment felt here at the slowness of your advance." Halleck claimed that "the patience of the authorities here has been completely exhausted," and only Halleck himself had stopped William from being fired. William sought reinforcements, but Stanton finally decided that "he shall not have another damned man." William proceeded with the troops he had. For the second time, William faked out Bragg, deceiving him about the positions of the major Union army troops. Once Bragg realized the difficult position into which he had been maneuvered, he again retreated. Chattanooga fell into federal hands, leaving most of Tennessee under Union occupation.[11]

Perhaps because of William's state of manic excitement in the heat of battle, there were people who passed on rumors that the general was a drunkard. Emerson Opdycke did not see evidence of this, but passed on to his wife a rumor that Sylvester had "visited [William] last winter, and made him promise to refrain entirely until they should meet again." Opdycke's next comment suggested a possible reason for such hostile rumors: "There are many officers of high rank here, who do not esteem his generalship as highly as does the country; and I have it from pretty good authority that his army is soon to be dispersed, to other departments."[12]

In Ohio, John Hunt Morgan's raid, which could have threatened William's supply lines, was stopped by the state militia, and Morgan was captured. On the electoral front, Vallandigham the Peace Democrat lost to a War Democrat, John Brough, who became governor of Ohio with the support of Republicans and the more bellicose Democrats.[13]

Violence Comes to New York

Irish Catholic enthusiasm for the war had begun to fade. The slaughter among Irish units at battlefields like Antietam, Fredericksburg, and Gettysburg was sobering. The aims of the war seemed to have shifted from restoring the union to freeing the slaves, a prospect which many Irish Americans found distasteful. There was still potential for support for the war among many of the Irish, however. The Union honored Saint Patrick's day (March 17) in New York City by christening a new gunboat, the *Shamrock*. The Irish Brigade, much reduced, continued to fight.[14]

Another event a couple weeks before St. Patrick's day was more ill-omened for the Union cause. Irish longshoremen went on strike for higher pay, and black workers were brought in to replace the strikers. A crowd of what the *Tribune* called "two or three hundred vagabond Irishmen" assailed the black workers, attacking police who came to the rescue. The *Tribune* rejoiced that "the mob [was] speedily quelled."[15]

In March 1863, Congress adopted a Conscription Act. A follow-up to the Militia Act of the previous year, the new law was more explicitly a draft. Supervising the enforcement of New York's draft was an Irish Brigade veteran, Colonel Robert Nugent, who had been wounded at Fredericksburg.[16]

Democratic governor Horatio Seymour spoke at the city's Academy of Music on July 4, denouncing the alleged tyranny of the Lincoln administration. Lincoln was allegedly usurping power on the pretext of "public necessity," but "the bloody and treasonable and revolutionary doctrine of *public necessity* can be proclaimed by a mob as well as by a Government."[17]

On July 9, Horace Greeley's *Tribune* published an avowedly friendly appeal from the Republican editor to Archbishop John Hughes, taking him to task for his attitude toward black people. Blacks "have been hunted and harried as Christians in Japan or Jews in medieval Europe never could be." Greeley reviewed the legal, economic and social discrimination to which Northern blacks had been subjected. "Rev. Sir! Your people have been and today are foremost in the degredation and abuse of this persecuted race" in depriving them of civil rights and attacking them with mob violence. Greeley asked rhetorically if Hughes had done enough to fight "this most un–Christian, inhuman spirit of negro-hate and all its manifestations." He compared Hughes to the priest and the Levite in the parable of the good Samaritan, who had passed the wounded man on the road without turning aside to help him.[18]

Accompanying all the heated rhetoric then, was socially combustible material, preparing the ground for a violent upheaval. The working classes grumbled at the provision in the draft law by which conscripts could buy themselves out of service with a $300 fee. The *National Anti-Slavery Standard,* not exactly a Confederate-sympathizing paper, said that the exemption was "a virtual release from the draft for the comfortable class." Another objectionable feature of the draft, in New York, was that it failed to exempt firemen. Under the New York militia laws, the members of the city fire companies, which doubled as social and political clubs, had been exempt, so the new liability to conscription was a blow.[19] And the fire companies were in a position to resist it.

On Monday July 13, federal authorities began drawing names of draftees. In the district served by Volunteer Engine Company 33—an all-white company known as the Black Joke— the firemen attacked the draft office and destroyed the records. While the Black Joke soon shifted from rioting to trying to tamp down the rioters, it was too late. The firefighters had ignited a conflagration.[20]

Soon, predominantly Irish rioters were attacking property and setting fires throughout the city. Targets included the black population—twelve innocent black people were set upon and lynched. Rioters killed soldiers, cut telegraph lines, and severely beat up police commissioner John A. Kennedy, a Protestant Irish American. An Irish American colonel who tried to disperse rioters was murdered when he returned to his home in the Irish quarter. Those believed to be rich abolitionists were also targeted. Rioters burned the Colored Orphan Asylum, while an Irish American youth reportedly helped rescue the victims.[21]

New York's Catholic priests circulated among the rioters in an attempt to return them to the ways of peace. Dr. John Torrey, a prominent scientist, lived at Columbia University, and he saw a mob near his home. "The rioters were induced to go away by one or two Catholic priests, who made pacific speeches to them." Other priests went into the streets, said Torry, to calm the rioters and try to disperse them. Dr. Torrey wrote that, on the 14th, "just as we were expecting the mob to come howling along, a person came in with a confidential message from a Catholic priest, that Gov. Seymour had taken the responsibility of stopping the draft, & the chief rioters were to be informed of this measure."[22]

Police and federal troops, both from the forces garrisoning New York and from troops diverted from the recent Gettysburg battlefield, managed to put down the riots by Thursday, July 16. Irish police and soldiers participated in putting down their rioting countrymen.[23]

Horace Greeley, whose *Tribune* building was a target of the rioters, published an editorial on the 14th criticizing Archbishop Hughes, who had tried to distance himself from the draft. The prelate had advocated a draft in the previous year, so what had changed, Greeley wondered.[24]

Governor Seymour appealed to Archbishop John Hughes to calm the rioters. Hughes was growing ill and weak, a contrast to the vigorous prelate of earlier years. He was disinclined

For several terrifying days in July 1863, mobs of largely Irish draft rioters roamed the streets of New York City wreaking havoc (J. T. Headley, *Pen and Pencil Sketches of the Great Riots* [New York: E. B. Treat, 1882], opposite p. 193).

to pen a harsh rebuke of his own flock or seem to be knuckling under to nativism. Still, he published an article which appeared in James Gordon Bennett's *New York Herald* on Wednesday, July 15. The article said that any Catholics involved in the riots should "retire to their homes" and "dissolve their bad associations with reckless men." At the same time, Hughes attacked war profiteers and claimed that factory owners had fired Irish Catholic employees to force them to enlist. As to the draft, Hughes insisted that he supported only a draft which was voluntary, a confusing concept. On Thursday, the 16th, notices were posted throughout the city that the archbishop would speak to the people at his official home at the corner of 36th and Madison. When members of his flock showed up near his house, Hughes spoke to them. Surrounded by six priests and sitting down because of his growing weakness, the archbishop spoke gently, softening any rebuke to the rioters with appeals to their Irish heritage and praising the United States as a land of opportunity—thereby urging loyalty.[25]

About 400 people were killed and wounded, and the rioters inflicted $5 million worth of damage on the city. A labor union, the Democratic-Republican Workingmen's Association of New York, looked into the matter and said the culprits were not workers, but "a certain class of leaders" who had stirred up "a few reckless and dissolute men, who vibrate between, the penitentiary and the dark dens of crime."[26]

Mayor George Opdyke acted as if he were deliberately trying to affront the Irish poor by acting like the Republican plutocrat they thought him to be. After the riots, the city's common council, under the leadership of William M. Tweed, head of Tammany Hall, voted an appropriation to pay the commutation fees of poor draftees. Opdyke vetoed the measure: "Can any reason be given why a person who happens to be poor should be exempted from service to his country as he is able to render?" Then one of the mayor's sons paid the commutation fee and avoided the draft. Local authorities managed to appropriate the money over the mayor's objection, and coincidentally or not, rioting did not recur. In the 1863 mayoral election, the victorious candidate, supported by the Irish, was an antiwar Democrat, Charles Godfrey Gunther. Gunther was sufficiently pacifist as to refuse to celebrate Union victories in late 1864.[27]

The River of Death

William's advance raised fears in the Confederacy of a federal invasion of Confederate states outside Tennessee. Mother Baptiste Lynch, head of the Ursuline Convent and Academy in Columbia, South Carolina, was worried that the Union troops would reach her city and seize or destroy her convent. In addition to being a religious sister, Mother Lynch was the biological sister of Bishop Patrick Lynch of Charleston. Mother Baptiste wrote the bishop on September 4 about how she proposed to protect her institution if the Catholic general came. The letter showed the solidarity among Catholics across the battle lines as well as the prewar connections between the Rosecrans brothers and the Ursulines: "if Rosencrans [sic] comes, I will write to him & beg him by our mutual regard for Abp Purcell by the friendship existing between his brother & our community the Ursulines of B.C. & the prayers which we offered for his own recovery when by a sad accident he was almost deprived of life in Cincinnati, to show mercy to our Convent & its inmates & require the same of all his men."[28]

Charles A. Dana was sent by the War Department to watch over William. A former managing editor of the *New York Tribune,* Dana served as a civilian War Department aide. Having been assigned to Grant, he was now sent to William to see how the latter was doing, riding with him during his advance to Chattanooga. Some officers had contempt for Dana as a spy. William, however, confided in Dana about his plans. At the *Tribune,* Dana had not always shown himself to be the best judge of men. When touring Europe to cover the revolutions of 1848, Dana met a scruffy radical writer named Karl Marx whom he later hired as European correspondent for the *Tribune.* Marx served as the *Tribune's* European correspondent for about ten years starting in 1851. Greeley ultimately let Marx go, getting rid of Dana himself shortly thereafter. Now, rather than evaluating reporters, Dana was evaluating a general.[29]

Charles A. Dana was not the best judge of men. As a newspaper editor, he promoted the career of Karl Marx, and as a War Department official in the field he wrote dispatches exaggerating the failures of General William Rosecrans (Charles A. Dana, *Recollections of the Civil War* [New York, D. Appleton, 1913]).

Moving beyond Chattanooga, the Army of the Cumberland approached Bragg's army, positioned near Chickamauga Creek. A "tradition," perhaps dating *after* the battle, said that "Chickamauga" was an Indian word for "river of death." Be that as it may, on September 19 the encounter of the two armies began.[30]

Rosecrans's former West Point roommate James Longstreet, now a general, arrived with two divisions of infantry to serve as reinforcements for Bragg's troops. Longstreet had to bring his troops from the northern Virginia front to Tennessee in time to affect the forthcoming battle. The Confederates transferred Longstreet's forces by rail from one front to another, and Longstreet moved his forces into position on the Confederate left wing.[31]

A solemn council of war held in William's headquarters—the commandeered cabin of a widow named Glenn—lasted until near midnight. After orders were drafted and issued, William asked Major General Alexander McCook, of the famous fighting clan of that name, to sing the "Hymn of the Hebrew Maid," the song of the persecuted Jewess Rebecca in Sir Walter Scott's *Ivanhoe,* probably to a tune included in songbooks sold to Union troops. "When Israel, of the Lord beloved, Out of the land of bondage came," began McCook, calling on God to be "a burning and a shining light" in time of peril.[32]

The following day, September 20, was a Sunday. After a sleepless night, William went to Mass. The correspondent for the Cincinnati *Commercial* took note of the exhausted

Rosecrans, his guard down, thinking nobody was watching him: "He was enveloped in a blue army overcoat, his pantaloons stuffed in his boots, and a light brown felt hat, of uncertain shape, was drawn over his head. A cigar, unlit, was held between his teeth, and his mouth was tightly compressed as if he were sharply biting it.... Rosecrans is usually brisk, nervous, powerful of presence, and to see him silent or absorbed in what looked like gloomy contemplation, filled me with indefinable dread." Battle resumed, and William sent reinforcements to General Thomas on the north of the front. Then came one of the biggest mistakes of William's career. Believing that there was a gap in his line, William sent an officer to General Thomas Wood with an order to fill the gap. Wood and the officer were aware that the gap did not in fact exist, and that the redeployment was not necessary. The messenger pleaded with Wood to delay compliance with the order until William could update his command in light of the new information. Instead, Wood withdrew his men as commanded.[33]

As it happened, Longstreet launched an attack against the precise part of the Union lines which Wood had just left undefended. Some federals under General McCook tried to beat Longstreet back, but in vain.[34]

Charles Dana was awakened by the sounds of battle as Longstreet advanced toward William's headquarters and the Union troops fell back. "I was awakened by the most infernal noise I ever heard. I sat up on the grass, and the first thing I saw was General Rosecrans crossing himself.... Hello, I said to myself, if the general is crossing himself we are in a desperate situation."[35]

Longstreet drove the federal troops away. "Like magic," Longstreet wrote later, "the Union army had melted away in our presence." Dana used similar imagery as he wrote how the Union right "br[oke] and melt[ed] away like the leaves before the wind." Bragg decided not to press onward to Chattanooga, but William and other Union leaders did not know this, fearing for the vulnerable Union-held city.[36]

First Lieutenant Ambrose Bierce, on the staff of General William B. Hazen, was on the battlefield. Bierce had received a promotion after fighting bravely at Stones River. He worked as Hazen's chief cartographer, but during the battle he traveled from one part of the battlefield to the other, delivering messages. In a later short story about the battle, Bierce described a scene at the creek, which in reality may have taken place at a pond near William's headquarters at the widow Glenn's house. A group of wounded Union soldiers crawled away from the fighting toward the water. "They crept upon their hands and knees. They used their hands only, dragging their legs. They used their knees only, their arms hanging idle at their sides.... [T]he clumsy multitude dragged itself slowly and painfully along in hideous pantomime—moved forward down the slope like a swarm of great black beetles, with never a sound of going—in silence profound, absolute.... The water gleamed with dashes of red, and red, too, were many of the stones protruding above the surface. But that was blood; the less desperately wounded had stained them in crossing.... Three or four who lay without motion appeared to have no heads.... After slaking their thirst these men had not had the strength to back away from the water, or to keep their heads above it. They were drowned."[37]

At noon on the 20th, William left the battlefield and went to Chattanooga. On the way, he "repeated to our Holy Lady the prayer of the Church very often, Monstra te esse Matra." The phrase "Monstra te esse matrem," Latin for "show thyself a Mother," is from the liturgical hymn "Ave Maris Stella" ("Hail Star of the Ocean"), in a verse imploring the intercession of the Blessed Virgin with Christ. Captain Alfred Hough later claimed that he found the defeated general at the Chattanooga telegraph office, tearful, seeking consolation from Fr. Trecy. Hough's account may have been exaggerated, though at the very least William was distraught at the disaster which had befallen his army.[38]

Chief of staff James Garfield, with William's permission, and perhaps at Garfield's insistence, went to see General Thomas, who was still holding his position in the north of the battlefield. On William's command, Thomas's still-intact troops withdrew to the village of Rossville.[39]

On the evening of the defeat, Rosecrans informed Washington of this "serious disaster." Dana sent a report of his own to Stanton after he himself returned to Chattanooga, declaring that "Chickamauga is as fatal a name in our history as Bull Run." The Lincoln administration feared the loss of Chattanooga.[40]

With his supplies running low, William sought to put Chattanooga in a fit posture for defense. Meanwhile, barbed attacks on him flowed into Washington. Dana wrote that William had "no strength at all and no consciousness of purpose." Secretary Chase now gave Lincoln a letter from Chief of staff Garfield, who was about to leave his military post and return to Washington as a congressman. Garfield's letter, from back in July, complained that the Tullahoma campaign had started too late to destroy Bragg's army, and that William was "disinclined to grasp the situation with a strong hand." With all these negative reports, Lincoln, though he held a soft spot for William because of Stones River, concluded that William was now behaving "confused and stunned, like a duck hit on the head."[41]

Lincoln promoted General Grant, the victor of Vicksburg, to the command of the Northern armies, leaving Grant to decide what to do with William. Not surprisingly, Grant, no friend of William, relieved him of command, replacing him with "The Rock of Chickamauga," General Thomas. Ironically, Thomas, the man whose bravery and fortitude was contrasted with William's alleged timidity, believed that William's removal would be a "national injury." Thomas said he would rather be reassigned than replace William, who appreciated the "noble sincerity" of this sentiment. But William urged Thomas to accept the promotion, and Thomas took up his new duties. Later, Thomas said that the only blame William deserved for the Chickamauga disaster was in prematurely advancing under orders from Washington, rather than resigning in protest at being forced to move so early.[42]

William waxed Biblical concerning his firing: "I was removed by Stanton because he hates me. I am Mordecai whom the little Haman wants to hang on a gallows 'sixty cubits high.'"[43] The scriptural reference was from the book of Esther, in which the evil minister Haman tries to kill the virtuous Jew Mordecai as well as all other Jews, but has his plans thwarted—the king has Haman hanged on the gallows intended for Mordecai.

Some verses from Sir Walter Scott's "Hymn of the Hebrew Maiden," verses omitted from Northern military songbooks and perhaps from Alexander McCook's stirring rendition on the eve of the defeat, could have struck William as pertinent as he changed from favorite of the public to banished scapegoat:

> Our harps we left by Babel's streams,
> The tyrant's jest, the Gentile's scorn;
> No censer round our altar beams,
> And mute our timbrel, trump and horn.[44]

18

"A mere inferential recognition, unconnected with political action or the regular establishment of diplomatic relations"

Boston Draft Riots

Massachusetts Republican abolitionist governor, John Andrew, was dissatisfied with the draft. He did not believe that the draft law was an efficient means of recruiting soldiers, and he was worried about the opposition it would provoke. If Andrew was skeptical of the draft, many of the Boston Irish hated it. As wartime inflation raised the price of goods, women with their men off at the front were economically pinched.[1]

Things were especially tense in summer 1863. In early July, an Irish mob in East Boston tried to liberate one of their confreres who had been arrested for drunkenness, injuring three policemen in the process.[2]

The morning of July 14 was "foggy and unpleasantly warm, sort of a dog day," in the words of Major Stephen Cabot who commanded troops in nearby Fort Warren. There was a Requiem Mass for fallen soldiers. Bad weather kept attendance down, but those present were reminded of the war's costs. It's not clear if those in the pews in the morning overlapped with those in the streets later in the day.[3]

The Boston draft riot started in the North End around noon that day. It started with another attempted rescue. Two federal marshals visited homes on Prince Street around noon to deliver draft notices. A woman seems to have hit one of them while he was speaking to her. The women of the neighborhood surrounded the marshals, growing angrier and angrier. The employees of a nearby gas works got off work and came to the scene, attacking the marshals. As police and more crowds arrived, the mob attacked the police as well. Crowds of young men, women and even children assembled in the North End in a foul mood. They attacked another policeman, who escaped, followed by imprecations like "Kill the damned Yankee son-of-a-bitch."[4]

An angry crowd congregated on Haymarket Square. A woman in the crowd held up a photograph of a young man, supposedly her son who had been killed in the war. Some mob members broke into hardware stores and gun shops to loot the contents.[5]

Mayor Frederic W. Lincoln, Jr. (not to be confused with the Emancipator) called on

Governor Andrew to help put down the rioters. The governor was at Harvard University, assisting at its commencement, but when he heard the news from Boston he went back to the city to consider how to suppress the riot. The famous 55th Regiment was available nearby, but this was a black regiment, and the governor thought it was unwise to use black troops to suppress "free white American citizens." Instead, Andrew called in the First Battalion of Massachusetts Volunteer Heavy Artillery, stationed at Fort Warren and commanded by Major Stephen Cabot. Cabot and his men reached the state house in half an hour, and Andrew put the men under the authority of Mayor Lincoln. Cabot split his 166-strong force between two Boston federal armories, with 111 of the men going to the Cooper Street building near the scene of the riot. Some of the rioters trailed the troops on the way to the Cooper Street Armory, throwing taunts and a few stones. Cabot locked his troops in the building, "hoping that the crowd would disperse if the soldiers were out of sight."[6]

Cabot posted soldiers at the armory windows. He had two six-pound cannons, and he directed that each be pointed at one of the two armory doors. A Captain Jones arrived, urging Cabot to fire blanks if it came to a confrontation. Cabot replied that he would try to avoid firing, but if he did, he would use live ammunition. Rioters began shooting at the armory and throwing projectiles. Cabot held his fire. William Schouler, the state adjutant general, described the standoff in a subsequent report: "The mob increased in numbers and vehemence. The quiet inside was in strange contrast to the noise and excitement outside. It was a fearful moment."[7]

At 7:30, Major Cabot heard a report that the mob was beating a soldier who was trying to get to the armory, and Cabot sent twenty troops to rescue their comrade. The would-be rescuers were themselves assailed, so Cabot sent more men. The soldiers fired over the heads of the rioters and returned to the armory, bringing the wounded soldier with them. Cabot interposed himself between the mob and his retreating troops until they were back in the building, and Cabot then went back in as well.[8]

The rioters attacked the armory with stones and axes, ignoring (or not hearing) Cabot's call to disperse. Cabot had one cannon shot fired through the Cooper Street door, into the mob's ranks. This dispersed the crowd, leaving behind some dead or wounded—perhaps between eight and fourteen dead. The Boston *Advertiser* estimated that nineteen people were badly hurt, including police and soldiers.[9]

In many ways, this was a replay of the Anthony Burns riots of 1854, with the participants reversed. In each case, the federal government tried to seize men who had not been convicted of any crime in order to send them South into involuntary servitude. In each case, a mob rallied to the defense of the threatened men. In each case, the mobs attacked the officers who tried to enforce the law. In each case, the authorities called in military assistance to deal with the mob. The difference was that in the Burns case, the rioters were Yankees and the forces of order included Irishmen. In the North End riots, the mob was Irish and the forces of order were Yankee. This comparison would have been indignantly rejected by both sides, of course. The one common element in each case was that the Catholic authorities came down on the side of order and against street violence.

Fr. Healy was concerned that the trouble might flare up again. He was determined not to have a repeat of the weeklong, bloody draft riots in New York. To Healy, Archbishop Hughes had been soft and dilatory in his response to the mob element among his flock. This would not happen in Boston, Healy decided. The North End must be pacified to prevent another eruption.[10]

Fr. Healy issued a circular to his priests, telling them to get out in the neighborhoods and calm the people down. At first, "seeing the quiet state of things," Fr. Healy hesitated to send out the letter, but at the request of Mayor Lincoln, Healy issued it, so that the priests could get started on their peaceful work as soon as possible. The letter was also published in the papers. Fr. Healy wrote in the letter that priests were expected "to use their utmost efforts to preserve the public peace among their congregations—to caution them not only against taking part in fractious assemblies, but even against being present at them."[11]

Fr. Healy spoke to the Jesuit priest Fr. Robert Brady, pastor of St. Mary's Church around the corner from the armory which was the site of much of the rioting. Fr. Brady agreed to go through the Irish neighborhoods, defuse any militance, and keep the peace.[12]

Priests patrolled the North End streets, looking for loiterers and telling them to go back to their homes. As a contemporary news report said, "boys, girls and men by the score were admonished that there was no necessity for their [outdoor] presence, and a large number were led to disperse under the mild but firm and unceasing efforts of their priests." Fr. Healy was happy to note that Fr. Brady had stopped the formation of another mob by a "well-timed admonition," getting what may have been an incipient riot under control and the would-be rioters back to their homes.[13]

The *Boston Pilot* published an editorial reinforcing the calls for calm. Fr. Healy's call to peace was read out in Boston's parish churches during Sunday Mass. By this time, calm had been restored, and the rioting had been confined to the events of July 14. A relieved Mayor Lincoln, reporting these events later to the Boston City Council, gave Fr. Healy the credit he was due, citing "as worthy of applause the good influence exerted by Reverend Fathers Healy and

Massachusetts Civil War governor, John Albion Andrew, worked with the Catholic Church to bridge the gap of distrust between the Bay State's Protestant establishment and the Catholic community. When draft riots erupted in Boston's Irish quarter, Governor Andrew and the Church faced the crisis together. Statue of John Albion Andrew, by Thomas R. Gould, Hingham, Massachusetts (photograph by Timothy Valentine, Wikimedia Commons).

Brady and others of the Roman Catholic clergy, who labored to preserve quiet among their congregations."[14]

The Boston church leaders had done what the New York City church leaders had not done: prevent the violence from extending beyond one day. There was considerable damage to property and attacks on soldiers and law officers, but not wild lynchings of black people or government supporters as in New York.

European Vacation

Fr. Healy's intervention in his city's draft riots, along with his other duties, appears to have been quite draining. By July 19, he was writing to his friend Bishop McFarland to apologize for not meeting the bishop when the latter was in Boston. Fr. Healy had been busy and sick, which had kept him at home.[15]

In August, Fr. Healy took a break from the stresses of Boston by embarking for Europe. Patrick Donahoe's *Pilot* published an admiring editorial about Fr. Healy, who had "labored most zealously" and was "justly beloved by all, more particularly by the old Cathedral congregation." Fr. Healy, said the *Pilot,* was going to the continent "to recruit his health, which has been greatly impaired by hard labor in the services of the Catholics of New England." Family business also led Fr. Healy to Europe. He wanted to enroll his youngest brother Eugene in the English seminary in Douai, France. The seminary had been founded during the Counter-Reformation to give Catholics the education that was denied them in Elizabethan England. The institution graduated over 160 martyrs to the faith and produced the Catholic English translation of the Bible which Catholics insisted on their children reading rather than the King James.[16]

Fr. Healy's itinerary was extensive, taking in the sights of Europe. He first landed at Liverpool. He then went to Brussels, where Bishop Fitzpatrick was still working at the American embassy promoting the Union cause. The bishop was ready for a vacation, too, so Fitzpatrick and Fr. Healy went together, first to Douai where Eugene was left at the English College, then to Germany to boat down the Rhine River. The bishop and his trusted priest returned to Brussels where Fitzpatrick took up his mission again. By this time, Patrick Healy, studying at Louvain, Belgium, learned that his brother James was nearby, and the two brothers met.[17]

Fr. James and Patrick went to England, where James was shocked at the "gin palaces in full vigor" and the hookers in the poor areas of London. The brothers took a more welcome trip by ship to the Spanish Mediterranean coast. They admired the Spanish ladies, laughed at the British tourists, and entertained themselves with wine and cigars. At Marseilles, France, Patrick left to go back to school while Fr. James went to Italy. Touring major Italian cities, James saw the sights and met Fr. Isaac Hecker. James finally reached Rome, where he had an audience with Pius IX. The pontiff gave an indulgence to the Boston cathedral choir. James visited some famous tourist sites in Rome and returned to Brussels, whence he sailed back to the United States. He was in Boston shortly before Christmas. The cathedral priests shared some champagne to welcome back their rector.[18]

During this same period, other visitors were arriving in Rome, and not as tourists.

The Confederacy Seeks the Pope's Support

Bishop Martin John Spalding's memorandum on the Civil War got through the U.S. mail, avoiding federal censorship, and crossed the Atlantic to Rome. Pius studied the report with interest, and the quasi-official papal organ *L'Osservatore Romano* published it serially and pseudonymously, as the work of "A Kentucky Priest." Some passages which would have hinted strongly at Spalding's identity were edited out.[19]

Papal consul Binsse in New York had lost his earlier enthusiasm for the Northern cause. As New York erupted in the draft riots and the North suffered costly setbacks, Binsse's reports grew pessimistic about Northern prospects. Richard M. Blatchford, the U.S. government minister in Rome, explained that the North refused foreign mediation, including the pope's. *L'Osservatore Romano,* along with the Jesuit *Civiltà Cattolica,* criticized the Emancipation Proclamation as likely to a bloody slave revolt as part of a campaign of ruthless warfare against the South. The two papers also began praising the courage and effectiveness of the Confederate generals. Blatchford, seemingly oblivious to Rome's growing coolness toward the U.S. war effort, chose this time in mid–1863 to go on break.[20]

Blatchford's timing could not have been worse. The Confederate government was just then turning its attention toward Rome. The impetus for this outreach came from a colorful priest, Fr. John B. Bannon. Fr. Bannon, a Missourian and a fervent supporter of the Confederacy, left his St. Louis parish to serve as a volunteer chaplain for the Confederate-sympathizing Missouri State Guard, and then as a chaplain in the army of General Sterling Price, General Rosecrans's opponent in the battles of Iuka and Corinth. Fr. Bannon zealously ministered to Catholics of both armies on the battlefield and the hospitals, and he was well enough respected that he was seriously considered for the position of bishop of Little Rock, Arkansas (the vacancy remained unfilled until 1867). The Confederate government did not at first respect Fr. Bannon—the intervention of Bishop John Quinlan of Mobile, and of Confederate Secretary of the Navy Stephen Mallory, a Catholic, was necessary to get Fr. Bannon a chaplain's salary. Fr. Bannon served at Vicksburg during the siege, and surrendered with the other Confederate forces when the city was taken by General Grant. Released, the Missouri priest then went to the Confederate capital, Richmond, Virginia, in late August 1863.[21]

In Richmond, Fr. Bannon was introduced to the Confederate version of a multicultural group—Protestant President Jefferson Davis, Catholic Secretary of the Navy Stephen Mallory, and Jewish Secretary of State Judah Benjamin. Davis and Benjamin wanted a Catholic emissary to go to Ireland and discourage Irish immigrants from moving to the North, because such immigration helped swell the ranks of the Union army. Persuaded by Bishop John McGill of Richmond, Fr. Bannon agreed to go to Ireland as a secret operative of Benjamin's State Department.[22]

Discussing the proposed mission, Fr. Bannon suggested that the Confederacy make another appeal—to the pope himself. As the Missouri priest wrote to Benjamin, "The C.S.A. have neglected to enlist in their favor the sympathy of a power exerting a great moral influence on the peoples & governments of Europe." If the pope could be brought over to the Confederate side, this "may not only direct the opinion of the masses but influence the policy of governments." The Catholics in France, or at least in Belgium, might be prompted by a Confederate pope to recognize the Richmond government. Secretary Benjamin issued his instructions: the priest was to persuade the Irish not to emigrate to the North. Fr. Bannon was authorized to seek support from the pope, to get a friendlier reception in Ireland.[23]

Now that the Confederate government's attention had been drawn Romeward, it designated another agent to appeal to the pope. On September 24, shortly after the Confederate victory at Chickamauga, Davis instructed Dudley Mann, the South's representative in Belgium, to go to Rome and plead the South's cause. Mann bore a letter from Davis, a belated response to the pope's peace appeal of the previous year and probably written at Fr. Bannon's suggestion. The South, Davis wrote, wanted "to see the end of this impious war." The Confederates "f[ough]t merely to resist the devastation of our country and the shedding of our best blood," and wanted only to be left alone with "our own institutions" (the closest Davis got to mentioning slavery). When he met Pope Pius, Mann supplemented Davis's message. Mann hinted that the states of the Confederacy (each state acting individually) might adopt policies to free the slaves, perhaps over a period of ten to fifteen years, enough time to prepare the slaves for their new freedom.[24] This welcome message was in line with what Bishop Spalding had said in his report, that the Confederacy would adopt a policy of gradual emancipation in contrast to the North's revolutionary policy of immediate emancipation.

Pope Pius replied to Jefferson Davis' letter in a letter of his own, addressed to the "Illustrious and Hon. JEFFERSON DAVIS, President of the Confederate States of America, Richmond." The Pope said he was glad "that you and your people are animated by the same desire for peace and tranquility, which we had so earnestly inculcated in" Pius's peace appeal the previous year. "Oh, that the other people also of the States and their rulers, considering seriously how cruel and how deplorable is this internecine war, would receive and embrace the counsels of peace and tranquillity."[25]

Mann made much of the pope's letter, circulating it widely in Europe and representing it as a papal endorsement of the Confederacy. Secretary Benjamin was not so enthusiastic. He wrote Mann that the pope's letter was "a mere inferential recognition, unconnected with political action or the regular establishment of diplomatic relations." Still, it was a useful propaganda tool.[26]

Northern representatives received the same message from Rome about the letter's limited scope. Secretary Seward appointed a new minister, Rufus King, to replace Blatchford. While Rome awaited King's arrival, J. C. Hooker, who handled legation business in the interim, wrote Seward that the papal government would not "change its position regarding our country.... Archbishop Hughes had settled that question." About the pope's meeting with Mann, Hooker said the pope reportedly "told Mr. Mann to come to him whenever [h]e liked however I do not see that any umbrage can be taken though one would have been better pleased otherwise. The Pope however gives audiences very freely to the world in general."[27]

King took about a month to reach Rome, arriving in the city on December 23, 1863. King and Hooker met with Cardinal Antonelli, the secretary of state. Antonelli wanted a reunited United States to balance out Great Britain, but he deplored the bloodshed and destruction of the Civil War. As summed up by King, Antonelli said "there were those Powers ... who were not averse to seeing the United States weakened and wasted by internal strife." This was probably an allusion to the British and French. Antonelli then repeated what Mann had said during his Roman mission: that the South was prepared to liberate the slaves over a ten- to fifteen-year period. "To this I replied," King explained to Seward, "that the sentiments put forth by Mr. Mann were not those held and expressed by the Southern leaders.... Mr. Mann, in all probability, said what he did, rather in deference to the existing sentiment of Europe, than as reflecting public opinion at home."[28] In short, Mann was saying what the pope and his officials wanted to hear. And it seemed to be working, despite King's efforts. The Spalding report and Mann's assurances seem to have convinced many in Rome, perhaps the pope himself, that the Confederates would get rid of slavery in a gradual, nondisruptive manner, obviating the need for the North's revolutionary policy of military emancipation.

King met with the pope after Christmas. In an audience taking up about a half hour, Pius said he was sad that the bloody war was continuing. "He had nothing to complain of, on the part of America—nothing, nothing." As King summarized, the pope "and his people had always been most kindly treated" in the United States, "and should not forget it." "As to intervening in your affairs," added the pope, "I have no weapon left but this pen."[29]

A Pope's-Eye View of the World

Rome did not have a particularly friendly attitude toward great powers throwing their weight around at the expense of smaller, weaker countries or their own citizens. A pope's-eye view of the world situation at this time was of big countries acting oppressively in many contexts. It would be remarkable if this didn't affect Rome's perspective in witnessing a powerful central government in the U.S. bloodily warring against a portion of its own territory.

Even the pope's supposed allies among the great powers seemed willing to act oppressively. Louis Napoleon Bonaparte, the gouty, goatish intriguer who ruled France as Napoleon III, was supposed to be the guardian of Rome and its environs against the forces of Victor Emmanuel, who now controlled most of Italy and wanted Rome. But while protecting Rome with about 30,000 French troops, Louis Napoleon (in addition to trying to force unwelcome French bishops on the pope) supported Victor Emmanuel's aggression against other parts of Italy, including the largest and most populous parts of the papal domains. The only reason Louis Napoleon protected Rome against his ally Victor Emmanuel was in deference to his French Catholic voters and his Spanish Catholic empress. Embarrassed at being in the position of thwarting Italian "unification," the Emperor sought a way to wiggle out of his commitments to the Holy Father, cutting a troop-withdrawal deal behind Pius' back.[30]

While the pope was handling diplomacy and correspondence affecting the American Civil War, another crisis erupted, illustrating the oppression a central government could perpetrate in the name of stamping out rebellion. Russia occupied most of the old Polish kingdom, ruling it as a Russian province. In Warsaw and other cities, Catholic Poles began protesting Russian rule, often in their parish churches through nationalist sermons, hymns, prayers, and church-based demonstrations. Many priests joined this movement, to Rome's disapproval. Russian soldiers invaded Warsaw churches where Poles were peacefully protesting. In January 1863, in the wake of a conscription call, rebels launched an uprising against the Czar. The Czar banished the moderate archbishop of Warsaw, Zygmunt

Feliński, who was trying to steer a middle course during the turbulence, sending him into internal exile.³¹

Pius believed that the Poles ought to be faithful Russian subjects, so he opposed the rebellion. To the pope, the Poles were improperly mixing nationalism with religion. But at the same time, Pius was outraged when Czar Alexander heightened the persecution of the Church in the guise of putting down the rebellion. In March 1863 the pope sent a protest to Czar Alexander, bringing up longstanding complaints about persecution of the Polish Church while reiterating his opposition to the revolutionaries' political agenda. Far from improving the condition of the Church, the Czar tightened the restrictions on Catholics. The pope gave a public address blaming Alexander for provoking rebellion among his Catholic subjects, banishing their archbishop, and sowing bloodshed. "I do not want to be forced to cry one day in the presence of the eternal judge, Vae mihi quia tacui!" ("Woe is me, I said nothing!"). An anti–Russian encyclical followed in the next year, and then a break-off of relations between the czar and the papacy.³²

While Pius was turning against Russia, the United States grew closer to that country.

Pope Pius IX was indignant when Czar Alexander II used the pretext of a Polish rebellion to increase the repression of the Catholic Church. The Czar had friendly relations with the Lincoln administration. *Image:* Expulsion of the Russian envoy to the Holy See Felix von Meyendorff by Pope Pius IX in 1864 for insulting Catholic faith, by Jędrzej Brydak (1837–1876) ([http://jbc.bj.uj.edu.pl/wgr/work/show/id/56/ordr/1], Wikimedia Commons).

Re-enactors, dressed as southern Italian rebels from the early 1860s, stand next to a memorial to General José Borjes, December 9, 2012. Borjes, sent from Rome to organize rebel forces against northern Italian occupiers, was captured and shot in December 1861. Pope Pius IX would have noted the parallels between this Italian insurgency and another Southern rebellion across the Atlantic (photograph © Pietro Guida, reprinted by permission. Appeared online at http://www.marsicalive.it/?p=40639).

The situation of the Polish rebels was sufficiently similar to the situation of the Confederates as to prompt closer ties between the North and the Russian government. The American ambassador to Russia was Cassius Clay, a prominent abolitionist who admired the czar both in his capacity as an emancipator of the serfs and in his capacity as an anti–Catholic who fought the benighted Catholic Poles.[33]

To protect his navy from a possible Franco-British attack, Czar Alexander asked permission to park his navy in the harbors of San Francisco and New York. The Lincoln administration was quite happy to allow this. Much of the Northern press spoke glowingly of a Russian-American alliance. Nor was the alliance seen in solely secular terms. Protestant ministers published articles praising the Russians for fighting Catholic power in Poland. The Lincoln administration went so far as to seize a Polish sailor, Alexander Milewski, who had deserted the Russian fleet in New York and joined the Union army, and returned the sailor to his Russian masters. This was at a time when the Union government supposedly frowned on forcibly returning fugitives from compulsory labor.[34] It would hardly be surprising if the pope, like Northern leaders, drew a parallel between the North's behavior and the behavior of the tyrannical czar.

For another example of the bloody repression of a "rebellion," the pope needed only look next door. In 1860, the nationalist Giuseppe Garibaldi's forces had overthrown King Francis II of Naples and driven him into exile in Rome. Garibaldi had then handed the "liberated" Kingdom of Naples, consisting of the southern half of the Italian peninsula as well as the island of Sicily, over to Victor Emmanuel. Many of the southern peasants, oppressed by increased taxes and conscription imposed from the north, took up arms against the new government.[35]

The northern Italian armies waged a harsh war against the southern rebels throughout the first half of the 1860s. Victor Emmanuel's government sent 100,000 to 120,000 troops, about two-thirds of the Italian army, to stamp out the resistance. Repressive measures, which Victor Emmanuel's parliament codified in August 1863 in the so-called Pica Law, were the order of the day. The civil war in the South caused more deaths than all of Italy's "wars of liberation." The Victor Emmanuel government conducted reprisals against suspected guerrilla supporters, including entire villages, and detained and banished suspects to places like Elba, without trial. Firing squads were busy gunning down rebels and alleged rebels, including some whose only crime was voicing disrespect for the new Italian flag or Victor Emmanuel's family.[36]

The exiled King Ferdinand of Naples, while living as a guest of Pope Pius in Rome, ran a government in exile, one of whose members was the brother of a cardinal. Ferdinand tried to rally his supporters in his occupied territories, sending a Spanish officer, José Borjes, to help lead one of the anti–Italian guerrilla bands. Borjes was captured and executed, choosing to be shot while on his knees praying. Many Neapolitan clergy sympathized with the uprising, and the occupying authorities responded by locking many prelates and priests in prison, or banishing them. Pope Pius, then, had every reason to be sympathetic with this particular Southern rebellion, whose parallels to another rebellion by an agricultural people across the Atlantic must have been noticed.[37]

With these examples before him, the pope had understandable reasons to be somewhat skeptical about the centralizing ambitions of a modern nation.

19

"Judea produced but one Judas Iscariot"

To St. Louis

Though removed from command of the Army of the Cumberland and supposedly disgraced, General Rosecrans still had his defenders, and in unexpected quarters. His successor, General Thomas, was loyal. And the *Richmond Examiner* said that by dismissing William, "Lincoln is helping us. He has removed from command the most dangerous man in his army. Rosecrans thus retired is unquestionably the greatest captain the Yankee nation has yet produced."[1]

The former public hero now found his Catholic religiosity turned against him by the fickle media. The *Chicago Tribune* told its readers the fable that William lost at Chickamauga because "he was wasting time counting beads." The *New York Times,* even as it praised his earlier victories and predicted a useful future, said William was "subject to fits of religious depression of the profoundest character." A Protestant newspaper, *Zion's Herald and Wesleyan Journal,* reported that, after Chickamauga, William used the Protestant churches in Chattanooga as hospitals for the wounded while refusing to use the city's Catholic church for that purpose.[2]

William's friend the priest Fr. Jeremiah Trecy, writing Archbishop Purcell from Nashville, said that William's army friends, particularly the Catholic ones, were being deprived of their positions. Only the turncoats who went from praising to denouncing William were getting any consideration.[3]

Garfield, still on friendly terms with William (who did not know about the congressman's backbiting letter in July), advised his associate to "be careful not to inaugurate a contest with the War Department." It was good advice, but not something William was going to particularly take to heart. His hometown press supported him, as the *Cincinnati Times* wrote of "wailing and weeping in the Army of the Cumberland" after his removal. To Colonel Rutherford B. Hayes, formerly an officer of his, William wrote that "in the integrity of my conscience I stand quietly biding the call of Providence and the judgment of my country and of history."[4]

William's political sponsor, Treasury Secretary Salmon Chase, suggested to President Lincoln that William be given a command in Missouri. One benefit of such a move, Chase suggested, would be to placate "the friends of the Administration in Ohio and elsewhere," who among other things were bitter at William's removal from command of the Army of the Cumberland. Early in 1864, the War Department sent William to St. Louis to command the military district known as the Department of the Missouri. The state of Missouri was generally considered a backwater of the war, but it had its special challenges. Missourians were bitterly divided between Union and Confederate supporters. Pro-Confederate guerrillas made it their business to harass Unionists. Letters came to William outlining the suffering of loyal citizens. A general commanding near St. Joseph reported that "there is scarcely a citizen in the county but wants to kill someone of his neighbors for fear that said neighbor may kill him."[5]

William's army had become largely responsible for Missouri's internal security and crime control, and those suspected of aiding the enemy were often put on trial. William was comfortable calling on the despised bondmen to help pacify the state, using slave testimony against alleged guerrillas. Despite William's preferences, not all antiguerrilla activity was addressed through formal judicial procedure, however. Union irregulars, and even regular forces, sometimes slipped the leash of the laws of war. Some loyalist militia and guerrillas disguised themselves as Confederate supporters and, at the very least, robbed the citizens they thereby tricked into helping them. Sometimes Union troops would simply shoot captured Confederate bushwhackers (guerrillas) without trial, a policy denounced by some on William's staff but condoned by others. One of William's officers told the Union commander at Cape Girardeau that bushwhackers found in arms were to be killed. "It is best ... to take few prisoners," since the soft-hearted President Lincoln "rarely approves a sentence of death." While orders such as this did not lead to indiscriminate killing, Union forces unsurprisingly killed prisoners from time to time. Sometimes headquarters in St. Louis disciplined those who went too far, as when militia captain Eli Crandall said he had seized civilian hostages to be killed in retaliation for bushwhacker atrocities. Crandall's superiors promptly overruled him, ordering him to conform to William's policy, which was "to exterminate the desperadoes" but not to be "a party of murderers and plunderers under federal patronage." But officers who were not as candid as Crandall in describing their activities were sometimes allowed to go unpunished.[6] William had a fair to middling humanitarian record, certainly not worse than other Union generals in Missouri.

In addition to military and quasi-military operations, there was the issue of ordinary crime, spying, and hidden conspiracies. To handle these law-and-order matters, William wanted Colonel John Sanderson to serve as provost marshal (head of military police). Before the war Sanderson had been a journalist and a Know-Nothing, the latter circumstance apparently not affecting William's trust in him. When William sought to appoint Sanderson as his provost marshal, the appointment was held up in Washington. Reports circulated that Colonel Sanderson had shown cowardice at Chickamauga. Rosecrans sent an officer to Washington to see what the holdup was, but Secretary of War Stanton had the messenger arrested for coming to Washington without permission. Finally the problems with Sanderson's appointment were resolved and he took up his provost marshal duties.[7]

One early internal security problem faced by William and Sanderson was inherited from earlier commanders in Missouri, and led to a controversy within the midwestern Catholic Church. The Lincoln administration often did not respect the religious freedom of those it deemed Confederate supporters. During this period, for example, Bishop William

Elder of Natchez, Mississippi, Brownson's erstwhile correspondent and a Confederate sympathizer who refused to pray for the Union during Mass, was arrested by Union occupiers and held until public outcry prompted his release. In Missouri, Rosecrans inherited a problem involving administration suspicion of some Southern Protestants. The Methodist Episcopal Church South was itself divided into Northern and Southern factions. The War Department believed that the faction headed by a Northern bishop named Ames, being more loyal than the Southern faction, should control the church's property. On November 30, the War Department sent an order to several military departments, including that of the Missouri. The order required that the property of allegedly disloyal congregations in the Methodist Episcopal Church South be turned over to Bishop Ames. Lincoln wrote Stanton on February 11, 1864, expressing surprise that the War Department was interfering with the internal government of churches, contrary to certain assurances Lincoln had given "in good faith." On February 13, the War Department prepared what purported to be an explanatory memo to Rosecrans—actually an amendment of the previous order—specifying that the orders about Methodist Episcopal Church property applied only in the seceded states—Missouri had never seceded. Meanwhile, Bishop Ames had come to Rosecrans on February 12, with a copy of the War Department order of November 30. No sooner had he instructed his troops to hand over church property to Bishop Ames than Rosecrans received either the February 13 order or a copy of it, delivered to him by St. Louis politician John Hogan with a handwritten endorsement by President Lincoln specifying that the November 30 instruction was not applicable to Missouri. Faced with this bewildering succession of orders, Rosecrans wrote to Stanton on February 28, probably delighted to embarrass the secretary with his awkward position, asking for "more definite instructions" regarding church property. Lincoln's clarification took precedence, and Bishop Ames was not allowed to claim the disputed property in Missouri.[8]

This bureaucratic squabble over federal intervention in Protestant church affairs was in the background as William received reports of disloyal elements in certain Protestant churches, probably including at least the Methodist Episcopal Church South and the Presbyterian Church, Missouri Synod. The immediate problem was probably the Methodist Episcopal Church South, which was scheduled to have a meeting in St. Louis on March 23 and whose schism was the subject of the previous War Department correspondence. As William later wrote to a critic, "loyal church members" had "called my attention to the facts that many [religious] assemblages ... were to convene during the spring and summer, in which would doubtless be many persons openly and avowedly hostile to the National and State governments." In addition to his official responsibility to maintain security, William said that "as a Christian I feel bound to secure religion from the danger and disgrace of being used as the cloak of malice." On March 5, 1864, Rosecrans instructed Provost Marshal Sanderson to "take ... steps" to make sure that "religious congregations and other religious assemblages ... be required to give satisfactory evidence of their loyalty to the Government of the United States." Sanderson responded with an edict on March 7, declaring that delegates at religious gatherings would have to take a loyalty oath disavowing the Confederacy.[9]

The Methodist Episcopal Conference met on March 23 and sent a delegation to William, who said he would be satisfied if the attendees simply certified that they were

Missouri citizens who had already taken loyalty oaths. A radical pro-Union faction of the Presbyterians, who met in St. Louis in October, got the help of federal soldiers to cast out Presbyterian dissenters who refused to take the oath. Around this time, and perhaps in response to complaints from the Methodist Episcopalians, Lincoln wrote William a letter on April 4 "containing suggestions rather than orders," first about Sanderson's church decree. Even loyal citizens might object to such an oath and "the point will probably be made, that while men may without an oath, to [sic] assemble in a noisy political meeting, they must take the oath, to assemble in a religious meeting." Only after his discussion of religious affairs did Lincoln move to other topics, expressing concerns about "assassinations" of "returned rebels"—which the president didn't think William countenanced—and about disorderly and "provocative" methods of recruiting black soldiers. Lincoln ended the letter on a somewhat ambiguous note: "So far you have got along in the Department of the Missouri, rather better than I dared to hope; and I congratulate you and myself upon it."[10]

As Lincoln probably knew by now, William was not the sort of person to obey mere "suggestions" from his superiors. William stood by his provost marshal's church decree. Perhaps in response to Lincoln's suggestion that William was treating religious meetings more harshly than political meetings, William wrote that he was being *less* harsh to religious meetings, simply requiring assurances of loyalty from those attending, and otherwise leaving religious gatherings free from "irksome surveillance."[11]

William's actions in Missouri eventually echoed in the archdiocese of Cincinnati. Archbishop Purcell scheduled a provincial council of the archdiocese for April 24, 1864. The de facto bishop of Detroit, Peter Paul Lefevere, wrote with his concerns that the council would be politicized. Some expressions in the letter of convocation, prepared by Sylvester, seem to have triggered the Detroit bishop's sensitive antennae. By implication, given Purcell and Sylvester's militant Unionism and antislavery views, Bishop Lefevere seemed to fear the two heads of the archdiocese would turn a local church council into something like a Republican meeting. Purcell wrote Lefevere on February 19 that he and Bishop Rosecrans were shocked at Lefevere's letter, and Purcell gave what he believed were reassurances. There was no intention to bring politics into the provincial council's deliberations. Of course, opposition to slavery was not politics! Anyone who wanted to say that Catholic criticism of slavery was political would have to denounce some important Catholic figures, whom Purcell cited.[12]

Purcell's first example was Felix Dupanloup, bishop of Orleans, France, and a prominent figure in the French church. Bishop Dupanloup was considered a liberal, part of the movement in the Church to establish a climate of political liberty in which the Church could flourish. Dupanloup was also a defender of the pope's temporal authority over the Papal States. A letter from Dupanloup had recently appeared in the *Catholic Telegraph,* and Purcell referred Lefevere to this letter. As early as 1862, the French bishop had spoken out against slavery in a pastoral letter. Dupanloup acknowledged but dismissed the theological, theoretical defense of slavery in the abstract as a "hypothesis that can never be realized," because the real conditions of the slaves had always been worse than Catholic doctrine allowed in theory. The reality was that "there are, on the same earth with myself, children of God and children of men like myself, saved by the same blood that I am, destined to the same Heaven as I am, five or six millions of my fellow beings, in the United States, Brazil, Cuba, and Surinam, who are slaves; aged people, vigorous men, women, young girls, children. Just Heaven! Is it not yet time, after eighteen centuries of Christianity, for us all to begin to practice the ever enduring law, 'Do not to another that which you would not he should do to you; and that which your brothers should do for you, do ye for them'?"[13]

Archbishop Purcell's other example involved Charles Montalembert, Brownson's French friend and a lay leader of liberal French Catholicism. The previous year, in August 1863, Montalembert had delivered a discourse at a Catholic conference in Malines, Belgium, and Purcell mentioned to Bishop Lefevere that the speech had been given in the presence of cardinals, whose lack of objection, by implication, was a tacit endorsement of what Montalembert said. Montalembert's speech did not specifically allude to slavery, but made the case for Catholics to support civil liberties of citizens: "political equality ... freedom of worship ... [t]he repulse of state encroachments, the consecration of the rights of property, respect for individual liberty, the establishment and maintenance of the right of association." These freedoms were not contrary to Catholic doctrine, but derived from it, and the defense of these freedoms benefited the Church and held back anti–Catholic tyrants. "The mutual independence of Church and state," said Montalembert, "which is the great law of modern societies, does not entail their absolute separation, still less their mutual hostility.... The free Church in the free state does not signify the Church at war with the state, the Church hostile or alien to the state.... Between the two there is a possible, lawful and often necessary alliance." If Archbishop Purcell was tying Montalembert's remarks to slavery, it was presumably because he was agreeing with Montalembert on how the Church should be a champion of freedom.[14]

To call antislavery teaching political, Purcell was saying, was to accuse Montalembert and Bishop Dupanloup of being political in laying out their freedom-friendly interpretation of Catholic doctrine. God forbid that should be seen as political, Purcell indicated.[15]

After Archbishop Purcell sent his reassuring no-politics letter, Bishop Lefevere learned about William's loyalty-oath decree relating to religious meetings. Cincinnati, where the provincial council was to be held, was not in William's military district, but now Lefevere apparently started worrying that Bishop Rosecrans might impose a loyalty oath after the example of his brother. So Lefevere wrote Purcell again to repeat his concerns about politicized discussions at the council. If there was to be a loyalty oath, the bishops should know about it in advance and not have to take the oath until the council met. It would be better to postpone the council than to get into political discussions, which would contravene the prior statement of the 1861 provincial council disclaiming political involvement. Lefevere had spoken to Archbishop Peter Kenrick of St. Louis—who was now William's archbishop. Peter Kenrick had suggested postponing the Cincinnati council, thinking Rome would go along. Lefevere agreed with Kenrick but sought Purcell's advice. Lefevere's bitterness at the Rosecrans brothers boiled over, and Lefevere suggested to Purcell that the general was only a nominal Catholic and not a loyal son of the Church.[16]

Another bishop went even further in his animadversions against the general. The (accurate) scuttlebutt from Rome was that Bishop Martin John Spalding of Louisville was going to be made archbishop of Baltimore, to succeed Francis Patrick Kenrick (Peter Kenrick's brother) who had died the previous year, at the time of the Battle of Gettysburg. When he knew that his term of service as Purcell's suffragan in Louisville was coming to a close, Bishop Spalding seemed to feel freer to express himself to his soon-to-be-former superior. Pope Pius knew (even if Purcell didn't) about Spalding's authorship of the anonymous attack on the Lincoln administration, and inferentially Purcell himself, in *L'Osservatore Romano*. Now Spalding wrote openly to Archbishop Purcell on March 22 with some harsh comments. A fellow bishop had alerted Spalding to a loyalist editorial in the *Telegraph* of March 9. This editorial came at the same time as the loyalty-oath decree of General Rosecrans, whom Spalding bitterly described as Purcell's favorite general. The decree and editorial led Spalding to think that a loyalty oath would be imposed on the attendees of the forthcoming provincial council—an insult to good Catholics who didn't deserve to have their loyalty questioned, and "savor[ing] of a union of Church & state." It appears that Spalding saw the Rosecrans brothers working in unison to force Church leaders to toe the Lincoln administration line. Spalding wanted a postponement of the council and suggested others wanted this too.[17]

Archbishop Purcell apparently took no official notice of Bishop Spalding's insolence, but he delivered a rebuke to Bishop Lefevere for questioning William's faith. Purcell required Lefevere to make an act of contrition for such detraction before celebrating Easter Mass. William, said Purcell, had good reasons for his order in the Missouri Department, but General Sherman, who had military authority over Ohio, firmly denied that a similar order would be imposed on the proposed Cincinnati council. Nevertheless, yielding to Lefevere's scruples, Purcell cancelled the provincial council. The bishops of the Cincinnati archdiocese had an informal meeting in Lefevere's house in Detroit (apparently with the approval of Rome) to deal with some issues Rome wanted addressed—"spiritism" (spirit-rapping), Fenianism (militant Irish radicalism), and the appointment of a new bishop for Louisville.[18]

Back in Missouri, William faced a problem more sinister than Protestants. Provost Marshal Sanderson began to uncover evidence of a widespread conspiracy among many Northerners to obstruct the war effort. Sanderson came across a proclamation addressed to members of an outfit called the Order of American Knights. Amid thunderous denunciations of the Lincoln administration, this pseudonymous paper told its readers: "To be successful when the storm comes we must be watchful, patient, brave, confident, organized, armed." Other reports, testimony, and information gathered by Sanderson's detectives provided more evidence of a conspiracy. William was convinced that Sanderson had uncovered something big, and he wanted to alert President Lincoln. William asked the president for permission to send Sanderson over to Washington with the evidence the provost marshal had uncovered, but he didn't want Sanderson to be arrested for coming to Washington without permission, the fate of a previous emissary. Lincoln did not want to interefere with his secretary of war, so he asked William to mail the evidence to Washington by express. Not trusting that method, William balked. So since William's people wouldn't come to Lincoln, Lincoln sent one of his people to William. Lincoln's trusted aide, John Hay, came to St. Louis and returned with Sanderson's evidence.[19]

Some in Washington were skeptical about the reported conspiracy, which as Sanderson saw it involved a planned uprising in the northwestern states in aid of the Confederacy. As it turned out, though, there was a good deal of fire behind all the smoke.

Death of an Archbishop

William responded even to events in New York City, where disaffection continued after the suppression of the draft riots. New York laborers were riled up even more when they learned that General Rosecrans, in St. Louis, had banned unions, claiming a need to prevent obstruction of the war effort. A similar measure was considered in the New York state legislature, but met with labor opposition and was defeated.[20]

One defender of striking workingmen was John Mullaly's *Metropolitan Record,* which in the 1850s had replaced James McMaster's *Freeman's Journal* as the New York Archdiocese's official paper. McMaster had turned against the war, earning him imprisonment without trial at Fort Lafayette in New York. Archbishop Hughes had no better luck with the *Record*—he had run his anti–Brownson editorial in the *Record,* but the paper's antiwar stance induced Hughes, as with the *Freeman's Journal,* to distance himself from the paper. A *Record* editorial of March 1864 defended Confederate Virginia and hoped that it would never be "subdued and given over to the spoiler and the plunderer," that is, the Union. Shortly afterward, General Rosecrans banned the *Record* from the Department of the Missouri. This was a personal matter for William: in his March 26 suppression decree he declared that Northern Catholics were "loyal and national," and that the *Record* was defaming William's coreligionists by linking them to disloyalty. William also took pains to point out, in his proclamation, that the *Metropolitan Record* was published "without ecclesiastical sanction." Later that year, Mullaly was arrested by federal authorities in New York on charges of inciting resistance to the draft and brought before a military commission. The commission, unusual for such bodies, acquitted Mullaly, who was defended by Democratic attorney Charles O'Conor. But in Ohio, a military commission convicted an Irish American editor who had reprinted the *Record*'s antidraft editorial in his own paper.[21]

In early January 1864, Archbishop Hughes died after a protracted illness. Hughes was not only the most prominent prowar Catholic in the city, he was perhaps the most prominent Catholic in the United States. At his funeral on January 7, nearly two hundred priests, eight bishops, and an immense crowd attended.[22]

Some Conspirators Unmasked

Sanderson's investigation of subversion was coming across evidence of some antiwar Northern Democrats working, with dubious legality, against the Union war effort. The Confederates were turning their minds to activities behind Northern lines. The leaders of the Confederacy were indignant at what they considered Union war crimes against civilians, and they were shocked when, so they claimed, they found certain documents possessed by a party of federal raiders who attacked Richmond in February. These papers supposedly revealed a federal plot to destroy Richmond and kill the Confederate cabinet. Even without these papers, the federals were battering at the Confederacy and some Confederate leaders thought another, more unconventional front in the war needed to be established.[23]

President Jefferson Davis sent two commissioners to Canada in March 1864 to plot special operations against the North. Jacob Thompson of Mississippi was a former secretary of the interior under James Buchanan. Clement Clay was an Alabama politician. These two joined a third commissioner, law professor James P. Holcombe, who was already in Canada to handle some Confederate legal business.[24]

Many antiwar Northern Democrats—who were coming to be known as Copperheads by their opponents—had organized themselves into a group known as the Sons of Liberty. They knew who should lead their organization—the exiled antiwar Democrat leader Clement Vallandigham. Vallandigham agreed, though he insisted on modifying some of the rituals. Sons of Liberty leaders met their chief in Windsor, Canada in April 1864—Vallandigham was in Canada because of his exile from the Union. The Sons of Liberty had split over tactics. Vallandigham still clung to his idea of a cease-fire in the war followed by a negotiated reunion of the country, while others would simply stop the war and let the Confederacy leave the Union. Vallandigham got into an angry argument with the Missouri delegate, Charles L. Hunt, who wanted the Sons of Liberty to support the Confederacy outright, while James McMaster, the New York editor, denounced Lincoln and supported secession. It was not surprising that McMaster and Hunt were in sympathy. Hunt was a prominent Catholic citizen of St. Louis and head of the Sons of Liberty in Missouri, and he also served as Belgian consul. One of Sanderson's detectives observed McMaster and Hunt meeting in Detroit—Sanderson was more worried about Hunt than he was about McMaster, seeing the latter as hostile to the government but not a menace. Sanderson believed correctly that Hunt was part of the Sons of Liberty conspiracy and had him arrested, but Washington countermanded this order and had Hunt released. McMaster had probably been in contact with another Missouri Catholic, Emile Longuemare, sent by President Davis to contact Northern Democratic leaders. In December 1863, Longuemare wrote from Chicago to send McMaster some proposed organizational rules, probably for the Organization of American Knights or the Sons of Liberty. McMaster and Longuemare had lengthy postwar correspondence indicating a closeness between the two.[25]

Soon after the meeting where he called Hunt too extreme, Vallandigham met with the Confederate agents from Canada, initiating Thompson into the Sons of Liberty. Thompson said later he offered Vallandigham some money. While refusing to take the money himself, Vallandigham let James Barrett of Missouri, the Sons of Liberty adjutant general, take the Confederate gold. Barrett was another Missourian whom Sanderson had arrested in St. Louis, but Barrett was released on the intervention of a friend, General Grant, who believed in Barrett's innocence. Thompson and his associates wanted to spark a Northern rebellion, particularly in the midwestern states. The Copperhead conspirators were open to this possibility, but to them, Plan A was defeating Lincoln in the presidential election, and with the president's growing unpopularity, this peaceful option seemed quite feasible. A series of promised Northern insurrections never came off.[26]

In St. Louis, Sanderson, with William's support, tried to get people to take the Copperhead conspiracy seriously. Sanderson objected to Stanton's releasing Barret and Hunt, whom Sanderson characterized as "leaders" whose liberation would "endanger the public safety and defeat the ends of justice." Sanderson wrote an exposé of the information he had uncovered, and William released the report to the press. The newspapers divided along Republican/Democratic lines on the credibility of Sanderson's revelations. In Washington, Stanton told the judge advocate general, Joseph Holt, to prepare a report on Copperhead conspiracies based on information from three sources: Sanderson, an aide to the governor of Indiana named Henry Carrington, and Lafayette Baker, the Union's top detective. Of these three sources, Holt leaned most heavily on Sanderson's information. The report, which came out in October and was widely publicized, found that there was an extensive Copperhead conspiracy whose members cooperated with the Confederates. Objectives of the plot included resisting the draft, helping the Confederates with weapons and military information, murdering federal officials, and sparking a midwestern revolt leading to a new country. Holt concluded with some Biblical and classical allusions rarely found in government reports today: "Judea produced but one Judas Iscariot, and Rome, from the sinks of demoralization, produced but one Catiline; and yet, as events prove, there has arisen in our land an entire brood of such traitors, all animated with the same parricidal spirit, and all struggling with the same relentless malignity for the dismemberment of the Union." As with Sanderson's report, Republican and Democratic papers disagreed on the accuracy of the purported revelations.[27]

Invasion

The National Union Party, a wartime coalition of Republicans and war Democrats, convened in Baltimore in June. The convention renominated Lincoln and cast about for a vice presidential candidate, preferably a War Democrat, to replace Maine Republican Hannibal Hamlin and cement the union between Republicans and Democratic supporters of administration war policy. William fit the bill. Congressman James Garfield, who was head of the Ohio delegation, telegraphed William to ask: "Will you allow your name to be used for vice–President on the ticket with Mr. Lincoln?" In a return telegraph, William accepted in the convoluted way customary among politicians at the time, not betraying unseemly ambition but making himself available: "The convention must discharge its high and responsible duties, in view of our national exigencies, according to its judgment and

Confederate agent Jacob Thompson, who operated from Canada, tried to work with antiwar Northerners to hinder the Union war effort ("Hon. Jacob Thompson of Miss.," Library of Congress, Reproduction Number LC-DIG-cwpbh-02849 [digital file from original neg.]).

conscience, leaving me to the exercise of mine when I know its decision. The nomination of any man acceptable to the loyal people of the Union would satisfy me." In those days, that was enough to get the ball rolling. Except Garfield didn't get the telegraph—he later told William that, not hearing from him, he hadn't pressed the matter, even though there were delegates willing to support the movement.[28]

What stopped William's acceptance telegram from reaching Garfield? William and his supporters had a ready answer: Secretary Stanton had prevented the telegraph from reaching Baltimore. When he became secretary of war, one of Stanton's first acts was to take the military telegraph away from General McClellan's Army of Virginia and put it in the War Department building. There Stanton followed important news and decided which messages to censor before they reached the public. President Lincoln himself would often come by to learn the news from the telegraph. Rosecrans's reply to Garfield in Baltimore would have to go through Stanton's telegraph office. So Stanton had the *opportunity* to block William's acceptance telegram, and there is hardly any room to doubt his *motive*. In any case, the opportunity to nominate William for vice president was lost and William's former associate from Tennessee, military governor and ex–Senator Andrew Johnson, got the nod. Had he been chosen vice president, William probably would have succeeded to the presidency on Lincoln's assassination, making him the first Catholic president.[29]

Some Democrats wanted William to run as a candidate of their party, but he was not interested. The Peace Democrats had too much influence. As William later put it to Sylvester: "Certain it is I would allow no poor Copperhead traitor to define Democracy for me."[30]

The Democrats nominated McClellan, running as a war supporter, for president. Though the Democratic convention adopted a dovish plank in its platform and gave the vice presidential nomination to Copperhead George Pendleton of Ohio, McClellan took a more Unionist attitude than his party and repudiated the peace plank.[31]

Through Sanderson's counter-subversion investigations, William believed that Confederate general Sterling Price planned an invasion of Missouri. William and Price were not strangers to each other—they had confronted each other in Mississippi in 1862, and William had won. Now Price was, indeed, preparing an attack from Arkansas, an attack which he launched in September 1864. William was short of troops, and the forces he had were tied up in security duties. William got permission to recruit eleven regiments locally, and he managed to get General A. J. Smith, who was passing through Missouri on the way to the Georgia front, to give him a hand against the Confederates. Smith followed William's orders though he was not strictly under William's command.[32]

Price expected, and William feared, an uprising among the pro–Confederates of Missouri. Price destroyed property, burned bridges, and cut telegraph lines, so the Union forces could track him based on where communications were out. Price recruited pro–Confederate Missouri guerrillas ("bushwhackers") to join his invasion forces. The presence of the bushwhackers in Price's army prompted William to send a letter to Price through the lines, denouncing the bushwhackers and calling for observance of "the highest dictates of humanity and the laws of war among civilized nations."[33]

The federal forces drove Price's much-depleted, hungry troops out of Missouri, but William did not receive credit for the victory. Instead, the higher-ups blamed him for not destroying Price and for letting the invaders destroy considerable property in Missouri. General Grant overestimated the strength of William's forces, even believing that William was hiding high troop numbers. Grant thought William was poaching troops from the key Georgia and Virginia theaters, and wanted his old rival removed or arrested. Grant exploded: "I know no department or army commander deserving such punishment as the infliction of Rosecrans on them." A petition with 738 signatories accused William of softness on treason and turning a blind eye to Catholic traitors, and of remaining "quietly in his pew" when the Rev. Patrick J. Ryan, a supposed Confederate sympathizer in St. Louis who ministered to Confederate POWs, denounced the Union in a sermon. Only the last accusation was plausible—William's respect for the clergy would probably preclude disrupting Mass over politics. But William had shown no partiality for Catholic subversives; indeed, his superiors had ordered the release of suspects whom he held in prison—including the Catholic Charles Hunt. Nevertheless, the complaints had their effect—William was removed from his command on December 6. As with his removal from the Army of the Cumberland, there were still those who appreciated his accomplishments, such as the general above him, Edwin Canby, who praised the "happy results" of the Missouri campaign.[34]

William returned to Cincinnati and did not receive another command for the rest of the war. He was angry and wanted some answers about why he had been put to pasture.[35] He shot off to Congressman Garfield a letter which made up in detail and passion for what it lacked in modesty:

> I who began by drilling home guards in Cincinnati, teaching the first Ohio troops how to encamp at [Camp] Dennison, who fought the first successful battle involving important results in the War; made the first successful campaign against Lee; helped to lay the foundations of the first State made out of a slave State [West Virginia], receiving for my service a unanimous vote of thanks from the legislature; who invented and had built the first army ambulance now universally used; who first suggested and put into operation the plan of providing photographed information maps of the country for distribution among military commanders now regarded as almost indispensable to all the great military operations in which there are not good topographical maps; whose inspector-general's system has been adopted throughout the army; who built up the cavalry of Mississippi, giving Sheridan the opportunity of winning his first star; who won Iuka and Corinth against great odds; who built up the dispirited mounted force of Buell's Army and brought it to be the victorious cavalry of the Army of the Cumberland; who fought Stone's [sic] River; drove Bragg from Shelbyville, Tullahoma, and Chattanooga, wresting from a superior force the keys of East Tennessee, Georgia and the center of the Southern Confederacy; who struck the Ohio and other Copperheads a great blow, virtually killed the OAKS; drove Price from Missouri; and did much to give that state ... freedom; an officer of sobriety, morality, industry, abstinence from all intrigues military and political, I find myself put into retirement and apparent disgrace, while young men of less age and rank, services, men tainted with pecuniary speculation if not *peculation*, are in command and favor. I want to tax your friendship, in which I confide, to find out and give me an explanation of how and why this is.[36]

20

"The Bishop attributes to God what is an execrable violence of men"

In the October 1863 *Brownson's Quarterly Review,* Orestes Brownson used the occasion of the New York draft riots to address the issue of Catholics in the war. Brownson said that the rioters—the nonrespectable elements of the Irish population—had rioted in their capacity as Democrats, not as Catholics. Of course, Brownson could not resist getting in a dig at Archbishop Hughes. Citing the fact that his clergy were belatedly able to disperse the rioters, Brownson concluded that many rioters were church attenders who would have been open to proper catechesis, which Hughes had neglected. But he said that disloyalty was not primarily a Catholic problem, since the disloyal Peace Democrat leaders were Protestants, and the Irish Catholics were mere dupes.[1]

According to Brownson, the Democratic leaders were the true culprits. The rioters were seduced by "Democratic leaders and journalists." The (Democratic) leaders of the Confederacy were not Catholics, but were "all either Jews or followers of those renowned Secessionists in the sixteenth century, called THE REFORMERS," that is, Protestants. The Northern Catholic clergy, Democrats though they were, were not generally disloyal.[2]

And the Republicans were not blameless for Catholics' Democratic proclivities, said Brownson's article. "The Republican party owed its successes to its union with the Know-Nothing party." The Democrats had been better than Republicans at reaching out to the Catholics: the Democratic Party "has favored early naturalization, and it has had less of that Puritanic cant, rigidity and fanaticism so peculiarly offensive to Catholics." But Republicans were dropping some of their nativism. If Catholics supported the disloyalty of the Democrats, they would provoke an anti-Catholic backlash.[3]

As for Pope Pius's peace appeal of the previous year, the letter was either "forged" or based on "gross misrepresentation" of the facts by people around the pope. The Union could no more make peace with the secessionists than the pope could compromise with the rebels in his own domains.[4]

In an essay entitled "The New Brahminical Literature of New England," also in the October 1863 issue, Brownson returned to his ambiguous relationship with his home region. He didn't want to be associated with the extreme attacks on New England by other Catholic journals, which blamed the region for basically every political evil in the country. Yet he saw some evils there, such as the conditions of workers in the factories. Brownson asked, "When will the 'Uncle Tom's Cabin' of that species of slavery be written, and its misery and cruelty find their Wendell Phillips [referring to the prominent abolitionist leader]?" This denunciation of industrial conditions went back at least to Brownson's "Laboring Classes" essay in 1840, and showed some continuity in his critique of modern society. Yet Brownson believed there was more good than evil in the people of New England. "We see in them the convulsive movements of one of the most advanced communities on the earth, one with extraordinary capacities for the highest Christian development, striving blindly to attain the highest and most complete form of faith and virtue."[5]

Brownson's daughter Sarah also wrote for publication in 1863, telling the readers of the *National Anti-Slavery Standard* that the liberal Catholics, such as her father in America and Bishop Dupanloup and Augustin Cochin in France, stood for the true "Catholic spirit" in opposing slavery, despite most Catholic periodicals in the U.S. being "pro-slavery in the worst sense."[6]

Brownson's January 1864 issue included some criticism of an old friend of his, William Rosecrans. Particularly did he criticize William's actions at Chickamauga and accuse him of recklessness at Iuka, Corinth, and Stones River. William, an old friend of Brownson, responded on January 22 in what for him counted as a friendly letter. Renewing his subscription and praising other articles in the January *Review*, and praising Brownson as a battler against "political despotism and military despotism," William defended his military record against the criticisms in Brownson's article. "I could put up with the barking of the hounds of power who started at my heels as soon as I was relieved of the command of that army which under my guidance had done good work for the Union: I will not even complain of calumnies in the [Copperhead] *Freeman's Journal*. But I must say I do complain of you."[7]

In the April 1864 *Review*, Brownson retracted his comments about General Rosecrans. Brownson admitted his lack of military expertise and affirmed his old friendship with the general. The reason he had published his criticism, he said, was to rebut the claims of certain Catholics, including some Catholic journals, that the firing of General Rosecrans was owing to anti-Catholic prejudice. While not a big admirer of the Lincoln administration, Brownson wanted to avoid this kind of unwarranted religious conflict.[8]

In the same April issue, Brownson began betraying a grumpiness and sarcasm which probably reflected his growing exhaustion. His essay "Abolition and Negro Equality" signaled this. Reviewing an egalitarian speech by abolitionist Wendell Phillips, Brownson spoke of the country's "debt of gratitude to the abolitionists"; honoring their honesty while avowing his traditional disagreement with them. As for the Lincoln administration, it pursued an "indecisive and double faced and no faced policy" on slavery. A sound War Democrat, who acknowledged that slavery was doomed, would be preferable to Lincoln and would be a more reliable abolitionist—perhaps an allusion to William Rosecrans.[9]

While opposing slavery, Brownson reiterated his belief in black inferiority and his opposition to intermarriage. Addressing a hypothetical female abolitionist who had a purely emotional commitment to racial equality, Brownson said he himself had given up his youthful romantic dreams along that line. "Our romance, my dear madam, has fled with our once dark, thick, glossy locks, and remains not with our dimmed eye and white hair." Another respect in which Brownson proclaimed he had lost his youthful idealism was in the area of voting rights, which Phillips was urging for the freed blacks. Voting was a privilege and not a right—"society in her own way elects the voters," said Brownson. Voting was not the way to improve one's condition in life—white voters were managed and manipulated so that voting was useless to them, "but it may serve to amuse them." Blacks, manipulated by their preachers, would abuse the vote at least as much as whites did.[10]

But, Brownson added, now that blacks had been admitted to the armed forces on equal terms with whites—foolish as that equality had been, they had become "nationalized and naturalized." This precluded Brownson's formerly preferred solution to the situation: "deportation or forced colonization is henceforth out of the question." Brownson would have preferred to keep blacks as serfs, a step above slavery where they would have been able to enjoy familial rights by being tied to the land. But now, Brownson threw up his hands: "We are growing old and irritable; we dislike agitation, indeed never liked it; and we think, since we have gone so far, in order to avoid greater evil and have done with the negro, it may be the wisest and safest plan for the General [federal] Government to abolish within its jurisdiction all distinctions founded on color, and, so far as it is concerned, to give the negro a chance to compete successfully with the white man, if he can." Brownson thought that black people would not be able to do this, and would move elsewhere, out of the whites' way. Brownson suggested that the states, as well as the federal authorities, should accept equal rights, but New England states should not force other states do this: "we do not know that if we could, we would Yankeeize the whole nation."[11]

After these reflections, supporting equal rights with as much ill-natured, racist complaining as possible, Brownson turned to that year's coming elections in an essay called "The Next President." To Brownson, the Lincoln administration was a disaster, with ruinous spending, corruption, and neglect of the army. Other than "his patience, his good humor, and capacity to labor," Lincoln lacked presidential qualifications. Lincoln neglected the "heroic element" in human nature. "His soul seems made of leather, and incapable of any grand or noble emotion." There were candidates preferable to Lincoln—Samuel Chase, the secretary of the treasury; General Benjamin Butler, the conqueror of New Orleans; and general-without-portfolio John C. Frémont who, Brownson believed, could have won great victories if he had not been fired from his command. Yet all these candidates were politically vulnerable and unlikely to prevail against Lincoln. Brownson suggested that a War Democrat could beat Lincoln—a Democrat committed to fighting the war to the end and abolishing slavery would be preferable to the incumbent president.[12]

Soon after this April issue, Brownson got a letter from General Frémont. The general was glad to see Brownson run an anti-Lincoln article, and wanted to consult with the editor. Frémont was contemplating a run for the presidency. With his connections to the Brownson family through Brownson's son Ned, Frémont had personal ties to Orestes. Frémont also was a subscriber to the *Review*, buying 1,000 copies—enough to get a struggling editor's attention. Meeting in Cleveland on May 31, 1864, a convention of abolitionists and other radical Republicans, as well as German Americans who formed an important part of Frémont's constituency, nominated General Frémont on a pro–Union, antislavery platform. Meanwhile, the Republicans got together in Baltimore with some leading War Democrats under the name of the Union Party, and renominated Lincoln, with Rosecrans's old acquaintance from Tennessee, Andrew Johnson, for vice president.[13]

The Frémont platform averred that "the rebellion has destroyed slavery," so slavery should be formally forbidden by Constitutional amendment. The platform called for the distribution of rebel property among "soldiers and actual settlers." The Lincoln administration was denounced for spending excessively and corruptly. The platform criticized Lincoln's infringements on civil liberties "outside of districts where martial law has been proclaimed." A Constitutional amendment should limit the president to one term. Reconstructing the seceded states, said the platform, was the job of congress and not the president, the argument of Sumner and Brownson.[14]

The sixth platform plank was of special interest to Catholics, defending "the right for asylum, except for crime, and subject to law." This was probably a reference to the recent case of the Polish sailor Alexander Milewski, who had escaped the Russian fleet in New York and joined the Union army, only for the Lincoln administration to send him back to the Russians.[15] This plank would not only appeal to the German radicals, who had themselves in many cases taken asylum in American after the 1848 revolutions, but it would appeal to the Catholic Poles and Irish, immigrants from oppressive European regimes.

In the July 1864 issue of his *Review,* Brownson jumped on the Frémont bandwagon. In his essay "Lincoln or Frémont?" he showed newfound enthusiasm for the old general. "The re-election of Mr. Lincoln would be not less damaging, in our judgment, to the national cause, than would have been the capture of Washington last summer by the Rebel forces." The danger to the country came "almost exclusively" from corruption in the North. Lincoln never sought the "total extirpation" of slavery. He ran "a civil despotism more oppressive than that of the Grand Turk." And he would lose the war if re-elected. In contrast, Frémont and his supporters were honorable and dedicated. The Cleveland platform was largely to Brownson's taste except that it gave too wide a scope to civil liberties. Lincoln's problem wasn't that he failed to observe civil liberties in the North but that he wielded his emergency powers arbitrarily and unfairly, locking up innocent or harmless people while leaving dangerous subversives at large. Brownson admitted that splitting the Republican vote between Lincoln and Frémont could get a Democrat elected, but even a Democratic victory, would be preferable to Lincoln's re-election.[16]

The July issue tackled the growing conflict between the liberal and conservative groups in the Church, a battle which was at that time coming to a head. In the article "Civil and Religious Freedom," Brownson again endorsed the liberal side, reviewing his friend Charles de Montalembert's Malines speeches of the previous year. These were the speeches in which Montalembert supported "a free Church in a free state," or as Brownson put it, "the freedom of the Church in the freedom of the citizen." Concurring with Montalembert, Brownson said that the Church must be free of state control, and the authorities of the Church should not run the state. Non-Catholic religions should have equal status in the state with the Church. "Error has no rights," proclaimed Brownson, invoking a phrase often used to justify the suppression of non–Catholic religions, "but the man who errs has equal rights with him who errs not." "The spirit of Christ is the spirit of liberty," and this meant Catholic governments should respect "freedom of error no less than the freedom of truth—the precise order which obtains in the United States." Brownson contrasted this view with the repressive attitude of the "*oscurantisti,*" who wanted the suppression of non–Catholic religions in Catholic states and allowed for religious freedom only where (as in the United States) they lacked the power to impose their will. Brownson singled out the Jesuit order and its Roman newspaper, *Civiltà Cattolica,* as the prime upholder of the *oscurantisti* standpoint. Brownson

20. *"The Bishop attributes to God..."* 235

When General John C. Frémont ran against Lincoln in 1864 on a militant platform of fighting slavery, vigorous prosecution of the war, and upholding civil liberties, Brownson supported the controversial general. Campaign flyer showing Frémont (left, in uniform) and his running mate, John Cochrane, Currier and Ives (Library of Congress, Reproduction Number LC-USZC2–3351 [color film copy slide]).

said the Jesuits "make war *à outrance* on what is called modern civilization," assiduously opposing Montalembert's campaign "to place the Church in harmony with modern civilization."[17] Of course, Brownson's paean to civil liberties hadn't prevented him from supporting federal restriction on these freedoms in the name of fighting the Confederates.

Meanwhile, across the Atlantic, Fr. Bannon, the Confederate emissary in Ireland, worked hard to discourage poor Irishmen from seeking their fortunes in America, where they could end up swelling the ranks of the Union army. The rebel priest wrote pro–Confederate articles and circulated writings from James McMaster's *Freeman's Journal* to show the supposed wickedness of the war. Fr. Bannon publicized the pope's letter to Jefferson Davis in order to suggest that the pope recognized the Confederacy. Also coming to Europe was Bishop Patrick Lynch of Charleston, who lobbied the French emperor and the pope on behalf of the Confederate cause. When Bishop Lynch was in Rome, papal officials assured Union ambassador Rufus King that they were receiving the prelate only in his capacity as bishop, not recognizing him as a Confederate ambassador. They again assured King that the correspondence with Jefferson Davis implied no recognition of the Confederacy.[18]

In an August 1864 meeting with Rufus King, Cardinal Antonelli praised the United States. The papal government (in King's paraphrase) "had nothing to ask from the United States; as in that country alone, added the Cardinal with some warmth, does there exist perfect freedom and equality in the matter of Religion and the Catholic enjoys every right and privilege that is accorded to any citizen, whatever his creed, or condition." Antonelli boasted that he had researched the situation in the United States, including reading the federal Constitution, and that secession was unconstitutional just as Lincoln and the Union proclaimed.[19]

In American politics, events moved rapidly. The Democrats agreed on one issue only –white supremacy. Editor James McMaster of the Catholic *Freeman's Journal* was typical of Democratic rhetoric, railing against the "beastly doctrine of the intermarriage of black men with white women" and "filthy black niggers ... jostl[ing] white people and even ladies everywhere." It was on the war question that the party was split. When Democrats nominated McClellan, who was going through a hawkish phase, with a Copperhead vice presidential candidate and a peace platform, solid Union men became worried that the split between Lincoln and Frémont would assure that the president would lose to a doubtful Democrat. On September 22, Frémont agreed to withdraw from the presidential race in exchange for Lincoln's getting rid of an old enemy of the general, cabinet member Montgomery Blair. Lincoln did so. No further concessions—say, on civil liberties—were obtained.[20]

Now that Frémont had given up his campaign, Brownson reluctantly crawled back to Lincoln. In the October issue of the *Review,* Brownson threw his support to the incumbent president. Not that he was pleased to do so—he still believed Lincoln "has listened to the whisperings of Satan, has dreamed of Robert I, and of making himself a Napoleon, or at least a Cromwell," defying congress and wielding "dictatorial powers" in reconstructing the South.[21]

During this time, Brownson, Job-like, had several tragedies rain down upon him. His health continued to be very poor. The political and religious views he expressed caused the circulation of his *Review* to keep dropping. In July, his thirty-year old son William died in a carriage accident on the way to join the army. Meanwhile, his son Ned was in the thick of the fighting on the Northern Virginia front. Ned Brownson, serving on the staff of General Winfield Scott Hancock, wanted to keep up his good relations with General Frémont, writing in letters to his family in 1863 that while he didn't want to return to the general's staff, he didn't want to alienate him with a direct refusal. In August 1864, Hancock was involved in heavy fighting, with the Confederates driving back some of the troops. The Union forces reformed their lines, as General Hancock later wrote, "with such small parties as could be rallied and formed by staff officers." These staff officers apparently included Ned, who "was mortally wounded, dying during the night." Finally, Orestes's mother died in the month after Ned did.[22]

In "Some Explanations offered to our Catholic Readers," Brownson announced that his *Review* might be discontinued in the face of personal and public tragedies. "It is our consolation under our great personal loss that [William and Ned] were both Catholics, both true patriots, both ardent lovers of liberty, and neither desiring a more glorious death than that of dying in defence of the integrity and freedom of the land of their birth. We would not have our Catholic friends suppose for a moment that we are indifferent to the interests of that religion in which all our children have been carefully trained, and in which five sons out of seven have died, and without which we could have no sweet hope of meeting them again in the bosom of our God."[23]

Brownson then defended his July essay "Civil and Religious Freedom." He took this opportunity to defend himself against the various accusations of unorthodoxy which had been mounted against him lately. He reiterated his criticism of the Jesuit order, which had many members and institutions in the Union and the Confederacy, as out of harmony with the modern age and of doubtful loyalty to the Union. Brownson reiterated that while he hoped the pope would give up his territories, the final decision was the pope's, not Brownson's or the Italian government's. Brownson said his ultramontane views of the pope's power over secular rulers were still substantially the same, though he would now express himself more charitably toward the "Gallicans" (those with a restricted view of papal power). On his theological speculations, Brownson claimed a greater freedom than his critics claimed he was allowed. He had criticized immigrant Catholics, and perhaps he had gone overboard in this, but "the violent tone of the Catholic press toward us" and that press's misrepresentations, closed off the possibility of reconciliation even when Brownson realized he had not been fully just to the Catholic immigrants. "Though we do not regard every Catholic as a saint, our sympathies are with Catholics. They are our people, and we belong to them. I love my country, I love my countrymen, and I am ready to give my life for it and them, as my brave and noble son, whose body lies, while I am writing, in an adjoining room, waiting the funeral rites of his Church, freely and without a murmur gave his; but my Church is dearer, and my Catholic brethren are nearer; my non–Catholic countrymen are my kindred after the flesh; Catholics are my brothers in soul and spirit." Finally, Brownson defended his right to discuss theological issues—had he not been called to his role as a "Catholic publicist" by "the unanimous voice of the Ecclesiastical authorities of our own country"? He thanked his loyal readers, avowed that he never claimed infallibility and acknowledged that he might be wrong, but that he had never said anything he believed to be un–Catholic. "From our youth up we have loved Truth, and wooed her as a bride, and we wish to die in her embrace. We have never adhered from pride or obstinacy to any opinion we had once entertained, and have always been ready—some would say too ready—to abandon any opinion once held the moment we were satisfied of its unsoundness." He concluded by affirming his subjection to "the Supreme Authority at Rome" and said he would accept its judgment and correction of his work. "We never have been disobedient to authority, and we never shall be."[24]

The Syllabus of Errors *and the Errors of Slavery*

While Brownson was proclaiming his obedience to Rome, and while the voters of the North were re-electing Abraham Lincoln, the Roman authorities were preparing a shot across the bow of the liberal Catholic principles which Brownson had so vigorously defended. The times did not seem propitious for the pope. In September 1864, the French emperor Louis Napoleon agreed to withdraw his troops from Rome in exchange for Victor Emmanuel's promise not to invade. Pope Pius expected that this deal would soon be followed by aggression and conquest of the Eternal City, since he had no trust in Victor Emmanuel's willingness to keep his word. "I have placed all my trust in God," said Pius, "if he chooses to preserve me in peace, I will praise Him; if He chooses to prove [test] me with tribulations I will not cease to extol Him."[25]

While worrying about being stripped of French protection, Pope Pius took up his project of writing an encyclical protecting his flock from the errors of the modern world. The encyclical had been in the works for a couple of years, and despite the caution of some of his advisors, who thought that he would alienate his allies in liberal states, Pius ploughed on, releasing two important documents on December 8, 1864: an encyclical called *Quanta Cura* and in an accompanying *Syllabus of Errors*. In *Quanta Cura,* Pius rejected the idea that freedom of conscience should be "an absolute liberty, which should be restrained by no authority whether ecclesiastical or civil." The pope also condemned the idea that the government could do anything in the name of "the people's will," regardless of the restraints of religion. "Where religion has been removed from civil society, and the doctrine and authority of divine revelation repudiated, the genuine notion itself of justice and human right is darkened and lost, and the place of true justice and legitimate right is supplied by material force." The pope cited examples of governments repressing the Church. The bishops and the faithful should join in fervent prayers to counteract these tendencies, and the encyclical concluded by proclaiming a Jubilee, for up to a month in the year 1865, the details to be worked out by the bishops themselves.[26]

The *Syllabus of Errors* was a list of eighty propositions which, in previous declarations, Pope Pius had already denounced. Technically, then, the *Syllabus* simply summarized what the pope had said before, and contained no new matter. It was the combination of all these denunciations in one document, without the limited contexts in which the original denunciations had been made, which gave the *Syllabus* its power. First off were seven propositions under the heading of "Pantheism, Naturalism and Absolute Rationalism," propositions which would be considered erroneous by liberal and conservative Catholics alike. Seven errors listed under "Moderate Rationalism" were somewhat closer to condemning the ideas of liberal Catholics, but the condemned propositions were far more extreme than what Montalembert, Brownson and other liberals would go for.[27]

Four condemned propositions under "Indifferentism, Latitudinarianism" were primarily offensive to Protestants, since they asserted the superiority of Catholicism to other religions, but they included a denunciation of the notion that "every man is free to embrace and profess that religion which, guided by the light of reason, he shall consider true," which could be seen as renouncing a key liberal Catholic belief.[28]

Of the errors concerning "Socialism, Communism, Secret Societies, Biblical Societies, Clerico-Liberal Societies," and "the Church and Her Rights," there were some potentially controversial denunciations. It was error to deny the right of the Church and its clergy to wield temporal power. One error, aimed at certain Catholic intellectuals (especially in Germany but probably elsewhere as well), claimed a freedom for "Catholic teachers and authors" to defy Roman authority in nondogmatic matters. Brownson had often been accused of this, but he had professed a willingness to be corrected by Rome.[29]

Numerous errors related to "Civil Society." Many of the errors involved the glorification of arbitrary state power. Among the ideas denounced were the claim that all rights come from the state, that the state could dictate to the Church on various matters, e.g., by deposing bishops and restricting monks and nuns, and that the state should run all the schools. The *Syllabus* also condemned various might-is-right doctrines, including the idea that people could do evil acts if motivated by patriotism. So far, most good Catholics would denounce these things (though Brownson, while denouncing state schooling, urged Catholics to send their children to state schools anyway). Condemned proposition 55 proved more controversial among some Catholics: "The Church ought to be separated from the State, and the State from the Church." As with the statement of the other errors, this sentence was put forth as wrong and heretical.[30] After the *Syllabus* came out, there was a bitter debate about whether the pope was condemning religious regimes like the United States, or whether he was condemning only the aggressive, repressive secularism of European regimes, while accepting, as Cardinal Antonelli did, the "perfect freedom and equality in the matter of Religion" which existed in the United States.

The final four propositions were read by many to suggest the former interpretation. As affirmed in the final propositions of the *Syllabus,* it was wrong to deny that "the Catholic religion should be held as the only religion of the State, to the exclusion of all other forms of worship." It was wrong that some Catholic countries allowed non–Catholic immigrants to worship in public. It was wrong to deny that complete religious freedom and freedom of expression "conduce more easily to corrupt the morals and minds of the people, and to propagate the pest [plague] of indifferentism." Proposition 80, the final error listed in the *Syllabus,* was "The Roman Pontiff can, and ought to, reconcile himself, and come to terms with progress, liberalism and modern civilization." This proposition referenced a prior declaration of the pope denouncing the usurping Italian government's pretense to uphold modern civilization. The pope's experience of modern liberalism included military aggression by a neighbor who suppressed religious institutions, as well as seizures of Church property and interference with Church government by other supposedly progressive governments. As expressed in the *Syllabus,* though, Proposition 80 appeared to many readers to encompass *all* modern progress and liberalism, not simply their abuses.[31]

Insofar as it denounced the pretensions of secular rules and rejected arbitrary and absolute state power, the *Syllabus* was quite forward looking, anticipating and warning against the centralized and totalitarian states of the coming centuries. But insofar as it appeared to contemplate Catholic states repressing non–Catholic religions, and insofar as it rejected "modern civilization," the *Syllabus* shocked not only the Protestant world, but liberal Catholics like Montalembert and Brownson.[32]

Bishop Felix Dupanloup of Orleans, France (whose sermon on slavery had earned the praise of Archbishop Purcell), tried to draw the sting of the *Syllabus* in a pamphlet arguing that he and his fellow Catholic liberals could continue to support civil liberties and religious freedom. The "progress" condemned by the *Syllabus* was only the false "progress" promoted by irreligious people and institutions. The picture of a Catholic-only society portrayed in the *Syllabus* was only an ideal, a "thesis," which contrasted with the "hypothesis" of what was practically achievable in real-world conditions. In a world of liberal institutions, where the ideal Catholic polity was not achievable, Catholics were allowed to work on behalf of religious freedom, free expression, and separation of Church and state. Pope Pius praised Dupanloup in a letter for rebutting false notions about his *Syllabus*. At the same time, though, the pope praised a book by Louis Veuillot pushing a more hard-core, reactionary version of the *Syllabus*. The liberal vs. conservative battle within the Church continued.[33]

Still, the liberal Catholic party was shocked and demoralized by the *Syllabus*. Montalembert wrote to Brownson to express his sorrow at the apparent triumph of religious reaction and to commiserate with the personal sorrows of his American counterpart. Montalembert was "grieved" at the closing of Brownson's *Review* and the "terrible domestic calamity" of the death of the two Brownson sons. The Frenchman agreed with everything in Brownson's valedictory article (except the denunciation of the Jesuits, which Montalembert considered too sweeping). The end of the *Review*, Montalembert said, was due to the same reactionary forces which he was fighting in Europe. Under the "pestilential ascendancy" of the "new inquisition," liberals like Bishop Dupanloup "have been more or less *excommunicated* just like you and me."[34]

Four days after the pope issued the *Syllabus*, the Congregation of the Index, responsible for censorship, met to consider another set of errors. The proslavery pastoral letter of Bishop Augustus Mary Martin of Natchitoches, Louisiana, had been under consideration for several years since it came out in August 1861. Now on December 12, 1864, the members of the Congregation of the Index denounced the pastoral as being inappropriately proslavery, thus approving the report of the consultor (expert) who had been assigned to investigate the orthodoxy of the pastoral. The consultor was Fr. Vincenzo M. Gatti, head of the Casanatense Library, and later a member of the Index's staff. Fr. Gatti was not the only one advising Rome on American slavery. Louis B. Binsse, the pope's consul in New York City, had written in September 1863 calling slavery "the sole cause of our terrible civil war" and denouncing American Catholics who not only opposed emancipation but in some cases "favor[ed] the cause of separation and … are hostile to the cause of our government."[35]

Fr. Gatti's report, dated November 15, 1864, set out the text of Bishop Martin's pastoral followed by the text of Pope Gregory XVI's 1839 encyclical *In Supremo*. Fr. Gatti then proceeded "to show the opposition of Bishop Martin's theory on slavery and the teaching of the Sovereign Pontiffs." Proceeding paragraph by paragraph through the bishop's pastoral, Fr. Gatti found doctrinal error in each paragraph.[36]

Bishop Martin's pastoral said that God had arranged to "snatch" black people "from the barbarity of their ferocious customs" by having them enslaved and brought to America and put under the care of "the privileged ones of the great human family"—the whites. Fr. Gatti remarked that by thus appearing to endorse the African slave trade, "the Bishop attributes to God what is an execrable violence of men." Bishop Martin also referred to blacks as "the children of the race of Canaan," referring to the book of Genesis, where Cham (Ham), the ancestor of the Canaanites, is cursed by his father Noah: "The lowest of slaves shall he be to his brothers." Bishop Martin was suggesting that black people were the descendants of Ham and subject to his curse of enslavement. Fr. Gatti questioned whether black people were actually descendants of Ham. In any case, "even if they were cursed by Noah, they are not cursed any longer after the coming of Jesus Christ when, as the Apostle says, there is no distinction between Jew and Gentile, between freeman and slave, between man and woman, since we are all sons of the same divine Father."37

Fr. Gatti indignantly rejected Bishop Martin's doctrines: "Did Jesus Christ say: 'Go and snatch them by force from their native country, drive them to your countries and convert them?'" Bishop Martin's pastoral said that God had arranged the enslavement of black people, depriving them of a freedom "which they are unable to defend and which will kill them," and compelling them to labor for their masters, in exchange for their masters giving them room and board and teaching them the Christian faith. Fr. Gatti denied that freedom would be deadly for blacks: "Will a Negro, especially when he becomes a Christian, not be able to live in society as other individuals, and will he be obliged to lose his freedom and become a slave?" Fr. Gatti invoked the examples of "religious orders for the redemption of slaves ... [and] saintly monarchs and masters who have freed them." He specifically cited Fr. Nicolò Olivieri, a contemporary priest who had dedicated his life to ransoming Sudanese and Egyptian slaves and, in many cases, finding them safe harbors in religious orders in Europe. Fr. Olivieri had, said Fr. Gatti, "recently led the Negroes from the markets of Cairo lest they be obliged to serve as slaves but instead ... let them become really free and and Christians like the others." This "belie[s] this theory of the bishop [Martin], though he has many supporters among all concerned in the Southern States.... Experience shows that Negroes, placed among Catholics and educated like them, can become learned and virtuous people, fit for moral dignity and freedom."38

Fr. Gatti acknowledged that the Church had endorsed some kinds of slavery, such as the slavery endorsed in the Old Testament and slavery derived from "just title" such as the ancient practice of enslaving prisoners of war in lieu of killing them. But modern American slavery "originat[ed] in violence and in the violation of the natural law" and as such had been denounced by the popes. Bishop Martin's pastoral "promotes the mistake of those who believe that the slave trade of the Negroes is lawful and who try to elude the condemnations of the Sovereign Pontiffs with every kind of cavil." Papal declarations, such as *In Supremo*, "have condemned not only the slave trade but slavery itself."39

For these reasons, Fr. Gatti concluded, Bishop Martin's pastoral was worthy of condemnation and "should not be read" by the faithful. Since the author was a bishop, though, he should be given the opportunity to correct the pastoral to conform with true doctrine, and the ban on the pastoral should only last until such corrections were made. After the Congregation of the Index approved these recommendations, Pope Pius gave his approval on December 17. The Congregation of the Index then wrote Cardinal Barbabo of Propaganda on December 30 to advise him of the Holy Father's decision: Bishop Martin had "to correct the errors and inaccuracies" in his pastoral "at the earliest possible time lest, should there be undue delay, further and harsher measures be taken by the Holy See." How Bishop Martin responded to this command is not recorded.[40]

In adopting Fr. Gatti's views, the pope and his Congregation of the Index had not only rebuked Bishop Martin, but had repudiated many of the views on slavery and race which had been endorsed by some American Catholics before and during the Civil War. Contrary to Bishop England and others, prior papal rulings on African slavery had condemned the institution itself, not simply the foreign slave traffic. Contrary to Brownson's racist pronouncements, black people were capable of achieving equality with white people, and as indicated by the work of Fr. Olivieri, which was specifically praised by Fr. Gatti, they could also live in peace among white people. To some modern ways of thinking, it could be deemed ironic that a pope who had just endorsed the supposedly reactionary doctrines of the *Syllabus of Errors* could declare against slavery, invoking the public declaration of a reactionary predecessor (Gregory XVI), while a liberal like Brownson trailed a baggage of proslavery and racist pronouncements. However, in truth there was no irony: The traditionalist Popes Pius and Gregory had simply ratified longstanding Church teachings and practices, which in the Middle Ages had largely resulted in the extirpation of slavery from Europe.

21

"The only country in which the Pope could seek and find a suitable and secure Asylum"

Assassination

The clergy and faithful of the American Catholic Church were divided over the Civil War, suffering internal conflicts they had been able to avoid before the war broke out. What with supporting one side or another, or in the North disagreeing over war versus peace and slavery versus freedom, Catholics took different sides and battled each other with weapons and words. But it scarcely ever reached the point of schism—that is, the various Catholic churches in the U.S. remained united with Rome and hence were in communion with each other. The faithful, regardless of politics, were being able to receive the sacraments anywhere in the country, even in local churches with different political orientations.[1]

Abraham Lincoln's assassination on April 14, 1865—Good Friday—shocked even Catholics who had opposed the president. In Boston, the Easter services on Sunday the 16th were more somber than usual. There was no triumphal singing of the Te Deum. Chancellor James Healy presided a Mass at the Washington Street Cathedral, voicing Bishop Fitzpatrick's grief, and his own. The churches were more crowded than usual on this day. The bishop decreed that penitential services should be held on the day of Lincoln's funeral. Chancellor Healy communicated this decree to the priests.[2]

Of the four people hanged on the order of a military commission for their alleged participation in the Lincoln assassination plot, Mary Surratt proved the most controversial. The Catholic owner of the boarding house where many of the conspirators lodged, Mrs. Surratt was accused by witnesses of involvement in their nefarious activities along with her son John, now a fugitive from justice. In her defense, Mrs. Surratt brought several priests as character witnesses, only one of whom had known her for any length of time, and he had not known her very well. Before her execution she met with another priest, Fr. John Walter, a stranger to her who nevertheless was convinced of her innocence and championed her cause afterwards, calling her execution a miscarriage of justice. John Brophy, an instructor at St. Aloysius College, also defended her and later her son John, claiming that a key witness against them, also Catholic, had admitted to making up his story.[3]

To many Americans, Protestant and Catholic, the execution of Mary Surratt was controversial. Not only was it rare for a woman to be executed, not only had the military commission recommended clemency, but critics assailed the evidence brought against Surratt, and to some extent against her codefendants. Fr. Walter, her priestly acquaintance who had been with her before her execution, wrote that he knew Mary Surratt was innocent. James McMaster, who continued to express Confederate sympathies after the war was over, called the assassination trial illegal and said Surratt was innocent and her execution was a "political murder."[4]

Mary Surratt's son John, another accused in the Lincoln assassination case, was Catholic like his mother, and his case also stirred the religious pot. After the assassination, John fled to French Canada, where many Catholics sympathized with the South. Pro-Confederate French Canadian priests sheltered Surratt and got him on a ship to Liverpool, England, where a French priest sheltered him in his rectory, perhaps on recommendation of the French Canadians. From Liverpool John Surratt went to Rome and joined the papal Zouaves, the troops recruited from Catholics throughout the world to defend the papal territories against invasion by Victor Emmanuel's Italian nationalist government or by Giuseppe Garibaldi's guerrillas.[5]

In late April 1866, one of John Surratt's fellow Zouaves, a Canadian, reported him to the American minister, Rufus King. With the assistance of Secretary of State Seward, King verified the fugitive's identity. The papal secretary of state, Cardinal Antonelli, agreed to extradite Surratt, even though there was no treaty of extradition between the United States and the pope, and Pius was generally hesitant about sending fugitives to countries where they faced the death penalty. But Pius had no love of assassins—his own minister, Pellegrino Rossi, had been assassinated in 1848 to the applause of many European liberals—and with the approval of the American consul, though this delicate latter point apparently didn't come up during the diplomatic discussion of Surratt. Rather than stand on the absence of an extradition treaty, the papal government responded to the U.S. government's request—which is certainly more than the U.S. would have done if asked to hand over one of Rossi's assassins—with the expectation that the United States would reciprocate in a similar case. Far from harboring any desire to insult the U.S. government, some in the papal administration were considering the U.S. as a haven of refuge for the pontiff. While Cardinal Antonelli told King that Pius meant to stay in Rome, other figures in the Roman government suggested that if Pius were forced to flee, his best destination would be the land of Uncle Sam. King paraphrased both Minister of War Hermann Kanzler and the pope's chaplain as claiming "that the only country in which the Pope could seek and find a suitable and secure Asylum was the great Republic of America." King in return, as he paraphrased it to Seward, told Kanzler that the pope would "meet with a kind welcome" in the United States and would be able to perform his duties "unquestioned and unmolested."[6]

On November 9, Antonelli gave King some unpleasant news—papal troops had arrested Surratt, but the prisoner had escaped from his guards by dramatically jumping into a deep ravine and fleeing. At least, this was the story the troop commander told—another soldier later told the American media that some of Surratt's fellow soldiers had contrived at his escape through a prison sewer. In any case, King got to work tracking Surratt, who was brought to ground in Alexandria, Egypt and returned to the United States for trial in a civil court in Washington, D.C. Unreliable government witnesses put Surratt in Washington on the day of President Lincoln's murder, while more plausible defense witnesses had him in New York. The jury hung, John Surratt didn't, and the charges were ultimately dismissed.[7]

Some of Pope Pius's ruminations about Canada were publicized in the press—rather than let the British-Canadian provinces fall to radical Irish Fenians, the pope thought the United States government should seize Canada. That this was a sincere statement, not crafted for diplomatic purposes, is shown by the embarrassment Pius got into by antagonizing the British and making remarks in support of U.S. expansionism, which seemed in tension with his opposition to Italian aggression.[8] In short, the pope's sympathies, now that the Civil War was over, were with the reunited United States and not with assassins.

Nonetheless, the Catholicism of the Surratts and some of their associates, such as Dr. Samuel Mudd, fed old Protestant suspicions of the Church. The most influential conspiracy theorist who tied the Church to the Lincoln assassination was a former priest named Charles P. T. Chiniquy, whose lengthy tome *Fifty Years in the Church of Rome* appeared in 1886. Before the war, Chiniquy had been a prominent priest in French Canada, famous as a temperance campaigner and a seducer of women. He moved to Illinois in the 1850s and became the pastor of a French Canadian parish but was ultimately defrocked by the bishop of Chicago. At the same time, one of his parishioners sued him for slander. Chiniquy hired a prominent Illinois lawyer named Abraham Lincoln to defend him against the slander charges, which were ultimately settled. Now alienated from the Church, Chiniquy ended up as a Presbyterian.[9]

In his 1886 book, Chiniquy claimed that during the slander case, Lincoln warned his ex-priest client about the ruthlessness of the Jesuits. Chiniquy also claimed to have met Lincoln three times during the Civil War. On two of these occasions, Chiniquy claimed, Lincoln spoke of a sinister Catholic and Jesuit conspiracy against himself and against America's free institutions. Lincoln supposedly said the pope and the Jesuits wanted to kill him and that he was ready to die for the sake of liberty. "It was Rome," wrote Chiniquy, "who directed [John Wilkes Booth's] arm, after corrupting his heart and damning his soul." Chiniquy's recollections are at odds with contemporaneous records. He misstated key elements of his slander case, and letters from Chiniquy to Lincoln during the Civil War do not show the level of acquaintanceship between the two men that Chiniquy later claimed. None of Lincoln's works contain any anti–Catholic sentiments like those attributed to him by Chiniquy, and the president's son Robert Todd said in 1922 that he did not know of any published Catholic-baiting quotes by Lincoln: "[Lincoln's] name has been a peg on which to hang many things."[10]

The fact-challenged nature of Chiniquy's narrative did not deter many people from accepting it, including one of the members of the military panel that condemned Mary Surratt and other conspirators. General Thomas Harris endured considerable abuse for his role in sending Mary Surratt to the gallows, and he found particularly galling the attacks from Fr. Walter and some Catholic publications. Several decades after his service on the military commission, he decided that the Catholic Church was to blame for Lincoln's assassination, and he privately published a book to this effect, which did not have the same circulation as

Chiniquy's book. In Harris' view, the American hierarchy probably persuaded the Confederate emissaries in Canada to carry out the assassination.[11]

One persistent myth has Pope Pius sending Jefferson Davis a crown of thorns while the latter was in a U.S. prison after the war, charged with treason. In reality, the pope sent a picture of himself to Davis around December 1866, with a Latin phrase based on Matthew 11:28, but there was no crown of thorns. Davis's wife, Varina, wove her husband a crown of thorns, and some sources erroneously reported this crown as a gift from the pope.[12]

Orestes Brownson

Without financial means, except some freelance journalism work, Orestes Brownson received a welcome gift in 1865. His friends Fr. Jeremiah Cummings and Fr. Isaac Hecker, along with Fr. Hecker's well-off brother George and other donors, established a $1,000 annuity for the editor-without-a-journal. Secure from destitution, Brownson continued writing. In 1866 he published his book *The American Republic,* trying to reconcile federal and state authority while avoiding on the one hand the Calhounism he had previously espoused but which he now blamed for the war, and on the other hand avoiding the centralization which he believed menaced the country from the other direction. Drawing careful distinctions about unity in diversity, reminiscent of nothing so much as Trinitarian theology, Brownson gave a vision of Constitutional government which he hoped would serve the country in its difficulties. In his Catholic journalism, Brownson tried to explain the 1864 *Syllabus of Errors* in terms compatible with his American Constitutional vision—the *Syllabus* had denounced the European version of militant antireligious liberalism, Brownson claimed, not the religion-friendly American version of liberalism. There were still errors of the modern world that the *Syllabus* rightly condemned, and, free from the wartime need to make Protestant allies, Brownson affirmed that it was again time to defend distinctively Catholic teachings.[13]

From his perch in America, Brownson tried to cover the Vatican Council, defending the doctrine of papal infallibility against hostile Protestants and dissident Catholics. In 1873 he revived *Brownson's Quarterly Review.* John McCloskey, Hughes's successor as archbishop of New York, was more supportive of the *Review* than Archbishop Hughes had been, seeing a need for Brownson's voice in defense of the Church. By this time, Brownson had become more supportive of the Irish. He wrote his old friend, Fr. Isaac Hecker, that "I think I am turning Paddy. I have lost confidence in my countrymen, and have become ashamed of them." A few years afterward, he wrote in his revived *Review* that the Irish were the hope for the future of the American Catholic Church, and that they "should retain their distinctive character as Irishmen."[14]

Brownson's wife died in 1872, leaving only two sons and his daughter Sarah. Sarah lived for a time at his Elizabeth, New Jersey, house, before and after her marriage and the birth of Orestes's granddaughter Mary. Sarah did not like what she saw as Orestes's excessive eating and drinking, which he seems to have persisted in despite his gout. He moved to Detroit in 1875 to live with his son Henry. He stopped publishing his *Review* in 1876. On

April 17, 1876, he died. Ten years later, his body was taken from its Detroit grave, brought to Notre Dame University, and buried in the Sacred Heart Chapel.[15]

Sylvester Rosecrans

Bishop Sylvester Rosecrans presided over the service which opened the archdiocesan synod in Cincinnati in September 1865. In 1867, he received a post as pastor of a Columbus, Ohio church, St. Patrick's. The previous pastor of St. Patrick's, Fr. Edward Fitzgerald, had just become bishop of Little Rock. Sylvester was appointed bishop of the new see of Columbus in 1868.[16]

Sylvester immediately got to work building up his new see. He was so busy establishing a new seminary and generally getting affairs in order that the pope excused him from coming to the Vatican Council meeting from 1869 to 1870. This spared Sylvester from the fight over the dogma of papal infallibility, which was discussed at the council. Archbishop Purcell attended the council, and initially fought against making a formal definition of the dogma. Ultimately, Purcell voted to affirm infallibility—only two of the world's bishops voted no, one of whom was Bishop Fitzgerald of Little Rock. When Purcell returned to Cincinnati he faced criticism in the secular press for allegedly changing his mind. The archbishop replied to these reports, affirming that the council's ultimate definition had met his initial objections. Brownson came to Purcell's defense in the *Tablet*, declaring that the archbishop had initially doubted the expediency of a dogmatic definition, not its accuracy, and that Purcell voted his approval after his reservations had been resolved. When, soon after the council, Italian troops conquered Rome and proclaimed it the capital of a united Italy, Catholics around the world rallied around their embattled pontiff; the American Catholic community continued its tradition of financial support for the papacy, becoming a financial mainstay of the institution.[17]

In Columbus, Sylvester was spared this drama as he focused single-mindedly on the work of governing his diocese. He brought in monks and nuns and began work on a new cathedral, to be called St. Joseph's. Busy with fundraising for the cathedral, he had to close his seminary. But the fundraising was a success. In a controversial move, Sylvester even advertised masses to be performed on behalf of donors. Less problematically, he retained an experienced engineer to help in the construction—General William Rosecrans. Sylvester performed his other priestly and episcopal labors while supervising the construction. As a newspaper later put it, "to accomplish all this [work], his hours of labor were from four in the morning until half-past nine at night."[18]

The cathedral was complete in 1878. The dedication was on Sunday, October 20. Sylvester was joined by Archbishop Purcell and by bishops from throughout the archdiocese. About four thousand of the laity attended. That afternoon, Sylvester suffered a serious attack, perhaps a stroke, and was taken to the nearby Sacred Heart Convent. The attacks redoubled, and Sylvester received the last rites. He died on Monday, October 21. His funeral was held in the new cathedral the following Saturday, again attended by several bishops and a large crowd of people. Sylvester had literally killed himself with overwork, holding on only long enough to see the completion of his important project. The shepherd had laid down his life for his sheep, as Sylvester had intimated that he might. Meanwhile, Pius IX, under whose pontificate Sylvester had spent most of his Catholic life, including the dramatic years in Rome, had predeceased the bishop of Columbus only a few months earlier, in February.[19]

Shortly after Sylvester's death, the Cincinnati archdiocese was hit with a disaster. Sylvester's former colleague, and Archbishop Purcell's brother, Fr. Edward Purcell, had served as banker for many people in the archdiocese, violating Church law against clerics lending at interest. Fr. Edward was honest but incompetent, and now the whole thing came crashing down. A crowd of people made a run on the bank—the Cincinnati Cathedral—in December 1878, only to be told there was not enough money. This began a lengthy period of financial and spiritual woes for the archdiocese, which was engulfed in litigation and—worse—hit by defections from a disillusioned, impoverished flock. Sylvester's good management of the Columbus Diocese formed a striking contrast with his former Metropolitan's leader-ship after Sylvester left Cincinnati. Indeed, the absence of Sylvester's guiding hand as auxiliary bishop after he went to Columbus may have deprived Purcell of the help he needed to perform the duties of the position from which he had unsuccessfully attempted to resign.[20]

William Rosecrans

William outlived his younger brother Sylvester by many years. He also outlived his son Louis, a priest, and his daughter Mary, a nun. He did not spend all his time mourning. After the war, William left the army and tried several business ventures in oil, railways, and blasting-powder manufacture. He patented a fuse cutter. He was always in a financially precarious position. Notwithstanding this, William managed to build himself an estate in California known as Rancho Sausal Redondo.[21]

Civic affairs also took up his attention. In summer 1868, William met the general he once defeated, Robert E. Lee, in the state where Lee suffered his defeat—West Virginia. In Sulphur Springs, West Virginia, Lee, along with other former Confederates, drafted a conciliatory letter to the North accepting the results of the war, pledging good treatment to the former slaves while refusing to accept "political power" for them, and pleading for an end to Reconstruction. William wanted Southern legislatures to endorse this letter in order to promote Democratic candidates at the polls, in particular to support the Democratic nominee, former New York governor Horatio Seymour. William coauthored a book *Popular Government*, advocating various government reforms. He served as minister to Mexico during the closing years of the Andrew Johnson administration, losing his job, naturally enough, when Johnson's successor Ulysses Grant defeated Horatio Seymour and became president in 1869. The two former generals remained foes. On several occasions, friends and supporters offered William government jobs or nominations to elective office—director of the San Francisco mint, Democratic nominee for governor of California, nominee for governor of Ohio, Democratic nominee for congressman from Nevada. He declined all these proffered appointments and nominations, achieving the nickname of "The Great Decliner."[22]

William finally accepted a Democratic nomination to Congress for the First District in California. His old friend James Garfield was nominated for president at the same time by the Republican Party. During the campaign, bitterness over the war years, exacerbated by recent revelations about Garfield's anti–Rosecrans letter of summer 1863, caused a break between the two men. Both William and Garfield were elected, the latter soon dying at the hands of an assassin. In 1882, William was elected to a second and final congressional term. He became chair of the Military Affairs Committee, and thus was in a position to oppose a bill granting Ulysses Grant a retroactive pension. Grant was financially strapped even after an administration in which his friends and colleagues had enriched themselves. William did not think Grant deserved a pension, and declared on the House floor that Grant's military reports in the Civil War were knowingly false and contradicted by William's own true reports. The pension bill passed anyway.[23]

Grant had his revenge. He was working on his memoirs, assisted by a writer/ businessman named Samuel ("Mark Twain") Clemens. The two-volume work came out at the time of Grant's death in 1885, and sold very well. The memoirs were widely read and studied by the general public. Grant avowed "the sincere desire to avoid doing injustice to any one whether on the National or Confederate side," but when it came to William, the account was strictly one-sided. Grant denounced just about everything about William's generalship. Rather than give William credit for his victories at Iuka, Corinth, and Stones River, or acknowledge his (Grant's) own failings in those battles, Grant blamed William for failing to exploit his advantages to inflict greater harm on the Confederates. And Chickamauga was of course William's fault. Grant's memoirs have been an important source for historians of the Civil War, unfortunately for William's reputation.[24]

As it had done with Grant, Congress awarded William a pension. William was willing to share some of what wealth he possessed with veterans and beggars, on one occasion giving a beggar who came to his hotel room several gold coins he had received as a gift from Mexico's latest president, Porfirio Diaz. He received honors from Catholic institutions: an honorary doctorate of laws from Georgetown University, and Notre Dame University's Laetare Medal.[25]

He spent his last years on his ranch, entertaining old colleagues with stories of the war. By 1898, his pilgrimage of life was nearing its end. Sorrowing at the news of the death of a beloved grandson, he died on March 11. Ten years later, his body was moved from its California grave to Arlington National Cemetery.[26]

James Longstreet, William's old troublemaking West Point roommate and the only Confederate general who had actually defeated him, made an unexpected postwar pilgrimage. Longstreet had always possessed an independent streak—the same sort of independent streak which he had manifested in West Point and on the battlefield—and now it manifested again. The war over, Longstreet moved to New Orleans to set up in business. He scandalized diehard former Confederates by joining the Republican party and defending blacks from riotous assaults by whites. He was shunned in the Episcopal church he attended. As a local Jesuit priest later put it, "Pain to the General's heart from the familiar voices opened his eyes to vanity of the world and to supernatural grace." Longstreet joined the Catholic Church on March 7, 1877. He remained a faithful Catholic for the remainder of his life, most of which he spent in Georgia. In 1897, at the age of seventy-six, Longstreet married a fellow–Catholic, Helen Dortch, who was born five months before Longstreet defeated William at Chickamauga. Longstreet died seven years later. His widow worked to vindicate his reputation—trashed by diehards who scapegoated Longstreet for Lee's defeat at Gettysburg—until her death in 1962.[27]

James Healy

At the Second Plenary Council of Baltimore, in 1866, the assembled prelates took up the situation of the newly freed slaves. Rome was interested in the question; Propaganda had endorsed a proposal by Archbishop Spalding of Baltimore that a single official—a prefect apostolic—be made responsible for evangelizing black people in America. The bishops voted against this infringement of their territorial prerogatives, deciding to leave the matter to each bishop, but they decreed that bishops should work at educating and providing services to black and white alike—failure to do so would "merit the strongest reproach." The prelates sent a pastoral letter that called on European religious orders to help in the task of education and evangelization of blacks. In regard to slavery, the council took a position approximating that of Spalding—regretting that slavery had not been abolished gradually, thus giving the slaves time to be educated up to understand freedom's responsibilities. The ex-slaves were not neglected, though. Bishop Verot of Savannah, who as vicar-apostolic of Florida had both attacked abolition and denounced the abuses of slavery (and whose priests had ministered to Union prisoners at the infamous Andersonville camp when Protestant ministers stayed away), launched major initiatives in educating and helping the freed people, appealing to Europe for aid.[28]

When Bishop Fitzpatrick of Boston died and was replaced by Fr. John J. Williams in 1866, Fr. James Healy left his position as chancellor of the Boston diocese to serve in Bishop Williams's old parish—St. James. Fr. Healy worked to build up his new church and retire the debt which it had racked up in those days of rapid expansion of religious institutions. In 1874, the bishopric of Portland, Maine, responsible for the states of Maine and New Hampshire, fell vacant. One candidate, Fr. John Barry, was hampered by reports of his illegitimacy—he was reported to be the offspring of an adulterous relationship. The appointment went to Fr. Healy himself; he began his service as bishop in 1875.[29]

A couple of priests grumbled about having a black bishop over them, though they found there was not much point in complaining. The new bishop took tours of the diocese, performed sacraments and got to know his people, supporters or otherwise. Bishop Healy took an interest in the Irish and French-Canadian workers and the Catholic-evangelized Indians in his diocese. The eloquence he had acquired as a student and as a priest served him in good stead, as he was called on to give homilies in other parts of the U.S. He worked to establish Indian schools for his Native American parishioners as well as several new parishes. Priests were pressured to be bilingual—English/French—and to give their homilies in both languages. Bishop Healy had to contend with revived anti–Catholicism in these predominantly Protestant states.[30]

Although solicited to support black-only ministries in the Church, Bishop Healy declined. His multiculturalism focused on his Irish, Indian, and French flocks, not on the black community. In the intra–Church quarrels of the time, Bishop Healy showed himself a worthy disciple of Fr. Joseph Carrière at St. Sulpice. Like Fr. Carrière, Bishop Healy supported the traditionalist side in Church controversies. When Catholic workers in Maine began showing an interest in a labor organization called the Knights of Labor, Bishop Healy was appalled by the group's secret-society trappings of oaths and initiation rites. None of these disputes kept the bishop from a long term of service. He continued in his ministry until his death in August 1900.[31]

Conclusion

Joining the Catholic Church marked the beginning, not the end, of our four converts' spiritual journeys. They converted in the mid–1840s, just in time to get involved in the great issues of the ensuing twenty years.

Catholic leaders in the U.S. were focused on building up the Church, and defending themselves as a community against nativism was a constant concern for Catholics, sapping energy which a more self-confident, less marginal community could have applied to reform in the broader society. While this was a heroic age for the American Church in terms of institutional development, it was not an age when the Church hierarchy boldly faced up to human rights issues in the broader community. Of most concern to modern Catholics and observers is examining how the American Church faced the question of slavery. Cardinal Timothy Dolan of New York recently deplored the hierarchy's being MIA on slavery. This neutrality did not stop our converts—especially through the pages of the *Catholic Telegraph,* and *Brownson's Quarterly Review*—from devoting attention to broader issues as well as handling the institutional defense and upbuilding of the Church. Foreign and domestic matters were commingled in the public mind, and Catholic publicists realized the impact in America of revolutions in Europe as well as of riots in Cincinnati; of the pope's affairs on the Italian peninsula as well as of the Know-Nothing upsurge in the country—among New Englanders in particular. To Catholics, the issue of American slavery was distorted by all these other events. To this day, Catholics in the United States debate their Church's history regarding slavery. American Catholic leaders tried to squeeze doctrines justifying slavery in certain circumstances into a justification of African slavery as practiced in the United States. It is true that the Church accepted the validity of slavery under certain conditions: self-sale, conviction of crime, capture in a just war, or birth to slave parents. Even now, many countries subject convicted criminals to compulsory labor. The modern Geneva Conventions limit, but do not abolish, the traditional right of belligerent powers to put POWs to work (while allowing the captor powers to keep their captured enemies indefinitely in tropical prisons). Self-sale and inherited slavery are now frowned upon, but were understandable doctrines at the time they were applied. What the popes *never* sanctioned was the enslavement of innocent Africans and their descendants, the system which existed in the antebellum United States. Nor did Catholic doctrine allow for certain key elements of American slavery, such as the separation of families, the disregard of slave marriages, the interstate slave traffic, and the persecution (including enslavement) of free people of African descent. American bishops misapplied their own Church's doctrines when they decided before the war to stay out of issues, such as slavery, which went beyond the requirements of the Church's institutional self-defense. The bishops did not remind slaveholding Catholics of their duties to their slaves, nor did they urge slaveholders to work toward freeing their bondmen. The episcopal stand was not to take a stand. Rome's Congregation of the Propaganda, which screened episcopal candidates and supervised the behavior of the American episcopacy, likewise failed to insist on observance of Catholic doctrine on slavery. And American Catholic intellectuals, despite the good example of Catholic abolitionists in Europe, chose instead to give reasons for leaving American slavery alone. When the war began, Catholics in America and abroad split on whether the war provided the occasion to eliminate what was admittedly a harmful institution.[1]

During this same period in which the United States blundered toward its Civil War, in several Catholic lands in the Americas, slavery was dying a slow death which didn't require bloody conflict. In the Spanish- and Portugese-speaking areas of Latin America, most of the descendants of African slaves had been freed by the actions of their former masters. As for the remaining slaves, the newly independent states of Latin America passed gradual-emancipation laws, putting slavery "on the course of ultimate extinction" as advocated by Abraham Lincoln. Faced with this sort of gradual abolition, many Catholics both in Europe and the United States did not see the need for immediate, military emancipation.[2]

At least mitigating some Catholics' failure to join the antislavery movement is the fact that this movement was top heavy with the sort of Puritan element which was trying to refashion the nation in a Protestant Yankee mold, not only with antislavery but with Prohibition, nativism, and the "reform" of citizens by force. Just as Catholics warned, the activities of these neo–Puritans contributed to the tensions and hostilities which led to a fratricidal Civil War. As Brownson warned, once dominant, the Puritan crusaders did not stop with attacks on slavery but went on to expand dubious crusades, at home and abroad, against perceived evils, crusades which had the effect of enhancing government powers and making them more arbitrary. Even in Europe, zealous Catholics—whether Roman officials, editors, or public intellectuals—differed over whether to support the North's war effort or to distance themselves from a Northern regime embodying those elements of state worship and militant liberalism which had wreaked so much harm in other contexts. The neo–Puritan ascendancy may have been an inevitable reaction to Southern stubbornness and defiance, but Catholics were understandably reluctant to embrace that ascendancy.[3]

The war brought about what Catholic leaders had tried to avoid for their Church—division. Those like Brownson, the Rosecrans brothers, and Fr. Healy supported emancipation at the hands of Union troops—while others opposed emancipation. In the middle were prowar prelates who looked forward to a gradual emancipation while opposing immediate freedom. But as before the war, gradual emancipation was hard to distinguish from a vague, noncommittal *manana*.

As she grew stronger and more self-confident in the United States, the Church showed a greater willingness to stand up and be counted on issues of human rights, not only on matters of race, but on matters like the right to life and justice for the poor.

Chapter Notes

Preface

1. John Slattery, "The Untold Story of Harriet Thompson in the Battle for Racial Equality in Catholicism," *Daily Theology*, January 23, 2014, http://dailytheology.org/2014/01/23/the-untold-story-of-harriet-thompson-in-the-battle-for-racial-equality-in-catholicism-tbt/.
2. For an example of clerics ministering to black people even in difficult circumstances, consider the case of Bishop William Elder of Natchez, Mississippi, who during the chaos of the Civil War travelled extensively through the diocese administering the sacraments to black and white Catholics. Bishop Elder supervised many black conversions, ministered to a slave who had been beaten for refusing to violate the Sabbath, and in general brought the sacraments to the scattered black Catholic population throughout the diocese (including black soldiers of the occupying Union army). William Elder (R. O. Gerow, ed.), *Civil War Diary (1862–1865) of Bishop William Henry Elder Bishop of Natchez* (Most Reverend R. O. Gerow, 1960), 9, 22, 23, 24, 56–57, 59, 62–63, 64, 65, 66, 67, 69, 73, 82, 109.

Chapter 1

1. Rev. W. Corby, *Memoirs of Chaplain Life* (Chicago: LaMonte, O'Donnell, 1893), 181–84.
2. "The Battle of Gettysburg—Thursday July 2, 1863—The Irish Brigade & 5th New Hampshire in the Wheatfield," http://www.brotherswar.com/Gettysburg-2g.htm.
3. "The Irish Brigade," http://www.history.com/topics/american-civil-war/the-irish-brigade; "The Irish Brigade Endures More Hard Fighting at Gettysburg," https://historyengine.richmond.edu/episodes/view/5338; "69th Infantry Regiment Civil War, First Regiment Irish Brigade," New York State Military Museum and Veterans' Research Center, http://dmna.ny.gov/historic/reghist/civil/infantry/69thInf/69thInfMain.htm.
4. See, generally, Iver Bernstein, *The New York City Draft Riots: Their Significance for American Society and Politics in the Age of the Civil War* (New York: Oxford University Press, 1990); Barnet Schecter, *The Devil's Own Work: The Civil War Draft Riots and the Fight to Reconstruct America* (New York: Walker, 2005).
5. Bernstein; Schechter; "Draft Riots Chronology," http://www.nydivided.org/popup/Documents/DraftRiotsTimeline.php et. seq.
6. Brian Steel Wills, *George Henry Thomas: As True as Steel* (Lawrence: University Press of Kansas, 2012), 189–90, 196, 304. See, generally, William M. Lamers, *The Edge of Glory: A Biography of General William S. Rosecrans, U.S.A.* (New York: Harcourt, Brace, 1961).
7. Allan Peskin, *Garfield: A Biography* (Kent, OH: Kent State University Press, 1978), 169, 170; William B. Kurtz, "'The Perfect Model of a Christian Hero': The Faith, Anti-Slaveryism and Postwar Influence of William S. Rosecrans," *U.S. Catholic Historian* 31, no. 1 (Winter 2013), pp. 73–96, at 84.
8. John T. McGreevy, *Catholicism and American Freedom: A History* (New York: W.W. Norton, 2003), 83–84, 86; Kurtz, "Perfect Model," 87–88.
9. Joseph Taggart, *Biographical Sketches of the Eminent American Patriots, Charles Carroll of Carrollton, Roger Brooke Taney, William Starke Rosecrans, John Barry, Philip Henry Sheridan, and a Sketch of the Early History of Maryland* (Kansas City: The Burton Company, 1907), 298–99. See, generally, Lamers.
10. Wills, 194, 414–15.
11. James Gilmore, *Personal Recollections of Abraham Lincoln and the Civil War* (Boston: L.C. Page, 1898), 97, 100.
12. Gilmore, 100–02.
13. Ibid., 104–13, 117–18, 120; Peskin 177.
14. Peskin, 178; Gilmore, 145.
15. Gilmore, 145–46.
16. Frank L. Klement, *The Limits of Dissent: Clement L. Vallandigham and the Civil War* (Lexington: University Press of Kentucky, 1970), 191–94.
17. Ibid., 194, 125; James L. Vallandigham, *A Life of Clement L. Vallandigham* (Baltimore: Turnbull Bros., 1872), 297–98.
18. Klement, *Limits of Dissent*, 125, 194–95, Vallandigham, 298–99.
19. McGreevy, *Catholicism and American Freedom*, 82; Judith Metz, S.C., *Women of Faith and Service: The Sisters of Charity of Cincinnati* (Sisters of Charity of Cincinnati, 2009), 13–14; David J. Endres, "Rectifying the Fatal Contrast: Archbishop John Purcell and the Slavery Controversy among Catholics in Civil War Cincinnati," *Ohio Valley History* 2, no. 2 (Fall 2002), 23–33, 28.
20. "The Church and Slavery," *Catholic Telegraph*, April 8, 1863, online at http://cdm16007.contentdm.oclc.org/cdm/compoundobject/collection/p267401coll36/id/2971/rec/7. The reference to Louisiana was possibly a dig at Judah Benjamin, the Jewish former Louisiana senator and current Confederate secretary of state.
21. Ibid.
22. Ibid.
23. Ibid.
24. Endres, "Fatal Contrast," 29.

25. John H. LaMott, *History of the Archdiocese of Cincinnati, 1821–1921* (New York: Frederick Pustet, 1921), 102, 103, 214, 215; David Spalding, "Martin John Spalding's 'Dissertation on the American Civil War,'" *The Catholic Historical Review* 52, no. 1 (April 1966), 67.

26. David Spalding, 66–85.

27. Ibid., 66; John O'Shea, *The Two Kenricks* (Philadelphia: John J. McVey, 1904); Joseph Brokhage, *Francis Patrick Kenrick's Opinion on Slavery* (Washington, D.C.: Catholic University of America Press, 1955); Leonard B. Riforgiato, "John Timon and the Succesion to the See of Baltimore in 1851," *Vincentian Heritage Journal* 8, no. 1 (April 1, 1987), 41, 42.

28. David Spalding, 66–67; J. J. O'Shea, "Francis Patrick and Peter Richard Kenrick," *Catholic Encyclopedia*, vol. 8, 1910, http://www.newadvent.org/cathen/08618a.htm.

29. David Spalding, 70–73.

30. Ibid., 74–79; Martin John Spalding, *Miscellanea: Comprising Reviews, Lectures and Essays, on Historical, Theological and Miscellaneous Subjects*, 4th ed. (Baltimore: John Murphy, 1895) (original edition 1855), 139.

31. David Spalding, 79–81.

32. Ibid., 82–85.

33. David J. Alvarez, "The Papacy in the Diplomacy of the American Civil War," *Catholic Historical Review*, 69, no. 2 (April 1983), 227–41; David Spalding, 68.

34. Klement, *Limits of Dissent*, 230, 245; Frank L. Klement, "Sound and Fury: Civil War Dissent in the Cincinnati Area," *Cincinnati Historical Society Bulletin* 35 (1977), 99, 100; Frank L. Klement, "Catholics as Copperheads," *The Catholic Historical Review* 80, no. 1 (January 1994), 36–57, 39. For Vallandigham's Protestantism, see Vallandigham, 492–514.

35. Klement, *The Limits of Dissent*, 237; Klement, "Catholics as Copperheads," 40.

36. Thomas H. O'Connor, *Fitzpatrick's Boston, 1846–1866: John Bernard Fitzpatrick, Third Bishop of Boston* (Boston: Northeastern University Press, 1984), 204–05, 209–11; James M. O'Toole, *Passing for White: Race, Religion and the Healy Family* (Amherst: University of Massachusetts Press, 2002), 96; William F. Hanna, "The Boston Draft Riot," *Civil War History* 36, no. 3 (September 1990), 262–273, 262–273; Ian Jesse, "In Search of Excitement: Understanding Boston's Civil War 'Draft Riot,'" *NeoAmericanist* 5, no. 2 (Fall/Winter 2011–2012).

37. James M. O'Toole, 97.

38. O'Connor, *Fitzpatrick's Boston*, 211–13; James M. O'Toole, 1–16; Hanna, 271; Fintan O'Toole, "Green, White and Black: Race and Irish Identity," in *Emerging Irish Identities*, ed. Ronit Lentin (Dublin: Dept. of Sociology, Trinity College Dublin, 2000) 22–23; Timothy L. Wesley, *The Politics of Faith During The Civil War* (Baton Rouge: Louisiana State University Press, 2013), 41.

39. O'Connor, *Fitzpatrick's Boston*, 171–78, 186.

40. Ibid., 195–97, 199.

41. Ibid., 203, 205; James M. O'Toole, 67, 71, 87–88.

42. James M. O'Toole, 90–95; James Hitchcock, "Race, Religion, and Rebellion: Hilary Tucker and the Civil War," *Catholic Historical Review* 80, no. 3 (July 1994), 497–507.

43. Hitchcock, 498, 500, 301, 502.

44. James M. O'Toole, 90–95; Hitchcock, 499, 507.

45. James M. O'Toole, 96; Hitchcock, 498, 504.

46. "Catholics and the Anti-Draft Riots," *Brownson's Quarterly Review*, October 1863, reprinted in Henry Brownson, ed., *The Works of Orestes A. Brownson* XVII (Detroit: Thorndike Nourse, 1885), 412–47.

47. Patrick W. Carey, *Orestes A. Brownson: American Religious Weathervane* (Grand Rapids: William B. Eerdmans, 2004), 275–77.

48. Robert Francis Hueston, *The Catholic Press and Nativism, 1840–1860* (New York: Arno Press 1976), 180, 239–255; Arthur M. Schlesinger, Jr., *Orestes A. Brownson: A Pilgrim's Progress* (Boston: Little, Brown, 1939), 213–15.

49. McGreevy, *Catholicism and American Freedom*, 48; Thomas T. McAvoy, "Orestes A. Brownson and Archbishop John Hughes in 1860," *The Review of Politics* 24, no. 1 (January 1962), 19–47; Carey, *Religious Weathervane*, 254–63; summary of Barnabo correspondence, University of Notre Dame Archives web site, http://archives.nd.edu/calendar/c186001.htm.

50. McAvoy, 46; Carey, *Religious Weathervane*, 261–63. Cullen to Barnabo, February 18, 1861 (summary), "Mount St. Mary's Seminary of the West," *American Ecclesiastical Review* XVIII, no. 6 (June 1898); University of Notre Dame Archives web site; Edward J. Power, *Religion and the Public Schools in 19th Century America: The Contribution of Orestes A. Brownson,* (New York: Paulist Press, 1996), 63.

51. Robert K. Summers, *The Fall and Redemption of Dr. Samuel A. Mudd* (self-published, 2008), 96–98.

52. McGreevy, *Catholicism and American Freedom*, 67.

53. "Catholics and the Anti-Draft Riots," 414–16.

54. Ibid.

Chapter 2

1. Allen Rosenkrans, *The Rosenkrans Family in Europe and America* (Newton: New Jersey Herald Press, 1900), 8, 39, 40–43; Rosenkrantz Tower—Bergen City Museum—http://www.visitbergen.com/en/Product/?TLp=412969.

2. Rosenkrans, 43, 48–49, 86–89, 132–33; Polly Horn, "Major General William Starke Rosecrans," Rosecrans Headquarters, http://www.rosecransheadquarters.org/. Ohio county map, http://www.digital-topo-maps.com/county-map/ohio-county-map.gif.

3. David G. Moore, *William S. Rosecrans and the Union Victory* (Jefferson, NC: McFarland, 2014); 5; Lamers, 10; Rosenkrans, 89, 220, 133; Horn, Part 1; Horn, "The Rosecrans Family," http://www.rosecransheadquarters.org/; "The Rosecrans Family at Homer, Licking County, Ohio," Diocese of Columbus, *Catholic Record Society Bulletin* VII, no. 3 (March 1981), 18; "Sylvester Horton Rosecrans—The 'Other' Rosecrans from Homer," Granville, Ohio, Historical Society, *The Historical Times* XV, no. 3 (Summer 2001), 1; "Jemima Hopkins Rosecrans," http://www.findagrave.com/cgi-bin/fg.cgi?page=gr&GRid=100530126; The name Starke is said to have been inspired by General John Stark, a hero of the American Revolution then in retirement in New Hampshire. On the other hand, Crandall's great-aunt Catharine had married a man named Paul Stark, and there were several Starks near Crandall's farm, some of whom could have been on friendly terms with Crandall. "Framers of Freedom—John Stark," http://www.seacoastnh.com/framers/stark.html; Rosenkrans, 133.

4. Lamers, 12; Moore, 5–6; Rosenkrans, 132–33, 220; Horn, Part 1; "The 'Other' Rosecrans," 2; Charles Wesley, http://www.christianitytoday.com/ch/131christians/poets/charleswesley.html.

5. Lamers, 12; Moore, 5; Horn, Part 1.

6. Mulhane, 50.

7. Lamers, 11; Horn, Part 1.

8. Horn, Part 1.

9. Moore, 6; Horn, Part 1.

10. Maciej Laskowski, "Jane Porter's *Thaddeus of Warsaw* as Evidence of Polish–British Relationships" (Posnan: Instytucie Filologii Angielskiej, 2012), 71; Jane Porter,

Thaddeus of Warsaw (London: Colburn and Bentley, 1831), x, xxi, 189–90, 204, 220–21, 308, 310, 381; Laskowski, 62, 68, 12, 26.

11. Porter, 37, 251, 305, 307, 358, 378.
12. Ibid., 120, 240, 342.
13. Lamers, 12; Moore, 6; Horn, Part 1.
14. Joseph James, "Life at West Point One Hundred Years Ago," *The Mississippi Valley Historical Review* 31, no. 1 (June 1944), 21–40, at 28.
15. Moore, 6; Horn, Part 1; "Poinsett, Joel Roberts," http://sc150civilwar.palmettohistory.org/edu/people/Poinsett-JoelR.htm.
16. James, 30; James L. Morrison, Jr.,*"The Best School in the World": West Point, the Pre–Civil War Years, 1833–1866* (Kent, OH: Kent State University Press, 1986), 160–63.
17. Norman K. Risjork, *Representative Americans: Populists and Progressives* (Lanham, MD: Rowman & Littlefield, 2004), 100; Morrison, 25, 44, 47, 49, 59–60, 70, 94–95; Russell F. Weigley, *Towards an American Army: Military Thought from Washington to Marshall* (New York: Columbia University Press, 1962), 42–47; Eugene C. Tidball, *No Disgrace to My Country: The Life of John C. Tidball* (Kent, OH: Kent State University Press, 2002), 45–46; Jeffry D. Wert, *General James Longstreet: The Confederacy's Most Controversial Soldier* (New York: Touchstone, 1993), 26–27. While William was at West Point, Dennis Mahan's son Alfred was born. Alfred Thayer Mahan became an admiral and a famous advocate of American naval greatness. "Rear Admiral Alfred Thayer Mahan—U.S. History," http://www.history.navy.mil/bios/mahan_alfred.htm.
18. Weigley, 44–52, 77.
19. Moore, 6.
20. Wert, 29–31, James, 27.
21. Lamers, 14; Horn, Part 2.
22. Morrison, 66–69.
23. Louis Garesché, *Biography of Lieut. Col. Julius P. Garesché, Assistant Adjutant General, U.S. Army* (Philadelphia: J. B. Lippincott, 1887 [printed for private circulation]), 19–20, 23, 27, 32, 35, 41–42, 49–50.
24. Ibid., 50–53; William Rosecrans to Major Alex. J. Dallas, January 21, 1880, Box 1, Folder 2, Julius Garesché papers, Special Collections, Georgetown University.
25. Moore, 6–7; Morrison, 88; Horn, Part 2.
26. Moore, 7–8; Horn, Part 2; Taggart, 271.
27. Anne C. Rose, "Some Private Roads to Rome: The Role of Families in American Victorian Conversions to Catholicism," *The Catholic Historical Review* 85, no. 1 (January 1999), 35–57, at 41; Moore, 7.
28. Peskin, 169; Moore, 7.
29. Kurtz, "'Perfect Model,'" 75.
30. John Milner, *The End of Religious Controversy in a Friendly Correspondence Between a Religious Society of Protestants and a Catholic Divine* (Baltimore: Metropolitan Press, 1844), 1; Bernard Ward, "John Milner," *Catholic Encyclopedia*, vol. 10, 1911, http://www.newadvent.org/cathen/10315a.htm; John Gerard and Edward D'Alton, "Roman Catholic Relief Bill," *Catholic Encyclopedia*, vol. 13, 1912, http://www.newadvent.org/cathen/13123a.htm; "Guy Fawkes Day: A Brief History," http://www.history.com/news/guy-fawkes-day-a-brief-history.
31. Milner, 33–34.
32. Ibid., 34.
33. Ibid., 142, 148–53, 157.
34. Ibid., 157–60.
35. Ibid., 40, 160.
36. Ibid., 207–09.
37. Ibid., 305–21. For the overthrow of James II and the "Glorious Revolution," see Michael Barone, *Our First Revolution: The Remarkable British Upheaval That Inspired America's Founding Fathers* (New York: Crown, 2007).
38. Milner, 73–74. The italicized phrase is from Ephesians 4:14 (Douay-Rheims translation).
39. Garesché, 66, 393; Very Rev. George M. Searle, "The Very Reverend George Deshon, C.S.P.," *The Catholic World* LXXVII, no. 467 (February 1904), 569–73; George Searle, "George Deshon," *Catholic Encyclopedia*, vol. 4, 1908, http://www.newadvent.org/cathen/04750b.htm. It was while witnessing a British attack on Fort McHenry that Francis Scott Key composed "The Star Spangled Banner." http://www.nps.gov/fomc/historyculture/the-star-spangled-banner.htm.
40. Garesché, 393.
41. Mulhane, 50; William Fanning, "Baptism," *Catholic Encyclopedia*, vol. 2, 1907, http://www.newadvent.org/cathen/02258b.htm; Kurtz, "Perfect Model," 75.
42. Horn, Part 2.
43. Horn, Part 2; Wert, 37–45; Kurtz, "'Perfect Model,'" 75; John F. Quinn, "'Where Religious Freedom Runs in the Streams': Catholic Expansion in Antebellum Newport," in Kevin Schmiesing, ed., *Catholicism and Historical Narrative: A Critical Engagement with Historical Scholarship* (Lanham, MD: Rowman & Littlefield, 2014), 139–42; Moore, 79; "Congress declares war on Mexico, May 13, 1846," http://www.politico.com/news/stories/0509/22418.html.
44. Rose, 41–42; Kurtz, "'Perfect Model,'" 77.

Chapter 3

1. Rose, 41–42.
2. Ibid., 42.
3. Sylvester's journal, *Catholic Record Society Bulletin* 2, no. 5 (May 1976), 124.
4. Sylvester's journal, *C.R.S.* 2, no. 5 (May 1876), 124–25; M. J. Spalding, *The History of the Protestant Reformation, vol. I (Reformation in Germany and Switzerland)*, 4th ed. (Baltimore: John Murphy, 1865).
5. Sylvester's journal, *Catholic Record Society Bulletin* 2, no. 5 (May 1976), 125.
6. Ibid., 125–26.
7. Ibid., 126.
8. Sylvester's journal, *Catholic Record Society Bulletin* 2, no. 6 (June 1976), 134–35.
9. Ibid., 135.
10. Ibid., 136.
11. Ibid.
12. Ibid.; Ray Allen Billington, *The Protestant Crusade 1800–1860: A Study of the Origins of American Nativism* (New York: Macmillan, 1938), 47; Jenny Franchot, *Roads to Rome: The Antebellum Protestant Encounter with Catholicism* (Berkeley: University of California Press, 1994), 101, 107.
13. Sylvester's journal, *Catholic Record Society Bulletin* 2, no. 6 (June 1976), 137
14. Lamott, 73.
15. Ibid., 172–75; Billington, 121.
16. Lamott, 184–85, 188; Billington, 121; William Jason Wallace, *The Medieval Specter: Catholics, Evangelicals, and the Limits of Political Protestantism: 1835–1860* (Dissertation, University of Virginia, January 2005), 70.
17. Billington, 126; Franchot, 100; Wallace, 70; Lyman Beecher, *A Plea for the West* (Cincinnati: Truman and Smith, 1835).
18. Billington, 85–89; Philip Hamburger, *Separation of Church and State* (Cambridge: Harvard University Press, 2002), 216.

19. Lyman Beecher, 9, 10, 55–56, 58, 61–62, 69, 82, 111, 117, 131.
20. Ibid., 24, 30, 53, 61, 70, 108, 164–65; Wallace, 62.
21. Billington, 126–27; Wallace, 71–73; Kenneth Silverman, *Lightning Man: The Accursed Life of Samuel F. B. Morse* (Boston: Da Capo Press, 2009), 134–39; Franchot, 105–06.
22. Joan D. Hedrick, *Harriet Beecher Stowe: A Life* (New York: Oxford University Press, 1994), 92; Sister Mary Agnes McCann, *The Sisters of Charity in Cincinnati, Ohio* (London: Longman's, Green, 1916), 129.
23. Billington, 65; Lamott, 78; *A Debate on the Roman Catholic Religion Between Alexander Campbell, Bethany, Va., and the Right Reverend John B. Purcell, Bishop of Cincinnati, Held in the Sycamore Street Meetinghouse, Cincinnati, From the 13th to the 21st of January 1837. Taken Down by Reporters, and Revised by the Parties* (Nashville: McQuiddy, 1914).
24. Sylvester's journal, *Catholic Record Society Bulletin* 2, no. 6 (June 1976), 137.
25. Ibid.
26. Owen Chadwick, *A History of the Popes 1830–1914* (Oxford: Clarendon Press, 1998), 54; E. E. Y. Hales, *Pio Nono: A Study of Pius IX and His Role in European Politics and Religion in the Nineteenth Century* (Garden City, NY: Image, 1962), 37–43, 60–70, 75; Mike Rapport, *1848: Year of Revolution* (New York: Basic Books, 2009), 28; Peter R. D'Agostino, *Rome In America: Transnational Catholic Ideology from the Risorgimento to Fascism* (Chapel Hill: University of North Carolina Press, 2004), 24.
27. Committee of Arrangements, *Proceedings of the Public Demonstration of Sympathy With Pope Pius IX, and with Italy, In the City of New York, On Monday, November 29, A.D. 1847* (New York: William van Norden, 1847).
28. *Public Demonstration*; Shaw, 239–40; Dale B. Light, *Rome and the New Republic: Conflict and Community in Philadelphia Catholicism Between the Revolution and the Civil War* (Notre Dame: University of Notre Dame Press, 1996), 312–13.
29. Sylvester's journal, *Catholic Record Society Bulletin* 2, no. 6 (June 1976), 137–38; Sylvester's journal, *Catholic Record Society Bulletin*, 2, no. 5 (May 1849), 123.
30. Hales, 72, 78; Rapport, 39–41, 96–97, 109, 151.
31. Hales, 37–43; Chadwick, 75; Frank J. Coppa, *Pope Pius IX: Crusader in a Secular Age* (Boston: Twayne, 1979), 29–30.
32. Sylvester's journal, *Catholic Record Society Bulletin* 2, no. 5 (May 1976), 123.
33. Sylvester's journal, *Catholic Record Society Bulletin* 2, no. 6 (June 1976), 136, 137.
34. G. F.-H. Berkeley and J. Berkeley, *Italy in the Making: January 1st 1848 to November 16 1848* (Cambridge: Cambridge University Press, 1968), 128, 130, 164–66, 169–71, 176; Hales, 78–81, 93–94; Rapport, 152–53, 162–63; George Macaulay Trevelyan, *Garibaldi's Defense of the Roman Republic* (London: Longman's, Green, 1908), 66–67.
35. Berkeley, 177–91; Chadwick, 76–80; Hales, 81–83; Rapport, 163.
36. George Barany, "A Note On the Prehistory of American Diplomatic Relations with the Papal States," *Catholic Historical Review* 47, no. 4 (January 1962), 508–13; Shaw, 239–40; Leo Francis Stock, *Consular Relations Between the United States and the Papal States* (Washington, D.C.: American Catholic Historical Association, 1945), xxx; Leo Francis Stock, *United States Ministers to the Papal States: Instructions and Despatches 1848–1968* (Washington, D.C.: American Catholic Historical Association, 1933), xxii, xxiii.

37. Sylvester's journal, September 15, 1848, *Catholic Record Society Bulletin* 2, no. 6 (June 1976), 137.
38. Ibid., 138.
39. Berkeley, 395–99, 410–15, 420–23; Chadwick, 80–81; Hales, 87–92; Rapport, 318–21; Trevelyan, *Defense*, 72, 74–75, 80–82.
40. Berkeley, 429–33, 440–41; Chadwick, 81–82; Hales, 96; Rapport, 321–22; Trevelyan, *Defense*, 80–82, 306.
41. Berkeley, 441, 447–49, 452–60; Chadwick, 82–83; Hales, 97–99.
42. Sylvester's journal, *Catholic Record Society Bulletin* 2, no. 6 (June 1976), 138.
43. Berkeley, 460; Hales, 99–101; Rapport, 322–23.
44. Brown to Buchanan, December 12, 1848, in Stock, *Consular Relations*, 129–36; Trevelyan, *Defense*, 82–83.
45. *A Handbook of Rome and Its Environs* (London: John Murray, 1871), 312–13.
46. Sylvester's journal, December 11 and 27, 1849, *Catholic Record Society Bulletin* 2, no. 8 (August 1976), 150.
47. *Rome and Its Environs*, 312–13; Hales, 102–04.
48. Trevelyan, *Defense*, 192.
49. Sylvester's journal, January 9, February 8, March 6, 1849, *C.R.S. Bulletin* 2, no. 8 (August 1976), 150; Hales, 104; Brown to Buchanan, February 1, 1849, in Stock, *Consular Relations*, 152; Rapport, 326–27, 350.
50. Brown to Buchanan, February 12, 1849, Brown to Msgr. Muzzarelli, February 11, 1849, Brown to Sr. Rusconi, February 21, 1849, in Stock, *Consular Relations*, 156–58, 161–62; Hales, 105; Rapport, 350–51; Trevelyan, *Defense*, 91–92.
51. Hales, 120, 123; Rapport, 253, 348, 353; Trevelyan, *Defense*, 95.
52. Hales, 40, 71, 106, 108–10, 113–18, 130–32; Rapport, 18–20, 355; Trevelyan, *Defense*, 93–94, 97–98; Bolton King, *Mazzini* (London: E. P. Dent, 1903), 126–30; R. M. Johnston, 239; Giuseppe Mazzini, *Thoughts upon Democracy in Europe (1846–1847)*, ed. Salvo Mastellone (Firenze: Centro Editoriale Toscano, 2001), 2–3, 8–9, 30–33, 37–42, 65, 79–81.
53. Brown to John M. Clayton, March 27, 1849, in Stock, *Consular Relations*, at 173; Stock, *Court of Pius IX*, 209; Megan Marshall, *Margaret Fuller: A New American Life* (Boston: Mariner Books, 2013), 332.
54. James F. Connelly, *The Visit of Archbishop Gaetano Bedini to the United States of America (June 1853-February 1854)* (Analecta Gregoriana, vol. 109, Rome, 1960), 4.
55. Sylvester's journal, Holy Week 1849, *Catholic Record Society Bulletin* 2, no. 8 (August 1976), 150.
56. Rapport, 325; John Francis Maguire, *Rome: Its Ruler and Its Institutions* (London: Longman, 1857), 119; King, 131.
57. Hales, 124; Rapport, 357; Trevelyan, *Defense*, 105, 109; Sylvester's journal, April 24, 1849, *Catholic Record Society Bulletin* 2, no. 8 (August 1976), 150–51.
58. Sylvester's journal, April 24, 1849, *Catholic Record Society Bulletin* 2, no. 8 (August 1976), 150–51; Trevelyan, *Defense*, 102, 197–98; Bolton King, 131; Brown to Buchanan, February 23, 1849, in Stock, *Consular Relations*, at 160.
59. Megan Marshall, 301, 329, 334, 337, 338, 341, 343, 356–57; D'Agostino, 30–31; Philip F. Gura, *American Transcendentalism: A History* (New York: Hill and Wang, 2007), 235–36.
60. Richard Shaw, 342–45; D'Agostino, 12, 24–31; Howard R. Marraro, "The Religious Problem of the Italian Risorgimento as Seen by Americans," *Church History*, 25, no. 1 (March 1956), 41–62, at 46–47.
61. Sylvester's journal, April 24, 1849, *Catholic Record*

Society Bulletin 2, no. 8, (August 1976), 150–51; Hales, 124; Trevelyan, *Defense*, 111, 116.

62. Sylvester's journal, April 29, 1849, *Catholic Record Society Bulletin* 2, no. 8 (August 1976), 151–52.

63. Sylvester's journal, April 30, 1849, *Catholic Record Society Bulletin* 2, no. 8 (August 1976), 152; Hales, 125; Rapport, 357; Trevelyan, *Defense*, 127–33.

64. Hales, 129; King, 130–31.

65. Rapport, 356; Trevelyan, *Defense*, 61, 102–04; King, 130.

66. Hales, 129; Rapport, 356; Reilly, *Life*, 287–88; Maguire, *Rome*, 120–22; Trevelyan, *Defense*, 75–78, 103, 149–50.

67. Sylvester's journal, May 2, 4, 7, 8, 1849, *Catholic Record Society Bulletin* 2, no. 8 (August 1976), 152–53.

68. Sylvester's journal, May 9, 1849, *Catholic Record Society Bulletin* 2, no. 8 (August 1976), 153–54.

69. Sylvester's journal, May 11, 1849, *Catholic Record Society Bulletin* 2, no. 8 (August 1976), 154.

70. Hales, 125; Trevelyan, *Defense*, 145–46.

71. Hales, 125; Trevelyan, *Defense*, 105.

72. Sylvester's journal, June 4, 1849, *Catholic Record Society Bulletin* 2, no. 8 (August 1976), 154; Hales, 125–26; Trevelyan, *Defense*, 161–187.

73. Trevelyan, *Defense*, 151.

74. Sylvester's journal, June 17, 1849, *Catholic Record Society Bulletin* 2, no. 8 (August 1976), 159–60.

75. Trevelyan, *Defense*, 194–97; Marshall, 347.

76. Sylvester's journal, *Catholic Record Society Bulletin* 2, no. 9 (September 1976), 159; King, 136.

77. Sylvester's journal, June 21, 1849, *Catholic Record Society Bulletin* 2, no. 9 (September 1976), 160.

78. Sylvester's journal, June 24, 1849, *Catholic Record Society Bulletin* 2, no. 9 (September 1976), 161; *Rome and Its Environs*, 312–13.

79. Sylvester's journal, June 25 and 29, 1849, *Catholic Record Society Bulletin* 2, no. 9 (September 1976), 161.

80. Nicholas Brown to Zachary Taylor, June 29, 1849, in Stock, *Consular Relations*, 178.

81. Sylvester's journal, June 30, 1849, *Catholic Record Society Bulletin*, 2, no. 9 (September 1976), 162.

82. Sylvester's journal, July 1, 2 and 3, 1849, in *Catholic Record Society Bulletin* 2, no. 10 (October 1976), 165–66; Hales, 126; Rapport, 252–53; Trevelyan, *Defense*, 217–28; King, 136.

83. Chadwick, 91; Hales, 126; Rapport, 229, 253; Trevelyan, *Defense*, 233, 241–308, 323.

84. Chadwick, 90; Hales, 126; Trevelyan, *Defense*, 234–35; King, 138; Marshall, 349–50.

85. McGreevy, *Catholicism and American Freedom*, 22; Marshall, 335, 348, 374–77, 382; Gura, *Transcendentalism*, 238; Marraro, 47–48.

86. Sylvester's journal, July 10, 1849, *Catholic Record Society Bulletin* 2, no. 10 (October 1976), 166; Chadwick, 91–92; Cass to Clayton, September 4, 1849, and March 9, 1850, in Stock, *United States Ministers*, 55, 65.

87. See, generally, Rapport for the rise and fall of the European revolutionary movements in 1848–49.

88. Sylvester's journal, July 11, July 12, July 13, August 9, August 28, August 29, September 7, 1849, *Catholic Record Society Bulletin* 2, no. 10 (October 1976), 167–68.

89. Cass to Clayton, April 20, 1850 in Stock, *United States Ministers*, 66–67; Chadwick, 92; Coppa, 30, 112–15, 125.

90. Chadwick, 92; Coppa, 114.

91. Sylvester's journal, Palm Sunday, 1851, *Catholic Record Society Bulletin* 2, no. 10 (October 1976), 169; Hales, 111–12, 145–48; Coppa, 115; Lamott, 101–02.

92. Sylvester's journal, May 17 and May 27, 1852, *C.R.S. Bulletin* 2, no. 10 (October 1976), 169–70.

93. Granville, Ohio, Historical Society, "Sylvester Rosecrans, The 'Other' Rosecrans from Homer," *The Historical Times* XV, no. 3 (Summer 2001), 3–4.

Chapter 4

1. James O'Toole, 25.

2. James O'Toole, 25; O'Connor, *Fitzpatrick's Boston*, 14–15, 41–42.

3. James O'Toole, 14; Bernie D. Jones, *Fathers of Conscience: Mixed-Race Inheritance in the Antebellum South* (Athens: University of Georgia Press, 2009), 53–54; *Georgia Telegraph*, November 9, 1847, 3; November 12, 1847, 1.

4. J. Q. Adams, "Misconceptions of Shakespeare, Upon the Stage," in James Henry Hackett, ed., *Notes and Comments Upon Certain Plays and Actors of Shakespeare*, 3d ed. (New York: Carleton, 1864), 224; Elise Lemire, *Miscegenation: Making Race in America* (Philadelphia: University of Pennsylvania Press, 2002), 57, 85, 168n36.

5. Brokhage, 187–99.

6. Lydia Maria Child, *A Romance of the Republic* (Boston: Ticknor and Fields, 1867), 186.

7. Adele Alexander, *Ambiguous Lives: Free Women of Color in Rural Georgia, 1789–1879* (Fayetteville: University of Arkansas Press, 1991), 40–41, 50, 57, 60–61, 85; David J. Grindle, "Manumission: The Weak Link in Georgia's Law of Slavery," *Mercer Law Review* 41 (1990), at 704–05; "An Act to add an additional section to the twelfth division of the Penal Code of this State.—Approved Dec. 24, 1836," in *A Digest of the Statute Laws of the State of Georgia, in Force Prior to the Session of the General Assembly of 1851* (Athens: Christy, Kelsey and Burke, 1851), 103ff; "Act prescribing the mode of manumitting slaves in this State.—Approved Dec. 5, 1801," *Georgia Statutes*, vol. 2, 27; "Act of December 18, 1818, supplementing the foregoing Act," *Georgia Statutes*, at 990; "An Act to repeal all laws and parts of laws which authorize selling into slavery of free persons of color.—Approved Dec. 20, 1824," *Georgia Statutes*, vol. 4, 411, at 996; "An Act to amend the several laws now in force in relation to Slaves and free persons of color.—Approved Dec. 26, 1835," *Georgia Statutes*, at 1008.

8. James O'Toole, 22; Bernie D. Jones, 52–53; Alexander, 91–93; Andrew Fede, *Roadblocks to Freedom: Slavery and Manumission in the United States South* (New Orleans: Quid Pro Books, 2011), 227, 232; Grindle, 705–06. In 1859, the Georgia legislature prohibited masters from freeing their slaves "within or without the State" by "any deed, will, or other instrument." *An Act to prohibit the post mortem manumission of slaves*, Assented to Dec. 14th, 1859.

9. James O'Toole, 23–24.

10. James O'Toole, 26–29; Thomas O'Connor, *Fitzpatrick's Boston*, 50–51.

11. James O'Toole, 38.

12. Articles in the *Georgia Telegraph*, for the indicated dates, are all taken from the *Georgia Telegraph* Archive, http://telegraph.galileo.usg.edu/telegraph/search). The *Georgia Telegraph* was later renamed the *Macon Telegraph*. Michael advertised in the paper's columns, and the editors sometimes included him or Eliza in the list of people whose mail was waiting for them at the post office, so he seems likely to have been a *Telegraph* reader (on the other hand, the postal officials sometimes handed favored newspapers the contract for advertising undelivered letters). Dorothy Ganfield Fowler, *Unmailable: Congress and the Post Office* (Athens: University of Georgia Press, 1977), 22.

13. Joseph Kelly, *America's Longest Siege: Charleston,*

Slavery, and the Slow March Toward Civil War (New York: The Overlook Press, 2013), 206-13; "A Citizen," *Georgia Telegraph,* April 21, 1846.

14. Kelly, 215; Brokhage, 98-99.

15. J. Herman Schauinger, *William Gaston: Carolinian* (Milwaukee: Bruce, 1949), 145-46, 157-62, 159, 165-71, 173-74, 176, 184-85, 188-95, 202-06, 208, 210-11, 224; Robert Emmett Curran, "Rome, the American Church, and Slavery," in Joseph C. Linck and Raymond J. Kupke, eds., *Building the Church in America: Studies in Honor of Monsignor Robert F. Trisco on the Occasion of his Seventieth Birthday* (Washington, D.C.: Catholic University of American Press, 1999), 39-40; William Gaston, "Address Delivered Before the Philanthropic and Dialectic Societies at Chapel Hill—June 20, 1832" (Raleigh: Jos. Gales, 1832).

16. Kelly, 204-06, 217; Caravaglios, *Negro Problem,* 84-85.

17. Kelly, 218, 220; Kenneth J. Zanca, ed., *American Catholics and Slavery: 1789-1866: An Anthology of Primary Documents* (Lanham, MD: University Press of America, 1994), 146-47.

18. "In Supremo Apostolatus," http://www.ewtn.com/library/papaldoc/g16sup.htm; John F. Quinn, "'Three Cheers for the Abolitionist Pope!' American Reactions to Gregory XVI's Condemnation of the Slave Trade, 1840-1860," *The Catholic Historical Review* 90, no. 1 (January 2004), 67-93, at 68-70; Curran, "Rome, the American Church, and Slavery," 30; Cyprian Davis, O.S.B., "Freedom and Slavery: The American Catholic Church Before the Civil War," in Clayton N. Jefford, ed., *Christian Freedom: Essays by the Faculty of the Saint Meinrad School of Theology* (New York: Peter Lang, 1993), 84-85. Jeremy Watt, an undergraduate at Indiana University who wrote a prize-winning senior thesis about *In Supremo,* finds it incongruous that Pope Gregory, who opposed liberalism, should have taken such a "liberal" stance against slavery, and concludes that the pope opposed the slave trade as part of an agenda to oppose the Industrial Revolution. Jeremy Watt, "The Incongruous Bull: *In Supremo Apostolatus,*" 2006. Prize announcement at http://www.indiana.edu/~libadmin/annual/2006/04a.html.

19. Quinn, "Three Cheers," 67-93, at 74-80; Curran, 30-32.

20. Brokhage, 130; Quinn, "Three Cheers," 68, 78; John England, *Letters of the Late Bishop England to the Hon. John Forsyth, on the Subject of Domestic Slavery,* ed. George Read (Baltimore: John Murphy, 1844), 21.

21. John F. Quinn, "Three Cheers," 74-80; Cyprian Davis, "Freedom and Slavery," 89-90; *Letters of the Late Bishop England,* 39-40; Kelly, 220, 253.

22. Kelly, 209-10; John Francis Maxwell, *The History of Catholic Teaching Concerning the Moral Legitimacy of Slavery* (Chichester: Barry Rose, 1975), 101-07; Quinn, "Three Cheers," 72.

23. Kelly, 251.

24. Quinn, "Three Cheers," 72-74, 80-81; Michael Ignatiev, *How the Irish Became White* (New York: Routledge Classics, 2008), 9-13.

25. James O'Toole, 36.

26. Quinn, "Three Cheers," 82; Ignatiev, 15-16; Richard Shaw, *Dagger John: The Unquiet Life and Times of Archbishop John Hughes of New York* (New York: Paulist Press, 1977), 22-23, 75-76, 109-10, 137; Thomas Fleming, *A Disease in the Public Mind: A New Understanding of Why We Fought the Civil War* (New York: Da Capo Press, 2013), 67-70, 73-77. The island of Santo Domingo, before the slave uprising, was divided into a French-controlled area in the west and a Spanish-controlled area in the east. Today, these areas have become respectively the republics of Haiti and the Dominican Republic. For Catholics in the South, see generally, Andrew H. M. Stern, *Southern Crucifix, Southern Cross: Catholic-Protestant Relations in the Old South* (Tuscaloosa: University of Alabama Press, 2012).

27. Quinn, "Three Cheers," 83-84; Ignatiev, 18-20, 29-32, 34.

28. Quinn, "Three Cheers," 84-85; Ignatiev, 35-36; Brokhage, 130; Steven Deyle, *Carry Me Back: The Domestic Slave Trade In American Life* (New York: Oxford University Press, 2005), 17, 20, 36, 72-73, 114, 145, 149-50, 177, 178, 184-87, 191, 193-95. For the campaign by the anti-slavery movement against the internal trade, see David L. Lightner, *Slavery and the Commerce Power: How the Struggle Against the Interstate Slave Trade Led to the Civil War* (New Haven: Yale University Press, 2006).

29. Quinn, "Three Cheers," 81-82, 85-86; Arthur Jones, *Pierre Toussaint: A Biography* (New York: Doubleday, 2003), 257-58, 297; "Venerable Immigrant," *America,* February 9, 2004.

30. Kelly, 208-09; "Introductory Notice" by Read, in *Letters of the Late Bishop England;* John F. Quinn, "Three Cheers," 87, 92-93; Ignatiev, 37-38, 72, 87.

31. Ignatiev, 37.

32. Ibid., 88-89, 114-15.

33. *Georgia Telegraph,* March 21, 1848, 3.

34. Shaw, 195-97; Hamburger, *Separation of Church and State,* 217.

35. Shaw, 195. For Moscow, see, generally, Alexander Mikaberidze, *The Burning of Moscow: Napoleon's Trial By Fire 1812* (Barnsley, South Yorkshire: Pen and Sword, 2014).

36. Brokhage, 1-3, 43.

37. Maxwell, 15, 17, 32-34, 39-41, 44-46, 79, 86; Brokhage, 54-55, 115; Maria Genoino Caravaglios, *The American Catholic Church and the Negro Problem in the XVIII-XIX Centuries* (Charleston: Caravaglios, 1974), 43-47.

38. Brokhage, 70-71, 86-87, 172-73, 184-87, 199-203.

39. Ibid., 64-65, 205.

40. Ibid., 140-41, 150, 235-43.

41. Ibid., 122-24, 162.

42. Kate Mason Rowland, *The Life of Charles Carroll of Carrolton 1737-1832,* vol. II (New York: G. P. Putnam's Sons, 1898), 9, 22, 24, 33, 178-80.

43. McDermott, 243-44; Zanca, *American Catholics and Slavery,* 87-88.

44. Rowland, 143-44; Scott McDermott, *Charles Carroll of Carrolton: Faithful Revolutionary* (New York: Scepter Pubs, 2001), 210-11.

45. Curran, "Rome, the American Church, and Slavery," 33-39; R. Emmett Curran, S. J., "'Splendid Poverty: Jesuit Slaveholding in Maryland," in Randall M. Miller and Jon L. Wakelyn, eds., *Catholics in the Old South: Essays on Church and Culture* (Macon: Mercer University Press, 1983), 125-146.

46. W.P. Strickland, *The Life of Jacob Gruber* (New York: Carlton and Porter, 1860), 145, 155-57, 166-68, 248. For a discussion of Taney's views, see, generally, Josephine C. Taheny, *Chief Justice Roger Brooke Taney's Attitude Toward Slavery* (Loyola University, M.A. Thesis, February 1942).

47. Stafford Poole and Douglas J. Slawson, *Church and Slave in Perry County, Missouri, 1818-1865* (Lewiston, NY: Edwin Mellen Press, 1986), 50-52, 61, 74, 80-85, 89, 90-91, 113-15, 129-30, 164-65, 175-76, 193; Deyle, 52-53; Brokhage, 75; Caravaglios, *Negro Problem,* 92-93; Curran, "Splendid Poverty," 132.

48. James O'Toole, 26-28; John L. Myers, *Henry Wilson and the Coming of the Civil War* (Lanham, MD: University Press of America, 2005), 255.

49. James O'Toole, 27, 31.

50. Ibid., 35-36.

51. Ibid., 30.
52. Ibid., 63–64.
53. Ibid., 38–39; Thomas O'Connor, *Fitzpatrick's Boston*, 51–52.
54. Fede, 224–25, 229–31, 321–22; Adele Alexander, 40–41, Law of 1818, in *Georgia Statutes*. Georgia statutes prohibited a master from emancipating his slaves without specific legislative approval, but despite the fairly rigorous terms of this anti-emancipation law, the courts had carved out a loophole. Masters could free their slaves by sending them to live in a state or country where slavery was prohibited, as Michael had done with most of his children by sending them to Northern states. The Georgia Supreme Court repeatedly, if relectantly, allowed this loophole. There was a particular problem, grumbled Chief Justice Lumpkin, in sending freed blacks to "our northwestern frontier," where "in case of civil war, they would become an element of strength to the enemy, as well as of annoyance to ourselves." Lumpkin was partially prophetic, because James (albeit in the Northeast rather than the Northwest) would later help out the Northern cause in the Civil War. James M. O'Toole, biographer of James and the Healy family, claims that, in the eyes of Georgia law, the Healy children were seen as slaves. If this were so, then for Michael to bring back his sons would lead to very bad consequences—male slaves who had lived in free states were not allowed to return, and not only would the master be punished for bringing his slaves back, but the slaves themselves would be seized and sold to new owners. As an incentive, informers who uncovered such goings-on would be entitled to half the money earned from the slave sale. James O'Toole, 49. However, the legal explanation given in the text is probably the better one.
55. Alexander, 62–63, 72–73, 81–83, 88–91. An example of a prosecution of a person of color protected by a white patron is *The State vs. Lavinia and Wilkes*, 25 Ga. 311 (1858). This case happened after Michael Healy's death, but the trial judge was named Hardeman, probably the same Robert Hardeman who served as Michael's executor. Judge Hardeman, upheld by the state high court, acquitted the defendants.
56. James O'Toole, 38–39.
57. Ibid., 40.
58. Ibid.; John Francis Maguire, *Father Mathew: A Biography* (London: Burns and Oates, 1882), 76–84; John F. Quinn, "Father Mathew's Disciples: American Catholic Support for Temperance, 1840–1920," *Church History* 65, no. 4 (December 1996), 624–640, 625–27. Not all Catholics were enthusiastic about Fr. Mathew—especially given his collaboration with Protestants. Also, Garrison's abolitionists were not particularly happy about the priest's newfound silence on slavery.
59. James O'Toole, 40; Anthony J. Kuzniewski, S.J. *Thy Honored Name: A History of the College of the Holy Cross, 1843–1994* (Washington, D.C.: Catholic University of America Press, 1999), 69.
60. Ibid., 69–70, 118–19.
61. James O'Toole, 36, 40.
62. Brokhage, 187–99.
63. http://friendsofcems.org/Jones/default1.htm?SQL HancockSelect2.asp?key=2040000001&CemName=Heal y+Cemetery&,2.

Chapter 5

1. Kevin Phillips, *The Cousins' Wars: Religion, Politics, & the Triumph of Anglo-America* (New York: Basic Books, 1999), 410–11; Steven Mintz, *Moralists and Modernizers: America's Pre-Civil War Reformers* (Baltimore: Johns Hopkins University Press, 1995), 30; Carey, *Religious Weathervane*, 4–5.
2. Carey, 1–4; Arthur M. Schlesinger, *Orestes A. Brownson: A Pilgrim's Progress* (Boston: Little, Brown, 1939), 5; Orestes Brownson, *Charles Elwood: Or The Infidel Converted* (Boston: Little, Brown, 1840), 89. In the preface to this novel, Brownson wrote, "I am willing the public should take the book as an account which I have thought proper to give of my own former unbelief and present belief." Ibid., vi-vii.
3. Orestes Brownson, *The Spirit-Rapper: An Autobiography* (Boston: Little, Brown, 1854), 264–67.
4. Brownson, *Charles Elwood*, 31; Carey, *Religious Weathervane*, 5–11; Reuben Smith, "Brownson's Development of Himself" (letter to the editor), *Princeton Review* 30 (April 1858), 390–92; Nathaniel Bartlett Sylvester, *History of Saratoga County, New York* (Philadelphia: Everts and Ensign, 1878), 236, 254.
5. Carey, *Religious Weathervane*, 8–9, 11–12; Schlesinger, *Pilgrim's Progress*, 12; Mintz, 23.
6. Carey, *Religious Weathervane*, 12, 14; Gura, *Transcendentalism*, 72.
7. Carey, *Religious Weathervane*, 13, 15 19–20; Schlesinger, *Pilgrim's Progress*, 15.
8. Carey, *Religious Weathervane*, 22–25; Mintz, 144, 151; Gura, *Transcendentalism*, 73; Brownson, *The Convert*, 95. In *The Spirit-Rapper*, the narrator works closely with a female reformer named Priscilla, though apparently without having any sexual relationship. Nonetheless, Priscilla's husband misunderstands the situation and fatally stabs the narrator. Brownson, *The Spirit-Rapper*, 255–56.
9. Brownson, *The Convert*, 99–101; "The Higher Law," *Brownson's Quarterly Review*, July 1851, in Brownson, *Works*, vol. XVII, 13.
10. Carey, *Religious Weathervane*, 26–29.
11. T. Gregory Garvey, *Creating the Culture of Reform in Antebellum America* (Athens: University of Georgia Press, 2006), 54; Brownson, *Charles Elwood*, 41–42; Carey, *Religious Weathervane*, 32–34; Schlesinger, *Pilgrim's Progress*, 22–23.
12. Carey, *Religious Weathervane*, 34–35; Schlesinger, *Pilgrim's Progress*, 50–51; Mintz, 21–23; Garvey, 51; Gura, 32–38.
13. Carey, *Religious Weathervane*, 48–59; *Pilgrim's Progress*, 26–28, 33, 64.
14. Carey, *Religious Weathervane*, 71; Chadwick, 15–17, 25–28; Antoine Dégert, "Félicité Robert de Lamennais," *Catholic Encyclopedia*, vol. 8, 1910, http://www.newadvent.org/cathen/08762a.htm; Gura, *Transcendantalism*, 74, 76–79, 95.
15. Schlesinger, *Pilgrim's Progress*, 44; Garvey, 68; Mintz, 22, 58; Gura, *Transcendantalism*, 75, 86–89.
16. Gura, *Transcendentalism*, 74.
17. Harriet Martineau, *Society in America*, vol. II (New York: Saunders and Otley, 1837), 357–58.
18. Rose, 46.
19. Carey, *Religious Weathervane*, 80–81; Schlesinger, *Pilgrim's Progress*, 71, 85, 72; Garvey, 20–21; Gura, *Transcendentalism*, 120, 137.
20. Carey, *Religious Weathervane*, 62, 68–69; Schlesinger, *Pilgrim's Progress*, 134–36; Gura, *Transcendentalism*, 9, 69–71; 116–19, 141–49.
21. Brownson, *Spirit-Rapper*, 85, 91; William McFeely, *Frederick Douglass* (New York: W. W. Norton, 1991), 71; Mintz, 140–41.
22. Schlesinger, *Pilgrim's Progress*, 124–31; Gura, *Transcendentalism*, 65–67, 200; Beverly Wilson Palmer, ed., *The*

Selected Letters of Charles Sumner, vol. 1 (Boston: Northeastern University Press, 1990), 77-78.

23. Carey, *Religious Weathervane*, 59; Schlesinger, *Pilgrim's Progress*, 73; Gura, *Transcendentalism*, 120.

24. Calhoun to George Bancroft, April 14, 1838, Calhoun to James Edward Colhoun, October 3, 1838, in Clyde N. Wilson, ed., *The Papers of John C. Calhoun*, vol. XIV (Columbia: University of South Carolina Press, 1981), 262, 434; Clyde N. Wilson, ed., *The Papers of John C. Calhoun*, vol. XIV (Columbia: University of South Carolina Press, 1981) 4, 26; Eric H. Walther. *The Fire-Eaters* (Baton Rouge: Louisiana State University Press, 1992), 18-22; "Was John C. Calhoun a Unitarian?" http://www.famoususus.com/bios/john_calhoun.htm. Calhoun explained his doctrine of nullification and the concurrent majority in John C. Calhoun, *A Disquisition on Government and a Discourse on the Constitution and Government of the United States* (Columbia, SC: A. S. Johnston, 1851).

25. Schlesinger, *Pilgrim's Progress*, 76-78, 113, 121; Calhoun to Brownson, December 30, 1939 (with accompanying note), Brownson to Calhoun, October 13, 1841, in Calhoun *Papers*, vol. XV (1983), 24-26, 790-92.

26. Carey, *Religious Weathervane*, 84-85; Schlesinger, *Pilgrim's Progress*, 79, 90.

27. Mintz, 141; Ignatiev, 124-26. The situation may have been more complicated than the abolitionists' critics indicated. The abolitionist William Lloyd Garrison, while supporting the Northern capitalist system, published criticism of the exploitation of some of the Northern workers, in one case calling for a ten-hour day. Henry Mayer, *All on Fire: William Lloyd Garrison and the Abolition of Slavery* (New York: W. W. Norton, 1998), 117.

28. Carey, *Religious Weathervane*, 90-92; Gura, *Transcendentalism*, 137-39.

29. Schlesinger, *Pilgrim's Progress*, 106; "Mr. Calhoun and the Baltimore Convention," *Brownson's Quarterly Review*, vol. XV (April 1844), 473-483.

30. Robert D. Sampson, *John L. O'Sullivan and His Times* (Kent, OH: Kent State University Press, 2003), 115; Schlesinger, *Pilgrim's Progress*, 110-11; Marshall, 145-57.

31. Sampson, 114, 113-15, 192-95, 202.

32. Ibid; Carey, *Religious Weathervane*, 125-26; Schlesinger, *Pilgrim's Progress*, 155-60.

33. Carey, *Religious Weathervane*, 100-12; Schlesinger, *Pilgrim's Progress*, 138-49, 173, 175-76; Garvey, 161-63; Gura, *Transcendentalism*, xiv, 14-17, 90-96, 116, 120-22, 214-15.

34. David J. O'Brien, *Isaac Hecker: An American Catholic* (New York: Paulist Press, 1992), 18-19, 20-23, 28-30, 49, 51.

35. Carey, *Religious Weathervane*, 138-39; O'Brien, *Hecker*, 32-34, 49, 53, 75.

36. O'Brien, *Hecker*, 54, 55, 60-61, 64.

37. Dixon H. Lewis to Richard K. Crallé, June 10, 1842, in Calhoun *Papers*, vol. XVI (1985), 274-78; "The Life and Speeches of John C. Calhoun," *Brownson's Quarterly Review*, vol. XV (January 1844), 451-72.

38. Calhoun to "the Rev. Orestes A. Brownson," February 1, 1844, Brownson to Calhoun, February 5, 1844, in Clyde N. Wilson, ed., *The Papers of John C. Calhoun*, vol. XVII (Columbia: University of South Carolina Press, 1987); 743-44; "Mr. Calhoun and the Baltimore Convention," *Brownson's Quarterly Review*, April 1844. "'98" was an allusion to the Virginia and Kentucky Resolutions of that year, opposing the federal Alien and Sedition Acts as unconstitutional. States'-rights supporters cited these resolutions as precedents for states protesting against federal usurpation.

39. O'Connor, *Fitzpatrick's Boston*, 43-47.

40. Carey, *Religious Weathervane*, 141-42; Schlesinger, *Pilgrim's Progress*, 175-76, 181.

41. "Sparks on Episcopacy," *Brownson's Quarterly Review*, July 1844.

42. Carey, *Religious Weathervane*, 142; Rose, 43-44; Schlesinger, *Pilgrim's Progress*, 182, 185-86. Orestes reconsidered the name he had given his third son, William Ellery Channing Brownson, now that the Unitarian leader was no longer a suitable role model. William's new name became William Ignatius, probably after Ignatius Loyola the founder of the Jesuits. The sons were sent to various Catholic schools, with John graduating from Holy Cross with honors inferior to those of James Augustine Healy. Rose, 44-45.

43. Franchot, 302-03, 306-07, 319-20, 321; Gura, *Transcendentalism*, 154-60, 164-68, 264.

44. Carey, *Religious Weathervane*, 157-64; Schlesinger, *Pilgrim's Progress*, 189, 194-95, 197; Gura, *Transcendentalism*, 198.

45. Ravitch, 22-23, 30-31, 34-35, 37, 40-41, 44, 58-59, 61, 67-70, 74-76, 79-84; Billington, 151-53.

46. Shaw, 195-98; Hueston, 89; Appollinaris W. Baumgartner, *Catholic Journalism: A Study of Its Development in the United States, 1789-1930* (New York: Columbia University Press, 1931), 14; Diane Ravitch, *The Great School Wars: A History of the New York City Public Schools* (New York: Basic Books, 1988), 36.

47. Clarke, *Lives*, 54-55; Sister Mary Augustine Kwitchen, *James Alphonsus McMaster: A Study in American Thought* (Washington, D.C.: Catholic University of America Press, 1949), 53-54; Walter Elliott, *The Life of Father Hecker* (New York: Columbus Press, 1891), viii, 198; John Murray, "Start of the Redemptorists in the United States," *Redemptorist North American Historical Bulletin*, Eighteenth Issue, December 2002, 2-3; Duanesburg Historical Society, *Duanesburg and Princeton (NY)* (Charleston: Arcadia, 2005), 24; "The autobiography of Rev. Gilbert M'Master D.D.," Clements Library, University of Michigan, Ann Arbor, 41-42, 46; George P. Hutchinson, *The History Behind the Reformed Presbyterian Church, Evangelical Synod* (Cherry Hill, NJ: Mack, 1974), 1-29; W. Melancthon Glasgow, *History of the Reformed Presbyterian Church in America* (Baltimore: Hill and Harvey, 1888). For the origins of the Covenanters, see Raymond Campbell Paterson, *A Land Afflicted: Scotland and the Covenanter Wars 1638-1690* (Edinburgh: John Donald, 1998).

48. Kwitchen, 83-85.

49. Ibid., 85-86.

50. Schlesinger, *Pilgrim's Progress*, 209; Blied, 12; Robert Morgan, *Lions of the West: Heroes and Villains of the Westward Expansion* (Chapel Hill: Algonquin, 2012), 254-55, 276, 294, 297, 300; William B. Kurtz, "Let us Hear no More 'Nativism': The Catholic Press in the Mexican and Civil Wars," *Civil War History* 60, no. 1, March 2014, 6-31, at 13-14, 17. For a discussion of the San Patricio Batallion, see Michael Hogan, *The Irish Soldiers of Mexico* (Intercambio Press, 2011).

51. Blied, 12-13; Gura, *Transcendentalism*, 208-09.

52. "Hon. J.C. Calhoun's Account for Salary," circa March 10, 1845, Calhoun to Dixon H. Lewis, May 16, 1845, in Clyde N. Wilson, ed., *The Papers of John C. Calhoun*, vol. XXI (Columbia: University of South Carolina Press 1993), 417, 556-58; bill for *Brownson's Quarterly Review*, December 11, 1845, in Calhoun *Papers*, vol. XXII (1995); Clyde N. Wilson, ed., *The Papers of John C. Calhoun*, vol. XXI (Columbia: University of South Carolina Press, 1993), 508; David M. Potter, *The Impending Crisis*, ed. Don G. Fehrenbacker (New York: Harper and Row, 1976), 1-6, 76; William W. Freehling. *The Road to Disunion: Volume I—secessionists at bay 1776-1854* (New York: Oxford University Press, 1990), 459.

53. Potter, 103.
54. Potter, 102; Kenneth M. Stampp, ed., *The Causes of the Civil War*, 3d rev. ed. (New York: Touchstone, 1991), 111–16, 137–39; Fehrenbacher, 161–163, 167, 171, 174; Scott J. Basinger, "Regulating Slavery: Deck-Stacking and Credible Commitment in the Fugitive Slave Act of 1850," *The Journal of Law, Economics & Organization* 19, no. 2, 307–342, 321–324; Freehling, 501, 503, 508–09, 536; Alvin M. Josephy, Jr., *The American Heritage History of the Congress of the United States* (New York: American Heritage, 1975), 207; Stanley W. Campbell, *The Slave Catchers: Enforcement of the Fugitive Slave Law, 1850–1860* (Chapel Hill: University of North Carolina Press, 1970), 18–25; Gary Lee Collison. *Shadrach Minkins: From Fugitive Slave to Citizen* (Cambridge: Harvard University Press, 1997), 75; Nat Brandt, *The Town that Started the Civil War* (New York: Dell, 1991), 17.
55. "The Higher Law," in *Brownson's Quarterly Review*, July 1851, in Brownson, *Works*, vol. XVII, 1–17.
56. Stanley W. Campbell, *The Slave Catchers: Enforcement of the Fugitive Slave Act, 1850–1860* (Chapel Hill: University of North Carolina Press, 1970), 117–21; "The Fugitive Slave Law," in *Brownson's Quarterly Review*, July 1851, in Brownson, *Works*, vol. XVII, 17–18.
57. "The Fugitive Slave Law," 17–20, 28, 33, 35.
58. Ibid., 22–23, 25–27.
59. Mike Rapport, *1848: Year of Revolution* (New York: Basic Books, 2008), 30, 40–41, 66–67, 142–47, 180–86, 302–07, 365–80; Gura, *Transcendentalism*, 208.
60. Andre M. Fleche, *The Revolution of 1861: The American Civil War in the Age of Nationalist Conflict* (Chapel Hill: University of North Carolina Press, 2012), 19–22; McGreevy, *Catholicism and American Freedom*, 45; Henry Brownson, *Orestes A. Brownson's Middle Life: From 1845 to 1855* (Detroit: H. F. Brownson, 1899), 418–24; Schlesinger, *Pilgrim's Progress*, 207.
61. Orestes Brownson, *The Convert: Or, Leaves from My Experience* (New York: Edward Dunigan and Brother [James B. Kirker], 1857), dedication page, 70–71.

Chapter 6

1. James T. O'Toole, 49–50.
2. James T. O'Toole, 50.
3. Anne Lohrli, "The Madiai: A Forgotten Chapter in Church History," *Victorian Studies*, Autumn 1989, 30–38. The case was publicized in Francesco Madiai and Rosa Madiai, *Letters of the Madiai, and Visits to their Prisons*, ed. "the Misses Senhouse" (Philadelphia: Presbyterian Board of Publication, 1853); American and Foreign Christian Union, *The Story of the Madiai* (New York: The Society, 1853); Pierce Connelly, *A Letter to the Rt. Hon. The Hon. The Earl of Aberdeen, First Lord of the Treasury* (London, T. Hatchard, 1853); Protestant Alliance, *The Madiai Case* (London: Protestant Alliance, 1853).
4. Billington, 267–68; John Hughes, "The Madiai Affair," in *The Metropolitan*, vol. I (Baltimore: John Murphy, 1853), 103–08, at 105.
5. Billington, 268–69.
6. "The Madiai Affair," at 103–06.
7. Ibid., 106–108.
8. Ibid., 104.
9. Lohrli, 39–50.
10. Clarke, 251; Lamott, 214
11. Connelly, 3–7.
12. Billington, 301–302.
13. Connelly, 33–35; Billington, 301–02, 303–04.
14. Connelly, 38–39; Billington, 302.
15. Connelly, 39–40.
16. Ibid., 33–34, 40.
17. Ibid., 21–33.
18. Fr. Rosecrans to Brownson, October 25, 1853, UNDA.
19. Connelly, 9.
20. Ibid., 98–100.
21. Ibid., 100–03; Billington, 302–03; *Diocese of Columbus: The History of Fifty Years, 1868–1918*, 1918, 26–27.
22. Connelly, 103–04; Billington, 302–03.
23. Connelly, 143–144.
24. Ibid., 200–27.

Chapter 7

1. Craig Wesley Pilant, *Inward promptings: Orestes Augustus Brownson, outsidership and Roman Catholicism in the United States* (Dissertation, Fordham University, 1996), 187.
2. Billington, 304–13; Hamburger, *Separation of Church and State*, 216–17; V. O. Chan, "The Riots of 1856 in British Guiana," *Caribbean Quarterly* 16, no. 1 (March 1970), 39–50.
3. "Louis Veuillot," in Reuben Parsons, *Studies in Church History* VI, Cent. XIX (Part II) (New York: Fr. Pustet, 1900), 427–440; Chadwick, 110–111.
4. Chadwick, 170–71; Montalembert to Brownson, November 12, 1852; Montalembert to Brownson, December 28, 1854, Notre Dame Calendar; "Charles Le Comte de Montalembert," http://www.acton.org/pub/religion-liberty/volume-3-number-4/charles-le-comte-de-montalembert.
5. "Ethics of Controversy," BQR, April 1853; "Charles Le Comte de Montalembert," http://www.acton.org/pub/religion-liberty/volume-3-number-4/charles-le-comte-de-montalembert.
6. Brownson to McMaster, July 9/July 12, 1853, UNDA.
7. Hecker to Brownson, August 23, 1853, UNDA.
8. Carey, *Religious Weathervane*, 222, 256, 270; "Schools and Education," BQR, July 1854, *Works*, vol. X, 567–70; *Spirit-Rapper*, 359.
9. *Spirit-Rapper*, 174.
10. "Temporal and Spiritual," BQR January 1854, *Works*, vol. XI, 6, 9; Thomas Keneally, *The Great Shame and the Triumph of the Irish in the English-Speaking World* (New York: Anchor Books, 2000), 247–52; Joseph Jude Rzeppa, *Thomas Francis Meagher and John Mitchell: Two Irishmen, Two Irish-Americans, One American* (MA Thesis, Texas Christian University, 2007), 40–52.
11. Lyon, 273–78; Rzeppa, 53–54.
12. "Temporal and Spiritual," *Works*, vol. XI; Michael Andrews, *American-Papal Relations from 1848 to 1867* (Dissertation, St. John's University, 2007), 145.
13. Carey, *Religious Weathervane*, 193.
14. Garrett Mattingly, *The Armada* (Boston: Houghton Mifflin, 1962), 59, 61, 345; "The Gunpowder Plot," http://www.newadvent.org/cathen/07081b.htm.
15. Andrews, *American-Papal Relations*, 138–39; "Pio Nono, the Washington Monument and the Purloined Block of Marble," *The American Catholic*, January 25, 2010, http://the-american-catholic.com/2010/01/25/pio-nono-the-washington-monument-and-the-purloined-block-of-marble/.
16. Billington, 304–13; Andrews, *American-Papal Relations*, 120; Donald A. Kopp, "Do school boards have academic freedom? Yes, they still do!" *School Law Advisory*, Spring 1998, at 1–2; "St. Mary's Church Sacked—1854," http://bit.ly/1cGBi0D.

17. Andrews, *American-Papal Relations*, 121; Wallace, 34, 48, 52; Phillips, 368, 398.

18. Wallace, 49; Fleming, 89, 93, 102–03. For discussion of the aggressive new form of Puritan nationalism, see Richard Franklin Bensel, *Yankee Leviathan: The Origins of Central State Authority, 1859–1877* (Cambridge: Camridge University Press, 1990); Susan Mary Grant, *North Over South: Northern Nationalism and American Identity in the Antebellum Era* (Lawrence: University Press of Kansas, 2000); David Goldfield, *America Aflame: How the Civil War Created a Nation* (New York: Bloomsbury Press, 2011). William Lloyd Garrison, a sincere and passionate abolitionist from Massachusetts, started his career as a Federalist Party editor. Henry Mayer, *All on Fire: William Lloyd Garrison and the Abolition of Slavery* (New York: W. W. Norton, 1998).

19. William Jason Wallace, *The Medieval Specter: Catholics, Evangelicals, and the Limits of Political Protestantism: 1835–1860* (Dissertation, University of Virginia, January 2005), 68, 91; Hamburger, *Separation of Church and State*, 193–95, 201–03, 211, 23–33.

20. Wallace, 32. For the origins of the Protestant-led prohibition movement, see Ken Burns, *Prohibition* (DVD), released October 4, 2011.

21. *Spirit-Rapper*, 182.

22. Dolan, 15; Hueston, 138; Rzeppa, 52.

23. Dolan, 36–39.

24. Ibid.

25. "Schools and Education," 573–77.

26. Ibid., 577–81, 584.

27. Ibid., 583; O'Connor, *Fitzpatrick's Boston*, 100–101.

28. Hueston, 248.

29. Ibid., 241–42.

30. Ibid., 244, 264.

31. Ibid., 254; Brownson to Hughes, July 3, 1854, UNDA, Hughes to Brownson, July 7, 1854, UNDA. For more Catholic criticism of Brownson, see Rt. Rev. Doctor O'Connor, Bishop of Pittsburg, *Celts and Saxons, Nativism and Naturalization: A Complete Refutation of the Nativism of Dr. Orestes A. Brownson, In the Catholic Press of the United States. Also, a Refutation of Mr. Brownson's Extravagant Theory of the (so called) Temporal Powers of the Popes* (Boston: Thomas Sweeney, 1854).

32. John Hughes, *Complete Works*, vol. II, ed. Lawrence Kehoe (New York: The Catholic Publication House, 1864), 688, 691.

33. David S. Reynolds, *Mightier Than the Sword: Uncle Tom's Cabin and the Battle for America* (New York: W. W. Norton, 2011), 32; Andrews, *American-Papal Relations*, 98; Wallace, 49; Tom Heneghan, "Secrets Behind the Forbidden Books," *America*, February 7, 2005, http://americamagazine.org/issue/517/article/secrets-behindthe-forbidden-books; "Vatican 'Opens' Forbidden Books, *Hindustan Times*, Dec. 24, 2005, http://www.hindustantimes.com/News-Feed/NM4/Vatican-opens-Forbidden-Books/Article1–4 2012.aspx.

34. Myers, 249, 250. Northern Whigs blamed the Irish voters for the victory of Franklin Pierce at the polls in 1852, and were suspicious of President Pierce's Catholic postmaster general, James Campbell, believing that Campbell used his patronage powers to shore up his support among the Irish. Pierce wouldn't have contradicted his image of catering to Catholics when he upgraded the status of the American minister in Rome, Lewis Cass, Jr., to Minister Resident. Myers, 249, 250; Andrews, *American-Papal Relations*, 115.

35. Von Frank, 13–14, 194; Campbell, 85; Fehrenbacher, 286; James L. Huston, "Democracy by Scripture Versus Democracy by Process: A Reflection on Stephen A. Douglas and Popular Sovereignty," *Civil War History: A Journal of the Middle Period* XLIII, no. 3 (September 1997), 189–200, at 190–91, 194–95; Timothy L. Wesley, *The Politics of Faith During The Civil War* (Baton Rouge: Louisiana State University Press, 2013), 17–20, 23; Hamburger, *Separation of Church and State*, 243–46.

36. Albert J. von Frank, *The Trials of Anthony Burns: Freedom and Slavery in Emerson's Boston* (Cambridge: Harvard University Press, 1998), 1, 17, 32, 53, 63, 65–70, 174–175, 190, 197–219; Stanley W. Campbell, *The Slave Catchers: Enforcement of the Fugitive Slave Law, 1850–1860* (Chapel Hill: University of North Carolina Press, 1970), 124–30; Carey, *Religious Weathervane*, 227–29; David Joseph Voelker, *Orestes Brownson and the Search for Authority in Democratic America* (Dissertation, University of North Carolina at Chapel Hill, 2003), 227. To this day, the U.S. Department of Justice honors Batchelder as a martyr to the cause of law and order—with respect to him and other marshals and possemen who died in the line of duty, the its web site says it "honor[s] their memory and their sacrifice." "Department of Justice Honors Slave Catchers for their Service to the Law," http://reason.com/blog/2013/07/29/department-of-justice-honors-slave-catch.

37. "Sumner on Fugitive Slaves," BQR, October 1854, *Works*, vol. XVII, 39–53.

38. Charles Sumner, *Defence of Massachusetts. Speeches of Hon. Charles Sumner, on the Boston memorial for the repeal of the fugitive slave bill, and in reply to Messrs. Jones of Tennessee, Butler of South Carolina, and Mason of Virginia. In Senate of United States, June 26 and 28, 1854* (Washington, D.C.: Buell & Blanchard, 1854); "Sumner on Fugitive Slaves"; Carey, *Religious Weathervane*, 225.

39. *Speeches of Sumner*, June 26, 4; "Sumner on Fugitive Slaves," 47.

40. *Speeches of Sumner*, June 26, 4.

41. "Remarks and Resolution Introduced in United States House of Representatives Concerning Abolition of Slavery in the District of Columbia," January 10, 1849, http://quod.lib.umich.edu/l/lincoln/lincoln2/1:21?rgn=div1;view=fulltext; "Featured Document: The D.C. Emancipation Act," http://www.archives.gov/exhibits/featured_documents/dc_emancipation_act/; Abraham Lincoln, Second Annual Message to Congress, December 1, 1862, http://www.presidency.ucsb.edu/ws/?pid=29503; Joel S. Panzer, *The Popes and Slavery* (Staten Island: Alba House, 1996).

42. Charles Emery Stevens, *Anthony Burns: A History* (Boston: John P. Jewett, 1856); Frank, 1, 17, 32, 53, 63, 65–70, 174–175, 190, 197–219; Cambell, 124–30.

43. Fede, 140–41, 262; Julie Winch, "Philadelphia and the Other Underground Railroad," *The Pennsylvania Magazine* CXI, no. 1 (January 1987), 3–25. See, generally, Deyle, *Carry Me Back*.

44. Solomon Northrup, *Twelve Years a Slave*, ed. Henry Louis Gates, Jr. (New York: Penguin, 2013), 6, 23–26, 32, 34, 43–44, 57–58, 120–21, 151–55, 164, 180–84, 188–89, 194–201, 208, 210, 214–15, 219–29.

45. Franchot, 346–47; *Spirit-Rapper*, 305–15; 160–61.

46. *Spirit-Rapper*, 46, 50, 68, 93, 106, 129.

47. *Spirit-Rapper*, 71, 172, Voelker, 227.

48. *Spirit-Rapper*, 199–213.

49. Ibid., 220–24, 229–34, 255, 400–01.

Chapter 8

1. T. J. O'Mahony, *Joseph Carriere, St Sulpice and the Church of France in His Time* (Dublin: J. Mullany, 1865), 45; Compagnie de Saint Sulpice, "Travel notes of the Saint-

Sulpice seminary," http://sulpiciens.fr/?page_id=140&lang_view=en, retrieved November 18, 2013.

2. O'Mahony, 37, 80, 85, 86, 124–25, 135.

3. Ibid., 143–44, 154; 155–58; J.F. Fenlon, "Sulpicians in the United States," *Catholic Encyclopedia*, vol. 14, 1912, http://www.newadvent.org/cathen/14329d.htm.

4. O'Mahony, 78–79, 136–39.

5. Ibid., 69–70, 75–76, 80, 85, 90, 98–99; Zanca, *American Catholics and Slavery*, 43, 143–46; "The Sulpicians—Province of the U.S.—History—http://www.sulpicians.org/history/, accessed November 18, 2013.

6. O'Mahony, 41–42, 59, 61–62, 111–12, 121; Chadwick, 25–28; Antoine Dégert, "Félicité Robert de Lamennais," *Catholic Encyclopedia*, vol. 8, 1910, http://www.newadvent.org/cathen/08762a.htm; John Francis Fenlon, "Joseph Carrière," *Catholic Encyclopedia*, vol. 3, 1908, http://www.newadvent.org/cathen/03379a.htm; Chadwick, 170–71; Montalembert to Brownson, November 12, 1852; Montalembert to Brownson, December 28, 1854, UNDA; "Charles Le Comte de Montalembert," http://www.acton.org/pub/religion-liberty/volume-3-number-4/charles-le-comte-de-montalembert.

7. Augustin Cochin. *The Results of Slavery*, trans. Mary Booth (Boston: Walker, Wise, 1863), 359.

8. James M. O'Toole, 58–59.

9. O'Connor, *Fitzpatrick's Boston*, 154; John Houlihan, "Portland," *Catholic Encyclopedia*, vol. 12, 1911, http://www.newadvent.org/cathen/12287a.htm; Nicholas Weber, "Marie-Dominique-Auguste Sibour," *Catholic Encyclopedia*, vol. 13, 1912, http://www.newadvent.org/cathen/13769a.htm.

10. O'Connor, *Fitzpatrick's Boston*, 154–55; James M. O'Toole, 63.

11. O'Connor, *Fitzpatrick's Boston*, 154.

12. O'Connor, *Fitzpatrick's Boston*, 154–55; James M. O'Toole, 64–65.

13. Chapter 3, op. cit.; *An Act to prevent free persons of color, commonly known as free negroes, from being brought or coming into the State of Georgia*, December 17, 1859.

14. James M. O'Toole, 46–48.

15. *Knight v. Hardeman*, 14 Ga. 253 (1855), 1855 Ga. Lexis 102; Fede, 322–24. Fede, and the headnote to the *Knight* opinion, refer to Michael Healy as "Michael J. Healy," but the text of the *Knight* opinion correctly names him Michael M. Healy. Hardeman, the trial judge who first heard the case, was the same person who managed the Healy estate, and unsurprisingly ruled against Phillips and her children when the case was at the trial stage.

16. William E. Gienapp, "Nativism and the Creation of a Republican Majority in the North before the Civil War," *The Journal of American History* 72, no. 3 (December 1985), 530–31.

17. O'Connor, *Fitzpatrick's Boston*, 152; Myers, 265.

18. Tyler G. Anbinder, *Nativism and Slavery: The Know-Nothings and the Politics of the 1850s* (New York: Oxford University Press, 1992), 137.

19. Anbinder, 136; Billington, 411–12.

20. Anbinder, 136–37; Steven Taylor, "Progressive Nativism: The Know-Nothing Party in Massachusetts," *Historical Journal of Massachusetts* 28, no. 2 (Summer 2000), 169; O'Connor, *Fitzpatrick's Boston*, 153.

21. Anbinder, 137–38.

22. Myers, 265, O'Connor, *Fitzpatrick's Boston*, 152–53.

23. O'Connor, *Fitzpatrick's Boston*, 114, 158.

24. Article XVIII of the Amendments to the Massachusetts Constitution, adopted May 19, 1855, https://malegislature.gov/Laws/Constitution (modified in the 1920s). "The purpose of the constitutional amendment was to prohibit the use of public funds for the education of the children of the Commonwealth in any institution, however conducted, and whether sectarian or not, the control of which is not in the municipal authorities." Opinion of the Attorney General of Massachusetts, March 18, 1896, Commonwealth of Massachusetts, *Report of the Attorney General for the Year Ending January 19, 1898*, (Boston: Wright & Potter, 1898).

25. O'Connor, *Fitzpatrick's Boston*, 158, Taylor, 169; Myers, 255, 284; Gienapp, 534.

26. Taylor, 171–76; Myers, 282–83.

27. Myers, 283; Thomas D. Morris, *Free Men All: The Personal Liberty Laws of the North, 1780–1861* (Baltimore: Johns Hopkins University Press, 1974), 168–173; *Acts and Resolves Passed by the General Court of Massachusetts in the Years 1854–5* (Boston, 1855), pp. 924–29; http://www.answers.com/topic/massachusetts-personal-liberty-act; Von Frank, 121; O'Connor, *Fitzpatrick's Boston*, 171–78.

28. O'Connor, *Fitzpatrick's Boston*, 149–52; David Jerome Callon, *Converting Catholicism: Orestes A. Brownson, Anna H. Dorsey, and Irish America, 1840–1896* (Dissertation, Washington University in St. Louis, 2008), 191, 194.

29. Billington, 414; O'Connor, *Fitzpatrick's Boston*, 153.

30. Billington, 414–15; O'Connor, *Fitzpatrick's Boston*, 153–54.

31. Billington, 415.

32. Gienapp, "Nativism," 531; Anbinder, 139.

33. Connelly, 52–73; Dolan, 48ff; *Brooksiana; or, The Controversy Between Senator Brooks and Archbishop Hughes, Growing out of the Recently Enacted Church Property Bill* (New York: Edward Dunigan, 1855), 5, 7, 9, 14, 45–48, 49–50, 62.

34. Most of *Brooksiana* is devoted to this quarrel, and to another newspaper controversy between Hughes and a St. Louis trustee.

35. *Brooksiana*, 53, 54, 57–58, 55; Hamburger, *Separation of Church and State*, 240–43.

36. Francis Patrick Kenrick, *A Vindication of the Catholic Church, In a Series of Letters Addressed to the Rt. Rev. John Henry Hopkins, Protestant Episcopal Bishop of Vermont* (Baltimore: John Murphy, 1855), 225, 226–27; M'Clintock, 22–23.

37. Kenrick, 217, 218, 221, 223, 224–25.

38. Carey, *Religious Weathervane*, 219; Frank Gerrity, "The Disruption of the Philadelphia Whigocracy: Joseph R. Chandler, Anti-Catholicism, and the Congressional Election of 1854," *The Pennsylvania Magazine of History and Biography* 111, no. 2 (April 1987), 161–194; Frank Gerrity, "Joseph Ripley Chandler and 'The Temporal Power of the Pope,'" *Pennsylvania History* 49, no. 2 (April 1982), 106–20; "Chandler, Joseph Ripley—Biographical Information," http://bioguide.congress.gov/scripts/biodisplay.pl?index=C000292; John M'Clintock, *The Temporal Power of the Pope, Containing the Speech of the Hon. Joseph R. Chandler, Delivered in the House of Representatives of the United States, January 11, 1855. With Nine Letters, Stating the Prevailing Roman Catholic Theory in the Language of Papal Writers* (New York: Carlton & Phillips, 1855), 9–59.

39. M'Clintock, 76–77, 92.

40. Carey, *Religious Weathervane*, 217–18.

41. Edward Beecher, *The Papal Conspiracy Exposed, and Protestantism Defended, in the Light of Reason, History and Scripture* (Boston: Stearns & Co, 1855); Rufus W. Clark, *Romanism in America* (Boston: S.K. Whipple, 1855).

42. "Romanism in America," BQR, April 1855, in *Works*, vol. VII, 508–10, 514 517–18, 520.

43. "Papal Conspiracy Exposed," BQR, April 1855, in *Works*, vol. VII, 544, 546, 549, 550.

44. BQR, vol. VII, 553, 556.

45. BQR, vol. VII, 547–49.

46. Martin John Spalding, *Miscellanea: Comprising Reviews, Lectures and Essays, on Historical, Theological and Miscellaneous Subjects*, 4th ed. (Baltimore: John Murphy & Co., 1895) (original edition 1855), 144–45.
47. Spalding, *Miscellanea*, xlii-xlv, liv.
48. Spalding, *Miscellanea*, xxiv, xxv, xxxviii, xxxix-xl, 137–40; David Spalding, "Martin John Spalding's 'Dissertation on the American Civil War,'" *The Catholic Historical Review* 52, no. 1 (April 1966), pp. 66–85.
49. Gerrity, "Joseph Ripley Chandler," 116, 118, 120 n55.

Chapter 9

1. Carey, *Religious Weathervane*, 232, 242–43.
2. Ibid; "Map of New Jersey compiled from the latest authorities, 1856," http://mapmaker.rutgers.edu/NJ_1856.jpg; "Elizabeth through the ages," http://www.visithistoricalelizabethnj.org/timeline.htm.
3. Clarke, 55–56, 57; John Gilmary Shea, *History of the Catholic Church in the United States from the Fifth Provincial Council of Baltimore, 1843, to the Second Plenary Council of Baltimore, 1866* (New York: John G. Shea, 1892), 121; *Howland v. Union Theological Seminary*, 3 Sand. 82 (1849), *Howland v. Union Theological Seminary*, 5 N.Y. 1 Seld 193 (1853).
4. Clarke, 60; "Roman Catholic Archdiocese of Newark: James Roosevelt Bayley, D.D." http://www.rcan.org/index.cfm?fuseaction=feature.display&feature_id=110.
5. Lamers, 17.
6. Ibid.; Lamott, 123, 190, 195, 205–06; Kurtz, "'Perfect Model,'" 78.
7. Kurtz, "'Perfect Model,'" 77.
8. Lamers, 17.
9. Ibid; Leland R. Johnson, *Men Mountains and Rivers: An Ilustrated History of the Huntington District, U.S. Army Corps of Engineers* (Washington, D.C.: U.S. Government Printing Office, 1977), 59; "Coal River Navigation Company," http://www.wvencyclopedia.org/articles/1368, "William Starke Rosecrans," http://www.wvencyclopedia.org/articles/130.
10. Lamers, 17; Leland R. Johnson, 61; "Coal River Navigation Company."
11. Kurtz, "Perfect Model," 82.
12. Clarke, 251–52.
13. Tracy Fessenden, "The Nineteenth-Century Bible Wars and the Separation of Church and State," *Church History* 74, no. 4 (December 2005), 784–811, at 798; Shea, *History 1843–1866*, 542–43.
14. Mischa Honeck, *We Are the Revolutionists: German-Speaking Immigrants & American Abolitionists After 1848* (Athens: University of Georgia Press, 2011), 17–18; George Henry Porter, *Ohio Politics During the Civil War Period* (Boston: Columbia University dissertation, 1911).
15. Bruce Levine, *The Spirit of 1848: German Immigrants, Labor Conflict, and the Coming of the Civil War* (Urbana: University of Illinois Press, 1992), 186; Honeck, 18–19; Hussey, "Some Notes," 3.
16. "Das Lied der Deutschen," http://www.brandenburghistorica.com/page5.html.
17. Levine, 91, 94–95; Lamott, 295.
18. Levine, 187.
19. Anbinder, 69–70.
20. Dann Woellert, *Cincinnati Turner Societies: The Cradle of an American Movement* (Charleston: The History Press, 2012), 32; John Kiesewetter, "Civil unrest woven into city's history," *Cincinnati Enquirer*, Sunday, July 15, 2001.
21. Shea, *History 1843–1866*, 542–43.
22. Anbinder, 175–77; Gienapp, "Nativism," 538; Porter, 17–18.
23. Gienapp, "Nativism," 538–39.
24. Campbell, 141–42; Warren, 262–62, 269–270; Fehrenbacher, 291, 310; Brandt, 22; Morris, 180–82. The Margaret Garner case inspired Toni Morrison's novel *Beloved*, see "Who is Margaret Garner?" http://www.ohiohistoryhost.org/ohiomemory/archives/876; Toni Morrison, *Beloved* (New York: Vintage, 2004).
25. Wallace S. Hutcheon, "The Louisville Riots of August 1855," *The Register of the Kentucky Historical Society* 69, no. 2 (April 1971), 150–172, at 152–53, 155; Charles E. Deusner, "The Know Nothing Riots in Louisville," *The Register of the Kentucky Historical Society* 61, no. 2 (April 1963), 122–147, at 123, 125–26, 127–28, 129, 134; Levine, 102; Thomas W. Spalding, *Martin John Spalding: American Churchman* (Washington, D.C.: Catholic University of American Press, 1973), 104–10; Kurtz, "'Perfect Model,'" 79.
26. Hutcheon, 156–57; Deusner, 137, 138–39.
27. Hutcheon, 158, Deusner, 144. In those days, voters used ballots printed up by the various parties, so poll-watchers could identify a voter's party affiliation.
28. Hutcheon, 158–59; Deusner, 140–43.
29. Hutcheon, 159–60; Deusner, 143–45; Spalding, *Spalding*, 109.
30. Anbinder, 167–70; Myers, 288–90.
31. Henry Wilson, *History of the Rise and Fall of the Slave Power in America*, vol. II (Boston: Houghton, Osgood, 1879), 432.
32. Ivory Chamberlain and Thomas Moses Foote, *Biography of Millard Fillmore* (Buffalo: Thomas & Lathrops, 1856), 87–88; Hutcheon, 155; Anbinder, 202–04; Paul Finkelman, *Millard Fillmore* (New York: Times Books, 2011), 23–24, 48, 133–34, 137; "United States Political Parties: The Liberty Party (1839–48)," http://histclo.com/country/us/hist/pp/ppi-lib.html.
33. Anbinder, 206–209; Dagmar Renshaw LeBreton, "Orestes Brownson's Visit to New Orleans in 1855," *American Literature* 16, no. 2 (May 1944), pp. 110–114, at 111.
34. Myers, 329, Anbinder, 209; Gienapp, 541–42.

Chapter 10

1. Philip Shriver Klein, *President James Buchanan: A Biography* (University Park: Pennsylvania State University Press, 1962), 260; Daniel W. Crofts, *Reluctant Confederates: Upper South Unionists in the Secession Crisis* (Chapel Hill: University of North Carolina Press, 1989), 52.
2. "Slavery and the Incoming Administration," *BQR*, January 1857, *Works*, vol. XVII, 54–77; Carey, *Religious Weathervane*, 265–66.
3. "The Slavery Question Once More," *BQR*, April 1857, vol. XVII, 77–89.
4. *Dred Scott v. Sandford*, 19 How. 393 (1857); Warren, pp. 300–319, 324–333; Fehrenbacher, 315–21, 324, 327, 551–58; Kenneth M. Stampp, *America in 1857* (New York: Oxford University Press, 1990), 93–99; Eaton, 131–33.
5. "The Slavery Question Once More," 89–94.
6. "The Great Rebellion," *BQR*, July 1861, *Works*, vol. XVII, 127–28; "Politics at Home," *BQR*, July 1860, *Works*, vol. XVII, 94–95; O'Connor, *Fitzpatrick's Boston*, 171–78; Stampp, *America in 1857*, 221–38.
7. Stampp, *America in 1857*, 324–25; Klein, *President James Buchanan*, 302, 308–09, 311–12; Fehrenbacher, 469, 479–81, 538–40; Potter, 422–29; "Chronology of the Secession Crisis," "Republican Party National Platform, 1860,"

http://www.cprr.org/Museum/Ephemera/Republican_Platform_1860.html.

8. Henry Brownson, *Orestes A. Brownson's Later Life: From 1856 to 1876* (Detroit: H.F. Brownson, 1900), 84–86, 88, 91–92.

9. Gienapp, "Nativism," 549.

10. McGreevy, *Catholicism and American Freedom*, 64.

11. David Herbert Donald, *Lincoln* (New York: Simon & Schuster, 1995), 169–70, 191; Orville Vernon Burton, *The Age of Lincoln* (New York: Hill and Wang, 2007), 65; Gienapp, "Nativism," 448.

Lincoln basically made an "if by whiskey" speech, a political straddle whereby a politician speaks conditionally, so as to take both sides of an issue. The speech is attributed to various politicians trying to equivocate on the issue of alcohol prohibition, and it goes something like this:

If by whisky, you mean the Devil's brew, the Poison scourge, the bloody monster that defies innocence, dethrones reason, creates misery and poverty, yea, literally takes the bread out of the mouths of babes; if you mean the Evil Drink that topples men and women from pinnacles of righteous, gracious living into the bottomless pit of despair, degradation, shame, helplessness and hopelessness—then certainly I am against it with all my power.

But if by whisky, you mean the oil of conversation, the philosophic wine and ale that is consumed when good fellows get together, that puts a song in their hearts, laughter on their lips and the warm glow of contentment in their eyes; if you mean that sterling drink that puts the spring in an old man's steps on a frosty morning; if you mean that drink, the sale of which pours into our treasury untold millions of dollars which are used to provide tender care for our little crippled children, our pitifully aged and infirm and to build our highways, hospitals and schools—then, Brother, I am for it. This is my stand [William Safire, "ON LANGUAGE; It's a Rain Forest Out There," *New York Times Magazine*, December 22, 1991].

12. Donald, 189; Burton, 65; Gienapp, "Nativism," 555.

13. James M. O'Toole, 71–72; Thomas H. O'Connor, *The Athens of America: Boston 1825–1845* (Boston: University of Massachusetts Press, 2006), 17.

14. James M. O'Toole, 64.

15. Shea, *History 1843–1866*, 368; James M. O'Toole, 65–66.

16. Anbinder, 243, 248–51; Myers, 326–27; James M. O'Toole, 67; Gienapp, "Nativism," 550.

17. "In the Police Court of Boston, Massachusetts. April 1859. Commonwealth, on Complaint of Wall vs. M'laurin F. Cooke," *The American Law Register (1852–1891)* 7, no. 7 (May 1859), 417–426; McGreevy, *Catholicism and American Freedom*, 7–8.

18. McGreevy (Kindle edition).

19. *Commonwealth v. Cooke*, 422–24, 426.

20. McGreevey, 8–11, 13.

21. Shea, *History 1843–1866*, 513–14; David W. Galenson, "Neighborhood Effects on the School Attendance of Irish Immigrants' Sons in Boston and Chicago in 1860," *American Journal of Education* 105, no. 3 (May 1997), pp. 261–293, at 280–82.

22. Galenson, 261–86.

23. Anbinder, 251–52.

24. Irving Herriott, "The Premises and Significance of Abraham Lincoln's Letter to Theodore Canisius," reprinted from *Deutsch-Amerikanische Geschichtsblatter Jahrbuch der Deutsch-Amerikanischen Historischen Gesellschaft von Illinois*—Jahrgang 1915 (Volulme XV), 181–254, 2–3, 19, 25–30, 37–39; Phillips, 421.

25. James M. O'Toole, 67.

26. See chaper 9.

27. Gareschè, 96, 110–11; 180, 212, 217.

28. Ibid., 55, 118, 313, 315–16. 318–326.

29. Ibid., 318–326.

30. Ibid., 140, 195, 244, 326–41, 261, 265. The article is by J. A. G. (probably a misprint for J.P.G.), "Divorce and Divorce Laws," BQR, October 1859, 473–92. The article concludes with a chilling warning: "The family, in its old sense, is disappearing from our land, and not only our free institutions are threatened but the very existence of our society is endangered." Many scholars have cited this sentence in order to mock it, and to show that modern concerns about the family are just as overblown and hysterical today as in 1859. The quotation is generally misattributed to the *Boston Quarterly Review*, which Brownson hadn't published for over a decade. See, e.g., Robert J. Brym and John Lie, *Sociology: Your Compass for a New World*, 2d ed. (Boston: Cengage Learning, 2010), 294 ("This alarm, or one much like it, is sounded whenever the family undergoes rapid change, and particularly when the divorce rate increases"). The misattribution seems to trace back to Herman Lantz, Martin Schultz, and Mary O'Hara, "The Changing American Family from the Preindustrial to the Industrial Period: A Final Report," *American Sociological Review* 42 (June 1977), 406–421, at 413.

31. Gareschè, 326–41.

32. David I. Kertzer, *The Kidnapping of Edgardo Mortara: The Extraordinary Story of How the Vatican's Imprisonment of a Six-Year-Old Jewish Boy in 1858 Helped Bring about the Collapse of the Popes' Worldly Power in Italy* (New York: Alfred A. Knopf, 1997), 3–12, 119–22, Hales, 161, 166–170.

33. Kertzer, 124–27; Bertram Wallace Korn, *The American Reaction to the Mortara Case: 1858–1859* (Cincinnati: The American Jewish Archives, 1957), 22–25, 29, 37–39.

34. Korn, 30–31, 40.

35. Ibid., 58–60; Anbinder, 257.

36. Brownson, *Later Life*, 83, 86–90.

37. "The Mortara Case," BQR, vol. VII (third series) (London: Catholic Publishing and Bookselling, 1859) April 1859, 226–246, at 228–31, 233–35, 237 (this volume, unlike the other volumes of Brownson's work I have quoted, is not part of Henry Brownson's series published in the 1880s, but was published contemporanously). Available online at https://archive.org/stream/brownsonsquarter07browuoft#page/226/mode/2up, et. seq.

38. "The Mortara Case," 228–31, 237.

39. Ibid., 236, 238–39.

40. Ibid., 239–41. On page 238, the article is marked with the letter "Z," possibly ending a section of the article written by Brownson's collaborators and commencing a section written solely by Brownson himself, although this is not certain. The passages after the letter "Z" include the discussion of the Papal States, see below.

41. Korn, 148, 153–54.

42. Lamers, 17–18; Madame Baptiste Lynch to Bishop Patrick Lynch—September 4, 1863 (p. 9), Lowcountry Digital Archives, Family Letters, 1858–1866 http://lcdl.library.cofc.edu/lcdl/catalog/lcdl:42038.

43. Lamers, 18.

44. William Rosecrans to McMaster, January 10, 1858, UNDA.

45. William Rosecrans to McMaster, August 1, 1859.

46. Gareschè, 217, 347.

47. Anbinder, 258–60.

48. Philip Gleason, "Boundlessness, Consolidation, and

Discontinuity Between Generations: Catholic Seminary Studies in Antebellum America," *Church History* 73, no. 3 (September 2004), 583–612, at 585, 592.

49. Gleason, 597; Thomas Meehan, "Caspar Henry Borgess," *Catholic Encyclopedia*, vol. 2, 1907, http://www.newadvent.org/cathen/02684c.htm.

50. Gleason, 596, 598–600, 602–03; Joseph M. White, "Perspectives on the Nineteenth-Century Diocesan Seminary in the United States," *U.S. Catholic Historian* 19, no. 1; The American Catholic Experience: Essays in Honor of Jay P. Dolan (Winter 2001), 21–35.

51. Gleason, 607; Lamott, 292; Clarke, 251–52.

52. Connelly, *Bedini*, 200–287; White, 21–35, 26, 28–29; Henry A. Branid, *History of the American College of the Roman Catholic Church of the United States Rome, Italy* (New York: Benziger Brothers, 1910), 24, 32–34.

53. White, 29; Lamott, 216.

54. Branid, 24, 85–86; Francis Kenrick to Peter Kenrick, July 14, 1859, *Kenrick-Frenaye Correspondence*, 422–23.

55. Thomas T. McAvoy, "Orestes A. Brownson and Archbishop John Hughes in 1860," *The Review of Politics* 24, no. 1 (January 1962), 19–47; 23, 26, 29, 39; White, 26; Gleason, 589–90, 609.

56. Kertzer, 295–98. In 2001, the International Catholic-Jewish Liaison Committee, representing the Vatican and various Jewish organizations, issued a statement which alluded to the papacy's treatment of Edgardo Mortara. The Committee "affirm[ed] that this episode exemplifies the historical problem which Nostra Aetate and subsequent statements of the Holy See have solved 'in our time.'" http://www.vatican.va/roman_curia/pontifical_councils/chrstuni/relations-jews-docs/rc_pc_chrstuni_doc_20010504_new-york-meeting_fr.html. *Nostra Aetate* is a Declaration issued by the Second Vatican Council in 1965 stating that anti-Jewish discrimination and anti-Semitism are unacceptable for Catholics and calling for better relations between the Church and the Jewish community. See Austin Flannery, O.P., ed., *Vatican Council II: The Conciliar and Post-Conciliar Documents* (Northport, NY: Costello, 1975), 738–743.

57. Hales, 166–170.

58. Paola Gemme, *Domesticating Foreign Struggles* (Athens: University of Georgia Press, 2005), 140–42, 145–46.

59. Gemme, 144, Marraro, 51–52.

60. John Gooch, *The Unification of Italy* (London: Lancaster Pamphlets, 2004), xii; Edward Cadogan, *The Life of Cavour* (London: Smith, Elder 1907), 310; Hales, 199–201, 169, 181; George Trevelyan, *Garibaldi and the Thousand: May 1860* (London: Thomas Nelson and Sons, 1921); George Trevelyan, *Garibaldi and the Making of Italy: June-November 1860* (London: Longman's, Green, 1914).

61. Chadwick, 174; Hales, 179, 186–88, 206.

62. McAvoy, 25–26.

63. Gooch, xii-xiv; Cadogan, 311–12; Charles A. Coulombe, *The Pope's Legion: The Multinational Fighting Force That Defended the Vatican* (New York: Palgrave Macmillan, 2008), 88, 95, 205; Hales, 327–30. One of the defeated Zouave volunteers at Castelfidardo was an American, Louis Louistman, who went on to serve in his country's Civil War. Another American Zouave was Myles Keogh, who went on to serve in the Civil War and ended his life at Custer's Last Stand—when mutilating the corpses of the defeated Americans, the Catholic Indian warriors saw that Keogh had a Papal medal, so they spared Keogh's body and gave it a proper burial.

64. Hales, 207, 209.

65. Marraro, 48–49, 52–53; Kenrick to Kenrick, July 13, 1860, in *The Kenrick-Frenaye Correspondence*, 447; Kenrick to Kenrick, November 13, 1860, in *The Kenrick-Frenaye Correspondence*.

66. Marraro, 52–53.

67. John P. Stockton to Lewis Cass, November 15, 1860, in Stock, *Ministers*, 211.

68. Potter, 369–71, 375–80; Renehan, 210–11, 212, 222, 226–27, 231, 233–35, 250; Fehrenbacher, p. 527–28; Crofts, 72–75; Walther, pp. 179, 184. For Senator Broderick, see David A. Williams, *David C. Broderick—A Political Portrait* (The Huntingdon Library, 1969).

Chapter 11

1. Phillips, 405, 432, 437–48.

2. Anbinder, 247; Phillips, 428; Potter, 416–17; Bonham, 135; Douglas R. Egerton, *Year of Meteors: Stephen Douglas, Abraham Lincoln, and the Election That Brought on the Civil War* (New York: Bloomsbury Press, 2010). "Chronology of the Secession Crisis," http://civilwarcauses.org/secesh.htm; "Constitutional Union (Bell-Everett) Platform, http://eweb.furman.edu/~benson/docs/conuplat.htm; Green, locations 305–32.

3. Anbinder, 255, 260, 264–65; Frank L. Klement, "Catholics as Copperheads During the Civil War," *The Catholic Historical Review* 80, no. 1 (January 1994), 36–57, at 36.

4. Anbinder, 265–66.

5. Potter, 422–29; Fehrenbacher, 538–40; "Chronology of the Secession Crisis," http://civilwarcauses.org/secesh.htm; "Republican Party National Platform, 1860," http://www.cprr.org/Museum/Ephemera/Republican_Platform_1860.html; Anbinder, 267–68.

6. Potter, 409–10, 412–13; Fehrenbacher, 533–35; Walther, 74–75, 151–54; Hubbard, 57; "Chronology of the Secession Crisis," http://civilwarcauses.org/secesh.htm. For Douglas Democrat platform, see http://avalon.law.yale.edu/19th_century/bm1860.asp and http://civilwarcauses.org/demo_d.htm. For Breckenridge Democrat platform, see http://civilwarcauses.org/demo_b.htm.

7. "Politics at Home," *BQR*, July 1860, vol. XVII, 94–95.

8. Ibid., 95.

9. Ibid., 96–100.

10. Ibid., 112–14.

11. Ibid., 106, 119–20.

12. Voelker, 241–42; "Politics at Home," 118.

13. McAvoy, 27–28.

14. Ibid., 28, 31; Henry Brownson, *Later Life*, 184–87, 225–26.

15. McAvoy, 28–29; Carey, *Religious Weathervane*, 194–95; Umberto Benigni, "Vincenzo Gioberti," *Catholic Encyclopedia*, vol. 6. 1909, http://www.newadvent.org/cathen/06562b.htm.

16. McAvoy, 29–33; Carey, *Religious Weathervane*, 251–52, 260.

17. Carey, *Religious Weathervane*, 248–49; McAvoy, 33–34.

18. McAvoy, 34–35.

19. Ibid., 35–37; David Fox, "John Mullaly," http://atlantic-cable.com/CablePioneers/Mullaly/index.htm; Mullaly had publicized Samuel Morse's telegraphic cable on the Atlantic Ocean floor. John Mullaly, *The Laying of the Cable, or, the Ocean Telegraph* (New York: D. Appleton, 1858).

20. Henry Brownson, *Later Life*, 198–99; McAvoy, 40.

21. McAvoy, 35, Henry Brownson, *Later Life*, 199–202, 221–25.

22. Eliza Starr to her cousin George, February 17, 1859, in James J. McGovern, ed., *The Life and Letters of Eliza Allen Starr,* introd. William Stetson Merrill (Chicago: Lakeside Press, 1905), 109–10; Henry Brownson, *Later Life,* 206–18.
23. McAvoy, 40.
24. Potter, 436; Arthur M. Schlesinger, et al., eds., *The Coming to Power: Critical Presidential Elections in American History* (New York: Chelsea House, 1972), 506; Phillips, 414.
25. Phillips, 299, 411–12; 418, 421, 428–30, 435–36; Anbinder, 263–64; Gienapp, 556–58.
26. Gienapp, 559; George W. Julian, "The Death-Struggle of the Republican Party," *North American Review* 126 (March-April 1878), 265–66.
27. Potter, 436–39; Schlesinger, et. al., *Coming to Power,* 506; Crofts, 90, 123–24, 164, 313–15, 329, 330, 334–352; Walther, 263; Ralph Newman and E. B. Long, *Civil War Digest* (New York: Grosset and Dunlap, 1956), 5–7; Chris Bishop and Alan Drury, *1400 Days: The Civil War Day by Day* (New York: Gallery Books, 1990), 24.
28. Henry Brownson, *Later Life,* 219–221.
29. McAvoy, 40–41.
30. Ibid., 37–40; Henry Brownson, *Later Life,* 228.
31. Kenrick to Kenrick, March 7, 1859, in *The Kenrick-Frenaye Correspondence,* 431; same to same, October 25, 1859, 430; same to same, February 8, 1860, 435; same to same, September 16, 1860, 449; *The Pentateuch. Translated from the Vulgate, and Diligently Compared with the Original Text, Being a Revised Edition of the Douay Version,* trans. Patrick Kenrick (Baltimore: Kelly, Hedian & Piett, 1860), ix-x.
32. O'Shea, *The Two Kenricks,* 199–200; James Hennesey, S.J., *American Catholics: A History of the Roman Catholic Community in the United States* (Oxford: Oxford University Press, 1981), 154; John Tracy Ellis, *American Catholicism* (Chicago: Unversity of Chicago Press, 1969), 96–97.
33. Newman and Long, 7; Bishop and Drury, 24; Kenrick to Kenrick, July 15, 1861, in *The Kenrick-Frenaye Correspondence,* 459–60; Mark E. Neely, Jr., *The Fate of Liberty: Abraham Lincoln and Civil Liberties* (New York: Oxford University Press, 1991), 4–8.
34. *Starr Life and Letters,* 15, 16, 33, 37, 71, 73, 74, 84, 96, 98.
35. Francis Kenrick to Starr, August 5, 1861, in *Starr Life and Letters,* 148; *Mirror* articles of November 24 and December 1, 1860, in Zanca, *American Catholics and Slavery,* 133–34.

Chapter 12

1. Michael V. Gannon, *Rebel Bishop: The Life and Era of Augustin Verot* (Milwaukee: Bruce, 1964), 21, 30–31, 49–50.
2. Gannon, 53. The Thirteenth Amendment, forbidding slavery, was ratified on December 6, 1865, see *The Constitution of the United States and Related Documents* (Melville, NY: Graphic Image, 2004).
3. Gannon, 51–52; Augustine Verot, *A Tract for the Times. Slavery & Abolitionism, being the Substance of a Sermon, Preached in the Church of St. Augustine, Florida, On the 4th Day of January 1861, Day of Public Humiliation, Fasting and Prayer* (no date or publisher given).
4. Verot, 6–8, 14.
5. Ibid., 7; "In Supremo Apostolatus," December 3, 1839, http://www.ewtn.com/library/papaldoc/g16sup.htm.
6. Verot, 10–14.
7. Gannon, 49–50.
8. Ibid., 63; Maria Genoino Caravaglios, "A Roman Critique of the Pro-Slavery Views of Bishop Martin of Natchitoches, Louisiana," *Records of the American Catholic Historical Society of Philadelphia* 83, no. 2 (1972), 68; Cyprian Davis, "Freedom and Slavery," 95.
9. William L. Burton, *Melting Pot Soldiers: The Union's Ethnic Regiments* (New York: Fordham University Press, 1998), 12, 25–26; Susannah Ural Bruce, *The Harp and The Eagle: The Impact of Civil War Military Service in the Union Army on The Irish in America* (Dissertation, Kansas State University, 2002), 5, 69, 91, 103; John A. French, *Irish-American Identity, Memory and Americanism During the Eras of the Civil War and First World War* (Dissertation, Marquette University, May 2012), 52–54; Cian Turlough McMahon, *Did the Irish "Become White"? Global Migration and National Identity, 1842–1877* (Dissertation, Carnegie Mellon University, 2010), 207.
10. Burton, 12, 127–31; Bruce, *Harp and Eagle,* 99; O'Connor, *Fitzpatrick's Boston,* 194–95; Shea, *History 1843–1866,* 515; William Byrne, et. al., *History of the Catholic Church in the New England States, Volume 1* (Boston: Kurd & Everts, 1899), 82.
11. Burton, 131–32; O'Connor, *Fitzpatrick's Boston,* 195–96; Shea, *History 1843–1866,* 515; Fitzpatrick to Andrew, June 18, 1861, John A. Andrew Papers, Reel 7, Massachusetts Historical Society.
12. Burton, 130–31, 132.
13. Bruce Catton, *This Hallowed Ground* (New York: Washington Square Press, 1961), 27; Burton, 127, 129.
14. Shea, *History 1843–1866,* 515; Brother Basil Leo Lee, *Discontent in New York City 1861–1865* (Dissertation, Catholic University of America Press, 1943), 73.
15. Healy to McFarland, May 3, 1861, UNDA; Shea, *History 1843–1866,* 516.
16. Luers to Lefevere, April 5, 1861, UNDA; Lamott, 83; "How Bishops Are Appointed," http://www.usccb.org/about//leadership/appointing-bishops.cfm; McCann, *Sisters of Charity,* 214–15.
17. Sister Mary Agnes McCann, "The Most Reverend John Baptist Purcell, D.D., Archbishop of Cincinnati (1800–1883)," *The Catholic Historical Review* 6, no. 2 (July 1920), 172–99, 190–91; McCann, *Sisters of Charity,* 214, 220.
18. McCann, *Sisters of Charity,* 217, 219; Lamott, 83; McCann, *Purcell,* 191; "How Bishops Are Appointed," http://www.usccb.org/about//leadership/appointing-bishops.cfm.
19. Lamers, 20–21; Whitelaw Reid, *Ohio in the War: Her Statesmen Generals and Soldiers, Volume 1* (Cincinnati: Robert Clarke, 1895), 30, 32–34; David J. Eicher, *The Longest Night: A Military History of the Civil War* (New York: Simon & Schuster, 2001), 84.
20. Lamers, 22–23; Reid, 36; Chase to James A. Garfield, August 17, 1863, in John Niven, ed., *The Salmon P. Chase Papers, Volume 4, Correspondence, April 1863–1864* (Kent, OH: Kent State University Press, 1997), 102. In the latter letter, while expressing disillusionment with William, Chase took credit for promoting his appointment, a plausible claim in light of the way patronage, especially patronage from the leaders of one's home state, worked at that time.
21. Lamers, 26; James Oakes, *Freedom National: The Destruction of Slavery in the United States, 1861–1865* (New York: W. W. Norton, 2013), 93, 95–99. Garesché singled out for criticism "*Militia* Generals, especially [Massachusetts politician-general Benjamin] B[utler]." Butler had recently lost a military skirmish. Indeed, throughout the war Butler would prove better as a politician than as a general.

22. Shea, *History 1843–1866*, 544–45; McCann, *Purcell*, 188; Lamott, 262–64.
23. McCann, *Sisters of Charity*, 125, 129, 201; Metz, 11; Bartholomew Randolph, "St. Elizabeth Ann Seton," *Catholic Encyclopedia*, vol. 13, 1912, http://www.newadven.org/cathen/13739a.htm. St. John's, for a few years in the early 1850s, was housed in a building formerly used for the Western Female Institute, where Harriet Beecher Stowe had taught. Joan D. Hedrick, *Harriet Beecher Stowe: A Life* (New York: Oxford University Press, 1994), 73.
24. McCann, *Sisters of Charity*, 213.
25. Ibid., 214–15.
26. Ibid., 216.
27. Kurtz, "'Perfect Model,'" 80.
28. Reid, 37, 49; Gerald D. Swick, "Virginia's Great Divorce," *America's Civil War*, May 2013, 66–73, 57–70; Mark A. Snell, *West Virginia and the Civil War: Mountaineers are Always Free* (Charleston: History Press, 2011), 35; *The Civil War Almanac* (New York: Bison Books, 1983), 56; Lamers, 26.
29. David M. Owens, *The Devil's Topographer: Ambrose Bierce and the American War Story* (Knoxville: University of Tennessee Press, 2006), 8–9, 22–23, 24–27; "On a Mountain," in Ambrose Bierce, *Ambrose Bierce's Civil War*, ed. William McCann (Washington, D.C.: Regnery Gateway, 1956), 1–9; "The Mocking-Bird," in Bierce, 220–227, 226; Bierce, "A Tough Tussle," http://www.eastoftheweb.com/short-stories/UBooks/TougTuss.shtml.
30. Clarke, 108–115; Shea, *History 1843–1866*, 436; Barbara J. Howe and Margaret A. Brennan, "The Sisters of St. Joseph in Wheeling, West Virginia, During the Civil War," *U.S. Catholic Historian* 31, no. 1 (Winter 2013), 21–49, at 23.
31. George C. Rable, *God's Almost Chosen Peoples: A Religious History of the American Civil War* (Chapel Hill: University of North Carolina Press, 2010), 61; Clarke, 115; Howe and Brennan, "Sisters of St. Joseph," 22, 24, 30, 32, 36, 39, 49; Whelan to McMaster, June 23, 1862, UNDA; Webb Garrison, *Civil War Hostages: Hostage Taking in the Civil War* (Shippensburg, PA: White Mane Books, 2000), 52–53, 106; Mark A. Snell, *West Virginia and the Civil War: Mountaineers are Always Free* (Charleston, SC: The History Press, 2011), 11, 12, 84.
32. Faye Royster Tuck, "Letters of a Halifax County Confederate soldier describe the July 1861 battle at Virginia's Rich Mountain," *America's Civil War*, July 2006, 18–21, 71; Lamers, 28–29; Reid, 50; Eicher, 85–86.
33. Lamers, 30–31; Peskin, 170.
34. Lamers, 32–333, 35; Snell, 35; Eicher, 86–87.
35. Eicher, 101; Lamers, 37; Donald Stoker, *The Grand Design: Strategy and the U.S. Civil War* (Oxford University Press, 2010), 52–53.
36. Eicher, 107–08; McCann, *Sisters of Mercy*, 224.
37. Eicher, 113–16; Lamers, 40–52; Snell, 47–49; Kurtz, "Perfect Model," 80; Swick, 70–73. After the war, a Jewish soldier, J. A. Joel, who had served in the 23rd Indiana Regiment in West Virginia, wrote a reminiscence of how he and other Jewish soldiers in the regiment obtained a leave from duty from "our commanding officer" to observe Passover in 1862, which fell that year on April 14, a month after William had been replaced by Frémont as commander in western Virginia. Joel did not specify whether the "commanding officer" was William, or Frémont, or Rutherford B. Hayes (future president), who commanded the 23d. But based on Joel's account, Bryna J. Fireside wrote a charming children's book which had William not only approve the Passover ceremony, but attend it, remarking how the matzah balls were hard enough to be used against the enemy—"you Hebrews have invented a new weapon" (in reality, William was talking to General Banks on the 14th). Fireside's book is a work of fiction which perhaps gives William too much credit for his multiculturalism, though if he had been asked for permission for the Seder before March 18, he would still have been in a position to grant permission, if not to attend the ceremony. If William was in fact the "commanding officer" who granted leave for the Jewish soldiers to observe the Seder, this would be additional evidence against the charge of favoritism to Catholics. J. A. Joel, "Passover: A Reminiscence of the War," *The Jewish Messenger*, April 1866, http://www.jewish-history.com/civilwar/union.htm; "Passover 1862: Exodus & Emancipation in Washington," http://civilwarwashingtondc1861-1865.blogspot.com/2012/04/passover-1862-exodus-emancipation-in.html; Moore, 21; Bryna J. Fireside, *Private Joel and the Sewell Mountain Seder* (Minneapolis: Kar-Ben, 2008).
38. McCann, *Sisters of Charity*, 217, 219–20, 225.
39. Ibid., 224.
40. McCloskey to Purcell, September 20, 1861, UNDA.
41. Spalding to Purcell, September 27, 1861, UNDA.
42. Zanca, *American Catholics and Slavery*, 242–44; Joseph Bell, *A Catholic Proslavery Perspective* (MA Thesis, California State University, Chico, Spring 2013), 1–2, 50, 51; David C. R. Heisser, "Bishop Lynch's Civil War Pamphlet on Slavery," *The Catholic Historical Review* 84, no. 4 (October 1998), 681–696, at 682; Kenrick to Kenrick, April 1, 1861, in *The Kenrick-Frenaye Correspondence*, 458–59.
43. "Letter to Bishop Lynch of Charleston, South Carolina," in John Hughes, *Complete Works*, ed. Lawrence Kehoe (New York: The Catholic Publication House, 1864), 513–14, 519.
44. "Letter to Bishop Lynch," 514–17.
45. Ibid.
46. Ibid., 518–19.
47. Caravaglios, *Roman Critique*, 68; Celestine Mahé, "Natchitoches," *Catholic Encyclopedia*, vol. 10, 1911, http://www.newadvent.org/cathen/10710a.htm; Clarke, vol. III, 397–400, 402; Shea, *History 1843–1866*, 675–77.
48. Caravaglios, *Roman Critique*, 71–72.
49. Ibid., 68–69; Benedetto Ojetti, "The Roman Congregations," *Catholic Encyclopedia*, vol. 13, 1912, http://www.newadvent.org/cathen/13136a.htm.

Chapter 13

1. Alan A. Siegel, *Beneath the Starry Flag: New Jersey's Civil War Experience* (New Brunswick: Rutgers University Press, 2001), 13, 14–15, 16.
2. Barnabo to Cummings, December 15, 1860, UNDA; Barnabo to Cummings, March 7, 1861, UNDA; Barnabo to Archbishop Paul Cullen, March 13, 1861, UNDA; McAvoy, 41.
3. McAvoy, 35; Brownson to Elder, in Henry Brownson, *Later Life*, 235–31.
4. Bayley to Brownson, January 29, 1861, UNDA; Brownson to Bayley, February 5, 1861, UNDA; Edward J. Power, *Religion and the Public Schools in 19th Century America: The Contribution of Orestes A. Brownson*, (New York: Paulist Press, 1996), 64, 70, 145; Clarke, 60; State of New Jersey, Division of Revenue and Enterprise Services, Business Records Service, https://www.njportal.com/DOR/businessrecords/, entry for "Seton Hall University," accessed January 22, 2014.
5. "The Great Rebellion," BQR, in *Works*, XVII, 121–22.
6. Ibid., 124–26, 130–32, 137, 142.

7. Ibid., 139, 141.
8. Ibid., 141–42.
9. Augustine Hewit to Brownson, June 24, 1861, UNDA; Henry Wyman, Henry, "Augustine Francis Hewit," *Catholic Encyclopedia*, vol. 7, 1910, http://www.newadvent.org/cathen/07309b.htm (accessed January 20, 2014); Augustine Hewit to Brownson, June 24, 1861, UNDA; Alvarez, 233; Robert Emmett Curran, *Shaping American Catholicism: Maryland and New York, 1805–1915* (Washington, D.C.: Catholic University of America Press, 2012), 106; Thomas F. Meehan, "Diplomatic Intercourse With the Pope," in United States Catholic Historical Association, *Historical Records and Studies* XI (December 1917), (New York: self-published, 1917), 88.
10. Henry Brownson, *Later Life*, 265–67; Barnabo to Cummings, June 25, 1861, UNDA; Cummings to Brownson, July 16, 1861, in Henry Brownson, *Later Life*, 254–55; Barnabo to Cummings, August 31, 1861, UNDA; McAvoy, 43. The current *Catechism* of the Catholic Church says: "To die in mortal sin without repenting and accepting God's merciful love means remaining separated from him for ever by our own free choice. This state of definitive self-exclusion from communion with God and the blessed is called 'hell.'...The teaching of the Church affirms the existence of hell and its eternity. Immediately after death the souls of those who die in a state of mortal sin descend into hell, where they suffer the punishments of hell, 'eternal fire.' The chief punishment of hell is eternal separation from God, in whom alone man can possess the life and happiness for which he was created and for which he longs." *Catechism of the Catholic Church* (New Orleans: Loyola University Press, 1994), 269–70.
11. Elder to Brownson, in Henry Brownson, *Later Life*, 231–41. "[W]e [Catholics] 'offer it up' by simply asking God in our own words to use a suffering as it occurs; we often do this for specific intentions (ex., 'Use this pain, Lord, for the salvation of my brother...')." http://www.fisheaters.com/offeringitup.html.
12. Barnabo to Cummings, June 25, 1861, UNDA; Cummings to Brownson, July 16, 1861, in Henry Brownson, *Later Life*, 254–55; Barnabo to Cummings, August 31, 1861, UNDA; Barnabo to Hughes, August 31, 1861, UNDA.
13. Barnabo to Cummings, August 31, 1861, UNDA; Barnabo to Hughes, September 12, 1861, UNDA to Barnabo, September 30, 1861, in McAvoy, 44–46; Hughes to Brownson, October 3, 1861, in Henry Brownson, *Later Life*, 257–68; Hughes to Barnabo, October 12, 1861, UNDA.
14. Rev. Charles Gresselin to Brownson, September 4, 1861, UNDA; O'Shea, 195–97; Marshall Delancey Haywood, *Lives of the Bishops of North Carolina* (Raleigh: Alfred Williams, 1910), 92, 113–137; James Emmett Ryan, *Faithful Passages: American Catholicism in Literary Culture, 1844–1931* (Madison: University of Wisconsin Press, 2013), 49, 85–103; Kenrick to Kenrick, August 17, 1860, in *The Kenrick-Frenaye Correspondence*, 447; same to same, September 16, 1860, 449; same to same, November 13, 1860, 450; same to same, April 1, 1861, 458–59; Francis Patrick Kenrick to Peter Kenrick, September 23, 1861, in *Kenrick-Frenaye Correspondence*, 462; Francis Kenrick to Archbishop Purcell, March 26, 1861, UNDA; Kenrick to Archbishop Odin, August 8, 1861, UNDA; Sarah Brownson to Mrs. Hewit, October 1, 1861, UNDA.
15. Oakes, 93–103, 137–39.
16. Andrew Rolle, *John Charles Frémont: Character as Destiny* (Norman: University of Oklahoma Press, 1991), 182–93, 197–201, 205; Oakes, 153–57; Alan Nevins, *Ordeal of the Union*, vol. 3, part 1 (*The Improvised War*) (New York: Collier, 1992), 309, 318, 326, 331–32, 333–34.
17. Rolle, 205–09; Alan Nevins, *Ordeal of the Union*, vol. 3, part 1 (*The Improvised War*) (New York: Collier, 1992), 224; Oakes, 157–58, 164–65.
18. Serge Gavronsky, "American Slavery and the French Liberals an Interpretation of the Role of Slavery in French Politics During the Second Empire," *The Journal of Negro History* 51, no. 1 (January 1966), 36–52; 40–45, 52; Samuel Bernstein, "The Opposition of French Labor to American Slavery," *Science & Society* 17, no. 2 (Spring 1953), 136–154, 137–39, 146–47; Cochin to Brownson, January 25, 1862, UNDA.
19. Samuel Bernstein, 144; John Delaunay, "Pierre-Suzanne-Augustin Cochin," *Catholic Encyclopedia*, vol. 4, 1908, http://www.newadvent.org/cathen/04078b.htm; Charles Poinsatte and Anne Marie Poinsatte, "Augustin Cochin's 'L'Abolition de l'esclavage' and the Emancipation Proclamation," *The Review of Politics* 46, no. 3 (July 1984), 410–427, at 410, 413; Cochin to Brownson, September 23, 1857, UNDA; Cochin to Brownson, July 21, 1861, UNDA.
20. Poinsatte and Poinsatte, 417; Augustin Cochin, *The Results of Emancipation*, trans. Mary Booth (Boston: Walker, Wise, 1863); Augustin Cochin, *The Results of Slavery*, trans. Mary Booth (Boston: Walker, Wise, 1863), 328, 333, 342, 347–350, 360. For Pope Gregory's encyclical, see Chapter 4.
21. "Slavery and the War," October 1861, BQR, 145–47, 152–56, 158–66, 171–76, 178.
22. "Slavery and the War," 159, 164.
23. Ibid., 167, 169.
24. Poinsatte and Poinsatte, 414, 425 (n12).
25. Rena Mazyck Andrews, "Slavery Views of a Northern Prelate," *Church History* 3, no. 1 (March 1934), 60–78, 62–63, 66.
26. Andrews, "Slavery Views," 64–65.
27. Ibid.
28. Ibid., 61–63.
29. John E. G. Hassard, *Life of the Most Reverend John Hughes, D.D., First Archbishop of New York. With extracts from his private correspondence* (New York: D. Appleton, 1866), 437; McGreevy, *Catholicism and American Freedom*, 80.
30. Hassard, 437, 447–51.
31. Andrews, "Slavery Views," 68–69.
32. Ibid., 70; Poinsatte and Poinsatte, 410; Hassard, 437–48; Cochin to Brownson, January 25, 1862, UNDA; Gavronsky, 48, 50; Patrick W. Carey, "Orestes Brownson and the Civil War," *U.S. Catholic Historian* 31, no. 1 (Winter 2013), 1–20, at 13.
33. Carey, *Religious Weathervane*, 42–43, 108–09, 224–25; Beverly Wilson Palmer, ed., *Guide and Index to the Papers of Charles Sumner* (Alexandria, VA: Chadwyck-Healey, 1988), 131; David Donald, *Charles Sumner and the Rights of Man* (New York: Alfred A. Knopf, 1970), 89, 98; Eric Foner, *Free Soil, Free Labor, Free Men: The Ideology of the Republican Party Before the Civil War* (New York: Oxford University Press, 1970), 119, 145; Oakes, 32–33; Sumner to Brownson, February 2, 1862, in *Selected Letters*, 99–100; Brownson to Sumner, April 11, 1862, UNDA. "Hughes on Slavery," 190–91. For John Brown and abolitionists, see generally, Edward J. Renehan, Jr., *The Secret Six: The True Tale of the Men Who Conspired With John Brown* (Columbia: University of South Carolina Press, 1997); Chester Hern, *Companions in Conspiracy: John Brown and Gerrit Smith* (Gettysburg, PA: Thomas Publications, 1996); Nevins, part 3, vol. 1, 333–34. As to Sumner and the French Revolution, Sumner later proposed a version of the Thirteenth Amendment which would forbid slavery based on the language of the 1789 French Declaration of Rights. His colleagues rejected this French Revolutionary phrasing and went with language based on America's Northwest Ordinance. Oakes,

441–42. In addition to lobbying Sumner, Orestes Brownson wrote Governor Andrew seeking an officer's commission for Ned, emphasizing that Ned was "Catholic" (underlined in original). Brownson to Andrew, July 25, 1862, John A. Andrew Papers, Reel 13, Massachusetts Historical Society.

34. "Archbishop Hughes on Slavery," January 1862, BQR, in *Works,* vol. XVII, 179–82.

35. "Hughes on Slavery," 184–85.

36. Ibid., 189.

37. Ibid., 192–96.

38. Ibid., 198–201.

39. Ibid., 203–05. Pope Gregory XVI's encyclical *In Supremo Apostolatus* concluded: "We prohibit and strictly forbid any Ecclesiastic or lay person from presuming to defend as permissible this traffic in Blacks under no matter what pretext or excuse, or from publishing or teaching in any manner whatsoever, in public or privately, opinions contrary to what We have set forth in this Apostolic Letter." http://www.ewtn.com/library/papaldoc/g16sup.htm. See Chapter 4.

40. H.S. Hewit to Brownson, February 21, 1861, UNDA; Fr. Augustine Hewit to Brownson, June 24, 1861, UNDA; H. S. Hewit to Brownson, September 16, 1861, UNDA; Mrs. Hewit to Brownson, September 25, 1861, UNDA; Sarah H. Brownson to Mrs. Hewit, October 1, 1861, UNDA; John H. Brinton, *Personal Memoirs of John H. Brinton, Major and Surgeon, U.S.V., 1861–1865* (New York: Neale Company, 1914), 26, 119, 122–23.

41. Rolle, 210–11, 216–18; Oakes, 166.

42. "State Rebellion, State Suicide," BQR, April 1861, in Brownson, *Works,* vol. XVII, 229–30, 232–36, 346–47, 250.

43. Eric Foner, 73–80, 85–87, 116–18, 144–45; Oakes, 7, 9, 23, 29, 200

44. "Emancipation and Colonization, BQR, April 1862, in *Works,* XVII, 259; Lester, 386; David von Drehle, *Rise to Greatness: Abraham Lincoln and America's Most Perilous Year* (New York: Henry Holt, 2012), 252; Foner, 266–69, 282–83, 293–94, Oakes, 274–75, 277–82.

45. "Emancipation and Colonization," 259–268, 270; Brownson to Sumner, April 11, 1862, UNDA; Louis Menand, "Morton, Agassiz, and the Origins of Scientific Racism in the United States," *The Journal of Blacks in Higher Education,* No. 34 (Winter, 2001–2002), 110–113; O'Connor, *The Athens of America,* 112.

46. John T. McGreevy, "Catholicism and Abolition: A Historican and Theological Problem," in Wilfred M. McClay, ed., *Figures in the Carpet,* (Grand Rapids, MI: William R. Eerdmans Publishing Company, 2007), 417; T. W. MacMahon, *Cause and Contrast: An Essay on the American Crisis* (Richmond: West and Johnston, 1862), electronic edition http://docsouth.unc.edu/imls/cause/cause.html; Bishop Elder to Archbishop Odin, March 24, 1862, UNDA; April 29, 1862: "Union Captures New Orleans," http://www.history.com/this-day-in-history/union-captures-new-orleans.

47. Sarah Brownson to Mrs. Hewit, May 20, 1862, UNDA; Brownson to Sumner, UNDA; May 21, 1862; Sumner to Brownson, February 2, 1862, in *Selected Letters,* 99–100; United States, Congress, Senate, *Journal of the Executive Proceedings of the Senate of the United States of America, From December 2, 1861, to July 17, 1862, inclusive, vol. XII* (Washington, D.C.: Government Printing Office, 1887), 422, 425, 427, 433–34; For Edward Brownson's assignment, see O.R., Series 1, vol. 11, Part 2 (Peninsular Campaign), Report of Captain John Edwards, July 5, 1862, 355–58, at 356.

48. Moore, *William S. Rosecrans and the Union Victory,* 21; Rolle, 218.

49. Rolle, 218–22, Henry Kyd Douglas, *I Rode With Stonewall* (St. Simon's Island, GA: Mockingbird Books, 1961), 73, 76–78, 85, 95, 97.

50. Edward Brownson to Sarah Brownson, June 16 and June 25, 1862, *in The Civil War Letters of Captain Edward "Ned" Patrick Brownson (1843–1864),* 1862 letters from the Mountain Department, Virginia, http://nedsletters.wordpress.com/chapters/1862-letters-from-the-mountain-department-virginia/.

51. Rolle, 222–25, 228; Ned Brownson to Sarah Brownson, July 2, 1862, Ned Brownson letters, http://nedsletters.wordpress.com/chapters/1862-letters-from-the-mountain-department-virginia/.

52. Henry Brownson, *Later Life,* 279–82.

Chapter 14

1. "Bishop Sylvester Horton Rosecrans, Deceased," http://www.catholic-hierarchy.org/bishop/brosec.html (accessed January 26, 2014); Clarke, 252–53; Sylvester's quote is from John 10:11.

2. Jack Tucker, *Innocents Return Abroad: Exploring Ancient Sites in Eastern Turkey (Volume 2)* (CreateSpace Independent Publishing Platform, 2013), 107–09; C. R. Cockerell, *Travels in Southern Europe and the Levant, 1810–1817,* ed. Samuel Pepys Cockerell (London: Longman's, Green, 1903), 189–90; John Carne, *Syria the Holy Land and Asia Minor Illustrated,* vol. II (London: Fisher, Son, [n.d., probably late 1830s]), 33–35; "Pompeiopolis in Cilicia (Titular See)," http://www.catholic-hierarchy.org/diocese/d3p04.html (accessed January 26, 2014).

3. Endres, "Fatal Contrast," 26–27.

4. *Diocese of Columbus: The History of Fifty Years, 1868–1918,* 1918, 30; Edward Riches de Levant, *Biblia Hexaglotta,* vol. v (New York: Funk and Wagnalls, 1901), 628–29; Clarke, 252–54.

5. Shea, *History 1843–1866,* 551; Sylvester to Purcell, May 18, 1862, and June 5, 1862, UNDA.

6. Mary Denis Maher, *To Bind Up the Wounds: Catholic Sister Nurses in the U.S. Civil War* (Baton Rouge: Louisiana State University Press, 1989), 36–38, 70, 74, 87, 101, 140; Margaret Humphreys, *Marrow of Tragedy: The Health Crisis of the American Civil War* (Baltimore: Johns Hopkins University Press, 2013), 34–35; Clarke, 254.

7. Maher, 39, 103, 111, 136–37, 139–40.

8. Barnabo to Purcell, February 15, 1862, in "Some Papers from the Purcell Collection," *The Catholic Historical Review* 1, no. 2 (July 1915), 199–201; Shea, *History 1843–1866,* 550; Bell Irvin Wiley, *The Life of Billy Yank: The Common Soldier of the Union* (Baton Rouge: Louisiana State University Press, 1971), 261–74.

9. Porter, 226, 238, 230.

10. George Henry Porter, 97, 103; Eugene H. Roseboom, "Southern Ohio and the Union in 1863," *The Mississippi Valley Historical Review* 39, no. 1 (June 1952), 29–44, at 33.

11. Oakes, 224, 235–36, 269–74, 285–88, 309; "An Act to Make An Additional Article of War," Freedmen and Southern Society Project, http://www.freedmen.umd.edu/artwar.htm; John S. Bowman, *The Civil War: Day by Day* (Greenwich, CT: Dorset, 1989), 92.

12. Louis P. Masur, *Lincoln's Hundred Days: The Emancipation Proclamation and the War for the Union* (Cambridge: Belknap Press, 2012), 153; Endres, 29, Reid, 84–86; Porter, 97; Bowman, 92.

13. Masur, 93–94; Oakes, 340–41; Joseph M. Laufer, "The Myth of the Excommunication of Comet Halley," *Halley's Comet Watch* IV, no. 1 (February 1985), available online at http://www.geocities.com/lauferworld.geo/HCexcomunication.htm (accessed January 26, 2014); W.F. Rigge, "The Pope and the Comet," *Popular Astronomy*, vol. 16 (1908), 481–83.

14. Oakes, 315–16.

15. Porter, *Ohio Politics*, 105; Oakes, 152–53.

16. Neely, 64–65; Porter, *Ohio Politics*, 107.

17. Weber, 36–37; 50–51; Porter, *Ohio Politics*, 105.

18. W. Jacque Voegeli, *Free But Not Equal: The Midwest and the Negro During the Civil War* (Chicago: University of Chicago Press, 1967), 95.

19. Lamers, 67.

20. Ibid., 68–83; Moore, *William S. Rosecrans and the Northern Victory*, 21–23.

21. Charles Whalen and Barbara Whalen, *The Fighting McCooks: America's Famous Fighting Family* (Bethesda, MD: Westmoreland Press, 2006), 98–99, 105; Honeck, 81–84, 98–100; Levine, 223–24.

22. Alan Nevins, *Ordeal of the Union*, vol. 3, Part II, *War Becomes Revolution* (New York: Collier, 1992), 372–73; Earl J. Hess, *Banners to the Breeze: The Kentucky Campaign, Corinth, and Stones River* (Lincoln: University of Nebraska Press, 2000), 129; Lamers, 92–96; Frank P. Varney, *General Grant and the Rewriting of History: How the Destruction of General William S. Rosecrans Influenced Our Understanding of the Civil War* (El Dorado Hills, CA: Savas Beatie, 2013), 110; Moore, 27.

23. Lamers, 104–05; Hess, 131–32; Varney, 40.

24. Lamers, 106–08; Varney, 48–49, 63–64; Moore, 29–31.

25. Lamers, 110–13; Hess, 133–37; Varney, 78; Moore, 32–33.

26. Varney, 54–58, 60.

27. Lamers, 120–21; 127–28; Moore, 35–36.

28. Hess, 141–42; Lamers, 131–35, 145; Varney, 83–84; Moore, 38.

29. Lamers, 132, 143–45; 148–49, 153–55; Hess, 146–61, 166–67, 172; Varney, 114–15; Moore, 38–43.

30. Lamers, 159–80; Varney, 103–07; Moore, 43–46.

31. Lamers, 181–84; Varney, 136–40; Moore, 49; William Rosecrans to Major General Wright, September 26, 1862, Abraham Lincoln Papers, War 1861 New York Historical Society.

32. David J. Endres and Jerrold P. Twohig, "'With a Father's Affection': Chaplain William T. O'Higgins and the Tenth Ohio Volunteer Infantry," *U.S. Catholic Historian* 31, no. 1 (Winter 2013), 97–127, at 97, 103–04, 120; Kurtz, "Let us Hear no More 'Nativism,'" 21.

33. Wiley, 165, 398 (n65). This song was recorded in a private soldier's diary in October 1863, probably in a retrospective mood after the song had reached its sell-by date in the wake of Chickamauga.

34. Ferdinand Heckmann, "Sts. Peter Baptist and Twenty-Five Companions," *Catholic Encyclopedia*, vol. 11, 1911, http://www.newadvent.org/cathen/11755b.htm; Daughters of St. Paul, "Prohibition of Christian Religion by Hideyoshi and 26 martyrs," http://english.pauline.or.jp/history/e-history03.php; Diego R. Yuki, S.J., "The Martyrs' Hill Nagasaki," Twenty-Six Martyrs Museum Home Page, http://210.136.236.116/MartyrsHP/Engmartstory.html; Emmanuel Kenners, *The Japanese Martyrs* (Manchester: Alex Ireland, 1862).

35. Chadwick, 170; Andrews, *American-Papal Relations*, 205; Hughes to Seward, June 12, 1862, in Hassard, 479; John L. Allen, Jr., *The Catholic Church: What Everyone Needs to Know* (New York: Oxford University Press, 2013), 139–41; Camillo Beccari, "Beatification and Canonizationm," *Catholic Encyclopedia*, vol. 2, 1907, http://www.newadvent.org/cathen/02364b.htm; Hughes to Seward, April 25, 1862, Seward Papers, Department of Rare Books and Special Collections, University of Rochester.

36. Stillman to Seward, January 3, 1862, January 23, in Stock, *Consular Relations*, 225–26, 228–29; Alvarez, 233–34, 236; Mary Salesia Martinkus, "Diplomatic Relations between the United States and the Vatican During the Civil War" (Master's Thesis, Loyola University, Chicago, 1953, 11–13, 32). For Stillman's life, see, generally, W.J. Stillman, *Autobiography of a Journalist, Volume I* (1901, reprinted by Project Gutenberg, March 11, 2004 [EBook #11546], http://www.gutenberg.org/files/11546/11546-8.txt).

37. Randall to Seward, June 11, June 18, 1862, in Stock, *United States Ministers*, 246–53; Alvarez, 235–37.

38. Fr. Matthew Hart to Bishop Francis McFarland, January 3 and January 12, 1862, UNDA; James Hennesey, S.J., *American Catholics: A History of the Roman Catholic Community in the United States* (Oxford: Oxford University Press, 1981), 164; Hales, 250–58; Chadwick, 169–70; Coppa, 143, 146; Allocution "Maxima quidem," June 9, 1862, in Monsignor Joseph Schroeder, *American Catholics and the Roman Question* (New York: Benziger Brothers, 1892), 38; certain key points of *Maxima Quidem* summarized in the *Syllabus of Errors*, propositions 1, 27, 39, 44, 49, 56, 59; http://www.papalencyclicals.net/Pius09/p9syll.htm, Papal Encyclicals Online; "A Brief History of the Diocese of Pittsburgh," http://www.diopitt.org/archives/this-day-in-diocesan-history.

39. Hales, 255–58; Alvarez, 236.

40. Alvarez, 237, 239; Anthony B. Lalli and Thomas H. O'Connor, "Roman Views on the American Civil War," *Catholic Historical Review* 57, no. 1 (April 1971), 21–41, 31.

41. Lalli and O'Connor, 31–34; Linck and Kupke, 42–43.

42. McGreevy, *Catholicism and American Freedom*, 87; Martinkus, 55–56.

43. Blatchford to Seward, November 29, 1862, in Stock, *United States Ministers*, 261–63.

44. Endres, 29; Shea, *History 1843–1866*, 551; Kurtz, "'Perfect Model,'" 81; Rosecrans to Purcell, August 10, 1862, UNDA; Kurtz, "Let us Hear no More 'Nativism,'" 24–26.

45. Lamers, 192–98; Hess, 177–78; Varney, 123–24.

46. Moore, 56; Garesché, 314, 315–16, 343–44, 349; Charles W. Eliot, ed., and Edward B. Pusey, trans., and William Benham, trans., *The Confessions of St Augustine—The Imitation of Christ (Kempis)* (Harvard Classics, 7) (New York: P. F. Collier and Sons, 1909). The reference to heaping coals of fire on an enemy's head by helping him is taken from Proverbs 25:22 and Romans 12:20.

47. Garesché, 355, 358, 363; Moore, 56.

48. Garesché, 352–53, 355–56. After the war, Julius' brother Alexander, an attorney, refused to take an oath imposed on attorneys and others by the new Unionist constitution in Missouri. *Missouri v. Garesché*, 36 Mo. 256, 1865 WL 2586 (Mo.). The oath required the affiant to swear that he had never aided the Confederacy or shown "sympathy" with it, and that he had "always been truly and loyally on the side of the United States." The United States Supreme Court later found this oath, which had also been imposed on the clergy and denounced as illegitimate by the Catholic Church, as constituting lay interference in Church affairs, unconstitutional, *Cummings v. Missouri*, 71 U.S. (4 Wall.) 277 (1867) (though the constitutional issue did not involve the First Amend-

ment rights of the Church but rather the fact that the law was a bill of attainder). Hiram Martin Chittenden, *Life, Letters and Travels of Father Pierre-Jean De Smet, S.J., 1801–1873,* Volume I (New York: Francis P. Harper, 1905), 134.

49. Gareschè, 19–20, 23, 351–52; Louis Gareschè to the French minister to the United States, August 28, 1889, Louis Gareschè papers, Rubenstein Library, Duke University.

50. Kurtz, "'Perfect Model,'" 81–82; Julius Gareschè to Mariquitta Gareschè, November 21, 1862, in Gareschè, 407.

51. Gareschè, 64, 65, 160.

52. Gareschè, 354–55; Homer Pittard, "The Strange Death of Julius Peter Gareschè: The Eccentric Officer 'Knew' He Would Die in his First Battle," http://www.latinamericanstudies.org/civil-war-cubans/Gareschè-death.htm.

53. Gareschè, 388.

54. Ibid., 396; Gareschè to McMaster, Sept. 30, 1882.

55. L. I. Gareschè to James McMaster, January 15, 1863, UNDA; General Orders, No. 31, Nashville, December 4, 1862, Julius P. Gareschè papers, Box 1, Folder 4, Georgetown University.

Chapter 15

1. O'Connor, *Fitzpatrick's Boston,* 198–99.

2. Samuel Windsor Brown, *The Secularization of American Education* (New York: Teachers College, Columbia, 1912), 78; Thomas H. O'Connor, *The Boston Irish: A Political History* (New York: Back Bay Books, 1997), 93; O'Connor, *Fitzpatrick's Boston,* 198–99; *Acts and Resolves Passed by the General Court of Massachusetts, in the years 1872, '73, Together With: The Constitution, the Messages of the Governor, List of the Civil Government, Changes in the Names of Persons, etc., etc., etc.* (Boston: Wright and Potter, 1873), 42–43, 47; Bruce, *Harp and Eagle,* 339–40; Thomas Harrington, "Massachusetts," *Catholic Encyclopedia,* vol. 10, 1911, http://www.newadvent.org/cathen/10024c.htm.

3. Bruce, *Harp and Eagle,* 184; Kerby A. Miller, *Emigrants and Exiles: Ireland and the Irish Exodus to North America* (New York: Oxford University Press, 1985), 74–77, 82–84, 86.

4. *Acts and Resolves Passed by the General Court of Massachusetts, in the years 1872, '73, Together With: The Constitution, the Messages of the Governor, List of the Civil Government, Changes in the Names of Persons, etc., etc., etc.* (Boston: Wright and Potter, 1873), 44; O'Connor, *The Boston Irish,* 93–94; Lawrence Friedman and Lynnea Thody, *The Massachusetts State Constitution* (New York: Oxford University Press, 2011), 174.

5. O'Connor, *Fitzpatrick's Boston,* 203; James M. O'Toole, 87; "Constitution of the Commonwealth of Massachusetts," https://malegislature.gov/Laws/Constitution.

6. O'Connor, *Fitzpatrick's Boston,* 203, 211; James M. O'Toole, 87; William L. Murfree, *The Justice of the Peace* (St. Louis: F. H. Thomas Law Book Company, 1886), 14; *Acts and Resolves Passed by the General Court of Massachusetts, in the years 1872, '73, Together With: The Constitution, the Messages of the Governor, List of the Civil Government, Changes in the Names of Persons, etc., etc., etc.* (Boston: Wright and Potter, 1873), 26.

7. McCloskey to Purcell, September 7, 1862, UNDA; McCloskey to Bishop Francis McFarland, November 29, 1862, UNDA.

8. McCloskey to Purcell, February 21, 1863, UNDA; O'Connor, *Fitzpatrick's Boston,* 203.

9. Joseph A. Fry, *Henry S. Sanford: Diplomacy and Business in Nineteenth-Century America* (Reno: University of Nevada Press, 1982), i, 1–2, 33, 35–59.

10. Fry, 59–65; Louis Gareschè, 361.

11. O'Connor, *Fitzpatrick's Boston,* 205.

12. Ibid., 204–05; Hubert Leroy, "Ambrose Dudley Mann: Diplomat of the Lost Cause," trans. Gerald Hawkins, Confederate Historical Association of Belgium, http://www.chab-belgium.com/pdf/english/Mann.pdf.

13. James M. O'Toole, 87–88.

14. 28th Massachusetts Regimental History, 1862, http://www.28thmass.org/history2.htm; Susannah Ural Bruce, "'Remember Your Country and Keep up Its Credit': Irish Volunteers and the Union Army, 1861–1865," *The Journal of Military History* 69, no. 2 (April 2005), 331–359, at 332–33.

15. Burton, 61, 130–31.

16. Corby, 42–43, 51–52, 73, 133.

17. Ibid., 113–14; Richard Slotkin, *The Long Road to Antietam: How the Civil War Became a Revolution* (New York: Liveright, 2012), 299–303.

18. Corby, 99–100.

19. Ibid., 57–58, 87, 90, 136.

20. Ibid., 122–27.

21. Bruce, *Harp and Eagle,* 175, 183; Burton, 133–34; Bruce, *Irish Volunteers,* 338–39.

22. Bruce, *Harp and Eagle,* 155; Corby, 62–63, 92, 112, 114; Bruce, *Irish Volunteers,* 346–47; Eicher, 379–80, 382–83, 395–405.

23. Bruce, *Irish Volunteers,* 339, 342–43.

24. Keneally, 367–68; Corby, 118; John Stauffer and Benjamin Soskis, *The Battle Hymn of the Republic: The Biography of a Song that Marches On* (New York: Oxford University Press, 2013), 9, 28, 46–48, 51–53. Keneally optimistically says: "The singing of an abolitionist song by largely Irish soldiers indicated that emancipation had achieved validity in the brigade" (368). Julia Ward Howe wrote new lyrics to "John Brown's Body" and the result was "The Battle Hymn of the Republic." See generally Stauffer and Soskis.

25. Bruce, *Irish Volunteers,* 344–45. One of the more moderate voices was Irish-American Rowland Redmond of New York, who wrote to a friend in the homeland that he supported gradual abolition but opposed the Lincoln administration's "exaggeration, unscrupulousness and lies." Immediate abolition meant "the destruction of the Blacks"—"Did I not often tell you that 'the north cared as little for poor Sambo as a pig did about the national debt!'"

26. Eicher, 401; Gerald F. Linderman, *Embattled Courage: The Experience of Combat in the American Civil War* (New York: The Free Press, 1987), 66.

27. Lindermann, 74; Bruce, 155–56; Craig A. Warren, "'O, God, What a Pity!' The Irish Brigade at Fredericksburg and the Creation of Myth," *Civil War History,* September 2001, http://vcwsg.com/PDF%20Files/Oh%20God%20What%20a%20Pity_The%20Irish%20Brigade%20at%20Fredericksburg%20and%20the%20Creation%20of%20Myth.pdf.

28. Bruce, *Irish Volunteers,* 344–45.

29. Hitchcock, 497–98, 502, 504, 507.

30. Lamers, 193; Earl J. Hess, *Banners to the Breeze: The Kentucky Campaign, Corinth, and Stones River* (Lincoln: University of Nebraska Press, 2000), 182

31. "W.D.B.," 52–54; Reid, 348.

32. Stephen E. Ambrose, *Halleck: Lincoln's Chief of Staff* (Baton Rouge: Louisiana State University Press, 1990), 107; Chase to James A. Garfield, August 17, 1863, in John Nive, ed., *The Salmon P. Chase Papers, Volume 4,*

Correspondence, April 1863–1864 (Kent, OH: Kent State University Press, 1997), 102; Moore, 57–58.
33. Kurtz, "'Perfect Model,'" 83.
34. Lamers, 198–201; Hess, 182–84.
35. Whalen and Whalen, 179–80; Hess, 193–96.
36. Garesché, 440; William Rosecrans to Major Alex. J. Dallas, January 21, 1880, Box 1, Folder 2, Julius Garesché papers, Special Collections, Georgetown University; Hess, 197–212; Lamers, 217–23; Whalen and Whalen, 181–85.
37. Lamers, 223–25; Hess, 212; Rosecrans to Dallas, Julius Garesché papers, Special Collections, Georgetown University.
38. Lamers, 225–26.
39. Ibid., 226–33; David Moore, 65.
40. Hess, 203–07; Lamers, 227; Thomas Meehan, "Philip Henry Sheridan," *Catholic Encyclopedia*, vol. 13, 1912, http://www.newadvent.org/cathen/13757a.htm.
41. Lamers, 225; Moore, 66.
42. Garesché, 440 (William Rosecrans recollections); Lamers, 232–33; Rosecrans to Dallas, Julius Garesché papers, Special Collections, Georgetown University.
43. Hess, 207–16–8; Peter Cozzens, *No Better Place to Die: The Battle of Stones River* (Urbana: University of Illinois Press, 1990), 171–74; Lamers, 235–37.
44. Oakes, 294–99.
45. Hess, 216–18, Lamers, 238–39; Oakes, 342–45.
46. Hess, 219–26; Lamers, 239–43; Kurtz, "'Perfect Model,'" 85; Moore, 71.
47. Cozzens, 206–07; von Drehle, 366–67; Lamers, 245.

Chapter 16

1. Edward Brownson to Sarah Brownson, July 2, 1862, http://nedsletters.wordpress.com/chapters/1862-letters-from-the-mountain-department-virginia/; Ned to Sarah, August 19, 1862, http://nedsletters.wordpress.com/chapters/1862-letters-from-the-military-district-of-washington/; Ned to Sarah, September 9 and September 12, 1862, http://nedsletters.wordpress.com/chapters/1862-letters-from-artillery-reserve-army-of-the-potomac/; Mrs. Brownson to Mrs. Hewit, May 20, 1862; UNDA.
2. Henry Brownson, *Later Life*, 376–77.
3. "Archbishop Hughes on Slavery," *BQR*, in *Works*, vol. XVII, 198–199; "Slavery and the War," in *Works*, vol. XVII, 158.
4. Brownson to Wood, May 2, 1862, Wood to Brownson, May 5, 1862, UNDA.
5. Hewit to Brownson, May 9, 1862, UNDA; Brownson to Sumner (draft), May 11, 1862, UNDA; Brownson to Sumner, May 12, 1862, UNDA; Brownson to Stanton, May 12, 1862, UNDA.
6. Hecker to Brownson, May 16, 1862, UNDA; Brownson to Simpson, May 21, 1862, UNDA; Herbert Thurston, "The Rambler," *Catholic Encyclopedia*, vol. 12, 1911, http://www.newadvent.org/cathen/12637b.htm; Edwin Burton, "Richard Simpson," *Catholic Encyclopedia*, vol. 14, 1912, http://www.newadvent.org/cathen/14004a.htm.
7. "What the Rebellion Teaches," July 1862, in *Works*, vol. XVII, 274–76.
8. Ibid., 277–78, 281.
9. Ibid., 279–80.
10. Ibid., 281–86, 291–92.
11. "Slavery and Emancipation," July 1862, *Works*, vol. XVII, 293–316.
12. Poinsatte and Poinsatte, 414–15, 423; Edwin G. Burrows and Mike Wallace, *Gotham: A History of New York City to 1898* (New York: Oxford University Press, 1999), 696; "Recent Publications," *The Christian Review* 28, January 1863, 155; "Reviews and Literary Notices," *Atlantic Monthly* 11, March 1863, 397.
13. Poinsatte and Poinsatte, 415, 425 (n20).
14. "Reviews and Literary Notices," *Atlantic Monthly* 11, March 1863, 397.

Chapter 17

1. Emerson Opdycke, *God and the Right*, ed. Glenn V. Longacre and John E. Haas (Urbana: University of Illinois Press, 2003), 49.
2. Lamers, 254–55.
3. Stoker, 238; Varney, 155–56.
4. Stoker, 238, 240; *God and the Right*, 62; Emerson Opdycke to Lucy Opdycke, April 26 1863 (incorrectly written "1864"), in *God and the Right*, 71; Moore, 75.
5. Emerson Opdycke to Lucy Opdycke, May 24, June 23, 1863, in *God and the Right*, 8.
6. Kurtz, "'Perfect Model,'" 85; "Father Emery," http://the-american-catholic.com/2008/10/09/father-emery/; "Father Emmeran Bliemel—Honoring a True American Hero," http://www.canadafreepress.com/index.php/article/13757.
7. Stoker, 239; *Freeman's Journal*, May 2, May 9, May 16, June 13, June 20, July 11, July 18, 1863.
8. General Rosecrans to Johnson, January 17, 1863, in Leroy P. Graf and Ralph W. Haskins, eds, *The Papers of Andrew Johnson, Volume 6, 1862–1864* (Knoxville: University of Tennessee Press, 1983), 123; Rosecrans to Johnson, April 4, 1863, in Graf. et. al., 205–06; Johnson to Rosecrans, June 1, 1863, in Graf., et al., 235. For Grant's actions against Jews, see Jonathan D. Sarna, *When General Grant Expelled the Jews* (New York: Nextbook, 2012).
9. Emerson Opdycke to Lucy Opdycke, June 2, 1863, July 1, 1863, in *God and the Right*, 82.
10. Lamers, 275–91; Peskin, 191–94; Moore, 88.
11. Eicher, 576–77; Varney, 178–79; Lamers, 295–96; Peskin, 197–200.
12. Emerson Opdycke to Lucy Opdycke, July 12, 1863, in *God and the Right*, 84–85
13. Reid, 138–47, 153–71; Vallandigham, 333–34.
14. Edward K. Spann, *Gotham at War: New York City 1861–1865* (Wilmington, DE: SR Books, 2001), 95–96, 114–19.
15. Florence Gibson, *The Attitudes of the New York Irish Toward State and National Affairs, 1848–1892* (New York: Columbia University Press, 1951), 143.
16. Schecter, 118–19.
17. Gibson, 151.
18. Horace Greeley, "A Friendly Letter to the Rt. Rev. John Hughes, R.C. Abp. Of NY," *New York Daily Tribune*, July 9, 1963, in Zanca, *American Catholics and Slavery*, 81–83.
19. Philip S. Foner, "Labor and the Copperheads," *Science & Society* 8, no. 3 (Summer 1944), 223–242, at 223; Spann, 96.
20. Toby Joyce, "The New York Draft Riots of 1863: An Irish Civil War?" *History Ireland* 11, no. 2 (Summer 2003), pp. 22–27, at 23–25.
21. Joyce, 24–27; Terry Golway, *Machine Made: Tammany Hall and the Creation of Modern American Politics* (New York: Liveright, 2014), 80.
22. Joyce, 25; A. Hunter Dupree and Leslie H Fishel, Jr., "An Eyewitness Account of the New York Draft Riots,

July 1863," *The Mississippi Valley Historical Review* 47, no. 3 (December 1960), pp. 472–479, 474, 477.

23. Joyce, 26–27.
24. Schecter, 207.
25. Gibson, 155–56; Schecter, 186, 206–08.
26. Foner, 225–26.
27. Brother Basil Leo Lee, *Discontent in New York City 1861–1865* (Dissertation, Catholic University of America Press, 1943), 108–10; Toby Joyce, "The New York Draft Riots of 1863: An Irish Civil War?" *History Ireland* 11, no. 2 (Summer 2003), 22–27, 25; Golway, *Machine Made*, 81–83; Clifton Hood, "An Unusable Past: Urban Elites, New York City's Evacuation Day, and the Transformations of Memory Culture," *Journal of Social History* 37, no. 4 (Summer 2004), 883–913, 883–84, 898; Gibson, 161–62; "Mayor Charles Godfrey Gunther, Coney Island Bound," August 20, 2009, http://theboweryboys.blogspot.com/2009/08/know-your-mayors-charles-godfrey.html.
28. Madame Baptiste Lynch to Bishop Patrick Lynch—September 4, 1863 (p. 9), Lowcountry Digital Archives, Family Letters, 1858–1866 http://lcdl.library.cofc.edu/lcdl/catalog/lcdl:42038; *Christian Record: Containing the History, Confession of Faith, and Statistics of Each Religious Denomination In the United States and Europe; A List of All Clergymen With their Post Office Address, etc., etc., etc.* (New York: W.R.C. Clark and Meeker, 1860), 387; David T. Gleeson, "No Disruption of Union," in Edward Blum and W. Scott Poole, *Vale of Tears: New Essays on Religion and Reconstruction* (Macon: Mercer University Press, 2005), 185. The Convent was later destroyed, but not by William. In 1865, during General Sherman's invasion, the city of Columbia burned and the convent and its valuables were consumed along with much of the town. The origins of the fire are uncertain to this day, though the Ursulines blamed the Northern invaders and Sherman. If it had been Rosecrans, rather than the vengeful Sherman, who led the federal invasion of South Carolina, it is possible that there wouldn't have been a fire, or if there had been, that the Ursulines would have been more willing to give the benefit of the doubt to their co-religionist. In the Court of Claims of the United States. Congressional No. 11075. The Ladies Ursuline Community of Columbia, S.C., v. The United States, United States Senate, 61st Congress, 3rd Session, Document 735, *The Ladies Ursuline Community, Columbia, S.C.,* 1911; Marion B. Lucas, *Sherman and the Burning of Columbia* (Columbia: University of South Carolina Press, 2000), 163–67.
29. Wiley Sword, *Mountains Touched With Fire: Chattanooga Besieged, 1863* (New York: St. Martin's Press, 1997), 11; Peskin, 201; Kevin Peraino, *Lincoln in the World: The Making of a Statesman and the Dawn of American Power* (New York: Crown, 2013), 180–89, 192–93.
30. Peskin, 202–04; Lamers, 325–335.
31. Wert, 28, 31, 303, 307–10.
32. Whalen and Whalen, 225; Sir Walter Scott, *Ivanhoe: A Romance* (New York: Signet Classic, 2001), 395–96; Andrew Dickson White, *The Soldier's Companion: Dedicated to the Defenders of Their Country in the Field by Their Friends at Home* (Boston: Walker, Wise, 1862), 9; *The Soldiers' Companion* (Boston: American Unitarian Association, 1865), 9; Theron Brown and Hezekiah Butterworth, *The Story of the Hymns and Tunes* (New York: George H. Doran, 1906), 240–41.
33. Sword, 12–13. A later story explained this sequence of events by reference to personality clashes. A few days before, says the story, William chewed Wood out in front of Wood's staff for disobeying an order. So when he got an order he knew to be based on bad information, Wood, resentful of his earlier upbraiding, supposedly decided to make a point of complying immediately.
34. Ibid., 13.
35. Ibid.; Lamers, 352.
36. Wert, 318–19; Sword, 13; Lamers, 351.
37. Owens, 9–10, 59, 95–98; "Chickagamauga," in *Ambrose Bierce's Civil War*, 102–03, 105.
38. Sword, 14, 18; Varney, 211–12; "Ave Maris Stella Hail Star of the Ocean," http://www.preces-latinae.org/thesaurus/BVM/AveMarisStella.html.
39. Sword, 14, 17–18.
40. Ibid., 15–17.
41. Ibid., 16, 44–45, 50; Lamers, 363.
42. Lamers, 386–87; Peskin, 216; Eicher, 595–96; Brian Steel Wills, *George Henry Thomas: As True as Steel* (Lawrence: University Press of Kansas, 2012), 414.
43. Peskin, 213.
44. Scott, *Ivanhoe*, 396; White (1862), 9; *The Soldiers' Companion* (1865), 9.

Chapter 18

1. Thomas H. O'Connor, *Civil War Boston: Home Front and Battlefield* (Boston: Northeastern University Press, 1997), 138–39; Judith Ann Giesberg, "'Lawless and Unprincipled': Women in Boston's Civil War Draft Riot," in James M. O'Toole and David Quigley, eds., *Boston's Histories: Essays in Honor of Thomas H. O'Connor* (Boston: Northeastern University Press, 2004), 79–80. Andrew did not think his state was getting enough credit for its volunteers. The more volunteers a state produced for the federal military, the lower its draft quotas were. Massachusetts' naval volunteers were the most numerous naval contingent of all states except New York. Yet only Army, not Navy, volunteers were set off against Massachusetts draft quotas. Also, Governor Andrew wanted to bring draftees into the Army as volunteers and pay them bounties, but the War Department nixed the idea.
2. Hanna, 272.
3. Giesberg, 80–81; Stephen Cabot, *Report of the "Draft Riot" in Boston, July 14, 1863, From the Diary of Major Stephen Cabot,* Printed by vote of the Veteran Association of Co. A, 1st Battalion of Massachusetts Heavy.
4. Hanna, 273; ; Giesberg, 71;"The Boston Draft Riot," http://www.ma150.org/day-by-day/1863-07-14/boston-draft-riot.
5. Giesberg, 272.
6. *Civil War Boston,* 140; Cabot, *Report*; "The Boston Draft Riot."
7. *Civil War Boston,* 140; Cabot, *Report*, "The Boston Draft Riot."
8. Cabot, *Report*.
9. Giesberg, 72; Cabot, *Report*.
10. Hanna, 271; James M. O'Toole, 97.
11. O'Connor, *Fitzpatrick's Boston,* 212; James M. O'Toole, 97–98; Hanna, 271.
12. James M. O'Toole, 97.
13. O'Connor, *Fitzpatrick's Boston,* 212; Geisber, 80; Hanna, 271.
14. Hanna, 271; James M. O'Toole, 98.
15. Healy to McFarland, July 19, 1863, UNDA.
16. James M. O'Toole, 99–100; Bernard Ward, "Douai," *Catholic Encyclopedia*, vol. 5, 1909, http://www.newadvent.org/cathen/05138a.htm.
17. McCloskey to McFarland, October 1, 1863, UNDA; James M. O'Toole, 100.
18. James M. O'Toole, 100–101.
19. Alvarez, 240–41.
20. Ibid., 239; Lalli and O'Connor, 31–32, 35.

21. William Barnaby Faherty, S.J., *Exile in Erin: A Confederate Chaplain's Story: The Life of Father John B. Bannon* (St. Louis: Missouri Historical Society Press, 2002), 38–39, 41, 43–51, 91–115, 98–99; Phillip Thomas Tucker, *The Confederacy's Fighting Chaplain: Father John B. Bannon* (Tuscaloosa: University of Alabama Press, 1992), 5, 20–21, 61–85, 87–158; Archbishop Francis Patrick Kenrick to Archbishop Odin, January 14, 1863, UNDA; Bishop Elder to Bishop Odin, May 21, 1863, UNDA; Bishop Elder to Bishop Odin, May 25, 1863, UNDA; Bishop Elder to Bishop Odin, July 6, 1863, UNDA; Bishop Elder to Bishop Odin, July 9, 1863, UNDA; Diocese of Little Rock, History of the Diocese, http://www.dolr.org/history/history.php Fr. Bannon initially served on an unpaid basis, surviving on borrowed money and aid from the officers. On one occasion, a mortally-wounded Confederate did not want to make his confession because he thought he was "not so bad." Fr. Bannon then pointed out that "your skull is split open, and your legs and arms are smashed." The soldier allowed as how he might need to confess, but he objected to the presence of a wounded Yankee next to him. This objection obviated, the rebel soldier made his confession, and the Yankee, who was also a Catholic, confessed to Fr. Bannon as well.
22. Tucker, 157–66.
23. Ibid., 161–63, 165–66.
24. Alvarez, 241–42; King to Seward, January 5, 1863, in Stock, *United States Ministers*, 281; Tucker, 166; "Letter to the Pope from Jefferson Davis," http://xpknights.net/images/lettertoJeffersonDavis.pdf.
25. "Correspondence between His Holiness Pope Pius IX and President Jefferson Davis," http://www.danvilleartillery.org/popeletter.htm.
26. Alvarez, 242–43.
27. Seward to King, October 15, 1863, J.C. Hooker to Seward, December 12, 1863, King to Seward, January 5, 1864, Seward to King, January 29, 1864, in Stock, *United States Ministers*, 278–80.
28. King to Seward, January 5, 1963, in Stock, *United States Ministers*, 280–81.
29. King to Seward, January 15, 1863, in Stock, *United States Ministers*, 281–82.
30. Joseph Cummins, *The War Chronicles: From Flintlocks to Machine Guns: A Global Reference of all the Major Modern Conflicts* (Beverly, MA: Fair Winds Press, 2009), 148; Chadwick, 162–65; John Bierman, *Napoleon III and His Carinval Empire* (New York: St. Martin's Press, 1988), 169–74, 193–94, 202, 204, 206, 229–30, 240; Hales, 262; "Louis Veuillot," 436–38. Louis Napoleon's loyalty to the pope was as fragile as his loyalty to his wife. He sought escape from his marital obligations in the arms of a series of mistresses, including a cousin of the Piedmontese premier Camille Cavour, who set up the relationship as an incentive for the French leader to stay on the Italian nationalist side.
31. Chadwick, 423–27, 429; Brian Porter-Szucs, *Faith and Fatherland: Catholicism, Modernity, and Poland* (New York: Oxford University Press, 2011), 225–29, 237–38. Archbishop Feliński spent twenty years in Siberian exile, still recognized by Rome as the archbishop of Warsaw. The pope arranged with the Russian government to give Felinski a titular bishopric outside the Russian empire, and to relax the terms of the prelate's exile. In 2009, Pope Benedict XVI canonized Felinski. http://www.vatican.va/news_services/liturgy/saints/ns_lit_doc_20020818_felinski_en.html.
32. Chadwick, 417, 419–23, 427–29; Brian Porter-Szucs, 215–22.
33. Joseph W. Wieczerzak, *A Polish Chapter in Civil War America: The Effects of the January Insurrection on American Opinion and Diplomacy* (Boston: Twayne, 1967), 39–40.
34. C. Douglas Kroll, *Friends in Peace and War: The Russian Navy's Landmark Visit to Civil War San Francisco* (Washington, D.C.: Potomac Books, 2007), 15–21, 55–56; Wieczerzak, *Polish Chapter*, 156–57, 170, 191–93, 247–48; M. Kaufman, "1863: Poland, Russia and the United States," *Polish American Studies* 21, no. 1 (January—June 1964), 10–15, 11, 13–16; J. Wieczerzak, "American Reactions to the Polish Insurrection of 1863," *Polish American Studies* 22, no. 2 (July—December 1965), 90–98. The Boston *Pilot*, in contrast, praised the Polish revolt as a just uprising against Czarist oppression. Like other Irish papers, the *Pilot* believed the Irish should draw inspiration from the Poles. Wieczerzak, *Polish Chapter*, 60–61, 135.
35. John A. Davis, *Conflict and Control: Law and Order in Nineteenth Century Italy* (New York: Macmillan Education, 1988) 168–72, 174–77, 183; Lucy Riall, *Sicily and the Unification of Italy: Liberal Policy and Local Power 1859–1866* (Oxford: Clarendon Press, 1998), 149–50, 163–64.
36. John Davis, 173, 175, 179–82, 184; Riall, 151, 156–58; Dickie, 10, 15; Guy Stair Sainty, "The Bourbons of Naples in Exile," in Philip Mansel and Torsten Riotte, eds., *Monarchy and Exile* (Basingstoke: Pagrave Macmillan, 2011), 261; Robert Pearce and Andrina Stiles, *The Unification of Italy 1815–70*, 3d ed. (Trans-Atlantic Publications, 2006 [Kindle Edition]).
37. Sainty, 263–64; 269; John Davis, 175; John Dickie, "A World at War: The Italian Army and Brigandage 1860–1870," *History Workshop* 33 (Spring 1992), 1–24, 16, 23 (n67); Riall, 149–50; Henry Winston Barron, *Results of Victor Emmanuel's Rule* (London: Harrison, 1863), 73, 83–86.

Chapter 19

1. Lamers, 395, 399, 401, 403.
2. Varney, 242; Lamers, 401–02; Kurtz, "'Perfect Model,'" 85.
3. Trecy to Purcell, November 18, 1863, UNDA.
4. Lamers, 401, 405.
5. Chase to Lincoln, October 31, 1863, in John Niven, et al., eds., *The Salmon P. Chase Papers, Volume 4, Correspondence, April 1863–1864* (Kent, OH: Kent State University Press, 1997), 163; Michael Fellman, *Inside War: The Guerrilla Conflict in Missouri During the American Civil War* (New York: Oxford University Press, 1989), 53, 54, 62.
6. Fellman, 29–31, 33, 34, 42, , 50–51, 71–72, 87, 92–93, 115–16, 118, 121.
7. Lamers, 395–96; Frank L. Klement, *Copperheads in the Middle West* (Chicago: University of Chicago Press, 1960), 176–77; Frank L. Klement, *Dark Lanterns: Secret Political Societies, Conspiracies, and Treason Trials in the Civil War* (Baton Rouge: Louisiana State University Press, 1984), 74–76.
8. McGreevy, *Catholicism and American Freedom*, 74; R. L. Stanton, *The Church and the Rebellion* (New York: Derby & Miller, 1864), 238–39; Lincoln to Stanton, February 11, 1864, in Roy P. Basler, ed., *The Collected Works of Abraham Lincoln*, vol. VII (New Brunswick: Rutgers University Press, 1953), 179–80, 182–83; "Let Us Hear No More 'Nativism,'" 29; Edward McPherson, *The Political History of the United States of America During the Great Rebellion* (Washington, D.C.: Philp and Solomons, 1865), 522; O.R., I, XXXIV, II, 452–53; Dennis K. Boman, *Lincoln and Citizens' Rights in Civil War Missouri: Balancing

Freedom and Security (Baton Rouge: Louisiana State University Press, 2011), 246–47; Worth E. "Woody" Norman, Jr., "Civil War, Church and State," July 4, 2013, http://www.livingchurch.org/civil-war-church-and-state; "Hogan, John," Biographical Directory of the United States Congress, http://bioguide.congress.gov/scripts/biodisplay.pl?index=H000691.

9. Rosecrans to J.P. Findley, Westminster College, Fulton, Missouri, April 29, 1864, O.R., Ser. 1, vol. 34, Part 3, 348–50; W. M. Leftwich, *Martyrdom in Missouri*, vol. II (St. Louis: Southwestern, 1870), 61–71; Boman, 247–48.

10. Leftwich, 67–70; Lincoln to WSR, April 4, 1864, in Basler, ed., *Collected Works of Abraham Lincoln*, vol. VII, 283–84, http://quod.lib.umich.edu/l/lincoln/lincoln7/1:619?rgn=div1;view=fulltext.

11. Rosecrans to Findley, April 29, 1864, O.R., Ser. 1, vol. 34, Part 3, 348–50.

12. Bishop Frederick Baraga to Purcell, January 16, 1864, UNDA; Purcell to the Bishops of the Province of Cincinnati, February 2, 1864, UNDA; Purcell to Lefevere, February 19, 1864, UNDA.

13. "From a Pastoral Letter of Bishop Dupanloup (Orleans, France) to His Clergy on the Subject of American Slaves, 1862," April 6, 1862, in Zanca, *American Catholics and Slavery*, 121–25; McGreevy, *Catholicism and American Freedom*, 50; Hales, 137, 210, 272–73; Coppa, 148; Joseph Sollier, "Felix-Antoine-Philibert Dupanloup," *Catholic Encyclopedia*, vol. 5, 1909, http://www.newadvent.org/cathen/05202a.htm.

14. Montalembert's Speech at the Malines Congress (Extracts), August 20–21, 1863, in J. F. MacLear, *Church and State in the Modern Age: A Documentary History* (New York: Oxford University Press, 1995), 156–63.

15. Purcell to Lefevere, February 19, 1864, UNDA; Carol E. Harrison, *Romantic Catholics: France's Postrevolutionary Generation in Search of a Modern Faith* (Ithaca: Cornell University Press, 2014), 103.

16. Lefevere to Purcell, March 15, 1864, UNDA; Kurtz, "'Perfect Model,'" 91.

17. McCloskey to Purcell, March 4, 1864, UNDA; Spalding to Purcell, March 22, 1864, UNDA; Spalding to Purcell, April 26, 1864, UNDA; Spalding to Purcell, May 19, 1864, UNDA; Spalding to Purcell, June 9, 1864, UNDA; Kurtz, "'Perfect Model,'" 91.

18. Fr. William McCloskey to Bishop McFarland, March 5, 1864, UNDA; Purcell to Lefevere, March 24, 1864, UNDA; Spalding to Purcell, June 14, 1864, UNDA; Spalding to Levevere, June 15, 1864, UNDA; Spalding to Lefevere, June 20, 1864, UNDA; Spalding to Purcell, June 20, 1864, UNDA; Spalding to Lefevere, June 23, 1864, UNDA.

19. Sanderson report, O.R., Series 2, vol. 7, Part 1, 233; Klement, *Midwest*, 177–83; Klement, *Dark Lanterns*, 76–84.

20. Basil Lee, 223–25.

21. Robert S. Harper, *Lincoln and the Press* (New York: McGraw-Hill, 1951), 127, 146; Spann, 168; Basil Lee, 250–51, 286–87; O.R., Series 2, vol. 2, Part 1 (Prisoners of War), 802, 804; Kwitchen, 126; U.S. Marshals Service, History, list of U.S. Marshals from New York, http://www.usmarshals.gov/readingroom/us_marshals/new_york.pdf; Rosecrans decree in the New York Times, April 6, 1864, http://www.nytimes.com/1864/04/03/news/gen-rosecrans-on-the-metropolitan-record-headquarters-department-of-the-missouri.html. For O'Conor, see Robert D. Sampson, "O'Conor (O'Connor), Charles," in Peter Eisenstadt and Laura-Eve Moss, eds., *The Encyclopedia of New York State* (Syracuse: Syracuse University Press, 2005), 1130; John D. Gordan III, "The Lemmon Slave Case," *Newsletter of the Historical Society of the Courts of the State of New York* 4, 2006, 1, 8–12. Charles Sloane, "Charles O'Conor," *Catholic Encyclopedia*, vol. 11, 1911, http://www.newadvent.org/cathen/11202a.htm; summary of *Jack v. Martin*, http://www.nycourts.gov/history/legal-history-new-york/legal-history-eras-02/history-new-york-legal-eras-jack-martin.html. After the war, O'Conor's clients included Jefferson Davis and Samuel Tilden. O'Conor fought lengthy legal proceedings against Boss Tweed for corruption. O'Conor ran for President in 1872, nominated by various disgruntled Democrats who refused to support the party's nominee, Horace Greeley. During a serious illness in the last years of his life, O'Conor received the last rites from Cardinal Archbishop John McCloskey.

22. Hassard, 502.

23. David Long, *The Jewel of Liberty: Abraham Lincoln's Re-Election and the End of Slavery* (Mechanicsburg, PA: Stackpole Books, 1994), 93–95.

24. John Boyko, *Blood and Daring: How Canada Fought the American Civil War and Forged a Nation* (Toronto: Alfred A. Knopf Canada, 2013), 160–61; Long, 102–03.

25. Robert H. Churchill, *To Shake Their Guns in the Tyrant's Face: Libertarian Political Violence and the Origins of the Militia Movement* (Ann Arbor: University of Michigan Press, 2012), 133; John Boyko, 175; Oscar A. Kinchen, *Confederate Operations in Canada and the North: A Little-Known Phase of the American Civil War* (North Quincy, MA: Christopher, 1970), 43; Klement, *Dark Lanterns*, 106–08; Mark A. Lause, *A Secret Society History of the Civil War* (Urbana: University of Illinois Press, 2011), 128–29; Kwitchen, 139–40; Longuemare to McMaster, December 4, 1863, April 26, 1865, September 20, 1865, October 18, 1865, [no month or day given] 1865, February 24, 1866, UNDA. For a discussion of the Confederacy's operations in the North, see Jane Singer, *The Confederate Dirty War: Arson, Bombings, Assassination and Plots for Chemical and Germ Attacks on the Union* (Jefferson, NC: McFarland, 2005).

26. Klement, *Middle West*, 184; David Long, 102–05; Boyko, 177; "U. S. Grant—Friends with foes," http://www.mocivilwar.org/u-s-grant-friends-foes/.

27. *Report of the Judge Advocate General* (Washington, D.C.: Government Printing Office, 1864); Klement, *Midwest*, 184–86; Klement, *Dark Lanterns*, 136–48. Klement believed that the Copperheads were loyal Americans who simply disagreed with the war, and that reports of conspiracies, such as Sanderson's report, were politically-motivated hack jobs. Some of the debate over the Copperheads is reviewed in Thomas E. Rodgers, "Copperheads or a Respectable Minority: Current Approaches to the Study of Civil War-Era Democrats," *Indiana Magazine of History* 109, no. 2 (June 2013), 114–146.

28. Lamers, 424–25; Varney, 250–51.

29. Lamers, 424–25; Varney, 250–51; Margaret Leech, *Reveille In Washington 1860–1865* (New York: Time Incorporated, 1962), 199–201.

30. Varney, 252.

31. John C. Waugh, *Reelecting Lincoln: The Battle for the 1864 Presidency* (Cambridge: Da Capo Press, 2001), 291–92, 300–01; James Grant Wilson and John Fiske, *Appleton's Cyclopædia of American Biography, Volume 4* (New York: D. Appleton, 1888), 554–55; Wilson and Fiske; Sloane.

32. Stephen Z. Starr, "Was There a Northwest Conspiracy?" *The Filson Club Historical Quarterly* 38, no. 4 (October 1964), 323–341, at 327–28; Lamers, 426–27; Varney, 253.

33. Fellman, 109, 111; Stephen Starr, 331; Varney, 253, 255.

34. Lamers, 427–29, 430–33, 435, 437; Varney, 253–58; Stephen Starr, 252–53, 331; Kurtz, "'Perfect Model,'" 91; "Father Patrick John Ryan," http://www.pricecamp.org/kelly.htm.
35. Lamers, 437–38.
36. Ibid., 4–5.

Chapter 20

1. BQR, Third New York Series, vol. IV (New York: D&J Sadlier, 1863), 385–93, 401.
2. Ibid., 403.
3. Ibid., 405–07.
4. Ibid., 409–11.
5. Ibid., 431–33.
6. McGreevy, *Catholicism and American Freedom*, 77.
7. Henry Brownson, 404–08.
8. BQR, National Series, vol. I (D&J Sadlier & Co., 1864), 243–45.
9. Ibid., 190–94.
10. Ibid., 196–200.
11. Ibid., 201–04, 207.
12. Ibid., 210–12, 214–15, 216–19.
13. Henry Brownson, 399–400, 437; Rolle, 230; James A. Rawley, *The Politics of Union: Northern Politics during the Civil War* (Hinsdale, IL: The Dryden Presss, 1974), 156; David Long, 180–81.
14. Michigan Historical Reprint Series, *The century of independence: Embracing a collection, from official sources, of the most important documents and statistics connected with the political history of America; also, a chronological record of the principal events ... with biographical and historical sketches* (Scholarly Publishing Office, University of Michigan Library, 2005), 342.
15. *The century of independence*, 342; Kaufman, "Poland, Russia and the United States"; Wieczerzak, "American Reactions."
16. BQR, vol. I, 340–41, 347, 350–69.
17. Ibid., 257–83.
18. Faherty, 130–36; Tucker, *Fighting Chaplain*, 172–80; Clarke, 73; King to Seward, July 30, August 16 and August 22, 1864, in Stock, *United States Ministers*, 313, 315.
19. King to Seward, August 22, 1864, in Stock, *United States Ministers*, 315–16.
20. David Long, 171, 236, 241–42; Rolle, 232; Catholic-baiting Unionist Samuel Morse sent out an SOS about the administration's emancipation policies—"*Slavery* to [black people] has been *Salvation*, and *freedom, ruin.*" Silverman, *Lightning Man*, 398–402.
21. BQR, vol. I, 420–50.
22. The Civil War Letters of Captain Edward "Ned" Patrick Brownson (1843–1864), 1863 Letters from the Artillery Reserve, Army of the Potomac, http://nedsletters.wordpress.com/chapters/1863-letters-from-the-artillery-reserve-army-of-the-potomac/; Ned Brownson letters, 1863, Letters from the 2nd Army Corps, Army of the Potomac, http://nedsletters.wordpress.com/chapters/1863-letters-from-the-2nd-army-corps-army-of-the-potomac/; General Hancock to General Humphreys, August 26, 1864, O.R., Series 1, vol. 42, Part 2, 525–26; Carey, *Religious Weathervane*, 280–81. Ned, while an abolitionist, had also somehow picked up some anti-black racism, preferring Irish servants to black ones and hanging up a black servant by the thumbs to punish him for stealing a horse. He later complained that a black servant had fled. "Civil War Letters."
23. BQR, National Series, vol. I, 470.
24. Ibid. 470–89.
25. Hales, 262–64.
26. Coppa, 145–46; Chadwick, 174–75; *Quanta Cura*, Papal Encyclicals online, http://www.papalencyclicals.net/Pius09/p9quanta.htm.
27. "Syllabus of Errors," Papal Encyclicals online, http://www.papalencyclicals.net/Pius09/p9syll.htm.
28. Ibid.
29. Ibid.; Avery Cardinal Dulles, S.J., *Church and Society: The Laurence J. McGinley Lectures, 1988–2007* (New York: Fordham University Press, 2008), 8.
30. "Syllabus of Errors."
31. Ibid.; Hales, 270–71.
32. Coppa, 147; Chadwick, 175–76.
33. Coppa, 148; Chadwick, 176–79.
34. Montalembert to Brownson, December 17, 1864, in Henry Brownson, *Later Life*, 439–41.
35. Caravaglios, *Roman Critique*, 68–69; Curran, in Linck and Kupke, 44–45.
36. Caravaglios, *Roman Critique*, 75.
37. Ibid., 75–76; Genesis 9:18, 21–26 (NAB).
38. Caravaglios, *Roman Critique*, 76–77, 79; Eve M. Troutt Powell, *Tell This in My Memory: Stories of Enslavement from Egypt, Sudan and the Ottoman Empire* (Redwood City, CA: Stanford University Press, 2012), 149; Jean Owen Maynard, *Josephine Bakhita: The Lucky One* (London: Catholic Truth Society, 2002), 21–22, 66–67.
39. Caravaglios, *Roman Critique*, 78–80.
40. Ibid., 69–70, 80.

Chapter 21

1. The one significant exception was in federally-occupied New Orleans, where a priest and his parishioners went into schism because of the war. A sketchy French parish priest, Claude Paschal Maistre, took up the cause of blacks, supporting abolitionism and the Northern war effort, and attracting fugitive slaves and free blacks to his parish. Archbishop Jean-Marie Odin, who opposed Maistre's politics, looked for an occasion to deal with the radical cleric, and found his chance with Maistre's French criminal record. Odin suspended Maistre, and when the latter continued his priestly ministry, Archbishop Odin put an interdict on his church. Maistre and his flock were formally in schism, and the priest got the support of radical Republicans in Louisiana. Cardinal Barnabo in Propaganda sustained Odin, and Maistre, whose congregation dwindled after the war, ultimately made peace with Odin's successor, Napoléon Perché, who as a priest-editor during the war had taken a pro-Confederate, anti-racist position. This took place in the context of a large community of Catholic "free persons of color" in New Orleans, free even before the war, who often didn't believe the local Church authorities were respecting their rights and dignity in the rapidly-changing circumstances of the war and the end of slavery. Stephen J. Ochs, *A Black Patriot and a White Priest: Andre Cailloux and Claude Paschal Maistre in Civil War New Orleans* (Baton Rouge: Louisiana State University Press, 2000), 1–2, 6–7, 95–99, 102–03, 106–07, 115–15, 132–37, 155–56, 190–97, 234–45, 250–61.
2. O'Connor, *Fitzpatrick's Boston*, 226–27.
3. Kate Clifford Larson, *The Assassin's Accomplice: Mary Surratt and the Plot to Kill President Lincoln* (New York: Basic Books, 2008), 13, 21, 25, 56, 157, 201–05.
4. H. E. Matheny, *Major General Thomas Maley Harris* (Parsons, WV: McClain, 1963), 198, 213–15; Andrews, *American-Papal Relations*, 259–60; Kenneth J. Zanca, The

Catholics and Mrs. Mary Surratt: How They Responded to the Trial and Execution of the Lincoln Conspirator (Lanham, MD: University Press of America, 2008), 95–96.

5. Andrew C. A. Jampoler, *The Last Lincoln Conspirator: John Surratt's Flight from the Gallows*, (Annapolis: Naval Institute Press, 2008), 45–46, 48–49, 68–69, 76, 87, 89–93, 95–97, 154; Boyko, 7, 137; Preston Jones, "Civil War, Culture War: French Quebec and the American War Between the States," *The Catholic Historical Review* 87, no. 1 (January 2001), 55–70; Kinchen, 46; Coulombe, 109–10.

6. Jampoler, 106–07, 112; King to Seward, April 23, 1866, Seward to King, April 30, 1866, King to Seward, May 11, 1866, F.W. Seward to King, May 21, 1866, F. W Seward to King, May 24, 1866, King to Seward, June 4, 1866, Seward to King, June 9, 1866, Seward to King, June 15, 1866, King to Seward, June 19, 1866, King to Seward, November 2, 1866, King to Seward, November 3, 1866, King to Seward, November 10, 1866, King to Seward, November 20, 1866, in Stock, *United States Ministers*, 359–65, 385–89, 394.

7. Jampoler, 112–13, 128–30, 141–52, 175–218, 250–64; King to Seward, November 10, 1866, King to Seward, November 19, 1866, King to Seward, November 20, 1866, Seward to King, November 26, 1866, King to Seward, November 26, 1866, Seward to King, November 30, 1866, King to Seward, December 1, 1866, in Stock, *United States Ministers*, 388–95.

8. Andrews, *American-Papal Relations*, 253–54.

9. Ibid., 259–60; Thomas A. Bogar, *Backstage at the Lincoln Assassination* (Washington: Regnery History, 2013); Paul Laverdure, "'The Jesuits Did It!' Charles Chiniquy's Theory of Lincoln's Assassination," *Historical Papers: Canadian Society of Church History* (2001): 125–139; Julie M. Fenster, *The Case of Abraham Lincoln: A Story of Adultery, Murder, and the Making of a Great President* (New York: Palgrave Macmillan, 2007), 86–89, 196–980; Joseph George, Jr., "The Lincoln Writings of Charles P. T. Chiniquy," *Journal of the Illinois State Historical Society* 69, no. 1 (February 1976), 17–25, at 22–23.

10. George, "Chiniquy," 18–25; William Hanchett, *The Lincoln Murder Conspiracies* (Urbana: University of Illinois Press, 1983), 233–41

11. Matheny, 198, 216–22; Thomas Harris, *Rome's Responsibility for the Assassination of Abraham Lincoln* (Tonasket, WA: Celestial Strains, 2005) (reprint of Williams edition, 1897), 20, 29–31, 36–38. For the perspective of a conspiracy theorist, see "THC 29: The Lincoln Assassination & the Catholic Church w/ Paul Serup," http://thehighersidechats.com/higherside-chats-podcast-29-lincoln-assassination-catholic-church-w-paul-serup/.

12. "Update on Jefferson Davis's Crown of Thorns," *Civil War Memory*, September 27, 2009, http://cwmemory.com/2009/09/27/update-on-jefferson-davis-crown-of-thorns/; "Jefferson Davis and the Crown of Thorns," *The American Catholic*, Tuesday, August 3, 2010, http://the-american-catholic.com/2010/08/03/jefferson-davis-and-the-crown-of-thorns/; Felicity Allen, "Jeff Davis's Crown of Thorns," July 24, 2014, http://www.abbevilleinstitute.org/blog/jeff-daviss-crown-of-thorns/.

13. Carey, *Religious Weathervane*, 284, 289, 291, 294, 338–343; Robert Emmet Moffit, "Orestes Brownson and the Political Culture of American Democracy," *Modern Age*, Summer 1978, 265–76.

14. Carey, *Religious Weathervane*, 285, 303–316; David Jerome Callon, *Converting Catholicism: Orestes A. Brownson, Anna H. Dorsey, and Irish America, 1840–1896* (Dissertation, Washington University, 2008), 14–15, 29.

15. Carey, *Religious Weathervane*, 380–85.

16. Lamott, 84, 109, 210; Clarke, "Bishops," 253; "The 'Other' Rosecrans," 4–5.

17. Clarke, "Bishops," 221–26, 253–55; Carey, *Religious Weathervane*, 306, 312–14; Jason Berry, *Render Unto Rome: The Secret Life of Money in the Catholic Church* (New York: Crown, 2011), 40–41, 48–49; Orestes Brownson, *The American Republic: Its Constitution, Tendencies and Destiny* (New York: P. O'Shea, 1866); Pat McNamera, "The Big Rock Versus the Little Rock: Bishop Edward M. Fitzgerald (1833–1907)," http://www.patheos.com/blogs/mcnamaras blog/2010/10/%E2%80%9Cthe-big-rock-versus-the-little-rock%E2%80%9D-bishop-edward-m-fitzgerald-1833-1907.html.

18. Clarke, "Bishops," 256–58; "The 'Other' Rosecrans," 5–7.

19. Clarke, "Bishops," 258–60; "The 'Other' Rosecrans," 6–7; Berry, 50.

20. Lamott, 82–83; 189–207.

21. Lamers, 440–43; Sylvester Rosecrans to Purcell, January 17, 1868, UNDA.

22. Ibid; William Rosecrans to Horatio Seymour, September 6, 1868, Seymour Papers, New York Historical Society; *Staunton Spectator*, September 8, 1868, available online at http://valley.lib.virginia.edu/news/ss1868/va.au.ss. 1868.09.08.xml.

23. Lamers, 443–46.

24. Varney, 1–2, 6–8, 42–44, 83–86, 133, 173, 269–70; Jerome Loving, *Confederate Bushwhacker: Mark Twain in the Shadow of the Civil War* (Hanover, NH: University Press of New England, 2013), 17, 52–53, 72–73, 85, 90, 138, 176–78; Lamers, 445.

25. Lamers, 446–48; Kurtz, "'Perfect Model,'" 92–93.

26. Lamers, 448–50.

27. Wert, 411–27; Joshua Canzona, "General James Longstreet in New Orleans," *The Loyola University Student Historical Journal* 34 (2002–2003), http://www.loyno.edu/~history/journal/documents/josh.PDF; Thomas Meehan, "James Longstreet," *Catholic Encyclopedia*, vol. 9, 1910, http://www.newadvent.org/cathen/09354a.htm; New Georgia Encyclopedia, "Helen Dortch Longstreet," http://www.georgiaencyclopedia.org/articles/history-archaeology/helen-dortch-longstreet-1863-1962.

28. Shea, *History 1843–1866*, 715–20; Ellis, 101–02; Benjamin J. Blied, *Catholics and the Civil War* (Milwaukee, 1945), 34; Cyprian Davis, 157–58; Gannon, 104–05, 128–31"; William Fanning, "Plenary Councils of Baltimore," *Catholic Encyclopedia*, vol. 2, 1907, http://www.newadvent.org/cathen/02235a.htm.

29. James M. O'Toole, 126–31; Wilfrid H. Paradis, *Upon This Granite: Catholicism in New Hampshire 1647–1997* (Portsmouth, NH: Peter E. Randall, 1998), 100.

30. James M. O'Toole, 138; Paradis, 100–02.

31. James M. O'Toole, 138–43, 150–51.

Conclusion

1. Cardinal Timothy Dolan and John L. Allen, Jr., *A People of Hope: The Challenges Facing the Catholic Church and the Faith that Can Save It* (New York: Image, 2011), 85; Michael J. Baxter, "Writing History in a World Without Ends: An Evangelical Catholic Critique of United States Catholic History," *Pro Ecclesia* V, no. 4 (Fall 1996); Joseph E. Capizzi, "For What Shall We Repent? Reflections on the American Bishops, Their Teaching, and Slavery in the United States, 1839–1861," *Theological Studies* 65 (2004); John T. Noonan, Jr., *A Church That Can and Cannot Change: The Development of Catholic Moral Teaching* (Notre Dame: University of Notre Dame Press, 2005), 17–123; Joel S. Panzer, *The Popes and Slavery* (Staten Island:

Alba House, 1996); Joseph Brokhage, *Francis Patrick Kenrick's Opinion on Slavery* (Washington, D.C.: Catholic University of America Press, 1955); Avery Cardinal Dulles, "Development or Reversal?" *First Things,* October 2005, available online at http://www.firstthings.com/article/2005/10/development-or-reversal. The Thirteenth Amendment to the U.S. Constitution, adopted after the end of the Civil War, allows the enslavement and forced labor of convicted criminals: "Neither slavery nor involuntary servitude, *except as a punishment for crime whereof the party shall have been duly convicted*, shall exist within the United States, or any place subject to their jurisdiction" (emphasis added). Concerning prisoners of war and the Geneva Convention: "In the context of international armed conflicts, the Third Geneva Convention provides that 'the Detaining Power may utilize the labour of prisoners of war who are physically fit, taking into account their age, sex, rank and physical aptitude, and with a view particularly to maintaining them in a good state of physical and mental health,'" provided the labor is not "unhealthy," "dangerous" or "humiliating." Also, "work done by prisoners of war shall have no direct connection with the operations of the war." International Committee of the Red Cross, "Customary IHL [International Humanitarian Law]," http://www.icrc.org/customary-ihl/eng/docs/v1_cha_chapter32_rule95.

2. Herbert S. Klein, *African Slavery in Latin America and the Caribbean* (New York: Oxford University Press, 1986), 217–271; Mark Noll, *The Civil War as a Theological Crisis* (Chapel Hill: University of North Carolian Press, 2006), 125–59. After the American Civil War, coindentally or not, the Spanish- and Portugese-speaking jurisdictions in Latin American hastened the emancipation process, but this does not change the fact that before the Civil War, when the United States were still struggling with the slavery issue, these Latin jurisdictions had already adopted gradual-emancipation policies. The Island of Santo Domingo (Haiti and the Dominican Republic) poses a special case, where the slaves liberated themselves through a bloody uprising against the whites, who feared any growth in the free black population and tried to limit any increase in that population.

3. Richard Franklin Bensel, *Yankee Leviathan*; Susan Mary Grant, *North Over South*; David Goldfield, *America Aflame*; Noll, 125–59.

Bibliography

Acts and Resolves Passed by the General Court of Massachusetts in the Years 1854–5. Boston, 1855.

Adams, J. Q. "Misconceptions of Shakespeare, Upon the Stage." in James Henry Hackett, ed., *Notes and Comments Upon Certain Plays and Actors of Shakespeare*, 3d ed. New York: Carleton, 1864.

Adams, Pauline. *English Catholic Converts and the Oxford Movement in Mid 19th Century Britain: The Cost of Conversion.* Bethesda, MD: Academica Press, 2010.

Alexander, De Alva Stanwood. *A Political History of the State of New York, vol. III, 1861–1882.* New York: Henry Holt, 1909.

Alexander, Adele. *Ambiguous Lives: Free Women of Color in Rural Georgia, 1789–1879.* Fayetteville: University of Arkansas Press, 1991.

Allen, John L., Jr. *The Catholic Church: What Everyone Needs to Know.* Oxford: Oxford University Press, 2013.

Allitt, Patrick. *Catholic Converts: British and American Intellectuals Turn to Rome.* Ithaca: Cornell University Press, 1997.

Alvarez, David J. "The Papacy in the Diplomacy of the American Civil War." *Catholic Historical Review* 69.2 (April 1983), 227–248.

Ambrose, Stephen E. *Halleck: Lincoln's Chief of Staff.* Baton Rouge: Louisiana State University Press, 1990.

American and Foreign Christian Union. *The Story of the Madiai.* New York: The Society, 1853.

Anbinder, Tyler G. *Nativism and Slavery: The Know-Nothings and the Politics of the 1850s.* New York: Oxford University Press, 1992..

John A. Andrew Papers. Massachusetts Historical Society.

Andrews, Michael. *American-Papal Relations from 1848 to 1867.* Dissertation, St. John's University, 2007.

Andrews, Rena Mazyck. "Slavery Views of a Northern Prelate." *Church History* 3, no. 1 (March 1934), 60–78.

"The autobiography of Rev. Gilbert M'Master D.D." Clements Library, University of Michigan, Ann Arbor.

Bainton, Roland Herbert. *Here I Stand: A Life of Martin Luther.* Nashville: Abingdon Press, 1978.

Barany, George. "On the Pre-history of American Diplomatic Relations with the Papal States." *Catholic Historical Review* 47, no. 4 (January 1962.

Barone, Michael. *Our First Revolution: The Remarkable British Upheaval that Inspired America's Founding Fathers.* New York: Crown, 2007.

Barron, Henry Winston. *Results of Victor Emmanuel's Rule.* London: Harrison, 1863.

Barthel, Joan. *American Saint: The Life of Elizabeth Seton.* New York: Thomas Dunne, 2014.

Basler, Roy P., ed. *The Collected Works of Abraham Lincoln*, vol. VII. New Brunswick: Rutgers University Press, 1953.

Baumgartner, Appollinaris W. *Catholic Journalism: A Study of Its Development in the United States, 1789–1930.* New York: Columbia University Press, 1931.

Baxter, Michael J. "Writing History in a World Without Ends: An Evangelical Catholic Critique of United States Catholic History." *Pro Ecclesia* V, no. 4 (Fall 1996).

Beecher, Edward. *The Papal Conspiracy Exposed, and Protestantism Defended, in the Light of Reason, History and Scripture.* Boston: Stearns, 1855.

Beecher, Lyman. *A Plea for the West.* Cincinnati: Truman and Smith, 1835.

Bell, Joseph. *A Catholic Proslavery Perspective.* MA Thesis, California State University, Chico, Spring 2013.

Bensel, Richard Franklin. *Yankee Leviathan: The Origins of Central State Authority, 1859–1877.* Cambridge: Cambridge University Press, 1990.

Berkeley, G. F. H., and J. Berkeley. *Italy in the Making: January 1st 1848 To November 16 1848.* Cambridge: Cambridge University Press, 1968.

Bernstein, Iver. *The New York City Draft Riots: Their Significance for American Society and Politics in the Age of the Civil War.* New York: Oxford University Press, 1990.

Bernstein, Samuel. "The Opposition of French Labor to American Slavery." *Science & Society* 17, no. 2 (Spring 1953), 136–154.

Berry, Jason. *Render Unto Rome: The Secret Life of Money in the Catholic Church.* New York: Crown, 2011.

Bierce, Ambrose. *Ambrose Bierce's Civil War.* Ed. William McCann. Washington, D.C.: Regnery Gateway, 1956.

Bierman, John. *Napoleon III and His Carnival Empire.* New York: St. Martin's Press, 1988.

Billington, Ray Allen. *The Protestant Crusade 1800–1860: A Study of the Origins of American Nativism.* New York: Macmillan, 1938.

Bishop, Chris, and Alan Drury. *1400 Days: The Civil War Day by Day.* New York: Gallery Books: 1990.

Blied, Benjamin J. *Catholics and the Civil War.* Milwaukee: Privately printed, 1945.

Blondheim, Menahem, ed. *Copperhead Gore: Benjamin Wood's Fort Lafayette and Civil War America.* Bloomington: Indiana University Press, 2006.

Bogar, Thomas A. *Backstage at the Lincoln Assassination.* Washington, D.C.: Regnery History, 2013.

Boman, Dennis K. *Lincoln and Citizens' Rights in Civil War Missouri: Balancing Freedom and Security.* Baton Rouge: Louisiana State University Press, 2011.

Bowman, John S. *The Civil War: Day by Day.* New York: Dorset, 1989.

Boyko, John. *Blood and Daring: How Canada Fought the American Civil War and Forged a Nation.* Toronto: Alfred A. Knopf Canada, 2013.

Branid, Henry A. *History of the American College of the Roman Catholic Church of the United States Rome, Italy.* New York: Benziger Brothers, 1910.

Brandt, Nat. *The Man Who Tried to Burn New York.* Syracuse: Syracuse University Press, 1986.

_____. *The Town That Started the Civil War.* New York: Dell, 1991.

Bremner, Robert H. *American Philanthropy.* Chicago: University of Chicago Press, 1988.

Brinton, John H. *Personal Memoirs of John H. Brinton, Major and Surgeon, U.S.V., 1861–1865.* New York: Neale, 1914.

British Parliament. "Eleventh General Report of the Colonial Land and Emigolumes I-XVII." Detroit: Thorndike Nourse, 1882–1885.

Brokhage, Joseph. *Francis Patrick Kenrick's Opinion on Slavery.* Washington, D.C.: Catholic University of America Press, 1955.

Brooksiana; or, The Controversy Between Senator Brooks and Archbishop Hughes, Growing out of the Recently Enacted Church Property Bill. New York: Edward Dunigan & Brother, 1855.

Brown, Samuel Windsor. *The Secularization of American Education.* New York: Teachers College, Columbia, 1912.

Brown, Theron, and Hezekiah Butterworth. *The Story of the Hymns and Tunes.* New York: George H. Doran, 1906.

Brownson, Henry. *Orestes A. Brownson's Later Life: From 1856 to 1876.* Detroit: H.F. Brownson, 1900.

_____. *Orestes A. Brownson's Middle Life: From 1845 to 1855* (Detroit: H. F. Brownson, 1899.

Brownson, Orestes. *The American Republic: Its Constitution, Tendencies and Destiny.* New York: P. O'Shea, 1866.

_____. *Brownson's Quarterly Review.* National Series, vol. I. D&J Sadlier & Co., 1864.

_____. *Charles Elwood: Or The Infidel Converted.* Boston: Little, Brown, 1840.

_____. *The Convert: Or, Leaves from My Experience.* New York: Edward Dunigan and Brother (James B. Kirker), 1857.

_____. *The Spirit-Rapper; An Autobiography* (Boston, Little, Brown and Company, 1854.

_____. *The Works of Orestes A. Brownson,* numerous vols. Ed. Henry Brownson. Detroit: Thorndike Nourse, various times during the 1880s.

Bruce, Susannah Ural. *The Harp and The Eagle: The Impact of Civil War Military Service in the Union Army on The Irish in America.* Dissertation, Kansas State University, 2002.

_____. "'Remember Your Country and Keep up Its Credit': Irish Volunteers and the Union Army,1861–1865." *The Journal of Military History* 69, no. 2 (April 2005), 331–359.

Brym, Robert J., and John Lie. *Sociology: Your Compass for a New World,* 2d ed. Belmont, CA: Cengage Learning, 2010.

Burnette, Patricia. *James F. Jaquess, Scholar, Soldier and Private Agent for President Lincoln.* Jefferson, NC: McFarland, 2013.

Burrows, Edwin G., and Mike Wallace. *Gotham: A History of New York City to 1898.* New York: Oxford University Press, 1999.

Burton, Orville Vernon. *The Age of Lincoln.* New York: Hill and Wang, 2007.

Burton, William L. *Melting Pot Soldiers: The Union's Ethnic Regiments.* New York: Fordham University Press, 1998.

Byrne, William, et al. *History of the Catholic Church in the New England States,* vol. 2. Boston: Kurd & Everts, 1899.

Cabot, Stephen. *Report of the '"Draft Riot" in Boston, July 14, 1863, From the Diary of Major Stephen Cabot.* Printed by vote of the Veteran Association of Co. A, 1st Battalion of Massachusetts Heavy Artillery.

Cadogan, Edward. *The Life of Cavour.* London: Smith, Elder, 1907.

Calhoun, John C. *A Disquisition on Government and a Discourse on the Constitution and Government of the United States* (Columbia, S.C.: printed by A. S. Johnston, 1851.

Callon, David Jerome. *Converting Catholicism: Orestes A. Brownson, Anna H. Dorsey, and Irish America, 1840–1896.* Dissertation, Washington University, 2008.

Campbell, Stanley W. *The Slave Catchers: Enforcement of the Fugitive Slave Law, 1850–1860.* Chapel Hill: University of North Carolina Press, 1970.

Canzona, Joshua. "General James Longstreet in New Orleans." *The Loyola University Student Historical Journal* 34 (2002–2003).

Capizzi, Joseph E. "For What Shall We Repent? Reflections on the American Bishops, Their Teaching, and Slavery in the United States, 1839–1861." *Theological Studies* 65 (2004.

Caravaglios, Maria Genoino. *The American Catholic Church and the Negro Problem in the XVIII-XIX Centuries.* Charleston, SC: Caravaglios, 1974.

_____. "A Roman critique of the pro-slavery views of Bishop Martin of Natchitoches, Louisiana." *Records of the American Catholic Historical Society of Philadelphia* 83, no. 2 (1972.

Carey, Patrick W. *Orestes A. Brownson: American Religious Weathervane.* Grand Rapids: William B. Eerdmans, 2004.

_____. "Orestes Brownson and the Civil War." *U.S. Catholic Historian* 31, no. 1 (Winter 2013), 1–20.

Carne, John. *Syria the Holy Land and Asia Minor Illustrated,* vol. II. London: Fisher, Son and Co., [n.d., probably late 1830s].

Catechism of the Catholic Church. New Orleans: Loyola University Press, 1994.

Catholic Encyclopedia, many vols. New York: Robert Appleton, 1905–1917.

Catholic Record Society Bulletin.

Catton, Bruce. *This Hallowed Ground*. New York: Washington Square Press, 1961.

The century of independence: Embracing a collection, from official sources, of the most important documents and statistics connected with the political history of America; also, a chronological record of the principal events ... with biographical and historical sketches. Michigan Historical Reprint Series, Scholarly Publishing Office, University of Michigan Library, 2005.

Chadwick, Owen. *A History of the Popes 1830–1914*. Oxford: Clarendon Press, 1998.

Chamberlain, Ivory, and Thomas Moses Foote. *Biography of Millard Fillmore*. Buffalo: Thomas & Lathrops, 1856.

Child, Lydia Maria. *A Romance of the Republic*. Boston: Ticknor and Fields, 1867.

Christian Record: Containing the History, Confession of Faith, and Statistics of Each Religious Denomination In the United States and Europe; A List of All Clergymen With their Post Office Address, etc., etc., etc. New York: W.R.C. Clark and Meeker, 1860.

The Civil War Almanac. New York: Bison Books, 1983.

Chan, V. O. "The Riots of 1856 in British Guiana." *Caribbean Quarterly* 16, no. 1 (March 1970.

Chittenden, Hiram Martin. *Life, Letters and Travels of Father Pierre-Jean De Smet, S.J., 1801–1873*, vol. I. New York: Francis P. Harper, 1905.

Churchill, Robert H. *To Shake Their Guns in the Tyrant's Face: Libertarian Political Violence and the Origins of the Militia Movement*. Ann Arbor: University of Michigan Press, 2012.

Clark, Rufus W. *Romanism in America*. Boston: S.K. Whipple, 1855.

Clarke, Richard H. *Lives of the Deceased Bishops of the Catholic Church in the United States*, vol. III. New York: Richard H. Clarke, 1888.

College of Charleston, Lowcountry Digital Archives. http://lcdl.library.cofc.edu/lcdl/catalog.

Cochin, Augustin. *The Results of Emancipation*. Trans. Mary Booth. Boston: Walker, Wise, 1863.

_____. *The Results of Slavery*. Trans. Mary Booth. Boston: Walker, Wise, 1863.

Cockerell, C. R. *Travels in Southern Europe and the Levant, 1810–1817*. Ed. Samuel Pepys Cockerell. London: Longman's, Green, 1903.

Collison, Gary Lee. *Shadrach Minkins: From Fugitive Slave to Citizen*. Cambridge: Harvard University Press, 1997.

Connelly, James F. *The Visit of Archbishop Gaetano Bedini to the United States of America (June 1853–February 1854*. Analecta Gregoriana 109. Rome 1960.

Connelly, Pierce. *The Madiai, A Letter To the Rt. Hon. The Earl of Aberdeen, First Lord of the Treasury*. London, T. Hatchard, 1853.

"Constitution of the Commonwealth of Massachusetts." https://malegislature.gov/Laws/Constitution.

The Constitution of the United States and Related Documents. Melville, NY: Graphic Image, 2004.

Coppa, Frank J. *Pope Pius IX: Crusader in a Secular Age*. Boston: Twayne, 1979.

Corby, Rev. W. *Memoirs of Chaplain Life*. Chicago: La-Monte, O'Donnell, 1893.

"Correspondence between His Holiness Pope Pius IX and President Jefferson Davis." http://www.danvilleartillery.org/popeletter.htm.

Coulombe, Charles A. *The Pope's Legion: The Multinational Fighting Force That Defended the Vatican*. New York: Palgrave Macmillan, 2008.

Cozzens, Peter. *No Better Place to Die: The Battle of Stones River*. Urbana: University of Illinois Press, 1990.

Crofts, Daniel W. *Reluctant Confederates: Upper South Unionists in the Secession Crisis*. Chapel Hill: University of North Carolina Press, 1989.

Cummings v. Missouri, 71 U.S. (4 Wall.) 277 (1867.

Cummins, Joseph. *The War Chronicles: From Flintlocks to Machine Guns*. Beverly, MA: Fair Winds Press, 2009.

Curran, Robert Emmett. "Rome, the American Church, and Slavery." in Joseph C. Linck and Raymond J. Kupke, eds., *Building the Church in America: Studies in Honor of Monsignor Robert F. Trisco on the Occasion of his Seventieth Birthday*. Washington, D.C.: Catholic University of American Press, 1999)

_____. *Shaping American Catholicism: Maryland and New York, 1805–1915*. Washington, D.C.: Catholic University of America Press, 2012.

_____. "'Splendid Poverty: Jesuit Slaveholding in Maryland." in Randall M. Miller and Jon L. Wakelyn, eds., *Catholics in the Old South: Essays on Church and Culture*. Macon: Mercer University Press, 1983.

D'Agostino, Peter R. *Rome in America: Transnational Catholic Ideology from the Risorgimento to Fascism*. Chapel Hill: University of North Carolina Press, 2004.

Davis, Cyprian. "Freedom and Slavery: The American Catholic Church Before the Civil War." in *Christian Freedom: Essays by the Faculty of the Saint Meinrad School of Theology*, Clayton N. Jefford, ed. New York: Peter Lang, 1993.

Davis, John A. *Conflict and Control: Law and Order in Nineteenth Century Italy*. New York: Macmillan Education, 1988.

A Debate on the Roman Catholic Religion Between Alexander Campbell, Bethany, Va., and the Right Reverend John B. Purcell, Bishop of Cincinnati, Held in the Sycamore Street Meetinghouse, Cincinnati, From the 13th to the 21st of January 1837. Taken Down by Reporters, and Revised by the Parties. Nashville: McQuiddy, 1914.

de Levant, Edward Riches. *Biblia Hexaglotta*, vol. v. New York: Funk and Wagnalls, 1901.

Deusner, Charles E. "The Know Nothing Riots in Louisville." *The Register of the Kentucky Historical Society* 61, no. 2 (April 1963), 122–147.

Deyle, Steven. *Carry Me Back: The Domestic Slave Trade in American Life*. New York: Oxford University Press, 2005.

Dickie, John. "A World at War: The Italian Army and Brigandage 1860–1870." *History Workshop* 33 (Spring 1992), 1–24.

A Digest of the Statute Laws of the State of Georgia, in Force Prior to the Session of the General Assembly of 1851. Athens, GA: Christy, Kelsey and Burke, 1851.

Diocese of Columbus: The History of Fifty Years, 1868–1918. 1918.

Dolan, Cardinal Timothy, and John L. Allen, Jr. *A People of Hope: The Challenges facing the Catholic Church and the Faith that Can Save It*. New York: Image, 2011.

Dolan, Jay P. *The Immigrant Church: New York's Irish and German Catholics, 1815–1865.* Notre Dame: University of Notre Dame Press, 1983.

Donald, David Herbert. *Charles Sumner and the Rights of Man.* New York: Alfred A. Knopf, 1970.

———. *Lincoln.* New York: Simon & Schuster, 1995.

Douglas, Henry Kyd. *I Rode with Stonewall.* St. Simon's Island, GA: Mockingbird Books, 1961.

Duanesburg Historical Society. *Duanesburg and Princeton (NY.* Charleston, SC: Arcadia, 2005.

Dulles, Avery Cardinal. *Church and Society: The Laurence J. McGinley Lectures, 1988–2007.* New York Province of the Society of Jesus, 2008.

———. "Development or Reversal?" *First Things,* October 2005, available online at http://www.firstthings.com/article/2005/10/development-or-reversal.

Dupree, A. Hunter, and Leslie H Fishel, Jr. "An Eyewitness Account of the New York Draft Riots, July 1863." *The Mississippi Valley Historical Review* 47, no. 3 (December 1960), 472–479.

Egan, Maurice Francis. "A Slight Appreciation of James Alphonsus McMaster." *Historical Records and Studies,* vol. xv, March 1921, United States Catholic Historical Society.

Egerton, Douglas R. *Year of Meteors: Stephen Douglas, Abraham Lincoln, and the Election That Brought on the Civil War.* New York: Bloomsbury Press, 2010.

Eicher, David J. *The Longest Night: A Military History of the Civil War.* New York: Simon & Schuster, 2001.

Eliot, Charles W., ed. *The Confessions of St. Augustine— The Imitation of Christ (Kempis.* Trans. Edward B. Pusey and William Beham. Harvard Classics 7. New York: P. F. Collier and Sons, 1909.

Elliott, Walter. *The Life of Father Hecker.* New York: Columbus Press, 1891.

Ellis, John Tracy. *American Catholicism.* Chicago: University of Chicago Press, 1969.

Endres, David J. "Rectifying the Fatal Contrast: Archbishop John Purcell and the Slavery Controversy among Catholics in Civil War Cincinnati." *Ohio Valley History* 2, no. 2 (Fall 2002), 23–33.

———, and Jerrold P. Twohig. "'With a Father's Affection': Chaplain William T. O'Higgins and the Tenth Ohio Volunteer Infantry." *U.S. Catholic Historian* 31, no. 1 (Winter 2013), 97–127.

England, John. *Letters of the Late Bishop England to the Hon. John Forsyth, on the Subject of Domestic Slavery.* Ed. George Read. Baltimore: John Murphy, 1844.

Fagerberg, David W. *On Liturgical Asceticism.* Washington, D.C.: Catholic University of America Press, 2013.

Faherty, William Barnaby. *Exile in Erin: A Confederate Chaplain's Story: The Life of Father John B. Bannon.* St. Louis: Missouri Historical Society Press, 2002.

"Father Patrick John Ryan." http://www.pricecamp.org/kelly.htm.

Fede, Andrew. *Roadblocks to Freedom: Slavery and Manumission in the United States South.* New Orleans: Quid Pro Books, 2011.

Fellman, Michael. *Inside War: The Guerrilla Conflict in Missouri During the American Civil War.* New York: Oxford University Press, 1989.

Fenster, Julie M. *The Case of Abraham Lincoln: A Story of Adultery, Murder, and the Making of a Great President.* New York: Palgrave MacMillan, 2007.

Fessenden, Tracy. "The Nineteenth-Century Bible Wars and the Separation of Church and State." *Church History* 74, no. 4 (December 2005), 784–811.

Finkelman, Paul. *Millard Fillmore.* New York: Times Books, 2011.

Fireside, Bryna J. *Private Joel and the Sewell Mountain Seder.* Minneapolis: Kar-Ben, 2008.

Flannery, Austin, ed. *Vatican Council II: The Conciliar and Post-Conciliar Documents.* Northport, NY: Costello, 1975.

Fleche, Andre M. *The Revolution of 1861: The American Civil War in the Age of Nationalist Conflict.* Chapel Hill: University of North Carolina Press, 2012.

Fleming, Thomas. *A Disease in the Public Mind: A New Understanding of Why We Fought the Civil War.* New York: Da Capo Press, 2013.

Foner, Eric. *Free Soil, Free Labor, Free Men: The Ideology of the Republican Party Before the Civil War.* New York: Oxford University Press, 1970.

Foner, Philip S. "Labor and the Copperheads." *Science & Society* 8, no. 3 (Summer 1944), 223–242.

Fowler, Dorothy Ganfield. *Unmailable: Congress and the Post Office.* Athens: University of Georgia Press, 1977.

Franchot, Jenny. *Roads to Rome: The Antebellum Protestant Encounter with Catholicism.* Berkeley: University of California Press, 1994.

Freehling, William W. *The Road to Disunion: Vol. I— Secessionists at Bay 1776–1854.* New York: Oxford University Press, 1990.

French, John A. *Irish-American Identity, Memory and Americanism During the Eras of the Civil War and First World War.* Dissertation, Marquette University, May 2012.

Friedman, Lawrence, and Lynnea Thody. *The Massachusetts State Constitution.* New York: Oxford University Press, 2011.

Fry, Joseph A. *Henry S. Sanford: Diplomacy and Business in Nineteenth-Century America.* Reno: University of Nevada Press, 1982.

Galenson, David W. "Neighborhood Effects on the School Attendance of Irish Immigrants' Sons in Boston and Chicago in 1860." *American Journal of Education* 105, no. 3 (May 1997), 261–293.

Gannon, Michael V. *Rebel Bishop: The Life and Era of Augustin Verot.* Milwaukee: Bruce Publishing Company, 1964.

Julius Garesché Papers. Georgetown University, Special Collections, Washington, D.C.

Garesché, Louis. *Biography of Lieut. Col. Julius P. Garesché, Assistant Adjutant General, U.S. Army.* Philadelphia: J. B. Lippincott, 1887 (printed for private circulation).

Louis Garesché Papers. Rubenstein Library, Duke University, Durham.

Garrison, Webb. *Civil War Hostages: Hostage Taking in the Civil War.* Shippensburg, PA: White Mane Books, 2000.

Garvey, T. Gregory. *Creating the Culture of Reform in Antebellum America.* Athens: University of Georgia Press, 2006.

Gaston, William. "Address Delivered Before the Philanthropic and Dialectic Societies at Chapel Hill— June 20, 1832." Raleigh: Jos. Gales & Son, 1832.

Gavronsky, Serge. "American Slavery and the French

Liberals an Interpretation of the Role of Slavery in French Politics During the Second Empire." *The Journal of Negro History* 51, no. 1 (January 1966), 36–52.

Gemme, Paola. *Domesticating Foreign Struggles.* Athens: University of Georgia Press, 2005.

George, Joseph, Jr. "The Lincoln Writings of Charles P. T. Chiniquy." *Journal of the Illinois State Historical Society* 69, no. 1 (February 1976), 17–25.

Gerrity, Frank. "The Disruption of the Philadelphia Whigocracy: Joseph R. Chandler, Anti-Catholicism, and the Congressional Election of 1854." *The Pennsylvania Magazine of History and Biography* 111, no. 2 (April 1987), 161–194.

_____. "Joseph Ripley Chandler and 'The Temporal Power of the Pope.'" *Pennsylvania History* 49, no. 2 (April 1982), 106–20.

Gibson, Florence. *The Attitudes of the New York Irish Toward State and National Affairs, 1848–1892.* New York: Columbia University Press, 1951.

Gienapp, William E. "Nativism and the Creation of a Republican Majority in the North before the Civil War." *The Journal of American History* 72, no. 3 (December 1985).

Giesberg, Judith Ann. "'Lawless and Unprincipled': Women in Boston's Civil War Draft Riot," in James M. O'Toole and David Quigley, eds., *Boston's Histories: Essays in Honor of Thomas H. O'Connor.* Boston: Northeastern University Press, 2004.

Gilmore, James. *Personal Recollections of Abraham Lincoln and the Civil War.* Boston: L.C. Page, 1898.

Glasgow, W. Melancthon. *History of the Reformed Presbyterian Church in America.* Baltimore: Hill and Harvey, 1888.

Gleason, Philip. "Boundlessness, Consolidation, and Discontinuity between Generations: Catholic Seminary Studies in Antebellum America." *Church History* 73, no. 3.

Gleeson, David T. "No Disruption of Union," in Edward Blum and W. Scott Poole, *Vale of Tears: New Essays on Religion and Reconstruction.* Macon: Mercer University Press, 2005.

Goldfield, David. *America Aflame: How the Civil War Created a Nation.* New York: Bloomsbury Press, 2011.

Golway, Terry. *Machine Made: Tammany Hall and the Creation of Modern American Politics.* New York: Liveright, 2014.

Gooch, John. *The Unification of Italy.* London: Lancaster Pamphlets, 2004.

Gordan, John D., III. "The Lemmon Slave Case." *Newsletter of the Historical Society of the Courts of the State of New York* 4 (2006).

Graf, Leroy P., and Ralph W. Haskins, eds. *The Papers of Andrew Johnson, vol. 6, 1862–1864.* Knoxville: University of Tennessee Press, 1983.

Grant, Susan Mary. *North Over South: Northern Nationalism and American Identity in the Antebellum Era.* Lawrence: University Press of Kansas, 2000.

Grindle, David J. "Manumission: The Weak Link in Georgia's Law of Slavery." *Mercer Law Review* 41 (1990), 701–722.

Gura, Philip F. *American Transcendentalism: A History.* New York: Hill and Wang, 2007.

Hales, E. E. Y. *Pio Nono: A Study of Pius IX and His Role in European Politics and Religion in the Nineteenth Century.* Garden City, NY: Image, 1962.

Hamburger, Philip. *Separation of Church and State.* Cambridge: Harvard University Press, 2002.

A Handbook of Rome and Its Environs. London: John Murray, 1871.

Hanley, Boniface. *Paulist Father Isaac Hecker: An American Saint.* Mahwah, NJ: Paulist Press, 2008.

Hanna, William F. "The Boston Draft Riot." *Civil War History* 36, no. 3 (September 1990), 262–273.

Harper, Robert S. *Lincoln and the Press.* New York: McGraw-Hill, 1951.

Harris, Thomas. *Rome's Responsibility for the Assassination of Abraham Lincoln.* Tonasket, WA: Celestial Strains Publications, 2005 (reprint of Williams edition, 1897).

Harrison, Carol E. *Romantic Catholics: France's Postrevolutionary Generation in Search of a Modern Faith.* Ithaca: Cornell University Press, 2014.

Hassard, John E. G. *Life of the Most Reverend John Hughes, D.D., First Archbishop of New York. With Extracts from His Private Correspondence.* New York: D. Appleton, 1866.

Haywood, Marshall Delancey. *Lives of the Bishops of North Carolina.* Raleigh: Alfred Williams, 1910.

Hedrick, Joan D. *Harriet Beecher Stowe: A Life.* New York: Oxford University Press, 1994.

Heisser, David C. R. "Bishop Lynch's Civil War Pamphlet on Slavery." *The Catholic Historical Review* 84, no. 4 (October 1998).

Hennesey, James. *American Catholics: A History of the Roman Catholic Community in the United States* London: Oxford University Press, 1981.

Hern, Chester. *Companions in Conspiracy: John Brown and Gerrit Smith.* Gettysburg, PA: Thomas, 1996.

Herndon, Joseph M., Jr. *Celts, Catholics & Copperheads: Ireland Views the American Civil War.* Columbus: Ohio State University Press, 1968.

Herriott, Irving. "The Premises and Significance of Abraham Lincoln's Letter to Theodore Canisius." Reprinted from *Deutsch-Amerikanische Geschichtsblatter Jahrbuch der Deutsch-Amerikanischen Historischen Gesellschaft von Illinois*—Jahrgang 1915, vol. XV.

Hess, Earl J. *Banners to the Breeze: The Kentucky Campaign, Corinth, and Stones River.* Lincoln: University of Nebraska Press, 2000.

Hitchcock, James. "Race, Religion, and Rebellion: Hilary Tucker and the Civil War." *Catholic Historical Review* 80, no. 3 (July 1994), 497–507.

Hofstra, Warren R., ed. *Ulster to America: The Scots-Irish Migration Experience, 1680–1830.* Knoxville: University of Tennessee Press, 2011.

Hogan, Michael. *The Irish Soldiers of Mexico.* Intercambio Press, 2011.

Holliday, Diane, and Chris Kretz, *Images of America: Oakdale.* Charleston, SC: Arcadia, 2010.

Honeck, Mischa. *We Are the Revolutionists: German-Speaking Immigrants & American Abolitionists after 1848.* Athens: University of Georgia Press, 2011.

Hood, Clifton. "An Unusable Past: Urban Elites, New York City's Evacuation Day, and the Transformations of Memory Culture." *Journal of Social History* 37, no. 4 (Summer 2004), 883–913.

Howe, Barbara J., and Margaret A. Brennan. "The Sisters of St. Joseph in Wheeling, West Virginia, during the Civil War." *U.S. Catholic Historian* 31, no. 1 (Winter 2013), 21–49.

Howland v. Union Theological Seminary, 3 Sand. 82 (1849).

Howland v. Union Theological Seminary, 5 N.Y. 1 Seld 193 (1853).

Hueston, Robert Francis. *The Catholic Press and Nativism, 1840–1860.* New York: Arno Press, 1976.

Hughes, John. *Complete Works*, 2 vols. Ed. Lawrence Kehoe. New York: Catholic Publication House, 1864.

_____. "The Madiai Affair," in *The Metropolitan*, vol. I. Baltimore: John Murphy and Company, 1853, 103–08.

Humphreys, Margaret. *Marrow of Tragedy: The Health Crisis of the American Civil War.* Baltimore: Johns Hopkins University Press, 2013.

Huston, James L. "Democracy by Scripture Versus Democracy by Process: A Reflection on Stephen A. Douglas and Popular Sovereignty." *Civil War History: A Journal of the Middle Period* XLIII, no. 3 (September 1997), 189–200.

Hutcheon, Wallace S. "The Louisville Riots of August 1855." *Register of the Kentucky Historical Society* 69, no. 2 (April 1971), 150–172.

Hutchinson, George P. *The History Behind the Reformed Presbyterian Church, Evangelical Synod.* Cherry Hill, NJ: Mack, 1974.

Ignatiev, Michael. *How the Irish Became White.* New York: Routledge Classics, 2008.

In the Court of Claims of the United States. Congressional No. 11075. The Ladies Ursuline Community of Columbia, S.C., v. The United States, United States Senate, 61st Congress, 3rd Session, Document 735, *The Ladies Ursuline Community, Columbia, S.C.*, 1911.

"In the Police Court of Boston, Massachusetts. April 1859. Commonwealth, on Complaint of Wall vs. M'laurin F. Cooke." *The American Law Register (1852–1891)* 7, no. 7 (May 1859), 417–26.

International Committee of the Red Cross. "Customary IHL [International Humanitarian Law]." http://www.icrc.org/customary-ihl/eng/docs/v1_cha_chapter32_rule95.

Jack v. Martin (summary). http://www.nycourts.gov/history/legal-history-new-york/legal-history-eras-02/history-new-york-legal-eras-jack-martin.html.

James, Joseph. "Life at West Point One Hundred Years Ago." *The Mississippi Valley Historical Review* 31, no. 1 (June 1944), 21–40.

Jampoler, Andrew C. A. *The Last Lincoln Conspirator: John Surratt's Flight from the Gallows.* Annapolis: Naval Institute Press, 2008.

Jesse, Ian. "In Search of Excitement: Understanding Boston's Civil War 'Draft Riot.'" *NeoAmericanist* 5, no. d. 2 (Fall/Winter 2011–2012).

Joel, J. A. "Passover: A Reminiscence of the War." *The Jewish Messenger*, April 1866. http://www.jewish-history.com/civilwar/union.htm.

Johnson, Leland R. *Men Mountains and Rivers: An Illustrated History of the Huntington District, U.S. Army Corps of Engineers.* Washington. D.C.: U.S. Government Printing Office, 1977.

Jones, Arthur. *Pierre Toussaint: A Biography.* New York: Doubleday, 2003.

Jones, Preston. "Civil War, Culture War: French Quebec and the American War Between the States." *The Catholic Historical Review* 87, no. 1 (January 2001), 55–70.

Jones, Bernie D. *Fathers of Conscience: Mixed-Race Inheritance in the Antebellum South.* Athens: University of Georgia Press, 2009.

Journal of the Congress of the Confederate States of America, 1861–1865, vol. I. Washington, D.C.: Government Printing Office, 1904.

Joyce, Toby. "The New York Draft Riots of 1863: An Irish Civil War?" *History Ireland*, 11, no. 2 (Summer 2003), 22–27.

Kaufman, M. "1863: Poland, Russia and the United States." *Polish American Studies* 21, no. 1 (January–June 1964), 10–15.

Kelly, Joseph. *America's Longest Siege: Charleston, Slavery, and the Slow March Toward Civil War.* New York: The Overlook Press, 2013.

Keneally, Thomas. *The Great Shame and the Triumph of the Irish in the English-Speaking World.* New York: Anchor Books, 2000.

Kenners, Emmanuel. *The Japanese Martyrs.* Manchester: Alex Ireland, 1862.

Kenrick, Francis Patrick. *Letters Chiefly of Francis Patrick Kenrick and Marc Anthony Frenaye, selected from the Cathedral Archives Philadelphia, Translated, Arranged and Annotated As Sources and Helps to the Study of Local Catholic History, 1830–1862.* Philadelphia: Wickersham, 1920.

_____. *A Vindication of the Catholic Church, In a Series of Letters Addressed to the Rt. Rev. John Henry Hopkins, Protestant Episcopal Bishop of Vermont.* Baltimore: John Murphy, 1855.

_____, tr. *The Pentateuch. Translated from the Vulgate, and Diligently Compared with the Original Text, Being a Revised Edition of the Douay Version.* Baltimore: Kelly, Hedian & Piett, 1860.

Kertzer, David I. *The Kidnapping of Edgardo Mortara: The Extraordinary Story of How the Vatican's Imprisonment of a Six-Year-Old Jewish Boy in 1858 Helped Bring About the Collapse of the Popes' Worldly Power in Italy.* New York: Alfred A. Knopf, 1997.

Kinchen, Oscar A. *Confederate Operations in Canada and the North: A Little-Known Phase of the American Civil War.* North Quincy, MA: Christopher Publishing House, 1970.

King, Bolton. *Mazzini.* London: E. P. Dent, 1903.

Kirkland, Edward Chase. *The Peacemakers of 1864.* New York: Macmillan, 1927.

Klein, Herbert S. *African Slavery in Latin American and the Caribbean.* New York: Oxford University Press, 1986.

Klein, Philip Shriver. *President James Buchanan: A Biography.* University Park: Pennsylvania State University Press, 1962.

Klement, Frank L. "Catholics as Copperheads During the Civil War." *The Catholic Historical Review* 80, no. 1 (January 1994).

_____. *Copperheads in the Middle West.* Chicago: University of Chicago Press, 1960.

_____. *Dark Lanterns: Secret Political Societies, Conspiracies, and Treason Trials in the Civil War.* Baton Rouge: Louisiana State University Press, 1984.

_____. *The Limits of Dissent: Clement L. Vallandigham and the Civil War.* Lexington: University Press of Kentucky, 1970.

———. "Sound and Fury: Civil War Dissent in the Cincinnati Area." *Cincinnati Historical Society Bulletin* 35 (1977).

Knight v. Hardeman, 14 Ga. 253 (1855), 1855 Ga. Lexis 102.

Kopp, Donald A. "Do school boards have academic freedom? Yes, they still do!" *School Law Advisory* (Spring 1998.

Korn, Bertram Wallace. *The American Reaction to the Mortara Case: 1858–1859.* Cincinnati: The American Jewish Archives, 1957.

Kroll, C. Douglas. *Friends in Peace and War: The Russian Navy's Landmark Visit to Civil War San Francisco.* Washington, D.C.: Potomac, 2007.

Kuzniewski, Anthony J. *Thy Honored Name: A History of the College of the Holy Cross, 1843–1994.* Washington, D.C.: Catholic University of American Press, 1999.

Kurtz, William B. "Let us Hear no More 'Nativism': The Catholic Press in the Mexican and Civil Wars." *Civil War History* 60, no. 1 (March 2014), 6–31.

———. "'The Perfect Model of a Christian Hero': The Faith, Anti-Slaveryism, and Post-War Legacy of William S. Rosecrans." *U.S. Catholic Historian* 31, no. 1 (Winter 2013), 73–96.

Kwitchen, Mary Augustine. *James Alphonsus McMaster: A Study in American Thought.* Washington, D.C.: Catholic University of America Press, 1949.

Lalli, Anthony B., and Thomas H. O'Connor, "Roman Views on the American Civil War." *Catholic Historical Review* 57, no. 1 (April 1971), 21–41.

Lamers, William M. *The Edge of Glory: A Biography of General William S. Rosecrans, U.S.A.* New York: Harcourt, Brace, 1961.

LaMott, John H. *History of the Archdiocese of Cincinnati, 1821–1921* (New York: Frederick Pustet Company, 1921.

Lantz, Herman, Martin Schultz, and Mary O'Hara. "The Changing American Family from the Preindustrial to the Industrial Period: A Final Report." *American Sociological Review* 42, no. 3 (June 1977), 406–21.

Larson, Kate Clifford. *The Assassin's Accomplice: Mary Surratt and the Plot to Kill President Lincoln.* New York: Basic Books, 2008.

Laskowski, Maciej. "Jane Porter's *Thaddeus of Warsaw* as evidence of Polish–British relationships." Instytucie Filologii Angielskiej (Poznan), 2012.

Laufer, Joseph M. "The Myth of the Excommunication of Comet Halley." *Halley's Comet Watch* IV, no. 1 (February 1985), available online at http://www.geocities.com/lauferworld.geo/HCexcomunication.htm.

Lause, Mark A. *A Secret Society History of the Civil War.* Urbana: University of Illinois Press, 2011.

Laverdure, Paul. "'The Jesuits Did It!' Charles Chiniquy's Theory of Lincoln's Assassination." *Historical Papers: Canadian Society of Church History* (2001): 125–39.

LeBreton, Dagmar Renshaw. "Orestes Brownson's Visit to New Orleans in 1855." *American Literature* 16, no. 2 (May 1944), 110–14.

Lee, Basil Leo. *Discontent in New York City 1861–1865.* Dissertation, Catholic University of America, 1943.

Leech, Margaret. *Reveille in Washington 1860–1865.* New York: Time, 1962.

Leftwich, W. M. *Martyrdom in Missouri,* vol. II. St. Louis: Southwestern, 1870.

Lemire, Elise. *Miscegenation: Making Race in America.* Philadelphia: University of Pennsylvania Press, 2002.

Levine, Bruce. *The Spirit of 1848: German Immigrants, Labor Conflict, and the Coming of the Civil War.* Urbana: University of Illinois Press, 1992.

Light, Dale B. *Rome and the New Republic: Conflict and Community in Philadelphia Catholicism Between the Revolution and the Civil War.* Notre Dame: University of Notre Dame Press, 1996.

Lightner, David L. *Slavery and the Commerce Power: How the Struggle Against the Interstate Slave Trade Led to the Civil War.* New Haven: Yale University Press, 2006.

Linderman, Gerald F. *Embattled Courage: The Experience of Combat in the American Civil War.* New York: The Free Press, 1987.

Lohrli, Anne. "The Madiai: A Forgotten Chapter in Church History." *Victorian Studies* (Autumn 1989), 30–38.

Long, David. *The Jewel of Liberty: Abraham Lincoln's Re-Election and the End of Slavery.* Mechanicsburg, PA: Stackpole Books, 1994.

Lucas, Marion B. *Sherman and the Burning of Columbia.* Columbia: University of South Carolina, 2000.

"Louis Veuillot," in Reuben Parsons, *Studies in Church History* VI, Cent. XIX (Part II). New York: Fr. Pustet, 1900, 427–40.

Loving: Jerome. *Confederate Bushwhacker: Mark Twain in the Shadow of the Civil War.* Hanover, NH: University Press of New England, 2013.

Madiai, Francesco, and Rosa Madiai. *Letters of the Madiai, and Visits to Their Prisons.* Ed. "The Misses Senhouse." Philadelphia: Presbyterian Board of Publication, 1853.

Maguire, John Francis. *Father Mathew: A Biography.* London: Burns and Oates, 1882.

———. *Rome: Its Ruler and Its Institutions.* London: Longman, Brown, Green, Longmans and Roberts, 1857.

Maher, Mary Denis. *To Bind Up the Wounds: Catholic Sister Nurses in the U.S. Civil War.* Baton Rouge: Louisiana State University Press, 1989.

Man, Albon P., Jr. "The Church and the New York Draft Riots of 1863." http://lachlan.bluehaze.com.au/books/albon_man/church_ny_irish/.

Manross, William Wilson. *A History of the American Episcopal Church.* New York: Morehouse, 1935.

Marraro, Howard R. "The Religious Problem of the Italian Risorgimento as Seen by Americans." *Church History* 25, no. 1 (March 1956), 41–62.

Martineau, Harriet. *Society in America,* vol. II. New York: Saunders and Otley, 1837.

Martinkus, Mary Salesia. "Diplomatic Relations Between the United States and the Vatican During the Civil War." Master's Thesis, Loyola University, 1953.

Masur, Louis P. *Lincoln's Hundred Days: The Emancipation Proclamation and the War for the Union.* Cambridge, MA: Belknap Press, 2012.

Matheny, H.E. *Major General Thomas Maley Harris.* Parsons, WV: McClain, 1963.

Matthews, Albert. "Origin of Butternut and Copperhead," in Colonial Society of Massachusetts, *Transactions: 1917–1919.* Boston: Published by the Society, 1919?.

Mattingly, Garrett. *The Armada*. Boston: Houghton Mifflin, 1962.

Maxwell, John Francis. *The History of Catholic Teaching Concerning the Moral Legitimacy of Slavery*. Chichester: Barry Rose, 1975.

May, Robert E. *Slavery, Race and Conquest in the Tropics: Lincoln, Douglas and the Future of Latin America*. Cambridge: Cambridge University Press, 2013.

Mayer, Henry. *All on Fire: William Lloyd Garrison and the Abolition of Slavery*. New York: W. W. Norton, 1998.

Maynard, Jean Owen. *Josephine Bakhita: The Lucky One*. London: Catholic Truth Society, 2002.

"Mayor Charles Godfrey Gunther, Coney Island Bound." August 20, 2009, http://theboweryboys.blogspot.com/2009/08/know-your-mayors-charles-godfrey.html.

Mazzini, Giuseppe. *Thoughts upon Democracy in Europe (1846–1847)*. Ed. Salvo Mastellone. Firenze: Centro Editoriale Toscano, 2001.

MacMahon, T. W. *Cause and Contrast: An Essay on the American Crisis*. Richmond: West and Johnston, 1862. Available online at http://docsouth.unc.edu/imls/cause/cause.html.

McAvoy, Thomas T. "Orestes A. Brownson and Archbishop John Hughes in 1860." *The Review of Politics* 24, no. 1 (January 1962), 19–47.

McCann, Mary Agnes. "The Most Reverend John Baptist Purcell, D.D., Archbishop of Cincinnati (1800–1883)." *The Catholic Historical Review* 6, no. 2 (July 1920), 172–99.

———. *The Sisters of Charity in Cincinnati, Ohio*. London: Longman's, Green, 1916.

M'Clintock, John. *The Temporal Power of the Pope, Containing the Speech of the Hon. Joseph R. Chandler, Delivered in the House of Representatives of the United States, January 11, 1855. With Nine Letters, Stating the Prevailing Roman Catholic Theory in the Language of Papal Writers*. New York: Carlton & Phillips, 1855.

McDermott, Scott. *Charles Carroll of Carrolton: Faithful Revolutionary*. New York: Scepter Pubs, 2001.

McFeely, William. *Frederick Douglass*. New York: W. W. Norton, 1991.

McGovern, James J., ed. *The Life and Letters of Eliza Allen Starr*. Introd. William Stetson Merrill. Chicago: Lakeside Press, 1905.

McGreevy, John T. "Catholicism and Abolition: A Historican and Theological Problem," in Wilfred M. McClay, ed., *Figures in the Carpet*. Grand Rapids: William B. Eerdmans, 2007.

———. *Catholicism and American Freedom: A History*. New York: W.W. Norton, 2003.

McJimsey, George T. *Genteel Partisan: Manton Marble, 1834–1917*. Ames: Iowa State University Press, 1971.

McKenna, Kevin E. *The Battle for Rights in the United States Catholic Church*. New York: Paulist Press, 2007.

McMahon, Cian Turlough. *Did the Irish "Become White"? Global Migration and National Identity, 1842–1877*. Dissertation, Carnegie Mellon University, 2010.

McNamera, Pat. "The Big Rock Versus the Little Rock: Bishop Edward M. Fitzgerald (1833–1907)." http://www.patheos.com/blogs/mcnamarasblog/2010/10/%E2%80%9Cthe-big-rock-versus-the-little-rock%E2%80%9D-bishop-edward-m-fitzgerald-1833–1907.html.

McPherson, Edward. *The Political History of the United States of America During the Great Rebellion*. Washington, D.C.: Philp and Solomons, 1865.Meehan, Thomas F. "Diplomatic Intercourse With the Pope," in United States Catholic Historical Association, *Historical Records and Studies,* vol. XI (December 1917).

Menand, Louis. "Morton, Agassiz, and the Origins of Scientific Racism in the United States." *The Journal of Blacks in Higher Education* 34 (Winter 2001–2002), 110–13.

Metz, Judith. *Women of Faith and Service: The Sisters of Charity of Cincinnati*. Sisters of Charity of Cincinnati, 2009.

Mikaberidze, Alexander. *The Burning of Moscow: Napoleon's Trial by Fire 1812*. Barnsley, South Yorkshire: Pen and Sword, 2014.

Miller, Kerby A. *Emigrants and Exiles: Ireland and the Irish Exodus to North America*. New York: Oxford University Press, 1985.

Milner, John. *The End of Religious Controversy in a Friendly Correspondence Between a Religious Society of Protestants and a Catholic Divine*. Baltimore: Metropolitan Press, 1844.

Mintz, Steven. *Moralists and Modernizers: America's Pre-Civil War Reformers*. Baltimore: Johns Hopkins University Press, 1995.

Mitchell, Stewart. *Horatio Seymour of New York*. Cambridge: Harvard University Press, 1938.

Moffit, Robert Emmet. "Orestes Brownson and the Political Culture of American Democracy." *Modern Age* (Summer 1978), 265–76.

Montalembert's Speech at the Malines Congress (Extracts), August 20–21, 1863, in J. F. MacLear, *Church and State in the Modern Age: A Documentary History*. New York: Oxford University Press, 1995.

Moore, David G. *William S. Rosecrans and the Union Victory*. Jefferson, NC: McFarland, 2014.

Morgan, Robert. *Lions of the West: Heroes and Villains of the Westward Expansion*. Chapel Hill: Algonquin, 2012.

Morris, Thomas D. *Free Men All: The Personal Liberty Laws of the North, 1780–1861*. Baltimore: Johns Hopkins University Press, 1974.

Morrison, James L., Jr. *"The Best School in the World": West Point, the Pre-Civil War Years, 1833–1866*. Kent, OH: Kent State University Press, 1986.

"The Mortara Case." *Brownson's Quarterly Review* VII (third series) (April 1859), 226–246.

"Mount St. Mary's Seminary of the West." *American Ecclesiastical Review* XVIII, no. 6 (June 1898.

Mullaly, John. *The Laying of the Cable, or, the Ocean Telegraph*. New York: D. Appleton, 1858.

Murfree, William L. *The Justice of the Peace*. St. Louis: F. H. Thomas Law Book Company, 1886.

Mushkat, Jerome. *Fernando Wood: A Political Biography*. Kent, OH: Kent State University Press, 1990.

Myers, John L. *Henry Wilson and the Coming of the Civil War*. Lanham, MD: University Press of America, 2005.

Neely, Mark E., Jr. *The Fate of Liberty: Abraham Lincoln and Civil Liberties*. New York: Oxford University Press, 1991.

Nevins, Alan. *Ordeal of the Union,* vol. 3. New York: Collier, 1992.
Newman, Ralph, and E. B. Long. *Civil War Digest.* New York: Grosset and Dunlap, 1956.
Nive, John, ed. *The Salmon P. Chase Papers, vol. 4, Correspondence, April 1863–1864.* Kent, OH: Kent State University Press, 1997.
Noll, Mark. *The Civil War as a Theological Crisis.* Chapel Hill: University of North Carolina Press, 2006.
Noonan, John T., Jr. *A Church That Can and Cannot Change: The Development of Catholic Moral Teaching.* Notre Dame: University of Notre Dame Press, 2005.
Northrup, Solomon. *Twelve Years a Slave.* Ed. Henry Louis Gates, Jr. New York: Penguin, 2013.
Norman, Worth E. "Woody" Jr. "Civil War, Church and State." July 4, 2013, http://www.livingchurch.org/civil-war-church-and-state.
O'Brien, David J. *Isaac Hecker: An American Catholic.* New York: Paulist Press, 1992.
O'Connor, Rt. Rev. Doctor, Bishop of Pittsburg, *Celts and Saxons, Nativism and Naturalization: A Complete Refutation of the Nativism of Dr. Orestes A. Brownson, In the Catholic Press of the United States. Also, a Refutation of Mr. Brownson's Extravagant Theory of the (so called) Temporal Powers of the Popes.* Boston: Thomas Sweeney, 1854.
O'Connor, Thomas H. *The Athens of America: Boston 1825–1845.* Boston: University of Massachusetts Press, 2006.
_____. *The Boston Irish: A Political History.* Boston: Back Bay Books, 1997.
_____. *Civil War Boston: Home Front and Battlefield.* Boston: Northeastern University Press, 1997.
_____. *Fitzpatrick's Boston, 1846–1866: John Bernard Fitzpatrick, Third Bishop of Boston.* Boston: Northeastern University Press, 1984.
O'Mahony, T. J. *Joseph Carriere, St Sulpice and the Church of France in His Time,* Dublin: J. Mullany, 1865.
O'Reilly, Bernard. *A Life of Pius IX. Down to the Episcopal Jubilee of 1877.* New York: P.F. Collier, 1877.
O'Shea, John. *The Two Kenricks.* Philadelphia: John J. McVey, 1904.
O'Toole, Fintan. "Green, White and Black: Race and Irish Identity," in *Emerging Irish Identities,* Proceedings of a Seminar Held in Trinity College Dublin, 27 November 1999, ed. Ronit Lentin, 2000, 22–23.
O'Toole, James M. *Passing for White: Race, Religion and the Healy Family.* Amherst: University of Massachusetts Press, 2002.
Oakes, James. *Freedom National: The Destruction of Slavery in the United States, 1861–1865.* New York: W. W. Norton, 2013.
Ochs, Stephen J. *A Black Patriot and a White Priest: Andre Cailloux and Claude Paschal Maistre in Civil War New Orleans.* Baton Rouge: Louisiana State University Press, 2000.
Opdycke, Emerson. *God and the Right.* Ed. Glenn V. Longacre and John E. Haas. Urbana: University of Illinois Press, 2003.
Opinion of the Attorney General of Massachusetts, March 18, 1896, Commonwealth of Massachusetts, *Report of the Attorney General for the Year Ending January 19, 1898.* Boston: Wright & Potter, 1898.
Owens, David M. *The Devil's Topographer: Ambrose Bierce and the American War Story.* Knoxville: University of Tennessee Press, 2006.
Palmer, Beverly Wilson, ed. *Guide and Index to the Papers of Charles Sumner* Alexandria, VA: Chadwyck-Healey, 1988.
_____, ed. *The Selected Letters of Charles Sumner,* vol. 1. Boston: Northeastern University Press, 1990.
Panzer, Joel S. *The Popes and Slavery.* Staten Island, NY: Alba House, 1996.
Paradis, Wilfrid H. *Upon This Granite: Catholicism in New Hampshire 1647–1997.* Portsmouth, NH: Peter E. Randall, 1998.
Paterson, Raymond Campbell. *A Land Afflicted: Scotland and the Covenanter Wars 1638–1690.* Edinburgh: John Donald, 1998.
Pearce, Robert, and Andrina Stiles. *The Unification of Italy 1815–70,* 3d ed. Trans-Atlantic, 2006. Kindle ed.
Peraino, Kevin. *Lincoln in the World: The Making of a Statesman and the Dawn of American Power.* New York: Crown, 2013.
Perry, Marvin, et al. *Western Civilization: Ideas, Politics and Society,* 10th ed. Belmont, CA: Cengage Learning, 2012.
Peskin, Alan. *Garfield: A Biography.* Kent, OH: Kent State University Press, 1978.
Phillips, Kevin. *The Cousins' Wars: Religion, Politics, & the Triumph of Anglo-America.* New York: Basic Books, 1999.
Pilant, Craig Wesley. *Inward promptings: Orestes Augustus Brownson, Outsidership and Roman Catholicism in the United States.* Dissertation, Fordham University, 1996.
Pittard, Homer. "The Strange Death of Julius Peter Garesché: The Eccentric Officer 'Knew' He Would Die in his First Battle." http://www.latinamericanstudies.org/civil-war-cubans/Garesché-death.htm.
"Pio Nono, the Washington Monument and the Purloined Block of Marble." *The American Catholic,* January 25, 2010. http://the-american-catholic.com/2010/01/25/pio-nono-the-washington-monument-and-the-purloined-block-of-marble/
Poinsatte, Charles, and Anne Marie Poinsatte. "Augustin Cochin's 'L'Abolition de l'esclavage' and the Emancipation Proclamation." *The Review of Politics* 46, no. 3 (July 1984), 410–27.
Poole, Stafford, and Douglas J. Slawson. *Church and Slave in Perry County, Missouri, 1818–1865.* Lewiston: Edwin Mellen Press, 1986.
Porter, George Henry. *Ohio Politics During the Civil War Period.* Boston: Columbia University dissertation, 1911)
Porter, Jane. *Thaddeus of Warsaw* (London, Henry Colburn and Richard Bentley, 1831.
Porter-Szucs, Brian. *Faith and Fatherland: Catholicism, Modernity, and Poland.* New York: Oxford University Press, 2011.
Potter, David M. *The Impending Crisis.* Don G. Fehrenbacker. New York: Harper and Row, 1976.
Powell, Eve M. Troutt. *Tell This in My Memory: Stories of Enslavement from Egypt, Sudan and the Ottoman Empire.* Redwood City, CA: Stanford University Press, 2012.
Power, Edward J. *Religion and the Public Schools in 19th*

Century America: The Contribution of Orestes A. Brownson. New York: Paulist Press, 1996.

Proceedings of the Public Demonstration of Sympathy With Pope Pius IX, and with Italy, in the City of New York, on Monday, November 29, A.D. 1847. New York: William van Norden, 1847.

Protestant Alliance. *The Madiai Case*. London: Protestant Alliance, 1853.

Purcell, J. A., and Alexander Cardinal Barnabo. "Some Papers from the Purcell Collection." *The Catholic Historical Review* 1, no. 2 (July 1915), 196–201.

Quinn, John F. "Father Mathew's Disciples: American Catholic Support for Temperance, 1840–1920." *Church History* 65, no. 4 (December 1996).

———. "'Three Cheers for the Abolitionist Pope!' American Reactions to Gregory XVI's Condemnation of the Slave Trade, 1840–1860." *The Catholic Historical Review* 90, no. 1 (January 2004), 67–93.

———. "'Where Religious Freedom Runs in the Streams': Catholic Expansion in Antebellum Newport," in Kevin Schmiesing, ed., *Catholicism and Historical Narrative: A Critical Engagement with Historical Scholarship*. New York: Rowman & Littlefield, 2014.

Rable, George C. *God's Almost Chosen Peoples: A Religious History of the American Civil War*. Chapel Hill: University of North Carolina Press, 2010.

Rapport, Mike. *1848: Year of Revolution*. New York: Basic Books, 2009.

Ravitch, Diane. *The Great School Wars: A History of the New York City Public Schools*. New York: Basic Books, 1988.

Rawley, James A. *The Politics of Union: Northern Politics during the Civil War*, Hinsdale, IL: The Dryden Presss, 1974.

"Recent Publications." *The Christian Review* 28 (January 1863), 155.

Reformation Principles Exhibited, by the Reformed Presbyterian Church in the United States of America. New York: Hopkins and Seymour, 1807.

Reid, Whitelaw. *Ohio in the War: Her Statesmen Generals and Soldiers, vol. 1*. Cincinnati: Robert Clarke, 1895.

Renehan, Edward J., Jr. *The Secret Six: The True Tale of the Men Who Conspired with John Brown*. Columbia, University of South Carolina Press, 1997.

Report of the Judge Advocate General. Washington, D.C.: Government Printing Office, 1864.

"Reviews and Literary Notices." *Atlantic Monthly* 11 (March 1863).

Reynolds, David S. *Mightier Than the Sword: Uncle Tom's Cabin and the Battle for America*. New York: W. W. Norton, 2011.

Riall, Lucy. *Sicily and the Unification of Italy: Liberal Policy and Local Power 1859–1866*. Oxford: Clarendon Press, 1998.

Riforgiato, Leonard B. "John Timon and the Succesion to the See of Baltimore in 1851." *Vincentian Heritage Journal* 8 no. 1 (April 1, 1987).

Rigge, W. F. "The Pope and the Comet." *Popular Astronomy* 16 (1908).

Risjork, Norman K. *Representative Americans: Populists and Progressives*. New York: Rowman and Littlefield, 2004.

Rodgers, Thomas E. "Copperheads or a Respectable Minority: Current Approaches to the Study of Civil War-Era Democrats." *Indiana Magazine of History* 109, no. 2 (June 2013), 114–46.

Rolle, Andrew. *John Charles Frémont: Character as Destiny*. Norman: University of Oklahoma Press, 1991.

Rose, Anne C. "Some Private Roads to Rome: The Role of Families in American Victorian Conversions to Catholicism." *The Catholic Historical Review* 85, no. 1 (January 1999), 35–57.

Roseboom, Eugene H. "Southern Ohio and the Union in 1863." *The Mississippi Valley Historical Review* 39, no. 1 (June 1952), 29–44.

"The Rosecrans Family At Homer, Licking County, Ohio." Diocese of Columbus, *Catholic Record Society Bulletin* VII, no. 3 (March 1981).

Rosecrans, William Starke. "King of the Hill, Part I." *Civil War Times Illustrated* 40, no. 3 (June 2001), reprinted from *National Tribune*, February 22, 1883.

Rosenkrans, Allen. *The Rosenkrans Family in Europe and America*. Newton, NJ: New Jersey Herald Press, 1900.

Rossi, Joseph. "Uncle Tom's Cabin and Protestantism in Italy." *American Quarterly* 11, no. 3 (Autumn 1959), 416–24.

Rowland, Kate Mason. *The Life of Charles Carroll of Carrolton 1737–1832*, vol. II. New York: G. P. Putnam's Sons, 1898.

Ryan, James Emmett. *Faithful Passages: American Catholicism in Literary Culture, 1844–1931*. Madison: University of Wisconsin Press, 2013.

Rzeppa, Joseph Jude. *Thomas Francis Meagher and John Mitchell: Two Irishmen, Two Irish-Americans, One American*. MA Thesis, Texas Christian University, 2007.

Safire, William. "ON LANGUAGE; It's a Rain Forest Out There." *New York Times Magazine*, December 22, 1991.

"St. Mary's Church Sacked." http://www.saintmarysabbey.org/about-us/abbey-history/st-marys-church-sacked/index.aspx.

Sainty, Guy Stair. "The Bourbons of Naples in Exile," in Philip Mansel and Torsten Riotte, eds. *Monarchy and Exile*. Basingstoke: Palgrave Macmillan, 2011.

Sampson, Robert D. *John L. O'Sullivan and His Times*. Kent, OH: Kent State University Press, 2003.

Sanders, Charles W., Jr. *In the Hands of the Enemy: Military Prisons of the Civil War*. Baton Rouge: Louisiana State University Press, 2005.

Sarna, Jonathan D. *When General Grant Expelled the Jews*. New York: Nextbook, 2012.

Schauinger, J. Herman. *William Gaston: Carolinian*. Milwaukee: Bruce, 1949.

Schecter, Barnet. *The Devil's Own Work: The Civil War Draft Riots and the Fight to Reconstruct America*. New York: Walker, 2005.

Shea, John Gilmary. *History of the Catholic Church in the United States from the Division of the Diocese of Baltimore, 1808, and Death of Archbishop Carroll, 1815, to the Fifth Provincial Council of Baltimore, 1843*. New York: John G. Shea, 1890.

———. *History of the Catholic Church in the United States from the Fifth Provincial Council of Baltimore, 1843, to the Second Plenary Council of Baltimore, 1866*. New York: John G. Shea, 1892.

Schlesinger, Arthur M., Jr. *Orestes A. Brownson: A Pilgrim's Progress*. Boston: Little, Brown, 1939.

Schlesinger, Arthur M., Jr., et al., ed. *The Coming to Power: Critical Presidential Elections in American History*. New York: Chelsea House, 1972.

Schouler, William. *A History of Massachusetts in the Civil War*. Boston: E.P. Dutton, 1868.

Schroeder, Joseph. *American Catholics and the Roman Question*. New York: Benziger Brothers, 1892.

Scott, Sir Walter. *Ivanhoe: A Romance*. New York: Signet Classic, 2001.

Searle, George M. "The Very Reverend George Deshon, C.S.P." *The Catholic World* LXXVII, no. 467 (February 1904), 569–73.

Sellery, George Clark. "Lincoln's Suspension of Habeas Corpus as Viewed by Congress." *Bulletin of the University of Wisconsin* 149, History Series 1, no. 3 (April 1907), 213–86.

Horatio Seymour Papers. New York Historical Society.

Shaw, Richard. *Dagger John: The Unquiet Life and Times of Archbishop John Hughes of New York*. New York: Paulist Press, 1977.

Siegel, Alan A. *Beneath the Starry Flag: New Jersey's Civil War Experience* (New Brunswick, NJ: Rutgers University Press, 2001.

Silbey, Joel H. *A Respectable Minority: The Democratic Party in the Civil War Era, 1860–1868*. New York: W. W. Norton, 1977.

Silverman, Kenneth. *Lightning Man: The Accursed Life of Samuel F. B. Morse*. New York: Da Capo Press, 2009.

Singer, Jane. *The Confederate Dirty War: Arson, Bombings, Assassination and Plots for Chemical and Germ Attacks on the Union*. Jefferson, NC: McFarland, 2005.

Slotkin, Richard. *The Long Road to Antietam: How the Civil War Became a Revolution*. New York: Liveright, 2012.

Smith, Reuben. "Brownson's Development of Himself" (letter to the editor). *Princeton Review*, vol. 30, April 1858, 390–92.

Snell, Mark A. *West Virginia and the Civil War: Mountaineers Are Always Free*. Charleston, SC: History Press, 2011.

Spalding, David. "Martin John Spalding's 'Dissertation on the American Civil War.'" *The Catholic Historical Review* 52, no. 1 (April 1966), 66–85.

Spalding, Martin John. *Miscellanea: Comprising Reviews, Lectures and Essays, on Historical, Theological and Miscellaneous Subjects*. Baltimore: John Murphy, 1895 (original edition 1855).

Spalding, Thomas W. *Martin John Spalding: American Churchman*. Washington, D.C.: Catholic University of American Press, 1973.

Spann, Edward K. *Gotham at War: New York City 1861–1865*. Wilmington, DE: SR Books, 2001.

Stampp, Kenneth M. *America in 1857*. New York: Oxford University Press, 1990.

Stanton, R. L. *The Church and the Rebellion*. New York: Derby & Miller, 1864.

Starr, Stephen Z. "Was There a Northwest Conspiracy?" *The Filson Club Historical Quarterly* 38, no. 4 (October 1964), 323–41.

_____, ed. *The Causes of the Civil War*, 3d rev. ed. New York: Touchstone, 1991.

The State vs. Lavinia and Wilkes, 25 Ga. 311 (1858).

Stauffer, John, and Benjamin Soskis. *The Battle Hymn of the Republic: The Biography of a Song That Marches On*. New York: Oxford University Press, 2013.

Stern, Andrew H. M. *Southern Crucifix, Southern Cross: Catholic-Protestant Relations in the Old South*. Tuscaloosa: University of Alabama Press, 2012.

Stillman, W. J. *Autobiography of a Journalist, vol. I*. 1901. Reprinted by Project Gutenberg, March 11, 2004 [EBook #11546], http://www.gutenberg.org/files/11546/11546-8.txt.

Stock, Leo Francis. *Consular Relations Between the United States and the Papal States*. Washington, D.C.: American Catholic Historical Association, 1945.

_____. *United States Ministers to the Papal States: Instructions and Despatches 1848–1968*. Washington, D.C.: American Catholic Historical Association, 1933.

Stoker, Donald. *The Grand Design: Strategy and the U.S. Civil War*. Oxford: Oxford University Press, 2010.

Strickland, W. P. *The Life of Jacob Gruber*. New York: Carlton and Porter, 1860.

Summers, Robert K. *The Fall and Redemption of Dr. Samuel A. Mudd*. Self-published, 2008.

Sumner, Charles. *Defence of Massachusetts. Speeches of Hon. Charles Sumner, on the Boston memorial for the repeal of the fugitive slave bill, and in reply to Messrs. Jones of Tennessee, Butler of South Carolina, and Mason of Virginia. In Senate of United States, June 26 and 28, 1854*. Washington, D.C.: Buell & Blanchard, 1854.

Swick, Gerald D. "Virginia's Great Divorce." *America's Civil War* (May 2013), 66–73.

Sword, Wiley. *Mountains Touched With Fire: Chattanooga Besieged, 1863*. New York: St. Martin's Press, 1997.

Sylvester, Nathanial Bartlett. *History of Saratoga County, New York*. Philadelphia: Everts and Ensign, 1878.

"Sylvester Horton Rosecrans—The 'Other' Rosecrans from Homer." Granville, Ohio, Historical Society. *The Historical Times* XV, no. 3 (Summer 2001).

Taggart, Joseph. *Biographical Sketches of the Eminent American Patriots, Charles Carroll of Carrollton, Roger Brooke Taney, William Starke Rosecrans, John Barry, Philip Henry Sheridan, and a Sketch of the Early History of Maryland*. Kansas City, MO: The Burton Company, 1907.

Taheny, Josephine C. *Chief Justice Roger Brooke Taney's Attitude Toward Slavery*. Loyola University, M.A. Thesis, February 1942.

Taylor, Steven. "Progressive Nativism: The Know-Nothing Party in Massachusetts." *Historical Journal of Massachusetts* 28, no. 2 (Summer 2000).

"THC 29: The Lincoln Assassination & the Catholic Church w/ Paul Serup." http://thehighersidechats.com/higherside-chats-podcast-29-lincoln-assassination-catholic-church-w-paul-serup/.

Tidball, Eugene C. *No Disgrace to My Country: The Life of John C. Tidball*. Kent, OH: Kent State University Press, 2002.

Trevelyan, George Macaulay. *Garibaldi and the Making of Italy: June–November 1860*. London: Longman's, Green, 1914.

_____. *Garibaldi and the Thousand: May 1860*. London: Thomas Nelson and Sons, 1921.

_____. *Garibaldi's Defense of the Roman Republic*. London: Longman's, Green, 1908.

Tuck, Faye Royster. "Letters of a Halifax County Confederate soldier describe the July 1861 Battle at Virginia's Rich Mountain." *America's Civil War* (July 2006), 18–21.

Tucker, Jack. *Innocents Return Abroad: Exploring Ancient Sites in Eastern Turkey*, vol. 2. CreateSpace Independent Publishing Platform, 2013.

Tucker, Phillip Thomas. *The Confederacy's Fighting Chaplain: Father John B. Bannon*. Tuscaloosa: The University of Alabama Press, 1992.

28th Massachusetts Regimental History, 1862. http://www.28thmass.org/history2.htm.

United States. Congress. Senate. *Journal of the Executive Proceedings of the Senate of the United States of America, From December 2, 1861, to July 17, 1862, inclusive*, vol. XII. Washington, D.C.: Government Printing Office, 1887.

University of Notre Dame Archives, online calendar (here described as UNDA). http://archives.nd.edu/search/calendar-search.htm.

Vallandigham, James L. *A Life of Clement L. Vallandigham*. Baltimore: Turnbull Bros., 1872.

Varney, Frank P. *General Grant and the Rewriting of History: How the Destruction of General William S. Rosecrans Influenced Our Understanding of the Civil War*. El Dorado Hills, CA: Savas Beatie, 2013.

Verot, Augustine. *A Tract for the Times. Slavery & Abolitionism, being the Substance of a Sermon, Preached in the Church of St. Augustine, Florida, On the 4th Day of January 1861, Day of Public Humiliation, Fasting and Prayer*.

Voegeli, W. Jacque. *Free But Not Equal: The Midwest and the Negro During the Civil War*. Chicago: University of Chicago Press, 1967.

Voelker, David Joseph. *Orestes Brownson and the Search for Authority in Democratic America*. Dissertation, University of North Carolina at Chapel Hill, 2003.

von Drehle, David. *Rise to Greatness: Abraham Lincoln and America's Most Perilous Year*. New York: Henry Holt, 2012.

von Frank, Albert J. *The Trials of Anthony Burns: Freedom and Slavery in Emerson's Boston*. Cambridge: Harvard University Press, 1998.

"W.D.B." (William D. Bickman). *Rosecrans' Campaign with the Fourteenth Army Corps*. Cincinnati: Moore, Wilstack.

Wallace, William Jason. *The Medieval Specter: Catholics, Evangelicals, and the Limits of Political Protestantism: 1835–1860*. Dissertation, University of Virginia, January 2005.

Walther, Eric H. *The Fire-Eaters*. Baton Rouge: Louisiana State University Press, 1992.

The War of the Rebellion. Official records of the Union and Confederate Armies (O.R.).

Warren, Craig A. "'O, God, What a Pity!' The Irish Brigade at Fredericksburg and the Creation of Myth." *Civil War History* (September 2001).

Watt, Jeremy. "The Incongruous Bull: *In Supremo Apostolatus*." Senior Thesis, Indiana University, 2006.

Waugh, John C. *Reelecting Lincoln: The Battle for the 1864 Presidency*. Cambridge, MA: Da Capo Press, 2001.

Weber, Jennifer L. *Copperheads: The Rise and Fall of Lincoln's Opponents in the North*. Oxford: Oxford University Press, 2006.

Weigley, Russell F. *Towards an American Army: Military Thought from Washington to Marshall*. New York: Columbia University Press, 1962.

Wert, Jeffry D. *General James Longstreet: The Confederacy's Most Controversial Soldier*. New York: Touchstone, 1993.

Wesley, Timothy L. *The Politics of Faith During The Civil War*. Baton Rouge: Louisiana State University Press, 2013.

Whalen, Charles, and Barbara Whalen. *The Fighting McCooks: America's Famous Fighting Family*. Bethesda, MD: Westmoreland Press, 2006.

Wheelan, Joseph. *Terrible Swift Sword: The Life of General Philip H. Sheridan*. New York: De Capo Press, 2012.

White, Andrew Dickson. *The Soldier's Companion: Dedicated to the Defenders of Their Country in the Field by Their Friends at Home*. Boston: Walker, Wise, 1862.

White, Joseph M. "Perspectives on the Nineteenth-Century Diocesan Seminary in the United States." *U.S. Catholic Historian* 19, no. 1, The American Catholic Experience: Essays in Honor of Jay P. Dolan (Winter 2001), 21–35.

Whittelsea, Charles Barney. *The Roosevelt Genealogy, 1649–1902*. Charles Barney Whittelsea, 1902.

Wieczerzak, Joseph W. "American Reactions to the Polish Insurrection of 1863." *Polish American Studies*, 22, no. 2 (July—December 1965).

_____. *A Polish Chapter in Civil War America: The Effects of the January Insurrection on American Opinion and Diplomacy*. Boston: Twayne, 1967.

Wiley, Bell Irvin. *The Life of Billy Yank: The Common Soldier of the Union*. Baton Rouge: Louisiana State University Press, 1971.

Williams, David A. *David C. Broderick—A Political Portrait*. The Huntingdon Library, 1969.

Wills, Brian Steel. *George Henry Thomas: As True as Steel*. Lawrence: University Press of Kansas, 2012.

Wilson, Clyde N., ed. *The Papers of John C. Calhoun*, several vols. Columbia: University of South Carolina Press, 1959–2003.

Wilson, James Grant, and John Fiske. *Appleton's Cyclopædia of American Biography*, vol. 4. New York: D. Appleton, 1888.

Wilson, Henry. *History of the Rise and Fall of the Slave Power in America*, vol. II. Boston: Houghton, Osgood, 1879.

Woellert, Dann. *Cincinnati Turner Societies: The Cradle of an American Movement*. Charleston, SC: The History Press, 2012.

Zanca, Kenneth J., *The Catholics and Mrs. Mary Surratt: How They Responded to the Trial and Execution of the Lincoln Conspirator*. Lanham, MD: University Press of America, 2008.

_____, ed. *American Catholics and Slavery: 1789–1866: An Anthology of Primary Documents*. Lanham, MD: University Press of America, 1994.

Index

Page numbers in ***bold italics*** indicate pages with illustrations.

"Abolition and Negro Equality" 232–33
L'Abolition de l'Esclavage 160, 199
abolitionism 8, 10, 13, 16–17, 52–56, 59, 64, 66, 69, 71, 78, 81, 95–96, 98, 102, 112, 115, 119, 121, 136, 139, 145–47, 150–51, 154, 159–66, 171–72, 179–83, 190, 196, 199–200, 204, 210, 218, 231–34, 250, 254, 279*n*22
Acton, John 91, 197
Adams, John Quincy 50
African Americans 2, 6, 13–15, 17, 49–50, 52–58, 60–63, 69, 71, 78, 80, 85, 96, 98, 102–03, 106, 122, 124, 130, 145–46, 156, 162, 165–66, 171–74, 180, 185, 192, 199, 203–04, 211, 213, 223, 232–33, 236, 240–42, 249–50, 255(Preface)*n*2, 261*n*54, 272*n*39, 274*n*25, 279*n*20, 279*n*22, 279*ch*21*n*1, 281*n*2
Agassiz, Louis 166
Alabama 143, 148, 175, 227; legislature 98
Albertus Magnus 132
alcohol, regulation of 90–91, 106, 116
Alexander, Edward Porter 190
Alexander II, Czar of Russia 216–18, 277*n*34
Alien and Sedition Acts (1798) 262*n*38
American and Foreign Christian Union 81, 83, 134
American College (Rome) 84, 132–34, 136, 153
American Colonization Society 59
The American Republic 246
Ames, Edward Raymond 222
Andersonville prison camp (Georgia) 250
Andrew, John Albion 15, 146–48, 184–185, 187, 190, 210–11, ***212***, 271–72*n*33, 276*n*1
"Angel Gabriel" *see* John S. Orr
Antietam (battle) 174, 177, 189
Antonelli, Cardinal Giacomo 13, 39, 136, 176–77, ***177***, 179, 215–16, 236, 239, 244
Arkansas 143, 214, 229
Arlington National Cemetary 249
Armstead, Rosetta 117
Army of the Cumberland 6–7, 175, 180–181, ***192***, 201–02, 207, 220–21, 230
Army of Virginia 229
Arnold, George 21
Association for the Propagation of the Faith 31
Athenaeum (Wheeling, Virginia/West Virginia) 151
Atlantic Monthly 199–200
Augustine, Saint 25
Austria 12, 31–32, 34–37, 39–40, 43, 45–47, 78–79, 83, 110, 128, 133–34
"Ave Maris Stella" 208–09
The Awful Disclosures of Maria Monk 32, 106, 134

Babst, Fr. John 90
Baker, Lafayette 228
Ballston Center (New York) 66
Ballston Center Reformed Presbyterian Church 66
Ballston Spa (New York) 66
Balmes, Jaime 54
Baltimore, Maryland 11, 26, 40, 52, 55, 57, 59, 83, 102, 108, 109, 123, 129, 136, 143–44, 146, 153, 159, 224, 228–29, 233
Baltimore, Second Plenary Council of 250
Bancroft, George 67–68
Banks, Nathaniel 108–09, 124, 270*n*37
Bannon, Fr. John B. 214–15, 236, 277*n*21
Baptism 20, 29
Baptists 175
Barbee, John 118
Barkley, T. W. 21
Barnabo, Allessandro 12, 142–43, 155, 158–59, 170, 279*ch*21*n*1
Barnum, P. T. 82, 90

Barrett, James 227
Barry, Fr. John 250
Barry, Fr. William 132–33, 140–41, 143, 150
Bassi, Ugo 41–42, 45–46, ***82***, 83
Batchelder, James 96, 264*n*36
Bath, Maine 85
"Battle Hymn of the Republic" 274*n*24
Bayley, Bishop James Roosevelt 75, 113, ***115***, 156
Bedini, Cardinal Gaetano 43, 46, 82–84, 150
Bedini riots (1853) 83–84
Beecher, Edward 90–91, 110; *Papal Conspiracy Exposed* 110, ***111***
Beecher, Harriet *see* Stowe, Harriet Beecher
Beecher, Henry Ward 110
Beecher, Lyman 31–32, 55, 90, 114; *A Plea for the West* 31–32
Belgium 110, 185, 187, 213–15, 224
Benedict XVI, Pope 277*n*31
Benjamin, Judah 196, 214–15, 255*n*20
Bennett, James Gordon 206
Bergier, Nicholas 54
Bible 8, 24–26, 57, 81–82, 105, 115, 117, 125–27, 143–45, 168–69, 184, 213
Bierce, Ambrose 150, 208
Binsse, Louis B 157, 214, 240
"Black Joke" *see* Volunteer Engine Company #33
Blair, Montgomery 236
Blanc, Bishop Anthony 33
Blatchford, Richard M. 179, 214–15
Bliemel, Fr. Emmeran 202
Bologna, Papal States 45, 83, 128
Bonaparte, Napoleon *see* Napoleon I
"Bonny Blue Flag" 193
Booth, John Wilkes 245
Booth, Mary Louise 199
Bordeaux province 102
Borjes, José ***218***, 219

295

Boston, Massachusetts 6, 14–16, 27, 31, 49, 50, 53, 55–56, 59, 61, 63, 67–69, 73–75, 78, 83–85, 92, 95–96, 98, 102–03, 105, 107, 113, 116, 122, 124–26, 146–48, 163–64, 169, 184, 185, 187, 190–91, 210–13, 243, 250; Cooper Street Armory 211; East Boston 210; North End 14–15, 125, 210–12
Boston City Council 212
Boston Daily Advertiser 207, 211
Boston, diocese of 14, 49–51, 116
Boston draft riot (1863) 14–16, 210–13
Boston Navy Yard 126
Boston Pilot 15, 30, 106, 122, 146–47, 184–85, 190, 212–13, 277n34
Boston Quarterly Review 69–71
Boston Reformer (magazine) 67, 69
Boston School Committee 105, 124–26
Bowling Green, Kentucky 175, 191
Boynton, Charles 90
Brady, Fr. Robert, S.J. 212–13
Brady, William 34
Bragg, Braxton 192–93, 195, 202–03, 209
"Brahmins" (Boston) 124, 184
Brazil 82
Breckenridge, John (anti-Catholic minister) 91
Breckenridge, John C. (politician) 139
British Guiana 85
Broadway Tabernacle 34
Broderick, David C. 136
Brook Farm 69, 73
Brooks, Erastus 107
Brooksiana 265n34
Brophy, John 243
Brough, John 14, 203
Brown, John 136, 163, 190; "John Brown's Body" 190, 274n24
Brown, Nicholas 36–41, 44
Brownson, Edward ("Ned") 163–64, 166–67, 196, 233, 236–37, 271–72n33, 279n22
Brownson, Henry 63, 141, 166, 196, 246, 267n37
Brownson, John H. 63, 262n42
Brownson, Oran 65
Brownson, Orestes 1, 6, **16**, 16–18, 63–79, 84–89, 91–94, 96–100, 102, 106, 108–10, 112–14, 119, 121, 127, 133–34, 139–43, 155–67, 196–200, 231–33, 236, 239–40, 242, 246–47, 254, 262n42, 271–72n33; *Charles Elwood: Or the Infidel Converted* 65–66, 261n2; "Civil and Religious Freedom" 235–37; *The Convert* 66, 79; "The Laboring Classes" 71–72, 88, 232; "Lincoln or Fremont?" 234; *The Mediatorial Life of Jesus* 72; "The Mortara Case" 129, 267n37, 267n40; "The New Brahminical Literature of New England" 231–32; *New Views of Christianity, Society and the Church* 67–68; "The Next President" 233; "Rights of the Temporal" 140–41; *The Spirit-Rapper* 65–66, 87, 99–100, 261n8
Brownson, Orestes, Jr. 68
Brownson, Relief Metcalf 237
Brownson, Sarah (Sally) 66, 74, 159, 246
Brownson, Sarah (daughter of Orestes and Sarah) 167, 196, 199, 232, 246
Brownson, William 63, 67, 236–37, 262n42
Brownson's Quarterly Review 16–17, 72–74, 89, 94, 96–98, 109–10, 121–23, 127, 133–34, 139–42, 155–64, 167, 197–99, 231–33, 240, 246, 253
Brussels 185, 213
Buchanan, James 34, 38, 40, 121, 123, 128, 130, 227
Buell, Don Carlos 201, 230
Bull Run (battle) 152
"burned-over district" 65
Burns, Anthony 95–96, **97**, 98, 105, 211
Burnside, Ambrose 9, 14, 189
bushwhackers 229
Butler, Benjamin 34, 144, 233, 269n21

Cabot, Stephen 210–11
"caesarism" 87
Cairo, Egypt 241
Calhoun, John C. 69–73, 76–77, 96, 122, 156, 262n24
California 248–49
Callipolis (Gallipoli) 49
Callistus III, Pope 171–72
Calvin, John 16
Calvinism 66, 90
Cameron, Simon 162
Camp Dennison 149, 230
Campbell, Alexander 32–33
Campbell, James 264n34
Canaanites 154, 241
Canada 13, 25, 63–64, 83, 226–27, 244–46
Canal River Coal Company 114
Canby, Edwin 130
Canisius, Theodore 126
Cape Girardeau, Missouri 221
Carne, John 168
Carnifex Ferry (battle) 152
Carrick's Ford (battle) 152
Carrière, Joseph 102, 251
Carrington, Henry 228
Carroll, Charles (Charles Carroll of Carrolton) 59
Carroll, Bishop John 59
Casanatense Library 240
Cass, Lewis, Jr. 40, 44, 46, 264n34
Cass, Lewis, Sr. 40, 81, 128–29
Cass, Thomas 147, 184, 187
Castelfidardo (battle) 135, **135**
Catechism of the Catholic Church 271n10
Catholic Institute (Cincinnati) 114
Catholic Mirror 144
Catholic Miscellany 53, 89
Catholic Telegraph 48, 84, 92–94, 114, 116, 130, 145, 150, 152, 171, 179–80, 225, 253
Catholic Tribune 41
Catiline 128
Cavour, Camillo 135, 277n30
Chadwick, Owen 35
Challoner, Bishop Richard *see* *Grounds of Catholic Doctrine*
Cham *see* Ham
Chandler, Joseph 108–10, 112
Channing, William Ellery 55, 67–68, 72–73
chaplains (military) 5, **6**, 10, 40, 45, **82**, 83, 147, 150, 170, 175, 187–88, **189**, 202, 214
Charles Albert, King of Piedmont 35
Charles Elwood: Or the Infidel Converted 65–66, 261n2
Charleston, South Carolina 51–53, 59, 89, 109, 143, 153, 206, 236
Charleston Harbor *see* Fort Sumter
Charlestown (Massachusetts) riots 31–32, 81, 106
"Charlie" *see* E. E. Jones
Chase, Salmon P. 117, 119, 131, 149, 165, 182, 192, 209, 220–21, 233, 269n20
Chattanooga, Tennessee 203, 207–09, 220, 230
Cheat Mountain (battle) 152
Chelsea, Massachusetts 73; Marine Hospital 68–69, 71, 73
Chicago 114, 126, 141–42
Chicago Tribune 195, 220
Chickamauga (battle) 207–09, 249
Child, Lydia Maria 50
Chiniquy, Charles P.T. 245–46; *Fifty Years in the Church of Rome* 245
Cilicia, modern Turkey 168
Cincinnati, Ohio 6, 10–11, 14, 31–33, 55, 84, 114–15, 117, 130–31, 145, 148–149, 152, 171, 173, 207, 224, 230, 253, 247–48
Cincinnati Cathedral 10, 82, 248
Cincinnati Commercial 149, 174, 191, 195, 207–08
Cincinnati Gazette 195, 197
Cincinnati Platform 116
Cincinnati riots 116
Cincinnati Times 116, 220

Index

"Civil and Religious Freedom" 235–37
Civiltà Cattolica 214, 234
Clark, Richard H. 132
Clark, Rufus W. 110; *Romanism in America* 110
Clay, Cassius 218
Clay, Clement 227
Clemens, Samuel ("Mark Twain") 249
Clerk, George 93
Cleveland, Ohio 82
Clough, Arthur Hugh 43
Coal River 114
Cochin, Augustin 160–63, 199–200, 232; *L'Abolition de l'Esclavage* 160; *The Results of Emancipation* 199
Cochrane, John **235**
College of the Propaganda 33, 38–40, 42
colonization 59, 165–66, 233
Colored Orphan Asylum 6
Columbia, South Carolina 276n28
Columbia Association 147
Columbian Artillery/Columbian Rifles 96, **97**, 105–06, 127, 147
Columbus, Ohio 21, 117; Diocese of 247–48
Communist Manifesto 71
concurrent majority 262n24
Confederate States of America 5, 6, 8–10, 11–12, 14–15, 143–44, 151–53, 158–61, 164–65, 167, 169, 170–75, 179–83, 185, 187, 189, 190–95, 198, 201–04, 214–16, 218, 221, 226–30, 236–34, 237, 244, 246, 248–49
Confiscation Acts: 1861 Act 159–60; 1862 Act 171
"Confiscation and Emancipation" 199
Confraternity of the Sacred Heart 114
Congregation of the Index 2, 94, 154, 240–42
Congregation of the Propaganda 12, 33, 52, 142, 146, 154, 250, 254
Connecticut 105, 148, 185
Conscription: Conscription Act (1863) 204; Militia Act (1862) 172
Constant, Benjamin 67
Constantine (Emperor) 91
Constitution of the United States 71, 105, 110, 121–22, 129, 139, 144, 153–54, 161, 165, 179, 190, 198, 233–34, 236, 246
Constitutional Union Party 137
The Convert 66, 79
convert fund 159
Cook, McLaurin 125
"copperheads" 227–30, 232, 236, 278n27

Corby, Fr. William 5, **6**, 188
Corinth (battle) 173–75, **174**, 214, 249
Le Correspondant 163
Counter-Reformation 213
Cousin, Victor 67, 69
Covington, Kentucky 82, 125
Cox, Samuel 171
Crandall, Eli 221
Cromwell 236
Cullen, Archbishop Paul 17
Cummings, Fr. Jeremiah Williams 64, 112, 123, 141–43, 155, 158–59, 246
Custer's Last Stand 268n63

Daily Advertiser (Boston) 107
Dana, Charles A. 207–09, **207**
Davis, Jefferson 15, 114, 196, 198, 214–15, 226–27, 236, 246, 278n21
Davis, Varina 246
Declaration of Independence 19, 20, 59, 108, 179
de Lagnel, J. A. **151**
Delaware 165
Delaware County, Pennsylvania 19
de Lesseps, Ferdinand 43
Della Genga, Cardinal 46
Democratic Party 1, 8–9, 13, 16, 18, 53, 56, 68, 71, 73, 88, 91, 95, 104, 116, 121–23, 126, 129, 136–37, **138**, 139, 142–43, 153, 170–72, 179, 183, 190, 197, 203–04, 206, 226–29, 231–34, 236
Democratic-Republican Workingmen's Association 206
Democratic Review 72
Denmark 19
Dennison, William 148–49
deposing power, Papal 88–89, 109–10
Deshon, George 26
Detroit 225, 227
Díaz, Porfirio 249
divorce 127–28, 267n30
"Dixie" 193
Dolan, Cardinal Timothy 253
Domenec, Bishop Michael 177
Dominican Order 202
Dominican Republic 182, 260n26, 281n2
Donahoe, Patrick 147, 190, 213
Douglas, Stephen 95, 123, 139
Douglass, Frederick 69
Dred Scott decision 122–23
Ducat, Arthur 180
Dugoujon, Casimir 54
Dupanloup 223–24, 232, 240
Durando, Giacomo 36
Dwight, Theodore 134

Eccleston, Archbishop Samuel 40
Egan, Fr. Charles 147, 188
88th New York Regiment 190

Elder, Bishop William 141, 155, 157–58, 166, 221–22, 255n2
Eliot School 125–26
Elizabeth, New Jersey 113, 155
Elizabeth I, Queen of England 88, 108
Ellsworth, Maine 90
Emancipation Proclamation: 1862 (preliminary) 11, 17, 172, 178–79, 182, 190; 1863 (final) 6, 10–11, 183, 190, 195, 199, 214
Emerson, Ralph Waldo 68–69; *Nature* 68
The End of Religious Controversy 24–26
England (country) *see* Great Britain
England, Bishop John 51–54, 242
English Seminary (Douai, France) 213
Ethiopian Serenaders 63
"Executive Power over the Army" 127

Faneuil Hall (Boston, Massachusetts) 55
Faran, James J. 116
Feast of the Annunciation 149, 168
Federalist Party 91, 264n18
Feliński, Archbishop Zygmunt 216–17, 277n31
Fenianism 225, 245
Fenwick, Bishop Benedict 49, 51, 53, 59–61, 73
Fenwick, Bishop Edward 31
Fenwick, Fr. George 60–64, 103
Fifty Years in the Church of Rome 245
55th Massachusetts Regiment 211
Fillmore, Millard 79, **118**, 119, 121, 137–38, 142
fire companies (New York) 204
Fireside, Bryna J. 270n37
First Vatican Council *see* Vatican Council
Fitzgerald, Fr. Edward 247
Fitzpatrick, Bishop John 14–15, 27, 49, 51–52, 61, 63–64, 73–75, 84, 91–94, 101, 103–06, 113, 124–26, 147–48, 166, 184–87, 213, 250
Florida 145
Floyd, John B. 152, 198
Flushing, New York 50
Fordham University *see* Saint John's College
Forrest, Nathan Bedford 191
Forsyth, John 53
Fort Donelson (battle) 173
Fort McHenry (Maryland) 26
Fort Sumter (Charleston, South Carolina) 143
Fort Warren (Boston) 164, 210–11
Fort Wayne, Indiana, diocese of 143, 148, 168

Fortress Monroe (Virginia) 23
"forty-eighters" 84
France 22, 31, 39, 43–46, *45*, 59, 86, 89, 102, 110, 128–29, 134–35, 141, 154, 160, 162–63, 178–79, 185, 191, 200, 213–15, 216, 218, 223, 232, 238, 240
Francis, Simeon 123
Francis II, King of Naples 219
Fransoni, Cardinal Giacomo 114
Frascati, Papal States 34–37
Fredericksburg (battle) 177, 189–90, 203; Marye's Heights 190
Freeman's Journal 10, 74–76, *77*, 81, 83, 86, 107–08, 110, 127, 130–31, 141, 145, 151, 180, 182–83, 196, 202, 226, 232, 236, 253
Frémont, John C. 120–21, 159–60, 163–64, 166–67, 171–72, 196, 233–34, *235*, 236–37, 270*n*37
Frenaye, Mark 55
French-Canadians 250
French Revolution 87, 179, 271–72*n*33
Fugitive Slave Act of 1850 77, 97–98
Fuller, Arthur Buckminster 125
Fuller, Margaret 41, 45–46, 66, 69

gallicanism 89, 108–10, 112, 123, 237
Gardner, Henry 105, 127
Garesché, Alexander 181, 273–74*n*48
Garesché, Bauduy 181
Garesché, Ferdinand 181
Garesché, Frederick 182
Garesché, Julius 23, 26, 127–28, 149, 180–83, *180*, 186, 191–95, *192*, 269*n*21, 273–74*n*48; "Divorce and Divorce Laws" 267*n*30
Garesché, Louis 26, 180, 182, 186
Garesché, Mariquitta 182
Garfield, James 7–9, 24, 151, 202, 209, 220, 228–30, 248–49
Garibaldi, Giuseppe 12, 41–42, 44–46, 83, 133–36, 178, 185–86, *186*, 198, 219, 244
Garner, Margaret 117
Garrison, William Lloyd 55, 59, 71, 161, 261*n*58, 262*n*27, 264*n*18
Gaston, William 52
Gatti, Fr. Vincenzo M. 240–42
Gavazzi, Alessandro 40–42, 44, 46, 83, *83*
Genessee Republican and Herald of Reform (newspaper) 67
Geneva Conventions 253, 280–81*n*1
Georgetown College (later Georgetown University) 60
Georgia 49–50, 60–63, 103–04, 175, 229–30, 259*n*8, 261*n*54
Georgia Telegraph 51, 54, 64, 259*n*12

Germany/Germans 17, 29, 35, 46, 69, 84, 91–92, 112, 115–18, 123, 126, 129, 131, 137–38, 173, 180, 188, 192, 198, 213, 233–34, 239
Gettysburg (battle) 5–6, *6*, 12, 16, 203, 205, 224–25
Gilmore, James 8–9
Gioberti, Fr. Vincenzo 34, 140
"Glorious Revolution" (1688) 26
Good Friday 243
The Gospel Advocate and Impartial Investigator 66–67
Grand Turk 234
Grant, Ulysses 6, 8, 23, 173–75, 197, 202, 207, 209, 214, 227, 229–30, 248–49
Great Britain/England 13, 17, 24–25, 29, 35, 46–47, 54, 56–57, 81, 88, 93, 110, 112, 128–29, 137, 146–47, 154, 176, 179, 190–91, 197–98, 213, 215, 218, 244
"The Great Rebellion" 156, 158
Greeley, Horace 8, 9, 34, 41, 137, 161, 204–05, 207, 278*n*21
Gregory XVI, Pope 33–34, 52–53, 55–56, 67, 102, 145–46, 164, 240, 242, 260*n*18, 272*n*39
Gregory the Great, Pope 58
Grounds of Catholic Doctrine 29
Gruber, Jacob 60
la guerre du Sud pour son independence 154
Guiney, Patrick 189
Gunpowder Plot 88
Gunther, Charles Godfrey 206
Gura, Philip 68

habeas corpus 112, 172
"Hail Columbia" 193
Haiti 52, 182, 260*n*26, 281*n*2
Halleck, Henry Wager 191–92, 201, 203
Halley's Comet 171
Ham (Cham) 241
Haman 209
Hamilton, Frank H. 201–02
Hamlin, Hannibal 228
Hampton Roads 23
Hancock, Winfield Scott 236–37
Hardeman, Robert 80, 261*n*55, 265*n*15
Harper, Alexander 21
Harpers Ferry, Virginia/West Virginia 136, 190
Harris, Thomas 245–46
Harrison, William Henry 19, 71
Hart, David 151
Hartford, Connecticut 148, 185
Harvard University 67, 184, 211
Hatfield, David 155
Hay, John 225
Hayes, Rutherford B. 220, 270*n*37
hazing 23
Healy, Eliza 49, 62–64, 80, 259*n*12

Healy, Eugene 213
Healy, Hugh 63, 80, 102–04
Healy, Fr. James Augustine 1, 6, *14*, 14–16, 49–64, 80, 101–104, 106, 124–26, 146–48, 185, 187, 190–91, 211–13, 243, 250–51, 254, 261*n*54, 262*n*42
Healy, John 66
Healy, Michael 49–52, 56–57, 61, 63–64, 80, 103–04, 259*n*12, 261*n*54, 261*n*55, 265*n*15
Healy, Patrick 60–61, 63, 213
Healy, Sally *see* Brownson, Sally
Healy, Sherwood 55, 61, 63, 103
Heaven 19, 25, 44, 66, 96, 148, 157, 182, 196, 123–24
Hecker, George 246
Hecker, Fr. Isaac 72–74, *75*, 86, 157, 197, 213, 246
Heg, Hans 194
Hegeman, Adrian 23
hell 16–17, 27, 66, 96, 157–58, 271*n*10
Hewit, Fr. Augustine 157, 164
Hewit, Henry S. 164, 197
Hibernian Society 56–57
"higher law" doctrine 77–78
Hilton Head, South Carolina 187
Hiss, Joseph 107
Hochwächter (newspaper) 84, 116
Hogan, John 222
Holcombe, James P. 227
Holland 112
Holmes, Oliver Wendell, Sr. 124
Holt, Joseph 227–28
Holy Cross College 51, 60–64, 102, 106–07
Home and Foreign Review 197
"Home, Sweet Home" 193
Homer, Ohio 19
Hooker, J. C. 215
Hopkins, Francis 19
Hough, Alfred 209
House of Representatives, U.S. 62, 104–05, 137
House of the Angel Guardian (Boston) 103
Howe, Julia Ward 274*n*24
Hughes, Bishop (later Archbishop) John 17, 34, 41, 46, 55, 73–76, *76*, 81–82, 88–89, 92, 94, 107–08, 113, 132, 136, 138, 140–41, 143, 150, 153–54, 156, 158–59, 161–64, 176–77, 179, 186, 196, 204–06, 211, 215, 226, 231, 246, 265*n*34
Hugo, Victor 160
Hungary 46, 79
Hunt, Charles L. 227, 230
Huntington family 65
"Hymn of the Hebrew Maid" 207, 209

Illinois 104, 126, 245
Illinois State Journal 123

The Imitation of Christ 180, 193–94
Imola, Papal States 33
In Supremo Apostolatus 52–53, 145–46, 240–41, 260*n*18, 272*n*39
Index of Forbidden Books 140
Indiana 149, 173
Indians 96, 250
Inquisition 128
International Catholic- Jewish Liaison Committee 268*n*56
Ireland/Irish 2, 5, 17, 24, 46, 51, 54–57, 88, 91–94, 113, 140–42, 146–47, 149, 154, 187–90, 198, 203–06, **205**, 214–15, 225–26, 231, 234, 236, 246, 250, 264*n*34, 277*n*34, 279*n*22
Irish American 190
Irish Brigade 5–6, 187–90, 203–04
Irish Volunteers 52
"if by whiskey" speech 267*n*11
Iuka (battle) 173–75, 214, 230, 232, 249
Ivanhoe 207
Iversen, Eric 19
Iversen, Neils 19

Jackson, Andrew 20, 21
Jackson, Thomas ("Stonewall") 114, 167
James II, King of England 25–26
Japanese Martyrs, canonization of (1862) 176–77, **178**, 185
Jefferson, Thomas 57
Jesuits 29–30, 42, 46, 51, 59–61, 63, 116, 155–56, 182, 212, 214, 234–37, 240, 245
Jews 34, 128–30, 202, 204, 231, 241, 268*n*56, 270*n*37
Joel, J. A. 270*n*37
Johnson, Andrew 202, 229, 233, 248
Johnson, Samuel 113
Jones, E. E. ("Charlie") 202
Jonesboro, Georgia (battle) 202
Judas Iscariot 228
Julian, George W. 142–43
jury trial 97–99, 112

Kanawha River, Virginia/West Virginia 115
Kansas 95, 119, 123; *see also* Kansas-Nebraska Act
Kansas-Nebraska Act 95–96, 104, 112, 117
Kanzler, Hermann 244
Kennedy, John A. 204
Kenrick, Bishop Francis Patrick 11–12, 57–59, 64, 108–09, 112, 123, 129–30, 132–33, 136, 143–44, 146, 153, 159, 224
Kenrick, Bishop Peter 11, 136, 224
Kentucky 8, 11, 13, 31, 82, 117, 125, 153, 165, 175, 191

Kentucky Military Institute 150
Kentucky Resolution *see* Virginia and Kentucky Resolutions
Kenyon College 21, 28–30
Keogh, Myles 268*n*63
Key, Francis Scott 257*n*39
King, Rufus 176, 215–16, 236, 244–45
Klement, Frank L. 278*n*27
Knight, John 104
Knights of Labor 251
Know-Nothing Party 1, 15, 90, 93–96, 100, 103–08, 110, 112, 115–21, 123–24, 127, 129, 131, 137–38, **138**, 142–43, 146–47, 185, 221, 231, 253
Knox, John 16
Kościuszko, Tadeusz 20
Kossuth, Louis 12, 79

"The Laboring Classes" 71–72, 88, 232
Laetare Medal 249
Lamennais, Hugues-Félicité Robert de 67, 102, 154
Latin America 254, 281*n*2
law of nations 165
Lawson (no first name given) 29
Lee, Robert E. 152–53, 167, 174, 190, 230, 248, 250
Lefevere, Bishop Peter Paul 148, 223–25
Leopoldine Association 31–32
Liberator 71, 161
Licking County, Ohio 19
Lilienthal, Rabbi Max 34
Lincoln, Abraham 8–10, 12–13, 16–18, 98, 123–24, 126, 138–40, 142–44, 146, 152, 159–61, 163, 165–67, 170–72, 175–76, 178–79, 182–83, 186, 189–91, 195, 199, 201–02, 204, 209, 218, 220–23, 225, 227–29, 232–34, 236, 238, 243–45, 254, 267*n*11
Lincoln, Frederick 15, 210–12
Lincoln, Robert Todd 245
"Lincoln or Fremont?" 234
Little Rock, Arkansas 214, 247
Livermore, Mary 170
Liverpool (England) 213, 244
London (England) 213
Longstreet, Helen Dortch 249–50
Longstreet, James 22–23, 27, 180, 207–08, 249–50
Longuemare, Emile 227
Lord's Prayer 105
Loring, Edward Greely 95
L'Osservatore Romano 178–79, 214, 225
Louis XIV 198
Louis Napoleon *see* Napoleon III
Louisiana 10, 25, 51, 59–60, 99, 119, 131, 143, 154, 240, 255*n*20
Louisiana Military Institute 131

Louistman, Louis 268*n*63
Louisville, Kentucky 8, 11, 29, 82, 89, 112, 114, 117–19, 153, 168, 195, 224–25
Louisville Journal 118, 195
Louisville Platform 117
Louisville riots 118–19
Lowell, Massachusetts 106–07
Loyola, Ignatius 30, 262*n*42
Luers, Bishop J. H. 143, 148, 168
Lukens, Thomas 84
Lumpkin, Joseph Henry 49, 261*n*54
Lynch, Mother Baptiste 206–07, 276*n*28
Lynch, Bishop Patrick 153–54, 161, 187, 206–07, 236, 276*n*28

MacMahon, T. W. 166
Macon, Georgia 51
Macon Telegraph see *Georgia Telegraph*
Madiai, Francesco 80–82
Madiai, Rosa 80–82, **81**
Mahan, Alfred Thayer 257*n*27
Mahan, Dennis 22, 24, 202, 257*n*27
Maine 104–05
Maine, Sebeus 125
Maistre, Fr. Claude Paschal 279*ch*21*n*1
Malines, Belgium 224
Mallory, Stephen 214
Malvern Hill (battle) 187
"Manifest Destiny" 72
Mann, Ambrose Dudley 187, 215
Manning, John 80, 104
Marches, Papal States 134
Marseilles (France) 213
Martin, Bishop Augustus Mary 154, 240–42
Martin, Jacob L. 36
Martineau, Harriet 68
Marx, Karl 71, 173, 193, 207; *Communist Manifesto* 71
Mary I, Queen of England 25
Maryland 51, 55, 59–60, 104, 112, 121, 144, 165
Masonic Hall (Boston) 68
Massachusetts 6, 14–16, 34, 49–50, 60, 64, 67, 77–78, 81, 96, 104–06, 112, 124–27, 131, 146–48, 163, 184–85, 187–89, 190, 210–11, 264*n*18, 265*n*24, 276*n*1; General Court (legislature) 31, 104–06, 184
Massachusetts Volunteer Heavy Artillery 211
Mastai-Ferretti, Giovanni Maria *see* Pius IX
Mather, Cotton 90
Mathew, Fr. Theobald 62–63, 91–92, 101, 261*n*58
Mazzini, Giuseppe 40–46, 133, 198

McClellan, George B. 148, *151*, 151–52, 189–90, 229, 236
McCloskey, Bishop John 246, 278*n*21
McCloskey, Fr. William 133, 136, 153, 155, 185
McCook, Alexander 192–94, 207–09
McCook, Robert 173, 192
McDowell, Ervin 152
McFarland, Bishop Francis 148, 185, 213
McGill, John 214
M'Clintock, John 109
McMahon, Lawrence 147, 187–88
McMaster, James 8, 10, 75, *77*, 81, 83, 85–86, 93, 107, 127, 130–31, 141, 145, 182, 196, 226–27, 232, 244, 254
McMullen, Fr. John 141–42
Meagher, Thomas Francis 88, *89*, 100, 188–90
The Mediatorial Life of Jesus 72
Men's Catholic Literary Institute (Cincinnati) 84
Mesmerism *see* spiritualism
Methodist Episcopal Church South 222–23
Methodists 175
Metropolitan Hall (New York) 81
Metropolitan Record 141, 153, 161–63, 226
Metternich, Klemens von 32, 35
Mexican War 76–77, 122
Mexico 160, 248
Meyendorff, Felix von *217*
Miami-Erie Canal (Cincinnati) 116
Michigan 117
Middle Ages 52–53, 58, 72, 87, 89, 91, 108, 112, 160, 204, 242
Milewski, Alexander 218, 234
Milner, Bishop John 24; *The End of Religious Controversy* 24–26
Milwaukee, Wisconsin 114
Mirari Vos 67, 102
Miscellanea 117
Mississippi 175, 230
Missouri 11, 15, 59–60, 159–60, 164–65, 171–72, 181, 190, 214, 220–23, 225–27, 229–30; loyalty oath 273–74*n*48; State Guard 214
Missouri Compromise 95, 119, 122
Mobile, Alabama 114, 148, 214
Modena, Duchy of 35
Le Monde 162
Monk, Maria 32, 106, 134
Montalembert, Charles de 85–86, *86*, 102, 141, 154, 160, 224, 234, 236, 238, 240
Montreal, Canada 63
Mordecai 209
Morgan, John Hunt 14, 180, 191, 203

Mormonism 65, 81, 128
Morse, Samuel 32, 114, 118, 279*n*20
Mortara, Edgardo 128–30, 133–34, 268*n*56
Moscow (Russia) 75
Mount Jackson, Virginia 167
Mount St. Mary's of the West Seminary (Cincinnati) 82, 84, 131–32, 150, 169
Mount St. Mary's Seminary (Emmitsburg, Maryland) 55, 102
Mudd, Samuel 17–18, 245
Mulhane, Rev. L. W. 20
Mullaly, John 141, 226, 268*n*19
Mulledy, Thomas, S.J. 51
Murfreesboro, Tennessee 8–9, 192, 195, 201
Murfreesboro, Battle of *see* Stones River (battle)

Nagasaki, Japan 176
Nahant, Massachusetts 124
Naples, Kingdom of 35, 37, 39, 133–34, 218–19
Napoleon I 22, 75, 236
Napoleon III (Louis Napoleon) 46, 86, 101, 134–36, 160, 178, 216, 238, 277*n*30
Narváez, Ramón María 43–44
Nashua, New Hampshire 85
Nashville, Tennessee 191–92, 201–02, 220
Natchez, Mississippi 255*n*2
Natchitoches, Louisiana 154, 240
National Anti-Slavery Standard 204, 232
National Union Party 228, 233
Native American Party *see* Know-Nothing Party
nativism 57–58, 75, 89–91, 93, 94–95, 105–07, 109, 114, 116–17, 123–24, 131, 134, 137–38, 145–46, 154, 198, 206, 231, 253–54
natural law 58, 110, 165, 241
Nature 68
Nebraska 95, 119; *see also* Kansas-Nebraska Act
neo–Puritans *see* Puritans
Nevada 248
"The New Brahminical Literature of New England" 231–32
New Coal River-Slack Water Navigation Company 115
New England 1, 15–16, 65–66, 75–76, 78, 90–91, 95, 100, 119, 121, 142, 164, 196–98, 213, 231–33, 253
New Hampshire 105
New Jersey 16, 50, 90, 113, 115, 143, 155, 246
New Jersey Journal 155
New Orleans, Louisiana 20, 33, 47, 55, 89, 114, 119, 166, 179, 233, 249, 279*ch*21*n*1

New Views of Christianity, Society and the Church 67–68
New York (state) 19, 21, 99, 104, 107–08, 121, 129, 131, 137, 205
New York (city) 2, 5–6, 12, 14–15, 17, *76*, *77*, 80–81, 83, 85, 88, 92, 94, 99, 103–04, 109, 113, 116, 119–20, 127–28, 131, 136, 138, 141–42, 156–58, 167, 179, 186, 196, 199, 203–06, 211, 214, 213, 218, 226, 227, 231, 234, 240, 245–46, 248, 253; diocese/archdiocese of 47, 94, 113, 116, 136, 226
New York Court of Appeals 113
New York Daily Times see *New York Times*
New York draft riots (1863) 6, 7, 205, *205*, 231
New York Express 64
New York Herald 206
New York Times 16, 134, 199, 220
New York Tribune 6, 7, 41, 46, 161, 204–05, 207
Newark, New Jersey 90
Newark, diocese of 113
Newman, John Henry 17, 91, 144
Newport, Rhode Island 27, 131
Newton, Massachusetts 16
"The Next President" 233
Nightingale, Florence 150
9th Indiana Volunteer Regiment 150
9th Massachusetts Infantry Regiment 147, 184, 187, *189*
9th Ohio Infantry Regiment 173
North Carolina 143
Northup, Solomon 98–99; *Twelve Years a Slave* 98–99
Northwest Ordinance 271–72*n*33
Norway 19
Nostra Aetate 268*n*56
Notre Dame University 247, 249; Sacred Heart Chapel 247
Nugent, Robert 204
nullification 69, 73, 262*n*24
"Nunnery Committee" 106–07

Oblate Sisters of Providence 102
O'Brien, Fr. Nicholas 147
O'Connell, Sister Anthony 149–50, 170
O'Connell, Daniel 54–57
O'Connor, Bishop Michael 129
O'Conor, Charles 226, 278*n*21
Odin, Archbishop Jean-Marie 166, 179, 279*ch*21*n*1
O'Gorman, Richard 190
Ohio 9–12, 14, 19, 28, 30–31, 82, 104, 115–17, 149–50, 172, 119, 121, 131–33, 148–50, 170–72, 192, 202–03, 220–21, 225–26, 228–30, 248
Ohio River 150
O'Leary, Charles 148

Index

Olivieri, Fr. Nicolò 241–42
Onesimus 11
Ontario *see* Canada West
Opdycke, Emerson 201–03
Opdyke, George 206
Orangemen 90, 112
Ord, Edward 173–74
Order of American Knights 225, 230
Order of the Star-Spangled Banner *see* Know-Nothing Party
Orr, John S. ("Angel Gabriel") 85, 90
oscurantisti 197, 234
O'Sullivan, John 72
O'Toole, James M. 261*n*54
Oudinot, Charles Nicolas Victor 43
Over the Rhine (Cincinnati) 116

Paddington, Father George 56
Papal Conspiracy Exposed 110, *111*
Papal States 33–37, 39–41, 43–44, 46, 81, 83, 86, 89, 94, 109, 128–30, 133–36, 140–41, 143, 155, 157–58, 178, 223; insurrection in (1848–1849) *38*, *45*, 79, 133; Mortara case 128–30, 267*n*40
Paris 69, 85, 101–03, 158, 162
Parker, Theodore 69, 78
Parma 35
Pendleton, George 229
Pennington, William 137
Pennsylvania 5, 6, 15, 19, 83, 104, 108–09, 121, 138
People's Party (Indiana) 104
Perché, Napoléon 279*ch*21*n*1
Peter, Sarah 149, 169–70
Phalen (no first name given) 29
Philadelphia 55–56, 119, 144, 197; riots (1844) 57, 75, 112
The Philanthropist 67
Philemon, St. Paul's Epistle to 11
Phillip II, King of Spain 88
Phillips, Margaret 104, 265*n*15
Phillips, Wendell 55–56, 171, 232
Pica Law 219
Pickett, George 190
Piedmont, Kingdom of 35, 128–29, 134–36, 140, 143, 177, 198, 277*n*30
Pierce, Franklin 95, 264*n*34
Pillow, Gideon 198
Pittsburgh, Pennsylvania 83, 114, 169
Pius V, Pope 88
Pius IX, Bl., Pope 10–13, 33–43, 46–48, *47*, 56, 85–86, 90, 93, 100, 112, 128, 130, 132, 134–36, 146, 148–49, 176–80, 199, 213–19, *217*, 225, 231, 236, 238–42, 244–46, 248
A Plea for the West 31–32
Poinsett, Joel 21
Poland/Poles 20–21, 216–18, *217*, 234, 277*n*34

Pompeiopolis 168, *169*
Pompey (Roman general) 168
Popular Government 248
Porter, Jane 20–21
Portland, Maine (diocese) 250–51
Post Office 49, 52, 259*n*12
Potato Famine (Ireland) 56–57, 92–93
Presbyterian Church, Missouri Synod 222–23
Presbyterians 175
Price, Samuel W. 193–94
Price, Sterling 173–75, 214, 229–30
Propagateur Catholique (New Orleans) 89, 166
Public School Society 74–75
Purcell, Fr. Edward 114, 248
Purcell, Bishop John 10–11, 13, 31–33, 47, 82, 84, 89, 109, 114–15, 117, 131–33, 148–49, 153, 168–71, 176, 179, 182, 206, 220, 223–25, 240, 247–48
Puritans 1, 90–92, 94, 106, 154, 254
Putnam, James 107

Quakers 50–51, 60
Quanta Cura 238
Quinlan, Fr. John (later Bishop) 148, 214
Quinn's Row (Louisville, Kentucky) 118
Quirinal Palace (Rome) 37, *38*, 41

The Rambler 197
Rancho Sausal Redondo (California) 248
Randall, Alexander 176–77, 179
Reconstruction 248
"Red Triumvirate" 46
Redmond, Rowland 274*n*25
re-enactors (of the Italian civil war) *218*
Reformation, Protestant 15, 30, 39, 44, 47, 68, 87; in England 29; in Germany 29
Regnans in Excelsis 88
Reid, Whitelaw 152
Republican Party 1, 6, 8, 12, 14, 16–17, 95, 104–06, 117, 120–24, 126, 129, 136–40, *138*, 142–43, 146–47, 149–50, 153, 156, 159, 161, 165, 170–72, 179, 189, 197, 203–04, 206, 210, 223, 227–29, 231, 233–34, 249, 279*ch*21*n*1
The Results of Emancipation 199
Rhine (River) 213
Rhode Island 105, 155
Rich Mountain (battle) 151–52, *151*, 173
Richmond, Virginia 147, 150, 152, 166, 214–15, 226
Richmond Examiner 220
"Rights of the Temporal" 140–41

Ripley, George 68–69, 73–74
Robert I (king) 236
Roddan, Fr. John 106
Rodrigue, William 55
Romagna, Papal States 134
Roman Republic 39–46
Romanism in America 110
Rome 10–11, 13, 17, 28, 33–48, *38*, *45*, 52, 56, 69, 82–85, 90, 94, 98, 100, 102, 108, 110, 128, 131–35, 136, 140, 142–44, 148, 153–55, 157–59, 167, 170, 176–79, 185–86, 213–16, 219, 224–25, 236, 238–45, 247–48, 250, 254
Roosevelt, James 113
Rosecrans, Ann(e) 23–24, 27–29, 39, 114, 182, 192, 195
Rosecrans, Chauncey 19
Rosecrans, Crandall 19–20, 30–31
Rosecrans, Henry 27, 37
Rosecrans, Jemima 19, 30–31
Rosecrans, Louis 248
Rosecrans, Lydia 37
Rosecrans, Mary 248
Rosecrans, Fr. (later Bishop) Sylvester 1, 6, 10, *11*, 13–14, 20, 28–48, *45*, 82–85, 92–94, 114–15, 117, 130–34, 148, 153, 168–71, 174–76, 179, 190–91, 203, 206, 223–24, 229, 247–48, 254
Rosecrans, William 1, 6–10, *9*, 19–30, *26*, 34, 36–38, 43, 114–15, 118, 127, 130–31, 148–53, *151*, 164, 167, 169–70, 172–75, 180–83, 186, 191–95, *192*, *193*, 201–03, 206–09, 214, 220–30, 232, 247–50, 254, 269*n*20, 270*n*37, 276*n*28, 276*n*33; *Popular Government* 248
Rosecrans, William (Jr.) 27
Rosecrants, Daniel 19
Rosecrants, Thankful 19–20
Rosenkrans, Daniel, Sr. 19
Rosenkrans, Daniel, Jr. *see* Rosecrants, Daniel
Rosenkrantz, Harmon Hendrick 19
Rossi, Pellegrino 37, 244
Roxbury, Massachusetts 106–07
Royalton, Vermont 65
"Rum, Romanism and slavery" 1, 90–91, 106, 123, 125
Russia 216–18, *217*, 234
Ryan, Fr. Patrick J. 230

Sacred Heart of Jesus 169
Sailer, Bishop Johann 54
Saint Aloysius College 243
Saint Augustine, Florida 145
Saint Elizabeth Ann Seton 149
Saint Gregory of Nyssa 57
Saint James parish, Boston 250
Saint John Crysostom 57
Saint John's College (later Fordham University) 29–30, 113

St. John's Hotel/Hospital (Cincinnati) 149, 152, 170, 270n23
Saint Joseph, Missouri 221
Saint Joseph's Cathedral (Columbus, Ohio) 247–48
Saint Louis, Missouri 11, 47, 89, 136, 164, 214, 220–24, 225–227, 230
Saint Mary's Church (Boston) 212
Saint Mary's Church (Newport, Rhode Island) 27
Saint Mary's College (Cincinnati) 132
Saint Patrick's Church (Columbus, Ohio) 247
Saint Patrick's Day 203
Saint Paul's Episcopal Chapel (NY) 24
Saint Sulpice, Paris 101–02, 251
Saint Sylvester convent (Rome) 41
Saint Thomas Aquinas 58, 73, 132
Saint Thomas Church (Cincinnati) 82
Saint Vincent de Paul Society 180
San Francisco, California 88, 177, 218, 248
San Patricio Batallion 76
Sanderson, John 221–23, 225–28, 278n27
Sanford, Henry S. 185–87
Santo Domingo 260n26; uprising 55, 172, *181*, 182, 281n2
Scammon, E. P. 148
School for Human Culture (Boston) 68
Schools: Catholic schools 32, 52, 60, 63, 82, 84, 92–93, 105–07, 112–13, 117, 125–26, 132–33, 141, 143, 153, 202, 213, 250, 265n24; common schools 66–67, 84, 92–93, 105–06, 116–17, 133, 138, 184, 239
Schouler, William 211
Scotland 85
Scott, Sir Walter 207, 209
Scott, Winfield 27, 149
Scully, Fr. Thomas 147, 188
Second Manassas (battle) 177
Seminary of St. Sulpice (Montreal) 63
Seminary of St. Sulpice (Paris) 101
Semmes, Thomas 119
Senate, U.S. 62
serfdom 112
Seton, Elizabeth Ann *see* Saint Elizabeth Ann Seton
Seton Hall College 156
Seward, William Henry 75, 77, 137–38, 162–63, 176–77, 185–87, 215–16, 244
Seymour, Horatio 204–05, 248
Shamrock (gunboat) 203
Shelbyville 230
Shepherd of the Valley 89
Sheridan, Phillip Henry 194, 230

Sherman, William T. 131, 225, 276n28
Shiloh (battle) 169, 173
Sibour, Archbishop Marry-Dominique August 103
Sicily 219
Simpson, Richard 197
Sims, Thomas 78
Sisters of Charity (Cincinnati) 149–50, 152, 170
Sisters of Charity of St. Vincent de Paul 149
Sisters of Mercy (Cincinnati) 149
Sisters of Notre Dame 106–07
Sisters of Saint Joseph (Wheeling, Virginia/West Virginia) 151
Sisters of the Poor of St. Francis 169–70
69th New York Regiment 189
slavery 1–2, 7–13, 16–17, 31–33, 49–60, 62, 64, 66, 69–71, 76–78, 90–91, 94–99, 102–06, 112, 115, 117, 119, 121–24, 128–31, 133, 136–43, 145–47, 153–54, 156–57, 159–66, 171, 178–83, 189, 196, 199–200, 215–16, 221, 223–24, 230–34, 240–43, 250, 253–54, 259n8, 260n18, 261n54, 261n55, 279n20, 279n22, 280–81n1, 281n2
"Slavery and the War" 160–61, 269n2
Smith, A. J. 229
Smith, Gerrit 163
Smith, Joseph 65
Smith, Reuben 66
Society for the Propagation of the Faith of the American Missions *see* Leopoldine Association
Soli *see* Pompeiopolis
"Some Explanations Offered to Our Catholic Readers" 237–38
Sons of Liberty 227
South Carolina 51, 53, 69, 77, 130, 143, 153, 187, 206, 276n28
Spalding, Bishop Martin 8, 11–13, 29, 89, 112, 117–19, 125, 153, 168, 214–16, 224–25, 250
Spanish Armada 88
Speed, Joshua 124
Spirit of the Times 202
The Spirit-Rapper 65–66, 87, 99–100, 261n8
"spiritism" *see* spiritualism
spiritualism 99–100, 225
Staats-Anziger 126
Stallo, Johann 173, 192
Stanton, Edwin 8–9, 172, 195, 197, 201, 203, 209, 221–22, 227, 229
"The Star-Spangled Banner" 257n39
Stark, John 256n3
Starr, Eliza 141–42, 144
"State Rebellion, State Suicide" 164–65

The State v. Lavinia and Wilkes 261n55
Staten Island, New York 113
"statolatry" 87
Stevens, Thaddeus 138
Stillman, W. J. 176
Stockbridge, Vermont 65
Stockton, John P. 136
Stones River (battle) 191–95, *192, 193,* 201, 208–09, 232, 249
Stowe, Harriet Beecher 31–32, 67, 94–95, 110, 270n23
Sulphur Springs, West Virginia 248
Sulpicians 63, 101–02
Sumner, Charles 17, 69, 96–98, 106, 163–67, 186–87, 190, 197, 199, 234, 271–72n33
Surratt, John 243–45
Surratt, Mary 243–45
Sweeney's Shambles 92
Switzerland 82, 112, 125
Syllabus of Errors 238–40, 242, 246
Syracuse, New York 85

Tablet 247
Tammany Hall 206
Taney, Roger 15, 52, 60, 122
Taylor, James 116
Taylor, Zachary 27
Telegraph *see Catholic Telegraph; Georgia Telegraph*
Ten Commandments 105, 124–25
Tennessee 143, 170, 175; Supreme Court 98
Thaddeus of Warsaw (novel) 20–21
Thebaud, Fr. Augustus 30
Thirteenth Amendment 145, 269n2, 271–72n33, 280–81n1
Thomas, George Henry 208–09, 220
Thomas, Lorenzo 180–81
Thomas à Kempis 180, 194
Thompson, Harriet 2
Thompson, Jacob 226–27, *228*
Thoreau, Henry David 69, *70,* 76
Tilden, Samuel 278n21
Timon, Bishop John 123
Tod, David 170, 172
Torrey, John 204–05
Toucey, Isaac 126
Transcendentalism 69, 72–74
Trecy, Fr. Jeremiah 191, *192,* 193, 209, 220
Trent crisis 176
Truesdail, William 202
trusteeship issue 105–08, 131
Tuchman, Barbara 1
Tucker, Fr. Hilary 15–16, 190–91
Tullahoma, Tennessee 203
Turkey 79, 168, *169*
Turner, James B. 190
Turnverein (Turner) 116, 173

Tuscany, Grand Duchy of 35, 80–82
Twain, Mark *see* Clemens, Samuel
Tweed, William M. 206
Twelve Years a Slave 98–99
23rd Ohio Regiment 150
24th Ohio Regiment 150
25th Ohio Regiment 150
26th Ohio Regiment 150
28th Massachusetts Regiment 147, 187
29th Massachusetts Regiment 187, 189
"Two-Year Law" 124, 126, 146, 185

ultramontanism 43, 109–10, 112, 123, 130, 237
Umbria, Papal States 134
Uncle Tom's Cabin 2, 94, 110, 160, 231–32
Union Party (Ohio) 170–72
unions 226
Unitarianism 55, 66–69, 72–74, 76, 78, 125, 142
United States 5, 12–15, 19, 31, 33, 35, 36, 40, 45–46, 51–52, 54, 56, 58–59, 68, 77, 79–83, 87, 89–90, 92–93, 98–100, 102, 108, 116, 119, 122, 128–37, 139, 150, 154, 160–61, 164–65, 172, 174, 176–79, 183, 185–86, 198, 206, 213, 215–17, 222, 224, 226, 234, 236, 239, 244–45, 253–54, 273n48, 280–81n1, 281n2; Department of Justice 264n36; federal marshals 96, 264n36; Supreme Court 15, 52, 98, 122, 185
L'Univers 43, 85–86, 130, 160
Universalism 19, 66–67, 142, 157
University of North Carolina 52
Ursuline Convent (Charlestown, Massachusetts) 31, 112
Ursuline Convent and Academy (Columbia, South Carolina) 130, 206–07, 276n28

Vallandigham, Clement 9–10, 13, 171, 203, 227
van Buren, Martin 34, 68, 71
Van Dieman's Land, Australia 88
Van Dorn, Earl 174–75
Vatican 268n56
Vatican Council: First Vatican Council 246–47; Second Vatican Council 268n56
Vermont 65
Verot, Bishop Augustin 145–46, 154, 250
Veuillot, Louis 85–86, *87*, 130, 160, 240
Vicksburg, Mississippi (battle) 6, 192, 203, 209, 214
Victor Emmanuel, King of Piedmont 134–35, 177–78, 186, 198, 216, 219, 238, 244
Villani, Fr. (no first name given) 29
Vincennes, Indiana 82
Vincentians 60
A Vindication of the Catholic Church 108
Virgin Mary 24, 29, 100–01, 152, 192, 195, 208–09
Virginia 23, 27, 32, 83, 98, 114–15, 130, 136, 143, 150–52, 155, 164, 166–67, 172, 174, 177, 183, 187–89, 194–95, 207, 214, 226, 230, 236–37
Virginia and Kentucky Resolutions (1798) 262n38
Virginia Military Academy 114
Volunteer Engine Company 33 ("Black Joke") 204
voting rights 232–33

Walden Pond *70*
Walter, Fr. John 243–45
Warheits-Freund 116
Warsaw (Poland) 216–17
Washington, George 34
Washington, D.C. 52, 147, 165, 167, 171, 199
Washington Street Cathedral 243

Watt, Jeremy 260n18
West Point Military Academy (New York) 7, 9, 20–24, 26, 29–30, 127, 180, 202, 207, 249
West Virginia 114, 150, 152, 195, 230, 148
Western Female Institute (Cincinnati) 32, 270n23
Western Tablet 126
Whall, Thomas 124–26
"What the Rebellion Teaches" 197–98
Wheeling, Virginia/West Virginia 83
Wheeling, diocese of 150
Whelan, Bishop Richard W. 150–51
Whig Party 1, 68, 71, 75, 77, 88, 90, 95, 104, 109, 119, 123, 126, 137, 142–43, 264n34
The Widow Glenn 207
Wiget, Fr. Bernardine 125
Willard Hotel 17
Williams, Fr. John 15, 103, 185, 187; appointed bishop of Boston 250
Willich, August 173, 193
Wilson, Henry 60, 106, 120
Windsor, Canada 227
Wise, Rabbi Isaac Meyer 128
Wood, Bishop James Frederick 197
Wood, Thomas 208, 276n33
Worcester, Massachusetts 60–61, 63, 107
Workingman's Party 67–68, 72
Wright, Fanny 66, 100
Wyoming Valley, Pennsylvania 19

Xavier, St. Francis 25

"Yankee Doodle" 193

Zambianchi, Callimaco 42
Zion's Herald and Wesleyan Journal 220
Zouaves, Papal 135, 244, 268n63

www.ingramcontent.com/pod-product-compliance
Lightning Source LLC
Chambersburg PA
CBHW081540300426
44116CB00015B/2703